NINTH EDITION

Subjects/Strategies
A Writer's Reader

Paul Eschholz
Alfred Rosa

University of Vermont

BEDFORD / ST. MARTIN'S
Boston ◆ New York

For Bedford/St. Martin's
Developmental Editor: Mikola de Roo
Associate Editor: Gregory S. Johnson
Editorial Assistant, Publishing Services: Maria Teresa Burwell
Senior Production Supervisor: Joe Ford
Marketing Manager: Brian Wheel
Project Management: Books By Design, Inc.
Text Design: Books By Design, Inc.
Photo Research: Alice Lundoff
Cover Design: Lucy Krikorian
Cover Photo: © Erika Rank / Photonica
Composition: Pine Tree Composition
Printing and Binding: Haddon Craftsmen, an RR Donnelley & Sons Company

President: Charles H. Christensen
Editorial Director: Joan E. Feinberg
Editor in Chief: Nancy Perry
Director of Marketing: Karen R. Melton
Director of Editing, Design, and Production: Marcia Cohen
Manager, Publishing Services: Emily Berleth

Library of Congress Control Number: 2001090610

Manufactured in the United States of America.

7 6 5 4 3 2
f e d c b a

For information, write: Bedford/St. Martin's, 75 Arlington Street, Boston, MA 02116   (617-399-4000)

ISBN: 0-312-39109-9

Acknowledgments

Edward Abbey. "Aravaipa Canyon." From *Down River* by Edward Abbey. Copyright © 1982 by Edward Abbey. Used by permission of Dutton, a division of Penguin Putnam Inc.

Diane Ackerman. "The Face of Beauty." From *A Natural History of the Senses* by Diane Ackerman. Copyright © 1990 by Diane Ackerman. Reprinted by permission of Random House, Inc.

Mortimer Adler. "How to Mark a Book." From the *Saturday Review of Literature,* July 6, 1940. Reprinted by permission.

Julia Alvarez. "Snow." From *How the García Girls Lost Their Accents.* Copyright © 1991 by Julia Alvarez. Published by Plume, an imprint of Dutton Signet, a division of Penguin USA and originally in hardcover by Algonquin Books of Chapel Hill. Reprinted by permission of Susan Bergholz Literary Services, New York. All rights reserved.

Acknowledgments and copyrights are continued at the back of the book on pages 676–78, which constitute an extension of the copyright page.

Preface

Since *Subjects/Strategies* was first published in 1978, it has offered composition students timely and teachable selections that help them master the full range of rhetorical strategies they need for successful college writing. As always, we think the selections in the ninth edition of this rhetorically arranged reader will inform and entertain students, shaping their understanding of the world around them. But above all, the seventy-three selections—fifty-seven professional essays, twelve annotated student essays, and four short stories—were chosen to help students become better writers and especially to help them grasp and master nine widely used and versatile writing strategies.

Subjects/Strategies, as its title suggests, places equal emphasis on the content and form of an essay—that is, on what an essay has to say and on the techniques used to say it. All readers pay attention to content, to the substance of what writers are saying. Far fewer, however, notice the strategies that writers use to organize their writing and to make it understandable and effective. Because these strategies are such an essential element of the writer's craft, students need first to become more aware of these strategies—most of which they intuitively use already—and then to practice using them in order to write well. The most important purpose of *Subjects/Strategies* is to help students understand how a given strategy, alone or in combination, can be used most effectively to communicate a subject to an audience.

FAVORITE FEATURES OF *SUBJECTS/STRATEGIES*

A Comprehensive Four-Chapter Introduction

The first four chapters provide detailed guidelines and instruction on reading critically, writing essays, combining rhetorical strategies, and researching and documenting sources (including Web sources).

Compelling and Diverse Readings

Seventy-three readings, including twelve student essays and sixty-one professional essays and stories by some of the best classic and contemporary writers, offer a broad spectrum of subject matter, style, and cultural points of view. These engaging selections, by well-known writers including Mark Twain, Gore Vidal, Malcolm X, David Guterson, Nikki Giovanni, Gary Soto, Judith Ortiz Cofer, and Anne Lamott, demonstrate the versatility and strengths of the different rhetorical strategies for effective college writing.

Detailed Introductions to Each Rhetorical Strategy

The introduction to each rhetorical chapter opens with a definition of the rhetorical strategy under discussion and then examines examples of the strategy put into practice. Next, after discussing the various purposes for which writers use each strategy, a complete, annotated student essay employing the strategy is presented. Finally, sound, practical advice is offered on how to write an essay using that strategy. This edition includes updated guidelines on selecting topics, developing thesis statements, considering audiences, gathering evidence, choosing organizational patterns, and using other rhetorical strategies in support of the dominant strategy.

Annotated Student Essays

An annotated student essay appears in each chapter introduction, offering students realistic examples of how they can successfully incorporate rhetorical strategies into their own writing. In this edition, discussion questions have been added to follow each student essay, encouraging students to analyze and evaluate the overall effectiveness of the rhetorical strategies employed in the example.

Extensive Rhetorical Apparatus

The abundant study materials accompanying each essay in the book teach students how to use each strategy to make their writing more effective by linking their reading to their writing.

- *Journal writing activities* are provided before and after each professional selection. *Before You Read* prereading journal prompts ask students to write about their own experiences with the issues discussed in the selection. *Responding to Reading* postreading journal prompts ask students to analyze, elaborate on, or take issue with a key aspect of the selection. From time to time, discussion questions and writing assignments ask students to return to these journal writings to reflect on their early thinking before moving ahead with more formal writing tasks.

- *Questioning the Text* questions focus students' attention on the content of the selection as well as on the author's purpose. These questions help students check their comprehension of the selection, and they provide a basis for classroom discussion.

- *Understanding the Writer's Craft* questions direct students to the various rhetorical strategies and writing techniques that the writer has used. These questions encourage students to put themselves in the writer's place and to consider how they might employ the strategies in their own writing.

- *Exploring Language* questions emphasize the importance of diction, word choice, and verbal context. Each set of questions ends with a vocabulary-building exercise in which students are asked to use a dictionary to determine the meanings of certain words as they are used in the selection.

- *Combining Rhetorical Strategies* questions ask students to identify and analyze places where the author has used one or more rhetorical strategies to enhance or develop the essay's dominant strategy. For "Combining Rhetorical Strategies" essays, a number of questions are designed to reveal the rich, often complex orchestration of multiple strategies.

- *Writing Suggestions* following each professional selection are of three types. The first type focuses on the particular rhetorical strategy under discussion. The second type asks students to explore the topic of the essay or a related topic using a different strategy. The third type asks students to do some research, including research on the Internet.

End-of-Chapter Writing Suggestions

As in previous editions, there are a number of writing suggestions at the end of Chapters 5 through 13. These writing suggestions provide additional topics suitable to the strategy covered by the chapters. In preparing the suggestions, we made an effort to tie them to particular selections or pairs of selections in the chapter. Instructors can use these writing suggestions as complements or substitutes for the more focused writing topics that accompany individual selections.

Thematic Table of Contents

Immediately after the main table of contents, a second table of contents classifies the reading selections into general thematic categories. This thematic table of contents is designed to make it easier for instructors and students to identify groups of essays that have common subject matter, thus providing further opportunities for discussion and writing based on the content of individual selections and on various rhetorical approaches to common themes.

Glossary of Rhetorical Terms

The glossary at the end of *Subjects/Strategies* provides concise definitions of terms useful in working with the rhetorical strategies presented in the text. Wherever we thought that information in the glossary might assist students in answering a study question in the text, we placed a cross-reference to the appropriate glossary entry next to the question.

NEW TO THIS EDITION OF *SUBJECTS/STRATEGIES*

New Selections

Nearly half of the professional writing in *Subjects/Strategies* is new to this edition. These new selections represent an astounding variety of writers, topics, viewpoints, and rhetorical approaches. Among the twenty-five new professional essays and three new short stories are Gore Vidal's "Lincoln Up Close"; David Guterson's "San Piedro Island"; Nikki Giovanni's "Campus Racism 101"; Lorrie Moore's "How to Become a Writer"; Gary Soto's "Like Mexicans"; Judith Ortiz Cofer's "The Myth of the Latin Woman"; Maya Angelou's "Living Well. Living Good."; and Ellen Ullman's "Needed: Techies Who Know Shakespeare."

An Expanded Chapter on Argumentation

This chapter opens with classic essays by Maya Angelou, Richard Lederer, Thomas Jefferson, and Martin Luther King Jr. To respond to the changing interests and debates of students, the chapter also contains two argument pairs on current topics (one new to the ninth edition)—"Violence in the Movies and on Television" and "Computer Technology and Education"—and a brand new five-essay case study, "Justice and the Death Penalty."

An Expanded Four-Chapter Introduction to Reading, Writing, Combining Strategies, and Research

This unique four-chapter introduction has been substantially revised to include even more comprehensive coverage on reading, writing, combining strategies, and research and documentation. To make information easier for students to use, reading and writing tips have been added throughout all four chapters in the form of easy-to-find boxes and checklists, including such topics as "How to Annotate a Text," "Will Your Thesis Hold Water?," "A Brief Guide to Peer Critiquing," "Notes on Beginnings and Endings," and "Addressing Common Writing Problems and Errors."

- *Chapter 1, "Reading for Understanding and Meaning."* This chapter shows students how to become stronger critical readers. Equally important, it stresses the role of reading (particularly analytical reading and critical thinking) in the student writer's development. In response to instructors' requests for extra advice on how to mark up a text properly, this chapter has been expanded to include sample annotations of a brief professional essay.

- *Chapter 2, "Writing Essays."* This chapter provides students with an overview of all aspects of the writing process, using an actual student essay—from initial notes to completed final draft—as illustration. The chapter now includes a checklist for each step in the writing process, more coverage of choosing and supporting a thesis and evaluating and revising essays, and boxes on peer critiquing, introductions and conclusions, and common writing problems.

- *Chapter 3, "Combining Strategies."* This unique chapter on mixing rhetorical strategies shows students how to use more than one strategy to achieve their purpose. A sample student essay demonstrates the possibilities open to writers who understand the function and purpose of each strategy. This edition also now includes a brief professional essay that illustrates how a number of different strategies can be used, even in a concise piece of writing. Also included is a new section explaining the purpose and function of the photographs in the book, a new feature to this edition, as well as guidelines on how to read a visual text using a sample photograph.

- *Chapter 4, "Writing Documented Essays."* A chapter on the documented research essay includes up-to-date instruction on using print sources and electronic Internet sources, as well as guidelines for evaluating the authority and reliability of print and Internet sources and for using the most current MLA documentation style. This chapter now includes a sample Internet search, with screen shots, to show students not only how to conduct Internet searches, but how to *evaluate* the sources they gather from the Web.

New Visual Apparatus in Each Rhetorical Chapter

Visual exercises and activities—photos and cartoons—have been paired with twenty professional essays to demonstrate to students how strategies and themes work in visual and written formats.

- *Combining Subjects and Strategies: Photographs That Accompany the Combining Rhetorical Strategies Essays.* We have introduced each of the Combining Rhetorical Strategies essays in this book with a photograph that depicts one or more of the themes in the essay. Occasionally, the photographs also demonstrate the rhetorical mode of the chapter. The questions that follow the photographs are designed to encourage close observation and critical thinking.
- *Post-essay Writing Suggestions Paired with Cartoons and Visual Texts.* A second essay in each rhetorical chapter contains one writing suggestion that has been paired with a visual component—a cartoon or a photo. Like the pre-essay photos described above, these visuals demonstrate similar themes or strategies in the essay and offer students another way of thinking about how those themes and strategies work.

It is our hope that by adding a new, visual medium to the mix of written essays and text-based analytical activities and assignments, we can demonstrate not only another approach to the themes and strategies, but also how a different medium portrays these same themes and strategies.

Questions for Revision Boxes

These checklists, which conclude the introduction to each rhetorical chapter, summarize and reinforce the chapter's key concepts and guide students in revising their own essays with that particular strategy in mind.

A Greater Emphasis on Combining Strategies

More extensive coverage of combining rhetorical strategies helps students become more skillful and flexible writers. Building on Chapter 3, which explains how to use multiple strategies in support of the dominant method, the combining of strategies is emphasized throughout the text. Each rhetorical chapter contains one highlighted selection in which rhetorical strategies are effectively combined, and every selection is accompanied by questions and activities designed to help students put into practice what they have learned about combining strategies.

Updated Coverage of New Technologies

The coverage of new technologies throughout *Subjects/Strategies* helps students take advantage of the vast potential of the Internet. Chapter 4 on research and documentation includes guidelines for conducting research online and for evaluating the reliability and timeliness of Internet sources. It features two new sections, "Subject Directories and Keyword Searches" and "Refining Keyword Searches on the Web." In addition, *Subjects/Strategies* continues to be the only book of its kind to offer Internet research questions for every professional selection. These Internet assignments, complete with URLs, have been revised and updated to reflect the most current sites available on the Web.

Expanded Ancillary Package

The ancillary package available to instructors includes the following items:

- An *Instructor's Edition,* incorporating the *Instructor's Manual to Accompany Subjects/Strategies,* is packed with teaching tips and answers to end-of-selection questions, including new material that reflects all the changes in the apparatus that accompany each selection.
- A new companion Web site (www.bedfordstmartins.com/ subjectsstrategies) offers students the best and most current Internet links for further research. Bedford/St. Martin's TopLinks—a topical links database accessible through the site—guides students to the best links with the most useful information on the ideas presented in *Subjects/Strategies.*

ACKNOWLEDGMENTS

We are gratified by the reception and use of the eight previous editions of *Subjects/Strategies.* Composition teachers in hundreds of community colleges, liberal arts colleges, and universities have used the book. Many teachers responded to our detailed review questionnaire, thus helping us tremendously in conceptualizing the improvements to this edition. We thank Teague Bohlen, Front Range Community College; Arnold Bradford, Northern Virginia Community College; Larry Brunt, Northland Pioneer College; Kathryn Coker, Lindenwood University; Robert W. Croft, Gainesville College; Barbara J. Grossman,

Essex County College; Rita Higgins, Essex County College; Arden Jensen, Gulf Coast Community College; Patrick Joyner, Northern Virginia Community College; Monique Kluczykowski, Gainesville College; Pat Kramer, Kishwaukee College; Pat Madden, Front Range Community College; Patricia D. Maida, University of D.C.; Carolyn Miller, Kishwaukee College; Suzanne E. O'Hop, Northland Pioneer College; Stella Shepard, Henderson State University; and David Waskin, Washtenaw Community College.

We thank our longtime friend and editor, Nancy Perry, and our talented and enthusiastic developmental editor, Mikola de Roo, at Bedford/St. Martin's for their commitment to *Subjects/Strategies*. Together we have charted some new territories for this enduring text, and the process has been truly exciting. Thanks go also to the rest of the Bedford/St. Martin's team: Chuck Christensen, Joan Feinberg, Karen Melton, Brian Wheel, Emily Berleth, Greg Johnson, Joanna Imm, and Judith Mara Riotto. Special thanks go to Mark Wanner for his assistance in developing the questions and to Betsy Eschholz for preparing the *Instructor's Manual*. We are also happy to recognize those students whose work appears in *Subjects/Strategies* for their willingness to contribute their time and effort in writing and rewriting their essays: Keith Eldred, Tara E. Ketch, Melanie Milks, Shannon Long, James Blake Wilson, Andrew Kauser, William Peterson, Barbara Bowman, Gerald Cleary, Howard Solomon Jr., Kevin Cunningham, and Mark Jackson. We are grateful to our own writing students at the University of Vermont for their enthusiasm for writing and for their invaluable responses to materials included in this book. And we also thank our families for sharing in our commitment to quality teaching and textbook writing.

Finally, we thank each other. Beginning in 1971 we have collaborated on many textbooks on language and writing, all of which have gone into multiple editions. With this ninth edition of *Subjects/Strategies,* we enter the thirty-first year of working together. Ours must be one of the longest-running and most mutually satisfying writing partnerships in college textbook publishing. The journey has been invigorating and challenging as we have come to understand the complexities and joys of good writing and have sought out new ways to help students become better writers.

Paul Eschholz
Alfred Rosa

Contents

6 Description 154

ROGER ANGELL, *On the Ball*   165

"Any baseball is beautiful. No other small package comes as close to the ideal in design and utility. It is a perfect object for a man's hand. Pick it up and it instantly suggests its purpose."

EDWARD ABBEY, *Aravaipa Canyon*   170

"We will never get to the end of it, never plumb the bottom of it, never know the whole or even so small and trivial and useless and precious a place as Aravaipa. Therein lies our redemption."

GORE VIDAL, *Lincoln Up Close*   177

A popular novelist and essayist searches for the true nature of the man behind the romanticized and celebrated "national deity" that Abraham Lincoln has become.

CHEROKEE PAUL McDONALD, *A View from the Bridge*   187

A chance encounter between a jogger and a young boy out fishing teaches them both how to see.

CARTOON: Bill Watterson, *Gone Fishing (from "Calvin and Hobbes")*   **191**

COMBINING SUBJECTS AND STRATEGIES

PHOTO: Peter Menzel, *Barrio Mural*   **193**

ROBERT RAMÍREZ, *The Barrio*   194

A Hispanic writer paints a vivid and sensuous picture of the district called "the barrio."

DAVID GUTERSON, *San Piedro Island* (FICTION)   201

In this excerpt from his best-selling work *Snow Falling on Cedars,* a novelist portrays the joys and hardships of life in the Pacific Northwest through his description of the landscape and history of San Piedro Island.

7 Narration   207

12　Cause and Effect Analysis　506

Thematic Contents

Places

Education

The World of Work

Contemporary Social Issues

Women and Men

The Minority Experience

Historical Perspectives

Health and Medicine

The Natural World

Machines and Technology

Life and Death

Language, Reading, and Writing

CHAPTER 1

Reading for Understanding and Meaning

Subjects/Strategies is a reader for writers. The selections in this book will entertain you, inform you, and even contribute to your self-awareness and understanding of the world around you. In addition, they will help you grasp and master nine versatile and widely used writing strategies: exemplification, description, narration, process analysis, comparison and contrast, division and classification, definition, cause and effect analysis, and argumentation. *Subjects/Strategies* devotes one chapter to each of these strategies. In each chapter, an introduction defines the strategy, illustrates it with examples, presents an annotated student essay using the strategy, and offers suggestions for using the strategy in your own writing. Each chapter then offers selections from professional writers, chosen because they serve as excellent models of the strategy in question.

Subjects/Strategies places equal emphasis on the content and form of a selection — that is, on what an essay has to say and on the strategy used to say it. All readers pay attention to content, to the substance of what an author is saying. Far fewer, however, notice the strategies authors use to organize their writing, to make it clear, logical, and effective. Yet using these strategies is an essential element of the writer's craft, one that writers must master to write well. Because these strategies are such a vital component of the writer's craft, you will need first to become more aware of them in your reading and then to master your use of them to become a better writer.

As the readings in this text demonstrate, content and form are unified in all good writing. Indeed, the two actually help determine one another. A writer who wants to relate the details of an event, to "tell what happened," for example, will naturally choose narration; at the same time, the requirements of the narrative form will influence the content of the written story. On the other hand, if the writer wants to examine *why* something happened, storytelling alone will not do the job. It will be necessary to use the strategy of cause and effect analysis, and this strategy will determine the ultimate content. As you write, you will often tentatively plan your strategy before you start, consciously deciding which strategy or which combination of strategies best fits what you have to say and what you want to accomplish with your writing. Sooner or later, you will have to look back at what you have written, making sure that your choice of strategy serves the purpose of your writing and that it expresses your content accurately and effectively.

One good way for you to become a stronger writer is to become a stronger, more active reader. By becoming more familiar with different types of writing, you will sharpen your critical thinking skills and learn how good writers make decisions in their writing. After reading an article or essay, most people feel more confident talking about the content of the piece than about the writer's style. Content is more tangible than style, which always seems so elusive. In large part, this discrepancy results from our schooling. Most of us have been taught to read for ideas. Not many of us, however, have been trained to read with a writer's eye, to ask why we like one piece of writing and not another. Likewise, most of us do not ask ourselves why one piece of writing is more believable or convincing than another. When you learn to read with a writer's eye, you begin to answer these important questions, and in the process, you come to appreciate the craftsmanship involved in writing — how a writer selects descriptive details, uses an unobtrusive organizational strategy, opts for fresh and lively language, chooses representative and persuasive examples, and emphasizes important points with sentence variety.

We have designed this text to help you improve your reading and writing skills. The two processes go hand in hand and should be studied that way because writing, after all, is the making of reading. The more sensitive you become to the content and style decisions made by the writers in this text, the more skilled you will be at making similar decisions in your own writing.

READING AS A WRITER

You read for many reasons and in many different ways. Whatever your reason and method, reading should be viewed as an interactive process between a reader and a text. Reading is most rewarding when you do it with an alert and inquiring mind, preferably with a pencil or pen in hand to make marginal notations of your reactions to the text as they occur. Reading analytically in this way will help you get more out of your reading because you will remember and understand what you read more fully. You will also be equipped to respond articulately to the ideas presented in a selection, offering interpretations and reactions supported by passages from the text itself.

Analytical reading will be useful to you in all aspects of life; research shows that it will help you succeed in school, excel in the workplace, and better interact with the world around you. Among all these positive outcomes, one of the greatest benefits of analytical reading is that it can help you become a better writer by making you more conscious of the craft of writing itself.

To read as a writer, you must be able to discover what is going on in an essay, to figure out the writer's reasons for shaping the essay in a particular way, and to decide whether the result works well or poorly — and why. At first, such digging may seem odd, and for good reason: Like writing itself, active reading is a skill that takes time to acquire. But it is a skill you will need if you are to understand the content of a piece of writing as well as the craft that shapes the writer's ideas into a presentable form. Active reading will repay your efforts by helping you read more effectively and write more persuasively.

Another important reason to master the skills of analytical reading is that, for everything you write, you will be your own first reader and critic. How well you are able to scrutinize your own drafts will powerfully affect how well you revise them, and revising well is crucial to writing well. So reading others' writings with a critical eye is useful and important practice; the more you read, the more practice you will have at sharpening your skills.

Getting the Most Out of Your Reading

Practice in analytical reading requires, first, that you commit time and effort. Second, you should try to take a positive interest in the act of reading, even if the subject matter is not immediately appealing. Remember, you are reading not for content alone, but also to understand the writer's methods — the kinds of decisions writers constantly make.

Here are some further tips to follow.

Read and Reread. Always read the selection at least twice, no matter how long it is. The first reading gives you a chance to get acquainted with the essay and to form your first impressions of it. The essay will offer you information, ideas, and arguments — some you may have expected, some you may not have expected. As you read, you will find yourself continually modifying your sense of the writer's purpose and strategy.

Your second reading should be quite different from the first. You will know what the essay is about, where it is going, and how it gets there; now you can relate the parts of the essay more accurately to the whole. Use your second reading to test your first impressions against the words on the page, developing and deepening your sense of how the essay is written, and how well. Because you now have a general understanding of the essay, you can pay special attention to the author's purpose and means of achieving that purpose. You can look for features of organization and style that you can learn from and adapt to your own work.

Ask Yourself Questions. As you probe the essay, focus your attention by asking yourself some basic questions about its content and its form. Here are some questions you may find useful.

▶ *Questions to Ask Yourself as You Read*

1. What does the writer want to say? What is the writer's main point or thesis?
2. Why does the writer want to make this point? What is the writer's purpose?
3. What strategy or strategies does the writer use? Where in the text are these strategies used?
4. How does the writer's strategy suit his or her subject and purpose?
5. What, if anything, is noteworthy about the writer's use of the strategy?
6. How effective is the essay? Does the writer make his or her points clear?

Each essay in *Subjects/Strategies* is followed by study questions similar to the ones suggested here, but more specific. These questions help you analyze both the content of the essay and the writer's craft. Answer them as fully as you can, using details from the selection to support your conclusions.

Annotate the Text. To retain a text's most salient points and your reactions to these ideas and how they are presented, you will need a quick way to record your responses as you proceed: annotation. When you annotate a text, you should do more than simply underline or high-light what you think are important points to remember. It is easy to underline so much that the notations become almost meaningless be-cause you forget why you underlined passages in the first place. Instead, as you read and ask yourself questions, write down your thoughts in the margins or on a separate piece of paper. Mark the se-lection's main point when you find it stated directly. Look for the strategy or strategies the author uses to develop that point, and jot the information down. If you disagree with a statement or a conclusion, object in the margin: "No!" If you feel skeptical, indicate that re-sponse: "Why?" or "Explain . . ." If you are impressed by an argument or a turn of phrase, compliment the author: "Good!" Place vertical lines or a star in the margin to indicate important points.

> ### ▶ How to Annotate a Text
>
> To keep a record of your responses as you read, you may want to mark the following elements as you go along:
> - Phrases summing up important ideas
> - Key terms
> - Central issues or themes
> - Unfamiliar words
> - Especially interesting, well-written passages
> - Questions you have about a point or passage
> - Your responses to a specific point or passage
> - Examples that support a main point
> - Phrases or passages that embody the writer's style
> - Unclear or ineffective phrases, passages, or examples

Jot down whatever marginal notes come naturally to you. Most students combine brief responses written in the margins with under-lining, circling, highlighting, stars, or question marks. Remember that there are no hard-and-fast rules for which elements you underline, circle, highlight, or star. Choose the methods of annotation that work best for you and that will make sense to you when you go back to rec-ollect your thoughts and responses to the essay. These quick, brief re-sponses will help you later when you begin asking and answering more specific and analytical questions.

When annotating a text, don't be timid. Mark up your book as much as you like, or jot down as many responses in your notebook as you think will be helpful. Don't let annotating become burdensome.

It should be an aid, not a chore; a word or phrase is usually as good as a sentence. You may, in fact, want to delay much of your annotating until a second reading so that your first reading can be fast and free, enabling you to concentrate on the larger issues.

An Example: Annotating Laurence Perrine's "Paradox"

The following brief selection is from Laurence Perrine's engaging text *Sound and Sense: An Introduction to Poetry*. First published in 1956, this book has introduced generations of high school and college students to the excitement and art of poetry. Notice how one of our students recorded her responses to Perrine's text with marginal annotations.

PARADOX

Example 1 — traveler's confusing behavior

Aesop tells the tale of a traveler who sought refuge with a Satyr on a bitter winter night. On entering the Satyr's lodging, he blew on his fingers, and was asked by the Satyr what he did it for. "To warm them up," he explained. Later, on being served with a piping hot bowl of porridge, he blew also on it, and again was asked what he did it for. "To cool it off," he explained. The Satyr thereupon thrust him out of doors, for he would have nothing to do with a man who could blow hot and cold with the same breath.

Definition of paradox

Example 2 — two types of paradox?

A (paradox) is an apparent contradiction that is nevertheless somehow true. It may be either a situation or a statement. Aesop's tale of the traveler illustrates a paradoxical situation. As a figure of speech, paradox is a statement. When Alexander Pope wrote that a literary critic of his time would "damn with faint praise," he was using a verbal paradox, for how can a man damn by praising?

Explains Aesop example 1

Explains Pope example 2

When we understand all the conditions and circumstances involved in a paradox, we find that what at first seemed impossible is actually entirely plausible and not strange at all. The paradox of the cold hands and hot porridge is not strange to a man who knows that a stream of air directed upon an object of different temperature will tend to bring that object closer to its own temperature. And Pope's paradox is not strange when we realize the *damn* is being used figuratively, and that Pope means only that a too reserved praise may damage an author with the public almost as much as adverse criticism. In a paradoxical statement the contradiction usually stems from one of the words being used figuratively or in more than one sense.

Main point

The value of paradox is its shock value. Its seeming impossibility startles the reader into attention and, thus, by the fact of its apparent absurdity, it underscores the truth of what is being said.

An Example: Reading Thomas Friedman's "My Favorite Teacher"

The following essay appeared in the *New York Times* on January 9, 2001. As you read this piece for the first time, try not to stop; take it all in as if in one breath. The second time, however, pause to annotate the text in any way you like, keeping in mind the six basic questions we mentioned earlier:

1. What does Friedman want to say?
2. Why does he want to make this point?
3. What strategy or strategies does Friedman use?
4. How does Friedman's strategy suit his subject and purpose?
5. What is noteworthy about Friedman's use of the strategy?
6. How effective is the essay? Why?

MY FAVORITE TEACHER

Last Sunday's *New York Times Magazine* published its annual review of people who died last year who left a particular mark on the world. I am sure all readers have their own such list. I certainly do. Indeed, someone who made the most important difference in my life died last year — my high school journalism teacher, Hattie M. Steinberg.

I grew up in a small suburb of Minneapolis, and Hattie was the legendary journalism teacher at St. Louis Park High School, Room 313. I took her intro to journalism course in 10th grade, back in 1969, and have never needed, or taken, another course in journalism since. She was that good.

Hattie was a woman who believed that the secret for success in life was getting the fundamentals right. And boy, she pounded the fundamentals of journalism into her students — not simply how to write a lead or accurately transcribe a quote, but, more important, how to comport yourself in a professional way and to always do quality work. To this day, when I forget to wear a tie on assignment, I think of Hattie scolding me. I once interviewed an ad exec for our high school paper who used a four-letter word. We debated whether to run it. Hattie ruled yes. That ad man almost lost his job when it appeared. She wanted to teach us about consequences.

Hattie was the toughest teacher I ever had. After you took her journalism course in 10th grade, you tried out for the paper, *The Echo*, which she supervised. Competition was fierce. In 11th grade, I didn't quite come up to her writing standards, so she made me business manager, selling ads to the local pizza parlors. That year, though, she let me write one story. It was about an Israeli general who had been a hero in the Six-Day War, who was giving a lecture at the University of Minnesota. I covered his lecture and interviewed him briefly. His name was Ariel Sharon. First story I ever got published.

Those of us on the paper, and the yearbook that she also supervised, lived in Hattie's classroom. We hung out there before and after school. Now, you have to understand, Hattie was a single woman, nearing 60 at the time, and this was the 1960's. She was the polar opposite of "cool," but we hung around her classroom like it was a malt shop and she was Wolfman Jack. None of us could have articulated it then, but it was because we enjoyed being harangued by her, disciplined by her and taught by her. She was a woman of clarity in an age of uncertainty.

We remained friends for 30 years, and she followed, bragged about and critiqued every twist in my career. After she died, her friends sent me a pile of my stories that she had saved over the years. Indeed, her students were her family — only closer. Judy Harrington, one of Hattie's former students, remarked about other friends who were on Hattie's newspapers and yearbooks: "We all graduated 41 years ago; and yet nearly each day in our lives something comes up — some mental image, some admonition that makes us think of Hattie."

Judy also told the story of one of Hattie's last birthday parties, when one man said he had to leave early to take his daughter somewhere. "Sit down," said Hattie. "You're not leaving yet. She can just be a little late."

That was my teacher! I sit up straight just thinkin' about her.

Among the fundamentals Hattie introduced me to was *The New York Times*. Every morning it was delivered to Room 313. I had never seen it before then. Real journalists, she taught us, start their day by reading *The Times* and columnists like Anthony Lewis and James Reston.

I have been thinking about Hattie a lot this year, not just because she died on July 31, but because the lessons she imparted seem so relevant now. We've just gone through this huge dot-com-Internet-globalization bubble — during which a lot of smart people got carried away and forgot the fundamentals of how you build a profitable company, a lasting portfolio, a nation state or a thriving student. It turns out that the real secret of success in the information age is what it always was: fundamentals — reading, writing and arithmetic, church, synagogue and mosque, the rule of law and good governance.

The Internet can make you smarter, but it can't make you smart. It can extend your reach, but it will never tell you what to say at a P.T.A. meeting. These fundamentals cannot be downloaded. You can only upload them, the old-fashioned way, one by one, in places like Room 313 at St. Louis Park High. I only regret that I didn't write this column when the woman who taught me all that was still alive.

Once you have read and reread Friedman's essay, write your own answers to the six basic questions listed earlier. Then compare your answers with the set of answers that follows.

1. *What does Friedman want to say?*

Friedman wants to tell his readers about his high school journalism teacher, Hattie M. Steinberg, because she was "someone who made the most important difference in my life" (paragraph 1). His main point seems to be that "Hattie was a woman who believed that the secret for success in life was getting the fundamentals right" (3). Friedman himself believes that "the real secret of success in the information age is what it always was: fundamentals" (10).

2. *Why does he want to make this point?*

Friedman's purpose is to recognize Hattie Steinberg, his former journalism teacher, and to explain the importance of the fundamentals that she taught him more than thirty years ago. He wants his readers to appreciate the examples of fundamentals offered by his journalism teacher and to realize that there are no shortcuts or quick fixes on the road to success. Without the fundamentals, success often eludes people.

3. *What strategy or strategies does Friedman use?*

Overall, Friedman uses the strategy of exemplification. Hattie M. Steinberg is offered up as a well-developed example of Friedman's favorite teacher. Friedman fleshes out his example of Steinberg with specific examples of the fundamentals she instilled in her students (paragraphs 3 and 9). Friedman uses description and narration as well to develop his profile of Hattie Steinberg. We learn that she was Friedman's "toughest teacher" (4), that she was "a single woman, nearing 60 at the time," that she was "the polar opposite of 'cool,'" and that she was "a woman of clarity in an age of uncertainty" (5). Finally, Friedman's brief narratives about his interview of an advertising executive, his interview of Ariel Sharon, hanging out in Steinberg's classroom, and one of the teacher's last birthday parties give readers insight into her personality by showing us what she was like instead of simply telling us.

4. *How does Friedman's strategy suit his subject and purpose?*

Friedman selects exemplification as a strategy because his purpose is to explain why — out of all the teachers that he has had — Hattie M. Steinberg is his favorite, the one who has had the greatest impact on his life. Friedman knew that he was not telling Steinberg's story, a narration, so much as he was showing what a great teacher she was.

Friedman's examples of Steinberg in action in her classroom and of the fundamentals she insisted her students learn make her come alive for readers and illustrate the life-shaping impact she had on them.

5. *What is noteworthy about Friedman's use of the strategy?*

In developing his portrait of Hattie M. Steinberg, Friedman relies on the fundamentals of good journalism. He selects brief examples that give us insight into Steinberg's character and personality. When taken collectively, these examples create a poignant picture of this unforgettable teacher. One would have to think that Steinberg herself would have been proud to see how her former student demonstrates his journalistic skills in paying tribute to the woman who taught him his craft so long ago.

6. *How effective is the essay? Why?*

Friedman's essay is effective because it serves his purpose extremely well. He helps his readers visualize Hattie M. Steinberg and understand the gifts that she gave to each of her journalism students. In his concluding two paragraphs, Friedman shows us that Steinberg's message is as relevant today as it was more than thirty years ago in St. Louis Park High School, Room 313.

USING READING IN THE WRITING PROCESS

What does reading have to do with your own writing? Analytical reading is not simply an end in itself; it is also a means to help you become a better writer. At the simplest level, reading stimulates your thinking, providing you with information and ideas to enliven your writing and subjects to write about. In fact, you might be surprised at how your reading can show itself in your writing. In a more subtle way, analytical reading can increase your awareness of how others' writing affects you, and thus can make you more sensitive to how your own writing will affect your readers. If you've ever been impressed by an author who uses convincing supporting evidence to document each of his or her claims, you might be more likely to back up your own claims carefully. If you've been impressed by an apt turn of phrase or been absorbed by a new idea, you may be less inclined to feed your readers clichés and platitudes. Gradually, you will discover yourself becoming more sensitive to how readers will be likely to respond to your ideas and your style of conveying them.

More to the point, however, analytical reading of the kind you'll be encouraged to do in this text will help you master important strategies of thinking and writing that you can use very specifically throughout the writing process. During the early stages of writing, you will need to focus on the large issues of choosing a subject, gathering information, planning a strategy suited to your purpose, and organizing your ideas. As you move from a first draft through revisions, your concerns will become more focused, and you will concentrate on making your writing clearer and more polished. In conference with your instructor, you may discover a faulty beginning or ending, or realize that your tone is inappropriate, or see that the various parts of your essay are not quite connected, or notice awkward repetitions in your choice of words and phrases. Analytical reading can lead you to solutions for such problems at every stage of the writing process: prewriting, writing a draft, and revising.

CHAPTER 2

Writing Essays

There is nothing mysterious or difficult about the nine rhetorical strategies discussed in this book. You're probably familiar with some of them already. When you want to tell a story, for example, you naturally use the strategy of narration. When you want to make a choice, you naturally compare and contrast the things you must choose between. When you want to explain how to make a pizza, you fall automatically into the strategy of process analysis. These and other strategies are ways we think about the world and our experiences in it. What might make these strategies seem unfamiliar, especially in writing, is that most people use them more or less intuitively, with little awareness of their use. Sophisticated thinking and writing do not come from simply using these structures — everyone does that — but from using them consciously and purposefully.

Writing strategies, however, are not like blueprints or plaster molds that determine in advance exactly how the final product will be shaped. Good essays usually employ components of more than one strategy, and the options for how to use them effectively are numerous. Rather, these strategies are flexible and versatile, with only a few fundamental rules or directions to define their shape — like the rules for basketball, chess, or other strategic games. Such directions leave plenty of room for all the imagination and variety you can put into your writing and for all the many things you may want to write about. In addition, because these strategies are fundamental ways of thinking, they will help you in all stages of the writing process — from prewriting and writing a first draft through revising and editing your piece.

THE WRITING PROCESS

Prewriting

Writers rarely rely on inspiration to produce an effective piece of writing. Good writers plan or prewrite, write, revise and edit, and proofread. It is worth remembering, however, that the writing process is rarely as simple and as straightforward as this. Often the process is recursive, moving back and forth among the four stages. Moreover, writing is personal — no two people go about it exactly the same way. Still, it is possible to describe the steps in the writing process and thereby have a reassuring and reliable method for undertaking a writing task and a good composition.

Your reading can give you ideas and information, of course. But reading also helps expand your knowledge of the writing strategies available to you, and consequently, it can help direct all your prewriting activities. In *prewriting*, you select your subject and topic, gather ideas and information, and determine the thesis, strategy, and organization you will use. Once you've worked through the prewriting process, you will be ready to start on your first draft. Let's explore how this works.

Understand Your Assignment. When you first receive an assignment, read it over several times to be sure you understand what you are being asked to do. For example, consider each of the following assignments:

- Tell about an experience that led you to a new understanding of relationships.
- Discuss the concept of supply and demand in the marketplace.
- Leading environmentalists agree that effective recycling efforts must be both economically and environmentally sustainable. Write an essay in which you analyze the prospects for recycling Styrofoam products.

The first assignment asks you to identify an experience that gave you some insight into human relationships and to narrate that experience. You might choose simply to narrate the experience, or you might choose to analyze it; in either case, you would have to explain to your reader what new understanding you gained. In the second assignment, you would need to define or explain exactly what is meant by supply and demand and then give several examples of how this concept applies to the marketplace. Finally, the third assignment asks you to do a number of things. First, you would need to define the concepts of economic and environmental sustainability. Second, you would probably research and explore the pros and cons of recycling Styrofoam products. Third, based on your understanding of sustainability as well as the issues involved with recycling Styrofoam, you need to speculate on the chances for setting up successful Styrofoam recycling programs.

If, after rereading the assignment several times, you are still unsure about what is being asked of you or of any additional requirements of the assignment, such as length or format, be sure to consult with your instructor. He or she should be willing to clear up any confusion before you start writing.

Determine Your Purpose. All effective writing is written with a purpose. Good writing seeks to accomplish any one of three purposes:

- To express thoughts and feelings about life experiences
- To inform readers by explaining something about the world around them
- To persuade readers to adopt some belief or action

Your purpose will often determine which strategy you choose to employ in your writing. For example, if you wish to express thoughts and feelings, a personal narrative is appropriate. If, on the other hand, you wish to persuade your readers to adopt a certain belief, you will probably choose to write an argument.

In *expressive writing*, or writing from experience, you put your thoughts and feelings before all other concerns. When Annie Dillard reacts to being caught throwing a snowball at a car (Chapter 7), when Malcolm X shows his frustration at not having appropriate language to express himself (Chapter 7), and when Edward Abbey describes a hike in Aravaipa Canyon with two friends (Chapter 6), each one is writing from experience. In each case, the writer has clarified an important life experience and has conveyed what he or she learned from it.

Informative writing focuses on telling the reader something about the outside world. In informative writing, you report, explain, analyze, define, classify, compare, describe a process, or examine causes and effects. When Kennedy P. Maize explains what happens when the residents of Kern County declare war on the mouse population (Chapter 12) and when Deborah Tannen discusses examples of orders given and received in the workplace (Chapter 5), each one is writing to inform.

Argumentative writing seeks to influence readers' thinking and attitudes toward a subject or issue and in some cases to move them to a particular course of action. Such persuasive writing uses logical reasoning, authoritative evidence, and testimony and sometimes includes emotionally charged language and examples. In selections reprinted in this book, Richard Lederer uses numerous examples to show us the power of short words (Chapter 13), and Barbara Hattemer uses evidence to link media violence and violent behavior by our youth (Chapter 13).

Find a Subject Area and Topic. Although you will usually be given specific assignments in your writing course, you may sometimes be given the freedom to choose your subject matter and topic. In either case, when selecting your specific topic you should determine whether you know something about it and also whether it interests you.

When your instructor leaves you free to choose your own topic, begin by determining a broad subject that you like to think about and might enjoy writing about — a general subject like virtual reality, biomedical ethics, amateur sports, or foreign travel. Something you've recently read — one of the essays in *Subjects/Strategies,* for example — may help bring particular subjects to mind. You might consider a subject related to your career ambitions — perhaps business, journalism, law, medicine, architecture, or computer programming. Another option is to list some subjects you enjoy discussing with friends: food, motorcycles, television programs, or politics. Select several likely subjects, and let your mind explore their potential for interesting topics. Your goal is to arrive at an appropriately limited topic.

Suppose, for example, you select as possible subject areas journalism, foreign travel, and television programs. You could develop the following focused topics:

General Subject Area	Limited Topic	More Limited Topic
Journalism	Investigative reporting	Protecting sources
Foreign travel	Study-abroad programs	Learning language by immersion
Television programs	Sitcoms	Comic devices on *Will & Grace*

Know Your Audience. The best writers always keep their audience in mind. Once they have decided upon a purpose and a topic, writers present their material in a way that empathizes with their readers, addresses their difficulties and concerns, and appeals to their rational and emotional faculties. Based on knowledge of their audience, writers make conscious decisions on content, sentence structure, and word choice.

An audience might be an individual (a parent), a group (the students in your class), a specialized group (heart surgeons), or a general readership (readers of your local newspaper). To help identify your audience, ask yourself the following questions:

- Who are my readers?
- Are they a specialized or a general group?
- What do I know about my audience's age, gender, education, religious affiliation, economic status, and political attitudes?
- What does my audience know about my subject? Are they experts or novices?
- What does my audience need to know that I can tell them?
- Will my audience be interested, open-minded, resistant, or hostile to what I have to say?
- Do I need to explain any specialized language so that my audience can understand my subject? Is there any language that I should avoid?
- What do I want my audience to do as a result of reading this piece?

Keep a Journal. Many writers keep a journal in which they record thoughts and observations that might be mined for future writing projects. They've learned not to rely on their memories to retain ideas, facts, and statistics they have heard or read about. Writers also use journals to keep all kinds of lists: lists of questions they would like answers to; lists of issues that concern them; lists of topics that they would like to write about someday.

Journals are also a great place to do *freewriting* — to run with an idea and to see where it leads. Writers often use these freewriting sessions — five to ten minutes of uninterrupted writing — to discover new materials, new strategies, and, perhaps most important, new topics. By writing about a topic before you have done any reading or research, not only will you discover what you already know about the topic, but you will find out what you think and how you feel about it. For each professional selection in *Subjects/Strategies,* we have provided a Before You Read question that offers you an opportunity to do some journal writing before you read the selection. After you have read a selection, it is a good practice to reflect in writing on what the author has said; to this end we provide a Responding to Reading question immediately after each professional selection.

Brainstorm for New Material. Another good way to generate ideas and information about your topic is to *brainstorm.* Simply list everything you know about your topic, freely associating one idea with another. At this point, order is not important. Let your mind range widely over the topic. Try to capture everything that comes to mind because you never know what might prove valuable later. Write quickly, but if you get stalled, reread what you have written; doing so will jog your mind in new directions. Keep your list handy so that you can add to it over the course of several days. Here, for example, is a student's brainstorming list on why Martin Luther King Jr.'s "I Have a Dream" speech (page 602) is enduring:

WHY "I HAVE A DREAM" IS MEMORABLE

- Civil rights demonstration in Washington, D.C.
- Delivered on the steps of Lincoln Memorial
- Repetition of "I have a dream"
- Allusions to the Bible, spirituals
- "Bad check" metaphor
- Other memorable figures of speech
- Crowd of more than 200,000 people
- Echoes other great American writings — Declaration of Independence and Gettysburg Address
- Refers to various parts of the country
- Embraces all races and religions
- Sermon format
- Displays energy and passion

Generate Ideas Using Rhetorical Strategies. Even the most experienced writers need to generate ideas and to find information to use in their writing. Use the rhetorical strategies to get your mind working, to make associations, and to discover meaningful things to say about your topic. Remember that writing strategies are more than techniques for composition; they are basic ways of thinking.

Suppose that you like to watch television news programs and you think you would like to write about some aspect of TV news. First, you might use the strategy of *division* to identify the most common genres, or types, of news programs.

Network evening news shows
Network morning news shows
Headline news shows
Newsmagazines
News talk shows
News interview shows
Tabloid news shows

To get to the next level of specificity about your subject, you might want to use the strategy of *classification* and supply examples for each of your established categories.

> Network evening news shows: *CBS Evening News, NBC Nightly News, ABC World News Tonight*
>
> Network morning news shows: *Early Show, Today, Good Morning America*
>
> Headline news shows: *CNN Headline News*
>
> Newsmagazines: *20/20, 60 Minutes, 48 Hours, Nightline*
>
> News talk shows: *NewsHour with Jim Lehrer, Crossfire, Hardball with Chris Matthews*
>
> News interview shows: *Meet the Press, Larry King Live*
>
> Tabloid news shows: *Entertainment Tonight, Inside Edition, Hard Copy*

With these examples clearly in mind, the next step would be to describe a typical program for each of your categories, trying to capture specific representative details of each category.

> *CBS Evening News:* Major network news program anchored by a well-known and respected reporter. Relies on a broad range of reports from around the world on news items and subjects of interest to the general public. Is broadcast once a day and is supported by commercials.
>
> *Today*: Latest overnight news roundup, weather, sports, interviews with major newsmakers, and human interest features. Is interrupted periodically by local updates.
>
> *CNN Headline News:* Capsule summaries of international, national, financial, sports, and entertainment news delivered at pre-set intervals each half-hour — 24 hours a day, every day.
>
> *60 Minutes*: Presents three in-depth stories based on investigative reporting. Usually includes a ten-minute commentary by Andy Rooney.
>
> *NewsHour with Jim Lehrer*: Focused and in-depth news analysis with a reserved and quiet tone. Not commercially supported.
>
> *Larry King Live*: Interview program with major personalities and newsmakers. Noted for being a great interviewer, King also tends to be somewhat sensational and controversial.
>
> *Entertainment Tonight*: Developing and breaking news stories in the entertainment world, very often characterized by up-to-the-minute reports. Borders on the gossipy.

Other strategies you might choose include *comparison and contrast,* showing the relative amounts of hard and soft news on each type of program; *definition,* defining the niche, vision, and purpose of each type of show; and *cause and effect,* analyzing the effects of various types of program formats on viewing audiences.

Of course, when you write your essay, you probably won't use all the material you gather, and you won't necessarily organize your writing using the same strategies that helped you find your ideas. At this stage, your goal should be to search your memory for material. After choosing a subject and topic and generating ideas and information, you are ready to make connections within the material you have collected and to organize your thoughts.

Formulate a Thesis Statement. You should now be ready to commit to a controlling idea, a *thesis.* The thesis of an essay is its main idea, the point the writer is trying to make. The thesis is often expressed in one or two sentences called a *thesis statement.* Here's an example.

> The so-called serious news programs are becoming too much like tabloid news shows in both their content and their presentation.

The thesis statement should not be confused with your purpose for writing. While a thesis statement makes an assertion about your topic and actually appears in your essay as such, your purpose is what you are trying to do in the paper — to express, to explain, or to argue — and should not be stated explicitly. For example, the purpose behind the preceding thesis statement might be expressed as follows.

> By comparing the transcripts of news shows like *The CBS Evening News* and tabloid shows like *Entertainment Tonight,* I will show alarming parallels in what the two genres of programs find "newsworthy."

Again, this type of purpose statement should not appear in your essay.
A thesis statement should be

- The most important point you make about your topic
- More general than the ideas and facts used to support it
- Focused enough to be covered in the space allotted for the essay

A thesis statement should not be a question but an assertion. If you find yourself writing a question for a thesis statement, answer the question first, and then write your statement.

An effective strategy for developing a thesis statement is to begin by writing, "What I want to say is that . . ."

> *What I want to say is that* unless language barriers between patients and health care providers are bridged, many patients' lives in our most culturally diverse cities will be endangered.

Later, you can delete the formulaic opening, and you will be left with a thesis statement.

> Unless language barriers between patients and health care providers are bridged, many patients' lives in our most culturally diverse cities will be endangered.

A good way to determine whether your thesis is too general or too specific is to think hard about how easy it will be to present information and examples to support it. If you stray too far in either direction, your task will become much more difficult. A thesis statement that is too general will leave you overwhelmed by the number of issues you must address. For example, the statement "Malls have ruined the fabric of American life" would lead to the question "How?" To answer it, you would probably have to include information about traffic patterns, urban decay, environmental damage, economic studies, and so on. You would obviously have to take shortcuts, and your paper would be ineffective. On the other hand, too specific a thesis statement will leave you with too little information to present. "The Big City Mall should not have been built because it reduced retail sales at existing Big City stores by 21.4%" does not leave you with any opportunity to develop an argument.

▶ *Will Your Thesis Hold Water?*

Once you have a possible thesis statement in mind for an essay, ask yourself the following questions:

- Does my thesis statement take a clear stance on an issue? If so, what is that stance?
- Is my thesis too general?
- Is my thesis too specific?
- Does my thesis apply to a larger audience than myself? If so, what is the audience, and how does the thesis apply?

The thesis statement is usually set forth near the beginning of the essay, although writers sometimes first offer a few sentences that establish a context for the piece. One common strategy is to position the thesis statement as the final sentence of the first paragraph. In the opening paragraph of an essay on the harmful effects of quick weight-loss diets, student Marcie Turple builds a context for her thesis statement, which she presents in her last sentence:

> Americans are obsessed with thinness--even at the risk of dying. In the 1930s, people took dinitrophenol, an industrial poison, to lose weight. It boosted metabolism but caused blindness and some deaths. Since then dieters have used thyroid hormone injections, amphetamines, liquid protein diets, and, most recently, the controversial fen-phen. What most dieters need to realize is that there is no magic way to lose weight--no pill, no crash diet plan. *The only way to permanent weight loss is through sensible eating and exercise.*

Determine Your Strategy. Once you decide what you want to write about and you come up with some ideas about what you might like to say, your next task is to jot down the main ideas for your essay in an order that seems both natural and logical to you. In other words, make a scratch outline. In constructing this outline, you might discover that one of the rhetorical strategies will help you approach your topic. If a particular strategy was especially helpful to you in generating ideas, you might consider using that as your overall organizing principle.

If you're still undecided about what strategy to use for your essay, try the following steps:

1. Summarize the point you want to make in a single phrase or sentence.
2. Restate the point as a question — in effect, the question your essay will answer.
3. Look closely at both the summary and the question for key words or concepts that go with a particular strategy.
4. Consider other strategies that would support your primary strategy.

Here are some examples:

SUMMARY: Michael Jordan was — and still is — the best player in basketball history.

QUESTION: How did Michael Jordan compare with other basketball players?

STRATEGY: Comparison and contrast. The writer must compare Jordan with other players and provide evidence to support the claim that Jordan was — and still is — "the best," even years after his initial retirement from basketball.

SUPPORTING STRATEGIES: Exemplification and description. Good evidence includes statistics, examples, and descriptions of Jordan's, and others', athletic feats.

SUMMARY: How to make chili.

QUESTION: How do you make chili?

STRATEGY: Process analysis. The word *how*, especially in the phrase *how to*, implies a procedure that can be explained in steps or stages.

SUPPORTING STRATEGY: Description. It is necessary to describe the dish at some points in the process — its taste, smell, texture, and appearance.

SUMMARY: The El Niño phenomenon has changed global weather patterns and has affected the safety of people around the world.

QUESTION: What are the effects of the El Niño phenomenon?

STRATEGY: Cause and effect. The word *what* asks for a listing of the effects.

SUPPORTING STRATEGY: Exemplification. The best presentation of effects is through vivid examples.

SUMMARY: Petroleum and natural gas prices should be federally controlled.

QUESTION: What should be done about petroleum and natural gas prices?

STRATEGY: Argument or persuasion. The word *should* signals an argument, calling for evidence and reasoning in support of the conclusion.

SUPPORTING STRATEGIES: Comparison and contrast and cause and effect analysis. Evidence comes from a comparison of federally controlled pricing with deregulated pricing as well as from a discussion of the effects of deregulation.

These are just a few examples of how to decide on a writing strategy and supporting strategies that are suitable for your topic and what you want to say about it. In every case, your reading can guide you in recognizing the best plan to follow. In the next chapter, you will learn more about combining strategies.

Organize Your Paper. Before you start a draft, it's a good idea to orga-nize your material according to the strategy you will use — that is, to create a working plan. Different strategies, of course, will suggest dif-ferent kinds of working plans. A process analysis essay, in which you provide directions for someone to follow, for example, might be mapped out in this way:

Step 1: _____

Step 2: _____

Step 3: _____

Step 4: _____

A working plan for an essay using comparison and contrast, however, would look quite different — perhaps like this:

Object A	**Object B**
Point 1: _____	Point 1: _____
Point 2: _____	Point 2: _____
Point 3: _____	Point 3: _____
Point 4: _____	Point 4: _____

A working plan for an argumentative essay might look like this:

Point to be proved: _____

Supporting arguments:

1. _____

2. _____

3. _____

Opposing argument(s):_____

Rebuttal:_____

Final argument: _____

A working plan is similar to a scratch outline; it is determined, however, much more specifically by the requirements of a particular writing strategy. You have a great deal of flexibility in determining your working plan's format. The models provided here are only sug-gestions. Your reading will help you understand the kinds of modifica-tions that are acceptable and useful for a given strategy.

Writing Your First Draft

First drafts are exploratory and sometimes unpredictable. While writing your first draft, you may find yourself getting away from your original plan. What started as a definition essay may develop into a process analysis or an effort at argumentation. For example, a definition of "school spirit" could turn into a process analysis of how a pep rally is organized or an argument about why school spirit is important (or detrimental). A definition of "manners" could become an instructive process analysis on how to be a good host, or it could turn into an argument that respect is based on the ways people treat one another. A definition of "democracy" could evolve into a process analysis of how democracy works in the United States or into an argument for democratic forms of government. If your draft is leaning toward another strategy, don't force yourself to revert to your original plan. Allow your inspiration to take you where it will. Later, when you finish your draft, you can see whether the new strategy works better than the old one or whether it would be best to go back to your initial strategy. Use your first draft to explore your ideas; you will always have a chance to revise later.

It may also happen that while writing your first draft, you run into a difficulty that prevents you from moving forward. For example, suppose you want to tell the story of something that happened to you, but you aren't certain whether you should be using the pronoun *I* so often. If you turn to the essays in Chapter 7 to see how authors of narrative essays handle this problem, you will find that it isn't necessarily a problem at all. For an account of a personal experience, it's perfectly acceptable to write *I* as often as you need to. Or suppose that after writing several pages describing someone you think is quite a character, you find that your draft seems flat and doesn't express how lively and funny your friend really is. If you read the introduction to Chapter 6, you will be told that descriptions need lots of factual, concrete detail, and the selections in that chapter give further proof of this. You suddenly realize that just such detail is what's missing from your draft. Reading, then, is helpful because it enables you to see how other writers successfully dealt with problems similar to yours.

If you do run into difficulties writing your first draft, don't worry or get upset. Even experienced writers run into problems at the beginning. Just try to keep going and take pressure off yourself. Think about your topic, and consider your details and what you want to say. You might even want to go back and look over the ideas and information you've gathered.

Revising

Once you have completed your first draft, you are ready for revision. During the revision stage of the writing process, you will focus on the large issues of thesis, purpose, content, organization, and paragraph structure to make sure that your writing says what you want it to say. But first, it is crucial that you set your draft aside and give yourself a rest. Then you can come back to it with some freshness and objectivity. When you do, resist the temptation to plunge immediately into a second draft. Scattered changes will not necessarily improve the piece. Try to look at your writing as a whole and to tackle your writing problems systematically. Use the following guidelines.

- Triple-space your draft so that you can make changes more easily.
- Make revisions on a hard copy of your paper.
- Read your paper aloud, listening for parts that do not make sense.
- Review your essay using the six basic questions for analyzing other people's essays (see Chapter 1, page 4).
- Have a fellow student read your essay and critique it.

When you work with other students on critiquing papers — yours or theirs — it is important to do so in ways that maximize the effectiveness and efficiency of the exercise. Whether you are revising your own paper or someone else's, the tips outlined in the box on page 26 will help you get the most out of peer critiques.

One way to begin the revision process is to make an informal outline of your first draft — not as you planned it, but as it actually came out. What does your outline tell you about the strategy you used? Does this strategy suit your purpose? Perhaps you meant to compare your two grandmothers, but you have not clearly shown their similarities and differences. Consequently, your draft is not one unified comparison and contrast essay but two descriptive essays spliced together. Or perhaps your outline will show you that you set out to write about your grandmothers, but you never had a definite purpose in mind. Outlining your rough draft helps you see that, despite some differences in looks and habits, both grandmothers are essentially alike in all the ways that matter. This gives you both a point to make and a strategy for making it: comparison and contrast.

Even if you are satisfied with the overall strategy of your draft, an outline can still help you make improvements. Perhaps your directions for preparing a pizza leave out an important step in the process — adding oregano to the tomato sauce, for example. Or perhaps your classification essay on types of college students is confusing because you create overlapping categories: computer science majors, athletes, and foreign students (a computer science major could, of course, be an athlete, a foreign student, or both). You may uncover a flaw in your organization, such as a lack of logic in an argument or a parallelism in a

▶ *A Brief Guide to Peer Critiquing*

When critiquing someone else's paper:

- Read the essay carefully. Read it to yourself first, and then, if possible, have the writer read it to you at the beginning of the session. Some flaws become obvious when read aloud.
- Ask the writer to state his or her purpose for writing and to identify the thesis statement within the paper itself.
- Be positive, but be honest. Never denigrate the paper's content or the writer's effort, but do your best to identify how the writer can improve the paper through revision.
- Try to address the most important issues first. Think about the thesis and the organization of the paper before moving on to more specific topics like word choice.
- Do not be dismissive, and do not dictate changes. Ask questions that encourage the writer to reconsider parts of the paper that you find confusing or ineffective.

When someone critiques your work:

- Give your reviewer a copy of your paper before your meeting.
- Listen carefully to your reviewer, and try not to discuss or argue each issue. Record comments, and evaluate them later.
- Do not get defensive or explain what you wanted to say if the reviewer misunderstands what you meant. Try to understand the reviewer's point of view, and learn what you need to revise to clear up the misunderstanding.
- Consider every suggestion, but only use the ones that make sense to you in your revision.
- Be sure to thank your reviewer for his or her effort on your behalf.

comparison and contrast. Now is the time to discover these problems and to fix them.

Another method you can use in revising is to start with large-scale issues, such as your overall structure, and then concentrate on finer and finer points. As you examine your essay, ask yourself questions about what you have written. The following list of questions addresses the large elements of your essay: thesis, purpose, organization, paragraphs, and evidence.

- Have I focused my topic?
- Does my thesis statement identify my topic and make an assertion about it?
- Is my organization pattern the best one, given my purpose?
- Are my paragraphs adequately developed, and does each support my thesis?
- Have I accomplished my purpose?
- How effective is my beginning? My ending?
- Do I have a good title?

Having addressed these questions, you might consider constructing a formal outline of your paper, one that reflects all the changes you want to make and the anticipated organization of the finished piece. At the beginning of this outline, include your title, a brief statement of your purpose, and your thesis statement. As a general rule, it is advisable to write in complete sentences unless your meaning is immediately clear from a phrase. If you wish to divide any of your main categories into subcategories, make sure that you have at least two subcategories; if not, a division is not necessary. Finally, you should observe the conventions of formal outlining. Notice how each new level of specificity in the pattern below is given a new letter or number designation.

Title: _____

Purpose: _____

Thesis: _____

  I. _____

    A. _____

    B. _____

      1. _____

      2. _____

    C. _____

  II. _____

    A. _____

      1. _____

        a. _____

        b. _____

      2. _____

    B. _____

  III. _____

Once you have addressed the major problems in your essay by writing a second draft, you should be ready to turn your attention to the finer elements of sentence structure, word choice, and usage. The following questions focus on these concerns.

- Do my sentences convey my thoughts clearly, and do they emphasize the most important parts of my thinking?
- Are my sentences stylistically varied?
- Is my diction fresh and forceful, or is my writing weighed down by unnecessary wordiness?
- Have I committed any errors of usage?

Finally, if you find yourself dissatisfied with specific elements of your draft, look at several essays in *Subjects/Strategies* to see how other writers have dealt with the particular situation you are confronting. For example, if you don't like the way the essay starts, find some

---

▶ *Notes on Beginnings and Endings*

Beginnings and endings are very important to the effectiveness of an essay, but they can be daunting to write. Inexperienced writers often feel they must write their essays sequentially when, in fact, it is usually better to write both the beginning and the ending after you have completed most or all of the rest of your paper. Once you see how your essay develops, you will know better how to catch your reader's attention and introduce the rest of the paper. Particular attention should be paid to both parts during the revision process. Ask yourself:

- Does my introduction grab the reader's attention?
- Is my introduction confusing in any way? How well does it relate to the rest of the essay?
- If I state my thesis in the introduction, how effectively is it presented?
- Does my essay come to a logical conclusion or does it seem to just stop?
- How well does the conclusion relate to the rest of the essay? Am I careful not to introduce new topics or issues that I did not address in the essay?
- Does my conclusion help to underscore or illuminate important aspects of the body of the essay, or is it redundant, a mechanical rehashing of what I wrote earlier?

beginnings you think are particularly effective. If your paragraphs don't seem to flow into one another, examine how various writers use transitions. If an example seems unconvincing, examine the way other writers include details, anecdotes, and facts and statistics to strengthen their illustrations. Remember that the readings in this text are here as a resource for you as you write.

Editing and Proofreading

Now that you have made your essay "right," it is time to think about making it "correct." During the *editing* stage of the writing process, you check your writing for errors in grammar, punctuation, capitalization, spelling, and manuscript format. The questions in the following box will guide you in the editing of your essay. Both your dictionary and your college handbook will help you in answering specific editing questions about your paper.

▶ *Addressing Common Writing Problems and Errors*

- Do my verbs agree in number with their antecedents?
- Do my pronouns have clear antecedents — that is, do they clearly refer to specific nouns earlier in my sentences?
- Do I have any sentence fragments, comma splices, or run-on sentences?
- Have I made any unnecessary shifts in person, tense, or number?
- Have I used the comma properly in all instances?
- Have I checked for misspellings, mistakes in capitalization, and typos?
- Have I inadvertently confused words like *their, they're,* and *there* or *it's* and *its*?
- Have I followed the prescribed guidelines for formatting my manuscript?

Having revised and edited your essay, you are ready to print out your final copy. Always proofread your work before submitting it to your instructor. Even though you may have used your computer's spell-check, you might find that you have typed *worm* instead of *word* or *form* instead of *from*. Check also to be sure that your essay is properly line-spaced and that the text is legible.

WRITING AN EXPOSITORY ESSAY: A STUDENT ESSAY IN PROGRESS

When he was a first-year student at the University of Vermont, Keith Eldred was asked to write an essay using the strategy of definition; he was able to choose whatever topic he wished. Eldred began by reading the entire chapter on definition in an earlier edition of this text. He had recently been introduced to the Hindu concept of the mantra, and he decided that he would like to explore this concept as it pertained to the secular world. Having made this decision, he began to generate some notes that would help him get started. These notes provided him with several examples of what he intended to call "secular mantras"; a dictionary definition of the word *mantra*; and the idea that a good starting point for his rough draft might be the story of "The Little Engine That Could." Here are the notes he jotted down.

> *Mantra:* "a mystical formula of invocation or incantation" (*Webster's*)
>
> Counting to ten when angry
>
> "Little Engine That Could" (possible beginning)
>
> "Let's Go Bulls" → action because crowd wants players to say it to themselves
>
> Swearing (not always a mantra)
>
> Tennis star — "Get serious!"
>
> "Come on, come on" (at traffic light)
>
> "Geronimo" "Ouch!"
>
> Hindu mythology

After mulling over his list, Eldred began to organize his ideas with the following scratch outline:

1. Begin with story of "Little Engine That Could"
2. Talk about the magic of secular mantras
3. Dictionary definition and Hindu connections
4. Examples of individuals using mantras
5. Crowd chants as mantras — Bulls
6. Conclusion — talk about how you can't get through the day without using mantras

Based on this outline, as well as on what he had learned through his reading about definition as a writing strategy, Eldred came up with the following rough draft.

Secular Mantras: Magic Words
Keith Eldred

Remember "The Little Engine That Could"? That's the   1
story about the tiny locomotive that pulled the train
over the mountain when the big locomotives wouldn't. Remember how the Little Engine strained and chugged, "I
think I can -- I think I can -- I think I can" until she
reached the top of the mountain? That's a perfect example
of a secular mantra in action.

A secular mantra (pronounced man-truh) is any word   2
or group of words that helps a person use his or her energy. The key word here is "helps" -- repeating a secular
mantra doesn't <u>create</u> energy; it just makes it easier to
channel a given amount. The Little Engine, for instance,
obviously had the strength to pull the train up the mountain; apparently, she could have done it without saying a
word. But we all know she wouldn't have been able to, any
more than any one of us would be able to sky-dive the
first time without yelling "Geronimo" or not exclaim
"Ouch" if we touched a hot stove. Some words and phrases
simply have a certain magic that makes a job easier or
that makes us feel better when we repeat them. These are
secular mantras.

It is because of their magical quality that these   3
expressions are called "secular mantras" in the first
place. A mantra (Sanskrit for "sacred counsel") is "a
mystical formula of invocation or incantation" used in
Hinduism (Webster's). According to Hindu mythology, Manu,
lawgiver and progenitor of humankind, created the first
language by teaching people the thought-forms of objects
and substances. "VAM," for example, is the thought-form
of what we call "water." Mantras, groups of these ancient
words, can summon any object or deity if they are miracu-
lously revealed to a seer and properly repeated silently
or vocally. Hindus use divine mantras to communicate with
gods, acquire superhuman powers, cure diseases, and for
many other purposes. Hence, everyday words that people
concentrate on to help themselves accomplish tasks or
cope with stress act as secular mantras.

All sorts of people use all sorts of secular mantras   4
for all sorts of reasons. A father counts to 10 before
saying anything when his son brings the car home dented.

A tennis player faults and chides himself, "Get serious!"
A frustrated mother pacing with her wailing baby mutters,
"You'll have your own kids someday." A college student
writhing before an exam instructs himself not to panic. A
freshly spanked child glares at his mother's back and repeatedly promises never to speak to her again. Secular
mantras are everywhere.

   Usually, we use secular mantras to make ourselves   5
walk faster or keep silent or do some other act. But we
can also use them to influence the actions of other persons. Say, for instance, the Chicago Bulls are behind in
the final minutes of a game. Ten thousand fans who want
them to win scream, "Let's go, Bulls!" The Bulls are
roused and win by 20 points. Chalk up the victory to the
fans' secular mantra, which transferred their energy to
the players on the court.

   If you're not convinced of the power of secular   6
mantras, try to complete a day without using any. Don't
mutter anything to force yourself out of bed. Don't utter
a sound when the water in the shower is cold. Don't
grumble when the traffic lights are long. Don't speak to
the computer when it's slow to boot up. And don't be surprised if you have an unusually long, painful, frustrating day.

Eldred read his paper aloud in class, and other students had an opportunity to ask him questions about secular mantras. As a result of
this classroom experience, Eldred had a good idea of what he needed
to do in subsequent drafts, and he made the following notes to himself so that he wouldn't forget.

- Get more examples, especially from everyday experiences
- Class thought Bulls example didn't work — expand or cut
- Be more specific in my definition of secular mantra — maybe tell
  what secular mantras are *not*
- Make use of "The Little Engine That Could" example in the body
  of the paper
- Get new conclusion — present conclusion doesn't follow from
  paper
- Explain how mantras might work and why they are important
- Don't eliminate background information about mantras

In subsequent drafts, Eldred worked on each of the areas he had listed. While revising, he found it helpful to reread particular portions of the selections in the definition chapter. His reading led him to new insights about how to change and strengthen his essay. As he revised his paper further, he found that he needed to make yet other changes that he had not anticipated. For example, once he made his definition more specific, he found that he then needed to do some reorganization (for example, moving the background information on mantras to a position later in the paper) and to develop a new paragraph. By the deadline, Eldred had completed the following final draft. Marginal annotations point to the revisions and comment on the paper's overall structure.

Secular Mantras

Keith Eldred

Introductory example (from first draft)

1   Remember "The Little Engine That Could"? That's the story about the tiny locomotive that hauled the train over the mountain when the big, rugged locomotives wouldn't. Remember how the Little Engine strained and heaved and chugged, "I think I can -- I think I can -- I think I can" until she reached the top of the mountain? That's a perfect example of a secular mantra in action.

Thesis: formal definition (revised)

Transitional/ organizational sentence (new)

2   You probably have used a secular mantra -- pronounce it "mantruh" -- already today. It's any word or group of words that helps you use your energy when you consciously repeat it to yourself. You must understand two things about secular mantras to be able to recognize one.

Qualifier no. 1 (new)

3   First of all, a secular mantra is not simply any word or phrase you say to yourself. It must help you use your energy. Thus, "I wish I were home" is not a secular mantra if you just think the words. But the sentence is a secular mantra if, walking home on a cold day, you repeat it each time you take a step, willing your feet to move in a fast rhythm. By the same token, every swear word you mutter to bear down on a job

is a secular mantra, while every one you un-
thinkingly repeat is simple profanity.

*Qualifier no. 2
(revised)*

Secondly, secular mantras only help   4
you use your energy. They don't create
energy. The Little Engine, for instance,
obviously had enough power to pull the
train up the mountainside -- she could have
done it without a peep. But we all know that
puffing "I think I can" somehow made her job
easier, just like, say, chanting "left-
right-left" makes it easier for us to march
in step. Any such word or phrase that magi-
cally seems to help you perform an action
when you purposefully utter it is a secular
mantra.

In fact, it is to highlight this appar-   5
ent magic that I dubbed these expressions
with so odd a title as "secular mantras."

*Historical
definition of
mantra (revised)*

"Mantra" means "sacred counsel" in San-   6
skrit. The term refers to a "mystical formula of invocation or incantation" used in
Hinduism (Webster's). According to Hindu
mythology, the god Manu created the first
language by teaching humans the thought-form
of every object and substance. "VAM," for
example, was what he told them to call the
stuff we call "water." But people altered or
forgot most of Manu's thought-forms. Followers of Hinduism believe mantras, groups of
these ancient words revealed anew by gods to
seers, can summon specific objects or
deities if they are properly repeated,
silently or vocally. Hindus repeat mantras
to gain superhuman powers, cure diseases,
and for many other purposes. Sideshow fakirs
chant "AUM" ("I agree" or "I accept") to become immune to pain when lying on beds of
nails.

*Definition of
secular (expanded)*

Our "mantras" are "secular" because,   7
unlike Hindus, we do not attribute them to
gods. Instead, we borrow them from tradition

or invent them to fit a situation, as the Little Engine did. They work not by divine power but because they help us, in a way, to govern transmissions along our central nervous systems.

Explanation (new)

Secular mantras give our brains a sort   8 of dual signal-boosting and signal-damping capacity. The act of repeating them pushes messages, or impulses, with extra force along our nerves or interferes with incoming messages we would rather ignore. We can then perform actions more easily or cope with stress that might keep us from functioning the way we want to. We may even accomplish both tasks at once. A sky-diver might yell

Example (elaborated)

"Geronimo," for example, both to amplify the signals telling his legs to jump and to drown out the ones warning him he's dizzy or scared.

More examples

Any one of us can use any words in this   9 way to help himself or herself to any task. A father might count to ten to keep from bellowing when junior brings the car home dented. A tennis player who faults may chide himself "Get serious!" as he swings, to concentrate harder on directing the ball. A sleepy mother pacing with her wailing baby can make her chore less painful by mutter-

Personal example (new)

ing, "You'll have kids someday." Chanting "Grease cartridge" always cools my temper because doing that once kept me from exploding at my father when we were working on a cantankerous Buick.

Revised conclusion (more positive)

You probably have favorite secular   10 mantras already. Think about it. How about those phrases you mumble to force yourself from your warm bed on chilly mornings? And those words you chant to ease your impatience when the traffic lights are endless? And the reminders you mutter so you'll remember to buy bread at the store? You know

what I'm talking about. And you must see how
much less painful and frustrating your life
is because of those magic words and phrases.

"Secular Mantras" is a fine essay of definition. Eldred provides a
clear explanation of the concept, offers numerous examples to illustrate
it, and suggests how mantras work and how we use them. More important, Eldred's notes and the two drafts of his paper show how writing is
accomplished. By reading analytically — both his own writing and the
writing of others more experienced than he — Eldred discovered and
understood the requirements of the strategy of definition. An honest
and thorough appraisal of his rough draft led to thoughtful revisions, resulting in a stronger and more effective piece of writing. Finally, note
how Eldred's essay combines the strategies of exemplification and definition to make his essay more interesting and convincing.

CHAPTER 3

Combining Strategies

Each of the last nine chapters of *Subjects/Strategies* emphasizes a particular rhetorical mode or writing strategy: exemplification, description, narration, process analysis, and so forth. The essays and selections within each of these chapters use the given strategy as the dominant method of development. It is important to remember, however, that the dominant strategy is rarely the only one used to develop a piece of writing. To fully explore their topics, writers find it useful and necessary to use other strategies in combination with the dominant strategy. Very seldom does an essay use only one strategy exclusively. To highlight and reinforce this point, we focus on the use of multiple strategies in the Combining Rhetorical Strategies section following each professional selection. For example, in Paul Roberts's "How to Say Nothing in 500 Words," an essay demonstrating process analysis, we ask about how he uses narration and exemplification to enhance his explanation of the process. In Nancy Mairs' "On Being a Cripple," an essay of definition, we ask about Mairs' use of comparison and contrast. She reorders her narrative sequence and bases the new arrangement on the contrast between the past and the present.

While some essays are developed *primarily* through the use of a single mode, it is more the norm in good writing that writers take advantage of the options open to them, using multiple strategies in artful combinations to achieve memorable results. It is to this end that we have highlighted one professional essay in each chapter as a Combining Rhetorical Strategies essay and have asked additional questions on the author's use of multiple strategies. These essays illustrate the ways that writers use a number of strategies to support the dominant strategy. You will encounter such combinations of strategies in the reading and writing you do in other college courses. Beyond the classroom, you might write a business proposal using both description and cause and effect to make an argument for a new marketing plan. Or you might use narration, description, and exemplification to write a news story for a company newsletter or a letter to the editor of your local newspaper.

WHAT DOES IT MEAN TO COMBINE STRATEGIES?

The following essay by Sydney Harris illustrates how several strategies can be used effectively, even in a brief, concise piece of writing. Although primarily a work of definition, notice how "A Jerk" also uses exemplification and personal narrative to engage the reader and achieve Harris's purpose.

A JERK

I don't know whether history repeats itself, but biography certainly does. The other day, Michael came in and asked me what a "jerk" was — the same question Carolyn put to me a dozen years ago.

At that time, I fluffed her off with some inane answer, such as "A jerk isn't a very nice person," but both of us knew it was an unsatisfactory reply. When she went to bed, I began trying to work up a suitable definition.

It is a marvelously apt word, of course. Until it was coined, not more than 25 years ago, there was really no single word in English to describe the kind of person who is a jerk — "boob" and "simp" were too old hat, and besides they really didn't fit, for they could be lovable, and a jerk never is.

Thinking it over, I decided that a jerk is basically a person without insight. He is not necessarily a fool or a dope, because some extremely clever persons can be jerks. In fact, it has little to do with intelligence as we commonly think of it; it is, rather, a kind of subtle but persuasive aroma emanating from the inner part of the personality.

I know a college president who can be described only as a jerk. He is not an unintelligent man, nor unlearned, nor even unschooled in the social amenities. Yet he is a jerk *cum laude*, because of a fatal flaw in his nature — he is totally incapable of looking into the mirror of his soul and shuddering at what he sees there.

A jerk, then, is a man (or woman) who is utterly unable to see himself as he appears to others. He has no grace, he is tactless without meaning to be, he is a bore even to his best friends, he is an egotist without charm. All of us are egotists to some extent, but most of us — unlike the jerk — are perfectly and horribly aware of it when we make asses of ourselves. The jerk never knows.

WHY DO WRITERS COMBINE STRATEGIES?

Essays that employ thoughtful combinations of rhetorical strategies have some obvious advantages for the writer and the reader. By reading the work of professional writers, you can learn how multiple strategies can be used to advantage — how a paragraph of narration, a vivid description, a clarifying instance of comparison and contrast, or a helpful definition can vary the interest level or terrain of an essay. More important, they answer a reader's need to know, to understand your purpose and thesis.

For example, let's suppose you wanted to write an essay on the college slang you heard being used all around you on campus. You might find it helpful to use a variety of strategies.

- *Definition* — to explain what slang is
- *Exemplification* — to give examples of slang
- *Comparison and contrast* — to differentiate slang from other types of speech, such as idioms or technical language
- *Division and classification* — to categorize different types of slang or different topics that slang terms are used for, such as courses, students, food, grades

Or let's say you wanted to write a paper on the Japanese Americans who were sent to internment camps during World War II while the United States was at war with Japan. The following strategies would be available to you.

- *Exemplification* — to illustrate several particular cases of families that were sent to internment camps
- *Narration* — to tell the stories of former camp residents, including their first reaction to their internment and their actual experiences in the camps
- *Cause and effect* — to examine the reasons why the United States government interned Japanese Americans and the long-term effects of this policy

When you rely on a single mode or approach to an essay, you may limit yourself and lose the opportunity to come at your subject from a number of different angles, all of which complete the picture and any one of which might be the most insightful or engaging and, therefore, the most memorable for the reader. This is particularly the case with essays that attempt to persuade or argue. So strong is the need, and so difficult the task, of changing readers' beliefs and thoughts that writers look for any combination of strategies that will make their arguments more convincing.

SUGGESTIONS FOR COMBINING RHETORICAL STRATEGIES

Before you can start combining strategies in your writing, it's essential that you have a firm understanding of the purpose and workings of each strategy.

Strategy of Development	Purpose
Exemplification	To provide examples or cases in point
Description	To detail sensory perceptions of a person, place, or thing
Narration	To recount an event
Process analysis	To explain how to do something or how something happens
Comparison and contrast	To show similarities and differences
Division and classification	To divide a whole into parts or to sort related items into categories
Definition	To provide the meaning of a term
Cause and effect analysis	To analyze why something happens and to describe the consequences of a string of events
Argumentation	To convince others through reasoning

Once you have become familiar with how the strategies work, you should be able to recognize ways to use and combine them in your own writing. Sometimes you will find yourself using a particular strategy almost intuitively. When you encounter a difficult or abstract term or concept — liberal, for example — you will define it almost as a matter of course. If you become perplexed because you are having trouble getting your readers to appreciate the severity of a problem, a quick review of the strategies will remind you that you could use description and exemplification. Knowledge of the individual strategies is crucial because there are no formulas or prescriptions for combining strategies. The more you write and the more aware you are of the options available to you, the more skillful you will become at thinking critically about your topic, developing your ideas, and conveying your thoughts to your readers (see box on page 41).

ABOUT THE PHOTOGRAPHS AND VISUAL TEXTS IN THIS BOOK

We have introduced each of the Combining Rhetorical Strategies essays with a photograph that depicts one or more of the themes in the

▶ *Would Another Strategy Be Useful?*

The questions listed below — broken up by rhetorical strategy — may help you decide whether a given essay might benefit from the use of additional strategies.

- *Exemplification.* Are there examples — facts, statistics, cases in point, personal experiences, interview quotations — that you could add to help you achieve the purpose of your essay?

- *Description.* Does a person, place, or object play a prominent role in your essay? Would the tone, pacing, or overall purpose of your essay benefit from sensory details?

- *Narration.* Are you trying to report or recount an anecdote, an experience, or an event? Does any part of your essay include the telling of a story (either something that happened to you or to a person you include in your essay)?

- *Process analysis.* Would any portion of your essay be more clear if you included concrete directions about a certain process? Are there any processes that readers would like to understand better? Are you evaluating any processes?

- *Comparison and contrast.* Does your essay contain two or more related subjects? Are you evaluating or analyzing two or more people, places, processes, events, or things? Do you need to establish the similarities and differences between two or more elements?

- *Division and classification.* Are you trying to explain a broad and complicated subject? Would it benefit your essay to reduce this subject to more manageable parts to focus your discussion?

- *Definition.* Who is your audience? Does your essay focus on any abstract, specialized, or new terms that need further explanation so your readers understand your point? Does any important word in your essay have many meanings and need to be clarified?

- *Cause and effect analysis.* Are you examining past events or their outcomes? Is your purpose to inform, speculate, or argue about why an identifiable fact happens the way it does?

- *Argumentation.* Are you trying to explain aspects of a particular subject, and are you trying to advocate a specific opinion on this subject or issue in your essay?

essay. Occasionally, the photographs also demonstrate the rhetorical mode of the chapter. Think of these photographs, then, as another type of Before You Read journal exercise. The questions that follow the photographs are designed to encourage close observation and critical thinking. It is our hope that, by adding a new, visual medium to the mix of written essays and text-based analytical activities and assignments, we can demonstrate not only another approach to themes and strategies but also how a different medium portrays these themes and strategies.

There's nothing unnatural or wrong about looking at a photograph and naming its subject or giving it a label. For example, summarizing the content of the following photograph by Sean Sprague of a village scene in Gujarat, India, is easy enough. We'd simply say, *"Here's a photograph of a woman in native dress."*

The problem comes when we mistake *looking* for *seeing*. If we think we are seeing and truly perceiving but are only looking, we miss a lot. Our visual sense can become uncritical and nonchalant, perhaps even numbed to what's going on in a photograph.

To reap the larger rewards, we need to move in more closely on an image. If we take a closer look, we will see all kinds of important details that we missed the first time around.

If we dig a little deeper and apply our critical faculties, we can see photographs as dynamic, visual works that play with some important concepts. We see some elements in a photograph as parts of something larger. We see elements in harmony as well as conflict. We see comparisons and contrasts. We see storytelling. We see process and change. We see highlights and shadows, foreground and background, light and dark, and a myriad of shades in between. There is movement — even in still photographs. There is tension and energy, peace and harmony, and line and texture. We see all this because we are seeing and not merely looking.

For example, we can examine the photograph of the woman again and quickly generate numerous observations that go beneath the surface and help exercise our critical reasoning faculties about what's going on in the photo.

1. The woman is holding a child. It looks as if the child is wearing a necklace but is otherwise naked. The woman is barefoot, but she's also wearing jewelry; a necklace and a bracelet. She is not necessarily poor. She is in some kind of native dress — the skirt goes down to her ankles, and there is some kind of scarf that goes over the back of her hair.

2. The woman is focusing on something to the photographer's right (her left). She is looking into the sun, which is low on the horizon. We know this because there is a large shadow behind her.

3. The second primary subject in the photograph is the satellite dish on the roof of the building the woman is standing beside. It is neither a huge dish indicating early technology nor a relatively small one indicating recent digital satellite technology. On the peak of the roof of the building is a cross.

4. There is nonwestern writing on the wall of the building. Some of the writing is smudged. The writing doesn't appear to be graffiti because it is very neatly rendered.

5. At what looks like the entrance to the building are two large sacks of what may be grain, still tied at their tops.

6. There's no paving or concrete apparent, simply dirt and stone. There is some tension in the fact that the woman is standing barefoot on this surface.

7. There are trees poking out from behind the building. They are not palm trees, and it is difficult to determine exactly what kind they are.
8. The most tension in the photograph lies in the juxtaposition of the high-tech satellite dish in what appears to be a third world setting.

In short, there is more in the photograph than we suspected. Based upon these detailed observations, we can begin to identify a number of themes at work in the photo: cultural diversity, cultural contradictions, culture clashes (Eastern world versus Western world), technology, and imperialism. Likewise, we can see that several rhetorical strategies are at work: comparison and contrast predominantly, with the juxtaposition of old- and new-world images, but also description and exemplification. A similar close analysis of the other photographs in this book will enhance your understanding of how themes and strategies work in these visual texts.

This exercise in visual analysis will, in turn, add to your understanding of how the same types of themes and strategies work in the reading selections. When it comes to reading, we need to train ourselves to pay close attention to catch all nuances and implications and to be attuned to what is not said as well as what is made clear. By sharpening our observational skills, we penetrate to another level of meaning in our reading — a level not apparent to a casual reader — and we enable ourselves to interact with essential facts and truths. For writers, the world does not exist so much in abstractions as it does in specifics — not trees but this particular tree, not leaves but this one I am holding in my hand. We need to see first, clearly and in detail, before we attempt as writers to find the proper words to make others see.

For all these reasons, then, there is value in analyzing photographs and other visual texts, just as there is value in analyzing life, as a way of understanding the processes of reading and writing.

AN ANNOTATED STUDENT ESSAY USING A COMBINATION OF STRATEGIES

While a senior at the University of Vermont, English major Tara E. Ketch took a course in children's literature and was asked to write a term paper on some aspect of the literature she was studying. She knew that she would soon be looking for a teaching position and realized that any teaching job she accepted would bring her face-to-face with the difficult task of selecting appropriate reading materials. Ketch understood, as well, that she would have to confront criticism of her choices, so she decided to delve a little deeper into the subject of censorship, particularly as it relates to children's and adolescent literature. She was interested in learning more about why people want to censor certain books so that she could consider an appropriate response to their efforts. In a way, she wanted to begin to develop her own teaching philosophy with respect to text selection. Her essay naturally incorporated several rhetorical modes working in combination. As you read Ketch's essay, notice how naturally she has used the supporting strategies of definition, cause and effect, and exemplification to enhance the dominant strategy of argumentation.

Kids, You Can't Read That Book!

Tara E. Ketch

Definition of censorship and censors' activities

Censorship is the restriction or suppression of speech or writing that is thought to have a negative influence. In the case of children's and adolescent literature the censors are very often school officials, parents, or adults in the community who wish to monitor and influence what children are reading. For whatever reason, they are saying, "Kids, you can't read that book; it is not fit for your eyes." To ensure that these books do not end up in the schools, pressure groups influence school boards not to purchase them or to restrict their use if they have already been purchased. Such actions present serious questions for educators. Who will decide what materials are fit for American schoolchildren?

Cause and effect: Pressure is put on school boards, and questions are raised.

Argumentation: Who will decide on censorship issues?

The federal government has set limits on censorship and encouraged local communities to make educational decisions. In the 1968 case of <u>Emerson v. Arkansas</u>, the Supreme Court stated, "Public education in our nation is committed to the control of state and local authorities. Courts do not and cannot intervene in the resolution of conflicts which arise in the daily operation of school systems and which do not directly and sharply implicate basic constitutional values" (Reichman 3). In 1982, the Supreme

Exemplification: Supreme Court decisions

1

2

Cause and effect: result of Supreme Court decisions

Court ruled that "local school boards may not remove books from school library shelves simply because they dislike the ideas contained in those books and seek by their removal to prescribe what shall be orthodox in politics, nationalism, religion, or other matters of opinion" (Reichman 3). These two rulings contradict each other. The outcome is that children's books continue to be banned in school systems for many reasons.

Cause and effect: first reason why children's and adolescents' books are banned

One important reason books are banned 3 is family values. The censor may attack a book because it goes against his or her personal values. For example, it may contain "offensive" language. Most problems with books seem to come out of the author's use of language. This is especially true of adolescent literature. In a list of the most frequently banned books in the 1990s, J. D. Salinger's Catcher in the Rye took the number three slot because of objections to its language. A parent found words such as hell, Chrissakes, bastard, damn, and crap to

Exemplification: authors' use of language that affronts family values

be unacceptable (Foerstel 147). The fear was that such language was being condoned by the school when such a book was taught. In a debate about Katherine Paterson's Bridge to Terabithia, a woman protested the use of the words snotty and shut up along with Lord and damn. She said, "Freedom of speech was not intended to guarantee schools the right to intrude on traditional family values without warning and regardless of the availability

Argumentation: Counterargument about redeeming social value is presented.

of non-offensive alternatives" (Reichman 38). The school board in this case decided that the book had a value that transcended the use of the few offensive words. That a book has redeeming value is the primary argument against such censorship. If we ignore all books that contain profanity, we are missing out on a lot of valuable literature.

Cause and effect: second reason why children's and adolescents' books are banned

Other people hold dear the value that children should not be exposed to anything depressing or violent. Not surprisingly, several communities have tried to get certain fairy tales banned because they are violent in nature. Jack and the Beanstalk and

Exemplification: violence in fairy tales

Little Red Riding Hood came under attack for this reason. In both cases the books were kept in the school system (Burress 283-91). The argument against their removal involved the fact that the violence was tied to fantasy. It was not in the child's everyday realm and therefore not threatening. Judy Blume's Blubber has been questioned for its

Exemplification: unhappy child characters

portrayal of unhappy child characters. Some parents refuse to recognize the fact that not all children have a happy and carefree existence. Judy Blume has her own ideas about childhood that she uses as an attack against such censorship. She argues, "Chil-

Argumentation: Counterargument by Judy Blume is presented.

dren have little control over their lives, and this causes both anger and unhappiness. Childhood can be a terrible time of life. No kid wants to stay a kid. . . . The fantasy of childhood is to be an adult" (West 12). Bridge to Terabithia has also been seen as a harsh portrayal of life because it deals

Exemplification: death of a child character

with the death of a child. Some parents want to shelter their children from the reality of death. Others find that a book such as Bridge to Terabithia is a natural way for children to be exposed to that sensitive topic.

Cause and effect: third reason why children's and adolescents' books are banned

Another family value that comes into play in censorship is the idea that children should be protected from sexuality. Maurice Sendak's In the Night Kitchen shows a naked little boy, and although there is no sexual connotation, many people were incensed by the book. In New York, in 1990, parents tried to have the book removed from an

4

5

elementary school. In Maine, a parent wanted the book removed because she felt it encouraged child molestation (Foerstel 201). Many of Judy Blume's books have also come under fire for their portrayal of sexual themes in adolescence. <u>Are You There, God? It's Me, Margaret</u> has been blacklisted for its frank discussion of menstruation and adolescent development. <u>Forever</u> is even worse to some because it mentions intercourse and abortion. As topics of discussion, these subjects are alien to many adults who grew up in environments where sex was not talked about; therefore, they try to perpetuate the cycle of silence by keeping these kinds of books from children. They may also worry that these books will encourage sexual activity. This fear extends to textbooks that educate children and adolescents about their bodies and sexual reproduction. Many try to ban gay and lesbian literature because they feel that homosexuality is obscene and that books about these subjects might encourage homosexual behavior and lifestyles. <u>All-American Boys</u> was donated to a California high school, but when administrators realized that it discussed homosexuality, the book was seized and then "lost" (Reichman 43). Alyson Wonderland Publications has also published two children's books to explain the gay lifestyle to children: Michael Willhoite's <u>Daddy's Roommate</u> and Leslea Newman's <u>Heather Has Two Mommies</u>. These, not surprisingly, have met with a lot of opposition.

Often there are religious concerns as well. Religion is in many cases the foundation for people's moral beliefs. Censorship of books because of their language, violence, and sexuality happens as much in the name of religion as family values. Religion is also used as an issue in censorship for

Exemplification: sexuality as topic

Cause and effect: explanation of reasons for banning books with sexual topics

Exemplification: books that discuss gay and lesbian themes

Cause and effect: fourth reason why children's and adolescents' books are banned

6

other reasons. Some people want the Bible when used as literature banned from class-rooms. Not only does teaching the Bible as literature present a problem for parents who want the Bible focused on as sacred mater-ial, but it is equally offensive to people who feel that religious documents should be kept out of the classroom (Burress 219). Sometimes religious considerations take the form of censorship of books that in any way involve the occult. The picture book Witches, Pumpkins, and Grinning Ghosts was considered inappropriate because it "inter-ests little minds into accepting the Devil with all his evil works" (Reichman 51). Ironically, "witches" sought the banning of Hansel and Gretel because it portrayed their religion in a negative light (Reichman 50). Greek and Roman mythology has also been at-tacked by religious groups because it dis-cusses gods other than the Christian one. Christians also fought to ban books on evo-lution that called into question their reli-gious beliefs.

Exemplification: books banned for religious reasons

Yet another reason for the censorship of children's books is concern over racism and sexism. Minority groups have often made efforts to combat stereotypes and racial prejudices through censorship. The idea is that if children are exposed to sexism and racism in books, they will learn it. Mark Twain's The Adventures of Huckleberry Finn is a good example of a text that has been banned because of its racist language. The use of the term nigger has offended many African Americans. The problem with this criticism is that the novel was not examined for its intention, which was to question the racist attitude of the South. Twain was not a racist. Nevertheless, Huckleberry Finn has become one of the most frequently banned

Cause and effect: fifth reason why children's and adolescents' books are banned

7

Exemplification: books banned for racial reasons

Argumentation: Counterargument is presented.

Exemplification: books banned for gender bias

books in the United States. Women have also tried to censor nursery rhymes and children's stories that reinforce negative images of women. Some have argued in opposition that to remove all books that are sexist and racist would be to remove a piece of our history that we can learn from.

Argumentation: Counterargument is presented.

Central question is raised: Should we censor children's books? Answers are given.

With this brief background and a review of some of the reasons used to ban children's books, how might the question "Should we censor children's books?" be answered? On the one hand, we should realize that there are age-appropriate themes for children. For example, elementary school children should not be exposed to the ideas of rape and abortion that occur in some young adult novels. Young adults should not be exposed to extremely violent novels like Anthony Burgess's <u>A Clockwork Orange</u>, which they may not understand at such a young age. Does this mean these books should be removed from school libraries? Perhaps not. Libraries should be resources for children to broaden their horizons. If a child independently seeks out a controversial novel, the child should not be stopped from doing so. Exposure to a rich diversity of works is always advisable. A good way to decide if a book should be taught is if its message speaks to the children. What if this message is couched in profanity? If it is in a character representation, kids can understand the context without feeling compelled to emulate the behavior. If children are constantly exposed to books that throw reality in their faces in a violent way, then their attitudes will reflect it. So, it is the job of educators to present different types of materials to balance the children's exposure.

Argumentation: The writer provides various criteria for making decisions about what is appropriate reading for children. Discussion of these criteria generally follows the writer's sequencing of the reasons why people attempt to censor children's and adolescents' books.

8

As far as sexuality goes, it's fine for libraries to include children's books that focus on this subject if the objective is to

9

educate or make transitions easier for the child. Religion, however, should not be focused on in the classroom because it causes too much conflict for different groups. This does not mean that religious works should be banned from school libraries. Children should have access to different religious materials to explore world religions and various belief systems. Lastly, if sexism and racism appear in books, those books should not automatically be banned. They can be useful tools for increasing understanding in our society.

Argumentation: Concluding statement calls for understanding and sensitivity in dealing with censorship and book selection for children and adolescents.

The efforts to censor what our children are reading can turn into potentially explosive situations and cause a great deal of misunderstanding and hurt feelings within our schools and communities. If we can gain an understanding of the major reasons why people have sought to censor what our kids are reading, we will be better prepared to respond to those efforts in a sensitive and reasonable manner. More importantly, we will be able to provide the best educational opportunity for our children through a sensible approach, one that neither overly restricts the range of their reading nor allows them to read any and all books no matter how inappropriate they might be for them.   10

Works Cited

Burress, Lee. Battle of the Books: Literary Censorship in the Public Schools, 1950–1985. New York: Scarecrow, 1989.

Foerstel, Herbert. Banned in the U.S.A.: A Reference Guide to Book Censorship in Schools and Public Libraries. London: Greenwood, 1994.

Reichman, Henry. Censorship and Selection: Issues and Answers to Schools. Chicago: American Library Association, 1993.

West, Mark. Trust Your Children: Voices against Censorship in Children's Literature. London: Neal-Schuman, 1988.

CHAPTER 4

Writing Documented Essays

A documented paper is not very different from the other writing that you will be doing in your college writing course. You will find yourself drawing heavily on what you learned in Chapter 2 (pages 12–36). First you determine what you want to say, then you decide on a purpose, consider your audience, develop a thesis, collect your evidence, write a first draft, revise and edit, and prepare a final copy. What differentiates the documented paper from other kinds of papers is your use of outside sources and how you acknowledge them. In this chapter, you will learn how to locate and use print and Internet sources, how to evaluate these sources, how to take useful notes, how to summarize, paraphrase, and quote your sources, how to integrate your notes into your paper, how to acknowledge your sources, and how to avoid plagiarism. You will also find extensive guidelines for documenting your essay in Modern Language Association (MLA) style.

Your library research will involve working with both print and electronic sources. In both cases, however, the process is essentially the same. Your aim is to select the most appropriate sources for your research from the many that are available on your topic.

PRINT SOURCES

In most cases, you should use print sources (books, newspapers, periodicals, encyclopedias, pamphlets, brochures, and government publications) as your primary tools for research. Most print sources, unlike many Internet sources, are reviewed and refereed by experts in the field, are approved and overseen by a reputable publishing company or organization, and are examined by editors and fact checkers for accuracy and reliability. Unless you are instructed otherwise, you should always use print sources in your research.

To find print sources, search through your library's reference works, card catalog, periodical indexes, and other databases to generate a preliminary listing of books, magazine and newspaper articles, public documents and reports, and other sources that look as if they might help you explore or answer your research question. At this early stage, it is better to err on the side of listing too many sources rather than finding yourself trying later to relocate those you discarded too hastily.

Previewing Print Sources

Although you want to be thorough in your research, you will soon realize that you do not have time to read every source you collect. Rather, you must preview your sources to decide what you will read, what you will skim, and what you will simply eliminate. Here are some suggestions for previewing your print sources.

QUESTIONS FOR PREVIEWING PRINT SOURCES

1. Is the book or article directly related to the specific research question you are trying to answer?
2. Are any of the books or articles obviously outdated (for example, a source on nuclear energy published in the 1960s)?
3. Have you checked tables of contents and indexes in books to locate the material that is important and relevant to your topic?
4. If an article appears to be what you are looking for, have you read the abstract or the opening paragraphs?
5. Is it necessary to quickly read the entire article to be sure that it is relevant?

Developing a Working Bibliography

For each work that you think might be helpful, make a separate bibliography card, using a 3- by 5-inch index card. As your collection of bibliography cards grows, alphabetize the cards by the authors' last names. By using a separate card for each book or article, you can continually edit your working bibliography, dropping sources that are not helpful and adding new ones.

Make sure you record all the necessary information about each source for which you make a bibliography card. You will use the cards to compile the final bibliography, or the list of works cited, for your paper.

For books, record the following information:

- All authors; any editors or translators
- Title and subtitle
- Edition (if not the first)
- Publication data: city, publishing company, and date
- Call number

For periodical articles, record the following information:

- All authors
- Title and subtitle
- Title of journal, magazine, or newspaper
- Volume and issue numbers
- Date
- Page numbers

Using correct bibliographic form ensures that your entries are complete, reduces the chance of introducing careless errors, and saves time when you prepare your final list of works cited. You will find MLA style guidelines for your list of works cited on pages 73–79.

Evaluating Print Sources

Before beginning to take notes, you should read your sources and evaluate them for their reliability and relevance in helping you answer your research question. Examine your sources for the writers' main ideas. Pay particular attention to abstracts or introductions, tables of contents, section headings, and indexes. Also, look for information about the authors themselves — information that will help you determine their authority and perspective on the issues.

QUESTIONS FOR EVALUATING PRINT SOURCES

1. Is your source focused on your particular research question?
2. Is your source too abstract, too general, or too technical for your needs?
3. Does your source build on current thinking and existing research in the field?
4. Does your source promote a particular view, or is it meant to inform?

5. What biases, if any, does your source exhibit?
6. Is the author of your source an authority on the issue? Do other writers mention the author of your source in their work?

INTERNET SOURCES

You will find that Internet sources can be informative and valuable additions to your research; for example, you might find a just-published article from a university laboratory or a news story in your local newspaper's online archives. Generally, however, Internet resources should be used alongside print sources and not as a replacement for them. While print sources are published under the guidance of a publisher or an organization, anyone with access to a computer and a modem can put text and pictures on the Internet; there is no governing body that checks for content or accuracy. The Internet offers a vast number of useful and carefully maintained resources, but it also contains many bogus facts and many examples of rumor, conjecture, and unreliable information. It is your responsibility to evaluate whether you can trust a given Internet source.

Your Internet research will almost certainly produce many more sources than you can reasonably use. By carefully previewing Web sites and other Internet sources, developing a working bibliography of potentially useful ones, and evaluating them for their reliability, you will ensure that you are making the best use of Internet sources in researching your topic.

If you do not know how to access the Internet, or if you need more instruction on conducting Internet searches, go to your campus computer center for more information, or consult one of the many books written for Internet beginners. You can also access the links to Internet information offered by Bedford/St. Martin's at <http://www.bedfordstmartins.com/online/>.

Previewing Internet Sources

The key to successful Internet research is being able to identify the sites that will help you the most. The following questions will help you weed out the sources that hold no promise.

QUESTIONS FOR PREVIEWING
INTERNET SOURCES

1. Scan the Web site. Do the contents and links appear to be related to your research topic?

2. Can you identify the author of the site? Are the author's credentials available?
3. Has the site been updated within the last six months? This information is usually provided at the bottom of the Web page. Updating is not always necessary, especially if your topic is not a current one and information about it is deemed to be somewhat stable.

If you answer "No" to any of these questions, you should consider eliminating the source from further consideration.

Developing a Working Bibliography

Just as for print sources, you must maintain accurate records for the Internet sources you use. Here is what you need for each source:

- All authors or sponsoring agents
- Title and subtitle of document
- Title of complete work (if applicable)
- Document date (or date "last modified")
- Date you accessed the site
- Publishing data for print version (if available)
- Address of the site, URL (uniform resource locator), or network path

See pages 76–79 for the latest MLA guidelines for electronic sources.

Evaluating Internet Sources

Because the quality of sources on the Internet varies tremendously, you will need guidelines for evaluating the information you find there. Here are some techniques to help you evaluate the validity of the sites you have included in your working bibliography.

QUESTIONS FOR EVALUATING INTERNET SOURCES
- Type of Web page
  Who hosts the Web site? Often the URL (the Internet version of an address) domain name suffix can give you an indication of the type of information provided and the type of organization that hosts the site.
  Common top-level domain names include these:
  .com — business/commercial
  .edu — educational institution

.gov — government sponsored
.mil — military
.net — various types of networks
.org — nonprofit organization

- Authority/author

    Is it clear what individual or company is responsible for the site?

    Can you verify if the site is official, actually sanctioned by an organization or company?

    What are the author's or company's qualifications for writing on this subject?

    Is there a way to verify the legitimacy of this individual or company? Are there links to a home page or résumé?

- Purpose and audience

    What appears to be the author's or sponsor's purpose or motivation?

    Who is the intended audience?

- Objectivity

    Are advertising, opinion, and factual information clearly distinguished?

    What biases, if any, can you detect?

- Accuracy

    Is important information documented through links so that it can be verified or corroborated in other sources?

    Is the text well written and free of careless errors in spelling and grammar?

- Coverage and currency

    Is there any indication that the site is still under construction?

    For sources with print equivalents, is the Web version more or less extensive than the print version?

    How detailed is the treatment of the topic?

    Is there any indication of the currency of the information (date of last update or statement regarding frequency of updates)?

- Ease of use

    Is the design and navigation of the site user-friendly? Do all the links work, and do they take you to relevant information? Can you return to the home page easily? Are the graphics helpful, or are they simply window dressing?

You can also find sources on the Internet itself that offer useful guidelines for evaluating electronic sources. One excellent example was created by reference librarians at the Wolfgram Memorial Library of Widener University; see <http://wwwZ.widener.edu/Wolfgram-Memorial-Library/webevaluation/webeval.htm>.

Internet Research: Subject Directories and Keyword Searches

Using Subject Directories to Refine Your Research Topic. The subject directories on the home pages of search engines make it easy to browse various subjects and topics, a big help if you are undecided about your exact research question or if you simply want to see if there is enough material to supplement your research work with print sources. Often the most efficient approach to Web research is to start with the subject directories provided by most search engines. Once you choose a subject area in the directory, you can click your mouse to narrow the subdirectories and eventually arrive at a list of sites closely related to your topic.

Suppose you want to research bilingualism in American schools, and you are using the search engine Google (<http://www.google.com>). Below is the "Web Directory" screen where you would start your search. Your first task would be to choose, from the 16 topics listed, the subject area most likely to contain information on bilingualism in education. Remember that just as you often need to browse through the tables of contents and indexes of numerous books on a given subject to uncover the three or four that will be most useful to you, more than one general subject area in a Web directory may seem appropriate on the surface.

The most common question students have at this stage in a Web search is, How can I tell if I'm looking in the right place? If more than one subject area sounds plausible, you will have to dig more deeply into each of their subdirectories, using logic and the process of elimination to determine which one is likely to produce the best Web site listings for your topic. In most cases, it doesn't take long — usually just one or two clicks — to figure out whether you're searching in the right subject area. If you click on a subject area and none of the topics listed in its subdirectories seems to pertain even remotely to your research topic, try a different subject area. For example, on the preceding screen on page 58, you might be tempted to click on "News," which has a "Current Events" link. If you do, you'll find that none of the current events topics listed seems to relate to language, education, or bilingualism, which is a strong sign that "News" is the wrong subject area for your topic. Similarly, although the "Reference" subject area contains an "Education" link, you'll find that the subdirectories listed there do not pertain to language in schools or bilingualism. The third, most logical, possibility in this case is "Society." Clicking on this subject area takes you to a screen that lists forty more subject areas, including one for "Language and Linguistics," a logical place to find sites on bilingualism in education (see the screen below). For "Language and Linguistics" alone, there are 3,766 Web sites listed, so chances are good that some of those sites address your subject.

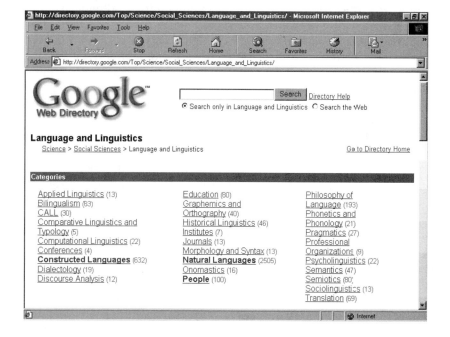

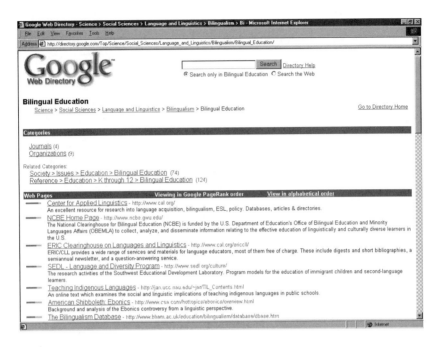

When you click on "Language and Linguistics," you arrive at a screen listing categories of sites related to language study. Because you are interested in bilingualism, the "Bilingualism" option is a natural (see the screen above). Clicking on this link takes you to a screen where you find three directory entries, including "Bilingual Education," and a listing of Web sites for bilingualism. By clicking on "Bilingual Education," you arrive at a screen that lists potentially valuable Web sites, including the NCBE home page (the description for this site identifies NCBE as the National Clearinghouse for Bilingual Education), the Center for Applied Linguistics, "American Shibboleth: Ebonics" posted by Cambridge Scientific Abstracts, and "Teaching Indigenous Languages" posted by Northern Arizona University. In some cases, clicking on a Web site link may bring you directly to a page containing an article on your topic. For example, clicking on "American Shibboleth: Ebonics" takes you directly to a ten-page overview and linguistic analysis of the Ebonics controversy, released online in September 2000.

Using Keyword Searches to Find Specific Information. When you type in a keyword in the "Search" box on a search engine's home page, the search engine goes looking for Web sites that match your term. One problem with keyword searches is that they can produce tens of thousands of matches, making it difficult to locate sites of immediate value. For that reason, make your keywords as specific as you can, and

▶ *Refining Keyword Searches on the Web*

While some variation in command terms and characters exists among electronic databases and popular search engines on the Internet, the following functions are almost universally accepted. If you have a particular question about refining your keyword search, seek assistance by clicking on "Help" or "Advanced Search."

- Use quotation marks or parentheses to indicate that you are searching for words in exact sequence — e.g., "whooping cough"; (Supreme Court).
- Use AND or a plus sign (+) between words to narrow your search by specifying that all words need to appear in a document — e.g., tobacco AND cancer; Shakespeare + sonnet.
- Use NOT or a minus sign (–) between words to narrow your search by eliminating unwanted words — e.g., monopoly NOT game, cowboys–Dallas.
- Use OR to broaden your search by requiring that only one of the words need appear — e.g., buffalo OR bison.
- Use an asterisk (*) to indicate that you will accept variations of a term — e.g., "food label*."

make sure that you have the correct spelling. It is always a good idea to consult the help screens or advanced search instructions for the search engine you are using before initiating a keyword search. Once you start a search, you may want to narrow or broaden it depending on the number of hits, or matches, you get.

When using a keyword search, you need to be careful about selecting the keywords that will yield the best results. If your word or words are too general, your results can be at best unwieldy and at worst not usable at all. During her initial search for her paper on cougars, an endangered cat indigenous to North America, student Dorothy Adams typed in "cougar" (see top screen, page 62). To her surprise, this produced 189,830 hits, mostly for products carrying the name or for teams with cougars as mascots. After surveying the suggested "Related Searches," Adams decided to type in "mountain lion cougar" (bottom screen, page 62). This search yielded 4,140 hits, still too many for Adams's purposes. In an effort to narrow her search even more, she tried "mountain lion cougar AND endangered" — a search that yielded a far more manageable forty-eight hits. Among these hits, she located a Web page entitled "Puma, Mountain Lion, Cougar, Catamount," produced by the Natural History Museum of Los Angeles

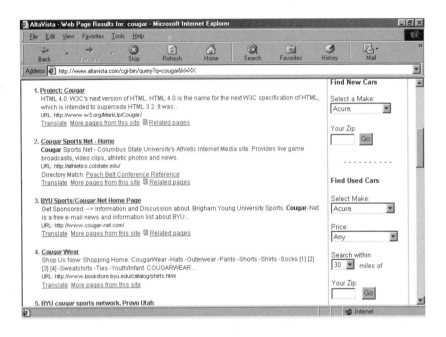

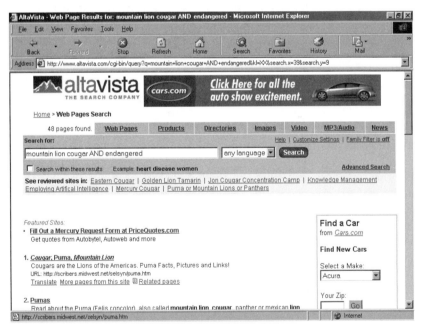

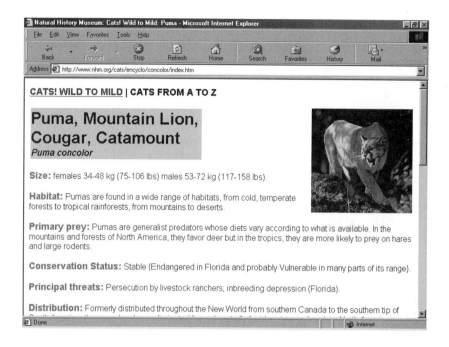

County (see above). This site was a perfect starting point for Adams; it provided her with sound information about cougars and related big cats.

About the Web Exercises in This Book

Along with each professional selection in this book you will find a research writing exercise that encourages the use of both print and Internet sources. Each of these exercises offers a set of suggested Web sites to help you direct your Internet research. These Web sites have all been evaluated and updated for the current edition of *Subjects/ Strategies*, using the guidelines for evaluating Internet sources described in this chapter. Each Web site entry in the book offers the name of the Web site, the URL, and a brief description.

NOTE TAKING

As you read, take notes. You're looking for ideas, facts, opinions, statistics, examples, and evidence that you think will be useful in writing your paper. As you work through the articles, look for recurring themes, and mark the places where the writers are in agreement and where they differ in their views. Try to remember that the effectiveness of your paper is largely determined by the quality — not necessarily the quantity — of your notes. The purpose of a research paper is not to present a collection of quotes that show you've read all the material and can report what others have said about your topic. Your goal is to analyze, evaluate, and synthesize the information you collect — in other words, to enter into the discussion of the issues and thereby take ownership of your topic. You want to view the results of your research from your own perspective and arrive at an informed opinion of your topic.

Now for some practical advice on taking notes: First, be systematic. As a rule, write one note on a card, and use cards of uniform size, preferably 4- by 6-inch cards because they are large enough to accommodate even a long note on a single card and yet small enough to be easily handled and carried. More important, when you get to the planning and writing stage, you will be able to sequence your notes according to the plan you have envisioned for your paper. Furthermore, should you decide to alter your organizational plan, you can easily reorder your cards to reflect those revisions.

Second, try not to take too many notes. One good way to help decide whether to take a note is to ask yourself, "How exactly does this material help prove or disprove my thesis?" You might even try envisioning where in your paper you could use the information. If it does not seem relevant to your thesis, don't bother to take a note.

Once you decide to take a note, you must decide whether to summarize, paraphrase, or quote directly. The approach that you take is largely determined by the content of the passage and the way you envision using it in your paper. All of the examples in the following discussion are taken from articles in *Subjects/Strategies.*

Summary

When you *summarize* material from one of your sources, you capture in condensed form the essential idea of a passage, article, or entire chapter. Summaries are particularly useful when you are working with lengthy, detailed arguments or long passages of narrative or descriptive background information where the details are not germane to the overall thrust of your paper. You simply want to capture the essence of the passage while dispensing with the details because you are confident that your readers will readily understand the point being made or do not need to be convinced about the validity of the point. Because you are distilling information, a summary is always shorter than the original; often a chapter or more can be reduced to a paragraph, or several paragraphs to a sentence or two. Remember, in writing a summary you should use your own words.

Consider the following paragraphs in which Richard Lederer compares big words with small words.

> When you speak and write, there is no law that says you have to use big words. Short words are as good as long ones, and short, old words — like *sun* and *grass* and *home* — are best of all. A lot of small words, more than you might think, can meet your needs with a strength, grace, and charm that large words do not have.
>
> Big words can make the way dark for those who read what you write and hear what you say. Small words cast their clear light on big things — night and day, love and hate, war and peace, and life and death. Big words at times seem strange to the eye and the ear and the mind and the heart. Small words are the ones we seem to have known from the time we were born, like the hearth fire that warms the home.

— RICHARD LEDERER,
"The Case for Short Words," page 590

A student wishing to capture the gist of Lederer's point without repeating his detailed contrast wrote the following summary.

Summary Note Card

Short words

Lederer favors short words for their clarity, familiarity, durability, and overall usefulness.

Lederer, 590

Paraphrase

When you *paraphrase* a source, you restate the information in your own words instead of quoting directly. Unlike a summary, which gives a brief overview of the essential information in the original, a paraphrase seeks to maintain the same level of detail as the original to aid readers in understanding or believing the information presented. A paraphrase presents the original information in approximately the same number of words, but in the paraphraser's own wording. To put it another way, your paraphrase should closely parallel the presentation of ideas in the original but should not use the same words or sentence structure as the original. Even though you are using your own words in a paraphrase, it's important to remember that you are borrowing ideas and therefore must acknowledge the source of these ideas with a citation.

How would you paraphrase the following passage from a speech by Martin Luther King Jr.?

> But one hundred years later [after the Emancipation Proclamation], the Negro is still not free. One hundred years later, the life of the Negro is still sadly crippled by the manacles of segregation and the chains of discrimination. One hundred years later, the Negro lives on a lonely island of poverty in the midst of a vast ocean of material prosperity. One hundred years later, the Negro is still anguished in the corners of American society and finds himself an exile in his own land.
>
> — MARTIN LUTHER KING JR.,
> "I Have a Dream," page 602

The following note card illustrates how one student paraphrased the passage from King's speech.

Paraphrase Note Card

Unfulfilled promises

On the one hundredth anniversary of the Emancipation Proclamation, African Americans find themselves still a marginalized people. African Americans do not experience the freedom that other Americans do. In a land of opportunity and plenty, racism and poverty affect the way they live their lives, separating them from mainstream society.

King, 602

In most cases, it is better to summarize or paraphrase materials — which by definition means using your own words — instead of quoting verbatim (word for word). Capturing an idea in your own words ensures that you have thought about and understood what your source is saying.

Direct Quotation

When you directly *quote* a source, you copy the words of your source exactly, putting all quoted material in quotation marks. When you make a quotation note card, carefully check for accuracy, including punctuation and capitalization. Be selective about what you choose to quote; reserve direct quotation for important ideas stated memorably, for especially clear explanations by authorities, and for arguments by proponents of a particular position in their own words.

Consider, for example, Deborah Tannen's powerful contrast between the ways boys and girls communicate:

> The girls in my study tended to talk at length about one topic, but the boys tended to jump from topic to topic. The second-grade girls exchanged stories about people they knew. The second-grade boys teased, told jokes, noticed things in the room, and talked about finding games to play. The sixth-grade girls talked about problems with a mutual friend. The sixth-grade boys talked about 55 different topics, none of which extended over more than a few turns.
>
> — DEBORAH TANNEN,
> "Sex, Lies, and Conversation," page 370

Quotation Note Card

Conversation differences

"The girls in my study tended to talk at length about one topic, but the boys tended to jump from topic to topic. The second-grade girls exchanged stories about people they knew. The second-grade boys teased, told jokes, noticed things in the room, and talked about finding games to play. The sixth-grade girls talked about problems with a mutual friend. The sixth-grade boys talked about 55 different topics, none of which extended over more than a few turns."

Tannen, 370

On occasion, you'll find a useful passage with some memorable wording in it. Avoid the temptation to quote the whole passage; instead you can combine summary or paraphrase with direct quotation.

Consider the following paragraph from Barbara Hattemer's essay on violence in the media.

> Television and violence have been almost synonymous since television became a part of nearly every home. As far back as 1977, 9 of every 10 TV programs contained violence. Today, while there is more variety, there are more sources of violence than ever before. In addition to violent action-adventure movies and television dramas, violence pervades music videos, rap songs, documentaries, commercials, and news broadcasts. The networks provide up to 10 violent acts per hour; cable, up to 18 violent acts per hour; and children's cartoons, 32 violent acts per hour. Movies like *Teenage Mutant Ninja Turtles* raise the count to 133 violent acts per hour. The body count is rising, too: *Total Recall,* 74 dead; *Robocop 2,* 81 dead; *Rambo III,* 106 dead; and *Die Hard 2,* 264 dead.

> — BARBARA HATTEMER,
> "Cause and Violent Effect:
> Media and Our Youth," page 617

Note how the student who took the following note was careful to put quotation marks around all words that have been borrowed directly.

Quotation and Summary Note Card

Violent acts

The link between television and violence has always existed, but today it's more varied. "The networks provide up to 10 violent acts per hour; cable, up to 18 violent acts per hour; and children's cartoons, 32 violent acts per hour. Movies like Teenage Mutant Ninja Turtles raise the count to 133 violent acts per hour. The body count is rising, too: Total Recall, 74 dead; Robocop 2, 81 dead; Rambo III, 106 dead; and Die Hard 2, 264 dead."

Hattemer, 617

Taking Notes on Internet Sources

Working from the computer screen or from a printout of it, you can take notes just as you would with print sources. You will need to decide whether to summarize, paraphrase, or quote directly the information you wish to borrow. Use the same 4- by 6-inch index card system that you use with print sources. The medium of the Internet, however, has an added advantage. An easy and accurate technique for capturing passages of text from the Internet is to copy the material into a separate computer file on your hard drive or diskette. In Netscape, for example, you can use your mouse to highlight the portion of the text you want to save and then use the Copy and Paste features to add it to your file of research notes. You can also use the same commands to capture the bibliographic information you will need later.

INTEGRATING QUOTATIONS INTO YOUR TEXT

Whenever you want to use borrowed material, be it a summary, paraphrase, or a quotation, it's best to introduce the material with a *signal phrase* — a phrase that alerts the reader that borrowed information is to follow. A signal phrase usually consists of the author's name and a verb. Well-chosen signal phrases help you integrate quotations, paraphrases, and summaries into the flow of your paper. Besides, signal phrases let your reader know who is speaking and, in the case of summaries and paraphrases, exactly where your ideas end and someone else's begin. Never confuse your reader with a quotation that appears suddenly without introduction in your paper. Unannounced quotations leave your reader wondering how the quoted material relates to the point you are trying to make.

UNANNOUNCED QUOTATION

In America, physically attractive people often have unspoken advantages. In spite of claims to the contrary, "attractive people do better in school, where they receive more help, better grades, and less punishment [and] at work, where they are rewarded with higher pay, more prestigious jobs, and faster promotions" (Ackerman, 541).

In the following revision, the writer has integrated the quotation into the text not only by means of a signal phrase, but in a number of other ways as well. By giving the name of the speaker, referring to her credentials, and noting that she "knows well the importance of beauty," the writer provides more context so that the reader can better understand how the writer meant for the quotation to fit into the discussion.

INTEGRATED QUOTATION

In America, physically attractive people often have unspoken advantages in spite of claims to the contrary. Diane Ackerman, author of *A Natural History of the Senses*, knows well the importance of beauty; she has seen that "attractive people do better in school, where they receive more help, better grades, and less punishment [and] at work, where they are rewarded with higher pay, more prestigious jobs, and faster promotions" (541).

How well you integrate a quote, paraphrase, or summary into your paper depends partly on varying your signal phrases and, in particular, choosing a verb for the signal phrase that accurately conveys the tone and intent of the writer you are citing. If a writer is arguing, use the verb *argues* (or *asserts, claims,* or *contends*); if the writer is contesting a particular position or fact, use the verb *contests* (or *denies, disputes, refutes,* or *rejects*). In using verbs that are specific to the situation in your paper, you bring your readers into the intellectual debate as well as avoid the monotony of repeating such all-purpose verbs as *says* or *writes*.

You should always try to use a signal phrase that fits the situation in your essay. The following are just a few examples of how you can vary signal phrases to add interest to your paper.

Malcolm X confesses that . . .
As linguist Deborah Tannen has observed, . . .
According to television watchdog Marie Winn, . . .
Bruce Catton, noted historian, emphasizes . . .
Judith Ortiz Cofer rejects the widely held belief that . . .
Gore Vidal enriches our understanding of . . .

Here are other verbs that you might use when constructing signal phrases.

acknowledges	declares	points out
adds	endorses	reasons
admits	grants	reports
believes	implies	responds
compares	insists	suggests
confirms		

DOCUMENTING SOURCES

Whenever you summarize, paraphrase, or quote a person's thoughts and ideas, and when you use facts or statistics that are not commonly known or believed, you must properly acknowledge the source of your information. You must document the source of your information whenever you

- Quote a source word for word
- Refer to information and ideas from another source that you present in your own words as either a paraphrase or a summary
- Cite statistics, tables, charts, or graphs

You do not need to document

- Your own observations, experiences, and ideas
- Factual information available in a number of reference works (known as "common knowledge")
- Proverbs, sayings, and familiar quotations

A reference to the source of your borrowed information is called a *citation*. There are many systems for making citations, and your citations must consistently follow one of these systems. The documentation style recommended by the Modern Language Association (MLA) is commonly used in English and the humanities and is the style used throughout this book. Another common system is American Psychological Association (APA) style, which is used in the social sciences. In general, your instructor will tell you which system to use. For more information on documentation styles, consult the appropriate manual or handbook. For MLA style, consult the *MLA Handbook for Writers of Research Papers,* 5th ed. (New York: MLA, 1999) and the most current *MLA Style Manual and Guide to Scholarly Publishing.* For guidelines for documenting Internet sources, check the MLA Web site: <http://www.mla.org>.

There are two components of documentation in a research paper: the *in-text citation,* placed in the body of your paper, and the *list of works cited,* which provides complete publication data on your sources and is placed at the end of your paper.

In-Text Citations

Most in-text citations, also known as parenthetical citations, consist of only the author's last name and a page reference. Usually, the author's name is given in an introductory or signal phrase at the beginning of the borrowed material, and the page reference is given in parentheses at the end. If the author's name is not given at the beginning, it belongs in the parentheses along with the page reference. The parenthetical reference signals the end of the borrowed material and directs your readers to the list of works cited should they want to pursue a source. You should treat electronic sources as you would print sources; keep in mind that some electronic sources use paragraph numbers instead of page numbers.

Consider the following examples of in-text citations from a student paper that borrows information from essays in *Subjects/Strategies*.

IN-TEXT CITATIONS (MLA STYLE)

The death penalty is in the news again, but this time the focus is not on whether we should have such a penalty. Some people question the medical and ethical consequences of the tools we use for executions.

Citation with author's name in the signal phrase

Surgeon and medical ethicist Sherwin B. Nuland, for example, argues persuasively that "electrocution is a barbaric way to kill someone" and therefore that "the electric chair should be forbidden" (647). Others believe that because "DNA tests have provided stone-cold proof that 69 people were sent to prison and death row in North America for crimes they did not commit"

Citation with authors' names in parentheses

(Dwyer, Neufeld, and Scheck 661), such tests ought to be administered routinely for persons standing trial for a capital offense.

LIST OF WORKS CITED (MLA STYLE)

Dwyer, Jim, Peter Neufeld, and Barry Scheck. "When Justice Lets Us Down." Subjects/Strategies. 9th ed. Ed. Paul Eschholz and Alfred Rosa. New York: Bedford/St. Martin's, 2002. 660-62.

Nuland, Sherwin B. "Cruel and Unusual." Subjects/ Strategies. 9th ed. Ed. Paul Eschholz and Alfred Rosa. New York: Bedford/St. Martin's, 2002. 646-47.

In the preceding example, page references are to the articles as they appear here in *Subjects/Strategies*. For articles and books located in the library, consult the following MLA guidelines for the list of works cited or the appropriate manual or handbook.

List of Works Cited

In this section, you will find general guidelines for creating a list of works cited, followed by sample entries designed to cover the citation situations you will encounter most often. Make sure that you follow the formats as they appear on the following pages.

General Guidelines

- Begin the list on a fresh page following the last page of text.
- Organize the list alphabetically by the author's last name. If the entry has no author name, alphabetize by the first major word of the title.
- Double-space the list.
- Begin each entry at the left margin. If the entry is longer than one line, indent the second and subsequent lines five spaces or one-half inch.
- Do not number the entries.

Books

BOOK BY ONE AUTHOR

List the author's last name first, followed by a comma and the author's first name. Underline the title, which goes next. Follow with the city of publication and a shortened version of the publisher's name — for example, *Houghton* for Houghton Mifflin, or *Cambridge UP* for Cambridge University Press. End with the year of publication.

Pynchon, Thomas. <u>Mason & Dixon</u>. New York: Henry Holt, 1997.

BOOK BY TWO OR THREE AUTHORS

List the first author (following the order on the title page) in the same way as for a single-author book; list subsequent authors first name first in the order in which they appear on the title page.

Gates, Henry Louis, Jr., and Cornell West. <u>The Future of the Race</u>. New York: Vintage, 1996.

BOOK BY FOUR OR MORE AUTHORS

List the first author in the same way as for a single-author book, followed by a comma and the abbreviation *et al.* ("and others").

Chomsky, Noam, et al. <u>Acts of Aggression</u>. New York: Seven
    Stories, 1999.

SEVERAL WORKS BY THE SAME AUTHOR

List two or more books by the same author in alphabetical order by title. List the first book by the author's name. After the first book, in place of the author's name substitute three unspaced hyphens followed by a period.

Stone, Robert. <u>Damascus Gate</u>. Boston: Houghton, 1998.
---. <u>Dog Soldiers, A Novel</u>. Boston: Houghton, 1974.

REVISED EDITION

Hassan, Ihab. <u>The Dismemberment of Orpheus: Toward a
    Postmodern Literature</u>. 2nd ed. Madison: U of
    Wisconsin P, 1982.

EDITED BOOK

Douglass, Frederick, <u>Narrative of the Life of Frederick
    Douglass, an American Slave, Written by Himself</u>.
    Ed. Benjamin Quarles. Cambridge: Belknap, 1960.

TRANSLATION

Oe, Kenzaburo. <u>A Personal Matter</u>. Trans. John Nathan. New
    York: Grove, 1968.

ANTHOLOGY

Eschholz, Paul, and Alfred Rosa, eds. <u>Subjects/
    Strategies</u>. 9th ed. New York: Bedford/St. Martin's,
    2002.

SECTION IN AN ANTHOLOGY

James, Samuel W. "Oligochaeta: Megascolecidae and Other
    Earth Worms from Southern and Midwestern North

America." <u>Soil Biology Guide</u>. Ed. Daniel L. Dindal.
New York: Wiley, 1990. 379–86.

SECTION OR CHAPTER IN A BOOK

Carver, Raymond. "Kindling." <u>Call If You Need Me: The
Uncollected Fiction and Other Prose</u>. New York:
Vintage, 2001.

Periodicals

ARTICLE IN A JOURNAL WITH CONTINUOUS PAGINATION THROUGHOUT AN ANNUAL VOLUME

Some journals paginate issues continuously, by volume; that is, the page numbers in one issue pick up where the previous issue left off. For these journals, the year of publication, in parentheses, follows the volume number.

Howard, June. "Unraveling Regions, Unsettling Periods:
Sara Orne Jewett and American Literary History."
<u>American Literature</u> 68 (1996): 365–84.

ARTICLE IN A JOURNAL WITH SEPARATE PAGINATION IN EACH ISSUE

Some journals paginate by issue; each issue begins with page 1. For these journals, follow the volume number with a period and the issue number. Then give the year of publication in parentheses.

Douglas, Ann. "The Failure of the New York
Intellectuals." <u>Raritan</u> 17.4 (1998): 1–23.

ARTICLE IN A MONTHLY MAGAZINE

Keizer, Garret. "Sound and Fury: The Politics of Noise in a
Loud Society." <u>Harper's Magazine</u> Mar. 2001: 39-48.

ARTICLE IN A WEEKLY OR BIWEEKLY MAGAZINE

Hamill, Pete. "On Lars-Erik Nelson." <u>New York Review of
Books</u> 11 Jan. 2001: 4.

ARTICLE IN A NEWSPAPER

If an article in a newspaper or magazine appears discontinuously — that is, if it starts on one page and skips one or more pages before continuing — include only the first page, followed by a plus sign.

Donnelly, John. "In the South, Deadly Silence." <u>Boston
     Globe</u> 1 June 2001: A1+.

EDITORIAL OR LETTER TO THE EDITOR
"The Return of Fuzzy Math." Editorial. <u>New York Times</u>
     1 Mar. 2001, late ed.: A32.
Norman, Naomi. Letter. <u>New York Times</u> 2 Mar. 2001, late
     ed.: A22.

Internet Sources
The following guidelines and models for citing information retrieved
from the World Wide Web are the very latest advice of the MLA, as
borrowed from the *MLA Handbook for Writers of Research Papers*, 5th
ed. (1999) and from the MLA's Web site <http://www.mla.org>. When
listing an electronic source in your list of works cited, include the following elements if they are available and relevant.

- Name of the author, editor, compiler, or translator of the source,
  reversed for alphabetizing and followed by an abbreviation, such
  as *ed.*, if appropriate
- Title of the poem, short story, article, essay, or similar short work
  within a scholarly project, database, or periodical (in quotation
  marks) or title of a posting to a discussion list or forum (taken
  from the subject line and put in quotation marks), followed by the
  description *Online posting*
- Title of book (underlined)
- Name of the editor, compiler, or translator of the text (if relevant
  and if not cited earlier), preceded by the appropriate abbreviation,
  such as *Ed.*
- Publication information for any print version of the source
- Title of the scholarly project, database, periodical, or professional
  or personal site (underlined) or, for professional or personal sites
  with no title, a description, such as *Home page*
- Name of the editor of the scholarly project or database (if available)
- Version number of the source (if not part of the title) or, for a
  journal, the volume number, issue number, or other identifying
  number
- Date of electronic publication, of the latest update, or of posting
- For a posting to a discussion list or forum, the name of the list or
  forum

- The number range or total number of pages, paragraphs, or other sections, if they are numbered
- Name of the institution or organization sponsoring or associated with the Web site, if any
- Date when you accessed the source
- Electronic address, or URL of the source (in angle brackets)

MLA style requires that you break URLs extending over more than one line only after a slash. Do *not* add hyphens, spaces, or any other punctuation to indicate the break.

SCHOLARLY PROJECT

Project Gutenberg. Ed. Michael Hart. 23 Feb. 2001. 6 Mar.
      2001 <http://promo.net/pg>.

PROFESSIONAL SITE

MLA on the Web. Modern Language Association. 20 Sept.
      2000. 1 Mar. 2001 <http://www.mla.org>.

PERSONAL SITE

Levi, Asher. Literary Kicks. 28 Feb. 2001
      <http://www.charm.net/~brooklyn/LitKicks.html>.

BOOK

Whitman, Walt. Leaves of Grass. 1900. Bartleby.com: Great
      Books Online. 6 Mar. 2001 <http://www.bartleby.com/
      142>.

POEM

Blake, William. "London." The William Blake Page. Ed.
      Richard Record. 14 Feb. 2001 <http://
      members.aa.net/~urizen/experience/soe.html>.

ARTICLE IN A JOURNAL

Cummings, William. "Interdisciplinary Social Science."
      Electronic Journal of Sociology 5.2 (2000) 12 Jan.
      2001 <http://www.sociology.org/content/vol005.002/
      cummings.html>.

ARTICLE IN A NEWSPAPER

Kessler, Glenn. "Committee Approves Reduction in
    Individual Tax Rates." Washington Post 1 Mar. 2001.
    13 Mar. 2001 <http://washingtonpost.com/wp-dyn/
    articles/A8679-2001Mar1.html>.

ARTICLE IN AN ONLINE REFERENCE WORK

"e. e. cummings." Encyclopedia.com. 1994. The Concise
    Columbia Electronic Encyclopedia. 3rd ed. 12 Sept.
    2000 <http://www.encyclopedia.com/articles/
    03328.htm>.

WORK FROM AN ONLINE SUBSCRIPTION SERVICE

Kappel-Smith, Diana. "Fickle Desert Blooms: Opulent One
    Year, No-Shows the Next." Smithsonian Magazine Mar.
    1995. 9 pp. America Online. 18 April 2000. Keyword:
    desert.

E-MAIL

De Roo, Mikola. E-mail to the author. 20 May 2001.

POSTING TO A DISCUSSION LIST

Preston, Dennis R. "Re: Basketball Terms." Online
    posting. 8 Nov. 1997. American Dialect Society.
    10 Jan. 2000 <http://www2.et.byu.edu/~lilliek/ads/
    indes.htm>.

SYNCHRONOUS COMMUNICATION

Jensen, Carlos. "MediaMOO Symposium: Using 3D Graphics in
    Online Communities." 20 Mar. 2000. MediaMOO. 2 Feb.
    2001 <http://www.cc.gatech.edu/~carlosj/
    MediaMOO.html>.

Other Nonprint Sources

SOURCE ON A PERIODICAL CD-ROM

James, Caryn. "An Army Family as Strong as Its Weakest
    Link." New York Times 16 Sept. 1994, late ed.:
    C8. New York Times Ondisc. CD-ROM. UMI-Proquest.
    Oct. 1994.

SOURCE ON A NONPERIODICAL CD-ROM

Sheehy, Donald, ed. Robert Frost: Poems, Life, Legacy.
    CD-ROM. New York: Holt, 1997.

TELEVISION OR RADIO PROGRAM

The American Experience: Chicago 1968. Writ. Chana Gazit.
    Narr. W.S. Merwin. PBS. WNET, New York. 13 Nov.
    1997.

MOVIE, VIDEOTAPE, RECORD, OR SLIDE PROGRAM

Gladiator. Dir. Ridley Scott. Perf. Russell Crowe,
    Joaquin Phoenix, Connie Nielsen, Oliver Reed, Derek
    Jacobi, Djimon Hounsou, and Richard Harris.
    DreamWorks Pictures, 2000.

PERSONAL INTERVIEW

Alameno, Joseph. Personal interview. 15 April 1998.

LECTURE

Menand, Louis. Lecture. English 802. CUNY Graduate
    School, New York. 14 Nov. 1995.

A NOTE ON PLAGIARISM

The importance of honesty and accuracy in doing library research
can't be stressed enough. Any material borrowed word for word must
be placed within quotation marks and be properly cited; any idea, explanation, or argument you have paraphrased or summarized must be
documented, and it must be clear where the paraphrased material begins and ends. In short, to use someone else's ideas, whether in their
original form or in an altered form, without proper acknowledgment
is to be guilty of plagiarism. And plagiarism is plagiarism even if it is
accidental. A little attention and effort at the note-taking stage can go
a long way toward eliminating the possibility of inadvertent plagiarism. Check all direct quotations against the wording of the original,
and double-check your paraphrases to be sure that you have not used
the writer's wording or sentence structure. It is easy to forget to put
quotation marks around material taken verbatim or to use the same
sentence structure and most of the same words — substituting a synonym here and there — and record it as a paraphrase. In working

closely with the ideas and words of others, intellectual honesty demands that we distinguish between what we borrow — and therefore acknowledge in a citation — and what is our own.

While writing your paper, be careful whenever you incorporate one of your notes into your paper: Make sure that you put quotation marks around material taken verbatim, and double-check your text against your note card — or, better yet, against the original if you have it on hand — to make sure that your quotation is accurate. When paraphrasing or summarizing, make sure you haven't inadvertently borrowed key words or sentence structures from the original.

Using Quotation Marks for Language Borrowed Directly

Whenever you use another person's exact words or sentences, you must enclose the borrowed language in quotation marks. Without quotation marks you give your reader the impression that the wording is your own. Even if you cite the source, you are guilty of plagiarism if you fail to use quotation marks. The following example demonstrates both plagiarism and a correct citation for a direct quotation.

ORIGINAL SOURCE

There are plenty of good television programs and movies that aim higher and do well at the box office. Since the market is master, people need not be passive about expressing their tastes.

— ROBERT SCHEER,
"Violence Is Us," page 613

PLAGIARISM

There are plenty of good television programs and movies that, according to Robert Scheer, aim higher and do well at the box office. Since the market is master, people need not be passive about expressing their tastes (613).

CORRECT CITATION OF BORROWED WORDS IN QUOTATION MARKS

"There are plenty of good television programs and movies that aim higher and do well at the box office," according to Robert Scheer. "Since the market is master," he says, "people need not be passive about expressing their tastes" (613).

Using Your Own Words and Word Order
When Summarizing and Paraphrasing

When summarizing or paraphrasing a source you need to use your own language. Pay particular attention to word choice and word order, especially if you are paraphrasing. Remember, it is not enough simply to use a synonym here or there and think you have paraphrased the source; you *must* restate the idea from the original in your own words, using your own style and sentence structure. In the following example, notice how plagiarism can occur when care is not taken in the wording or sentence structure of a paraphrase. Notice that in the acceptable paraphrase, the student writer uses her own language and sentence structure.

ORIGINAL SOURCE

As family ties grow weaker and vaguer, as children's lives become more separate from their parents', as parents' educational role in their children's lives is taken over by television and schools, family life becomes increasingly more unsatisfying for both parents and children.

— MARIE WINN,
"Television and Family Life," page 512

UNACCEPTABLY CLOSE WORDING

According to Winn, family life becomes increasingly less satisfying for all concerned when family ties weaken, children begin to lead lives separate from their parents', and television and schools take over the educational role in children's lives formerly fulfilled by parents (512).

UNACCEPTABLY CLOSE SENTENCE STRUCTURE

Winn believes that as family bonds become less defined, as young people begin to lead lives independent of their folks', and as TV and schools assume the instructional role formerly delegated to parents, family life becomes less rewarding for all concerned (512).

ACCEPTABLE PARAPHRASE

Winn reports that life at home for many American families is becoming less rewarding or gratifying. She attributes this state of affairs to three basic causes: (1) the breakdown of family bonds, (2) the widening gap between children's lives and those of their parents, and (3) television and schools assuming a dominant instructional role in the lives of children (512).

▶ *Preventing Plagiarism*

Questions to Ask about Direct Quotations

- Do quotation marks clearly indicate the language that I borrowed verbatim?
- Is the language of the quotation accurate, with no missing or misquoted words or phrases?
- Do brackets or ellipsis marks clearly indicate any changes or omissions I have introduced?
- Does a signal phrase naming the author introduce each quotation? Does the verb in the signal phrase help establish a context for each quotation?
- Does a parenthetical page citation follow each quotation?

Questions to Ask about Summaries and Paraphrases

- Is each summary and paraphrase written in my own words and style?
- Does each summary and paraphrase accurately represent the opinion, position, or reasoning of the original writer?
- Does each summary and paraphrase start with a signal phrase so that readers know where my borrowed material begins?
- Does each summary and paraphrase conclude with a parenthetical page citation?

Questions to Ask about Facts and Statistics

- Do I use a signal phrase or some other marker to introduce each fact or statistic that is not common knowledge so that readers know where the borrowed material begins?
- Is each fact or statistic that is not common knowledge clearly documented with a parenthetical page citation?

Finally, as you proofread your final draft, check all your citations one last time. If at any time while you are taking notes or writing your paper you have a question about plagiarism, consult your instructor for clarification and guidance before proceeding.

A DOCUMENTED STUDENT ESSAY

Melanie Milks's essay grew out of her reading of *Subjects/ Strategies*. Her assignment was to write an essay in response to one that she had read.

She knew from past experience that to write a good essay, she would have to write on a topic she cared about. She also knew that she should allow herself a reasonable amount of time to gather her ideas and to focus her topic. After reading Marie Winn's "Television and Family Life" in Chapter 12, Milks knew that she'd found her topic — television and how it affects the family. She started to see this paper as an opportunity to become more informed about the issue, to articulate her own position on it, and to explore her childhood experiences.

Milks began by brainstorming about her topic. She made lists of all the ideas, facts, questions, arguments, opposing arguments, and refutations that came to mind as a result of her own reflections about television viewing. She then went to the library to find additional information and was successful in locating several helpful sources. Once she was confident that she had enough information to begin writing, she made a rough outline of an organizational pattern she believed would work for her. Keeping this pattern in mind, Milks wrote a first draft of her essay. Later she went back and examined it carefully, assessing how it could be improved.

Milks was writing this essay in the second half of the semester after she had read and written a number of essays and had learned the importance of such matters as good paragraphing, unity, and sound organization. In revising her first draft, Milks realized that a chronological organizational pattern would best suit her purpose, and she rearranged her discussion of family experiences accordingly. She also found places where phrases and even whole sentences could be added to make her meaning clearer. She repositioned some sentences, added key transitions, and rewrote her concluding paragraphs to make them more forceful and more persuasive. As you read Milks's final draft, notice how she develops each of her paragraphs, how she uses specific information and examples to support her thesis and purpose, and how she has used the MLA in-text citation system to acknowledge her sources. Finally, notice how Milks uses her opening paragraph to establish a context for her essay and how she uses her concluding paragraph to bring her essay back full circle to her parents' decision not to have television in their home.

The Absence of Television in My Family

Melanie Milks

I believe television is going to be the test of   1
the modern world, and that in this new opportunity
to see beyond the range of our vision we shall discover either a new and unbearable disturbance of
the general peace or a saving radiance in the sky.

We shall stand or fall by television -- of that I am
quite sure.

                              -- E. B. White, from "One Man's Meat,"
                                 Harper's (October 1938)

About two months ago at a dinner for the runners in   2
the Montreal Marathon, my father and I had a discussion
with a woman concerning the effects of television on family life. At one point in our conversation, my father
mentioned to her that I grew up in a television-free
environment. This woman, Elizabeth, looked at my father
and asked, "How did you do it?" Elizabeth said she would
prefer not having a television in her home but she relies
on television for her own stimulation as well as an
outlet for her children. Admitting that television dis-
rupted her family harmony, Elizabeth confessed it would
be nearly impossible to eliminate television from her
daily routine. Nevertheless she applauded the decision my
parents made in 1973 to exclude television from our home.
In The New Read-Aloud Handbook, Jim Trelease reports,
"Both children and adults average nearly four hours a day
[in front of the television] passively letting someone
else do all the thinking, speaking, imagining, and exploring" (118). Another study confirms Trelease's startling conclusions (Russell A1). My parents feared that a
television would dominate our lives and provide an unnecessary disruption of family.

As a child, I never developed a real appetite for   3
television; I had too many things to keep me occupied.
If I wasn't looking through a stack of books, I could
be found cutting purses out of colorful sheets of construction paper, singing to my favorite records, or
coloring with my crayons. There was never enough time,
or need, to fit television programs like Mr. Rogers,
Sesame Street, or The Electric Company into my day. My
mother shuddered at the thought of relying on these
programs to teach me how to count from one to ten and
recite my ABC's. She and my father gladly undertook this
project themselves. We used flashcards and pieces of
paper labeling every inch of our house to begin my reading instruction.

Story time became a nightly ritual for both my par- 4
ents and me. Cuddling up next to them was the best part
of my day. I could have spent hours listening to them
read while I gazed at the illustrations in front of me.
The beautiful drawings pulled me into the story, mesmer-
izing me. My favorite read-aloud books were the Beatrix
Potter series, The Little Princess and The Secret Garden
by Frances Hodgson Burnett, and Anne of Green Gables by
Lucy M. Montgomery. Each story contained lovely illustrations that made my imagination soar.

Reading became a pleasure for me, and consequently I 5
never considered it a chore in school. In second and
third grade the public library became my second home.
With encouragement from my parents I got my first library
card. While many of my friends sat in front of the television after school, I roamed every aisle in the children's section. I read everything from the Anastasia
Krupnik series to Superfudge. In third grade I begged my
teacher, Mrs. Coombs, to be allowed to read from the
fourth grade book section. After two or three sample novels, I was permitted to choose my first novel from the
coveted shelves. I proudly chose a book entitled Roll of
Thunder Hear My Cry, one of the best young adult books I
have ever read. While my friends were busy reenacting
their favorite episodes of Chips or The Dukes of Hazzard,
I lingered on every word in my book.

As I got older, I'd often postpone bedtime reading 6
to play checkers or backgammon with my dad. We spent
hours huddled over game boards, waiting in silence as the
other person developed a strategy for the next move. The
silence was always broken by a story or a question. We
exchanged details from our day that we failed to mention
at the dinner table, and often my dad would tell hilari-
ous stories from his childhood. Laughter continually rang
throughout our house. Marie Winn, a nationally recognized
television critic and author of The Plug-In Drug, asserts
that there are "decreased opportunities for simple conversation between parents and children in a television-
centered home" (510). I believe this. My dad and I might
not have done so many things together if we had a television in our house.

Without a television to turn on, I had to use my   7
imagination to its fullest. When we lived in Illinois, I
had access to the local library, great playground structures to explore at my elementary school, and friends'
houses close by. When we moved to rural Vermont, all my
freedoms slipped away from me. I found it difficult ac-
climating myself to my new surroundings. My parents
showed me that Vermont had as much to offer as our urban
community in Illinois. Our weekends were packed with
camping trips in the Green Mountains and biking along the
shores of Lake Champlain. In the winter we cross-country
skied in the pastures behind our house. I don't remember
having many dull moments growing up.

Nevertheless, at the age of nine I had my own battle   8
with television. Without the accessibility to the local
library in our little Vermont town, I would race to my
friend Julie's house after school. Instead of enjoying a
beautiful fall day outside discovering a new corner of
the woods, we sat glued in front of her television watching the last twenty-five minutes of Guiding Light, a soap
opera I became hooked on. Looking back now, I realize how
true Urie Bronfenbrenner's statement about television is.
He said, "The television set casts its magic spell,
freezing speech and action, turning the living into
silent statues as long as the enchantment lasts. . . .
Turning on the television set can turn off the process
that transforms children into people" (qtd. in Winn 505).
Never before did I actually realize the addicting qualities of television. I know watching television requires
no intelligence because the mind is engaged in the activity on the screen.

Eventually my parents would not let me go to Julie's   9
after school. They witnessed a deterioration in my attention span because of too many afternoons spent in front
of what Marie Winn calls the "plug-in drug." In the
evenings I would be somewhat dazed from hours of watching
television. My parents constantly reminded me why they
chose not to purchase one. But I did not want to listen
to their explanations. Sometimes I felt like an outsider
at school because I had not seen a particular episode of
Silver Spoons or Who's the Boss? However, my parents

would not give in to my pestering. They did not want me
to grow up like they did, spending beautiful afternoons
in front of the television. At my grandparents' house the
television was always on. My father's parents ran a store
and my mother's parents both worked. Much of the time my
parents spent with their families was done silently,
watching evening sitcoms. Jim Trelease states that "conversation during [a television] program is seldom if ever
encouraged by the child or the parents" (122). Parenting
becomes easy without much interaction between parent and
child. Family activities have diminished since the development of television. My parents were afraid of falling
into this trap.

At college, my roommate and I have a television in   10
our apartment, and even though it is hardly on, we have
favorite shows we occasionally sit down to watch, or
catch during dinner -- 60 Minutes on Sunday, Melrose
Place on Monday, 90210 and Party of Five on Wednesday,
Seinfeld and ER on Thursday, and of course CNN. I rarely
have time to watch all of these shows in a given week,
but there are many people who do. I have found that after
a full day of work the lure of the television presents a
distraction, and sometimes it is very difficult to turn
it off and do my work. Growing up I never had the desire
to spend hours in front of the television following a
certain show or avoiding something that I had to do. Now,
I realize the challenge my parents had keeping the television out of our home and that they were very courageous
to raise two children in a television-free environment. I
wish I still lived there.

Works Cited

Russell, Christine. "Study: Teens Sitting through Life."
     Burlington Free Press 8 Nov. 1994: A1.
Trelease, Jim. The New Read-Aloud Handbook. New York:
     Penguin, 1989.
White, E. B. "One Man's Meat." Harper's Oct. 1938:
     553-56.
Winn, Marie. "Television and Family Life." Subjects/
     Strategies. 8th ed. Ed. Paul Eschholz and Alfred
     Rosa. New York: Bedford/St. Martin's, 1999. 504-12.

CHAPTER 5

Exemplification

WHAT IS EXEMPLIFICATION?

Exemplification is the use of examples — facts, opinions, samples, and anecdotes or stories — to make a generalization more vivid, understandable, and persuasive. Saying that "Kris did a wonderful job of managing her roommate's campaign for Student Government Association president" is not nearly as effective as providing concrete reasons that support this statement. For example, consider the following rewrite: "Kris did a wonderful job of managing her roommate's campaign for Student Government Association president because she kept her roommate up to date on students' concerns about parking and a proposed increase in student fees. In addition, Kris made posters to advertise her roommate's candidacy, set up dormitory meetings so that students could meet her, and then, on election day, went through the dorms reminding students to vote for her." Examples serve to illustrate the truth or validity of the generalization you make.

In the following paragraph from "Wandering through Winter," notice how naturalist Edwin Way Teale uses examples to support his generalization that "country people" have many superstitions about how harsh the coming winter will be.

Topic sentence about weather superstitions frames the entire paragraph.
    In the folklore of the country, numerous superstitions relate to winter weather. Back-country farmers examine their husks — the thicker the husk, the colder the winter. They watch the acorn crop — the more acorns, the more severe the season. They observe where white-faced hornets

Series of examples that amplify and elucidate the topic sentence

place their paper nests — the higher they are, the deeper will be the snow. They examine the size and shape and color of the spleens of butchered hogs for clues to the severity of the season. They keep track of the blooming of the dogwood in the spring — the more abundant the blooms, the more bitter the cold in January. When chipmunks carry their tails high and squirrels have heavier fur, the superstitious gird themselves for a long, hard winter. Without any specific basis, a wider-than-usual black band on a woolly-bear caterpillar is accepted as a sign that winter will arrive early and stay late. Even the way a cat sits beside the stove carries its message to the credulous. According to the belief once widely held in the Ozarks, a cat sitting with its tail to the fire indicates very cold weather is on the way.

— Edwin Way Teale

Teale uses nine separate examples to illustrate and explain his topic sentence about weather-related superstitions. These examples demonstrate his knowledge of folk traditions and entertain us at the same time. As readers, we come away from Teale's paragraph thinking that he is an authority on his subject.

Teale's examples are a series of related but varied illustrations of his main point. Not only are there many examples, but the examples are representative because they illustrate the main generalization and are typical or characteristic of the topic. Sometimes just one sustained example is more effective if the example is representative and the writer develops it well. Here is one such example by basketball legend Bill Russell from his autobiographical *Second Wind:*

Topic sentence about athletes slipping into an unknown gear

Extended example of Bob Beamon's record-shattering day exemplifies Russell's topic sentence.

Example illustrates that even Beamon did not anticipate his own performance.

Every champion athlete has a moment when everything goes so perfectly for him he slips into a gear that he didn't know was there. It's easy to spot that perfect moment in a sport like track. I remember watching the 1968 Olympics in Mexico City, where the world record in the long jump was just under 27 feet. Then Bob Beamon flew down the chute and leaped out over the pit in a majestic jump that I have seen replayed many times. There was an awed silence when the announcer said that Beamon's jump measured 29 feet 2¼ inches. Generally world records are broken by fractions of inches, but Beamon had exceeded the existing record by more than two feet. On learning what he had done, Beamon slumped down on the ground and cried. Most viewers' image of Beamon ends with the picture of him weeping on the ground, but in fact he got up and took some more jumps that day. I like to think that he did so because he had jumped for so long at his best that *even then* he didn't know what might come

> out of him. At the end of the day he wanted to be ab-
> solutely sure that he'd had his perfect day.

Few readers have experienced that "extra gear" that Russell describes, so he illustrates what he means with a single, extended example — in this case, an anecdote that gives substance to the idea he wants his readers to understand. Russell's example of Bob Beamon's record-breaking jump is not only concrete and specific; it is memorable because it so aptly captures the essence of his topic sentence about athletic perfection. Without this extended example, Russell's claim that every athlete "slips into a gear that he didn't know was there" would simply be a hollow statement.

WHY DO WRITERS USE EXEMPLIFICATION?

Exemplifying a point with examples is a basic strategy of human communication, and it serves several purposes for writers. First, examples make writing more vivid and interesting. Writing that consists of loosely strung generalizations is lifeless and difficult to read, regardless of the believability of the generalizations or our willingness to accept them. Good writers try to provide just the right kind and number of examples to make their ideas clear and convincing. For example, an essay about television bloopers will be dull and pointless without some examples of on-screen blunders — accidents, pratfalls, and "tips of the slongue," as one writer calls them. Likewise, a more serious essay on the dangers of drunk driving will have more impact if it is illustrated with descriptions of the victims' suffering and the grief and outrage of their family and friends.

Writers also use exemplification to explain or clarify their ideas. All readers want specific information and feel that it is the writer's responsibility to provide it. Even if readers are capable of providing examples themselves, they want to see what kind of evidence the writer is able to provide. In an essay on political leadership, for instance, the assertion "Successful leaders are often a product of their times" will certainly require further explanation. Such explanation could be provided very effectively through examples: Franklin D. Roosevelt, Winston Churchill, Charles de Gaulle, Corazon Aquino, and Nelson Mandela all rose to power because their people were looking for leadership in a time of national crisis. Keep in mind, however, that the use of these specific examples paints a different picture of the term "successful leaders" than a different set of examples would; unlike leaders like Joseph Stalin, Adolf Hitler, and Benito Mussolini, who rose to power under similar circumstances, the first group of leaders exercised their power in the interest of the people. The importance of carefully selected examples cannot be overemphasized. Good examples always clearly illustrate the writer's point or idea.

All of the selections in this chapter use exemplification to add interest and substance. The chapter's opening essay is Natalie Goldberg's "Be Specific," which itself uses a number of specific examples to illustrate a writer's need to be specific. She asserts, "Be specific. Don't say 'fruit.' Tell what kind of fruit — 'It is a pomegranate.' " In "An Audience with Dolly," Charles Siebert reflects on the meaning and impact of biotechnology by showing us the surprisingly unremarkable example of Dolly the sheep, an icon of the world of cloning. Mark Twain uses a variety of examples in "Corn-pone Opinions" to illustrate the power of social and economic factors on a person's opinions. In her essay "How to Give Orders like a Man," language expert Deborah Tannen uses different types of examples of the ways orders are given and received — gender-related, cross-cultural, and situational — to challenge the idea that indirectness in one's interpersonal communications necessarily conveys an undesirable powerlessness and a self-deprecating attitude. Alice Walker, in the essay "In Search of Our Mothers' Gardens," gives us poignant examples of the artistic expressions of the oppressed black women who went before her. These women carried the spark of creativity that is now Walker's cherished legacy. Leslie Marmon Silko, in her essay "Yellow Woman and a Beauty of the Spirit," uses narration and comparison and contrast in support of exemplification to illustrate the way her Pueblo people accommodated differences among themselves. As she writes, "In the old Pueblo world, differences were celebrated as signs of the Mother Creator's grace."

Exemplification is so useful and versatile a strategy that it is found in different kinds of writing, such as reports, cover letters, editorials, applications, proposals, law briefs, and reviews. In fact, there is hardly an essay in this book that does not use exemplification in one way or another.

AN ANNOTATED STUDENT ESSAY
USING EXEMPLIFICATION

Shannon Long wrote the following essay while she was a student at the University of Kentucky in Lexington. Confined to a wheelchair herself, Long knows firsthand the problems of accessibility on her campus. She uses this personal experience to show her readers that the physical improvements made at her university simply do not go far enough in solving the problems of wheelchair accessibility. Her examples of particular problems in specific buildings are intended to persuade readers that additional improvements are necessary.

Wheelchair Hell: A Look at

Campus Accessibility

Shannon Long

Opening example is a personal one and gives an excellent illustration of the problem of inaccessibility.

It was my first week of college, and I was going to the library to meet someone on the third floor and study. After entering the library, I went to the elevator and hit the button calling it. A few seconds later the doors opened, I rolled inside, and the doors closed behind me. Expecting the buttons to be down in front, I suddenly noticed that they were behind me -- and too high to reach. There I was stuck in the elevator with no way to get help. Finally, somebody got on at the fourth floor. I'd been waiting fifteen minutes.

1

Author shows that the problem of campus accessibility is a widespread issue.

I'm not the only one who has been a victim of inaccessibility. According to Jake Karnes, the Assistant Dean of Students and the Director of Handicapped Student Services, the University of Kentucky currently has eleven buildings that are inaccessible to students in wheelchairs. Many other buildings, like the library, are accessible, but have elevators that are inoperable by handicapped students. Yet, Section 504 of the Rehabilitation Act of 1973 states,

2

Explanation of the federal law regarding accessibility and financial assistance to the university

> No qualified handicapped person shall, because a recipient's facilities are inaccessible to or unusable by handicapped persons, be denied the benefits of, be excluded from participation in, or otherwise be subjected to discrimination under any program or activity receiving Federal financial assistance (Federal 22681).

When this law went into effect in 1977, 3
the University of Kentucky started a renovation process in which close to a million
dollars was spent on handicap modifications
(Karnes). But even though that much money
has been spent, there are still many more

Examples of
buildings that are
still inaccessible

modifications needed. Buildings still inaccessible to wheelchair students are the Administration Building, Alumni House, Barker
Hall, Bowman Hall, Bradley Hall, Engineering
Quadrangle, Gillis Building, Kinkead Hall,
Miller Hall, Safety and Security Building,
and Scovell Hall ("Transition Plan").

Examples of
problems created
by inaccessibility

So many inaccessible buildings create 4
many unnecessary problems. For example, if a
handicapped student wants to meet an administrator, he or she must make an appointment
to meet somewhere more accessible than the
Administration Building. Making appointments
is usually not a problem, but there is still
the fact that able-bodied students have no
problem entering the Administration Building
while handicapped students cannot. Though
handicapped students can enter the Gillis
Building, they cannot go above the ground
floor and even have to push a button to get
someone to come downstairs to help them.
Finally, for handicapped students to get
counseling from the Career Planning Center,
they must set up an appointment to meet with
someone at another place. In this case, some
students might not use the Center's services
because of the extra effort involved
(Croucher).

Examples of
problems for the
handicapped even
in buildings that
are accessible

Even many of the accessible buildings 5
have elevators, water fountains, and door
handles that are inoperable by handicapped
students (Karnes). Elevators in the Library
and Whitehall Classroom Building, for instance, have buttons too high for wheelchair
students, forcing them to ask somebody else

to hit the button. If there is nobody around to ask, the handicapped person simply has to wait. In the Chemistry and Physics Building, a key is needed to operate the elevator, forcing wheelchair students to ride up and down the hall to find somebody to help. Many water fountains are inaccessible to people in wheelchairs. Some buildings have only <u>one</u> accessible water fountain. Finally, hardly any buildings have doorknobs that students with hand and arm impairments can operate.

Examples of inaccessibility in residence halls

Many residence halls, such as Boyd Hall, Donovan Hall, Patterson Hall, and Keenland Hall, are also completely inaccessible. If a handicapped student wanted to drop by and see a friend or attend a party in one of these dorms, he or she would have to be carried up steps. Kirivan and Blanding Towers have bathrooms that are inaccessible. Also, in Kirivan Tower the elevator is so small that someone has to lift the back of the chair into the elevator. The complex lowrises -- Shawnee-town, Commonwealth Village, and Cooperstown Apartments -- are also inaccessible. Coopers-town has some first-floor apartments that are accessible, but a handicapped student couldn't very well live there because the bathrooms are inaccessible. All eleven soror-ities are inaccessible, and only five of the sixteen fraternities are accessible. Since the land sororities and fraternities are on is owned by UK, Section 504 does require that houses be accessible ("Transition Plan" 14, 15). Clearly, many UK places are still inaccessible. 6

Author argues that the university should make more changes to improve accessibility.

June 1980 was the deadline for meeting the requirements of Section 504 (Robinson 28). While the University of Kentucky has made significant changes to make campus buildings more accessible, many more changes are needed. Handicapped students often work to overachieve to prove their abilities. All 7

they ask for is a chance, and that chance
should not be blocked by high buttons, heavy
doors, or steps.

Works Cited

Croucher, Lisa. "Accessibility at U.K. for Handicapped
    Still Can Be Better." Kentucky Kernal. Date unknown.
Federal Register. Volume 42 (4 May 1977): 22681.
Karnes, Jake. Personal interview. 17 Oct. 1989.
Robinson, Rita. "For the Handicapped: Renovation Report
    Card." American School & University (Apr. 1980): 28.
"University of Kentucky -- Transition Plan" [report].
    Date unknown.

Analyzing Shannon Long's Essay of Exemplification: Questions for Discussion

1. What different types of examples does Long use in her essay?
2. What points do her examples serve to illustrate or support?
3. Which examples did you find most effective? Least effective? Explain why.

SUGGESTIONS FOR WRITING AN ESSAY OF EXEMPLIFICATION

Begin by thinking of ideas and generalizations about your topic that you can make clearer and more persuasive by illustrating them with facts, anecdotes, or specific details. You should focus primarily on your main point, the central generalization that you will develop in your essay. But also be alert for other statements or references that may benefit from exemplification. You will find that examples add clarity, color, and weight to what you say.

Consider the following generalization:

Americans are a pain-conscious people who would rather get rid of pain than seek and cure its root causes.

This assertion is broad and general; it raises the following questions: How so? What does this mean exactly? Why does the writer think so? The statement could be the topic sentence of a paragraph or perhaps even the thesis of an essay or of an entire book. As a writer, you could make it stronger and more meaningful through exemplification. You might support this statement by pointing to the sheer number of painkillers available and the different types of pain they address or by citing specific situations or specific cases in which Americans have gone to the drugstore instead of to a doctor. In addition, you might compare sales figures per capita of painkillers in the United States and in other countries.

Gather Your Examples

Before you begin to write, bring together as many examples as you can think of that are related to your subject — more even than you can possibly use. An example may be anything from a fact or a statistic to an anecdote or a story; it may be stated in a few words — "India's population is now approaching 900 million people" — or it may go on for several pages of elaborate description or explanation.

The kinds of examples you look for and where you look for them will depend, of course, on your subject and the point you want to make about it. If you plan to write about all the quirky, fascinating people who make up your family, you can gather your examples without leaving your room: descriptions of their habits and clothing, stories about their strange adventures, facts about their backgrounds, quotations from their conversations. If, however, you are writing an essay on book censorship in American public schools, you will need to do research in the library or perhaps on the Internet and read many sources to supply yourself with examples. Your essay might well include accounts drawn from newspapers; statistics published by librarians' or teachers' professional organizations; court transcripts and judicial opinions on censorship; and interviews with school board members, parents, book publishers, and even the authors whose work has been pulled off library shelves or kept out of the classroom.

The range of sources and the variety of examples are limited only by your imagination and the time you can spend on research. One student who was trying to answer the question "Do diets really work?" remembers her research in the library very clearly: "It's really not that difficult if you stay organized. I started with *The Readers' Guide to Periodical Literature*. I also thought it was wise to use a variety of magazines, starting with popular newsmagazines such as *Time* and *U.S. News & World Report*. After this, I consulted scholarly journals in order to get a better understanding of the short- and long-term effects of diets." As she puts it, "I collected all kinds of examples because I did not know at that point which ones would be most useful when I got to actually writing my paper, and I wanted to make sure that I had more than enough to choose from."

Shannon Long, in gathering examples for her "Wheelchair Hell" essay, relied on her own experiences on the University of Kentucky campus. She had been a "victim of inaccessibility," and she had interviewed the director of Handicapped Student Services to help her identify the buildings where problems existed and the exact nature of the problems for those in wheelchairs (problems such as inoperable door handles, locked elevators or elevators with hard-to-reach buttons, and inaccessible water fountains and bathrooms). In addition to her interview with the director, Long also consulted several public documents that addressed her problems — documents she includes in her Works Cited list.

Collecting an abundance of examples will allow you to choose the strongest and most representative ones for your essay, not merely the first ones that come to mind. Having enough material will also make it less likely that you will have to stop in mid-draft and hunt for further examples, losing the rhythm of your work or the thread of your ideas. Moreover, the more examples you gather, the more you will learn about your subject and the easier it will be to write about it with authority.

Test Your Examples

You must make sure that your examples are relevant. Do they clarify and support the points you want to make? Suppose the main point of your planned essay is that censorship runs rampant in American public education. A newspaper story about the banning of *Catcher in the Rye* and *The Merchant of Venice* from the local high school's English curriculum would clearly be relevant because it concerns book censorship at a public school. The fact that James Joyce's novel *Ulysses* was first banned as obscene and then vindicated in a famous trial, although a landmark case of censorship in American history, has nothing to do with books in public schools. While the case of *Ulysses* might be a useful example for other discussions of censorship, it would not be relevant to your essay.

Sometimes more than one of your examples will be relevant. In such cases, choose the examples that are most closely related to your main idea or generalization. If you were working on the pain essay mentioned earlier, a statistic indicating the sales of a particular drug in a given year might be interesting; a statistic showing that over the past ten years painkiller sales in America have increased more rapidly than the population would be relevant to the idea that Americans are a pain-conscious people, and so this statistic could be used to support your assertion. In other words, examples may be interesting in and of themselves, but they only really come alive when they illustrate and link important ideas that the writer is trying to promote.

Be Sure Your Examples Are Representative

Besides being relevant, to be most effective an example should also be representative. The story it tells or the fact it presents should be typical of the main point or concept, an example indicative of a larger pattern rather than an uncommon or isolated occurrence. Figures showing how many people use aspirin, and for what purposes, would be representative because aspirin is the most widely used painkiller in America. Statistics about a newly developed barbiturate (a highly specialized kind of painkiller) might show a tremendous increase in its use compared with the use of other barbiturates, but the example would not be very representative because not very many people use barbiturates compared with other kinds of painkillers. In fact, giving the barbiturate as an example might even cause readers to wonder why aspirin, which is better known, was not used as an example.

If, while working on the censorship paper, you found reports on a dozen quiet administrative hearings and orderly court cases, but only one report of a sensational incident in which books were actually burned in a school parking lot, the latter incident, however dramatic, is clearly not a representative example. You might want to mention the book burning in your essay as an extremist viewpoint, but you should not present it as typical of how censorship is handled.

What if your examples do not support your point? Perhaps you have missed some important information and need to look further. It may be, though, that the problem is with the point itself. For example, suppose you intend your censorship paper to illustrate the following thesis: "Book censorship has seriously impacted American public education." However, you have not found very many examples in which specific books were actually censored or banned outright. While many attempts at censorship have been made, most were ultimately prevented or overturned in the courts. You might then have to revise your original thesis: "Although there have been many well-publicized attempts to censor books in public schools, actual censorship is relatively rare."

Organize Your Examples

It is important to arrange your examples in an order that serves your purpose, is easy for readers to follow, and will have maximum effect. Some possible patterns of organization include chronological order and spatial order. Others include moving from the simplest example to the most difficult to understand, as in Russell Baker's "The Plot against People" (page 399); from the least controversial to the most controversial, as in Martin Luther King Jr.'s "The Ways of Meeting Oppression" (page 411); or from the least important to the most important, as in Jo Goodwin Parker's "What Is Poverty?" (page 467). Or you may hit upon an order that "feels right" to you, as Edwin Way Teale did in his paragraph about winter superstitions. How many examples you include depends, of course, on the length and nature of the assignment. Before starting the first draft, it may be helpful to work out your pattern of organization in a rough outline, using only enough words so that you will be able to tell which example each entry refers to.

Use Transitions

While it is important to give the presentation of your examples an inherent logic, it is also important to link your examples to the topic sentences in your paragraphs and, indeed, to the thesis of your entire paper by using transitional words and expressions, such as *for example, for instance, therefore, afterward, in other words, next,* and *finally*. Such structural devices will signal your use of examples and will make the sequencing of the examples easy to follow.

Share Your Work with Others

Students often find it particularly helpful to share the drafts of their essays with other students in their writing class. One of our students commented, "In total, I probably wrote five or six different versions of this essay. I shared them with members of the class, and their comments were extremely insightful. I remember one student's question in particular because she really got me to focus on the problems with fad diets. The students also helped me to see where I needed examples to explain what I was talking about. The very first draft that I wrote is completely different from the one I submitted in class."

> ▶ *Questions for Revision: Exemplification*
>
> 1. Is my topic well focused?
> 2. Does my thesis statement clearly identify my topic and make an assertion about it?
> 3. Are my examples well chosen to support my thesis? Are there other examples that might work better?
> 4. Are my examples representative? That is, are they typical of the main point or concept, rather than bizarre or atypical?
> 5. Do I have enough examples to be convincing, or do I have too many examples?
> 6. Have I developed my examples in enough detail so as to be clear to readers?
> 7. Have I organized my examples in some logical pattern, and is that pattern clear to readers?
> 8. Does the essay accomplish my purpose?

Be Specific

Natalie Goldberg

Author Natalie Goldberg has made a specialty of writing about writing. Her first and best-known work, Writing Down the Bones: Freeing the Writer Within, *was published in 1986. Goldberg's advice to would-be writers is, on the one hand, practical and pithy; on the other, it is almost mystical in its call to know and appreciate the world. "Be Specific," the excerpt that appears below, is representative of the book as a whole. Amid widespread acclaim for the book, one critic commented, "Goldberg teaches us not only how to write better, but how to live better."* Writing Down the Bones *was followed by three more successful books about writing:* Wild Mind: Living the Writer's Life *(1990),* Living Color: A Writer Paints Her World *(1996), and* Thunder and Lightning: Cracking Open the Writer's Craft *(2000). Altogether, more than half a million copies of these books are now in print. Goldberg has also written fiction; her first novel,* Banana Rose, *was published in 1994.*

Notice the way in which Goldberg demonstrates her advice to be specific in the following selection.

BEFORE YOU READ

Suppose someone says to you, "I walked in the woods." What do you envision? Write down what you see in your mind's eye. Now suppose someone says, "I walked in the redwood forest." Again, write what you see. What's different about your two descriptions, and why?

Be specific. Don't say "fruit." Tell what kind of fruit — "It is a pomegranate." Give things the dignity of their names. Just as with human beings, it is rude to say, "Hey, girl, get in line." That "girl" has a name. (As a matter of fact, if she's at least twenty years old, she's a woman, not a "girl" at all.) Things, too, have names. It is much better to say "the geranium in the window" than "the flower in the window." "Geranium" — that one word gives us a much more specific picture. It penetrates more deeply into the beingness of that flower. It immediately gives us the scene by the window — red petals, green circular leaves, all straining toward sunlight.

About ten years ago I decided I had to learn the names of plants and flowers in my environment. I bought a book on them and walked down the tree-lined streets of Boulder, examining leaf, bark, and seed, trying to match them up with their descriptions and names in the book. Maple, elm, oak, locust. I usually tried to cheat by asking people working in their yards the names of the flowers and trees growing there. I was amazed how few people had any idea of the names of the live beings inhabiting their little plot of land.

When we know the name of something, it brings us closer to the ground. It takes the blur out of our mind; it connects us to the earth. If I walk down the street and see "dogwood," "forsythia," I feel more friendly toward the environment. I am noticing what is around me and can name it. It makes me more awake.

If you read the poems of William Carlos Williams, you will see how specific he is about plants, trees, flowers — chicory, daisy, locust, poplar, quince, primrose, black-eyed Susan, lilacs — each has its own integrity. Williams says, "Write what's in front of your nose." It's good for us to know what is in front of our noses. Not just "daisy," but how the flower is in the season we are looking at it — "The dayseye hugging the earth / in August . . . brownedged, / green and pointed scales / armor his yellow."[1] Continue to hone your awareness: to the name, to the month, to the day, and finally to the moment.

Williams also says: "No idea, but in things." Study what is "in front of your nose." By saying "geranium" instead of "flower," you are penetrating more deeply into the present and being there. The closer we can get to what's in front of our nose, the more it can teach us everything. "To see the World in a Grain of Sand, and a heaven in a Wild Flower . . ."[2]

In writing groups and classes too, it is good to quickly learn the names of all the other group members. It helps to ground you in the group and make you more attentive to each other's work.

Learn the names of everything: birds, cheese, tractors, cars, buildings. A writer is all at once everything — an architect, French cook, farmer — and at the same time, a writer is none of these things.

RESPONDING TO READING

Natalie Goldberg found that she wasn't the only one in her neighborhood who didn't know the names of local trees and flowers. Are you unable to name individual members of some categories of things that you encounter often? What are these categories? What are some that would be pleasing or useful for you to learn? How might you go about learning them? (Consider

---

[1] William Carlos Williams, "Daisy," in *The Collected Earlier Poems* (New York: New Directions, 1938).

[2] William Blake, "The Auguries of Innocence."

why Goldberg says it was "cheating" to ask people the names of their flowers and trees.) What would you gain by knowing them?

QUESTIONING THE TEXT

1. In paragraphs 3, 5, and 6, Goldberg cites a number of advantages to be gained by knowing the names of things. Review these advantages. What are they? Do they ring true?

2. Throughout the essay, Goldberg instructs the reader to be specific and to be aware of the world all around. Of what besides names is the reader advised to be aware? Why?

UNDERSTANDING THE WRITER'S CRAFT

1. How does Goldberg "specifically" follow the advice she gives writers in this essay?

2. Goldberg makes several lists of the names of things. What purpose do these lists serve? How does she use these specifics to exemplify her point?

3. What specific audience is Goldberg addressing in this essay? (Glossary: *Audience*) How do you know?

EXPLORING LANGUAGE

1. Goldberg says that to name an object gives it dignity (paragraph 1) and integrity (4). What does she mean in each case?

2. In paragraph 1, Goldberg writes, "It [the word *geranium*] penetrates more deeply into the beingness of that flower." The word *beingness* does not appear in the dictionary. Where does it come from? Why does Goldberg use it, and what does she mean by her statement?

3. In his poem "Daisy," quoted in paragraph 4, William Carlos Williams calls the flower "dayseye." How does this spelling reinforce the central idea of the paragraph? Of the essay as a whole?

4. Refer to your desk dictionary to determine the meanings of the following words as Goldberg uses them in this selection: *pomegranate* (paragraph 1), *integrity* (4).

COMBINING RHETORICAL STRATEGIES

The strategies of definition and exemplification are closely intertwined in this essay; to name a thing precisely, after all, is to take the first step in defining it. (Glossary: *Definition*) What central concept is defined by Goldberg's many illustrations of naming? How might a writer use exemplification to make definitions richer and more meaningful?

WRITING SUGGESTIONS

1. **(Exemplification)** Write a brief essay advising your readers of something they should do. Title your essay, as Goldberg does, with a directive ("Be Specific"). Tell your readers how they can improve their lives by taking your advice, and give strong examples of the behavior you are recommending.

2. **(Other Strategies)** "No idea, but in things," says William Carlos Williams. Read a collection of his short poems and a few good critical studies of his poetry. Write a paper in which you analyze Williams's statement by exploring how it is illustrated by his poems.

3. **(Research)** In the final paragraph, the three occupations that Goldberg names are probably familiar to you, but many of the tools and products connected to them may not be familiar at all. With several classmates, brainstorm an expanded list of such occupations. Choose one that interests you and learn about the activities and functions served by a person in that profession. You might also consider using the Internet to help you with brainstorming and research; below you will find career-oriented Web sites that describe many occupations and offer job listings. Write a report to share what you have learned.

- **Job Descriptions**
  <http://www.system.missouri.edu/hrs/comp/contents.htm>

  Maintained by the University of Missouri, this site provides an extensive listing of job titles and descriptions.

- **JobGenie**
  <http://www.stepfour.com/jobs>

  JobGenie features an alphabetical index of job titles and descriptions that are certified by the U.S. Department of Labor.

- **Job Listings**
  <http://www.workers.gov>

  Cosponsored by the U.S. Department of Labor and the National Partnership for Reinventing Government, FirstGov for Workers contains exhaustive information and links on finding and keeping a job.

  <http://directory.google.com/Top/Business/Employment>

  Google.com sponsors this employment Web Directory, which includes links to job databases and recruiting and career consultant services for a huge spectrum of employment fields ranging from agriculture and forestry to translation services.

An Audience with Dolly

Charles Siebert

Poet, essayist, and novelist, Charles Siebert is a native of Brooklyn, New York. In his memoir Wickerby: An Urban Pastoral *(1998), Siebert describes his old Brooklyn neighborhood and how he forsook the city to move to a cabin in the wilds of rural Quebec. After only five months in the woods, he returned to Brooklyn, where he and his wife currently reside in Crown Heights. His most recent book is* Angus *(2000), a novel narrated by a Jack Russell terrier. Siebert's articles, essays, and poems regularly appear in* Esquire, The New Yorker, Audubon, Vanity Fair, *and* Harper's.

In the following essay, first published in the New York Times Magazine *on September 24, 2000, Siebert uses the example of Dolly, the famous cloned sheep, to reflect on the impact and meaning of biotechnology in our age.*

BEFORE YOU READ

How do you feel about cloning? Does the fact that scientists can create genetic duplicates of existing creatures raise ethical or moral issues for you? Explain.

Recently, I marked the dawn of the new millennium by making a peculiarly postmodern pilgrimage. I journeyed across the Atlantic to the little town of Roslin, Scotland, to see Dolly, the world-renowned clone, the most photographed, fretted over and philosophized about farm animal in the history of civilization. Two thousand years ago, as the New Testament tells it, wise men traveled great distances to see the Christ Child in his manger outside Bethlehem. Now we come from all corners of the globe to visit with a distant relative of one of that manger's bit players.

She hasn't been in the headlines much these days, having been shepherded into a side paddock of our consciousness by more recent biotechnological breakthroughs, like the completed mapping of the human genome — the so-called Book of Life — and by some of the very developments that scientists at the Roslin Institute insisted Dolly augered when they first announced her existence, to much hue and cry, back in February 1997. As the first known mammal to be cloned from a fully developed adult cell, Dolly instantly spawned in the collective consciousness nightmarish scenarios of cookie-cutter people and headless human clones reared for organ harvesting. To date however, we have gotten only ongoing healthy debate about the potential uses of cloning technology and intriguing new barnyard mates for Dolly: Polly and Molly, for example, transgenic clones, or pharm animals, as they have come to be called, because their DNA has been fitted with a human gene that produces proteins in their milk that help combat human diseases.

Still, while Dolly's moment may seem to have passed, she has already achieved iconic status. She's an icon of what can arguably be called the present era's pre-eminent mystery cult: biotechnology. The decidedly unspiritual nature of her immaculate conception notwithstanding, there is an aura of otherworldliness about Dolly: a sheep, the quintessence of creaturely nondescriptness, shepherded by the increasingly deft hand of science, not only into the world's spotlight but, when her 12- to 13-year life span is complete, into a kind of immortality: a taxidermist is to dispatch Dolly to her own private diorama at the Museum of Scotland in Edinburgh. I, however, wanted to see her in the flesh, wanted, for whatever it might yield, to lock eyes with this unwitting pioneer, the curly coated harbinger of either humanity's greatest potential or, as some view it, our ultimate perversion. 3

And so it was that I found myself being escorted to Dolly's living quarters by the Roslin Institute's assistant director, Harry Griffin, a bearded, crinkly eyed Scotsman. Behind the institute's office complex, we approached a semicircular cluster of farm sheds. Just ahead, I could see a small flock of sheep being led out to pasture. I asked Griffin if he could tell which one was Dolly. 4

"Yes, actually," he answered, bypassing that flock. "Dolly makes the most noise and is the quickest to come to camera." 5

I had to hurry to catch up with Griffin, distracted as I was by the revelation that Dolly is in fact something of a publicity hound, the first ingenue ewe. 6

"There's an embargo on Dolly visits just now," Griffin said, stepping toward what he called the celebrity sheep shed, "but you have come all this way." 7

With that he pulled open the shed door. Lying there, at the front of a five-tiered array of adjacent, hay-lined stalls, was Dolly, that stuck, beatific sheep smile on her face, and just beneath her, half lost in her breast wool, two white dewdrops of baby lamb, blinking. 8

"I'd greatly appreciate it if you wouldn't make a headline of them," Griffin said in a near whisper. "We'll be besieged by photographers." 9

I stood in silence, trying to focus my attention on the object of my journey, trying, rather absurdly, to plumb every last second of Dolly's blank, far-off stare for an inner nudge of our shared DNA, some subliminal wink. 10

"Pretty dull, eh?" Griffin said, already moving to close the shed door. "A sheep's life." 11

Thousands of miles for 10 seconds with a sheep, and yet, I felt I'd   12
gotten what I'd come for. It came to me, I think, in the vast disjunc-
ture between the myth of Dolly and the plain sight of her there
munching away in sheeply oblivion. Her only heresy, it occurred to
me, is that she too much reminds us of who we are; outcasts from the
common biology we share with all creatures. Dolly's very existence
underscores what modern biological science has pointed up to us for
well over a century, the undeniable tenet that — to borrow the language of an earlier Book of Life — there but for the grace of a few
strands of DNA go we. In effect, biotechnology, for all of its perceived
threats and seeming supernaturalness, has merely brought us back
around to a more thorough recognition of the same terrifying paradox
that inspired civilization's earlier books of life, the creation myths and
sacred texts with which we first tried to reconcile the fact that we are
at once a part of, and yet seem so apart from, all of nature. Dolly reminds us that we alone have the gift — or is it a curse? — of being
able to look upon our fellow creatures and name and shepherd and
now even subtly reshape them.

In effect, Dolly and the genome map complete a stunning histori-   13
cal arc in which we have gone from being fearful wonderers at seemingly otherworldly, unknowable phenomena, to fearful creators of
them. Creators who, by our very nature, must mythologize our deeds
and exaggerate their potentially disastrous consequences by way of
avoiding outcomes we instinctually abhor.

Walking back to his car, I asked Griffin what he and the other sci-   14
entists were intending to name Dolly's latest lambs. "We're not," he
told me. "It makes it easier to turn them out to pasture."

RESPONDING TO READING

After visiting with Dolly for what seemed like ten seconds, Siebert announces that "I'd gotten what I'd come for" (paragraph 12). What did he
learn about Dolly? What did he learn about himself?

QUESTIONING THE TEXT

1. Why does Siebert make the pilgrimage to the Roslin Institute in Roslin,
   Scotland? What does he hope to gain by visiting with Dolly in the
   flesh?

2. According to Siebert, what were people afraid of when they first heard
   that Dolly had been cloned in February 1997?

3. What connections does Siebert see between Dolly and civilization's earlier "creation myths and sacred texts" (paragraph 12)?

UNDERSTANDING THE WRITER'S CRAFT

1. Siebert argues that Dolly is an icon of biotechnology, and as such he uses her as the lone example in his reflections on modern science. As a reader, were you satisfied with Siebert's use of Dolly as a representative example, or did you find yourself wishing that he had developed several of the other examples of biotechnological miracles he mentions in paragraph 2 to support his insights? Explain.

2. In this essay, Siebert includes dialogue from his meeting with the Roslin Institute's assistant director, Harry Griffin. What purpose does this dialogue serve? What does it add to the essay? What effect, if any, did it have on you as a reader?

3. Identify the transitions that Siebert uses to connect each of his paragraphs with the one preceding it. (Glossary: *Transitions*) Which transitions do you think work best? Explain.

EXPLORING LANGUAGE

1. In his opening paragraph, Siebert explicitly associates the New Testament story of the wise men and the Christ Child with today's story of people traveling great distances to visit Dolly. Why do you suppose Siebert makes this connection? Identify the diction Siebert uses to maintain a spiritual or mystical aura about Dolly throughout the essay.

2. Refer to your dictionary to determine the meanings of the following words as Siebert uses them in this selection: *postmodern* (paragraph 1), *paddock* (2), *genome* (2), *augered* (2), *icon* (3), *quintessence* (3), *diorama* (3), *ingenue* (6), *subliminal* (10), *tenet* (12), *abhor* (13).

COMBINING RHETORICAL STRATEGIES

After three introductory paragraphs, Siebert narrates his brief visit with Dolly in paragraphs 4 through 14. In what ways does Siebert's attention to and selection of detail reflect his reason for telling this story? What function does Harry Griffin, the Roslin Institute's assistant director, serve?

WRITING SUGGESTIONS

1. **(Exemplification)** While new technological inventions — electronic gadgets like Palm™Pilot, cell phones, computers, and video game systems — have made certain aspects of our lives more convenient, efficient, and fun, these creations are not without their critics, who fear that technology isolates people and fragments community. Where do you stand on this issue? Do the positive effects of technological innovations outweigh the negative? Using well-developed examples from your own experiences, observations, or reading, write an essay in which you defend your position.

2. **(Other Strategies)** Consider the following cartoon by Lee Lorenz.

"Ewe again?"

What point about cloning does the cartoon make? How do you think Siebert would react to the cartoon? Siebert reminds us that when Dolly was cloned from a fully developed adult cell, she "instantly spawned in the collective consciousness nightmarish scenarios of cookie-cutter people and headless human clones reared for organ harvesting" (paragraph 2). What effects, if any, do you think biotechnological discoveries such as cloning will have on society? What moral or ethical issues are involved? Do you think people are taking breakthroughs like cloning seriously, or do you think the public is generally apathetic, paying little heed to the profound implications of this discovery? Using Siebert's essay and Lorenz's cartoon as resources, write an essay in which you speculate about the possible positive and negative effects of cloning — or another recent biotechnological breakthrough — on humankind.

3. **(Research)** Scientists around the world have hailed the mapping of the human genome as one of the major scientific feats of the twentieth century. While most people know of this accomplishment, few of us know many of the particulars about "the so-called Book of Life" (paragraph 2). After researching this topic in your library and on the Internet, prepare a report on the human genome mapping project. You may find it helpful to consider one or more of the following questions: What was involved in mapping the human genome? How long did it take? Why was this project considered so important within the scientific community? What are some possible applications of this new knowledge?

- **The New Scientist: Human Genome Special**
  <http://www.newscientist.com/news/genome.jsp>

  This page is a special collection of articles and frequently asked questions (FAQs) about the human genome and the Human Genome Project, answering questions about the genome's potential uses and ethical dilemmas.

- **Division of Extramural Research: Human Genome Project**
  <http://www.nhgri.nih.gov/HGP>

  This is the official site of the Human Genome Project.

- **About the Human Genome Project**
  <http://www.ornl.gov/hgmis/project/about.html>

  This site offers a comprehensive look at the Human Genome Project, with sections on the project, news, basic information, medicine and new genetics, ethical and legal issues, research in progress, and publications.

Corn-pone Opinions

Mark Twain

Mark Twain, the pen name for Samuel L. Clemens (1835-1910), was born in Florida, Missouri, and grew up in nearby Hannibal. One of America's most popular writers, Twain is generally regarded as an important practitioner of realism, a style that emphasizes observable details. He wrote Tom Sawyer *(1876),* Huckleberry Finn *(1884), and* A Connecticut Yankee in King Arthur's Court *(1889), among other classics. Twain's humor is legendary, both in his writing and in his public lectures, which the actor Hal Holbrook has captured in the show* An Evening with Mark Twain.*

"Corn-pone Opinions" was probably written in 1901 and first appeared after Twain's death in a volume entitled Europe and Elsewhere *(1923), edited by his longtime friend Albert Bigelow Paine. As you read this selection, notice how Twain deftly uses humorous examples to make a serious point about public opinion.*

BEFORE YOU READ

What has been your experience with peer pressure? How does it work? Have you ever done something that you later regretted because of the pressure your friends exerted upon you? Is all peer pressure bad? Explain.

Fifty years ago, when I was a boy of fifteen and helping to inhabit a   1
Missourian village on the banks of the Mississippi, I had a friend whose society was very dear to me because I was forbidden by my mother to partake of it. He was a gay and impudent and satirical and delightful young black man — a slave — who daily preached sermons from the top of his master's woodpile, with me for sole audience. He imitated the pulpit style of the several clergymen of the village, and did it well, and with fine passion and energy. To me he was a wonder. I believed he was the greatest orator in the United States and would some day be heard from. But it did not happen; in the distribution of rewards he was overlooked. It is the way, in this world.

He interrupted his preaching, now and then, to saw a stick of   2
wood; but the sawing was a pretense — he did it with his mouth; exactly imitating the sound the bucksaw makes in shrieking its way through the wood. But it served its purpose; it kept his master from coming out to see how the work was getting along. I listened to the sermons from the open window of a lumber room at the back of the house. One of his texts was this:

110

"You tell me whar a man gits his corn pone, en I'll tell you what   3
his 'pinions is."

I can never forget it. It was deeply impressed upon me. By my   4
mother. Not upon my memory, but elsewhere. She had slipped in
upon me while I was absorbed and not watching. The black philosopher's idea was that a man is not independent, and cannot afford
views which might interfere with his bread and butter. If he would
prosper, he must train with the majority; in matters of large moment,
like politics and religion, he must think and feel with the bulk of his
neighbors, or suffer damage in his social standing and in his business
prosperities. He must restrict himself to corn-pone opinions — at least
on the surface. He must get his opinions from other people; he must
reason out none for himself; he must have no first-hand views.

I think Jerry was right, in the main, but I think he did not go far   5
enough.

1. It was his idea that a man conforms to the majority view of his   6
locality by calculation and intention.

This happens, but I think it is not the rule.   7

2. It was his idea that there is such a thing as a first-hand opinion;   8
an original opinion; an opinion which is coldly reasoned out in a
man's head, by a searching analysis of the facts involved, with the
heart unconsulted, and the jury room closed against outside influences. It may be that such an opinion has been born somewhere, at
some time or other, but I suppose it got away before they could catch
it and stuff it and put it in the museum.

I am persuaded that a coldly-thought-out and independent verdict   9
upon a fashion in clothes, or manners, or literature, or politics, or religion, or any other matter that is projected into the field of our notice
and interest, is a most rare thing — if it has indeed ever existed.

A new thing in costume appears — the flaring hoopskirt, for ex-   10
ample — and the passers-by are shocked, and the irreverent laugh. Six
months later everybody is reconciled; the fashion has established itself; it is admired, now, and no one laughs. Public opinion resented it
before, public opinion accepts it now, and is happy in it. Why? Was
the resentment reasoned out? Was the acceptance reasoned out? No.
The instinct that moves to conformity did the work. It is our nature to
conform; it is a force which not many can successfully resist. What is
its seat? The inborn requirement of self-approval. We all have to bow
to that; there are no exceptions. Even the woman who refuses from
first to last to wear the hoopskirt comes under that law and is its slave;
she could not wear the skirt and have her own approval; and that she
must have, she cannot help herself. But as a rule our self-approval has
its source in but one place and not elsewhere — the approval of other
people. A person of vast consequences can introduce any kind of nov-
elty in dress and the general world will presently adopt it — moved to

do it, in the first place, by the natural instinct to passively yield to that vague something recognized as authority, and in the second place by the human instinct to train with the multitude and have its approval. An empress introduced the hoopskirt, and we know the result. A nobody introduced the bloomer, and we know the result. If Eve should come again, in her ripe renown, and reintroduce her quaint styles — well, we know what would happen. And we should be cruelly embarrassed, along at first.

The hoopskirt runs its course and disappears. Nobody reasons 11 about it. One woman abandons the fashion; her neighbor notices this and follows her lead; this influences the next woman; and so on and so on, and presently the skirt has vanished out of the world, no one knows how nor why, nor cares, for that matter. It will come again, by and by and in due course will go again.

Twenty-five years ago, in England, six or eight wine glasses stood 12 grouped by each person's plate at a dinner party, and they were used, not left idle and empty; to-day there are but three or four in the group, and the average guest sparingly uses about two of them. We have not adopted this new fashion yet, but we shall do it presently. We shall not think it out; we shall merely conform, and let it go at that. We get our notions and habits and opinions from outside influences; we do not have to study them out.

Our table manners, and company manners, and street manners 13 change from time to time, but the changes are not reasoned out; we merely notice and conform. We are creatures of outside influences; as a rule we do not think, we only imitate. We cannot invent standards that will stick; what we mistake for standards are only fashions, and perishable. We may continue to admire them, but we drop the use of them. We notice this in literature. Shakespeare is a standard, and fifty years ago we used to write tragedies which we couldn't tell from — from somebody else's; but we don't do it any more, now. Our prose standard, three quarters of a century ago, was ornate and diffuse; some authority or other changed it in the direction of compactness and simplicity, and conformity followed, without argument. The historical novel starts up suddenly, and sweeps the land. Everybody writes one, and the nation is glad. We had historical novels before; but nobody read them, and the rest of us conformed — without reasoning it out. We are conforming in the other way, now, because it is another case of everybody.

The outside influences are always pouring in upon us, and we are 14 always obeying their orders and accepting their verdicts. The Smiths like the new play; the Joneses go to see it, and they copy the Smith verdict. Morals, religions, politics, get their following from surrounding influences and atmospheres, almost entirely; not from study, not from thinking. A man must and will have his own approval first of all, in each and every moment and circumstance of his life — even if he must repent of a self-approved act the moment after its commission, in order to get his self-approval *again:* but, speaking in general terms, a man's self-approval in the large concerns of life has its source in the approval of the peoples about him, and not in a searching personal examination of the matter. Mohammedans are Mohammedans because they are born and reared among that sect, not because they have thought it out and can furnish sound reasons for being Mohammedans; we know why Catholics are Catholics; why Presbyterians are Presbyterians; why Baptists are Baptists; why Mormons are Mormons; why thieves are thieves; why monarchists are monarchists; why Republicans are Republicans and Democrats are Democrats. We know it is a matter of association and sympathy, not reasoning and examination; that hardly a man in the world has an opinion upon morals, politics, or religion which he got otherwise than through his associations and sympathies. Broadly speaking, there are none but corn-pone opinions. And broadly speaking, corn-pone stands for self-approval. Self-approval is acquired mainly from the approval of other people. The result is conformity. Sometimes conformity has a sordid business interest — the bread-and-butter interest — but not in most cases, I think. I think that in the majority of cases it is unconscious and not calculated; that it is born of the human being's natural yearning to stand well with his fellows and have their inspiring approval and praise — a yearning which is commonly so strong and so insistent that it cannot be effectually resisted, and must have its way.

A political emergency brings out the corn-pone opinion in fine force 15 in its two chief varieties — the pocketbook variety, which has its origin in self-interest, and the bigger variety, the sentimental variety — the one which can't bear to be outside the pale; can't bear to be in disfavor; can't endure the averted face and the cold shoulder; wants to stand well with his friends, wants to be smiled upon, wants to be welcome, wants to hear the precious words, *"He's* on the right track!" Uttered, perhaps by an ass, but still an ass of high degree, an ass whose approval is gold and diamonds to a smaller ass, and confers glory and honor and happiness, and membership in the herd. For these gauds many a man will dump his life-long principles into the street, and his conscience along with them. We have seen it happen. In some millions of instances.

Men think they think upon great political questions, and they do; 16 but they think with their party, not independently; they read its literature, but not that of the other side; they arrive at convictions, but they are drawn from a partial view of the matter in hand and are of no particular value. They swarm with their party, they feel with their party, they are happy in their party's approval; and where the party leads they will follow, whether for right and honor, or through blood and dirt and a mush of mutilated morals.

In our late canvass half of the nation passionately believed that in   17
silver lay salvation, the other half as passionately believed that that
way lay destruction. Do you believe that a tenth part of the people, on
either side, had any rational excuse for having an opinion about the
matter at all? I studied that mighty question to the bottom — came
out empty. Half of our people passionately believe in high tariff, the
other half believe otherwise. Does this mean study and examination,
or only feeling? The latter, I think. I have deeply studied that question, too — and didn't arrive. We all do no end of feeling, and we mistake it for thinking. And out of it we get an aggregation which we consider a boon. Its name is Public Opinion. It is held in reverence. It
settles everything. Some think it the Voice of God.

RESPONDING TO READING

What relevance does this essay, written one hundred years ago, have for
readers today? What, for Twain, is the relationship among public opinion,
self-approval, and conformity? Do you agree with Twain's reasoning? Why
or why not?

QUESTIONING THE TEXT

1. What is corn pone, and what, according to the young black man Jerry,
   is its relationship to opinions?

2. On what point(s) does Twain differ with Jerry? Why do you suppose he
   does? With whom do you tend to agree? Explain.

3. What is an "original opinion" (paragraph 8) or an "independent verdict" (9)? Why, according to Twain, are such opinions so rare?

UNDERSTANDING THE WRITER'S CRAFT

1. What is Twain's thesis, and where does he present it? (Glossary: *Thesis*)
   What kinds of supportive or illustrative examples does his thesis lead
   you to expect later in the essay?

2. What is Twain's purpose in writing about corn-pone opinions? What in
   this essay led you to your conclusion?

3. In paragraph 10, Twain discusses the world of fashion, or costume,
   using the examples of the hoopskirt and the bloomer. What generalization do these examples illustrate?

4. Twain, a celebrated humorist, often uses his humor to comment seriously on human behavior. What is the source of his humor in
   this essay? Why is humor appropriate given his subject and his audience?

EXPLORING LANGUAGE

1. Twain uses informal, almost conversational, diction in this essay. In what ways is such diction appropriate given his subject and purpose? Explain by citing examples from the text.

2. What is Twain's attitude toward public opinion? His attitude toward humankind? What in Twain's diction led you to these conclusions?

3. Refer to your desk dictionary to determine the meanings of the following words as Twain uses them in this selection: *impudent* (paragraph 1), *satirical* (1), *pretense* (2), *quaint* (10), *diffuse* (13), *gauds* (15), *canvass* (17), *aggregation* (17).

COMBINING RHETORICAL STRATEGIES

Twain uses a number of rhetorical strategies in combination with exemplification in this essay. For example, he opens the essay by narrating the story of Jerry, the black philosopher. Later he uses cause and effect analysis to explain how public opinion affects individuals, and he uses division and classification to discuss categories of corn-pone opinion. For you, how does Twain's use of these strategies help to both clarify and strengthen his examples and ultimately his argument? (Glossary: *Cause and Effect Analysis; Classification; Division; Narration*)

WRITING SUGGESTIONS

1. **(Exemplification)** Mark Twain states that "We are creatures of outside influences; as a rule we do not think, we only imitate" (paragraph 13). Do you agree or disagree? Using examples from your own experiences or observations, write an essay in which you present your position.

2. **(Other Strategies)** Write an essay in which you explore the concept of conformity and its relationship to self-approval. You may find it helpful to consider one or more of the following questions while planning your essay. How do you define conformity (Glossary: *Definition*)? What is its function within a community? Is conformity a good thing or a bad thing or both? What is Twain's attitude toward our tendency to conform, and how does his attitude compare with your own?

3. **(Research)** Some people believe that we are living in an age of public opinion polls. Community, business, and political leaders seem to make decisions only after reviewing the results of this poll or that survey. How important is public opinion in America today? What influence or effect does it have on important decisions that affect all of our lives? A century ago, Twain thought that public opinion "is held in reverence. It settles everything. Some think it the Voice of God" (paragraph 17). Does his assessment apply to today's society? After doing some research in the library or on the Internet, write an essay in which you discuss the

impact of public opinion polls on a recent election, court decision, business plan, or community issue.

- **PollingReport.com**

<http://www.pollingreport.com>

This "independent, nonpartisan" guide to public opinion in America covers topics from mad cow disease to President George W. Bush's most recent approval ratings.

- **The Gallup Association**

<http://www.gallup.com>

This is the home of the Gallup poll, one of the world's best-known public opinion guides. It lists polls in the categories of Business and the Economy, Politics and Elections, Social Issues and Policy, and Lifestyle.

- **Public Agenda Online**

<http://www.publicagenda.org>

This site lists public opinion polls by issue, along with an overview of the issue, articles, facts and statistics, perspectives on the debate, resources, and cautionary advice about how to read the poll's information.

How to Give Orders Like a Man

Deborah Tannen

Deborah Tannen, professor of linguistics at Georgetown University, was born in 1945 in Brooklyn, New York. Tannen received her B.A. in English from the State University of New York at Binghamton in 1966 and taught English in Greece until 1968. She then earned an M.A. in English literature from Wayne State University in 1970. While pursuing her Ph.D. in linguistics at the University of California, Berkeley, she received several prizes for her poetry and short fiction. Her work has appeared in New York, Vogue, *and the* New York Times Magazine. *In addition, she has authored three best-selling books on how people communicate:* You Just Don't Understand *(1990),* That's Not What I Meant *(1991), and* Talking from Nine to Five *(1994). The success of these books attests to the public's interest in language, especially when it pertains to gender differences. Tannen's most recent book is entitled* The Argument Culture: Stopping America's War of Words *(1998).*

In this essay, first published in the New York Times Magazine *in August 1994, Tannen looks at the variety of ways in which orders are given and received. Interestingly, she concludes that contrary to popular belief, directness is not necessarily logical or effective, and indirectness is not necessarily manipulative or insecure.*

BEFORE YOU READ

Write about a time in your life when you were ordered to do something. Who gave you the order — a friend, a parent, maybe a teacher? Did the person's relationship to you affect how you carried out the order? Did it make a difference to you whether the order giver was male or female? Why?

A university president was expecting a visit from a member of the board of trustees. When her secretary buzzed to tell her that the board member had arrived, she left her office and entered the reception area to greet him. Before ushering him into her office, she handed her secretary a sheet of paper and said: "I've just finished drafting this letter. Do you think you could type it right away? I'd like to get it out before lunch. And would you please do me a favor and hold all calls while I'm meeting with Mr. Smith?"

When they sat down behind the closed door of her office, Mr. Smith began by telling her that he thought she had spoken inappropriately to her secretary. "Don't forget," he said. *"You're* the president!"

Putting aside the question of the appropriateness of his admonishing the president on her way of speaking, it is revealing — and representative of many Americans' assumptions — that the indirect way in which the university president told her secretary what to do struck him as self-deprecating. He took it as evidence that she didn't think she had the right to make demands of her secretary. He probably thought he was giving her a needed pep talk, bolstering her self-confidence.

I challenge the assumption that talking in an indirect way necessarily reveals powerlessness, lack of self-confidence or anything else about the character of the speaker. Indirectness is a fundamental element in human communication. It is also one of the elements that varies most from one culture to another, and one that can cause confusion and misunderstanding when speakers have different habits with regard to using it. I also want to dispel the assumption that American women tend to be more indirect than American men. Women and men are both indirect, but in addition to differences associated with their backgrounds — regional, ethnic and class — they tend to be indirect in different situations and in different ways.

At work, we need to get others to do things, and we all have different ways of accomplishing this. Any individual's ways will vary depending on who is being addressed — a boss, a peer or a subordinate. At one extreme are bald commands. At the other are requests so indirect that they don't sound like requests at all, but are just a statement of need or a description of a situation. People with direct styles of asking others to do things perceive indirect requests — if they perceive them as requests at all — as manipulative. But this is often just a way of blaming others for our discomfort with their styles.

The indirect style is no more manipulative than making a telephone call, asking "Is Rachel there?" and expecting whoever answers the phone to put Rachel on. Only a child is likely to answer "Yes" and continue holding the phone — not out of orneriness but because of inexperience with the conventional meaning of the question. (A mischievous adult might do it to tease.) Those who feel that indirect orders are illogical or manipulative do not recognize the conventional nature of indirect requests.

Issuing orders indirectly can be the prerogative of those in power. Imagine, for example, a master who says "It's cold in here" and expects a servant to make a move to close a window, while a servant who says the same thing is not likely to see his employer rise to correct the situation and make him more comfortable. Indeed, a Frenchman raised in Brittany tells me that his family never gave bald commands to their servants but always communicated orders in indirect and highly polite ways. This pattern renders less surprising the finding of David Bellinger and Jean Berko Gleason that fathers' speech to their young children had a higher incidence than mothers' of both direct imperatives like "Turn the bolt with the wrench" *and* indirect orders like "The wheel is going to fall off."

The use of indirectness can hardly be understood without the cross-cultural perspective. Many Americans find it self-evident that directness is logical and aligned with power while indirectness is akin to dishonesty and reflects subservience. But for speakers raised in most of the world's cultures, varieties of indirectness are the norm in communication. This is the pattern found by a Japanese sociolinguist, Kunihiko Harada, in his analysis of a conversation he recorded between a Japanese boss and a subordinate.

The markers of superior status were clear. One speaker was a Japanese man in his late 40's who managed the local branch of a Japanese private school in the United States. His conversational partner was a Japanese-American woman in her early 20's who worked at the school. By virtue of his job, his age and his native fluency in the language being taught, the man was in the superior position. Yet when he addressed the woman, he frequently used polite language and almost always used indirectness. For example, he had tried and failed to find a photography store that would make a black-and-white print from a color negative for a brochure they were producing. He let her know that he wanted her to take over the task by stating the situation and allowed her to volunteer to do it: (This is a translation of the Japanese conversation.)

> On this matter, that, that, on the leaflet? This photo, I'm thinking of changing it to black-and-white and making it clearer. . . . I went to a photo shop and asked them. They said they didn't do black-and-white. I asked if they knew any place that did. They said they didn't know. They weren't very helpful, but anyway, a place must be found, the negative brought to it, the picture developed.

Harada observes, "Given the fact that there are some duties to be performed and that there are two parties present, the subordinate is supposed to assume that those are his or her obligation." It was precisely because of his higher status that the boss was free to choose whether to speak formally or informally, to assert his power or to play it down and build rapport — an option not available to the subordinate, who would have seemed cheeky if she had chosen a style that enhanced friendliness and closeness.

The same pattern was found by a Chinese sociolinguist, Yuling Pan, in a meeting of officials involved in a neighborhood youth program. All spoke in ways that reflected their place in the hierarchy. A subordinate addressing a superior always spoke in a deferential way, but a superior addressing a subordinate could either be authoritarian, demonstrating his power, or friendly, establishing rapport. The ones in power had the option of choosing which style to use. In this spirit, I have been told by people who prefer their bosses to give orders indirectly that those who issue bald commands must be pretty insecure; otherwise why would they have to bolster their egos by throwing their weight around?

I am not inclined to accept that those who give orders directly are 12 really insecure and powerless, any more than I want to accept that judgment of those who give indirect orders. The conclusion to be drawn is that ways of talking should not be taken as obvious evidence of inner psychological states like insecurity or lack of confidence. Considering the many influences on conversational style, individuals have a wide range of ways of getting things done and expressing their emotional states. Personality characteristics like insecurity cannot be linked to ways of speaking in an automatic, self-evident way.

Those who expect orders to be given indirectly are offended when 13 they come unadorned. One woman said that when her boss gives her instructions, she feels she should click her heels, salute, and say "Yes, boss!" His directions strike her as so imperious as to border on the militaristic. Yet I received a letter from a man telling me that indirect orders were a fundamental part of his military training. He wrote:

> Many years ago, when I was in the Navy, I was training to be a radio technician. One class I was in was taught by a chief radioman, a regular Navy man who had been to sea, and who was then in his third hitch. The students, about 20 of us, were fresh out of boot camp, with no sea duty and little knowledge of real Navy life. One day in class the chief said it was hot in the room. The students didn't react, except perhaps to nod in agreement. The chief repeated himself: "It's hot in this room." Again there was no reaction from the students.
>
> Then the chief explained. He wasn't looking for agreement or discussion from us. When he said that the room was hot, he expected us to do something about it — like opening the window. He tried it one more time, and this time all of us left our workbenches and headed for the windows. We had learned. And we had many opportunities to apply what we had learned.

This letter especially intrigued me because "It's cold in here" is the 14 standard sentence used by linguists to illustrate an indirect way of getting someone to do something — as I used it earlier. In this example, it is the very obviousness and rigidity of the military hierarchy that makes the statement of a problem sufficient to trigger corrective action on the part of subordinates.

A man who had worked at the Pentagon reinforced the view that 15 the burden of interpretation is on subordinates in the military — and he noticed the difference when he moved to a position in the private sector. He was frustrated when he'd say to his new secretary, for example, "Do we have a list of invitees?" and be told, "I don't know; we probably do" rather than "I'll get it for you." Indeed, he explained, at the Pentagon, such a question would likely be heard as a reproach that the list was not already on his desk.

The suggestion that indirectness is associated with the military must come as a surprise to many. But everyone is indirect, meaning more than is put into words and deriving meaning from words that are never actually said. It's a matter of where, when and how we each tend to be indirect and look for hidden meanings. But indirectness has a built-in liability. There is a risk that the other will either miss or choose to ignore your meaning. 16

On January 13, 1982, a freezing cold, snowy day in Washington, Air Florida Flight 90 took off from National Airport, but could not get the lift it needed to keep climbing. It crashed into a bridge linking Washington to the state of Virginia and plunged into the Potomac. Of the 79 people on board, all but 5 perished, many floundering and drowning in the icy water while horror-stricken bystanders watched helplessly from the river's edge and millions more watched, aghast, on their television screens. Experts later concluded that the plane had waited too long after deicing to take off. Fresh buildup of ice on the wings and engine brought the plane down. How could the pilot and co-pilot have made such a blunder? Didn't at least one of them realize it was dangerous to take off under these conditions? 17

Charlotte Linde, a linguist at the Institute for Research on Learning in Palo Alto, Calif., has studied the "black box" recordings of cockpit conversations that preceded crashes as well as tape recordings of conversations that took place among crews during flight simulations in which problems were presented. Among the black box conversations she studied was the one between the pilot and co-pilot just before the Air Florida crash. The pilot, it turned out, had little experience flying in icy weather. The co-pilot had a bit more, and it became heartbreakingly clear on analysis that he had tried to warn the pilot, but he did so indirectly. 18

The co-pilot repeatedly called attention to the bad weather and to ice building up on other planes: 19

> Co-pilot: Look how the ice is just hanging on his, ah, back, back there, see that?
> . . .
> Co-pilot: See all those icicles on the back there and everything?
> Captain: Yeah.

He expressed concern early on about the long waiting time be- 20
tween deicing:

> Co-pilot: Boy, this is a, this is a losing battle here on trying to
> de-ice those things, it [gives] you a false feeling of security, that's all
> that does.

Shortly after they were given clearance to take off, he again ex- 21
pressed concern:

> Co-pilot: Let's check these tops again since we been setting
> here awhile.
> Captain: I think we get to go here in a minute.

When they were about to take off, the co-pilot called attention to 22
the engine instrument readings, which were not normal:

> Co-pilot: That don't seem right, does it? [three-second pause]
> Ah, that's not right. . . .
> Captain: Yes, it is, there's 80.
> Co-pilot: Naw, I don't think that's right. [seven-second pause]
> Ah, maybe it is.
> Captain: Hundred and twenty.
> Co-pilot: I don't know.

The takeoff proceeded, and 37 seconds later the pilot and co-pilot 23
exchanged their last words.

The co-pilot had repeatedly called the pilot's attention to danger- 24
ous conditions but did not directly suggest they abort the takeoff. In
Linde's judgment, he was expressing his concern indirectly, and the
captain didn't pick up on it — with tragic results.

That the co-pilot was trying to warn the captain indirectly is sup- 25
ported by evidence from another airline accident — a relatively minor
one — investigated by Linde that also involved the unsuccessful use of
indirectness.

On July 9, 1978, Allegheny Airlines Flight 453 was landing at 26
Monroe County Airport in Rochester, when it overran the runway by
728 feet. Everyone survived. This meant that the captain and co-pilot
could be interviewed. It turned out that the plane had been flying too
fast for a safe landing. The captain should have realized this and flown
around a second time, decreasing his speed before trying to land. The
captain said he simply had not been aware that he was going too fast.
But the co-pilot told interviewers that he "tried to warn the captain in
subtle ways, like mentioning the possibility of a tail wind and the
slowness of flap extension." His exact words were recorded in the

black box. The crosshatches indicate words deleted by the National Transportation Safety Board and were probably expletives:

> Co-pilot: Yeah, it looks like you got a tail wind here.
> Captain: Yeah.
>   [?]: Yeah [it] moves awfully # slow.
> Co-pilot: Yeah the # flaps are slower than a #.
> Captain: We'll make it, gonna have to add power.
> Co-pilot: I know.

The co-pilot thought the captain would understand that if there was a tail wind, it would result in the plane going too fast, and if the flaps were slow, they would be inadequate to break the speed sufficiently for a safe landing. He thought the captain would then correct for the error by not trying to land. But the captain said he didn't interpret the co-pilot's remarks to mean they were going too fast.

Linde believes it is not a coincidence that the people being indirect in these conversations were the co-pilots. In her analyses of flight-crew conversations she found it was typical for the speech of subordinates to be more mitigated — polite, tentative or indirect. She also found that topics broached in a mitigated way were more likely to fail, and that captains were more likely to ignore hints from their crew members than the other way around. These findings are evidence that not only can indirectness and other forms of mitigation be misunderstood, but they are also easier to ignore.

In the Air Florida case, it is doubtful that the captain did not realize what the co-pilot was suggesting when he said, "Let's check these tops again since we been setting here awhile" (though it seems safe to assume he did not realize the gravity of the co-pilot's concern). But the indirectness of the co-pilot's phrasing certainly made it easier for the pilot to ignore it. In this sense, the captain's response, "I think we get to go here in a minute," was an indirect way of saying, "I'd rather not." In view of these patterns, the flight crews of some airlines are now given training to express their concerns, even to superiors, in more direct ways.

The conclusion that people should learn to express themselves more directly has a ring of truth to it — especially for Americans. But direct communication is not necessarily always preferable. If more direct expression is better communication, then the most direct-speaking crews should be the best ones. Linde was surprised to find in her research that crews that used the most mitigated speech were often judged the best crews. As part of the study of talk among cockpit crews in flight simulations, the trainers observed and rated the performances of the simulation crews. The crews they rated top in performance had a higher rate of mitigation than crews they judged to be poor.

This finding seems at odds with the role played by indirectness in   31
the examples of crashes that we just saw. Linde concluded that since
every utterance functions on two levels — the referential (what it says)
and the relational (what it implies about the speaker's relationships),
crews that attend to the relational level will be better crews. A similar
explanation was suggested by Kunihiko Harada. He believes that the
secret of successful communication lies not in teaching subordinates
to be more direct, but in teaching higher-ups to be more sensitive to
indirect meaning. In other words, the crashes resulted not only because the co-pilots tried to alert the captains to danger indirectly but
also because the captains were not attuned to the co-pilots' hints.
What made for successful performance among the best crews might
have been the ability — or willingness — of listeners to pick up on
hints, just as members of families or longstanding couples come to
understand each other's meaning without anyone being particularly
explicit.

It is not surprising that a Japanese sociolinguist came up with this   32
explanation; what he described is the Japanese system, by which good
communication is believed to take place when meaning is gleaned
without being stated directly — or at all.

While Americans believe that "the squeaky wheel gets the grease"   33
(so it's best to speak up), the Japanese say, "The nail that sticks out
gets hammered back in" (so it's best to remain silent if you don't want
to be hit on the head). Many Japanese scholars writing in English have
tried to explain to bewildered Americans the ethics of a culture in
which silence is often given greater value than speech, and ideas are
believed to be best communicated without being explicitly stated. Key
concepts in Japanese give a flavor of the attitudes toward language
that they reveal — and set in relief the strategies that Americans encounter at work when talking to other Americans.

Takie Sugiyama Lebra, a Japanese-born anthropologist, explains   34
that one of the most basic values in Japanese culture is *omoiyari,*
which she translates as "empathy." Because of *omoiyari,* it should not
be necessary to state one's meaning explicitly; people should be able
to sense each other's meaning intuitively. Lebra explains that it is
typical for a Japanese speaker to let sentences trail off rather than
complete them because expressing ideas before knowing how they
will be received seems intrusive. "Only an insensitive, uncouth person
needs a direct, verbal, complete message," Lebra says.

Sasshi, the anticipation of another's message through insightful   35
guesswork, is considered an indication of maturity.

Considering the value placed on direct communication by Ameri-   36
cans in general, and especially by American business people, it is easy
to imagine that many American readers may scoff at such conversa-

tional habits. But the success of Japanese businesses makes it impossible to continue to maintain that there is anything inherently inefficient about such conversational conventions. With indirectness, as with all aspects of conversational style, our own habitual style seems to make sense — seems polite, right and good. The light cast by the habits and assumptions of another culture can help us see our way to the flexibility and respect for other styles that is the only best way of speaking.

RESPONDING TO READING

In her essay, Tannen states that "indirectness is a fundamental element in human communication" (paragraph 4). Do you agree with Tannen on this point? What does she mean when she says that it is just as important to notice what we do not say as what we actually say?

QUESTIONING THE TEXT

1. How does Tannen define indirect speech? What does she see as the built-in liability of indirect speech? Do you see comparable liability inherent in direct speech?

2. Tannen doesn't contest a finding that fathers had a higher incidence of both direct imperatives and indirect orders than mothers. How does she interpret the meaning of these results?

3. Why doesn't Tannen tell her audience how to deal with an insecure boss?

4. Why is it typical for Japanese speakers to let their sentences trail off?

UNDERSTANDING THE WRITER'S CRAFT

1. What is Tannen's thesis, and where does she present it? (Glossary: *Thesis*)

2. Tannen mostly uses examples in which men give direct orders. In what ways do these examples support her thesis?

3. For what audience has Tannen written this essay? Does this help to explain why she focuses primarily on indirect communication? Why or why not? (Glossary: *Audience*)

4. Tannen gives two examples of flight accidents that resulted from indirect speech, and yet she then explains that top-performing flight teams used indirect speech more often than poorly performing teams. How do these seemingly contradictory examples support the author's argument?

5. Tannen uses several examples from other cultures. What do these examples help to show us about Americans?

EXPLORING LANGUAGE

1. In paragraph 13, what irony does Tannen point out in the popular understanding of the word *militaristic?*

2. How would you describe Tannen's diction in this essay? (Glossary: *Diction*) Does she ever get too scientific for the general reader? If so, where do you think her language gets too technical? Why do you think she uses such language?

3. Refer to your dictionary to determine the meanings of the following words as Tannen uses them in this selection: *admonishing* (paragraph 3), *self-deprecating* (3), *manipulative* (5), *prerogative* (7), *subservience* (8), *cheeky* (10), *deferential* (11), *imperious* (13), *liability* (16), *mitigated* (28), *broached* (28), *gleaned* (32), *relief* (33), *empathy* (34).

COMBINING RHETORICAL STRATEGIES

Explain how Tannen uses comparison and contrast to document the assertion that "indirectness is a fundamental element in human communication. (Glossary: *Comparison and Contrast*) It is also one of the elements that varies most from one culture to another, and one that can cause confusion and misunderstanding when speakers have different habits with regard to using it" (paragraph 4). How does this strategy enhance or support the dominant strategy in the essay?

WRITING SUGGESTIONS

1. **(Exemplification)** Tannen concludes that "the light cast by the habits and assumptions of another culture can help us see our way to the flexibility and respect for other styles that is the only best way of speaking" (paragraph 36). Write an essay in which you use concrete examples from your own experience, observation, or readings to agree or disagree with her conclusion.

2. **(Other Strategies)** Write an essay comparing the command styles of two people — either people you know or fictional characters. You might consider your parents, teachers, professors, coaches, television characters like Captain Picard and Captain Kirk from *Star Trek,* or characters from movies or novels. What conclusions can you draw from your analysis?

3. **(Research)** Tannen often refers to the communication practices of other cultures and the options these practices open for us. Do some research in the sociology and anthropology sections of your library and possibly on the Internet. Using your research, write an essay in which you illustrate the importance of understanding and learning from other cultures' communication habits, in terms of both speech and body language.

- **UCSB Cool Anthropology Web Links**
  <http://www.anth.ucsb.edu/links/pages>

This Web site offers an extensive list of anthropology links maintained by the University of California — Santa Barbara.

- **The WWW Virtual Library: Sociology**
  <http://www.ixpres.com/lunatic.soc.html>

  Links to resources on all aspects of sociology are included here.

- **Anthropology in the News**
  <http://www.tamu.edu/anthropology/news.html>

  This site, maintained by Texas A&M, offers links to recent anthropology-related articles.

- **<http://www.georgetown.edu/tannen>**

  This is Deborah Tannen's official Web page at Georgetown University.

In Search of Our Mothers' Gardens

Alice Walker

Best known for her Pulitzer Prize–winning novel, The Color Purple, *Alice Walker is a prolific writer of poetry, essays, and fiction. Walker was born in Georgia in 1944, the youngest of eight children in a share-cropping family. She took advantage of educational opportunities to escape a life of poverty and servitude, attending Spelman College in Georgia and then graduating from the prestigious Sarah Lawrence College in New York. An African American activist and feminist, Walker often deals with controversial subjects in her writing;* The Color Purple *(1982), the novel* The Secret of Joy *(1992), and the nonfiction* Warrior Works *(1993) are known for this characteristic. Other widely acclaimed works by Walker include her collected poems,* Her Blue Body Everything We Know: Earthling Poems, 1965–1990 *(1993); a memoir entitled* The Same River Twice: Honoring the Difficult *(1996); a collection of essays,* Anything We Love Can Be Saved: A Writer's Activism *(1997); and a collection of stories,* The Way Forward Is with a Broken Heart *(2000). Although much of her writing deals with pain and life's hardships, her work is not pessimistic; in the words of one reviewer, Walker's writing represents a "quest for peace and joy in a difficult world."*

In the following essay, the title piece from a collection of essays published in 1983, she explores what it has meant in the past — and, by implication, what it means today — to be a black woman in America.

BEFORE YOU READ

Is everyone born with creative impulses, with the urge to indulge artistic expression of some kind, or is creativity a special gift granted only to a few? Are there ways to satisfy creativity other than with art? What happens to a person whose artistic drive is discouraged? Can you think of examples from your own experience?

I described her own nature and temperament. Told how they needed a larger life for their expression. . . . I pointed out that in lieu of proper channels, her emotions had overflowed into paths that dissipated them. I talked, beautifully I thought, about an art that would be born, an art that would open the way for women the likes of her. I asked her to hope, and build up an inner life against the coming of that day. . . . I sang, with a strange quiver in my voice, a promise song.

— JEAN TOOMER,
"Avey," Cane

The poet speaking to a prostitute who falls asleep while he's talking — 1

When the poet Jean Toomer walked through the South in the early 2
twenties, he discovered a curious thing: black women whose spirituality
was so intense, so deep, so *unconscious,* that they were themselves unaware of the richness they held. They stumbled blindly through their
lives: creatures so abused and mutilated in body, so dimmed and confused by pain, that they considered themselves unworthy even of hope.
In the selfless abstractions their bodies became to the men who used
them, they became more than "sexual objects," even more than mere
women: they became "Saints." Instead of being perceived as whole persons, their bodies became shrines, what was thought to be their minds
became temples suitable for worship. These crazy Saints stared out at the
world, wildly, like lunatics — or quietly, like suicides; and the "God"
that was in their gaze was as mute as a great stone.

Who were these Saints? These crazy, loony, pitiful women? 3

Some of them, without a doubt, were our mothers and grand- 4
mothers.

In the still heat of the post-Reconstruction South, this is how they 5
seemed to Jean Toomer: exquisite butterflies trapped in an evil honey,
toiling away their lives in an era, a century, that did not acknowledge
them, except as "the *mule* of the world." They dreamed dreams that
no one knew — not even themselves, in any coherent fashion — and
saw visions no one could understand. They wandered or sat about the
countryside crooning lullabies to ghosts, and drawing the mother of
Christ in charcoal on courthouse walls.

They forced their minds to desert their bodies and their striving 6
spirits sought to rise, like frail whirlwinds from the hard red clay. And
when those frail whirlwinds fell, in scattered particles, upon the
ground, no one mourned. Instead, men lit candles to celebrate the
emptiness that remained, as people do who enter a beautiful but vacant space to resurrect a God.

Our mothers and grandmothers, some of them: moving to music 7
not yet written. And they waited.

They waited for a day when the unknown thing that was in them 8
would be made known; but guessed, somehow in their darkness, that
on the day of their revelation they would be long dead. Therefore to
Toomer they walked, and even ran, in slow motion. For they were
going nowhere immediate, and the future was not yet within their
grasp. And men took our mothers and grandmothers, "but got no
pleasure from it." So complex was their passion and their calm.

To Toomer, they lay vacant and fallow as autumn fields, with har- 9
vest time never in sight: and he saw them enter loveless marriages,

without joy; and become prostitutes, without resistance, and become mothers of children, without fulfillment.

For these grandmothers and mothers of ours were not Saints, but 10
Artists; driven to a numb and bleeding madness by the springs of creativity in them for which there was no release. They were Creators, who lived lives of spiritual waste, because they were so rich in spirituality — which is the basis of Art — that the strain of enduring their unused and unwanted talent drove them insane. Throwing away this spirituality was their pathetic attempt to lighten the soul to a weight their work-worn, sexually abused bodies could bear.

What did it mean for a black woman to be an artist in our grand- 11
mothers' time? In our great-grandmothers' day? It is a question with an answer cruel enough to stop the blood.

Did you have a genius of a great-great-grandmother who died 12
under some ignorant and depraved white overseer's lash? Or was she required to bake biscuits for a lazy backwater tramp, when she cried out in her soul to paint watercolors of sunsets, or the rain falling on the green and peaceful pasturelands? Or was her body broken and forced to bear children (who were more often than not sold away from her) — eight, ten, fifteen, twenty children — when her one joy was the thought of modeling heroic figures of rebellion, in stone or clay?

How was the creativity of the black woman kept alive, year after 13
year and century after century, when for most of the years black people have been in America, it was a punishable crime for a black person to read or write? And the freedom to paint, to sculpt, to expand the mind with an action did not exist. Consider, if you can bear to imagine it, what might have been the result if singing, too, had been forbidden by law. Listen to the voices of Bessie Smith, Billie Holiday, Nina Simone, Roberta Flack, and Aretha Franklin, among others, and imagine those voices muzzled for life. Then you may begin to comprehend the lives of our "crazy," "Sainted" mothers and grandmothers. The agony of the lives of women who might have been Poets, Novelists, Essayists, and Short-Story Writers (over a period of centuries), who died with their real gifts stifled within them.

And, if this were the end of the story, we would have cause to cry 14
out in my paraphrase of Okot p'Bitek's great poem:

O, my clanswomen
Let us all cry together!
Come,
Let us mourn the death of our mother,
The death of a Queen
The ash that was produced
By a great fire!

O, this homestead is utterly dead
Close the gates
With *lacari* thorns,
For our mother
The creator of the Stool is lost!
And all the young women
Have perished in the wilderness!

But this is not the end of the story, for all the young women —
our mothers and grandmothers, *ourselves* — have not perished in the
wilderness. And if we ask ourselves why, and search for and find the
answer, we will know beyond all efforts to erase it from our minds,
just exactly who, and of what, we black American women are.

One example, perhaps the most pathetic, most misunderstood
one, can provide a backdrop for our mothers' work: Phillis Wheatley,[1]
a slave in the 1700s.

Virginia Woolf,[2] in her book *A Room of One's Own*, wrote that in
order for a woman to write fiction she must have two things, certainly: a room of her own (the key and lock) and enough money to
support herself.

What then are we to make of Phillis Wheatley, a slave, who
owned not even herself? This sickly, frail black girl who required a servant of her own at times — her health was so precarious — and who,
had she been white, would have been easily considered the intellectual superior of all women and most of the men in the society of
her day.

Virginia Woolf wrote further, speaking of course not of our Phillis,
that "any woman born with a great gift in the sixteenth century [in-
sert "eighteenth century," insert "black woman," insert "born or made
a slave"] would certainly have gone crazed, shot herself, or ended her
days in some lonely cottage outside the village, half witch, half wizard
[insert "Saint"], feared and mocked at. For it needs little skill and psychology to be sure that a highly gifted girl who had tried to use her
gift for poetry would have been so thwarted and hindered by contrary
instincts [add "chains, guns, the lash, the ownership of one's body by
someone else, submission to an alien religion"], that she must have
lost her health and sanity to a certainty."

The key words, as they relate to Phillis, are "contrary instincts."
For when we read the poetry of Phillis Wheatley — and when we read
the novels of Nella Larsen or the oddly false-sounding autobiography

---

[1]Wheatley (1753?–1784) published several volumes of poetry and is considered the first important African American writer in the United States.

[2]Woolf (1882–1941) was an acclaimed English essayist and novelist.

15

16

17

18

19

20

of that freest of all black women writers, Zora Hurston[3] — evidence of "contrary instincts" is everywhere. Her loyalties were completely divided, as was, without question, her mind.

But how could this be otherwise? Captured at seven, a slave of wealthy, doting whites who instilled in her the "savagery" of the Africa they "rescued" her from . . . one wonders if she was even able to remember her homeland as she had known it, or as it really was.   21

Yet, because she did not try to use her gift for poetry in a world that made her a slave, she was "so thwarted and hindered by . . . contrary instincts, that she . . . lost her health. . . ." In the last years of her brief life, burdened not only with the need to express her gift but also with a penniless, friendless "freedom" and several small children for whom she was forced to do strenuous work to feed, she lost her health, certainly. Suffering from malnutrition and neglect and who knows what mental agonies, Phillis Wheatley died.   22

So torn by "contrary instincts" was black, kidnapped, enslaved Phillis that her description of "the Goddess" — as she poetically called the Liberty she did not have — is ironically, cruelly humorous. And, in fact, has held Phillis up to ridicule for more than a century. It is usually read prior to hanging Phillis's memory as that of a fool. She wrote: 23

> The Goddess comes, she moves divinely fair,
> Olive and laurel binds her *golden* hair.
> Wherever shines this native of the skies,
> Unnumber'd charms and recent graces rise. [My italics]

It is obvious that Phillis, the slave, combed the "Goddess's" hair every morning; prior, perhaps, to bringing in the milk, or fixing her mistress's lunch. She took her imagery from the one thing she saw elevated above all others.   24

With the benefit of hindsight we ask, "How could she?"   25

But at last, Phillis, we understand. No more snickering when your stiff, struggling, ambivalent lines are forced on us. We know now that you were not an idiot or a traitor; only a sickly little black girl, snatched from your home and country and made a slave; a woman who still struggled to sing the song that was your gift, although in a land of barbarians who praised you for your bewildered tongue. It is not so much what you sang, as that you kept alive, in so many of our ancestors, *the notion of song.*   26

---

[3]Larsen (1891–1964) wrote realistic novels about the relationships between different races; Hurston (1903–1960) is known for her folklore research, novels, and stories that convey the nuances of southern black speech.

Black women are called, in the folklore that so aptly identifies   27
one's status in society, "the *mule* of the world," because we have been
handed the burdens that everyone else — *everyone* else — refused to
carry. We have also been called "Matriarchs," "Superwomen," and
"Mean and Evil Bitches." Not to mention "Castrators" and "Sapphire's
Mama." When we have pleaded for understanding, our character has
been distorted; when we have asked for simple caring, we have been
handed empty inspirational appellations, then stuck in the farthest
corner. When we have asked for love, we have been given children. In
short, even our plainer gifts, our labors of fidelity and love, have been
knocked down our throats. To be an artist and a black woman, even
today, lowers our status in many respects, rather than raises it: and
yet, artists we will be.

Therefore we must fearlessly pull out of ourselves and look at and   28
identify with our lives the living creativity some of our great-
grandmothers were not allowed to know. I stress *some* of them because
it is well known that the majority of our great-grandmothers knew,
even without "knowing" it, the reality of their spirituality, even if
they didn't recognize it beyond what happened in the singing at
church — and they never had any intention of giving it up.

How they did it — those millions of black women who were not   29
Phillis Wheatley, or Lucy Terry or Frances Harper or Zora Hurston
or Nella Larsen or Bessie Smith; or Elizabeth Catlett, or Katherine
Dunham,[4] either — brings me to the title of this essay, "In Search of
Our Mothers' Gardens," which is a personal account that is yet shared,
in its theme and its meaning, by all of us. I found, while thinking about
the far-reaching world of the creative black woman, that often the
truest answer to a question that really matters can be found very close.

In the late 1920s my mother ran away from home to marry my fa-   30
ther. Marriage, if not running away, was expected of seventeen-year-
old girls. By the time she was twenty, she had two children and was
pregnant with a third. Five children later, I was born. And this is how I
came to know my mother: she seemed a large, soft, loving-eyed
woman who was rarely impatient in our home. Her quick, violent
temper was on view only a few times a year when she battled with the
white landlord who had the misfortune to suggest to her that her children did not need to go to school.

---

[4]Accomplished African American female artists; the first five were writers,
Smith was a singer and songwriter, Catlett a sculptor, and Dunham a choreog-
rapher and dancer.

She made all the clothes we wore, even my brothers' overalls. She 31
made all the towels and sheets we used. She spent the summers
canning vegetables and fruits. She spent the winter evenings making
quilts enough to cover all our beds.

During the "working" day, she labored beside — not behind — my 32
father in the fields. Her day began before sunup, and did not end until
late at night. There was never a moment for her to sit down, undisturbed, to unravel her own private thoughts; never a time free from interruption — by work or the noisy inquiries of her many children. And
yet, it is to my mother — and all our mothers who were not famous —
that I went in search of the secret of what has fed that muzzled and often
mutilated, but vibrant, creative spirit that the black woman has inher-
ited, and that pops out in wild and unlikely places to this day.

But when, you will ask, did my overworked mother have time to 33
know or care about feeding the creative spirit?

The answer is so simple that many of us have spent years discover- 34
ing it. We have constantly looked high, when we should have looked
high — and low.

For example: in the Smithsonian Institution in Washington, D.C., 35
there hangs a quilt unlike any other in the world. In fanciful, inspired,
and yet simple and identifiable figures, it portrays the story of the Cru-
cifixion. It is considered rare, beyond price. Though it follows no
known pattern of quilt-making, and though it is made of bits and
pieces of worthless rags, it is obviously the work of a person of powerful imagination and deep spiritual feeling. Below this quilt I saw a
note that says it was made by "an anonymous Black woman in Alabama, a hundred years ago."

If we could locate this "anonymous" black woman from Alabama, 36
she would turn out to be one of our grandmothers — an artist who
left her mark in the only materials she could afford, and in the only
medium her position in society allowed her to use.

As Virginia Woolf wrote further, in *A Room of One's Own:* 37

> Yet genius of a sort must have existed among women as it must
> have existed among the working class. [Change this to "slaves" and
> "the wives and the daughters of sharecroppers."] Now and again an
> Emily Brontë or a Robert Burns [change this to "a Zora Hurston or a
> Richard Wright"] blazes out and proves its presence. But certainly it
> never got itself on to paper. When, however, one reads of a witch
> being ducked, of a woman possessed by devils [or "Sainthood"], of a
> wise woman selling herbs [our root workers], or even a very remark-
> able man who had a mother, then I think we are on the track of a
> lost novelist, a suppressed poet, of some mute and inglorious Jane
> Austen. . . . Indeed, I would venture to guess that Anon, who wrote
> so many poems without signing them, was often a woman. . . .

And so our mothers and grandmothers have, more often than not   38
anonymously, handed on the creative spark, the seed of the flower
they themselves never hoped to see: or like a sealed letter they could
not plainly read.

And so it is, certainly, with my own mother. Unlike "Ma"   39
Rainey's[5] songs, which retained their creator's name even while blast-
ing forth from Bessie Smith's mouth, no song or poem will bear my
mother's name. Yet so many of the stories that I write, that we all
write, are my mother's stories. Only recently did I fully realize this:
that through years of listening to my mother's stories of her life, I
have absorbed not only the stories themselves, but something of the
manner in which she spoke, something of the urgency that involves
the knowledge that her stories — like her life — must be recorded. It is
probably for this reason that so much of what I have written is about
characters whose counterparts in real life are so much older than I am.

But the telling of these stories, which came from my mother's lips   40
as naturally as breathing, was not the only way my mother showed
herself as an artist. For stories, too, were subject to being distracted, to
dying without conclusion. Dinners must be started, and cotton must
be gathered before the big rains. The artist that was and is my mother
showed itself to me only after many years. This is what I finally
noticed:

Like Mem, a character in *The Third Life of Grange Copeland,* my   41
mother adorned with flowers whatever shabby house we were forced
to live in. And not just your typical straggly country stand of zinnias,
either. She planted ambitious gardens — and still does — with over
fifty different varieties of plants that bloom profusely from early
March until late November. Before she left home for the fields, she
watered her flowers, chopped up the grass, and laid out new beds.
When she returned from the fields she might divide clumps of bulbs,
dig a cold pit, uproot and replant rose, or prune branches from her
taller bushes or trees — until night came and it was too dark to see.

Whatever she planted grew as if by magic, and her fame as a   42
grower of flowers spread over three counties. Because of her creativity
with her flowers, even my memories of poverty are seen through a
screen of blooms — sunflowers, petunias, roses, dahlias, forsythia,
spirea, delphiniums, verbena . . . and on and on.

And I remember people coming to my mother's yard to be given   43
cuttings from her flowers; I hear again the praise showered on her because whatever rocky soil she landed on, she turned into a garden. A
garden so brilliant with colors, so original in its design, so magnificent
with life and creativity, that to this day people drive by our house in

---

[5]Rainey (1886–1939) was a famous blues singer and songwriter.

Georgia — perfect strangers and imperfect strangers — and ask to stand or walk in my mother's art.

I notice that it is not only when my mother is working in her 44 flowers that she is radiant, almost to the point of being invisible — except as Creator: hand and eye. She is involved in work her soul must have. Ordering the universe in the image of her personal conception of Beauty.

Her face, as she prepares the Art that is her gift, is a legacy of respect 45 she leaves to me, for all that illuminates and cherishes life. She has handed down respect for the possibilities — and the will to grasp them.

For her, so hindered and intruded upon in so many ways, being 46 an artist has still been a daily part of her life. This ability to hold on, even in very simple ways, is work black women have done for a very long time.

This poem is not enough, but it is something, for the woman who 47 literally covered the holes in our walls with sunflowers:

They were women then
My mama's generation
Husky of voice — Stout of
Step
With fists as well as
Hands
How they battered down
Doors
And ironed
Starched white
Shirts
How they led
Armies
Headragged Generals
Across mined
Fields
Booby-trapped
Kitchens
To discovery books
Desks
A place for us
How they knew what we
Must know
Without knowing a page
Of it
Themselves.

Guided by my heritage of a love of beauty and a respect for 48 strength — in search of my mother's garden, I found my own.

And perhaps in Africa over two hundred years ago, there was just 49 such a mother; perhaps she painted vivid and daring decorations in oranges and yellows and greens on the walls of her hut; perhaps she sang — in a voice like Roberta Flack's — *sweetly* over the compounds of her village; perhaps she wove the most stunning mats or told the most ingenious stories of all the village storytellers. Perhaps she was herself a poet — though only her daughter's name is signed to the poems that we know.

Perhaps Phillis Wheatley's mother was also an artist. 50

Perhaps in more than Phillis Wheatley's biological life is her 51 mother's signature made clear.

RESPONDING TO READING

Walker finds art in a quilt and a garden. Where have you encountered examples of artistic expression in unusual forms or in everyday places? Describe one or two. What do they suggest to you about the nature and motivation of the creators?

QUESTIONING THE TEXT

1. Why does Walker open her essay with a quote from Jean Toomer? What surprising discovery did he make many years ago about black women in America? Where did his understanding of them fall short?

2. Who was Phillis Wheatley? Why might modern blacks consider her a "traitor"? What is Walker's opinion of her? What does she exemplify?

3. Walker gives two examples of her mother's artistry. What are these examples? What is the impact of each upon Walker herself?

UNDERSTANDING THE WRITER'S CRAFT

1. Near the end of the essay, Walker includes a poem of her own, written in tribute to her mother and other black women of her mother's generation. Why is it appropriate here? What central idea does it support and exemplify? How does mixing two forms, prose and poetry, emphasize her main point?

2. Paragraph 11 uses a rhetorical question to introduce a turning point in the essay: "What did it mean for a black woman to be an artist in our grandmothers' time?" (Glossary: *Rhetorical Question*) What shift of emphasis does this question bring about? Although Walker says the answer is "cruel enough to stop the blood," she does not state it directly. In your own words, what is the answer?

3. Examples and illustrations have a purpose; usually they support an argument. (Glossary: *Argument*) Walker uses different types of examples throughout this essay. Find and identify several different kinds of examples. What idea or argument does each support?

EXPLORING LANGUAGE

1. In paragraph 44, what does Walker imply when she describes her mother as "radiant, almost to the point of being invisible"? What is the metaphor in this paragraph, and how does it relate to the earlier description of black women as "Saints"? Through these metaphors, what is Walker trying to express about the process of art? (Glossary: *Figures of Speech*)

2. What does Walker mean, in paragraph 34, when she says that "we should have looked high — and low" to find examples of the creative spirit? What kinds of places does she mean?

3. Walker, a poet, chooses words precisely. Be sure you know the meanings of these words as she uses them: *abstractions* (paragraph 2), *post-Reconstruction* (5), *revelation* (8), *depraved* (12), *precarious* (18), *doting* (21), *ambivalent* (26), *matriarchs* (27), *appellations* (27), *vibrant* (32).

COMBINING RHETORICAL STRATEGIES

1. Walker tells of her mother's natural gift for narrative. (Glossary: *Narration*) The only brief examples of narrative in this essay occur when Walker tells about her mother. Find these examples, and explain how and why they are effective in their context.

2. Walker quotes Virginia Woolf, a white author, to support her vision of the suppressed female artist, but she also draws a contrast between Woolf's ancestors and her own. (Glossary: *Comparison and Contrast*) How does she make the contrast explicit? Why does Walker use Woolf as an example?

WRITING SUGGESTIONS

1. **(Exemplification)** Walker equates creative artistry with spirituality. Do you agree with the connection she makes? What does she mean, exactly, by these two terms? How would you define them? What do you believe to be the wellspring of art? Write an essay in which you use numerous illustrations to define and exemplify the creative spirit. You might find it helpful to refer to your Before You Read and Responding to Reading entries.

2. **(Other Strategies)** Why are there so few women among the best-known writers in Western culture? Walker cites the work of Virginia Woolf and Zora Neale Hurston, one white woman and one black, who wrote their landmark works early in the twentieth century. Read either *A Room of One's Own* by Woolf or *Dust Tracks on a Road* by Hurston. Write an essay to discuss how the work you chose exemplifies the limits society laid on its author and the ways in which she overcame or sought to overcome those limits.

3. **(Research)** Interview a female artist (author, painter, singer, quilt maker, etc.) within your community. Before you conduct your inter-

view, you might want to check your library, local newspapers, or the Internet to find out what some female artists have to say about their lives. What were the advantages and limitations the artist experienced as an artist because of her gender? What does she believe to be the wellspring of the creative spirit? What role, if any, did her mother, grandmother, or other female relative play in her choice and pursuit of art? Write an essay profiling this artist.

- **The World's Women On-line! Electronic Art Networking**
  <http://wwol.inre.asu.edu>

This electronic art networking project includes works by thousands of female artists from around the world. Perhaps your interview subject already has work depicted on this site, or you might suggest that she submit some of her works to it.

- **Women Artists Archive**
  <http://libweb.sonoma.edu/special/waa>

This Web site, listing hundreds of female artists from around the world, is maintained by the Sonoma University Library.

- **WWWomen Search Directory for Women On-line: Arts**
  <http://www.wwwomen.com/category/arts1.html>

This site offers numerous links to Web resources concerning women in the arts.

COMBINING SUBJECTS AND STRATEGIES

The photograph below depicts many of the same themes and strategies as the Combining Rhetorical Strategies essay that follows. Your observations about the photograph will help guide you to the key themes and strategies in the essay. After you've read the essay, you may use your observations about both the photograph and the essay to examine how the overlapping themes and strategies work in each medium.

We've all posed for family portraits, those pictures often taken on special occasions or gatherings. People value these pictures because they create family histories, forming a permanent record of who we were at particular points in time. While in New Mexico, photographer Joel Gordon captured this shot of three generations of Taos Pueblo women near their home village. Look closely at the story that this photograph reveals.

© Joel Gordon 1993

For Discussion

How do you "read" this photograph depicting three generations of Native American women? What do you see in this grandmother's face? What, if anything, do you find that is beautiful about her? Which facial features do you find most expressive? Does her face tell you something about who this woman is? In a word or two, what qualities does this woman represent for you? Explain. Now ask these same questions about the daughter's face and the granddaughter's face. What similarities do you see among the three women? What differences?

Yellow Woman and a Beauty of the Spirit

Leslie Marmon Silko

Born in Albuquerque, New Mexico, in 1948 of Pueblo, Laguna, Mexican, and white ancestors and raised through her early years on the Laguna Pueblo reservation, Leslie Marmon Silko is now a professor of English at the University of New Mexico. Through both her writing and her teaching she has taken a leading role in raising consciousness and interest in Native American culture. Silko is unique in her ability to combine the oral traditions of a tribal storyteller with the literary traditions of Western civilization. She employs an unusually wide variety of genres to communicate her ideas, including essays, poetry, transcriptions of legends, photographic illustrations, screenplays, novels, and short fiction. As one critic observes, Silko writes of the conflicts between the white and Native American cultures with "fury, clear vision, and an eloquent voice." Her best-known works include the novels Ceremony *(1988),* Almanac of the Dead *(1991), and* Gardens in the Dunes *(1999);* Storyteller *(1989), a collection depicting Native American life; and* Sacred Water *(1993), an illustrated autobiographical narrative.*

The following essay is the title piece from Yellow Woman and a Beauty of the Spirit: Essays on Native American Life *(1996).*

BEFORE YOU READ

Every person is unique; every individual has qualities that set him or her apart from others. In what ways do you perceive yourself to be different from the norm of the culture in which you grew up? How do you feel about these differences — do they please or embarrass you? How do others respond to the qualities that make you different?

From the time I was a small child, I was aware that I was different. I looked different from my playmates. My two sisters looked different too. We didn't quite look like the other Laguna Pueblo children, but we didn't look quite white either. In the 1880s, my great-grandfather had followed his older brother west from Ohio to the New Mexico Territory to survey the land for the U.S. government. The two Marmon brothers came to the Laguna Pueblo reservation because they had an Ohio cousin who already lived there. The Ohio cousin was involved in sending Indian children thousands of miles away from their families to the War Department's big Indian boarding school in Carlisle, Pennsylvania. Both brothers married full-blood Laguna Pueblo women. My great-grandfather had first married my great-grandmother's older sister, but she died in childbirth and left two small children. My great-grandmother was fifteen or twenty years younger than my great-grandfather. She had attended Carlisle Indian School and spoke and wrote English beautifully.

I called her Grandma A'mooh because that's what I heard her say whenever she saw me. *A'mooh* means "granddaughter" in the Laguna language. I remember this word because her love and her acceptance of me as a small child were so important. I had sensed immediately that something about my appearance was not acceptable to some people, white and Indian. But I did not see any signs of that strain or anxiety in the face of my beloved Grandma A'mooh.

Younger people, people my parents' age, seemed to look at the world in a more modern way. The modern way included racism. My physical appearance seemed not to matter to the old-time people. They looked at the world very differently; a person's appearance and possessions did not matter nearly as much as a person's behavior. For them, a person's value lies in how that person interacts with other people, how that person behaves toward the animals and the earth. That is what matters most to the old-time people. The Pueblo people believed this long before the Puritans arrived with their notions of sin and damnation, and racism. The old-time beliefs persist today; thus I will refer to the old-time people in the present tense as well as the past. Many worlds may coexist here.

I spent a great deal of time with my great-grandmother. Her house was next to our house, and I used to wake up at dawn, hours before my parents or younger sisters, and I'd go wait on the porch swing or on the back steps by her kitchen door. She got up at dawn, but she was more than eighty years old, so she needed a little while to get dressed and to get the fire going in the cookstove. I had been carefully instructed by my parents not to bother her and to behave, and to try to help her any way I could. I always loved the early mornings when the air was so cool with a hint of rain smell in the breeze. In the dry New Mexico air, the least hint of dampness smells sweet.

My great-grandmother's yard was planted with lilac bushes and iris; there were four o'clocks, cosmos, morning glories, and hollyhocks, and old-fashioned rosebushes that I helped her water. If the garden hose got stuck on one of the big rocks that lined the path in the yard, I ran and pulled it free. That's what I came to do early every morning: to help Grandma water the plants before the heat of the day arrived.

Grandma A'mooh would tell about the old days, family stories about relatives who had been killed by Apache raiders who stole the sheep our relatives had been herding near Swahnee. Sometimes she read Bible stories that we kids liked because of the illustrations of Jonah in the mouth of a whale and Daniel surrounded by lions. Grandma A'mooh would send me home when she took her nap, but when the sun got low and the afternoon began to cool off, I would be back on the porch swing, waiting for her to come out to water the plants and to haul in firewood for the evening. When Grandma was eighty-five, she still chopped her own kindling. She used to let me carry it in the coal bucket for her, but she would not allow me to use the ax. I carried armloads of kindling too, and I learned to be proud of my strength.

I was allowed to listen quietly when Aunt Susie or Aunt Alice came to visit Grandma. When I got old enough to cross the road alone, I went and visited them almost daily. They were vigorous women who valued books and writing. They were usually busy chopping wood or cooking but never hesitated to take time to answer my questions. Best of all they told me the *hummah-hah* stories, about an earlier time when animals and humans shared a common language. In the old days, the Pueblo people had educated their children in this manner; adults took time out to talk to and teach young people. Everyone was a teacher, and every activity had the potential to teach the child.

But as soon as I started kindergarten at the Bureau of Indian Affairs day school, I began to learn more about the differences between the Laguna Pueblo world and the outside world. It was at school that I learned just how different I looked from my classmates. Sometimes tourists driving past on Route 66 would stop by Laguna Day School at recess time to take photographs of us kids. One day, when I was in the first grade, we all crowded around the smiling white tourists, who peered at our faces. We all wanted to be in the picture because afterward the tourists sometimes gave us each a penny. Just as we were all posed and ready to have our picture taken, the tourist man looked at me. "Not you," he said and motioned for me to step away from my classmates. I felt so embarrassed that I wanted to disappear. My classmates were puzzled by the tourists' behavior, but I knew the tourists didn't want me in their snapshot because I looked different, because I was part white.

In the view of the old-time people, we were all sisters and brothers   9
because the Mother Creator made all of us — all colors and all sizes. We are sisters and brothers, clanspeople of all the living beings around us. The plants, the birds, fish, clouds, water, even the clay — they all are related to us. The old-time people believe that all things, even rocks and water, have spirit and being. They understood that all things want only to continue being as they are; they need only to be left as they are. Thus the old folks used to tell us kids not to disturb the earth unnecessarily. All things as they were created exist already in harmony with one another as long as we do not disturb them.

As the old story tells us, Tse'itsi'nako, Thought Woman, the Spi-   10
der, thought of her three sisters, and as she thought of them, they came into being. Together with Thought Woman, they thought of the sun and the stars and the moon. The Mother Creators imagined the earth and the oceans, the animals and the people, and the *ka'tsina* spirits that reside in the mountains. The Mother Creators imagined all the plants that would flower and the trees that bear fruit. As Thought Woman and her sisters thought of it, the whole universe came into being. In this universe, there is no absolute good or absolute bad; there are only balances, and harmonies that ebb and flow. Some years the desert receives abundant rain, other years there is too little rain, and sometimes there is so much rain that floods cause destruction. But rain itself is neither innocent nor guilty. The rain is simply itself.

My great-grandmother was dark and handsome. Her expression in   11
photographs is one of confidence and strength. I do not know if white people then or now would consider her beautiful. I do not know if old-time Laguna Pueblo people considered her beautiful or if the old-time people even thought in those terms. To the Pueblo way of think-ing, the act of comparing one living being with another was silly, be-cause each living being or thing is unique and therefore incomparably valuable because it is the only one of its kind. The old-time people thought it was crazy to attach such importance to a person's appear-ance. I understood very early that there were two distinct ways of in-terpreting the world. There was the white people's way and there was the Laguna way. In the Laguna way, it was bad manners to make com-parisons that might hurt another person's feelings.

In everyday Pueblo life, not much attention was paid to one's   12
physical appearance or clothing. Ceremonial clothing was quite elabo-rate but was used only for the sacred dances. The traditional Pueblo societies were communal and strictly egalitarian, which means that no

matter how well or how poorly one might have dressed, there was no social ladder to fall from. All food and other resources were strictly shared so that no one person or group had more than another. I mention social status because it seems to me that most of the definitions of beauty in contemporary Western culture are really codes for determining social status. People no longer hide their face-lifts and they discuss their liposuctions because the point of the procedures isn't just cosmetic, it is social. It says to the world, "I have enough spare cash that I can afford surgery for cosmetic purposes."

In the old-time Pueblo world, beauty was manifested in behavior 13 and in one's relationships with other living beings. Beauty was as much a feeling of harmony as it was a visual, aural, or sensual effect. The whole person had to be beautiful, not just the face or the body; faces or bodies could not be separated from hearts and souls. Health was foremost in achieving this sense of well-being and harmony; in the old-time Pueblo world, a person who did not look healthy inspired feelings of worry and anxiety, not feelings of well-being. A healthy person, of course, is in harmony with the world around her; she is at peace with herself too. Thus an unhappy person or spiteful person would not be considered beautiful.

In the old days, sturdy women were most admired. One of my avid 14 preschool memories is of the crew of Laguna women, in their forties and fifties, who came to cover our house with adobe plaster. They handled the ladders with great ease, and while two women ground the adobe mud on stones and added straw, another woman loaded the hod with mud and passed it up to the two women on ladders, who were smoothing the plaster on the wall with their hands. Since women owned the houses, they did the plastering. At Laguna, men did the basket making and the weaving of fine textiles; men helped a great deal with the child care too. Because the Creator is female, there is no stigma on being female; gender is not used to control behavior. No job was a man's job or a woman's job; the most able person did the work.

My Grandma Lily had been a Ford Model A mechanic when she 15 was a teenager. I remember when I was young, she was always fixing broken lamps and appliances. She was small and wiry, but she could lift her weight in rolled roofing or boxes of nails. When she was seventy-five, she was still repairing washing machines in my uncle's coin-operated laundry.

The old-time people paid no attention to birthdays. When a person was ready to do something, she did it. When she was no longer 16 able, she stopped. Thus the traditional Pueblo people did not worry about aging or about looking old because there were no social boundaries drawn by the passage of years. It was not remarkable for young men to marry women as old as their mothers. I never heard anyone talk about "women's work" until after I left Laguna for college. Work was there to be done by any able-bodied person who wanted to do it. At the same time, in the old-time Pueblo world, identity was acknowledged to be always in a flux; in the old stories, one minute Spider Woman is a little spider under a yucca plant, and the next instant she is a sprightly grandmother walking down the road.

When I was growing up, there was a young man from a nearby   17
village who wore nail polish and women's blouses and permed his hair. People paid little attention to his appearance; he was always part of a group of other young men from his village. No one ever made fun of him. Pueblo communities were and still are very interdependent, but they also have to be tolerant of individual eccentricities because survival of the group means everyone has to cooperate.

In the old Pueblo world, differences were celebrated as signs of the   18
Mother Creator's grace. Persons born with exceptional physical or sexual differences were highly respected and honored because their physical differences gave them special positions as mediators between this world and the spirit world. The great Navajo medicine man of the 1920s, the Crawler, had a hunchback and could not walk upright, but he was able to heal even the most difficult cases.

Before the arrival of Christian missionaries, a man could dress as a   19
woman and work with women and even marry a man without any fanfare. Likewise, a woman was free to dress like a man, to hunt and go to war with the men, and to marry a woman. In the old Pueblo worldview, we are all a mixture of male and female, and this sexual identity is changing constantly. Sexual inhibition did not begin until the Christian missionaries arrived. For the old-time people, marriage was about teamwork and social relationships, not about sexual excitement. In the days before the Puritans came, marriage did not mean an end to sex with people other than your spouse. Women were just as likely as men to have a *si'ash,* or lover.

New life was so precious that pregnancy was always appropriate,   20
and pregnancy before marriage was celebrated as a good sign. Since the children belonged to the mother and her clan, and women owned and bequeathed the houses and farmland, the exact determination of paternity wasn't critical. Although fertility was prized, infertility was no problem because mothers with unplanned pregnancies gave their babies to childless couples within the clan in open adoption arrangements. Children called their mother's sisters "mother" as well, and a child became attached to a number of parent figures.

In the sacred kiva ceremonies, men mask and dress as women to   21
pay homage and to be possessed by the female energies of the spirit beings. Because differences in physical appearance were so highly valued, surgery to change one's face and body to resemble a model's face

and body would be unimaginable. To be different, to be unique was blessed and was best of all.

The traditional clothing of Pueblo women emphasized a woman's 22 sturdiness. Buckskin leggings wrapped around the legs protected her from scratches and injuries while she worked. The more layers of buckskin, the better. All those layers gave her legs the appearance of strength, like sturdy tree trunks. To demonstrate sisterhood and brotherhood with the plants and animals, the old-time people make masks and costumes that transform the human figures of the dancers into the animal beings they portray. Dancers paint their exposed skin; their postures and motions are adapted from their observations. But the motions are stylized. The observer sees not an actual eagle or actual deer dancing, but witnesses a human being, a dancer, gradually changing into a woman/buffalo or a man/deer. Every impulse is to reaffirm the urgent relationships that human beings have with the plant and animal world.

In the high desert, all vegetation, even weeds and thorns, becomes 23 special, and all life is precious and beautiful because without the plants, the insects, and the animals, human beings living here cannot survive. Perhaps human beings long ago noticed the devastating impact human activity can have on the plants and animals; maybe this is why tribal cultures devised the stories about humans and animals intermarrying, and the clans that bind humans to animals and plants through a whole complex of duties.

We children were always warned not to harm frogs or toads, the 24 beloved children of the rain clouds, because terrible floods would occur. I remember in the summer the old folks used to stick big bolls of cotton on the outside of their screen doors as bait to keep the flies from going in the house when the door was opened. The old folks staunchly resisted the killing of flies because once, long, long ago, when human beings were in a great deal of trouble, a Green Bottle Fly carried desperate messages from human beings to the Mother Creator in the Fourth World, below this one. Human beings had outraged the Mother Creator by neglecting the Mother Corn altar while they dabbled with sorcery and magic. The Mother Creator disappeared, and with her disappeared the rain clouds, and the plants and the animals too. The people began to starve, and they had no way of reaching the Mother Creator down below. Green Bottle Fly took the message to the Mother Creator, and the people were saved. To show their gratitude, the old folks refused to kill any flies.

The old stories demonstrate the interrelationships that the Pueblo 25 people have maintained with their plant and animal clanspeople. Kochininako, Yellow Woman, represents all women in the old stories.

Her deeds span the spectrum of human behavior and are mostly heroic acts, though in at least one story, she chooses to join the secret Destroyer Clan, which worships destruction and death. Because Laguna Pueblo cosmology features a female Creator, the status of women is equal with the status of men, and women appear as often as men in the old stories as hero figures. Yellow Woman is my favorite because she dares to cross traditional boundaries of ordinary behavior during times of crisis in order to save the Pueblo; her power lies in her courage and her uninhibited sexuality, which the old-time Pueblo stories celebrate again and again because fertility was so highly valued.

The old stories always say that Yellow Woman was beautiful, but 26 remember that the old-time people were not so much thinking about physical appearances. In each story, the beauty that Yellow Woman possesses is the beauty of her passion, her daring, and her sheer strength to act when catastrophe is imminent.

In one story, the people are suffering during a great drought and 27 accompanying famine. Each day, Kochininako has to walk farther and farther from the village to find fresh water for her husband and children. One day she travels far, far to the east, to the plains, and she finally locates a freshwater spring. But when she reaches the pool, the water is churning violently as if something large had just gotten out of the pool. Kochininako does not want to see what huge creature had been at the pool, but just as she fills her water jar and turns to hurry away, a strong, sexy man in buffalo-skin leggings appears by the pool. Little drops of water glisten on his chest. She cannot help but look at him because he is so strong and so good to look at. Able to transform himself from human to buffalo in the wink of an eye, Buffalo Man gallops away with her on his back. Kochininako falls in love with Buffalo Man, and because of this liaison, the Buffalo People agree to give their bodies to the hunters to feed the starving Pueblo. Thus Kochininako's fearless sensuality results in the salvation of the people of her village, who are saved by the meat the Buffalo People "give" to them.

My father taught me and my sisters to shoot .22 rifles when we 28 were seven; I went hunting with my father when I was eight, and I killed my first mule deer buck when I was thirteen. The Kochininako stories were always my favorite because Yellow Woman had so many adventures. In one story, as she hunts rabbits to feed her family, a giant monster pursues her, but she has the courage and the presence of mind to outwit it.

In another story, Kochininako has a fling with Whirlwind Man 29 and returns to her husband ten months later with twin baby boys. The twin boys grow up to be great heroes of the people. Once again, Kochininako's vibrant sexuality benefits her people.

The stories about Kochininako made me aware that sometimes an 30 individual must act despite disapproval, or concern for appearances or what others may say. From Yellow Woman's adventures, I learned to be comfortable with my differences. I even imagined that Yellow Woman had yellow skin, brown hair, and green eyes like mine, although her name does not refer to her color, but rather to the ritual color of the east.

There have been many other moments like the one with the camera-toting tourist in the schoolyard. But the old-time people always say, remember the stories, the stories will help you be strong. So all these years I have depended on Kochininako and the stories of her adventures. 31

Kochininako is beautiful because she has the courage to act in times of great peril, and her triumph is achieved by her sensuality, not through violence and destruction. For these qualities of the spirit, Yellow Woman and all women are beautiful. 32

RESPONDING TO READING

Consider several ways in which Tse'itsi'nako, Thought Woman, contrasts with the god of Judeo-Christian culture. What are some differences in cultural values or behavior that might be implied by the differences between these two creators?

QUESTIONING THE TEXT

1. In paragraph 3, Silko distinguishes between the old-time Laguna way of looking at the world and a modern way. What are the primary differences between these worldviews?

2. Why are old women so highly valued by the Pueblo people? Give a number of examples.

3. To what does Silko equate definitions of personal beauty in contemporary Western culture? Do you agree? Why or why not?

UNDERSTANDING THE WRITER'S CRAFT

1. Silko braids together numerous brief stories, some of which stem from Laguna mythology, some from her own experience. How do the stories relate to one another? Is there a common thread or purpose among them?

2. In what way is it ironic that Grandma A'mooh shared Bible stories with the Pueblo children? That the children enjoyed them? Can you think of ways that these stories were also useful? (Glossary: *Irony*)

3. Kochininako, the Yellow Woman of the title, does not appear until the last few paragraphs of the essay. Why, in your opinion, does Silko wait so long in introducing her to the reader?

EXPLORING LANGUAGE

1. Silko shows that the language of her tribe had no words or phrases to express such familiar Western cultural concepts as sin, racism, or woman's work. Why do these English terms have no Laguna equivalent? Does she mention other terms of which this is true?

2. In referring to the Pueblo culture at the end of paragraph 3, what does Silko mean when she writes, "Many worlds may coexist here"?

3. Refer to your dictionary to determine the meanings of the following words as Silko uses them in this selection: *communal* (paragraph 12), *egalitarian* (12), *liposuctions* (12), *aural* (13), *hod* (14), *yucca* (16), *mediators* (18), *cosmology* (25), *imminent* (26).

COMBINING RHETORICAL STRATEGIES

Throughout this essay, Silko contrasts the old Laguna beliefs with those of modern Western culture. In your own words, state her central thesis. How do the contrasts she draws support this thesis? (Glossary: *Comparison and Contrast*) Be specific; cite illustrations from the text.

WRITING SUGGESTIONS

1. **(Exemplification)** Silko challenges the reader to think about the multiple meanings of the word *beauty*. Are you able to see beauty in a person's passion, courage, daring, sensuality, and strength, or are you caught up in what Silko calls "physical appearances"? Using examples from Silko's essay, Joel Gordon's photograph, and your own experiences, write an essay in which you explore the meaning of *beauty*.

2. **(Other Strategies)** The education of a Laguna child emphasizes cooperation rather than competition. Is this emphasis always desirable? In what ways does competition benefit children and adults? Write an essay contrasting the effects of cooperation and competition in a learning or work environment.

3. **(Research)** Virtually all cultures have creation myths. Read in detail the creation stories of the Pueblo people; read also the creation myths of two or three other Native American tribes. What elements do the stories have in common? Research in the library and perhaps on the Internet. Write an essay in which you draw generalizations about the beliefs and values of different Native American tribes and exemplify these generalizations with specific examples from their creation stories.

   - **Aadizookaanag: Traditional Stories, Legends, and Myths**
     <http://indy4.fdl.cc.mn.us/~isk/stories/myths.html>

     This page offers links to myths and stories of various Native American tribes.

- **Native American Nations**
  <http://www.nativeculture.com/lisamitten/nations.html>

  Links to sites on many Native American nations, including many nations' official Web sites can be found at this site, maintained by Lisa Mitten, a librarian at the University of Pittsburgh. Also check out her general site at
  <http://www.nativeculture.com/lisamitten/indians.html>

- **Index of Native American Resources on the Internet**
  <http://hanksville.org/NAresources>

  This encyclopedic site has links organized by subject.

WRITING SUGGESTIONS FOR EXEMPLIFICATION

1. Write an essay on one of the following statements, using examples to illustrate your ideas. You should be able to draw some of your examples from personal experience and firsthand observations.

   a. Fads never go out of style.
   b. Television has produced a number of "classic" programs.
   c. Every college campus has its own unique slang terms.
   d. Making excuses sometimes seems like a national pastime.
   e. A liberal arts education can have many practical applications.
   f. All good teachers (*or* doctors, secretaries, auto mechanics, sales representatives) have certain traits in common.
   g. Television talk shows are an accurate (*or* inaccurate) reflection of our society.
   h. Good literature always teaches us something about our humanity.
   i. Grades are not always a good indication of what has been learned.
   j. Recycling starts with the individual.

2. Write an essay on one of the following statements, using examples to illustrate your ideas. Draw your examples from a variety of sources: your library's print and Internet resources, interviews, and information gathered from lectures and the media. As you plan your essay, consider whether you will want to use a series of short examples or one or more extended examples.

   a. Much has been (*or* should still be) done to eliminate barriers for the physically handicapped.
   b. Nature's oddities are numerous.
   c. Throughout history, dire predictions have been made about the end of the world.
   d. Boxing should be outlawed.
   e. The past predictions of science fiction are today's realities.
   f. The world has not seen an absence of warfare since World War II.
   g. The Japanese have developed many innovative management strategies.
   h. A great work of art may come out of an artist's most difficult period.
   i. The misjudgments of our presidents can be useful lessons in leadership.
   j. Genius is 10 percent talent and 90 percent hard work.
   k. Drugs have taken an economic toll on American business.
   l. Democracy has attracted renewed interest in countries outside of the United States.

3. College students are not often given credit for the community volunteer work they do. Write a letter to the editor of your local newspaper in which you demonstrate, with several extended examples, the beneficial impact that you and your fellow students have had on the community.

4. How do advertisers portray older people in their advertisements? Based on your analysis of some real ads, how fair are advertisers to senior citizens? What tactics do advertisers use to sell their products to senior citizens? Write an essay in which you use actual ads to illustrate two or three such tactics.

5. Most students would agree that in order to be happy and "well adjusted," people need to learn how to relieve stress and to relax. What strategies do you and your friends use to relax? What have been the benefits of these relaxation techniques for you? Write an article for the school newspaper in which you give examples of several of these techniques and encourage your fellow students to try them.

6. The Internet has profoundly altered the way people around the world communicate and share information. One area in which significant change is especially evident is education. While having so much information at your fingertips can be exciting, such technology is not without its problems. What are the advantages and disadvantages of the Internet for teachers and students? Write an essay in which you analyze its value for education. Document your assessment with specific examples.

7. Some people think it's important to look their best and, therefore, give careful attention to the clothing they wear. Others do not seem to care. How much stock do you put in the old saying, "Clothes make the person"? Use examples of the people on your own campus or in your community to argue your position.

8. By all accounts, *Frasier* is one of the most successful television comedies ever. Drawing on your knowledge of the show, how would you account for its popular acclaim? You might consider videotaping a number of episodes so that you can see them more than once. Gather examples to illustrate the many ways this show appeals to viewers. Write an essay in which you explain the show's popularity, drawing on selected examples of theme, characterizations, situations, stories, and dialogue in episodes that you have seen.

CHAPTER 6

Description

WHAT IS DESCRIPTION?

Description is conveying, through words, the perceptions of our five senses. We see, hear, smell, taste, and feel; and through description we try to re-create those sensations to share them with others. Some sensations are so basic that they almost precede thought: the color and dazzle of fireworks, the crunch of snow underfoot, the savory aroma of fried onion rings, the tartness of lemonade, the soothing coolness of aloe vera on sunburned skin, the pleasant tiredness of leg muscles after a brisk run. Other perceptions appeal more directly to the mind, like the intricate architecture of a spider web or the multilayered sounds of a symphony. All are the province of description.

It is often said that to describe is to paint a verbal picture — of a thing, a place, a person — and the analogy is a helpful one. Both description and painting seek to transform fleeting perceptions into lasting images through the use of a foreign medium: words in the case of description, oils or watercolors in the case of a painting. Although the original perception may have taken place in a flash, both description and painting are created bit by bit, word by word, or brush stroke by brush stroke. Yet while we can view a painting in a single glance (though appreciation may take longer), we take in a description only piece by piece, or word by word, just as the writer created it. And of course, a picture is purely visual and textural, while a description may draw on all of our sense perceptions, evoking not just sight, but also sound, texture, taste, and smell.

Consider, for example, the following description by Bernd Heinrich from his book *One Man's Owl* (1987). In this selection, Heinrich describes trekking through the woods in search of owls. First, allow the words of his description to build up a concrete mental image. Try to experience in your mind what Heinrich experienced firsthand; try to see, hear, smell, and feel what his words suggest. Form the jigsaw puzzle of words and details into a complete experience. Once you've built this mental image, define the dominant impression Heinrich creates.

Writer sets the scene with description of the landscape.

By mid-March in Vermont, the snow from the winter storms has already become crusty as the first midday thaws refreeze during the cold nights. A solid white cap compacts the snow, and you can walk on it without breaking through to your waist. The maple sap is starting to run on warm days, and one's blood quickens.

Writer describes the sights and sounds of the birds in early spring.

Spring is just around the corner, and the birds act as if they know. The hairy and downy woodpeckers drum on dry branches and on the loose flakes of maple bark, and purple finches sing merrily from the spruces. This year the reedy voices of the pine siskins can be heard everywhere on the ridge where the hemlocks grow, as can the chickadees' two-note, plaintive song. Down in the bog, the first red-winged blackbirds have just returned, and they can be heard yodeling from the tops of dry cattails. Flocks of rusty blackbirds fly over in long skeins, heading north.

Writer reveals his position and relies on auditory details as night approaches.

From where I stand at the edge of the woods overlooking Shelburne Bog, I feel a slight breeze and hear a moaning gust sweeping through the forest behind me. It is getting dark. There are eery creaking and scraping noises. Inside the pine forest it is becoming black, pitch black. The songbirds are silent. Only the sound of the wind can be heard above the distant honks of Canada geese flying below the now starry skies. Suddenly I hear a booming hollow "hoo-hoo-*hoo*-hoo-." The deep resonating hoot can send a chill down any spine, as indeed it has done to peoples of many cultures. But I know what the sound is, and it gives me great pleasure.

Heinrich could have described the scene with far fewer words, but that description would likely not have conveyed his dominant impression — one of comfort with the natural surroundings. Heinrich reads the landscape with subtle insight; he knows all the different birds and understands their springtime habits. The reader can imagine the smile (Heinrich's face when he hears the call of the owl.

WHY DO WRITERS USE DESCRIPTION?

Writers often use description to inform — to provide readers with specific data. You may need to describe the results of a chemical reaction for a lab report; the style of a Renaissance painting for an art history term paper; the physical capabilities and limitations of a stroke patient for a case study; or the acting of John Cusack in a movie you want your friends to see. Such descriptions will sometimes be scientifically objective, sometimes intensely impressionistic. The approach you use will depend on the subject itself, the information you want to communicate about it, and the format in which the description appears.

Another important use of description is to create a mood or atmosphere or even to convey your own views — to develop a *dominant impression*. In "The Barrio," Robert Ramírez reveals the contradictions within a neighborhood by juxtaposing positive and negative sensory details. For example, the barrio can be a vibrant place where "the denseness of multicolored plants and trees gives the house the appearance of an oasis or a tropical island hideaway," but it is also stricken by poverty, with "backyards [that] have well-worn paths to the outhouses." Each of the descriptions in this chapter, whether entertaining, informative, or both, is distinguished by the strong dominant impression the writer wishes to create.

There are essentially two types of description: objective and subjective. *Objective description* is as factual as possible, emphasizing the actual qualities of the subject being described while subordinating the writer's personal responses. For example, a holdup witness would try to give authorities a precise, objective description of the assailant, unaffected by emotional responses, so that positive identification could be made and an innocent person would not be arrested by mistake. In his essay "On the Ball," Roger Angell begins objectively and tells us not only about a baseball's obvious features — its weight, diameter, covering, stitching, and endorsements — but also about its innards. *Subjective* or *impressionistic description*, on the other hand, conveys the writer's personal opinion or impression of the object, often in language rich in modifiers and figures of speech. A food critic describing a memorable meal would inevitably write about it impressionistically, using colorful or highly subjective language; in fact, relatively few words in English can describe the subtleties of smell and taste in neutral terms. In "Aravaipa Canyon," Edward Abbey uses subjective description to capture the subtle beauty that he witnesses when walking through a desert canyon in America's Southwest. Notice that with objective description, it is usually the person, place, or thing being described that stands out, whereas with subjective description, the response of the person doing the describing is the most prominent feature. Most subjects, however, lend themselves to both objective and subjective description, depending on the writer's purpose. You could write, for example, that you had "exactly four weeks" to finish a history term paper (objective) or that you had "all the time in the world" or "an outrageously short amount of time" (subjective). Each type of description can be accurate and useful in its own way.

Although descriptive writing can stand alone, and often does, it is also used with other types of writing. In a narrative, for example, descriptions provide the context for the story — and make the characters, settings, and events come alive for us. Description may also help to define an unusual object or thing, such as a giraffe, or to clarify the steps of a process, such as diagnosing an illness or making butter. Wherever it is used, good description creates vivid and specific pictures that clarify, create a mood, build a dominant impression, and inform and entertain.

AN ANNOTATED STUDENT ESSAY USING DESCRIPTION

James Blake Wilson wrote the following essay while he was a student at the University of California–Riverside. Drawing details from his teenage memories of Crenshaw Boulevard in South Central Los Angeles, where he grew up, Wilson gives an insightful view of an infamous place — a place that has gotten much media attention, mostly negative and sensational. His observations offer readers a picture of the region that they won't see on the 11 o'clock news or on the front page of the *Los Angeles Times*.

The "Shaw"

James Blake Wilson

Writer sets context — Sunday afternoon walk down Crenshaw Boulevard in South Central Los Angeles.

Ah yes, my home. It feels good to be 1
back. It's just another Sunday afternoon in
the beautiful city of Los Angeles. As I walk
down the street I see all the little things
that make me remember all of the good times
I have had out here on this street, and all
the bad things that I wish I could put in
the back of my memory. I'm standing on the
corner of Slauson Avenue and Crenshaw Boulevard, the center of liveliness here on the

Writer focuses on details of sound.

"Shaw." As I stand here and close my eyes,
can hear many different noises and sounds

that would convince anyone that they were in
the big city. I hear the diesel exhaust of
the "108" metro bus line throttle up to take
its passengers up and down Crenshaw every
twenty minutes. I hear the mingling of car
horns honking from impatient drivers trying
to get from point A to point B in a matter
of minutes, squeaking wheels of a homeless
man's shopping cart that he uses to collect
cans. These cans, which to me conveniently
hold soda, are a source of income for him.
It's amazing to see that what one man takes
for granted, another man may cherish.

I open my eyes and see street vendors   2
of all shapes and sizes. I see little children trying to sell ten dollar cutlery sets
to every motorist that stops at a street
light, and grown adults selling the latest
in scandal fashion. With clothes bearing
slogans such as "Let the Juice Loose" or
"Free O.J.," you can't help but think that
people will try to make money off of anything these days. Alongside the street vendors, you can see members of The Nation of
Islam, dressed in their single breasted
suits with afrocentric bowties, selling bean
pies for five dollars and copies of the
Final Call for fifty cents. I walk up the
street and see Willie on the corner of Crenshaw and 54th Street. It is here that Willie
waits for his bus with a Walkman and his hy-
peractive body which dances, slides, and gy-
rates to the music that he hears in his own
world. People watch and laugh at the zany
actions of a man we call crazy. But who are
we to call someone crazy?

I look up the block and see the paint   3
on the Crenshaw "Wall of Fame" fading from
the sun. This wall symbolizes those in the
Black community who have struggled, fought
and sometimes died for the Black race in
America. With portraits of Martin Luther

*Writer selects
details to highlight
both sights and
sounds.*

*Writer's
description
portrays a sense
of movement.*

Well-selected details of the "Wall of Fame"

King Jr., Malcolm X, Louis Farrakhan, Frederick Douglass, and many others, this wall is highly respected and remains untouched by graffiti and vandalism all year round. Of course with every pro, there's a con. It only takes a glimpse down the street to see gang colors on the white walls of a neighborhood liquor store. It's heartbreaking to know that hundreds of kids, male and female,

Writer uses description to depict emotion.

mark up, fight and die over territory that isn't even theirs. I wonder what these kids could accomplish if their efforts were taken away from gang violence and put into something more productive. Maybe their efforts could go towards cleaning up the infamous Leimert Park, a home to many homeless people. The park is a truly diverse landmark, where one day you might see an organized marketplace of vendors selling clothing and food, and the next day the sirens and lights of police cars at the scene of a drug deal gone bad.

As the sun goes down, and the moon illuminates the dark gray, almost black, asphalt of the street, Crenshaw Boulevard turns into the "Shaw." It all starts with the first sonic thumps of bass extending from the oversized speakers of a car stereo. 4

"The name of the game is...Boom-Boom." 5

I hear the two thundering thumps muffle out the lyrics and hit me in my chest. Ten, twelve, or fifteen inches diameter speakers can be commonly found in the trunks of these attention hungry motorists. Out here there's no telling what kind of car you'll see: anything from a new 1995 Lexus to a fully restored 1964 Chevrolet Impala with hydraulic lifts on every wheel and axle. I've seen a lot of things on this street, some good, some bad. But no matter how hard I try, I can never repress my inner feeling that this is my home. 6

Analyzing James Blake Wilson's Essay of Description:
Questions for Discussion

1. What senses does Wilson call on to describe the "Shaw"?
2. Why is it significant that no graffiti mar the "Wall of Fame"? What does much of the graffiti elsewhere symbolize to Wilson?
3. Why is the "Shaw" a paradoxical place for Wilson? How does his description serve to strengthen his conflicted emotions about the place?

SUGGESTIONS FOR WRITING A DESCRIPTIVE ESSAY

Begin by fixing the subject of your description firmly in your mind. If it's an inanimate object, get it and keep it handy as you work on your essay; if it's a place, go there and spend some time taking in the sights, sounds, and smells; if it's a person, dig out old photographs and letters, or go visit. Observe, observe, observe, and make notes of your sensory impressions: not just what you can see, but also what you hear, smell, taste, touch, and feel. If you must work from memory — if, for example, you are describing your great-grandmother — try to "observe" with your mind's eye, to conjure up the half-forgotten face, the quirky way of talking, the special walk. If you must rely on others' writing (to describe Pompeii before the eruption of Mount Vesuvius, for example), try to imagine a picture of your own from the pieces you find in your sources. Without vivid perceptions of your own to work from, you can hardly create a detailed, accurate description. The way you develop your perceptions will depend, first, on your purpose for writing the description and on your audience.

Collect Sensory Details about Your Subject

Writing a description requires that you gather a great many details about your subject — more, in fact, than you are likely to use. Like a reporter at the scene of an accident, you will take notes about what you see and hear directly, but you may also need to list details that you remember or that you have learned from other sources.

When collecting descriptive details, it's easy to forget to use *all* your senses. Sight is so important that we tend to pay attention only to what we can see, and inexperienced writers often rely almost completely on visual detail. While observing an emergency room, for example, you would by all means take notes about the medical equipment, the blank white walls, the unnaturally brilliant lighting, and the efficient movements of the medical staff. But don't stop there. Keep your ears open for the hiss of trolley tires on linoleum and the odd, mechanical noises that interrupt the emergency room hush; sniff the hospital smells; touch the starched sheets on the stretchers and the cold stainless steel that seems to be everywhere. Your observations, and the notes you make about them, will give you the details you need when you write your description.

Select Descriptive Details with Your Purpose in Mind

Why you are writing will influence the kinds of descriptive details you use and the way you use them. In describing the emergency room, if your purpose is mainly to entertain, then you might want to create an atmosphere of intricate technology, as in a mad scientist's laboratory, or of controlled chaos, as in the operating room on *ER*. If your chief aim is to inform your readers, however, you will use a more objective approach, relying on factual descriptions of individual staff members and pieces of emergency equipment, as well as explaining the functions of each.

Identify Your Audience

Whom do you expect to read your essay? What do they know already, and what do they want to learn from you? If you are describing the hospital emergency room for an audience of medical professionals, you will only need to mention a nuclear magnetic resonance scanner for them to know what it looks like and what it does. A less specialized audience, however, will appreciate a more detailed description. In addition, the general audience will be more receptive to impressionistic description and to details like the color of the staff's uniforms and the strong antiseptic smell; professional readers will consider such things obvious or irrelevant.

Create a Dominant Impression

From the catalog of details that you have collected, select those that will be most helpful in developing a dominant impression. Suppose that you wish to depict the hospital emergency room as a place of great tension. You will then naturally choose details to reinforce that sense of tension: the worried looks on the faces of a couple sitting in the corner, the quick movements of the medical staff as they tend a patient on a wheeled stretcher, the urgent whisperings of two interns out in the hallway, the incessant paging of Doctor Thomas. If the dominant impression you want to create is of the emergency room's sterility, however, you will choose different details: the smell of disinfectant, the spotless white uniforms of the staff members, the stainless steel tables and chairs, the gleaming instruments the nurse hands to the physician. Building a convincing dominant impression depends on the selection of such details.

Of course, it is equally important to omit any details that conflict with the dominant impression. Perhaps there was an orderly lounging in a corner, chewing gum and reading a magazine, who did not feel the tension of the emergency room; perhaps the room's sterility was marred by several used Styrofoam coffee cups left on a corner table. Deciding which details to include and which to exclude is up to you.

Organize Your Details to Create a Vivid Picture

A photographer can capture a large, complicated scene with the press of a button. The writer has to put descriptive details down on paper one at a time. It's not enough to decide which details to include and which to leave out; you also need to arrange your chosen details in a particular order, one that serves your purpose and is easy for the reader to follow.

Imagine what the reader would experience first. A description of an emergency room could begin at the entrance, move through the waiting area, pass the registration desk, and proceed into the treatment cubicles. A description of a restaurant kitchen might conjure up the smells and sounds that escape through the swinging doors even before moving on to the first glimpse inside the kitchen.

Other patterns of organization include moving from general to specific, from smallest to largest, from least important to most important, or from the usual to the unusual. Roger Angell's description of a baseball moves from the objective to the impressionistic and subjective. Keep in mind that the very last details you present will probably stay in the reader's mind the longest and that the very first details will also have special force. Those in the middle of your description, though they will have their effect, may not have the same impact as those before and after them.

Before you begin your first draft, you may find it useful to sketch out an outline of your description. Here's a sample of such an outline for Bernd Heinrich's description earlier in this introduction:

Description of Shelburne Bog

Dominant impression: Comfort with the natural surroundings

Paragraph 1: Snow-crusted landscape in mid-March

Paragraph 2: Activity and sounds of the birds (e.g., woodpeckers, finches, chickadees, and red-winged blackbirds) described from the edge of the woods

Paragraph 3: Activity and sounds inside the pine forest behind the speaker, culminating with the call of the familiar owl

Such an outline can remind you of the dominant impression you want to create and can suggest which specific details may be most useful to you.

Use Specific Strong Nouns and Verbs

Inexperienced writers often believe that adjectives and adverbs are the basis for effective descriptions. They're right in one sense, but not wholly so. Although strong adjectives and adverbs are crucial, description also depends on well-chosen nouns and verbs. *Vehicle* is not nearly as descriptive as something more specific — *jeep, snowmobile,* or *Honda Civic.* Why write *see* when what you mean is *glance, stare, spy, gaze, peek, examine,* or *witness*? The more specific and strong you make your nouns and verbs, the more lively and interesting your descriptions will be.

When you have difficulty thinking of strong, specific nouns and verbs to use in your description, reach for a thesaurus. Inexpensive paperback editions are available at any bookstore, and most word-processing programs have a thesaurus utility built right in. A thesaurus will help you keep your descriptions from getting repetitive and will be invaluable when you need to find a specific word with just the right meaning.

Use Figurative Language to Add Freshness and Clarity

Although it is most often associated with poetry, figurative language is used widely in daily speech and in much contemporary nonfiction. Two of the most commonly used figures of speech are the simile and the metaphor. A *simile* is an explicit comparison between two essentially different ideas or things that uses the words *like* or *as* to link them.

The children flocked onto the bus like a gaggle of geese.

A *metaphor,* on the other hand, makes an implicit comparison between dissimilar ideas or things without using *like* or *as.*

Love is a red, red rose.

When used sparingly, similes and metaphors add a richness to the texture of your descriptions.

▶ *Questions for Revision: Description*

1. Is the subject of my description interesting and relevant to my audience?
2. What senses have I chosen to use to describe it? For example, what does it look like, sound like, or smell like? Does it have a texture or taste that is important to mention?
3. Which details must I include in my essay? Which are irrelevant or distracting to my purpose and should be discarded?
4. Have I achieved the dominant impression I wish to leave with my audience?
5. Does the organization I have chosen for my essay make it easy for the reader to follow my description?
6. How carefully have I chosen my descriptive words? Are my nouns and verbs strong and specific? Have I used figurative language, if appropriate, to further strengthen my description?

On the Ball

Roger Angell

Roger Angell, born in New York City in 1920, is a unique figure in the world of American letters, having made a career by writing about base-ball, the game called America's national pastime. Angell's earliest pub-lished works were pieces of short fiction and personal narratives. He first wrote professionally about baseball in 1962, when the New Yorker *mag-azine invited him to travel to Florida to write a few pieces about spring training. Since then, Angell has translated a lifetime passion for the sport into a steady stream of elegantly written essays, most of which were origi-nally published in the* New Yorker, *where he has worked as an editor since 1956. Many of these essays have been collected in a series of criti-cally acclaimed, best-selling books:* The Summer Game *(1972),* Five Seasons *(1977),* Late Innings *(1982),* Season Ticket *(1988), and* Once More around the Park *(1991). The stepson of renowned essayist E. B. White, who exerted a lasting influence on his writing, Angell has been called "the best baseball writer ever" for his stylish, intelligent prose.*

"On the Ball," the opening paragraph of Five Seasons, *begins a book about the game of baseball with a careful study of its most impor-tant component, the ball itself.*

BEFORE YOU READ

Most of us take for granted the ordinary things of everyday life — the tools, utensils, and equipment that we use over and over again as part of our regular activities. But most of us also have developed a fondness for some common object that seems especially well suited for its task, one that is a pleasure to handle and employ. Think of an object that you really enjoy using, and describe in full, careful detail the object itself, how you relate to it, and how it ful-fills its function.

It weighs just over five ounces and measures between 2.86 and 2.94 inches in diameter. It is made of a composition-cork nucleus encased in two thin layers of rubber, one black and one red, surrounded by 121 yards of tightly wrapped blue-gray wool yarn, 45 yards of white wool yarn, 54 more yards of blue-gray wool yarn, 150 yards of fine cotton yarn, a coat of rubber cement, and a cowhide (formerly horse-hide) exterior, which is held together with 216 slightly raised red cotton stitches. Printed certifications, endorsements, and outdoor adver-tising spherically attest to its authenticity. Like most institutions, it is considered inferior in its present form to its ancient archetypes, and in this case the complaint is probably justified; on occasion in recent years it has actually been known to come apart under the demands of its brief but rigorous active career. Baseballs are assembled and hand-stitched in Taiwan (before this year the work was done in Haiti, and before 1973 in Chicopee, Massachusetts), and contemporary pitchers claim that there is a tangible variation in the size and feel of the balls that now come into play in a single game; a true peewee is treasured by hurlers, and its departure from the premises, by fair means or foul, is secretly mourned. But never mind: any baseball is beautiful. No other small package comes as close to the ideal in design and utility. It is a perfect object for a man's hand. Pick it up and it instantly suggests its purpose; it is meant to be thrown a considerable distance — thrown hard and with precision. Its feel and heft are the beginning of the sport's critical dimensions; if it were a fraction of an inch larger or smaller, a few centigrams heavier or lighter, the game of baseball would be utterly different. Hold a baseball in your hand. As it happens, this one is not brand-new. Here, just to one side of the curved surgical welt of stitches, there is a pale-green grass smudge, darkening on one edge almost to black — the mark of an old infield play, a tough grounder now lost in memory. Feel the ball, turn it over in your hand; hold it across the seam or the other way, with the seam just to the side of your middle finger. Speculation stirs. You want to get outdoors and throw this spare and sensual object to somebody or, at the very least, watch somebody else throw it. The game has begun.

RESPONDING TO READING

Angell's essay shows a passion not just for the baseball itself, but for the game of which it is a crucial part. In this tiny selection filled with objective facts, how does he convey passion?

QUESTIONING THE TEXT

1. Why is the modern baseball considered inferior to earlier baseballs?

2. In what ways has the physical structure of the baseball changed over the years? How is it made differently?

3. What does Angell mean when he writes the single sentence, "Speculation stirs" toward the end of the selection?

UNDERSTANDING THE WRITER'S CRAFT

1. Why does Angell refer to the baseball as "it" for the first four sentences?

2. What is the purpose of enumerating the exact dimensions and components of the ball? Why do these objective figures precede Angell's subjective judgments that a baseball is "beautiful" and "close to the ideal,"

and how do they lend weight to these judgments? (Glossary: *Objective/Subjective*)

3. Why does Angell choose to include his information as a single paragraph?

4. Angell begins the selection by presenting the standard dimensions of a generic baseball and then moves on to write about a specific ball: "As it happens, this one is not brand-new." What effect does this have on the reader?

EXPLORING LANGUAGE

1. What humorous double meaning does Angell achieve when he refers to the ball's "departure from the premises, by fair means or foul"?

2. Angell refers to the baseball itself as an "institution." What insight does he provide with this surprising metaphor? (Glossary: *Figures of Speech*)

3. Angell's precise description of the ball and its uses depends on some extremely specific terms. Define the following words as he uses them: *spherically, authenticity, archetypes, rigorous, tangible, peewee, heft.*

COMBINING RHETORICAL STRATEGIES

In describing a baseball, Angell also defines it in terms of its history and function. (Glossary: *Definition*) Show where and how description and definition overlap in this essay.

WRITING SUGGESTIONS

1. **(Description)** Refer to your Before You Read response. Now, using "On the Ball" as a model, flesh out your description. Look at the inside of your chosen object as well as its outer appearance; capture it in all its detail of structure and purpose; tell how your object has changed and developed over time. You may need to do some research to give your object full justice. Like Angell, finish your description by moving from specifics to speculation.

2. **(Other Strategies)** What is it about baseball (or any other popular sport) that puts stars in children's eyes and captures the imagination of adults? Choose a sport you particularly like, and list the qualities that appeal to you; then interview a number of other fans to find out what they love about the game. In "Getting Caught" (Chapter 7), Annie Dillard tells us that she liked football because it is "all or nothing"; this is exactly the sort of comment you are looking for. Write an essay describing your sport in terms of its appeal to player, spectator, or both.

3. **(Research)** Team up with two or three classmates who enjoy either playing or watching the same sport you enjoy. Brainstorm a list of all the equipment the sport requires, including, if appropriate, the uniforms and playing field (basketball shoes, for instance, would make an

interesting study, as would the development of a golf course). Each person in the group may choose one or more items from the list as a subject for research; do your research in the library and possibly on the Internet. Describe in detail the history, composition, and purpose of the equipment. Compile your group's efforts, and create an impressive documentation of one sport's paraphernalia.

- **Wilson Sporting Goods Homepage**
  <http://www.wilsonsports.com>

  This international commercial site for Wilson Sporting Goods offers an inventory of the equipment and paraphernalia associated with professional and recreational sports.

PROFESSIONAL SPORTS LEAGUES

- **The Women's National Basketball Association**
  <http://www.wnba.com>

  The WNBA's official site features news, articles, schedules, and team and player profiles.

- **The National Basketball Association**
  <http://www.nba.com>

  The NBA's official site features chats, message boards, news, schedules, and team and player profiles.

- **The National Hockey League**
  <http://www.nhl.com>

  The NHL's official site features trivia games, news, and photo galleries.

- **Major League Baseball**
  <http://www.mlb.com>

  The MLB's official site features surveys, news, schedules, and team and player profiles.

- **The National Football League**
  <http://nfl.com>

  The NFL's official site features news, statistics, team rosters, scores, and standings.

SPORTS NEWS AND HISTORY

- **EXPN**
  <http://expn.com>

  ESPN's "Xtreme" sports page has information, interviews, and news on professional skateboarding, snowboarding, motocross, and freestyle BMX.

- **The Yahoo! Sports Index**
  <http://sports.yahoo.com>

  This site is a good starting point for finding sports news, scores, and sports-related chats and message boards.

- **Online Sports Home Page**
  <http://www.onlinesports.com>

  This site claims to be "the Internet's oldest and largest catalog of sports memorabilia, products and services." Browse for items from your favorite teams or players.

- **The *Sporting News* Online**
  <http://tsn.sportingnews.com>

  The *Sporting News* provides historical background and information for professional baseball, basketball, hockey, and football.

Aravaipa Canyon

Edward Abbey

Edward Abbey (1927–1989) wrote numerous novels, including two that were adapted for film: The Brave Cowboy *(1958), which was released as a film in 1962 under the title* Lonely Are the Brave, *and* Fire on the Mountain *(1962). He is best known, however, for his many volumes of nature writings. Variously called an ecologist, a naturalist, and an environmental activist, Abbey described himself simply as "one who loves the unfenced country." He had a particular love for the American Southwest, where he worked for many years as a ranger in the National Park Service. In his collections of nonfiction essays, including* Desert Solitaire *(1968),* The Journey Home *(1977), and* Abbey's Road *(1979), Abbey celebrated the Southwest and made a passionate case for the preservation of its natural wonders.*

"Aravaipa Canyon" is a strong example of the rich descriptive prose in which he expressed his belief in the sacred power of the landscape.

BEFORE YOU READ

Recall a natural setting that you found particularly beautiful, impressive, or awe-inspiring. Describe this setting using rich and evocative details.

Southeast of Phoenix and northeast of Tucson, in the Pinal Mountains, is a short deep gorge called Aravaipa Canyon. It is among the few places in Arizona with a permanent stream of water and in popular estimation one of the most beautiful. I am giving away no secrets here: Aravaipa Canyon has long been well known to hikers, campers, horsemen, and hunters from the nearby cities. The federal Bureau of Land Management (BLM), charged with administration of the canyon, recently decreed it an official Primitive Area, thus guaranteeing its fame. Demand for enjoyment of the canyon is so great that the BLM has been obliged to institute a rationing program: no one camps here without a permit and only a limited number of such permits are issued.

Two friends and I took a walk into Aravaipa Canyon a few days ago. We walked because there is no road. There is hardly even a foot trail. Twelve miles long from end to end, the canyon is mostly occupied by the little river which gives it its name, and by stream banks piled with slabs of fallen rock from the cliffs above, the whole overgrown with cactus, trees, and riparian desert shrubbery.

Aravaipa is an Apache name (some say Pima, some say Papago) and the commonly accepted meaning is "laughing waters." The name fits. The stream is brisk, clear, about a foot deep at normal flow levels, churning its way around boulders, rippling over gravelbars, plunging into pools with bright and noisy vivacity. Schools of loach minnow, roundtail chub, spike dace, and Gila mudsuckers — rare and endemic species — slip and slither past your ankles as you wade into the current. The water is too warm to support trout or other varieties of what are called game fish; the fish here live out their lives undisturbed by anything more than horses' hooves and the sneaker-shod feet of hikers. (PLEASE DO NOT MOLEST THE FISH.)

The Apaches who gave the name to this water and this canyon are 4 not around anymore. Most of that particular band — unarmed old men, women, children — huddled in a cave near the mouth of Aravaipa Canyon, were exterminated in the 1880s by a death squad of American pioneers, aided by Mexican and Papagos, from the nearby city of Tucson. The reason for this vigilante action is obscure (suspicion of murder and cattle stealing) but the results were clear. No more Apaches in Aravaipa Canyon. During pauses in the gunfire, as the pioneers reloaded their rifles, the surviving Indians could have heard the sound of laughing waters. One hundred and twenty-five were killed, the remainder relocated in the White Mountain Reservation to the northeast. Since then those people have given us no back talk at all.

Trudging upstream and over rocky little beaches, we are no more 5 troubled by ancient history than are the mudsuckers in the pools. We prefer to enjoy the scenery. The stone walls stand up on both sides, twelve hundred feet high in the heart of the canyon. The rock is of volcanic origin, rosy-colored andesites and buff, golden, consolidated tuff. Cleavages and fractures across the face of the walls form perfect stairways and sometimes sloping ramps, slick as sidewalks. On the beaches lie obsidian boulders streaked with veins of quartzite and pegmatite.

The walls bristle with spiky rock gardens of formidable desert veg- 6 etation. Most prominent is the giant saguaro cactus, growing five to fifty feet tall out of crevices in the stone you might think could barely lodge a flower. The barrel cactus, with its pink fishhook thorns, thrives here on the sunny side; and clusters of hedgehog cactus, and prickly pear with names like clockface and cows-tongue, have wedged roots into the rock. Since most of the wall is vertical, parallel to gravity, these plants grow first outward then upward, forming right-angled bends near the base. It looks difficult but they do it. They like it here.

Also present are tangles of buckhorn, staghorn, chainfruit, and 7 teddybear cholla; the teddybear cholla is a cactus so thick with spines it glistens under the sun as if covered with fur. From more comfortable niches in the rock grow plants like the sotol, a thing with sawtooth leaves and a flower stalk ten feet tall. The agave, a type of lily, is even bigger, and its leaves are long, rigid, pointed like bayonets. Near the summit of the cliffs, where the moisture is insufficient to support cactus, we see gray-green streaks of lichen clinging to the stone like a mold.

The prospect at streamside is conventionally sylvan, restful to desert-weary eyes. Great cottonwoods and sycamores shade the creek's stony shores; when we're not wading in water we're wading through a crashing autumn debris of green-gold cottonwood and dusty-red sycamore leaves. Other trees flourish here — willow, salt cedar, alder, desert hackberry, and a kind of wild walnut. Cracked with stones, the nuts yield a sweet but frugal meat. At the water's edge is a nearly continuous growth of peppery-flavored watercress. The stagnant pools are full of algae; and small pale frogs, treefrogs, and leopard frogs leap from the bank at our approach and dive into the water; they swim for the deeps with kicking legs, quick breaststrokes. 8

We pass shadowy, intriguing side canyons with names like Painted Cave (ancient pictographs), Iceberg (where the sun seldom shines), and Virgus (named in honor of himself by an early settler in the area). At midday we enter a further side canyon, one called Horse-camp, and linger here for a lunch of bread, cheese, and water. We contemplate what appears to be a bottomless pool. 9

The water in this pool has a dark clarity, like smoked glass, transparent but obscure. We see a waterlogged branch six feet down resting on a ledge but cannot see to the bottom. The water feels intensely cold to hand and foot; a few tadpoles have attached themselves to the stony rim of the pool just beneath the surface of the water. They are sluggish, barely animate. One waterbug, the kind called boatman, propels itself with limp oars down toward darkness when I extend my hand toward it. 10

Above the pool is a thirty-foot bluff of sheer, vesiculated, fine-grained, monolithic gray rock with a glossy chute carved down its face. Flash floods, pouring down that chute with driving force, must have drilled this basin in the rock below. The process would require a generous allowance of time — ten thousand, twenty thousand years — give or take a few thousand. Only a trickle of water from a ring of seeps enters the pool now, on this hot still blazing day in December. Feels like 80°F; a month from now it may be freezing; in June 110°. In the silence I hear the rasping chant of locusts — that universal lament for mortality and time — here in this canyon where winter seldom comes. 11

The black and bottomless pool gleams in the shining rock — a sinister paradox, to a fanciful mind. To any man of natural piety this pool, this place, this silence, would suggest reverence, even fear. But I'm an apostate Presbyterian from a long-ago Pennsylvania: I shuck my clothes, jump in, and touch bottom only ten feet down. Bedrock 12 bottom, as I'd expected, and if any Grendels dwell in this inky pool they're not inclined to reveal themselves today.

We return to the Aravaipa. Halfway back to camp and the canyon entrance we pause to inspect a sycamore that seems to be embracing a boulder. The trunk of the tree has grown around the rock. Feeling the tree for better understanding, I hear a clatter of loose stones, look up, and see six, seven, eight bighorn sheep perched on the rimrock a hundred feet above us. Three rams, five ewes. They are browsing at the local salad bar — brittlebush, desert holly, bursage, and jojoba — aware of us but not alarmed. We watch them for a long time as they move casually along the rim and up a talus slope beyond, eating as they go, halting now and then to stare back at the humans staring up at them.   13

Once, years before, I had glimpsed a mountain lion in this canyon, following me through the twilight. It was the only mountain lion I had ever seen, so far, in the wild. I stopped, the big cat stopped, we peered at each other through the gloom. Mutual curiosity: I felt more wonder than fear. After a minute, or perhaps it was five minutes, I made a move to turn. The lion leaped up into the rocks and melted away.   14

We see no mountain lions this evening. Nor any of the local deer, either Sonoran whitetail or the desert mule deer, although the little heart-shaped tracks of the former are apparent in the sand. Javelina, or peccary, too, reside in this area; piglike animals with tusks, oversized heads, and tapering bodies, they roam the slopes and gulches in family bands (like the Apaches), living on roots, tubers, and innards of barrel cactus, on grubs, insects, and carrion. Omnivorous, like us, and equally playful, if not so dangerous. Any desert canyon with permanent water, like Aravaipa, will be as full of life as it is beautiful.   15

We stumble homeward over the stones and through the ankle-bone-chilling water. The winter day seems alarmingly short; it is.   16

We reach the mouth of the canyon and the old trail uphill to the roadhead in time to see the first stars come out. Barely in time. Nightfall is quick in this arid climate and the air feels already cold. But we have earned enough memories, stored enough mental-emotional images in our heads, from one brief day in Aravaipa Canyon, to enrich the urban days to come. As Thoreau found a universe in the woods around Concord, any person whose senses are alive can make a world of any natural place, however limited it might seem, on this subtle planet of ours.   17

"The world is big but it is comprehensible," says R. Buckminster Fuller. But it seems to me that the world is not nearly big enough and that any portion of its surface, left unpaved and alive, is infinitely rich in details and relationships, in wonder, beauty, mystery, comprehensible only in part. The very existence of existence is itself suggestive of the unknown — not a problem but a mystery.   18

We will never get to the end of it, never plumb the bottom of it, 19 never know the whole of even so small and trivial and useless and precious a place as Aravaipa. Therein lies our redemption.

RESPONDING TO READING

Aravaipa Canyon is under the protection of the Bureau of Land Management. For what reasons should the government restrict land use in a nation with a relatively unrestricted economy? Given Abbey's commentary in this essay, how might he answer that question? What are some aspects of the question that he doesn't address?

QUESTIONING THE TEXT

1. Abbey writes that he and his companions "are no more troubled by ancient history than are the mudsuckers in the pools" (paragraph 5). Why not? What does he mean by this statement? If his assertion is true, why does he include a long paragraph telling the reader about the canyon's ancient history? Why is his tone in paragraph 4 ironic? (Glossary: *Irony*)

2. Why, in your opinion, does Abbey dive into the pool? (Before answering, consider the final sentence of paragraph 18.)

3. What does the last paragraph mean, particularly in regard to the word *redemption?* How does this paragraph contradict the Buckminster Fuller quotation in paragraph 18?

UNDERSTANDING THE WRITER'S CRAFT

1. Abbey gives a chronological account of his explorations of Aravaipa Canyon; that is, he narrates the events of the day in the order in which they happened. (Glossary: *Narration*) How does he organize his descriptions of what he experienced?

2. Abbey pays close attention to the sounds of words, using techniques such as the alliteration found in this sentence in paragraph 5: "Cleavages and fractures across the face of the walls form perfect stairways and sometimes sloping ramps, slick as sidewalks." How does the repeated sound of *s* add to the effectiveness of his description? Find other instances where the author uses repetition of sound to good effect.

3. Much of this essay is composed of objective, factual description, but Abbey also shares with the reader some subjective thoughts inspired by his exploration of Aravaipa Canyon. (Glossary: *Objective/Subjective*) Note the places where he expresses his own opinions. As a writer, what effect does he achieve through the contrast between objective and subjective detail?

EXPLORING LANGUAGE

1. Paragraph 3 ends with an unexpected warning: "(PLEASE DO NOT MOLEST THE FISH)." Why is it written in capitals and parenthesized? What is the effect on the reader?

2. The words *obscure* (paragraph 10) and *comprehensible* (18) bring strong connotations to the passages in which they are used. What multiple meanings are implied?

3. What similarities does Abbey perceive between the peccary and the human? Why does he choose to highlight these similarities? (Glossary: *Comparison and Contrast*)

4. Abbey uses a great deal of precise terminology in naming what he sees. The following descriptive words, all equally important to the essay, are not restricted to the land and wildlife of Aravaipa Canyon. Be sure you know their meanings to appreciate the description fully: *riparian* (paragraph 2), *vivacity* (3), *endemic* (3), *vigilante* (4), *formidable* (6), *sylvan* (8), *vesiculated* (11), *apostate* (12), *Grendel* (12).

COMBINING RHETORICAL STRATEGIES

This primarily descriptive essay makes clear the author's opinion about the relationship of humans to nature. What is his argument? Does it take the form of a thesis statement? Explain. Why does Abbey place the direct argument at the end of the piece rather than at the beginning, where arguments are usually stated?

WRITING SUGGESTIONS

1. **(Description)** Write about a trip you have taken into a natural setting. Using "Aravaipa Canyon" as a model, tell about the trip in chronological order, describing in detail what you saw and experienced. In your writing, make sure you convey the impact the natural setting had on you.

2. **(Other Strategies)** Refer to your Responding to Reading answer. Land-use restrictions are a matter of considerable controversy in America today. Which is more important, the development of natural resources or the preservation of wilderness? To reach a decision about any particular piece of land, what issues should be taken into consideration? Who should have the right to decide? Write an essay in support of your own stance toward land use.

3. **(Research)** We learn in this essay that the federal Bureau of Land Management decreed Aravaipa Canyon an official Primitive Area. What are the criteria by which a piece of land is named a Primitive Area? How does this designation differ from Wilderness Area or from National Park? Which human activities are permitted in a Primitive Area, and which are not? What are some other Primitive Areas in the United States? Use government publications and other relevant sources to

answer these questions and others that may occur to you on the subject; write a report to present your findings. You might also consider writing a research essay that explores the various designations that government agencies assign to protect natural resources in the United States.

- **The U.S. Department of the Interior Bureau of Land Management National Homepage**
  <http://www.blm.gov>

  This searchable Web site has links to government agencies, news, press releases, and more.

- **ParkNet — The National Park Service Homepage**
  <http://www.nps.gov>

  This Web site offers information about national parks across the United States, including information on various area designations.

Lincoln Up Close

Gore Vidal

Gore Vidal was born at West Point in 1925, where his father was an instructor at the U.S. Military Academy. Following his graduation from Phillips Exeter Academy in 1945, Vidal followed in his father's footsteps by enlisting in the Army. The next year, he published his first novel, Williwaw, *while serving as a warrant officer aboard an army supply ship. Vidal never did make it to college, but he went on to write dozens of novels, mysteries, and plays, as well as gaining recognition as perhaps America's finest contemporary essayist. He is a frequent contributor to* The *New York Review of Books,* from which the following selection is taken, and other magazines. His latest book is The Golden Age (2000), described as the latest in his seven-volume "artful, acidic history of the United States." Another volume,* Lincoln, *first published in 1984, recently became available in paperback.*

In "Lincoln Up Close," published in 1991, Vidal probes the nature of the man behind the "national deity" that Abraham Lincoln has become. Not surprisingly, he finds a man who is far more complex than most of us realize.

BEFORE YOU READ

It is difficult to grow up in our culture without acquiring a somewhat unrealistic, romanticized image of Abraham Lincoln. From his profile on pennies to his famous speeches, he has become more of a two-dimensional symbol than a three-dimensional historical figure. What is your image of Lincoln? What kind of statesman do you think he was? From where do you get your most powerful impressions of him?

Once, at the Library of Congress in Washington, I was shown the contents of Lincoln's pockets on the night that he was shot at Ford's Theater. There was a Confederate bank note, perhaps acquired during the president's recent excursion to the fallen capital, Richmond; a pocket knife; a couple of newspaper cuttings (good notices for his administration); and two pairs of spectacles. It was eerie to hold in one's hand what looked to be the same spectacles that he wore as he was photographed reading the Second Inaugural Address, the month before his murder. One of the wire "legs" of the spectacles had broken off and someone, presumably Lincoln himself, had clumsily repaired it with a piece of darning wool. I tried on the glasses: he was indeed farsighted, and what must have been to him the clearly printed lines "let us strive on to finish the work we are in; to bind up the nation's wounds" was to my myopic eyes a gray quartzlike blur.

Next I was shown the Bible which the president had kissed as he swore his second oath to preserve, protect, and defend the Constitution of the United States; the oath that he often used, in lieu of less spiritual argument, to justify the war that he had fought to preserve the Union. The Bible is small and beautifully bound. To the consternation of the custodian, I opened the book. The pages were as bright and clear as the day they were printed; in fact, they stuck together in such a way as to suggest that no one had ever even riffled them. Obviously the book had been sent for at the last moment; then given away, to become a treasured relic.

Although Lincoln belonged to no Christian church, he did speak of the "Almighty" more and more often as the war progressed. During the congressional election of 1846, Lincoln had been charged with "infidelity" to Christianity. At this time, he made a rather lawyerly response. To placate those who insist that presidents must be devout monotheists (preferably Christian and Protestant), Lincoln allowed that he himself could never support "a man for office, whom I knew to be an open enemy of, and scoffer at, religion." The key word, of course, is "open." As usual, Lincoln does not lie — something that the Jesuits maintain no wise man does — but he shifts the argument to his own advantage and gets himself off the atheistical hook much as Thomas Jefferson had done almost a century earlier.

Last, I was shown a life mask, made shortly before the murder. The hair on the head has been tightly covered over, the whiskers greased. When the sculptor Saint-Gaudens first saw it, he thought it was a *death* mask, so worn and remote is the face. I was most startled by the smallness of the head. In photographs, with hair and beard, the head had seemed in correct proportion to Lincoln's great height. But this vulpine little face seems strangely vulnerable. The cheeks are sunken in. The nose is sharper than in the photographs, and the lines about the wide thin mouth are deep. With eyes shut, he looks to be a small man, in rehearsal for his death.

Those who knew Lincoln always thought it a pity that there was never a photograph of him truly smiling. A non-user of tobacco, he had splendid teeth for that era, and he liked to laugh, and when he did, Philip Hone noted, the tip of his nose moved like a tapir's.

Gertrude Stein used to say that U. S. Grant had the finest American prose style. The general was certainly among our best writers, but he lacked music (Gertrude lacked it too, but she did have rhythm). Lincoln deployed the plain style as masterfully as Grant; and he does have music. In fact, there is now little argument that Lincoln is one of the great masters of prose in our language, and the only surprising aspect of so demonstrable a fact is that there are those who still affect surprise. Partly this is due to the Education Mafia that has taken over what little culture the United States has, and partly to the sort of cranks who maintain that since Shakespeare had little Latin and less Greek and did not keep company with kings, he could never have written so brilliantly of kings and courts, and so not he but some great lord wrote the plays in his name.

For all practical purposes, Lincoln had no formal education. But he studied law, which meant not only reading Blackstone (according to Jeremy Bentham, a writer "cold, reserved and wary, exhibiting a frigid pride") but brooding over words in themselves and in combination. In those days, most good lawyers, like good generals, wrote good prose; if they were not precisely understood, a case or a battle might be lost. 7

William Herndon was Lincoln's law partner in Springfield, Illinois, from 1844 to February 18, 1861, when Lincoln went to Washington to be inaugurated president. Herndon is the principal source for Lincoln's pre-presidential life. He is a constant embarrassment to Lincoln scholars because they must rely on him, yet since Lincoln is the national deity, they omit a great deal of Herndon's testimony about Lincoln. For one thing, Lincoln was something of a manic-depressive, to use current jargon. In fact, there was a time when, according to Herndon, Lincoln was *as 'crazy as a loon' in this city in 1841."* Since this sort of detail does not suit the history departments, it is usually omitted or glossed over, or poor Herndon is accused of telling lies. 8

The Lincoln of the hagiographers is forever serene and noble, in defeat as well as in victory. With perfect hindsight, they maintain that it was immediately apparent that the Lincoln-Douglas contest had opened wide the gates of political opportunity for Lincoln. Actually, after Lincoln's defeat by Douglas for the U.S. Senate, he was pretty loonlike for a time; and he thought that the gates of political opportunity had slammed shut for him. Lincoln's friend Henry C. Whitney, in a letter to Herndon, wrote: 9

> I shall never forget the day — January 6, 1859 — I went to your office and found Lincoln there alone. He appeared to be somewhat dejected — in fact I never saw a man so depressed. I tried to rally his drooping spirits . . . but with ill success. He was simply steeped in gloom. For a time he was silent . . . blurting out as he sank down: "Well, whatever happens I expect everyone to desert me now, but Billy Herndon."

Despite the busyness of the Lincoln priests, the rest of us can still discern the real Lincoln by entering his mind through what he wrote, a 10 seductive business, by and large, particularly when he shows us unexpected views of the familiar. Incidentally, to read Lincoln's letters in holograph is revelatory; the writing changes dramatically with his mood. In the eloquent, thought-out letters to mourners for the dead, he writes a clear firm hand. When the governor of Massachusetts, John A. Andrew, in the summer of 1862 wrote that he could not send troops because his paymasters were incapable of "quick work," Lincoln replied, "Please say to these gentlemen that if they do not work quickly I will make quick work of them. In the name of all that is reasonable, how long does it take to pay a couple of regiments?" The words tumble from Lincoln's pen in uneven rows upon the page, and one senses not only his fury but his terror that the city of Washington might soon fall to the rebels.

Since 1920 no American president has written his state speeches; 11 lately, many of our presidents seem to experience some difficulty in reading aloud what others have written for them to say. But until Woodrow Wilson suffered a stroke, it was assumed that the chief task of the first magistrate was to report to the American people, in their Congress assembled, upon the state of the union. The president was elected not only to execute the laws but to communicate to the people his vision of the prospect before us. As a reporter to the people, Lincoln surpassed all presidents. Even in his youthful letters and speeches, he is already himself. The prose is austere and sharp; there are few adjectives and adverbs; and then, suddenly, sparks of humor.

> Fellow Citizens — It will be but a very few words that I shall undertake to say. I was born in Kentucky, raised in Indiana and lived in Illinois. And now I am here, where it is my business to care equally for the good people of all the States. . . . There are but few views or aspects of this great war upon which I have not said or written something whereby my own opinions might be known. But there is one — the recent attempts of our erring brethren, as they are sometimes called — to employ the negro to fight for them. I have neither written nor made a speech on that subject, because that was their business, not mine; and if I had a wish upon the subject I had not the power to introduce it, or make it effective. The great question with them was, whether the negro, being put into the army, would fight for them. I do not know, and therefore cannot decide. They ought to know better than we. I have in my lifetime heard many arguments why the negroes ought to be slaves; but if they fight for those who would keep them in slavery it will be a better argument than any I have yet heard. He who will fight for that ought to be a slave. They have concluded at last to take one out of four of the slaves, and put them in the army; and that one out of the four who will fight to keep the others in slavery ought to be a slave himself unless he is killed in a fight. While I have often said

that all men ought to be free, yet I would allow those colored persons to be slaves who want to be; and next to them those white persons who argue in favor of making other people slaves. I am in favor of giving an opportunity to such white men to try it on for themselves.

Also, as a lawyer on circuit, Lincoln was something of a stand-up comedian, able to keep an audience laughing for hours as he appeared to improvise his stories; actually, he claimed no originality as "I am a re-tailer." 12

Lincoln did not depend very much on others for help when it came to the writing of the great papers. Secretary of State William Seward gave him a line or two for the coda of the First Inaugural Address, while the poetry of Shakespeare and the prose of the King James version of the Bible were so much in Lincoln's blood that he occasionally slipped into iambic pentameter. 13

The Annual Message to Congress, December 1, 1862, has echoes of Shakespeare's *Julius Caesar* and *Macbeth* (ominously, Lincoln's favorite play): 14

> We can not escape history. We of this Congress and this administration will be remembered in spite of ourselves. No personal significance, or insignificance, can spare one or another of us. The fiery trial through which we pass will light us down, in honor or dishonor, to the latest generation.

A few years earlier, at Brown University, Lincoln's young secretary, John Hay, wrote a valedictory poem. Of his class's common memories, "Our hearts shall bear them safe through life's commotion / Their fading gleam shall light us to our graves." But of course, Macbeth had said long before Hay, "And all our yesterdays have lighted fools / The way to dusty death."

Of Lincoln's contemporaries, William Herndon has given us the best close-up view of the man that he had shared an office with for seventeen years. "He was the most continuous and severest thinker in America. He read but little and that for an end. Politics were his Heaven, and his Hades metaphysics." As for the notion that Lincoln was a gentle, humble, holy man, even John Hay felt obliged to note that "no great man was ever modest. It was [Lincoln's] intellectual arrogance and unconscious assumption of superiority that men like Chase and Sumner could never forgive." Along with so much ambition and secretiveness of nature, Lincoln also had an impish sense of humor; he liked to read aloud comic writers like Petroleum V. Nasby, and he told comic stories to divert, if not others, himself from the ongoing tragedy at whose center he was. 15

What was it like to be in the audience when Lincoln made a speech? 16
What did he really look like? What did he sound like? To the first question we have the photographs; but they are motionless. He was six feet four, "more or less stoop-shouldered," wrote Herndon. "He was very tall, thin, and gaunt. . . . When he first began speaking, he was shrill, squeaking, piping, unpleasant; his general look, his form, his pose, the color of flesh, wrinkled and dry, his sensitiveness, and his momentary diffidence, everything seemed to be against him." Then, "He gently and gradually warmed up . . . voice became harmonious, melodious, musical, if you please, with face somewhat aglow. . . . Lincoln's gray eyes would flash fire when speaking against slavery or spoke volumes of hope and love when speaking of liberty, justice and the progress of mankind."

Of Lincoln's politics, Herndon wrote, he "was a conscientious 17
conservative; he believed in Law and Order. See his speech before Springfield Lyceum in 1838." This speech is indeed a key to Lincoln's character, for it is here that he speaks of the nature of ambition and how, in a republic that was already founded, a tyrant might be tempted to reorder the state in his own image. At the end Lincoln himself did just that. There is a kind of terrible Miltonian majesty in his address to the doubtless puzzled young men of the Springfield Lyceum. In effect, their twenty-nine-year-old contemporary was saying that for the ambitious man, it is better to reign in hell than serve in heaven.

In the end, whether or not Lincoln's personal ambition undid 18
him and the nation is immaterial. He took a divided house and jammed it back together. He was always a pro-Union man. As for slavery, he was averse, rather than adverse, to the institution but no Abolitionist. Lincoln's eulogy on Henry Clay (July 6, 1852) is to the point. Of Clay, Lincoln wrote,

> As a politician or statesman, no one was so habitually careful to avoid all sectional ground. Whatever he did, he did for the whole country. . . . Feeling as he did, and as the truth surely is, that the world's best hope depended on the continued union of the States, he was ever jealous of, and watchful for, whatever might have the slightest tendency to separate them.

He supports Clay's policy of colonizing the blacks elsewhere; today any mention of Lincoln's partiality for this scheme amuses black historians and makes many of the white ones deal economically with the truth.

Eight years later, the eulogist, now the president, promptly made 19
war on those states that had chosen to depart the Union on the same high moral ground that Lincoln himself had so eloquently stated at the time of the Mexican War in 1848: "Any people anywhere, being inclined and having the power, have the right to rise up, and shake off

the existing government, and form a new one that suits them better." Lawyer Lincoln would probably have said, rather bleakly, that the key phrase here was "and having the power." The Confederacy did not have the power; six hundred thousand men died in the next four years; and the Confederacy was smashed and Lincoln was murdered.

In a sense, we have had three republics. The first, a loose confeder-   20 ation of former British colonies, lasted from 1776 to 1789, when the first Congress under the Constitution met. The second republic ended April 9, 1865, with the South's surrender. In due course Lincoln's third republic was transformed (inevitably?) into the national security state where we have been locked up for forty years. A fourth republic might be nice.

In any event, for better or worse, we still live in the divided house   21 that Lincoln cobbled together for us, and it is always useful to get to know through his writing not the god of the establishment-priests but a literary genius who was called upon to live, rather than merely to write, a high tragedy. I can think of no one in literary or political history quite like this essential American writer.

RESPONDING TO READING

What are the precise definitions of *averse* and *adverse?* Why are they so important to Vidal's impression of Lincoln and the way he viewed slavery? Did this distinction surprise you, based on your previous knowledge of Lincoln? Why do you think most Lincoln scholars overlook or dismiss this distinction?

QUESTIONING THE TEXT

1. Why is Vidal surprised by Lincoln's life mask? What impression of Lincoln does it convey?

2. Why is Lincoln's associate, William Herndon, described as "a constant embarrassment to Lincoln scholars" (paragraph 8)?

3. Vidal points out some of Lincoln's shortcomings that historians prefer to gloss over, but he states that in at least one way, Lincoln "surpassed all presidents" (paragraph 11). What was his special skill? Why was it so important to both him and his situation?

4. What does Vidal mean by his statement, "A fourth republic might be nice" (paragraph 20)? What is he saying about Lincoln's legacy?

UNDERSTANDING THE WRITER'S CRAFT

1. What does Vidal accomplish by beginning his essay about Lincoln by describing the contents of Lincoln's pockets the night he was shot? (Glossary: *Beginnings/Endings*) The objects are rather mundane — what

makes them special? Does their description change the way the reader thinks about Lincoln? If so, how?

2. Vidal quotes Lincoln's writing at some length on three occasions, each to illustrate a different facet of Lincoln's character (paragraphs 11, 14, and 18). (Glossary: *Examples*) Identify what each quote accomplishes, and discuss how it contributes to the reader's understanding of Lincoln. Why do you think Vidal chose quotes that are likely to be unfamiliar to the average reader?

3. Vidal emphasizes Lincoln's lighter side, describing a man who liked to smile and laugh, who appreciated the humor of others, and who was something of a stand-up comedian himself. What is important about Lincoln's lighter side? How does revealing it serve Vidal's purpose? (Glossary: *Purpose*)

4. Vidal makes clear that historians have created an idealized Lincoln — serene, noble, wise beyond measure. Vidal's Lincoln is far more complex, and he begins his conclusion with the shocking statement, "In the end, whether or not Lincoln's personal ambition undid him and the nation is immaterial" (paragraph 18), a direct contradiction to the usual lesson that Lincoln was the one who *preserved* the Union, not undid it. In the end, what is Vidal's dominant impression of Lincoln? (Glossary: *Dominant Impression*) Explain your answer.

EXPLORING LANGUAGE

1. Vidal says (to paraphrase Lincoln himself), "It is better to reign in hell than serve in heaven" (paragraph 17). The distinction between the words *reign* and *serve* is of vital importance in this statement. Exactly what does each word mean? Why is this quote so appropriate to Lincoln's ultimate fate?

2. Although Vidal refers to Lincoln historians on numerous occasions, he crystallizes his feelings for them by calling them "Lincoln priests" (paragraph 10) when discussing Lincoln's writing. What connotations does the word *priest* possess when used in this context? (Glossary: *Connotation/Denotation*) What is Vidal saying about Lincoln scholars with his choice of this word?

3. Good description depends upon words that are exact in meaning, rich in nuance, or both. Be sure you understand the definition and, where it is significant, the emotional resonance of these words: *myopic* (paragraph 1), *placate* (3), *monotheists* (3), *atheistical* (3), *vulpine* (4), *hagiographers* (9), *holograph* (10), *coda* (13).

COMBINING RHETORICAL STRATEGIES

Vidal's description of Lincoln undermines the way historians have treated him, which has been more to establish him as a national deity than to describe him accurately. In a sense, Vidal contrasts the real, "private" Lincoln with the revered public figure. Write a short comparison and contrast piece about a person you know well — parent, sibling, friend, roommate — who has a private persona that is at odds with the public one. For example, he or she may be an excellent athlete or actor, confident and sure in front of large audiences, but tongue-tied in social settings. Or he or she may be both the life of the party as well as a quiet, reclusive person who likes to knit or read at home. Base your comparisons and contrasts on concise descriptions of each persona.

WRITING SUGGESTIONS

1. **(Description)** Write a descriptive essay about a well-known contemporary public figure you admire or have studied (politician, actor, athlete), based on what you have read, seen, and heard about this person. Do your best to convey a sense not just of the image projected in the media, but also of what the person is really like. Pay attention to any slant you give in your essay. How might your source materials have contributed to the dominant impression you convey about this person?

2. **(Other Strategies)** Question 4 in Understanding the Writer's Craft quotes Vidal's contention that Lincoln himself may have brought about much of the destruction and misery of the Civil War. Write a paper in which you argue for or against this statement. Was Lincoln's drive to preserve the Union based on egomania or a necessary, even heroic, sense of what the United States is all about? What other options might Lincoln have had following the secession of the southern states?

3. **(Research)** Choose a historical figure whose legacy has been strongly biased — whether for good or bad — to create a simple image or symbol, rather than a complex person. Some examples to think about are Nero, George Washington, Daniel Boone, Susan B. Anthony, and Adolf Hitler. Write a short description of the person you choose, using the perspective of the popular media accounts. Then, following Vidal's model, research and examine the human being behind the facade. Obviously, the biased perspective has some basis in fact, so in what way does your research agree with the well-known two-dimensional image? What contradictions can you find? What reasons might there be for the interpretations made by historians? In other words, why have most people sought to simplify the image of this person, rather than encourage a better understanding of him or her?

- **Biography.com**
<http://www.biography.com>

This site, from the A&E television show, has profiles of 25,000 personalities.

- **The *Time* 100**
<http://www.time.com/time/time100>

Time magazine's 100 Most Important People of the Twentieth Century Web site is organized into Leaders and Revolutionaries, Artists and

Entertainers, Builders and Titans, Scientists and Thinkers, Heroes and Icons, and the Person of the Century.

- **Lives, the Biography Resource**
  <http://www.amillionlives.com>

  You can search for individuals by surname, region, or profession in this directory of online biographical information.

A View from the Bridge

Cherokee Paul McDonald

A fiction writer and journalist, Cherokee Paul McDonald was raised and schooled in Fort Lauderdale, Florida. In 1970, he returned home from a tour of duty in Vietnam and joined the Fort Lauderdale Police Department, where he remained until 1980, resigning with the rank of sergeant. During this time, McDonald received a degree in criminal science from Broward Community College. He left the police department to become a writer and worked a number of odd jobs before publishing his first book, The Patch, *in 1986. McDonald has said that almost all of his writing comes from his police work, and his common themes of justice, balance, and fairness reflect his life as part of the "thin blue line" (the police department). In 1991, he published* Blue Truth, *a memoir. His first novel,* Summer's Reason, *was released in 1994. His most recent book is a memoir of his three years as an artillery forward observer in Vietnam,* Into the Green: Reconnaissance by Fire *(2001).*

"A View from the Bridge" was originally published in Sunshine *magazine in 1990. The essay shows McDonald's usual expert handling of fish and fishermen, both in and out of water, and reminds us that things are not always as they seem.*

BEFORE YOU READ

There's an old saying that "familiarity breeds contempt." We've all had the experience of becoming numb to sights or experiences that once struck us with wonderment; but sometimes, with luck, something happens to renew our appreciation. Think of an example from your own experience. What are some ways we can retain or recover our appreciation of the remarkable things we have come to take for granted?

I was coming up on the little bridge in the Rio Vista neighborhood of Fort Lauderdale, deepening my stride and my breathing to negotiate the slight incline without altering my pace. And then, as I neared the crest, I saw the kid.

He was a lumpy little guy with baggy shorts, a faded T-shirt and heavy sweat socks falling down over old sneakers.

Partially covering his shaggy blond hair was one of those blue baseball caps with gold braid on the bill and a sailfish patch sewn onto the peak. Covering his eyes and part of his face was a pair of those stupid-looking '50s-style wrap-around sunglasses.

He was fumbling with a beat-up rod and reel, and he had a little bait bucket by his feet. I puffed on by, glancing down into the empty bucket as I passed.

"Hey, mister! Would you help me, please?" 5

The shrill voice penetrated my jogger's concentration, and I was 6
determined to ignore it. But for some reason, I stopped.

With my hands on my hips and the sweat dripping from my nose 7
I asked, "What do you want, kid?"

"Would you please help me find my shrimp? It's my last one and 8
I've been getting bites and I know I can catch a fish if I can just find
that shrimp. He jumped outta my hand as I was getting him from the
bucket."

Exasperated, I walked slowly back to the kid, and pointed. 9

"There's the damn shrimp by your left foot. You stopped me for *that?*" 10

As I said it, the kid reached down and trapped the shrimp. 11

"Thanks a lot, mister," he said. 12

I watched as the kid dropped the baited hook down into the 13
canal. Then I turned to start back down the bridge.

That's when the kid let out a "Hey! Hey!" and the prettiest tarpon 14
I'd ever seen came almost six feet out of the water, twisting and turning as he fell through the air.

"I got one!" the kid yelled as the fish hit the water with a loud 15
splash and took off down the canal.

I watched the line being burned off the reel at an alarming rate. 16
The kid's left hand held the crank while the extended fingers felt for
the drag setting.

"No, kid!" I shouted. "Leave the drag alone . . . just keep that 17
damn rod tip up!"

Then I glanced at the reel and saw there were just a few loops of 18
line left on the spool.

"Why don't you get yourself some decent equipment?" I said, but 19
before the kid could answer I saw the line go slack.

"Ohhh, I lost him," the kid said. I saw the flash of silver as the fish 20
turned.

"Crank, kid, crank! You didn't lose him. He's coming back toward 21
you. Bring in the slack!"

The kid cranked like mad, and a beautiful grin spread across his 22
face.

"He's heading in for the pilings," I said. "Keep him out of those 23
pilings!"

The kid played it perfectly. When the fish made its play for the 24
pilings, he kept just enough pressure on to force the fish out. When
the water exploded and the silver missile hurled into the air, the kid
kept the rod tip up and the line tight.

As the fish came to the surface and began a slow circle in the 25
middle of the canal, I said, "Whooee, is that a nice fish or what?"

The kid didn't say anything, so I said, "Okay, move to the edge of 26
the bridge and I'll climb down to the seawall and pull him out."

When I reached the seawall I pulled in the leader, leaving the fish   27
lying on its side in the water.

"How's that?" I said.   28

"Hey, mister, tell me what it looks like."   29

"Look down here and check him out," I said, "He's beautiful."   30

But then I looked up into those stupid-looking sunglasses and it   31
hit me. The kid was blind.

"Could you tell me what he looks like, mister?" he said again.   32

"Well, he's just under three, uh, he's about as long as one of your   33
arms," I said. "I'd guess he goes about 15, 20 pounds. He's mostly
silver, but the silver is somehow made up of *all* the colors, if you
know what I mean." I stopped. "Do you know what I mean by
colors?"

The kid nodded.   34

"Okay. He has all these big scales, like armor all over his   35
body. They're silver too, and when he moves they sparkle. He has
a strong body and a large powerful tail. He has big round eyes, bigger than a quarter, and a lower jaw that sticks out past the upper
one and is very tough. His belly is almost white and his back is a
gunmetal gray. When he jumped he came out of the water about
six feet, and his scales caught the sun and flashed it all over the
place."

By now the fish had righted itself, and I could see the bright-red   36
gills as the gill plates opened and closed. I explained this to the kid,
and then said, more to myself, "He's a beauty."

"Can you get him off the hook?" the kid asked. "I don't want to   37
kill him."

I watched as the tarpon began to slowly swim away, tired but still   38
alive.

By the time I got back up to the top of the bridge the kid had his   39
line secured and his bait bucket in one hand.

He grinned and said, "Just in time. My mom drops me off here,   40
and she'll be back to pick me up any minute."

He used the back of one hand to wipe his nose.   41

"Thanks for helping me catch that tarpon," he said, "and for help-   42
ing me to see it."

I looked at him, shook my head, and said, "No, my friend, thank   43
you for letting *me* see that fish."

I took off, but before I got far the kid yelled again.   44

"Hey, mister!"   45

I stopped.   46

"Someday I'm gonna catch a sailfish and a blue marlin and a giant   47
tuna and *all* those big sportfish!"

As I looked into those sunglasses I knew he probably would. I   48
wished I could be there when it happened.

RESPONDING TO READING

The jogger and the kid are very different from each other, but they share a passionate interest in fishing. What role does the tarpon play in this story? What can a shared interest do for a relationship between two people?

QUESTIONING THE TEXT

1. What clues lead up to the revelation that the kid is blind? Why does it take the narrator so long to realize it?

2. "Why don't you get yourself some decent equipment?" the narrator asks the kid (paragraph 19). Why does McDonald include this question? Speculate about the answer.

3. Near the end of the story, why does the narrator say to the kid, "No, my friend, thank you for letting *me* see that fish" (paragraph 43)?

UNDERSTANDING THE WRITER'S CRAFT

1. Notice the way the narrator chooses and actually adjusts some of the words he uses to describe the fish to the kid. Why does he do this? What is McDonald's desired effect?

2. By the end of the essay, we know much more about the kid than the fact that he is blind, but after the initial description, McDonald characterizes him only indirectly. As the essay unfolds, what do we learn about the kid, and by what techniques does the author convey this knowledge?

3. Why does McDonald tell so much of his story through dialogue?

EXPLORING LANGUAGE

1. What is the metaphor in paragraph 24? Why is it apt? How does this metaphor enhance McDonald's description? (Glossary: *Figures of Speech*)

2. Reread the description of the kid (paragraphs 2 and 3). Which details gain significance as events unfold over the course of the essay?

3. What is the connotation of the word *view* in the title? Of the word *bridge?* (Glossary: *Connotation/Denotation*)

4. You may be unfamiliar with some of the fishing-related vocabulary in this essay. What sort of fish is a tarpon? In the context of fishing, define *drag* (paragraph 16), *pilings* (23), *seawall* (26), *leader* (27).

COMBINING RHETORICAL STRATEGIES

This essay, descriptive in theme and intent, is structured as a narrative. (Glossary: *Narration*) What makes the combination of story and description effective? Suppose McDonald had started his essay with a statement like this: "If you really want to see something clearly, try describing it to a blind child." How would such an opening change the impact of the piece? Which other rhetorical strategies might McDonald have used along with the new opening?

WRITING SUGGESTIONS

1. **(Description)** Divide the class into groups of three or four. In your group, take turns describing some specific beautiful or remarkable thing to the others as if they were blind. You may actually want to bring an object to observe while your classmates cover their eyes. Help each other find the best words to create a vivid verbal picture. Write your description in a couple of brief paragraphs, retaining the informal style of your speaking voice.

2. **(Other Strategies)** McDonald's "A View from the Bridge" and the Calvin and Hobbes cartoon reprinted below are just two "fish stories" in the long and rich tradition of that genre. In their own ways, both the essay and the cartoon play upon the ironic notion that fishing is a quiet sport but one in which participants come to expect the unexpected. For the narrator in McDonald's story, there is a lesson in not merely looking but truly seeing. For Calvin, there is the story of "latchin' on to the big one." It is interesting that a sport in which "nothing happens" can be the source of so much storytelling. Write an essay in which you tell a "fish story" of your own, making sure that it reveals a larger, significant truth or life lesson. Try as well to incorporate the element of surprise.

3. **(Research)** There are many services available to visually impaired people. Working with a classmate, have one partner learn about the accommodations and services for visually impaired students at your college or university, while the other partner searches the community and the Internet to learn about resources and adaptive technology for the blind in your area. Share your findings, and write a report to present them.

- **Blindness-Related Resources on the Web and Beyond**
   <http://www.hicom.net/~oedipus/blind.html>

   This comprehensive site offers numerous links to related pages.

- **The Blindness Resource Center**
  <http://www.nyise.org/blind.htm#index>

  Links for services and products for the visually impaired can be found here.

- **The American Printing House for the Blind, Inc.**
  <http://www.aph.org>

  This site features products, technologies, and services designed to help the visually impaired read and communicate with "written" language.

COMBINING SUBJECTS AND STRATEGIES

The photograph below depicts many of the same themes and strategies as the Combining Rhetorical Strategies essay that follows. Your observations about the photograph will help guide you to the key themes and strategies in the essay. After you've read the essay, you may use your observations about both the photograph and the essay to examine how the overlapping themes and strategies work in each medium.

The following photograph, "Barrio Mural," was taken by Peter Menzel in San Diego, California. A Hispanic woman, presumably going about her daily routine, ignores the striking mural honoring Hispanic heroes and revolutionaries. Figures like Cesar Chavez, who led migrant farmworkers in protest against terrible working conditions in California during the 1950s, '60s, and '70s, and Che Guevara, a revolutionary leader who played a key role in Fidel Castro's ascent to power in Cuba during the late 1950s and early '60s, offer a defiant backdrop to the everyday life of the community.

© Peter Menzel/Stock Boston

For Discussion

Based on the visual details within the photograph, what can you say about the community that lives in this neighborhood? Which details in the photograph tell you what kind of neighborhood it is? Which details suggest the socioeconomic struggles in the barrio? Why do you think portraits of such figures as Che Guevara, Cesar Chavez, and even the Virgin Mary are included on the mural? What does the mural suggest about the people who live in the neighborhood and the lives they lead?

The Barrio

Robert Ramírez

> *Robert Ramírez was born in 1949 and was raised in Edinburg, Texas, near the Mexican border. He graduated from the University of Texas — Pan-American, then worked in several communications-related jobs before joining KGBT-TV in Harlingen, Texas, where he was an anchor. He then moved to finance and worked for a time in banking and as a development officer responsible for alumni fund-raising for his alma mater.*
>
> *Ramírez's knowledge of the barrio allows him to paint an affectionate portrait of barrio life that nevertheless has a hard edge. His barrio is colorful but not romantic, and his description raises important societal issues as it describes the vibrant community within.*

BEFORE YOU READ

Describe the neighborhood in which you grew up or the most memorable neighborhood of your experience. Did you like it? Why or why not? How strong was the sense of community between neighbors? To your knowledge, how did it contrast with other neighborhoods nearby?

The train, its metal wheels squealing as they spin along the silvery tracks, rolls slower now. Through the gaps between the cars blinks a streetlamp, and this pulsing light on a barrio streetcorner beats slower, like a weary heartbeat, until the train shudders to a halt, the light goes out, and the barrio is deep asleep. 1

Throughout Aztlán (the Nahuatl term meaning "land to the north"), trains grumble along the edges of a sleeping people. From Lower California, through the blistering Southwest, down the Rio 2

Grande to the muddy Gulf, the darkness and mystery of dreams engulf communities fenced off by railroads, canals, and expressways. Paradoxical communities, isolated from the rest of the town by concrete columned monuments of progress, yet stranded in the past. They are surrounded by change. It eludes their reach, in their own backyards, and the people, unable and unwilling to see the future, or even touch the present, perpetuate the past.

Leaning from the expressway or jolting across the tracks, one enters a different physical world permeated by a different attitude. The physical dimensions are impressive. It is a large section of town which extends for fifteen blocks north and south along the tracks, and then advances eastward, thinning into nothingness beyond the city limits. Within the invisible (yet sensible) walls of the barrio, are many, many people living in too few houses. The homes, however, are much more numerous than on the outside.

Members of the barrio describe the entire area as their home. It is a home, but it is more than this. The barrio is a refuge from the harshness and the coldness of the Anglo world. It is a forced refuge. The leprous people are isolated from the rest of the community and contained in their section of town. The stoical pariahs of the barrio accept their fate, and from the angry seeds of rejection grow the flowers of closeness between outcasts, not the thorns of bitterness and the mad desire to flee. There is no want to escape, for the feeling of the barrio is known only to its inhabitants, and the material needs of life can also be found here.

The *tortillería* fires up its machinery three times a day, producing steaming, round, flat slices of barrio bread. In the winter, the warmth of the tortilla factory is a wool *sarape* in the chilly morning hours, but in the summer, it unbearably toasts every noontime customer.

The *panadería* sends its sweet messenger aroma down the dimly lit street, announcing the arrival of fresh, hot sugary *pan dulce*.

The small corner grocery serves the meal-to-meal needs of customers, and the owner, a part of the neighborhood, willingly gives credit to people unable to pay cash for foodstuffs.

The barbershop is a living room with hydraulic chairs, radio, and television, where old friends meet and speak of life as their salted hair falls aimlessly about them.

The pool hall is a junior level country club where '*chucos*, strangers in their own land, get together to shoot pool and rap, while veterans, unaware of the cracking, popping balls on the green felt, complacently play dominoes beneath rudely hung *Playboy* foldouts.

The *cantina* is the night spot of the barrio. It is the country club and the den where the rites of puberty are enacted. Here the young become men. It is in the taverns that the young dude shows his *machismo* through the quantity of beer he can hold, the stories of *rucas* he has had, and his willingness and ability to defend his image against hardened and scarred old lions.

No, there is no frantic wish to flee. It would be absurd to leave the familiar and nervously step into the strange and cold Anglo community when the needs of the Chicano can be met in the barrio.   11

The barrio is closeness. From the family living unit, familial relationships stretch out to immediate neighbors, down the block, around the corner, and to all parts of the barrio. The feeling of family, a rare and treasurable sentiment, pervades and accounts for the inability of the people to leave. The barrio is this attitude manifested on the countenances of the people, on the faces of their homes, and in the gaiety of their gardens.   12

The color-splashed homes arrest your eyes, arouse your curiosity, and make you wonder what life scenes are being played out in them. The flimsy, brightly colored, wood-frame houses ignore no neon-brilliant color. Houses trimmed in orange, chartreuse, lime-green, yellow, and mixtures of these and other hues beckon the beholder to reflect on the peculiarity of each home. Passing through this land is refreshing like Brubeck, not narcotizing like revolting rows of similar houses, which neither offend nor please.   13

In the evenings, the porches and front yards are occupied with men calmly talking over the noise of children playing baseball in the unpaved extension of the living room, while the women cook supper or gossip with female neighbors as they water their *jardines*. The gardens mutely echo the expressive verses of the colorful houses. The denseness of multicolored plants and trees gives the house the appearance of an oasis or a tropical island hideaway, sheltered from the rest of the world.   14

Fences are common in the barrio, but they are fences and not the walls of the Anglo community. On the western side of town, the high wooden fences between houses are thick, impenetrable walls, built to keep the neighbors at bay. In the barrio, the fences may be rusty, wire contraptions or thick green shrubs. In either case you can see through them and feel no sense of intrusion when you cross them.   15

Many lower-income families of the barrio manage to maintain a comfortable standard of living through the communal action of family members who contribute their wages to the head of the family. Economic need creates interdependence and closeness. Small barefooted boys sell papers on cool, dark Sunday mornings, deny themselves pleasantries, and give their earnings to *mamá*. The older the child, the greater the responsibility to help the head of the household provide for the rest of the family.   16

There are those, too, who for a number of reasons have not achieved a relative sense of financial security. Perhaps it results from   17 too many children too soon, but it is the homes of these people and their situation that numbs rather than charms. Their houses, aged and bent, oozing children, are fissures in the horn of plenty. Their wooden homes may have brick-pattern asbestos tile on the outer walls, but the tile is not convincing.

Unable to pay city taxes or incapable of influencing the city to live up to its duty to serve all the citizens, the poorer barrio families remain trapped in the nineteenth century and survive as best they can. The backyards have well-worn paths to the outhouses, which sit near the alley. Running water is considered a luxury in some parts of the barrio. Decent drainage is usually unknown, and when it rains, the water stands for days, an incubator of health hazards and an avoidable nuisance. Streets, costly to pave, remain rough, rocky trails. Tires do not last long, and the constant rattling and shaking grind away a car's life and spread dust through screen windows.   18

The houses and their *jardines,* the jollity of the people in an adverse world, the brightly feathered alarm clock pecking away at supper and cautiously eyeing the children playing nearby, produce a mystifying sensation at finding the noble savage alive in the twentieth century. It is easy to look at the positive qualities of life in the barrio, and look at them with a distantly envious feeling. One wishes to experience the feelings of the barrio and not the hardships. Remembering the illness, the hunger, the feeling of time running out on you, the walls, both real and imagined, reflecting on living in the past, one finds his envy becoming more elusive, until it has vanished altogether.   19

Back now beyond the tracks, the train creaks and groans, the cars jostle each other down the track, and as the light begins its pulsing, the barrio, with all its meanings, greets a new dawn with yawns and restless stretchings.   20

RESPONDING TO READING

Does Ramírez's essay leave you with a positive or negative image of the barrio? Is it a place you would like to live in, visit, or avoid? Explain your answer.

QUESTIONING THE TEXT

1. Based on Ramírez's essay, what is the barrio? Why do you think that Ramírez uses the image of the train to introduce and close his essay about the barrio?

2. In paragraph 4, Ramírez states that residents consider the barrio something more than a home. What does he mean? In what ways is it more than just a place where they live?

3. Why are the color schemes of the houses in the barrio striking? How do they contrast with houses in other areas of town? (Glossary: *Comparison and Contrast*)

4. Many of the barrio residents are able to achieve financial security. How are they able to do this? What is life like for those who cannot?

UNDERSTANDING THE WRITER'S CRAFT

1. Explain Ramírez's use of the imagery of walls and fences to describe a sense of cultural isolation. What might this imagery symbolize?

2. Ramírez uses several metaphors throughout his essay. (Glossary: *Figures of Speech*) Identify them, and discuss how they contribute to the essay.

3. Ramírez begins his essay with a relatively positive picture of the barrio but ends on a more disheartening note. Why has he organized his essay this way? What might the effect have been if he had reversed the images? (Glossary: *Beginnings/Endings*)

EXPLORING LANGUAGE

1. Ramírez uses Spanish phrases throughout his essay. Why do you suppose he uses them? What is their effect on the reader? He also uses the words *home, refuge, family*, and *closeness*. In what ways, if any, are they essential to his purpose? (Glossary: *Purpose*)

2. Ramírez calls barrio residents "the leprous people" (paragraph 4). What does the word *leprous* connote in the context of this essay? (Glossary: *Connotation/Denotation*) Why do you think Ramírez chose to use such a strong word to communicate the segregation of the community?

3. Refer to your desk dictionary to determine the meanings of the following words as Ramírez uses them in this selection: *paradoxical* (paragraph 2), *permeated* (3), *stoical* (4), *pariahs* (4), *complacently* (9), *Chicano* (11), *countenances* (12), *fissures* (17), *adverse* (19).

COMBINING RHETORICAL STRATEGIES

1. Use Ramírez's description to write a one-paragraph definition of the word *barrio*. Did reading the essay change the connotations of the word for you? (Glossary: *Connotation/Denotation*) If so, how?

2. Ramírez goes into detail about the many groups living in the barrio. How does his subtle use of division and classification add to his description of the barrio? In what ways do the groups he identifies contribute to the unity of life in the barrio?

3. Ramírez invokes such warm images of the barrio that his statement that its inhabitants do not wish to leave seems benign. In the end, however, it has a somewhat ominous ring. How does the description of the barrio

have two components, one good and one bad? What are the two sides of the barrio's embrace for the residents?

WRITING SUGGESTIONS

1. **(Description)** Ramírez frames his essay with the image of the train rumbling past the sleeping residents. Likewise, Peter Menzel's photograph juxtaposes contrasting images in a barrio — a huge outdoor mural that includes portraits of important political, social, and religious figures and a middle-aged woman trudging past it with her groceries on an otherwise deserted street — to create an overall picture of a place that is simultaneously vibrant and lively and run-down. Using Ramírez's essay and Menzel's photo as models, write a descriptive essay about where you currently live, whether it is a dorm, an apartment, or a neighborhood with an identity, such as a barrio. Use a metaphorical image to frame your essay. What image is both a part of life where you live and an effective metaphor for the life you lead there?

2. **(Other Strategies)** Write a comparison and contrast essay in which you compare where you live now with another residence. Where are you the most comfortable? What about your current surroundings do you like? What do you dislike? How does it compare with your hometown, your first apartment, or whatever place you choose to reference? If and when you move on, where do you hope to go?

3. **(Research)** Over the past few decades, there has been a lot of attention paid to Hispanic communities. Hispanic candidates have been elected to the U.S. Congress, there is a greater awareness of Hispanic issues, and the popular media have embraced many of the influences of Hispanic culture. There has also been some backlash, however, particularly in language issues. The English-only movement has largely sought to curtail the prevalence of the growing use of Spanish in official government functions and publications. Write an essay in which you address whether Hispanics, such as those described by Ramírez, are still functional "lepers," or outsiders, in American society. Base your argument on research you do into the language issues, life in communities that have a high percentage of Hispanic residents, and popular media accounts of Hispanic issues. How much progress is real, and how much is mainly show? Do children in Hispanic communities today have possibilities that extend beyond their "barrio" or not? Explain.

- **U.S. English**
  <http://www.us-english.org>

  This is the site of U.S. English, the largest citizens' action group trying to make English the nation's official language.

- **English Only?**
  <http://coloquio.com/english.html>

This Web site argues against making English the nation's official language.

- *Hispanic* **Online**
  <http://www.hispaniconline.com>

  The online version of *Hispanic* magazine includes areas on Education, Politics and Opinions, and Finance.

- **Bilingual Education**
  <http://www.edweek.org/context/topics/issuespage.cfm?id=8>

  The Bilingual Education page from *Education Week* lists articles, organizations, and Web sites about the debate.

San Piedro Island (FICTION)

David Guterson

David Guterson was born in Seattle, Washington, in 1956. He grew up in the area and received his M.A. from the University of Washington. Following the completion of his schooling, he taught English at a high school on Bainbridge Island in Puget Sound, where he began his writing career. His works include articles published in Sports Illustrated *and* Harper's *magazine and two books:* The Country Ahead of Us, the County Behind *(1989), a collection of short stories, and* Family Matters: Why Homeschooling Makes Sense *(1992), a work of nonfiction. His debut novel,* Snow Falling on Cedars *(1995) was a huge critical and commercial success. Among the many awards it received was the PEN/Faulkner Award for fiction, the largest annual juried prize in the United States. The novel spent a year on the national bestseller lists. Guterson's second novel,* East of the Mountains, *was published in 1999.*

In the following excerpt from Snow Falling on Cedars, *Guterson's understanding of, and appreciation for, the joys and difficulties of living in the Pacific Northwest are showcased in his description of San Piedro Island.*

BEFORE YOU READ

We all have places where we feel at home, whether it is where we grew up, where we have spent a lot of time, or a place that just felt "right," even at first glance. We find comfort in the way these places look, sound, even smell. On the other hand, there are places that we find hostile or disquieting in ways that are sometimes obvious, sometimes not. Nightfall in the country can be idyllic, but to a city dweller it can seem almost oppressively quiet. The unbroken horizon of the plains can unnerve someone who grew up in ski country. Write about a place where you find it disagreeable to spend a lot of time. How does this setting differ from where you feel at home? What about it bothers you in particular?

San Piedro was an island of five thousand damp souls, named by lost Spaniards who moored offshore in the year 1603. They'd sailed in search of the Northwest Passage, as many Spaniards did in those days, and their pilot and captain, Martín de Aquilar of the Vizcaíno expedition, sent a work detail ashore to cull a fresh spar pole from among the hemlocks at water's edge. Its members were murdered almost immediately upon setting foot on the beach by a party of Nootka slave raiders.

Settlers arrived — mostly wayward souls and eccentrics who had meandered off the Oregon Trail. A few rooting pigs were slaughtered in 1845 — by Canadian Englishmen up in arms about the border —

but San Piedro Island generally lay clear of violence after that. The most distressing news story of the preceding ten years had been the wounding of an island resident by a drunken Seattle yachtsman with a shotgun on the Fourth of July, 1951.

Amity Harbor, the island's only town, provided deep moorage for   3
a fleet of purse seiners and one-man gill-netting boats. It was an eccentric, rainy, wind-beaten sea village, downtrodden and mildewed, the boards of its buildings bleached and weathered, their drainpipes rusted a dull orange. Its long, steep inclines lay broad and desolate; its high-curbed gutters swarmed, most winter nights, with traveling rain. Often the sea wind made its single traffic light flail from side to side or caused the town's electrical power to flicker out and stay out for days. Main Street presented to the populace Petersen's Grocery, a post office, Fisk's Hardware Center, Larsen's Pharmacy, a dime-store-with-fountain owned by a woman in Seattle, a Puget Power office, a chandlery, Lottie Opsvig's apparel shop, Klaus Hartmann's real estate agency, the San Piedro Café, the Amity Harbor Restaurant, and a battered, run-down filling station owned and operated by the Torgerson brothers. At the wharf a fish packing plant exuded the odor of salmon bones, and the creosoted pilings of the state ferry terminal lay in among a fleet of mildewed boats. Rain, the spirit of the place, patiently beat down everything man-made. On winter evenings it roared in sheets against the pavements and made Amity Harbor invisible.

San Piedro had too a brand of verdant beauty that inclined its resi-   4
dents toward the poetical. Enormous hills, soft green with cedars, rose and fell in every direction. The island homes were damp and moss covered and lay in solitary fields and vales of alfalfa, feed corn, and strawberries. Haphazard cedar fences lined the careless roads, which slid beneath the shadows of the trees and past the bracken meadows. Cows grazed, stinking of sweet dung and addled by summer blackflies. Here and there an islander tried his hand at milling sawlogs on his own, leaving fragrant heaps of sawdust and mounds of cedar bark at roadside. The beaches glistened with smooth stones and sea foam. Two dozen coves and inlets, each with its pleasant muddle of sailboats and summer homes, ran the circumference of San Piedro, an endless series of pristine anchorages.

RESPONDING TO READING

San Piedro Island is a place of contrasts: a place of beauty and the pleasures found on an island, as well as a place of gloom, rain, and wind. Refer to your Before You Read answer. From Guterson's description of the island, how appealing do you think you would find it? Use specific passages from the description to explain your answer.

QUESTIONING THE TEXT

1. What happened to the first Spaniards who set foot on San Piedro Island? Has the luck of the island's inhabitants changed since then?

2. Why are Amity Harbor's buildings and other structures so run-down? Why does the climate have such a large influence on life in the town?

3. Where does the beauty of San Piedro Island lay? Guterson never explicitly says, but from his description, how big do you think the island is? Explain your answer.

UNDERSTANDING THE WRITER'S CRAFT

1. San Piedro Island acquires slightly absurd characteristics when Guterson describes it in terms of its place in the lives of people. Named by "lost Spaniards," the island was settled by "wayward souls and eccentrics" (paragraph 2), was the scene of a pig slaughter and a foolish firearm accident, and was inhabited by "five thousand damp souls" (1). What do these descriptions imply about the island and its inhabitants? How do they add to Guterson's dominant impression of the island? (Glossary: *Dominant Impression*)

2. What does Guterson mean when he identifies rain as "the spirit of the place" (paragraph 3)? How can rain serve as a metaphor for a place's "spirit"? (Glossary: *Figurative Language*) Why did he choose this identification instead of saying something more straightforward, such as "Rain beats down on the town relentlessly"?

3. Guterson provides an intimate look at the Main Street in Amity Harbor, naming proprietors of stores and detailing their functions. Why do you think he chooses to go into such detail about the businesses, especially when he uses a fairly broad brush to describe the rest of the island? What does his description gain from the precision of the list and the use of proper names?

EXPLORING LANGUAGE

1. Rain is, of course, an important component of life on San Piedro Island. According to Guterson, it swarms, roars, travels, and beats down manmade objects. What might be some more traditional adjectives he could have used to describe the rain? What connotations do such words as *swarm* and *travels* have for you in connection with the rain? (Glossary: *Connotation/Denotation*)

2. Guterson uses sometimes contradictory words to describe the island's "verdant beauty." Analyze his word choice in paragraph 4. How does his description present the "beauty" of the island?

3. Guterson uses precise terminology and strong, descriptive language to paint a picture of San Piedro Island. Make sure you understand the meanings of these words to fully appreciate the description: *spar* (paragraph 1), *wayward* (2), *seiners* (3), *chandlery* (3), *verdant* (4), *pristine* (4).

COMBINING RHETORICAL STRATEGIES

Guterson's description of San Piedro Island contains a strong cause and effect relationship. Rain is the cause, and the appearance of the island and the difficulties its inhabitants encounter are the effects. Write a short analysis of causes and effects to be found in a place you know well, choosing a cause that has important effects on people's lives. For example, extreme heat in the desert (the cause) may lead to overcrowding of town playgrounds during the morning and evening (the effect). Or wintry road conditions (the cause) may lead to brisk sales of four-wheel-drive vehicles (the effect). How do such causes and effects influence your description of the place you choose?

WRITING SUGGESTIONS

1. **(Description)** Write a description of the place you consider your hometown. Focus on the conditions that shape life there: weather, under- or overpopulation, topography, overall appearance, and so on. Identify what you like about the place and what you would change about it if you could. Does the place make you feel relaxed, invigorated, excited, bored, happy, or something else? Create a dominant impression that conveys this feeling.

2. **(Other Strategies)** Quality of life is important for everyone, yet it is a very subjective commodity. One person's paradise can be another's purgatory. What two or three factors are the most important for you in deciding where you want to live? Write a personal narrative essay in which you present the factors important to you and explain why they are so important for your quality of life.

3. **(Research)** Seattle has boomed in recent years, but not long ago it was known more for its constant rain than anything else. Research Seattle's early history on the Internet and in your library. How did the weather affect the lives of the Native Americans and early Europeans in the area? How did they adapt to accommodate it? Write a paper in which you present the early development of the region. How might its early history and location have contributed to its current popularity?

- **HistoryLink**
  <http://www.historylink.org>

  This site, which calls itself an "online encyclopedia of Seattle and King County history," was developed for the sesquicentennial of the establishment of King County and Seattle.

- **A History of the Northwest Coast**
  <http://www.hallman.org/indian/.www.html>

  This site records the early history of the Northwest coast from 1774 to 1962, with links to primary source accounts from settlers.

- **History of Washington State and the Pacific Northwest**
  <http://www.washington.edu/uwired/outreach/cspn/hstaa432>

  Read Professor John Findlay's account of the early history of Washington State at this site.

WRITING SUGGESTIONS FOR DESCRIPTION

1. Most description is predominantly visual; that is, it appeals to our sense of sight. Good description, however, often goes beyond the visual; it appeals as well to one or more of the other senses — hearing, smell, taste, and touch. One way to heighten your awareness of these other senses is purposefully to deemphasize the visual impressions you receive. For example, while standing on a busy street corner, sitting in a classroom, or shopping in a supermarket, carefully note what you hear, smell, taste, or feel. (It may help if you close your eyes to eliminate visual distractions as you carry out this experiment.) Use these sense impressions to write a brief description of the street corner, the classroom, the supermarket, or another spot of your choosing.

2. Select one of the following topics, and write an objective description of it. Remember that your task in writing objective description is to inform the reader about the object, not to convey to the reader the mood or feeling that the object evokes in you.

   a. a pine tree
   b. a personal computer
   c. a café
   d. a dictionary
   e. a fast-food restaurant
   f. a soccer ball
   g. the layout of your campus
   h. a stereo system
   i. a houseplant
   j. your room

3. Writers of description often rely on factual information to make their writing more substantial and interesting. Using facts, statistics, or other information found in standard reference works in your college library (encyclopedias, dictionaries, almanacs, atlases, biographical dictionaries, or yearbooks), write an essay of several paragraphs describing one of the people, places, or things in the following list. Be sure that you focus your description, that you have a purpose for your description, and that you present your facts in an interesting manner.

   a. the Statue of Liberty
   b. the telephone
   c. Gloria Steinem
   d. Niagara Falls
   e. the Great Wall of China
   f. Michael Jordan
   g. Aretha Franklin
   h. the Tower of London
   i. the sun
   j. Disney World
   k. John Glenn

l. Toni Morrison
m. Robin Williams
n. a local landmark

4. Select one of the following places, and write a multiparagraph description that captures your subjective sense impressions of that particular place.

   a. a busy intersection
   b. a bakery
   c. an auction house
   d. a factory
   e. a service station
   f. a zoo
   g. a cafeteria
   h. a farmers' market
   i. a concert hall
   j. a locker room
   k. a bank
   l. a library

5. At college you have the opportunity to meet many new people, students as well as teachers; perhaps you would like to share your impressions of these people with a friend or family member. In a letter to someone back home, describe one of your new acquaintances. Try to capture the essence of the person you choose and to explain why this person stands out from all the other people you have met at school.

6. As a way of getting to know your campus, select a building, statue, sculpture, or other familiar landmark, and research it. What's its significance or meaning to your college or university? Are there any ceremonies or college rituals associated with the object? What are its distinctive features? What's unusual about it? When was it erected? Who sponsored it? Is it currently being used as originally intended? Once you have completed your informal research, write a description of your subject in which you create a dominant impression of your landmark's importance to the campus community.

   You and your classmates may wish to turn this particular assignment into a collaborative class project: the compilation of a booklet of essays that introduces readers to the unique physical and historic features of your campus. To avoid duplication, the class should make a list of campus landmarks, and students should sign up for the one that they would like to write about.

CHAPTER 7

Narration

WHAT IS NARRATION?

We all love a good story. We want to find out what happens. The tremendous popularity of current fiction and biography reflects our avid interest in stories. Knowing of our interest in stories, many writers and speakers use them to their advantage. A science writer, for example, wishing to assert that many important scientific discoveries have been made by accident, could tell the story of how Sir Alexander Fleming discovered penicillin: Fleming noticed that a bit of mold had fallen into a culture plate in his laboratory and had destroyed bacteria around it. Or a religious leader writing a sermon about charity could illustrate the point that charity should not always be measured in monetary terms by telling the story of an old woman who spends hours every week visiting hospital patients. Or a politician giving a speech could engage the audience by starting off with a humorous anecdote.

Whenever you recount an event or tell a story or anecdote to illustrate an idea, you are using narration. In its broadest sense, narration includes all writing that gives an account of an event or a series of events in a logical sequence. Although you are already very familiar with narratives, you probably associate narration with novels, short fiction, poetry, and even movies. But narration is effective and useful in most nonfiction writing, such as biography, autobiography, history, and news reporting. A good narrative essay provides a meaningful account of some significant event — anything from an account of the United States' involvement with Iraq to a personal experience that gave you new insight about yourself or others.

Consider, for example, the following narrative by E. J. Kahn Jr., about the invention of Coca-Cola as both a medicine and a soft drink, from his book *The Big Drink: The Story of Coca-Cola.*

Writer establishes context for his narrative about Pemberton and Coca-Cola.

Writer uses third-person point of view.

Writer organizes the narrative chronologically, using time markers.

Writer focuses on the discovery that led to Coca-Cola's becoming a popular soft drink.

The man who invented Coca-Cola was not a native Atlantan, but on the day of his funeral every drugstore in town testimonially shut up shop. He was John Styth Pemberton, born in 1833 in Knoxville, Georgia, eighty miles away. Sometimes known as Doctor, Pemberton was a pharmacist who, during the Civil War, led a cavalry troop under General Joe Wheeler. He settled in Atlanta in 1869, and soon began brewing such patent medicines as Triplex Liver Pills and Globe of Flower Cough Syrup. In 1885, he registered a trademark for something called French Wine Coca — Ideal Nerve and Tonic Stimulant; a few months later he formed the Pemberton Chemical Company, and recruited the services of a bookkeeper named Frank M. Robinson, who not only had a good head for figures but, attached to it, so exceptional a nose that he could audit the composition of a batch of syrup merely by sniffing it. In 1886 — a year in which, as contemporary Coca-Cola officials like to point out, Conan Doyle unveiled Sherlock Holmes and France unveiled the Statue of Liberty — Pemberton unveiled a syrup that he called Coca-Cola. He had taken out the wine and added a pinch of caffeine, and, when the end product tasted awful, had thrown in some extract of cola (or kola) nut and a few other oils, blending the mixture in a three-legged iron pot in his back yard and swishing it around with an oar. He distributed it to soda fountains in used beer bottles, and Robinson, with his flowing bookkeeper's script, presently devised a label on which "Coca-Cola" was written in the fashion that is still employed. Pemberton looked upon his concoction less as a refreshment than as a headache cure, especially for people whose throbbing temples could be traced to overindulgence. On a morning late in 1886, one such victim of the night before dragged himself into an Atlanta drugstore and asked for a dollop of Coca-Cola. Druggists customarily stirred a teaspoonful of syrup into a glass of water, but in this instance the factotum on duty was too lazy to walk to the fresh-water tap, a couple of feet off. Instead, he mixed the syrup with some charged water, which was closer at hand. The suffering customer perked up almost at once, and word quickly spread that the best Coca-Cola was a fizzy one.

A good narrative essay, like the paragraph above, has four essential features. The first is *context*: The writer makes clear when the action happened, where it happened, and to whom. The second is *point of view*: The writer establishes and maintains a consistent relationship to the action, either as a participant or as a reporter looking on. The third is *selection of detail*: The writer carefully chooses what to include, focusing on those actions and details that are most important to the story while playing down or even eliminating others. The fourth is *organization*: The writer arranges the events of the narrative in an appropriate sequence, often a strict chronology with a clear beginning, middle, and end.

As you read the selections in this chapter, watch for these features and for how each writer uses them to tell his or her story. Think about how each writer's choices affect the way you reacted to the selections.

WHY DO WRITERS USE NARRATION?

Good stories are compelling; we're hungry for them. We read novels and short stories, and we watch dramatized stories on TV, at the movies, and in the theater because we're curious about others' lives. We want to know what happened to other people to gain insights into our own lives. The most basic and most important purpose of narration is to instruct, to share a meaningful experience with readers.

Another important purpose of narration is to report — to give the facts, to tell what happened. Journalists and historians, in reporting events of the near and more distant past, provide us with information that we can use to form opinions about a current issue or to better understand the world around us. In "The Great Kern County Mouse War" (Chapter 12), for example, Kennedy P. Maize tells of the disastrous consequences of the Kern County, California, residents' all-out war on the area's predators. Noted historian and biographer Bruce Catton ("Grant and Lee," Chapter 9) uses the occasion of Robert E. Lee's surrender at Appomattox Court House to sketch for us the lives of two great Civil War generals. Scientists like Diane Ackerman ("The Face of Beauty," Chapter 12) recount studies and experiments so that we may judge for ourselves whether their conclusions are to be believed. We expect writers to make these narratives as objective as possible and to try to distinguish between facts and opinions.

Narration is often used in combination with one or more of the other rhetorical strategies. In an essay that is written primarily to explain a process — reading a book, for example — a writer might find it useful to tell a brief story or anecdote demonstrating an instance when the process worked especially well (Mortimer Adler, "How to Mark a Book," Chapter 8). In the same way, a writer attempting to define the term *poverty* might tell several stories to illustrate clearly the many hard facets of poverty (Jo Goodwin Parker, "What Is Poverty?"

Chapter 11). Finally, a writer could use narrative examples to persuade —
for example, to argue for patients' rights and the right to die (Christine Mitchell, "When Living Is a Fate Worse Than Death," Chapter 13)
or to demonstrate for readers the power and clarity of monosyllabic
words (Richard Lederer, "The Case for Short Words," Chapter 13). Essays that use process analysis, definition, and argumentation as their
dominant strategies are addressed in detail in Chapters 8, 11, and 13,
respectively.

A narrative may present a straightforward moral, or it may make a
more subtle point about ourselves and the world in which we live.
In each of the narratives in this chapter, we witness a slice of the ongoing human drama. In "Coming to an Awareness of Language,"
Malcolm X tells of his discovery of the power of the written and spoken word. Annie Dillard reveals the surprising lesson learned from a
childhood prank in "Getting Caught." In "Stranger Than True," attorney Barry Winston tells a story to explain why he defends guilty
clients. Langston Hughes's autobiographical "Salvation" shows us the
heart-wrenching guilt that the twelve-year-old Langston experienced
when he lied about "being saved" at a church revival meeting. In
"Shooting an Elephant," George Orwell tells of a time when, in a position of authority, he found himself compelled to act against his convictions. And in "Snow," Julia Alvarez shows how a young immigrant's first experience with snow ironically becomes, in this age of
nuclear weapons, a moment of possible holocaust for the child.

AN ANNOTATED STUDENT ESSAY
USING NARRATION

Andrew Kauser, a student at the University of Vermont, was born in
Montreal, Canada, where he grew up and still makes his home. As a
youngster, he often went on weekend-long flying trips with his father,
who is a pilot; these experiences instilled in him a passion for flying
and a desire to get his own pilot's license one day. In the following
essay, Kauser writes how he felt as he took that most important step in
becoming a licensed pilot, the first solo flight.

Challenging My Fears

Andrew Kauser

Context set —
writer driving to
airport on chilly
autumn morning
for first solo flight

Cedars Airport, just off the western
tip of Montreal, is about a half-hour drive
from my house. Today's drive is boring as
usual except for the chill which runs up the

1

back of my legs because of the cold breeze
entering through the rusted floorboards. I
peer through the dew-covered windshield to
see the leaves changing color. Winter is on
its way.

Writer tells story in present tense and uses first-person point of view.

Finally, I arrive at the airport; while
my instructor waits, I do my aircraft check.
I curse as I touch the steely cold parts of
the aircraft. Even though the discomfort is
great, I do my check slowly. Hurrying could
make me miss a potential problem. It is better to find a problem on the ground instead
of in the air. The check takes about fifteen
minutes, and by this time my fingertips are

Writer presents events in chronological order.

white. Everything appears to be in order so
now it is time to start up.

My instructor and I climb into the
cockpit of the airplane and strap ourselves
in. The plane has been out all night, and it
is just as cold inside as it is outside. My
back shivers as I sit in the seat, and the
controls are painfully cold to touch. The
plane starts without a hint of trouble, and
in one continuous motion I taxi onto the
runway. At full throttle we begin to increase our speed down the runway. In a matter of seconds we leave the ground. The
winds are calm and the visibility is endless. It's a beautiful day to fly.

The object of today's lesson is to
practice taking off and landing. The first
"touch and go" is so smooth that I surprise
both myself and my instructor. Unfortunately, my next two attempts are more like
"smash and goes." I land once more; this
time it is not as jarring as my last two,
and my instructor gives me the O.K. to do a

Writer introduces central idea — solo flight.

circuit alone. We taxi to the hanger, and he
gets out.

Confined in the small cockpit with my
seatbelt strapped around me as tightly as it
will go, I look out the window and watch my

2

3

4

5

Writer uses figurative language to describe his feelings.

human security blanket walking back toward the hangars. The calm feeling with which I began the day quickly disappears. I feel like a soldier being sent to the front lines. I begin to feel smothered by the enclosed cockpit. My stomach tightens around the breakfast I ate and squeezes out my last breath. I gulp for air, and my breathing becomes irregular. My mind still functions, though, and I begin to taxi toward the runway.

Key word taxi repeated to make a transition

It is a long taxi, and I have ample time to think about what I am about to do. I remember the time when my father had to land on a football field when his engine quit. My eyes scan the instruments quickly in hope of finding something comforting in all the dials. My hands are still feeling quite cool. I reach out and pull the lever for

Writer's selection of detail reveals his state of mind.

cabin heat. A rush of warm air saturated with the smell of the engine fills the cockpit. This allows me some comfort as my mind begins to wander. The radio crackles and breaks my train of thought. A student pilot in the air with his instructor announces that he is on final approach for landing. While still taxiing, I look through the Plexiglas windscreen to watch him land. The plane hits hard and bounces right back into the air. It comes down again, and as though on springs, leaps back into the air. Once again it comes down and this time stays.

At the parking area off the runway, I close the throttle and bring the plane to a stop. I check the instruments and request clearance for take-off from the tower. While I wait, I try to calm down.

Now hold your breath and count to ten. Look, the chances of dying in a car accident are twenty times greater, I think to myself. Somehow that isn't very comforting. The radio crackles, and I exhale quickly. Permission is granted.

6

7

8

Dramatic short sentence announces the start of the solo.

Writer makes connection to title.

I taxi onto the runway and come to a stop. I mentally list my options, but they are very few. One is to get up the courage to challenge my fears; the other, to turn the plane around and shamefully go back to the hangar. Well, the choices are limited, but the ultimate decision seems fairly obvious. I reach out and push the throttle into the full open position. The engine roars to life. The decision to go has been made. The plane screams down the runway, and at fifty-five knots I pull back on the controls. In one clean movement, the plane and I leave the ground.

The noise of the engine is the only thing I can hear as the air pressure begins to clog my ears. My mind still racing, I check my instruments. The winds are still calm, and the plane cuts through the air without a hint of trouble. Warm gas-laden air streams through the vents as the sun streaks into the cockpit through the passenger window, and I begin to feel quite hot. At seven hundred feet above the ground, I turn left, check for any traffic, and continue climbing. At twelve hundred feet, I turn left onto the downward portion of the circuit which is parallel to the runway.

Writer's choice of details shows his growing calm once airborne.

This is a longer stretch, and I take a moment to gaze down at the ground below. The view is simply amazing. The trees are all rich bright colors, and I can see for miles. Then it hits me. I'm flying alone. It's great, almost tranquil, no instructor yelling things into my ear, just the machine and myself. A relaxed feeling comes over me, and I start to enjoy the flight. I check my instruments again and start to descend as I turn left.

Turning on the final approach, I an- 12
nounce my intentions on the radio. The nice
feeling of calm leaves me just as quickly as
it came. What is there to worry about, Andrew? All you have to do is land the airplane, preferably on the runway. My heart
starts to pound quickly, almost to the beat
of the motor. Where is my instructor? Why am
I alone?

Writer addresses himself directly as he once again challenges his fears.

Lower the nose, Andrew. Don't lose 13
speed. Give it some more power, maintain
your glidepath. That's it. Bank a little to
the left. Now you're doing it, just a little
further. My ears begin to pop as the pressure on them decreases, and the motor gets
quieter as I start to decrease power. The
plane passes over the threshold of the runway. I begin to raise the nose. The wheels
utter a squeal as they touch down, but the
impact quickly sends the plane back into the
air. The wheels hit again; this time they
stay down, and I roll to a stop.

Short sentences enhance tension and drama of landing.

Back at the hangar, I climb out of the 14
plane and shudder as the cool air hits me
again. A smile comes across my face, and it
persists. I told myself that I would just be
cool about it and not try to show any emotion, but it isn't going to work. I can't
stop smiling as my instructor congratulates
me. I smile because I know that I was successful in challenging and overcoming my
fears.

Writer comments on the meaning of his first solo flight.

Analyzing Andrew Kauser's Essay of Narration: Questions for Discussion

1. What context does Kauser provide for his narrative? What else, if anything, would you have liked to have known about the situation?

2. Kauser tells his story in the first person. How would the narrative have changed had he used a third-person point of view?

3. What details in Kauser's narrative did you find most effective? Are there places where you think he could have used more detail? Explain.

4. Kauser uses a straightforward chronological organization in his narrative. How might he have used flashback in his narrative? What would have been the effect?

5. What meaning or importance do you think this experience holds for Kauser?

SUGGESTIONS FOR WRITING A NARRATIVE ESSAY

Keep in mind the basic features of narration, and use them when planning, writing, and revising your narrative essay. How you use those features will depend on the story you have to tell and your purpose for telling it.

Select a Topic That Has Meaning for You

In your writing course, you may have the freedom to choose the story you want to narrate, or your instructor may give you a list of topics from which to choose. Instead of jumping at the first topic that looks good, brainstorm a list of events that have had an impact on your life and that you could write about. For example, such a list might include your first blind date, catching frogs as a child, making a team or a club, the death of a loved one, a graduation celebration, a trip to the Grand Canyon, the loss of a pet, learning to drive a car, or even the breakup of a relationship. As you narrow down your options, look for an event or an incident that is particularly memorable to you. Memorable experiences are memorable for a reason; they offer us important insights into our lives. Such experiences are worth narrating because people want to read about them. Before you begin writing, ask yourself why you consider meaningful the experience you have chosen. What did you learn from it? How are you different as a result of the experience? What has changed?

Determine Your Point and Purpose

Right from the beginning, ask yourself what is the significance of the event you are narrating and why you are telling your story. Your narrative point (the meaning of your narrative) and purpose in writing will influence which events and details you include and which you leave out. Suppose, for example, you choose to write about how you learned to ride a bicycle. If you mean mainly to entertain, you will probably include a number of unusual and amazing incidents unique to your experience. If your purpose is mainly to report or inform, it will make more sense to concentrate on the kinds of details that are common to most people's experience. However, if your purpose is to tell your readers step-by-step how to ride a bicycle, you should use process analysis, a strategy used by writers whose purpose is to give directions for how something is done or to explain how something works (see Chapter 8).

The most successful narrative essays, however, do more than entertain or inform. While narratives do not have a formal thesis statement, readers will more than likely expect your story to make a statement or to arrive at some meaningful conclusion — implied or explicit — about your experience. The student essay by Andrew Kauser, for example, shows how important it was for him to challenge his fears. In overcoming his fears of flying solo, he gains a measure of control over his life. Certainly, you will not be happy if your story is dismissed as essentially "pointless." As you prepare to write, then, look for the significance in the story you want to tell — some broader, more instructive points it could make about the ways of the world. Learning to ride a bicycle may not suggest such points to you, and it may therefore not be a very good subject for your narrative essay. However, the subject does have possibilities. Here's one: Learning to master a difficult, even dangerous, but definitely useful skill like riding a bike is an important experience to have in life. Here's another: Learning to ride a bicycle is an opportunity for you to acquire and use some basic physics, such as the laws of gravity and the behavior of a gyroscope. Perhaps you can think of others. If, however, you do not know why you are telling the story and it seems pointless even to you, your readers will pick up on the ambivalence in your writing, too, and you should probably find another, more meaningful, story to tell.

Establish a Context

Early in your essay, perhaps in the opening paragraphs, establish the context, or setting, of your story — the world within which the action took place:

When it happened — morning; afternoon; 11:37 on the dot; 1997; winter

Where it happened — in the street; at Wendy's; in Pocatello, Idaho

To whom it happened — to me; to my father; to the assistant to Teri Hopper

Without a clear context, your readers can easily get confused or even completely lost. And remember, readers respond well to specific contextual information because such details make them feel like they are present, ready to witness the narrative.

Choose the Most Appropriate Point of View

Consider what point of view to take in your narrative. Did you take part in the action? If so, it will seem most natural for you to use the first-person (*I, we*) point of view. On the other hand, if you weren't there at all and must rely on other sources for your information, you will probably choose the third-person (*he, she, it, they*) point of view, as did the author writing about the invention of Coca-Cola earlier in this chapter. However, if you were a witness to part or all of what happened but not a participant, then you will need to choose between the more immediate and subjective quality of the first person and the more distanced, objective effect of the third person. Whichever you choose, you should maintain the same point of view throughout your narrative.

Select Details of the Event

When writing your essay, you should include enough detail about the action, the people involved, and the context to let your readers understand what is going on. Start collecting details by asking yourself the traditional reporter's questions:

- Who was involved?
- What happened?
- Where did it happen?
- When did it happen?
- Why did it happen?
- How did it happen?

Generate as many details as you can because you never know which ones will prove valuable in developing your narrative point so that your essay *shows* and doesn't *tell* too much. For example, instead of telling readers that he is scared, Andrew Kauser shows us his irregular breathing and tightening stomach and lets us draw our own conclusion about his state of mind. As you write, you will want to select and emphasize details that support your point, serve your purpose, and show the reader what is happening. Above all, you should not get so carried away with details that your readers become confused or bored by excess information. In good storytelling, deciding what to leave out can be as important as deciding what to include. In his narrative about the discovery of Coca-Cola, E. J. Kahn gives us just enough information about inventor John Styth Pemberton to make him interesting but not so much as to distract readers from the story.

Organize Your Narrative

Storytellers tend to follow an old rule: Begin at the beginning, and go on till you come to the end; then stop. Chronological organization is natural in narration because it is a retelling of the original order of events; it is also easiest for the writer to manage and the reader to understand.

Some narratives, however, are organized using a technique common in movies and the theater called *flashback*: The writer may begin midway through the story, or even at the end, with an important or exciting event, then use flashbacks to fill in what happened earlier to lead up to that event. Some authors begin in the present and then use flashbacks to shift to the past to tell the story. Whatever organization pattern you choose, words and phrases like *for a month, afterward,* and *three days earlier* are examples of devices that will help you and your reader keep the sequence of events straight.

It may help you in organizing to jot down a quick outline before tackling the first draft of your narrative. Here's an outline that student Andrew Kauser used to order the events in his narrative chronologically.

Narration about My First Solo Airplane Flight
Point: You don't get anywhere by just sitting around being afraid.
Context: Cedars Airport outside Montreal, early morning, autumn.

1. Drive to airport sets scene.
2. Perform my aircraft safety check.
3. Practice takeoffs and landings with instructor.
4. Wait for clearance to take off on solo.
5. Decide to solo in spite of my fears.

6. Take off on my first solo.
7. Thrill at the reality of flying alone.
8. Fears return as I think about landing alone.
9. Celebrate my victory over my fears.

Such an outline can remind you of your point, your organization, and the emphasis you want when you write your first draft.

Keep Your Verb Tense Consistent

Most narratives are in the past tense, and this is logical: They recount events that have already happened, even if very recently. But writers sometimes use the present tense to create an effect of intense immediacy, as if the events were happening as you read about them. The essay by Andrew Kauser, "Challenging My Fears," is an example of a narrative using the present tense. The important thing to remember is to be consistent. If you are recounting an event that has already occurred, use the past tense throughout. For an event in the present, use the present tense consistently. If you find yourself jumping from a present event to a past event, as in the case of a flashback, you will need to switch verb tenses to signal the change in time.

Use Narrative Time for Emphasis

The number of words or pages you devote to an event does not usually correspond to the number of minutes or hours the event took to happen. You may require several pages to recount an important or complex quarter of an hour, but then pass over several hours or days in a sentence or two. Length has less to do with chronological time than with the amount of detail you include, and that's a function of the amount of emphasis you want to give to a particular incident.

Use Transitional Words to Clarify Narrative Sequence

Transitional words like *after, next, then, earlier, immediately,* and *finally* are useful, as they help your readers smoothly connect and understand the sequence of events that makes up your narrative. Likewise, a specific time mark like *on April 20, two weeks earlier,* and *in 2001* can indicate time shifts and can signal to readers how much time has elapsed between events. But inexperienced writers sometimes overuse these words; this makes their writing style wordy and tiresome. Use these conventional transitions when you really need them, but when you don't — when your readers can follow your story without them — leave them out.

Use Dialogue to Bring Your Narrative to Life

Having people in a narrative speak is a very effective way of showing rather than telling or summarizing what happened. Snippets of actual dialogue make a story come alive and feel immediate to the reader.

Consider the following passages from a student narrative, an early draft without dialogue:

```
    I hated having to call a garage, but I knew I
couldn't do the work myself and I knew they'd rip me off.
Besides, I had to get the car off the street before the
police had it towed. I felt trapped without any choices.
```

Now compare this early draft, in which the writer summarizes and tells us what happened in very general terms, with the revised draft below, in which the situation is revealed through dialogue.

```
    "University Gulf, Glen speaking. What can I do for
ya?"
    "Yeah, my car broke down. I think it's the timing
belt, and I was wondering if you could give me an esti-
mate."
    "What kind of car is it?" asked Glen.
    "A Ford Escort."
    "What year?"
    "1987," I said, emphasizing the 87.
    "Oh, those are a bitch to work on. Can ya hold on
for a second?"
    I knew what was coming before Glen came back on the
line.
```

With dialogue, readers can hear the direct exchange between the car owner and the mechanic. You can use dialogue in your own writing to deliver a sense of immediacy to the reader.

▶ *Questions for Revision: Narration*

1. Is my narrative well focused, or do I try to cover too long a period of time?

2. What is my reason for telling this story? Is that reason clearly stated or implied for readers?

3. Have I established a clear context for my readers? Is it clear when the action happened, where it happened, and to whom?

4. Have I used the most effective point of view to tell my story? How would my story be different had I used another point of view?

5. Have I selected details that help readers understand what is going on in my narrative, or have I included unnecessary details that distract readers or get in the way of what I'm trying to say? Do I give enough examples of the important events in my narrative?

6. Is the chronology of events in my narrative clear? Have I taken advantage of opportunities to add emphasis, drama, or suspense with flashbacks or other complications of the chronological organization?

7. Have I used transitional expressions or time markers to help readers follow the sequencing of events in my narrative?

8. Have I employed dialogue in my narrative to reveal a situation, or have I told about or summarized the situation too much?

9. Is the meaning of my narrative clear? Have I left my readers thinking, "So what?"

Coming to an Awareness of Language

Malcolm X

In the course of Malcolm X's brief life, he rose from a world of street crime to become one of the most powerful and articulate African American leaders in the United States during the 1960s. On February 21, 1965, his life was cut short at age thirty-nine; he was shot and killed as he addressed an afternoon rally in Harlem. Malcolm X told his life story in The Autobiography of Malcolm X *(1964), written with the assistance of* Roots *author Alex Haley. The book, a moving account of his life and his struggle for fulfillment, is still read by hundreds of thousands each year. In 1992, the life of this influential African American leader was reexamined in Spike Lee's film* Malcolm X.

The following selection from The Autobiography *refers to a period Malcolm X spent in federal prison. In the selection, Malcolm X explains how he was frustrated by his inability to express his ideas and how this frustration led him to a goal: acquiring the skills of reading and writing.*

BEFORE YOU READ

Our educational system places a great emphasis on our having a large and varied working vocabulary. Has anyone ever stressed to you the importance of developing a good vocabulary? What did you think when you heard this advice? In what ways can words be used as powerful tools? How would you judge your own vocabulary?

I've never been one for inaction. Everything I've ever felt strongly 1 about, I've done something about. I guess that's why, unable to do anything else, I soon began writing to people I had known in the hustling world, such as Sammy the Pimp, John Hughes, the gambling house owner, the thief Jumpsteady, and several dope peddlers. I wrote them all about Allah and Islam and Mr. Elijah Muhammad. I had no idea where most of them lived. I addressed their letters in care of the Harlem or Roxbury bars and clubs where I'd known them.

I never got a single reply. The average hustler and criminal was 2 too uneducated to write a letter. I have known many slick, sharp-looking hustlers, who would have you think they had an interest in Wall Street; privately, they would get someone else to read a letter if they received one. Besides, neither would I have replied to anyone writing me something as wild as "the white man is the devil."

What certainly went on the Harlem and Roxbury wires was that Detroit Red was going crazy in stir, or else he was trying some hype to shake up the warden's office.

During the years that I stayed in the Norfolk Prison Colony, never did any official directly say anything to me about those letters, although, of course, they all passed through the prison censorship. I'm sure, however, they monitored what I wrote to add to the files which every state and federal prison keeps on the conversion of Negro inmates by the teachings of Mr. Elijah Muhammad.

But at that time, I felt that the real reason was that the white man knew that he was the devil.

Later on, I even wrote to the Mayor of Boston, to the Governor of Massachusetts, and to Harry S. Truman. They never answered; they probably never even saw my letters. I handscratched to them how the white man's society was responsible for the black man's condition in this wilderness of North America.

It was because of my letters that I happened to stumble upon starting to acquire some kind of a homemade education.

I became increasingly frustrated at not being able to express what I wanted to convey in letters that I wrote, especially those to Mr. Elijah Muhammad. In the street, I had been the most articulate hustler out there — I had commanded attention when I said something. But now, trying to write simple English, I not only wasn't articulate, I wasn't even functional. How would I sound writing in slang, the way I would *say* it, something such as, "Look, daddy, let me pull your coat about a cat. Elijah Muhammad —"

Many who today hear me somewhere in person, or on television, or those who read something I've said, will think I went to school far beyond the eighth grade. This impression is due entirely to my prison studies.

It had really begun back in the Charlestown Prison, when Bimbi first made me feel envy of his stock of knowledge. Bimbi had always taken charge of any conversation he was in, and I had tried to emulate him. But every book I picked up had few sentences which didn't contain anywhere from one to nearly all of the words that might as well have been in Chinese. When I just skipped those words, of course, I really ended up with little idea of what the book said. So I had come to the Norfolk Prison Colony still going through only book-reading motions. Pretty soon, I would have quit even these motions, unless I had received the motivation that I did.

I saw that the best thing I could do was get hold of a dictionary — to study, to learn some words. I was lucky enough to reason also that I should try to improve my penmanship. It was sad. I couldn't even write in a straight line. It was both ideas together that moved me to request a dictionary along with some tablets and pencils from the Norfolk Prison Colony school.

I spent two days just riffling uncertainly through the dictionary's 12 pages. I'd never realized so many words existed! I didn't know *which* words I needed to learn. Finally, just to start some kind of action, I began copying.

In my slow, painstaking, ragged handwriting, I copied into my tablet 13 everything printed on that first page, down to the punctuation marks.

I believe it took me a day. Then, aloud, I read back, to myself, 14 everything I'd written on the tablet. Over and over, aloud, to myself, I read my own handwriting.

I woke up the next morning, thinking about those words — im- 15 mensely proud to realize that not only had I written so much at one time, but I'd written words that I never knew were in the world. Moreover, with a little effort, I also could remember what many of these words meant. I reviewed the words whose meanings I didn't remember. Funny thing, from the dictionary first page right now, that "aardvark" springs to my mind. The dictionary had a picture of it, a long-tailed, long-eared, burrowing African mammal, which lives off termites caught by sticking out its tongue as an anteater does for ants.

I was so fascinated that I went on — I copied the dictionary's next 16 page. And the same experience came when I studied that. With every succeeding page, I also learned of people and places and events from history. Actually the dictionary is like a miniature encyclopedia. Finally the dictionary's A section had filled a whole tablet — and I went on into the B's. That was the way I started copying what eventually became the entire dictionary. It went a lot faster after so much practice helped me to pick up handwriting speed. Between what I wrote in my tablet, and writing letters, during the rest of my time in prison I would guess I wrote a million words.

I suppose it was inevitable that as my word-base broadened, I 17 could for the first time pick up a book and read and now begin to understand what the book was saying. Anyone who has read a great deal can imagine the new world that opened. Let me tell you something: from then until I left that prison, in every free moment I had, if I was not reading in the library, I was reading on my bunk. You couldn't have gotten me out of books with a wedge. Between Mr. Muhammad's teachings, my correspondence, my visitors . . . and my reading of books, months passed without my even thinking about being imprisoned. In fact, up to then, I never had been so truly free in my life.

RESPONDING TO READING

We are all to one degree or another prisoners of our own language. Sometimes we lack the ability to communicate as effectively as we would like.

Why do you think this happens, and what do you think can be done to remedy it? How can improved language skills also improve a person's life?

QUESTIONING THE TEXT

1. In paragraph 8, Malcolm X refers to the difference between being "articulate" and being "functional" in his speaking and writing. What is the distinction he makes? In your opinion, is it a valid one?

2. Malcolm X offers two possible reasons for the warden's keeping track of African American inmates' conversion to the teachings of Elijah Muhammad. What are those two assertions, and what is their effect on the reader?

3. What is the nature of the freedom that Malcolm X refers to in the final sentence? In what sense can language be said to be liberating?

UNDERSTANDING THE WRITER'S CRAFT

1. Malcolm X narrates his experiences as a prisoner using the first-person *I*. Why is the first person particularly appropriate? What would be lost or gained had he narrated his story using the third-person pronoun *he?*

2. In the opening paragraph, Malcolm X refers to himself as a man of action and conviction. What details does he include to support this assertion?

3. Many people think of "vocabulary building" as learning strange, multisyllabic, difficult-to-spell words. But acquiring an effective vocabulary does not have to be so intimidating. How would you characterize Malcolm X's vocabulary in this narrative? Did you find his word choice suited to what he was trying to accomplish in this selection?

4. What is Malcolm X's narrative point in this passage? How do you know? What does he learn about himself as a result of this experience?

EXPLORING LANGUAGE

1. Although Malcolm X taught himself to be articulate, we can still "hear" a street-savvy voice in his writing. Cite examples of his diction that convey a streetwise sound.

2. What do you do when you encounter new words in your reading? Do you skip those words as Malcolm X once did, do you take the time to look them up in the dictionary, or do you try to figure out their meanings from the context? Explain the strategies you use to determine the meaning of a word from its context. Can you think of other strategies?

3. Refer to a desk dictionary to determine the meanings of the following words as Malcolm X uses them in this selection: *hustler* (paragraph 2), *slick* (2), *hype* (3), *frustrated* (8), *emulate* (10), *riffling* (12), *inevitable* (17).

COMBINING RHETORICAL STRATEGIES

In reflecting on his years in prison, Malcolm X comes to an understanding of the events that caused him to reassess his life and take charge of his own education. Identify those events, and discuss the changes that resulted from Malcolm X's actions. How does his inclusion of these causal links enhance the overall narrative? (Glossary: *Cause and Effect Analysis*)

WRITING SUGGESTIONS

1. **(Narration)** Using Malcolm X's essay as a model, write a narrative about some goal you have set and achieved in which you were motivated by a strong inner conflict. What was the nature of your conflict? What feeling did it arouse in you, and how did the conflict help you to accomplish your goal?

2. **(Other Strategies)** Malcolm X solved the problems of his own near-illiteracy by carefully studying the dictionary. Would this be a practical solution to the national problem of illiteracy? In your experience, what does it mean to be literate? Write a proposal on what can be done to promote literacy in this country. You might also consider what is being done now in your community.

3. **(Research)** Some newspapers and magazines carry regular "vocabulary building" columns. Locate several vocabulary building columns in magazines and newspapers at your library. How do you react to them? Characterize the kinds of words introduced in these columns. What does the continuing popularity of these features suggest about our fascination with words? Write an essay in which you explain the value to you and your peers of columns such as the ones you find in the library.

4. **(Research)** There are a tremendous number of language resources on the Internet. Explore the Web; what other language Web sites can you find besides the ones listed below? Do you think the Internet is a good medium for building a stronger vocabulary? Why or why not? Write an essay about how people can use the library and the Internet to improve their language skills.

   - **Onelook Dictionaries: The Faster Finder**
     <http://www.onelook.com>

     This site indexes over 1.5 million words in 223 dictionaries and includes links to dozens of online dictionaries in a number of languages.

   - **The Onelook Dictionaries Extras Page**
     <http://www.onelook.com/more.shtml>

     This site provides links to further language resources on the Internet. It is a good place for you to start "enriching your word power!"

   - **The Human-Languages Page**
     <http://www.june29.com/HLP>

Designed to be a "comprehensive catalog of language-related Internet resources," this site offers over 1,800 links in the HLP database.

- **The Semantic Rhyming Dictionary**
  <http://www.rhymezone.com>

  An interesting Internet rhyming dictionary based on syllables and phonemes can be found here.

- **A Collection of Word Oddities and Trivia**
  <http://members.aol.com/gulfhigh2/words.html>

  This site offers fascinating facts about word usage, origins, and more.

- ***The Elements of Style* Online**
  <http://www.bartleby.com/141>

  Read William Strunk Jr.'s classic *The Elements of Style* online in its entirety at this site.

Getting Caught

Annie Dillard

*Born in Pittsburgh, Pennsylvania, in 1945, Annie Dillard has written in
many genres. Her first two books were both published in 1974, before she
was thirty years old; the first was a collection of poems entitled* Tickets
for a Prayer Wheel *and the second was* Pilgrim at Tinker Creek, *a
Pulitzer Prize–winning book of essays based on her observations of and
reflections about nature. She has explored the world of fiction, writing
books of criticism (*Living by Fiction, *1982, and* Encounters with Chinese Writers, *1984) and a novel (*The Living, *1992). Most recently, she
published a collection of essays* For the Time Being *(2000).*

*In one of her early essays, Dillard expressed a mistrust of memoirs,
saying, "I don't recommend, or even approve, writing personally. It can lead
to dreadful writing." By 1987, however, she had put this warning aside to
publish an autobiography,* An American Childhood, *from which this selection is taken. The book details Dillard's memories of her years growing
up in Pittsburgh and is filled with the wonder and joy of living. "Getting
Caught" (the editors' title) reflects the tone of the book as a whole.*

BEFORE YOU READ

What activity are you passionate about — an activity that makes
you give your all? A sport is a good example of a pursuit that demands and rewards total involvement, but you might also want to
consider other types of activities. What satisfactions result from
wholehearted participation in the activity of your choice?

Some boys taught me to play football. This was fine sport. You
thought up a new strategy for every play and whispered it to the
others. You went out for a pass, fooling everyone. Best, you got to
throw yourself mightily at someone's running legs. Either you brought
him down or you hit the ground flat out on your chin, with your arms
empty before you. It was all or nothing. If you hesitated in fear, you
would miss and get hurt: you would take a hard fall while the kid got
away, or you would get kicked in the face while the kid got away. But
if you flung yourself wholeheartedly at the back of his knees — if you
gathered and joined body and soul and pointed them diving fearlessly — then you likely wouldn't get hurt, and you'd stop the ball.
Your fate, and your team's score, depended on your concentration and
courage. Nothing girls did could compare with it.

Boys welcomed me at baseball, too, for I had, through enthusiastic
practice, what was weirdly known as a boy's arm. In winter, in the
snow, there was neither baseball nor football, so the boys and I threw

snowballs at passing cars. I got in trouble throwing snowballs, and have seldom been happier since.

On one weekday morning after Christmas, six inches of new snow had just fallen. We were standing up to our boot tops in snow on a front yard on trafficked Reynolds Street, waiting for cars. The cars traveled Reynolds Street slowly and evenly; they were targets all but wrapped in red ribbons, cream puffs. We couldn't miss.   3

I was seven; the boys were eight, nine, and ten. The oldest two Fahey boys were there — Mikey and Peter — polite blond boys who lived near me on Lloyd Street, and who already had four brothers and sisters. My parents approved Mikey and Peter Fahey. Chickie McBride was there, a tough kid, and Billy Paul and Mackie Kean too, from across Reynolds, where the boys grew up dark and furious, grew up skinny, knowing, and skilled. We had all drifted from our houses that morning looking for action, and had found it here on Reynolds Street.   4

It was cloudy but cold. The cars' tires laid behind them on the snowy street a complex trail of beige chunks like crenellated castle walls. I had stepped on some earlier; they squeaked. We could have wished for more traffic. When a car came, we all popped it one. In the intervals between cars we reverted to the natural solitude of children.   5

I started making an iceball — a perfect iceball, from perfectly white snow, perfectly spherical, and squeezed perfectly translucent so no snow remained all the way through. (The Fahey boys and I considered it unfair actually to throw an iceball at somebody, but it had been known to happen.)   6

I had just embarked on the iceball project when we heard tire chains come clanking from afar. A black Buick was moving toward us down the street. We all spread out, banged together some regular snowballs, took aim, and, when the Buick drew nigh, fired.   7

A soft snowball hit the driver's windshield right before the driver's face. It made a smashed star with a hump in the middle.   8

Often, of course, we hit our target, but this time, the only time in all of life, the car pulled over and stopped. Its wide black door opened; a man got out of it, running. He didn't even close the car door.   9

He ran after us, and we ran away from him, up the snowy Reynolds sidewalk. At the corner, I looked back; incredibly, he was still after us. He was in city clothes: a suit and tie, street shoes. Any normal adult would have quit, having sprung us into flight and made his point. This man was gaining on us. He was a thin man, all action. All of a sudden, we were running for our lives.   10

Wordless, we split up. We were on our turf; we could lose ourselves in the neighborhood backyards, everyone for himself. I paused and considered. Everyone had vanished except Mikey Fahey, who was just rounding the corner of a yellow brick house. Poor Mikey, I trailed   11 him. The driver of the Buick sensibly picked the two of us to follow. The man apparently had all day.

He chased Mikey and me around the yellow house and up a back- 12
yard path we knew by heart: under a low tree, up a bank, through a hedge, down some snowy steps, and across the grocery store's delivery driveway. We smashed through a gap in another hedge, entered a scruffy backyard and ran around its back porch and tight between houses to Edgerton Avenue; we ran across Edgerton to an alley and up our own sliding woodpile to the Halls' front yard; he kept coming. We ran up Lloyd Street and wound through mazy backyards toward the steep hilltop at Willard and Lang.

He chased us silently, block after block. He chased us silently over 13
picket fences, through thorny hedges, between houses, around garbage cans, and across streets. Every time I glanced back, choking for breath, I expected he would have quit. He must have been as breathless as we were. His jacket strained over his body. It was an immense discovery, pounding into my hot head with every sliding, joyous step, that this ordinary adult evidently knew what I thought only children who trained at football knew: that you have to fling yourself at what you're doing, you have to point yourself, forget yourself, aim, dive.

Mikey and I had nowhere to go, in our own neighborhood or out 14
of it, but away from this man who was chasing us. He impelled us forward; we compelled him to follow our route. The air was cold; every breath tore my throat. We kept running, block after block; we kept improvising, backyard after backyard, running a frantic course and choosing it simultaneously, failing always to find small places or hard places to slow him down, and discovering always, exhilarated, dismayed, that only bare speed could save us — for he would never give up, this man — and we were losing speed.

He chased us through the backyard labyrinths of ten blocks before 15
he caught us by our jackets. He caught us and we all stopped.

We three stood staggering, half blinded, coughing, in an obscure 16
hilltop backyard: a man in his twenties, a boy, a girl. He had released our jackets, our pursuer, our captor, our hero: he knew we weren't going anywhere. We all played by the rules. Mikey and I unzipped our jackets. I pulled off my sopping mittens. Our tracks multiplied in the backyard's new snow. We had been breaking new snow all morning. We didn't look at each other. I was cherishing my excitement. The man's lower pants legs were wet; his cuffs were full of snow, and there was a prow of snow beneath them on his shoes and socks. Some trees bordered the little flat backyard, some messy winter trees. There was no one around: a clearing in a grove, and we the only players.

It was a long time before he could speak. I had some difficulty at 17
first recalling why we were there. My lips felt swollen; I couldn't see out of the sides of my eyes; I kept coughing.

"You stupid kids," he began perfunctorily.   18

We listened perfunctorily indeed, if we listened at all, for the   19
chewing out was redundant, a mere formality, and beside the point.
The point was that he had chased us passionately without giving up,
and so he had caught us. Now he came down to earth. I wanted the
glory to last forever.

But how could the glory have lasted forever? We could have run   20
through every backyard in North America until we got to Panama. But
when he trapped us at the lip of the Panama Canal, what precisely
could he have done to prolong the drama of the chase and cap its
glory? I brooded about this for the next few years. He could only have
fried Mikey Fahey and me in boiling oil, say, or dismembered us piece-
meal, or staked us to anthills. None of which I really wanted, and
none of which any adult was likely to do, even in the spirit of fun. He
could only chew us out there in the Panamanian jungle, after months
or years of exalting pursuit. He could only begin, "You stupid kids,"
and continue in his ordinary Pittsburgh accent with his normal righ-
teous anger and the usual common sense.

If in that snowy backyard the driver of the black Buick had cut off   21
our heads, Mikey's and mine, I would have died happy, for nothing
has required so much of me since as being chased all over Pittsburgh
in the middle of winter — running terrified, exhausted — by this
sainted, skinny, furious red-headed man who wished to have a word
with us. I don't know how he found his way back to his car.

RESPONDING TO READING

As a child, did you ever do something exhilarating, satisfying, or fun even
though you knew that it was "wrong"? Compare your experience to
Dillard's. To what extent should children be held responsible for their delib-
erate misbehaviors? What would have been an appropriate consequence for
Dillard and her companions? If you had chased them down, what would
you have done?

QUESTIONING THE TEXT

1. In this essay, Dillard separates the behavior of boys from that of both
   girls and adults. What characteristics does she identify that distinguish
   the actions of boys? Why is she able to play with them?

2. What is Dillard's main point? Where does she state it explicitly?

3. Why was the driver "sensible" to choose Mikey and the author as the
   targets of his chase?

4. What made the chase so unusual and exciting? Why was the end of the
   chase disappointing? Was there any way it could have ended that
   would have been more satisfying to the author? Why or why not?

UNDERSTANDING THE WRITER'S CRAFT

1. In an unusual rhetorical strategy, Dillard opens her essay in the first person but immediately switches to second person. (Glossary: *Point of View*) What is her purpose for using two points of view, and especially for shifting from one to the other? In what ways does Dillard's use of the second-person point of view evoke childhood?

2. This narrative essay begins with two nonnarrative introductory paragraphs whose connection to the rest of the story may not be immediately apparent. Note especially the apparently paradoxical sentence that closes the introduction: "I got in trouble throwing snowballs, and have seldom been happier since." (Glossary: *Paradox*) How do these paragraphs, and particularly this sentence, help the reader understand the story that follows?

EXPLORING LANGUAGE

1. In paragraph 14, Dillard describes the chase using parallel word structures: "He impelled us forward; we compelled him to follow our route." In paragraph 16, find the parallel noun phrases that Dillard uses to characterize the young man who chased them. What is the impact on the reader of these parallel word structures? (Glossary: *Parallelism*) This essay contains numerous examples of parallelism; find several others that add to the impact you have identified.

2. Notice the use of strong verbs (*flung, popped, smashed*) throughout the narrative. How do strong verbs work to enhance a narrative?

3. Dillard uses a great deal of description in her narrative essay. Look up and define these words, vital to her descriptions, as she uses them: *crenellated* (paragraph 5), *reverted* (5), *turf* (11), *impelled* (14), *compelled* (14), *labyrinths* (15), *obscure* (16), *perfunctorily* (18, 19), *exalting* (20). How do these words contribute to the impact of the finished piece?

COMBINING RHETORICAL STRATEGIES

The event that prompted this narrative was in itself small and seemingly insignificant, but Dillard describes it with such intensity that the reader is left in no doubt as to its tremendous significance for her. Show how she uses carefully crafted description to lift her story from the ordinary to the remarkable. (Glossary: *Description*)

WRITING SUGGESTIONS

1. **(Narration)** Children know what it means to plunge headlong, fearlessly and eagerly, into a challenging situation. One of the most wonderful encounters a child can have is with an adult who is still able to summon up that childlike enthusiasm — one who can put aside grown-up ideas of respectability and caution in order to accomplish something. In this narrative, Dillard reveres a man who is willing to pursue his young

tormentors until he catches them. Recall and write about an enthusiastic adult — a parent, a relative, a teacher, a chance acquaintance — who abandoned grown-up behavior to inspire you as a child. In what way did he or she do so? As Annie Dillard does, make your story lively and detailed.

2. **(Other Strategies)** Consider the following cartoon by Barbara Smaller. What do you think Smaller is saying here? After reading "Getting Caught," how do you think Annie Dillard would respond to Smaller's cartoon? Explain. Now review what you wrote in Responding to Reading. How accountable should children be for their misconduct or lack of performance? Using Smaller's cartoon, Dillard's essay, and your own experience, write an essay in which you look at the question of holding people responsible for their actions. Your essay could take the form of an argument in which you take a definite position or a narrative in which you tell the story of a childhood punishment that you received or witnessed. If you choose to narrate a childhood experience, be sure to be clear about your response to the punishment: Was it justified? Appropriate? Effective? Why or why not? It might be useful to trade stories with classmates and discuss the issues that arise before you start writing.

3. **(Research)** When Annie Dillard was a child, it was more unusual for girls to participate in athletic programs in schools and universities. This all changed in 1972 with the passage of Title IX, which legislated equal funding of school athletics for males and females. Since then, the involvement of girls and women in sports has grown tremendously. What

"What do I think is an appropriate punishment? I think an appropriate punishment would be to make me live with my guilt."

kind of impact have competitive sports had on the lives of female athletes? Interview some female athletes and their coaches about the effects of sports on the lives of girls and women. You might also consider doing research in the library and on the Internet to find out more about women in sports. Write an essay to present your findings; be sure to include appropriate quotations and examples.

- **Gender Equity in Sports Page**
  <http://www.bailiwick.lib.uiowa.edu/ge>

  This Web site, maintained at the University of Iowa, offers copious coverage of Title IX and other gender-related sports issues.

- **Just SPORTS for Women**
  <http://www.sportsforwomen.com/contents/index.html>

  This online resource for women in sports includes features on all-star female athletes, the latest headlines and stats on professional and Olympic women's sports, and a chatroom.

- **Title IX Library from the *Brown Daily Herald***
  <http://www.netspace.org/herald/library/titleix/homepage.html>

  This site offers articles and coverage of a Title IX dispute at Brown University that attained national prominence.

- **Women and Girls in Sports**
  <http://www.feminist.org/gateway/sp_exec2.html>

  Maintained by the Feminist Majority Foundation, this site lists Internet sources related to the topic of women's sports.

Stranger Than True

Barry Winston

Barry Winston is a practicing attorney in Chapel Hill, North Carolina. He was born in New York City in March 1934 and graduated from the University of North Carolina, from which he also received his law degree. His specialty is criminal law.

"Stranger Than True" was published in Harper's *magazine in December 1986. In the story, Winston recounts his experience defending a young college graduate accused of driving while under the influence of alcohol and causing his sister's death. The story is characterized by Winston's energetic and strong voice. In commenting on his use of narrative detail, Winston says, "I could have made it twice as long, but it wouldn't have been as good a story."*

BEFORE YOU READ

The American judicial system works on the basis of the presumption of innocence. In short, you are innocent until proven guilty. But what about a situation in which all the evidence seems to point to a person's guilt? What's the purpose of a trial in such a case?

Let me tell you a story. A true story. The court records are all there if anyone wants to check. It's three years ago. I'm sitting in my office, staring out the window, when I get a call from a lawyer I hardly know. Tax lawyer. Some kid is in trouble and would I be interested in helping him out? He's charged with manslaughter, a felony, and driving under the influence. I tell him sure, have the kid call me.

So the kid calls and makes an appointment to see me. He's a nice kid, fresh out of college, and he's come down here to spend some time with his older sister, who's in med school. One day she tells him they're invited to a cookout with some friends of hers. She's going directly from class and he's going to take her car and meet her there. It's way out in the country, but he gets there before she does, introduces himself around, and pops a beer. She shows up after a while and he pops another beer. Then he eats a hamburger and drinks a third beer. At some point his sister says, "Well, it's about time to go," and they head for the car.

And, the kid tells me, sitting there in my office, the next thing he remembers, he's waking up in a hospital room, hurting like hell, bandages and casts all over him, and somebody is telling him he's charged with manslaughter and DUI because he wrecked his sister's car, killed her in the process, and blew fourteen on the Breathalyzer. I ask him what the hell he means by "the next thing he remembers," and he looks me straight in the eye and says he can't remember anything from the time they leave the cookout until he wakes up in the hospital. He tells me the doctors say he has post-retrograde amnesia. I say of course I believe him, but I'm worried about finding a judge who'll believe him.

I agree to represent him and send somebody for a copy of the wreck report. It says there are four witnesses: a couple in a car going the other way who passed the kid and his sister just before their car ran off the road, the guy whose front yard they landed in, and the trooper who investigated. I call the guy whose yard they ended up in. He isn't home. I leave word. Then I call the couple. The wife agrees to come in the next day with her husband. While I'm talking to her, the first guy calls. I call him back, introduce myself, tell him I'm representing the kid and need to talk to him about the accident. He hems and haws and I figure he's one of those people who think it's against the law to talk to defense lawyers. I say the D.A. will tell him it's O.K. to talk to me, but he doesn't have to. I give him the name and number of the D.A. and he says he'll call me back.

Then I go out and hunt up the trooper. He tells me the whole story. The kid and his sister are coming into town on Smith Level Road, after it turns from fifty-five to forty-five. The Thornes — the couple — are heading out of town. They say this sports car passes them, going the other way, right after that bad turn just south of the new subdivision. They say it's going like a striped-ass ape, at least sixty-five or seventy. Mrs. Thorne turns around to look and Mr. Thorne watches in the rearview mirror. They both see the same thing: halfway into the curve, the car runs off the road on the right, whips back onto the road, spins, runs off on the left, and disappears. They turn around in the first driveway they come to and start back, both terrified of what they're going to find. By this time, Trooper Johnson says, the guy whose front yard the car has ended up in has pulled the kid and his sister out of the wreck and started CPR on the girl. Turns out he's an emergency medical technician. Holloway, that's his name. Johnson tells me that Holloway says he's sitting in his front room, watching television, when he hears a hell of a crash in his yard. He runs outside and finds the car flipped over, and so he pulls the kid out from the driver's side, the girl from the other side. She dies in his arms.

And that, says Trooper Johnson, is that. The kid's blood/alcohol content was fourteen, he was going way too fast, *and* the girl is dead. He had to charge him. It's a shame, he seems a nice kid, it was his own sister and all, but what the hell can he do, right?

The next day the Thornes come in, and they confirm everything Johnson said. By now things are looking not so hot for my client, and

I'm thinking it's about time to have a little chat with the D.A. But Holloway still hasn't called me back, so I call him. Not home. Leave word. No call. I wait a couple of days and call again. Finally I get him on the phone. He's very agitated, and won't talk to me except to say that he doesn't have to talk to me.

I know I better look for a deal, so I go to the D.A. He's very sympa-   8
thetic. But. There's only so far you can get on sympathy. A young woman is dead, promising career cut short, all because somebody has too much to drink and drives. The kid has to pay. Not, the D.A. says, with jail time. But he's got to plead guilty to two misdemeanors: death by vehicle and driving under the influence. That means probation, a big fine. Several thousand dollars. Still, it's hard for me to criticize the D.A. After all, he's probably going to have the MADD mothers all over him because of reducing the felony to a misdemeanor.

On the day of the trial, I get to court a few minutes early. There   9
are the Thornes and Trooper Johnson, and someone I assume is Holloway. Sure enough, when this guy sees me, he comes over and in- troduces himself and starts right in: "I just want you to know how se- rious all this drinking and driving really is," he says. "If those young people hadn't been drinking and driving that night, that poor young girl would be alive today." Now, I'm trying to hold my temper when I spot the D.A. I bolt across the room, grab him by the arm, and say, "We gotta talk. Why the hell have you got all those people here? That jerk Holloway. Surely to God you're not going to call him as a witness. This is a guilty plea! My client's parents are sitting out there. You don't need to put them through a dog-and-pony show."

The D.A. looks at me and says, "Man, I'm sorry, but in a case like   10
this, I gotta put on witnesses. Weird Wally is on the bench. If I try to go without witnesses, he might throw me out."

The D.A. calls his first witness. Trooper Johnson identifies himself,   11
tells about being called to the scene of the accident, and describes what he found when he got there and what everybody told him. After he finishes, the judge looks at me. "No questions," I say. Then the D.A. calls Holloway. He describes the noise, running out of the house, the upside-down car in his yard, pulling my client out of the window on the left side of the car and then going around to the other side for the girl. When he gets to this part, he really hits his stride. He de- scribes, in minute detail, the injuries he saw and what he did to try and save her life. And then he tells, breath by breath, how she died in his arms.

The D.A. says, "No further questions, your Honor." The judge   12
looks at me. I shake my head, and he says to Holloway, "You may step down."

One of those awful silences hangs there, and nothing happens for   13
a minute. Holloway doesn't move. Then he looks at me, and at the

D.A., and then at the judge. He says, "Can I say something else, your Honor?"

All my bells are ringing at once, and my gut is screaming at me, Object! Object! I'm trying to decide in three quarters of a second whether it'll be worse to listen to a lecture on the evils of drink from this jerk Holloway or piss off the judge by objecting. But all I say is, "No objections, your Honor." The judge smiles at me, then at Holloway, and says, "Very well, Mr. Holloway. What did you wish to say?" 14

It all comes out in a rush. "Well, you see, your Honor," Holloway says, "it was just like I told Trooper Johnson. It all happened so fast. I heard the noise, and I came running out, and it was night, and I was excited, and the next morning, when I had a chance to think about it, I figured out what had happened, but by then I'd already told Trooper Johnson and I didn't know what to do, but you see, the car, it was up-side down, and I did pull that boy out of the left-hand window, but don't you see, the car was upside down, and if you turned it over on its wheels like it's supposed to be, the left-hand side is really on the right-hand side, and your Honor, that boy wasn't driving that car at all. It was the girl that was driving, and when I had a chance to think about it the next morning, I realized that I'd told Trooper Johnson wrong, and I was scared and I didn't know what to do, and that's why" — and now he's looking right at me — "why I wouldn't talk to you." 15

Naturally, the defendant is allowed to withdraw his guilty plea. The charges are dismissed and the kid and his parents and I go into one of the back rooms in the courthouse and sit there looking at one another for a while. Finally, we recover enough to mumble some Oh my Gods and Thank yous and You're welcomes. And that's why I can stand to represent somebody when I know he's guilty. 16

RESPONDING TO READING

Much abuse is heaped on lawyers who defend clients whose guilt seems obvious. How does Winston's story help explain why lawyers need to defend "guilty" clients?

QUESTIONING THE TEXT

1. Why does the D.A. bring in witnesses for a case that has been plea-bargained? What is ironic about that decision? (Glossary: *Irony*)

2. Why was Holloway reluctant to be interviewed by Winston about what he saw and did in the aftermath of the accident? What might he have been afraid of?

3. Why did Holloway finally ask to speak to the court? Why do you suppose Winston chose not to object to Holloway's request?

4. What do you think is the point of Winston's narrative?

UNDERSTANDING THE WRITER'S CRAFT

1. Winston establishes the context for his story in the first three paragraphs. What basic information does he give readers?

2. What details does Winston choose to include in the story? Why does he include them? Is there other information that you would like to have had? Why do you suppose Winston chose to omit that information?

3. Explain how Winston uses sentence variety to pace his narrative. What effect do his short sentences and sentence fragments have on you?

4. What does Winston gain as a writer by telling us that this is "a true story," one that we can check out in the court records?

5. During the courtroom scene (paragraphs 9–15), Winston relies heavily on dialogue. What does he gain by using dialogue? Why do you suppose he uses dialogue sparingly in the other parts of his narrative? (Glossary: *Dialogue*)

EXPLORING LANGUAGE

1. How would you characterize Winston's voice in this story? How is that voice established?

2. What, if anything, does Winston's diction tell you about Winston himself? What effect does his diction have on the tone of his narrative? (Glossary: *Tone*)

3. Refer to your desk dictionary to determine the meanings of the following words as Winston uses them in this selection: *felony* (paragraph 1), *agitated* (7), *misdemeanor* (8), *probation* (8), *bolt* (9).

COMBINING RHETORICAL STRATEGIES

How does Winston use description to differentiate the four witnesses to the accident? Why is it important for him to give his readers some idea of their differing characters? (Glossary: *Description*)

WRITING SUGGESTIONS

1. **(Narration)** "Stranger Than True" is a first-person narrative told from the defense lawyer's point of view. Imagine that you are a newspaper reporter covering this case. What changes would you have to make in Winston's narrative to make it a news story? Make a list of the changes you would have to make, and then rewrite the story.

2. **(Other Strategies)** Holloway's revelation in the courtroom catches everyone by surprise. Analyze the chain of events in the accident and the assumptions that people made based on the accounts of those events. Write a cause and effect essay in which you explain some of the possible reasons why Holloway's confession is so unexpected.

3. **(Research)** Winston's purpose here is to tell a story and not to report on the investigation he himself undertook on the accident. Assume that you were the defense lawyer. How would you go about researching the facts in this case? Whom would you interview? What questions would you want answers to? How might you use the Internet to help you with your research? Write an essay explaining the strategy you would use to get at the truth.

- **Finding Law-Related Internet Resources**
  <http://www.llrx.com/sources.html>

  This site contains a thorough index for legal information.

- **The WWW Virtual Library: Law**
  <http://www.law.indiana.edu/law/v-lib>

  This Web site offers legal information grouped by organization type as well as by topic and provides links to other law sites.

- **The National Association of Criminal Defense Lawyers Home Page**
  <http://www.criminaljustice.org/public.nsf/freeform/publicwelcome?opendocument>

  This Web site offers information for defense attorneys.

Salvation

Langston Hughes

*Born in Joplin, Missouri, Langston Hughes (1902–1967) wrote poetry,
fiction, and drama and regularly contributed a column to the* New York
Post. *Although he began writing poetry at an early age, he was unable to
get his work published; he supported himself by traveling around the
country, doing whatever work he could find. While working as a busboy,
he was discovered by Vachel Lindsay, a famous poet of the Harlem Renaissance. Through his novels, plays, and a popular series of newspaper
sketches, Hughes explored common themes of African American life and
became a key figure in the Harlem Renaissance. Hughes is best known for*
Weary Blues *(1926),* Ask Your Mama *(1961), and* The Negro Mother
*(1971), collections of poetry that reflect his deep understanding of
African American traditions and his incorporation of jazz rhythms into
poetry.*

In this selection, taken from his autobiography, The Big Sea *(1940),
Hughes narrates his unsettling experiences at a church revival meeting he
attended when he was twelve years old.*

BEFORE YOU READ

Write about a time in your life when outside pressures forced you
to do something you didn't want to do. You might consider pressure you felt from family members, friends, or peers. How did you
feel about the situation? What could you have done differently? Or
maybe the action you took turned out to be for the best.

I was saved from sin when I was going on thirteen. But not really   1
saved. It happened like this. There was a big revival at my Auntie
Reed's church. Every night for weeks there had been much preaching,
singing, praying, and shouting, and some very hardened sinners had
been brought to Christ, and the membership of the church had grown
by leaps and bounds. Then just before the revival ended, they held a
special meeting for children, "to bring the young lambs to the fold."
My aunt spoke of it for days ahead. That night I was escorted to the
front row and placed on the mourners' bench with all the other young
sinners, who had not yet been brought to Jesus.

My aunt told me that when you were saved you saw a light, and   2
something happened to you inside! And Jesus came into your life!
And God was with you from then on! She said you could see and hear
and feel Jesus in your soul. I believed her. I have heard a great many
old people say the same thing and it seemed to me they ought to

know. So I sat there calmly in the hot, crowded church, waiting for Jesus to come to me.

The preacher preached a wonderful rhythmical sermon, all moans   3
and shouts and lonely cries and dire pictures of hell, and then he sang a song about the ninety and nine safe in the fold, but one little lamb was left out in the cold. Then he said: "Won't you come? Won't you come to Jesus? Young lambs, won't you come?" And he held out his arms to all us young sinners there on the mourners' bench. And the little girls cried. And some of them jumped up and went to Jesus right away. But most of us just sat there.

A great many old people came and knelt around us and prayed,   4
old women with jet-black faces and braided hair, old men with work-gnarled hands. And the church sang a song about the lower lights are burning, some poor sinners to be saved. And the whole building rocked with prayer and song.

Still I kept waiting to *see* Jesus.   5

Finally all the young people had gone to the altar and were saved,   6
but one boy and me. He was a rounder's son named Westley. Westley and I were surrounded by sisters and deacons praying. It was very hot in the church, and getting late now. Finally Westley said to me in a whisper: "God damn! I'm tired o' sitting here. Let's get up and be saved." So he got up and was saved.

Then I was left all alone on the mourners' bench. My aunt came   7
and knelt at my knees and cried, while prayers and songs swirled all around me in the little church. The whole congregation prayed for me alone, in a mighty wail of moans and voices. And I kept waiting serenely for Jesus, waiting, waiting — but he didn't come. I wanted to see him, but nothing happened to me. Nothing! I wanted something to happen to me, but nothing happened.

I heard the songs and the minister saying: "Why don't you come?   8
My dear child, why don't you come to Jesus? Jesus is waiting for you. He wants you. Why don't you come? Sister Reed, what is this child's name?"

"Langston," my aunt sobbed.   9

"Langston, why don't you come? Why don't you come and be   10
saved? Oh, Lamb of God! Why don't you come?"

Now it was really getting late. I began to be ashamed of myself,   11
holding everything up so long. I began to wonder what God thought about Westley, who certainly hadn't seen Jesus either, but who was now sitting proudly on the platform, swinging his knickerbockered legs and grinning down at me, surrounded by deacons and old women on their knees praying. God had not struck Westley dead for taking his name in vain or for lying in the temple. So I decided that maybe to save further trouble, I'd better lie, too, and say that Jesus had come, and get up and be saved.

So I got up.   12

Suddenly the whole room broke into a sea of shouting, as they   13
saw me rise. Waves of rejoicing swept the place. Women leaped in the
air. My aunt threw her arms around me. The minister took me by the
hand and led me to the platform.

When things quieted down, in a hushed silence, punctuated by a   14
few ecstatic "Amens," all the new young lambs were blessed in the
name of God. Then joyous singing filled the room.

That night, for the last time in my life but one — for I was a big boy   15
twelve years old — I cried. I cried, in bed alone, and couldn't stop. I
buried my head under the quilts, but my aunt heard me. She woke up
and told my uncle I was crying because the Holy Ghost had come into
my life, and because I had seen Jesus. But I was really crying because I
couldn't bear to tell her that I had lied, that I had deceived everybody in
the church, that I hadn't seen Jesus, and that now I didn't believe there
was a Jesus any more, since he didn't come to help me.

RESPONDING TO READING

In this story, Hughes misunderstood the meaning of the word *see* in a religious context. Why do you think he misunderstood the word? Have you
ever had an experience in which you really didn't "see"?

QUESTIONING THE TEXT

1. Why does the young Langston expect to be saved at the revival meeting? Once the children are in church, what appeals are made to them to
   encourage them to seek salvation?

2. Trace the various pressures working on Hughes that lead to his decision
   to "get up and be saved" (paragraph 11). What realization finally convinces him to lie about being saved?

3. Even though Hughes's account of the events at the revival is at points
   humorous, the experience was nonetheless painful for him. Why does
   he cry on the night of his "salvation"? Why does his aunt think he is
   crying? Why does Hughes no longer believe in Jesus?

UNDERSTANDING THE WRITER'S CRAFT

1. What paradox or apparent contradiction does Hughes present in the
   first two sentences of the narrative? Why do you think he uses this device? (Glossary: *Paradox*)

2. Hughes consciously varies the structure and length of his sentences to
   create different effects. What effect does he create through the short
   sentences in paragraphs 2 and 3? What is the effect of the long sentence

that concludes the final paragraph? Throughout the selection, how do the short, one-sentence paragraphs aid the author in telling his story?

3. Although Hughes tells most of the story himself, he allows Auntie Reed, the minister, and Westley to speak for themselves. What does Hughes gain by including his characters' dialogue?

EXPLORING LANGUAGE

1. How does Hughes's word choice help establish a realistic atmosphere for a religious revival meeting? Does he use any traditional religious figures of speech? If so, identify them. (Glossary: *Figures of Speech*)

2. Why does Hughes italicize the word *see* in paragraph 5? What do you think he means by *see*? What do you think his aunt means by *see* (2)? Explain your answer.

3. Refer to your desk dictionary to determine the meanings of the following words as Hughes uses them in this selection: *dire* (paragraph 3), *gnarled* (4), *vain* (11), *punctuated* (14), *ecstatic* (14).

COMBINING RHETORICAL STRATEGIES

Explain how Hughes uses comparison and contrast to differentiate between the people who "see" Jesus and the young Langston himself, who does not. (Glossary: *Comparison and Contrast*)

WRITING SUGGESTIONS

1. **(Narration)** Like the young Langston Hughes, we sometimes find ourselves in situations in which, for the sake of conformity, we say or do things we do not believe in. Consider one such experience you have had. What is it about human nature that makes us occasionally act in ways that contradict our inner feelings? Write an essay in which you explore your experience through narration.

2. **(Other Strategies)** In Hughes's essay, the reader gets the impression that the young Langston is stifled by his surroundings. Reflect on an environment in which you have felt stifled. Write an essay that explains the causes of your discomfort. Include ways you tried to deal with this difficult situation.

3. **(Research)** Any narrative requires that the writer gather information about a particular incident from his or her own experience or from other reliable sources. Interview a member of your class; obtain enough information to write a brief narrative about a significant, influential, or life-shaping spiritual event in that person's life. You might also consider researching similar experiences in your library, or perhaps on the Internet, to add detail to your understanding of the event or to find out more information on how people think about spirituality. Write your narrative from the third-person point of view.

- **Religion and Philosophy Resources on the Internet**
  <http://www.bu.edu/sth/library>

  This comprehensive Web site is maintained by the Boston University School of Theology Library.

- **Religion/Religions/Religious Studies**
  <http://www.clas.ufl.edu/users/gthursby/rel>

  This site offers information and links for the study and interpretation of religions.

- **The WWW Virtual Library: Philosophy**
  <http://www.bris.ac.uk/Depts/Philosophy/VL>

  This site offers links to resources on all aspects of philosophy.

-

COMBINING SUBJECTS AND STRATEGIES

The photograph below depicts many of the same themes and strategies as the Combining Rhetorical Strategies essay that follows on the next page. Your observations about the photograph will help guide you to the key themes and strategies in the essay. After you've read the essay, you may use your observations about both the photograph and the essay to examine how the overlapping themes and strategies work in each medium.

Any time the police are called in to investigate a crime scene, settle a domestic argument, calm an unruly crowd, or arrest a criminal suspect, they are on stage. Their actions can be captured by a local citizen armed with a camcorder or by a television or newspaper cameraman. While on assignment in Austin, Texas, photographer Bob Daemmrich captured local police officers arresting and handcuffing a suspect.

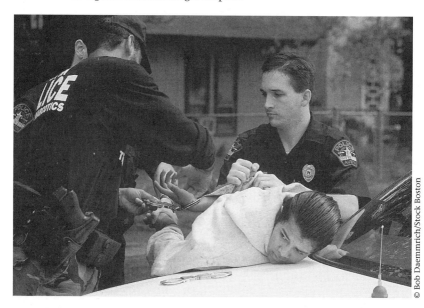

© Bob Daemmrich/Stock Boston

For Discussion

What do you see happening in this photograph? What story has the photographer captured? Whose story is being told, and how do you know? For you, what are the most telling details in the picture? Explain. Who is the leader? What emotions do you "read" on the face of the other police officer?

Shooting an Elephant

George Orwell

George Orwell (1903–1950) was capable of capturing the reader's imagination as few writers have ever done. Born in Bengal, India, but raised and educated in England, he chose to work as a civil servant in the British colonies after his schooling and was sent to Burma at nineteen as an assistant superintendent of police. Disillusioned by his firsthand experiences of public life under British colonial rule, he resigned in 1929 and returned to England to begin a career in writing. He captured the exotic mystery of life in the colonies, along with its many injustices and ironies, in such works as Down and Out in Paris and London *(1933) and* The Road to Wigan Pier *(1937). His most famous books are, of course,* Animal Farm *(1945), a satire on the Russian Revolution, and* 1984 *(1949), a chilling novel set in an imagined totalitarian state of the future. Orwell maintained a lifelong interest in international social and political issues.*

"Shooting an Elephant" was published in the British magazine New Writing *in 1936. Adolf Hitler, Benito Mussolini, and Joseph Stalin were in power, building the "younger empires" that Orwell refers to in the second paragraph, and the old British Empire was soon to decline, as Orwell predicted. In this essay, Orwell tells of a time when, in a position of authority, he found himself compelled to act against his convictions.*

BEFORE YOU READ

Have you ever acted against your better judgment to save face with your friends or relatives? What motivated you to take the action that you did, and what did you learn from the experience?

In Moulmein, in Lower Burma, I was hated by large numbers of people — the only time in my life that I have been important enough for this to happen to me. I was subdivisional police officer of the town, and in an aimless, petty kind of way anti-European feeling was very bitter. No one had the guts to raise a riot, but if a European woman went through the bazaars alone somebody would probably spit betel juice* over her dress. As a police officer I was an obvious target and was baited whenever it seemed safe to do so. When a nimble Burman tripped me up on the football field and the referee (another Burman) looked the other way, the crowd yelled with hideous laughter. This happened more than once. In the end the sneering yellow

1

---

*The juice of an Asiatic plant whose leaves are chewed to induce narcotic effects. (Ed.)

faces of young men that met me everywhere, the insults hooted after me when I was at a safe distance, got badly on my nerves. The young Buddhist priests were the worst of all. There were several thousands of them in the town and none of them seemed to have anything to do except stand on street corners and jeer at Europeans.

All this was perplexing and upsetting. For at that time I had already made up my mind that imperialism was an evil thing and the sooner I chucked up my job and got out of it the better. Theoretically — and secretly, of course — I was all for the Burmese and all against the oppressors, the British. As for the job I was doing, I hated it more bitterly than I can perhaps make clear. In a job like that you see the dirty work of Empire at close quarters. The wretched prisoners huddling in the stinking cages of the lockups, the grey, cowed faces of the long-term convicts, the scarred buttocks of the men who had been flogged with bamboos — all these oppressed me with an intolerable sense of guilt. But I could get nothing into perspective. I was young and ill-educated and I had had to think out my problems in the utter silence that is imposed on every Englishman in the East. I did not even know that the British Empire is dying, still less did I know that it is a great deal better than the younger empires that are going to supplant it. All I knew was that I was stuck between my hatred of the empire I served and my rage against the evil-spirited little beasts who tried to make my job impossible. With one part of my mind I thought of the British Raj* as an unbreakable tyranny, as something clamped down, in *saecula saeculorum,*** upon the will of prostrate peoples; with another part I thought that the greatest joy in the world would be to drive a bayonet into a Buddhist priest's guts. Feelings like these are the normal by-products of imperialism; ask any anglo-Indian official, if you can catch him off duty.

One day something happened which in a roundabout way was enlightening. It was a tiny incident in itself, but it gave me a better glimpse than I had had before of the real nature of imperialism — the real motives for which despotic governments act. Early one morning the subinspector at a police station the other end of town rang me up on the phone and said that an elephant was ravaging the bazaar. Would I please come and do something about it? I did not know what I could do, but I wanted to see what was happening and I got on to a pony and started out. I took my rifle, an old .44 Winchester and much too small to kill an elephant, but I thought the noise might be useful *in terrorem.* Various Burmans stopped me on the way and told me about the elephant's doings. It was not, of course, a wild elephant, but

---

*British rule, especially in India. (Ed.)
**From time immemorial. (Ed.)

a tame one which had gone "must."* It had been chained up, as tame elephants always are when their attack of "must" is due, but on the previous night it had broken its chain and escaped. Its mahout,** the only person who could manage it when it was in that state, had set out in pursuit, but had taken the wrong direction and was now twelve hours' journey away, and in the morning the elephant had suddenly reappeared in the town. The Burmese population had no weapons and were quite helpless against it. It had already destroyed somebody's bamboo hut, killed a cow and raided some fruit stalls and devoured the stock; also it had met the municipal rubbish van and, when the driver jumped out and took to his heels, had turned the van over and inflicted violences upon it.

The Burmese subinspector and some Indian constables were wait- 4
ing for me in the quarter where the elephant had been seen. It was a very poor quarter, a labyrinth of squalid bamboo huts, thatched with palmleaf, winding all over a steep hillside. I remember that it was a cloudy, stuffy morning at the beginning of the rains. We began questioning the people as to where the elephant had gone and, as usual, failed to get any definite information. That is invariably the case in the East; a story always sounds clear enough at a distance, but the nearer you get to the scene of events the vaguer it becomes. Some of the people said that the elephant had gone in one direction, some said that he had gone in another, some professed not even to have heard of any elephant. I had almost made up my mind that the whole story was a pack of lies, when we heard yells a little distance away. There was a loud, scandalized cry of "Go away, child! Go away this instant!" and an old woman with a switch in her hand came round the corner of a hut, violently shooing away a crowd of naked children. Some more women followed, clicking their tongues and exclaiming; evidently there was something that the children ought not to have seen. I rounded the hut and saw a man's dead body sprawling in the mud. He was an Indian, a black Dravidian coolie,*** almost naked, and he could not have been dead many minutes. The people said that the elephant had come suddenly upon him round the corner of the hut, caught him with its trunk, put its foot on his back and ground him into the earth. This was the rainy season and the ground was soft, and his face had scored a trench a foot deep and a couple of yards long. He was lying on his belly with arms crucified and head sharply twisted to one side. His face was coated with mud, the eyes wide open, the teeth bared and grinning with an expression of unendurable agony. (Never

---

*That is, gone into an uncontrollable frenzy. (Ed.)
**The keeper and driver of an elephant. (Ed.)
***An unskilled laborer. (Ed.)

tell me, by the way, that the dead look peaceful. Most of the corpses I have seen looked devilish.) The friction of the great beast's foot had stripped the skin from his back as neatly as one skins a rabbit. As soon as I saw the dead man I sent an orderly to a friend's house nearby to borrow an elephant rifle. I had already sent back the pony, not wanting it to go mad with fright and throw me if it smelled the elephant.

The orderly came back in a few minutes with a rifle and five cartridges, and meanwhile some Burmans had arrived and told us that the elephant was in the paddy fields below, only a few hundred yards away. As I started forward practically the whole population of the quarter flocked out of the houses and followed me. They had seen the rifle and were all shouting excitedly that I was going to shoot the elephant. They had not shown much interest in the elephant when he was merely ravaging their homes, but it was different now that he was going to be shot. It was a bit of fun to them, as it would be to an English crowd; besides they wanted the meat. It made me vaguely uneasy. I had no intention of shooting the elephant — I had merely sent for the rifle to defend myself if necessary — and it is always unnerving to have a crowd following you. I marched down the hill, looking and feeling a fool, with the rifle over my shoulder and an ever-growing army of people jostling at my heels. At the bottom, when you got away from the huts, there was a metalled road* and beyond that a miry waste of paddy fields a thousand yards across, not yet ploughed but soggy from the first rains and dotted with coarse grass. The elephant was standing eight yards from the road, his left side towards us. He took not the slightest notice of the crowd's approach. He was tearing up bunches of grass, beating them against his knees to clean them and stuffing them into his mouth. 5

I had halted on the road. As soon as I saw the elephant I knew with perfect certainty that I ought not to shoot him. It is a serious matter to shoot a working elephant — it is comparable to destroying a huge and costly piece of machinery — and obviously one ought not to do it if it can possibly be avoided. And at that distance, peacefully eating, the elephant looked no more dangerous than a cow. I thought then and I think now that his attack of "must" was already passing off; in which case he would merely wander harmlessly about until the mahout came back and caught him. Moreover, I did not in the least want to shoot him. I decided that I would watch him for a little while to make sure that he did not turn savage again, and then go home. 6

But at that moment, I glanced round at the crowd that had followed me. It was an immense crowd, two thousand at the least and growing 7

---

*A road made of broken or crushed stone. (Ed.)

every minute. It blocked the road for a long distance on either side. I looked at the sea of yellow faces above the garish clothes — faces all happy and excited over this bit of fun, all certain that the elephant was going to be shot. They were watching me as they would watch a conjuror about to perform a trick. They did not like me, but with the magical rifle in my hands I was momentarily worth watching. And suddenly I realized that I should have to shoot the elephant after all. The people expected it of me and I had got to do it; I could feel their two thousand wills pressing me forward, irresistibly. And it was at this moment, as I stood there with the rifle in my hands, that I first grasped the hollowness, the futility of the white man's dominion in the East. Here was I, the white man with his gun, standing in front of the unarmed native crowd — seemingly the leading actor of the piece; but in reality I was only an absurd puppet pushed to and fro by the will of those yellow faces behind. I perceived in this moment that when the white man turns tyrant it is his own freedom that he destroys. He becomes a sort of hollow, posing dummy, the conventionalized figure of a sahib.* For it is the condition of his rule that he shall spend his life in trying to impress the "natives," and so in every crisis he has got to do what the "natives" expect of him. He wears a mask, and his face grows to fit it. I had got to shoot the elephant. I had committed myself to doing it when I sent for the rifle. A sahib has got to act like a sahib; he has got to appear resolute, to know his own mind and do definite things. To come all that way, rifle in hand, with two thousand people marching at my heels, and then to trail feebly away, having done nothing — no, that was impossible. The crowd would laugh at me. And my whole life, every white man's life in the East, was one long struggle not to be laughed at.

But I did not want to shoot the elephant. I watched him beating his bunch of grass against his knees, with that preoccupied grandmotherly air that elephants have. It seemed to me that it would be murder to shoot him. At that age I was not squeamish about killing animals, but I had never shot an elephant and never wanted to. (Somehow it always seems worse to kill a *large* animal.) Besides, there was the beast's owner to be considered. Alive, the elephant was worth at least a hundred pounds; dead, he would only be worth the value of his tusks, five pounds, possibly. But I had got to act quickly. I turned to some experienced-looking Burmans who had been there when we arrived, and asked them how the elephant had been behaving. They all said the same thing: He took no notice of you if you left him alone, but he might charge if you went too close to him.

8

---

*A title of respect when addressing Europeans in colonial India. (Ed.)

It was perfectly clear to me what I ought to do. I ought to walk up 9 to within, say, twenty-five yards of the elephant and test his behavior. If he charged, I could shoot; if he took no notice of me, it would be safe to leave him until the mahout came back. But also I knew that I was going to do no such thing. I was a poor shot with a rifle and the ground was soft mud into which one would sink at every step. If the elephant charged and I missed him, I should have about as much chance as a toad under a steamroller. But even then I was not thinking particularly of my own skin, only of the watchful yellow faces behind. For at that moment, with the crowd watching me, I was not afraid in the ordinary sense, as I would have been if I had been alone. A white man mustn't be frightened in front of "natives"; and so, in general, he isn't frightened. The sole thought in my mind was that if anything went wrong those two thousand Burmans would see me pursued, caught, trampled on, and reduced to a grinning corpse like that Indian up the hill. And if that happened it was quite probable that some of them would laugh. That would never do. There was only one alternative. I shoved the cartridges into the magazine and lay down on the road to get a better aim.

The crowd grew very still, and a deep, low, happy sigh, as of 10 people who see the theater curtain go up at last, breathed from innumerable throats. They were going to have their bit of fun after all. The rifle was a beautiful German thing with cross-hair sights. I did not then know that in shooting an elephant one would shoot to cut an imaginary bar running from ear-hole to ear-hole. I ought, therefore, as the elephant was sideways on, to have aimed straight at his ear-hole; actually I aimed several inches in front of this, thinking the brain would be further forward.

When I pulled the trigger I did not hear the bang or feel the kick — 11 one never does when a shot goes home — but I heard the devilish roar of glee that went up from the crowd. In that instant, in too short a time, one would have thought, even for the bullet to get there, a mysterious, terrible change had come over the elephant. He neither stirred nor fell, but every line of his body had altered. He looked suddenly stricken, shrunken, immensely old, as though the frightful impact of the bullet had paralyzed him without knocking him down. At last, after what seemed a long time — it might have been five seconds, I dare say — he sagged flabbily to his knees. His mouth slobbered. An enormous senility seemed to have settled upon him. One could have imagined him thousands of years old. I fired again into the same spot. At the second shot he did not collapse but climbed with desperate slowness to his feet and stood weakly upright, with legs sagging and head drooping. I fired a third time. That was the shot that did for him. You could see the agony of it jolt his whole body and knock the last remnant of strength from his legs. But in falling he seemed for a moment to rise, for as his hind legs collapsed beneath him he seemed to tower upward like a huge rock toppling, his trunk reaching skywards like a tree. He trumpeted, for the first and only time. And then down he came, his belly towards me, with a crash that seemed to shake the ground even where I lay.

I got up. The Burmans were already racing past me across the mud. It was obvious that the elephant would never rise again, but he was not dead. He was breathing very rhythmically with long rattling gasps, his great mound of a side painfully rising and falling. His mouth was wide open. I could see far down into caverns of pale pink throat. I waited a long time for him to die, but his breathing did not weaken. Finally I fired my two remaining shots into the spot where I thought his heart must be. The thick blood welled out of him like red velvet, but still he did not die. His body did not even jerk when the shots hit him, the tortured breathing continued without a pause. He was dying, very slowly and in great agony, but in some world remote from me where not even a bullet could damage him further. I felt I had got to put an end to that dreadful noise. It seemed dreadful to see the great beast lying there, powerless to move and yet powerless to die, and not even to be able to finish him. I sent back for my small rifle and poured shot after shot into his heart and down his throat. They seemed to make no impression. The tortured gasps continued as steadily as the ticking of a clock.

In the end I could not stand it any longer and went away. I heard later that it took him half an hour to die. Burmans were bringing dahs* and baskets even before I left, and I was told they had stripped his body almost to the bones by the afternoon.

Afterwards, of course, there were endless discussions about the shooting of the elephant. The owner was furious, but he was only an Indian and could do nothing. Besides, legally I had done the right thing, for a mad elephant has to be killed, like a mad dog, if its owner fails to control it. Among the Europeans opinion was divided. The older men said I was right, the younger men said it was a damn shame to shoot an elephant for killing a coolie, because the elephant was worth more than any damn Coringhee coolie. And afterwards I was very glad that the coolie had been killed; it put me legally in the right and it gave me sufficient pretext for shooting the elephant. I often wondered whether any of the others grasped that I had done it solely to avoid looking a fool.

---

*Heavy knives. (Ed.)

RESPONDING TO READING

Even though Orwell does not want to shoot the elephant, he does. How does he rationalize his behavior? On what grounds was Orwell legally in the right? What alternatives did he have? What do you think Orwell learned from this incident?

QUESTIONING THE TEXT

1. What do you suppose would have happened had Orwell not sent for an elephant rifle?

2. What is imperialism, and what discovery about imperialism does Orwell make during the course of the event he narrates?

3. What does Orwell mean when he says, "I was very glad that the coolie had been killed" (paragraph 14)?

4. What is the point of Orwell's final paragraph? How does that paragraph affect your response to the whole essay?

UNDERSTANDING THE WRITER'S CRAFT

1. Why do you think Orwell is so meticulous in establishing the setting for his essay in paragraphs 1 and 2?

2. What do you think was Orwell's purpose in telling this story? Cite evidence from the text that indicates to you that purpose. Does he accomplish his purpose in your opinion? (Glossary: *Purpose*)

3. Orwell is quick to capitalize on the ironies of the circumstances of the events he narrates. Identify any circumstances you found ironic, and explain what this irony contributes to Orwell's overall purpose. (Glossary: *Irony*)

4. What part of the essay struck you most strongly? The shooting itself? Orwell's feelings? The descriptions of the Burmans and their behavior? What is it about Orwell's prose that enhances the impact of that passage for you? Explain.

5. Orwell wrote "Shooting an Elephant" some years after the event occurred. What does his account of the event gain with the passage of time? Explain.

EXPLORING LANGUAGE

1. A British citizen, Orwell uses British English. Cite several examples of this British diction. How might an American say the same thing?

2. Identify several of the metaphors and similes that Orwell uses, and explain what each adds to his descriptions in this essay. (Glossary: *Figures of Speech*)

3. Orwell advocates using strong action verbs because they are vivid and eliminate unnecessary modification. For example, in paragraph 1 he uses the verb *jeer* instead of the verb *yell* plus the adverb *derisively*. Identify other strong verbs that you found particularly striking. What do these strong verbs add to Orwell's prose style?

4. Orwell chooses words with precision to bring an extraordinary scene to life. Refer to your dictionary to determine the meanings of the following words as Orwell uses them in this selection: *baited* (paragraph 1), *intolerable* (2), *supplant* (2), *tyranny* (2), *despotic* (3), *ravaging* (3), *labyrinth* (4), *squalid* (4), *miry* (5), *garish* (7), *squeamish* (8), *devilish* (11), *senility* (11).

COMBINING RHETORICAL STRATEGIES

"Shooting an Elephant" is, first of all, a narrative; Orwell has a story to tell. But Orwell uses other strategies in support of narration to help develop and give meaning to his story. Identify passages in which Orwell uses description, exemplification, and cause and effect analysis, and explain how each enhances the incident he narrates.

WRITING SUGGESTIONS

1. **(Narration)** Write an essay in which you recount a situation in which you felt compelled to act against your convictions. Before you start writing, you may find it helpful to consider one or more of the following questions and to review what you wrote in response to the Before You Read section for this essay. How can you justify your action? How much freedom of choice did you actually have, and what were the limits on your freedom? On what basis can you refuse to subordinate your convictions to others' or to society's?

2. **(Other Strategies)** Consider situations in which you have been a leader, like Orwell or the narcotics policeman securing the handcuffs in the photograph at the beginning of this essay, or part of a crowd, like the Burmans or the other officer in the photograph. As a leader, what was your attitude toward your followers? As a follower, what did you feel toward your leader? Using Orwell's essay, Bob Daemmrich's photograph, and your own experiences, what conclusions can you draw about leaders and followers? Write an essay in which you explore the relationship between leaders and followers.

3. **(Research)** Hardly a week goes by that some government official, community leader, or businessperson does not make the local or national news for some face-saving action. Collect and analyze several examples of public leaders caught in the act of covering for themselves. What, in your opinion, is the real story in each case? How successful was each person in his or her attempts to save face? What is your opinion of these people now that you understand what they have been up to? Explain.

- **Capitol Hill Blue**

<http://www.capitolhillblue.com/home.pl>

This site features breaking political news and commentary about the people and politics of Capitol Hill.

- **The Skeleton Closet**

<http://www.realchange.org>

Maintained by Real People for Real Change, "an independent, nonpartisan political group," this site contains extensive information on scandals and politicians' ethical missteps. Links to similar sites are also included.

- **The Drudge Report**

<http://www.drudgereport.com>

This site, maintained by reporter Matt Drudge, broke the Clinton/Lewinsky story. With links to major U.S. and British newspapers and columnists' sites, this is a compendium of pop culture scandal and controversy.

- **Mr. Show Biz: Celebrities**

<http://www.mrshowbiz.go.com/celebrities/index.html>

This site offers short bios and links to recent news stories about actors, writers, musicians, athletes, and TV personalities.

Snow (FICTION)

Julia Alvarez

Julia Alvarez was born in New York City in 1950, but soon after her birth, her family moved to the Dominican Republic, where she spent the first ten years of her childhood. Her return to the United States in 1960 brought her into contact with a new language and a culture steeped in the anxieties of the cold war.

Alvarez, who teaches creative writing at Middlebury College, is the author of poetry, essays, short fiction, and autobiographical novels, including How the García Girls Lost Their Accents *(1992) and* In the Time of the Butterflies *(1994). More recently, she wrote* Yo! *(1997) and* In the Name of Salome *(2000), two novels;* Something to Declare *(1998), a collection of autobiographical essays; and* The Secret Footprints *(2000), a children's story.*

"Snow" was published in a collection of pieces by various authors on the Nuclear Age. Its tone of fear and anxiety may seem strange to readers of typical college age today, but such memories are very familiar to anyone who grew up in the America of the late 1950s and early 1960s, when the threat of nuclear war prompted Americans to build backyard bomb shelters and stage community air-raid drills.

BEFORE YOU READ

Whether you called it the bogeyman, the monster under the bed, or the thing in the closet, classic childhood fear takes many forms. What warnings or threats from adults really scared you when you were a child? Describe them, tell why they were so frightening, and show how you responded.

O ur first year in New York we rented a small apartment with a Catholic school nearby, taught by the Sisters of Charity, hefty women in long black gowns and bonnets that made them look peculiar, like dolls in mourning. I liked them a lot, especially my grandmotherly fourth grade teacher, Sister Zoe. I had a lovely name, she said, and she had me teach the whole class how to pronounce it. *Yo-lan-da.* As the only immigrant in my class, I was put in a special seat in the first row by the window, apart from the other children so that Sister Zoe could tutor me without disturbing them. Slowly, she enunciated the new words I was to repeat: *laundromat, cornflakes, subway, snow.*

Soon I picked up enough English to understand holocaust was in the air. Sister Zoe explained to a wide-eyed classroom what was happening in Cuba. Russian missiles were being assembled, trained supposedly on New York City. President Kennedy, looking worried too, was on the television at home, explaining we might have to go to war against the Communists. At school, we had air-raid drills: an ominous bell would go off and we'd file into the hall, fall to the floor, cover our heads with our coats, and imagine our hair falling out, the bones in our arms going soft. At home, Mami and my sisters and I said a rosary for world peace. I heard new vocabulary: *nuclear bomb, radioactive fallout, bomb shelter.* Sister Zoe explained how it would happen. She drew a picture of a mushroom on the blackboard and dotted a flurry of chalkmarks for the dusty fallout that would kill us all.

The months grew cold, November, December. It was dark when I 3 got up in the morning, frosty when I followed my breath to school. One morning as I sat at my desk daydreaming out the window, I saw dots in the air like the ones Sister Zoe had drawn — random at first, then lots and lots. I shrieked, "Bomb! Bomb!" Sister Zoe jerked around, her full black skirt ballooning as she hurried to my side. A few girls began to cry.

But then Sister Zoe's shocked look faded. "Why, Yolanda dear, 4 that's snow!" She laughed. "Snow."

"Snow," I repeated. I looked out the window warily. All my life I 5 had heard about the white crystals that fell out of American skies in the winter. From my desk I watched the fine powder dust the sidewalk and parked cars below. Each flake was different, Sister Zoe said, like a person, irreplaceable and beautiful.

RESPONDING TO READING

In the person of Sister Zoe, Alvarez depicts a teacher who truly cares about her young students, but one whose benevolence bears sinister overtones. The reader first gets a hint of this early in the story, starting with the description of the Sisters of Charity as "dolls in mourning" (paragraph 1). In what other subtle ways does Alvarez portray Sister Zoe as a herald or personification of death?

QUESTIONING THE TEXT

1. Why was Yolanda seated by the window, apart from the others in her class?

2. What does Alvarez mean by the phrase in paragraph 2, "holocaust was in the air"? Explain how the phrase "in the air" is particularly apt for the purposes of this story.

3. What is the significance of the story's final sentence? How does it relate to the central theme?

UNDERSTANDING THE WRITER'S CRAFT

1. In literature, snow is often used as a metaphor for death because it is cold and can be a symbol for barren winter. (Glossary: *Figures of Speech*) Show how this implied metaphor serves to underscore the author's message about the threat of nuclear war. In the final paragraph, snow becomes a metaphor for something else; what does it represent at the end of the essay?

2. This very short narrative touches on more than one issue important to the American culture of the early 1960s. Try to identify these issues. Which of these issues are presented directly, and which are presented indirectly? How does Alvarez pack so much content into five paragraphs?

EXPLORING LANGUAGE

1. Note the words *dusty* (paragraph 2) and *dust* (5). How do they relate to and differ from each other? What distinction does Alvarez make through this difference?

2. Contrast the vocabulary Yolanda was learning from Sister Zoe in paragraph 1 (*laundromat, cornflakes, subway, snow*) with the vocabulary words in paragraph 2 (*nuclear bomb, radioactive fallout, bomb shelter*). Sister Zoe must have taught her many new words; why do you think Alvarez chose these particular words for the first and second lists?

3. The vocabulary of this short piece is generally simple and direct. Be sure you know the meaning of each of the following words: *enunciated* (paragraph 1), *holocaust* (2), *fallout* (2), *flurry* (2), *random* (3), *warily* (5).

COMBINING RHETORICAL STRATEGIES

In commenting on how she chose to write "Snow," Alvarez said, "Rather than becoming polemical or railing against nuclear weapons, I thought I might best 'prove' the destructiveness of nuclear weapons if I showed how a simple, poignant, and 'natural' moment becomes in this nuclear age a moment of possible holocaust for a child." How did Alvarez turn a straightforward narrative of an event into a powerful argument? Besides narration, what other rhetorical strategies does she use?

WRITING SUGGESTIONS

1. **(Narration)** "Snow" is a very short narrative; the details have been selected carefully to support Alvarez's theme, and much that might have been said is left out. Recall a moment in your life when something happened to make you sharply aware that every person is "irreplaceable and beautiful." Briefly write the story of that moment, being sure that each detail is important. To do this, look for any details that might be distracting, and leave them out, thereby distilling your story.

2. **(Other Strategies)** Attempts are now being made to reduce the number of nuclear weapons worldwide. Should the United States continue to stockpile nuclear weapons? Why or why not? Write a paper to argue your point of view. (You may want to do some research to support your opinions.)

3. **(Research)** The cold war held the United States in the grip of fear for years, especially in the late 1950s and early 1960s. In the library, look for some directives published during those years detailing how to construct and equip a backyard bomb shelter or how to behave during an air raid. You might also consider interviewing a parent, grandparent, or other person who has firsthand memories of this time period. Were these directives expressions of wisdom or of paranoia? Bring your findings together in a brief essay. You might also consider doing research in the library as well as on the Internet and writing about the difficult task of worldwide nuclear disarmament in our post–cold war era, especially as more nations, such as India and Pakistan, demonstrate nuclear capabilities.

- **Trinity Atomic Web Site**
  <http://www.envirolink.org/issues/nuketesting>

  This site offers copious information on all aspects of nuclear weapons.

- **Federation of American Scientists**
  <http://www.fas.org/nwp>

  A "Cooperative Research Program on Nuclear Non-Proliferation and Disarmament" is described here.

- **Coalition to Reduce Nuclear Dangers**
  <http://www.clw.org/pub/clw/coalition/index.html>

  This is the Web site for a coalition of organizations devoted to nuclear disarmament.

- **United Nations Institute for Disarmament Research (UNIDIR)**
  <http://www.unog.ch/UNIDIR>

  UNIDIR is an autonomous institution within the framework of the United Nations devoted to disarmament and related problems.

- **The Bulletin of the Atomic Scientists**
  <www.bullatomsci.org>

  This Web site reports on "international security, military affairs, and social issues."

WRITING SUGGESTIONS FOR NARRATION

1. Using Malcolm X's essay as a model, narrate an experience that gave you a new awareness of yourself. Use enough telling detail in your narrative to help your reader visualize your experience and understand its significance for you. You may find the following suggestions helpful in choosing an experience to narrate in the first person:

   a. my greatest success
   b. my biggest failure
   c. my most embarrassing moment
   d. my happiest moment
   e. a truly frightening experience
   f. an experience that, in my eyes, turned a hero or idol into an ordinary person
   g. an experience that turned an ordinary person I know into one of my heroes
   h. the experience that was the most important turning point in my life

2. Each of us can tell of an experience that has been unusually significant in teaching us about our relationship to society or to life's institutions — schools, social or service organizations, religious groups, government. Think about your past, and identify one experience that has been especially important for you in this way. After you have considered this event's significance, write an essay recounting it. In preparing to write your narrative, review Langston Hughes's experience at a revival meeting in his essay "Salvation" and George Orwell's account of acting against his better judgment in Burma in "Shooting an Elephant," as well as your journal responses to both essays. To bring your experience into focus and to help you decide what to include in your essay, ask yourself, Why is this experience important to me? What details are necessary for me to re-create the experience in an interesting and engaging way? How can my narrative be most effectively organized? What point of view will work best?

3. As a way of gaining experience with third-person narration, write an article intended for your school or community newspaper in which you report on what happened at one of the following:

   a. the visit of a state or national figure to your campus or community
   b. a dormitory meeting
   c. a current event of local, state, or national significance
   d. an important sports event
   e. a current research project of one of your professors
   f. a campus gathering or performance
   g. an important development at a local business or at your own place of employment

4. Imagine that you are a member of a campus organization that is seeking volunteers for a community project. Your job is to write a piece for the

school newspaper to solicit help for your organization. To build support for the project, narrate one or more stories about the rewards of lending a hand to others within the community.

5. Many people love to tell stories (that is, they use narration!) to illustrate an abstract point, to bring an idea down to a personal level, or to render an idea memorable. Often, the telling of such stories can be entertaining as well as instructive. Think about a belief or position that you hold dear (for example: every individual deserves respect, recycling matters, voluntarism creates community, people need artistic outlets, nature renews the individual), and try to capture that belief in a sentence or two. Then, narrate a story that illustrates your thesis. Before you start writing, you may want to read Christine Mitchell's essay "When Living Is a Fate Worse Than Death" in Chapter 13. Consider how she uses narration to illustrate her belief in maintaining the dignity of terminally ill patients.

6. Like Annie Dillard in "Getting Caught," we have all done something we know we should not have done. Sometimes we have gotten away with our transgressions, sometimes not. Sometimes our actions have no repercussions; sometimes they have very serious ones. Tell the story of one of your escapades, and explain why you have remembered it so well.

7. Sometimes a personal story can be set against or interwoven with events that are similar but of greater magnitude, perhaps national or global in their scope. For example, in the novel *The War between the Tates*, Alison Lurie tells the story of the breakup of a marriage. She sets the story against the backdrop of the Vietnam War in such a way as to impart valuable insights into both events. Julia Alvarez takes a similar approach in "Snow" when she sets the story of a child's first encounter with snow against the highly charged atmosphere of the Cuban missile crisis. Select an event that you are familiar with (a disagreement, a reconciliation, a breakdown in communication, the unraveling of trust), and write an essay in which you tell the story against the backdrop of a national news event (a war, a peace accord, a breakdown in negotiations, a border skirmish) so that each event affects the way the reader views the other. Concentrate on the details and dynamics of each retelling, as well as on the best way to interweave the events, so as to show that the global often mirrors the personal and vice versa.

CHAPTER 8

Process Analysis

WHAT IS PROCESS ANALYSIS?

A process is a series of actions or stages that follow one another in a specific order and that lead to a particular end. People have invented many processes, like assembling pickup trucks or making bread; others occur naturally, like the erosion of a coastline or the development of a fetus in its mother's womb. All are processes because, if each step occurs correctly and in the right order, the results will be predictable: A completed pickup will roll off the assembly line, or a healthy baby will be born. Process analysis essays involve separating an event, an operation, or a cycle of development into distinct steps, describing each step precisely, and arranging the steps in their proper order.

Whenever you explain how something occurs or how it can (and should) be done — how plants create oxygen, how to make ice cream, or merely how to get to your house — you are using process analysis. Each year, thousands of books and magazine articles tell us how to make home repairs, how to lose weight and get physically fit, how to improve our memories, how to play better tennis, how to manage our money. They try to satisfy our curiosity about how television shows are made, how jet planes work, and how monkeys, bees, or whales mate. People simply want to know how things work and how to do things for themselves, so it's not surprising that process analysis is one of the most widespread and popular forms of writing today.

Process analysis resembles narration because both strategies present a series of events occurring over time. But a narration is the story of how things happened in a particular way during one particular period of time; process analysis relates how things always happen — or always should happen — in essentially the same way time after time.

Here is a process analysis written by Bernard Gladstone to explain how to light a fire in a fireplace.

Writer tells us this will be an explanation of a method for building a fire in a fireplace

Though "experts" differ as to the best technique to follow when building a fire, one generally accepted method consists of first laying a generous amount of crumpled newspaper on the hearth between the andirons. Kindling wood is then spread generously over this layer of newspaper and one of the thickest logs is placed across the back of the andirons. This should be as close to the back of the fireplace as possible, but not quite touching it. A second log is then placed an inch or so in front of this, and a few additional sticks of kindling are laid across these two. A third log is then placed on top to form a sort of pyramid with air space between all logs so that flames can lick freely up between them.

In one paragraph the writer takes us through six steps: the result is a wood-and-paper structure.

The next three paragraphs present three common mistakes.

A mistake frequently made is in building the fire too far forward so that the rear wall of the fireplace does not get properly heated. A heated back wall helps increase the draft and tends to suck smoke and flames rearward with less chance of sparks or smoke spurting out into the room.

Another common mistake often made by the inexperienced fire-tender is to try to build a fire with only one or two logs, instead of using at least three. A single log is difficult to ignite properly, and even two logs do not provide an efficient bed with adequate fuel burning capacity.

Writer reinforces his direction by telling us what not to do.

Use of too many logs, on the other hand, is also a common fault and can prove hazardous. Building too big a fire can create more smoke and draft than the chimney can safely handle, increasing the possibility of sparks or smoke being thrown out into the room. For best results, the homeowner should start with three medium-sized logs as described above, then add additional logs as needed if the fire is to be kept burning.

WHY DO WRITERS USE PROCESS ANALYSIS?

There are essentially two major reasons for writing a process analysis: to give directions, known as *directional process analysis*, and to inform, known as *informational process analysis*. Writers often combine one of these reasons with other rhetorical strategies to evaluate the process in question; this is known as *evaluative process analysis*. Let's take a look at each of these forms of process analysis more closely.

Directional Process Analysis

Writers use directional process analysis to provide readers with the necessary steps to achieve a desired result. The directions may be as simple as the instructions on a frozen-food package ("Heat in microwave on high for 6–8 minutes. Rotate ¼ turn halfway through cooking time, stir, and serve") or as complex as the operator's manual for a personal computer. In his student essay on juggling, William Peterson takes us through the process of learning how to juggle one step at a time. Mortimer Adler proposes a method for getting the most out of reading in his essay "How to Mark a Book." First he compares what he sees as "the two ways one can own a book" and classifies book lovers into three categories. Then he presents his directions for how one should make marginal comments to get the most out of a book. In his "How to Say Nothing in 500 Words," Paul Roberts lays out the steps by which a writer can turn a dull subject into a lively, interesting one. No matter their length or complexity, however, all directions have the same purpose: to guide the reader through a clear and logically ordered series of steps toward a particular goal.

Informational Process Analysis

This strategy deals not with processes that readers are able to perform for themselves, but with processes that readers are curious about or would like to understand better: how presidents are elected, how plants reproduce, how an elevator works, how the brain processes and generates language. In "Inside the Engine," Tom and Ray Magliozzi (the hosts of the nationally syndicated radio show *Car Talk*), use simple, straightforward language to break down a process that is baffling to most of us, even those of us who own and drive cars every day: how oil works inside a car engine. In the following selection from his *Lives Around Us*, Alan Devoe explains what happens to an animal when it goes into hibernation.

> The woodchuck's hibernation usually starts about the middle of September. For weeks he has been foraging with increased appetite among the clover blossoms and has grown heavy and slow-moving. Now, with the coming of mid-September, apples and corn and yarrow tops have become less plentiful, and the nights are cool. The woodchuck moves with slower gait, and emerges less and less frequently for feeding trips. Layers of fat have accumulated around his chest and shoulders, and there is thick fat in the axils of his legs. He has extended his summer burrow to a length of nearly thirty feet, and has fashioned a deep nest-chamber at the end of it, far below the level of the frost. He has carried in, usually, a little hay. He is ready for the Long Sleep.

When the temperature of the September days falls below 50 degrees or so, the woodchuck becomes too drowsy to come forth from his burrow in the chilly dusk to forage. He remains in the deep nest-chamber, lethargic, hardly moving. Gradually, with the passing of hours or days, his coarse-furred body curls into a semicircle, like a fetus, nose-tip touching tail. The small legs are tucked in, the hand-like clawed forefeet folded. The woodchuck has become a compact ball. Presently the temperature of his body begins to fall.

In normal life the woodchuck's temperature, though fluctuant, averages about 97 degrees. Now, as he lies tight-curled in a ball with the winter sleep stealing over him, this body heat drops ten degrees, twenty degrees, thirty. Finally, by the time the snow is on the ground and the woodchuck's winter dormancy has become complete, his temperature is only 38 or 40. With the falling of the body heat there is a slowing of his heartbeat and his respiration. In normal life he breathes thirty or forty times each minute; when he is excited, as many as a hundred times. Now he breathes slower and slower: ten times a minute, five times a minute, once a minute, and at last only ten or twelve times in an hour. His heartbeat is a twentieth of normal. He has entered fully into the oblivion of hibernation.

The process Devoe describes is natural to woodchucks but not to humans, so obviously he cannot be giving instructions. Rather, he has created an informational process analysis to help us understand what happens during the remarkable process of hibernation. As Devoe's analysis reveals, hibernation is not a series of well-defined steps but a long, slow change from the activity of late summer to the immobility of a deep winter's sleep. The woodchuck does not suddenly stop feeding, nor do his temperature, pulse, and rate of respiration plummet at once. Using a transitional expression and time markers, Devoe shows us that the process lasts for weeks, even months. He connects the progress of hibernation with changes in the weather because the woodchuck's body responds to the dropping temperature as autumn sets in rather than to the passage of specific periods of time.

Evaluative Process Analysis

People often want to understand processes in order to evaluate them — to make improvements in how things are done, to better understand how events occur — and usually to improve those processes or to profit from their increased understanding. They want to improve processes by making them simpler, quicker, safer, or more efficient. They may also wish to analyze processes to understand them more deeply or accurately in order to base subsequent actions on more reliable information. An evaluative process analysis might give the reader insight into the writer's thinking about the pros and cons, the pitfalls, and the rewards of altering a widely understood and accepted process. In other words, an evaluative process analysis may offer a reconsideration of our understanding of a known process. If we look at Paul Roberts's "How to Say Nothing in 500 Words," we see that throughout the essay he describes an ineffective writing process used by some students and then compares and contrasts it with a more effective process. The evaluative function of process analysis is also evident in Lars Eighner's "On Dumpster Diving," wherein he continually assesses his scavenging strategies as a homeless person on his way to making a provocative point in his final three paragraphs about the values of the rich, the poor, and those in between — the "millions who have confounded their selves with the objects they grasp." Here, process and argument are intimately connected. Whether used to direct, inform, or evaluate, process analysis is an invaluable critical thinking skill.

AN ANNOTATED STUDENT ESSAY USING PROCESS ANALYSIS

Bill Peterson grew up in New Hartford, New York. After completing a business major at the University of Vermont, he entered the music business and now works as a booking agent. He had extensive experience organizing campus concerts for his university's student association. Peterson is also an avid juggler, and he enjoys teaching others the craft. In "I Bet You Can," he shares with us, step-by-step, the basics of how to juggle. Try it.

I Bet You Can

William Peterson

Introduction invites reader to learn how to juggle.

Have you ever seen Michael Davis on television? He's a standup comic and a juggler. His antics got me interested in learning how to juggle. Several years ago after watching his act on "Saturday Night Live" I went out to my garage and started to experiment with some tennis balls. At first I felt helpless after tossing and chasing the balls for what seemed like countless hours. However, I actually did start to learn how to juggle. To my surprise I discovered that juggling is much easier than it had at first

1

Transition

appeared. If you'd like to learn how to juggle, I recommend that you find some tennis balls or lacrosse balls and continue reading.

First step in process: the simple toss

Step one is the simple toss. Stand erect and hold one ball in your right hand. Carefully toss the ball up to approximately an inch above your head and to about half an arm's length in front of you. The ball should arch from your right hand across to your left. This step should now be repeated, starting with your left hand and tossing to your right. Be sure that the ball reaches the same height and distance from you and is not simply passed from your left hand to

2

Recommendation to practice first step until perfected

your right. Keep tossing the ball back and forth until you have become thoroughly disgusted with this step. If you have practiced this toss enough, we can now call this step

Labeling of step one as "the perfect toss"

"the perfect toss." If it is not quite perfect, then you have not become disgusted enough with the step. We'll assume that

Transition

you've perfected it. Now you're ready to take a little breather and move on.

Second step in process: the toss and return

Step two is the toss and return. Get back on your feet and this time hold a ball in each hand. Take a deep breath and make a perfect toss with the ball in your right hand. As that ball reaches its peak make another perfect toss with the ball in your left hand. The second ball should end up passing under the first one and reaching approximately the same height. When the second ball peaks, you should be grabbing -- or already have grabbed, depending on timing -- the first ball. The second ball should then gently drop into your awaiting right hand. If it was not that easy, then don't worry about the "gently" bit. Most people do not

3

Emphasis on need to practice step two

achieve perfection at first. Step two is the key factor in becoming a good juggler and should be practiced at least five times as much as step one.

4

Helpful suggestion

Don't deceive yourself after a few successful completions. This maneuver really must be perfected before step three can be approached. As a way to improve dexterity, you should try several tosses and returns starting with your left hand. Let's call step two "the exchange." You're now ready for another well-deserved breather before you proceed.

Labeling of step two as "the exchange"

5

Third step in process: addition of third ball

Ready or not, here it goes. Step three is merely a continuum of "the exchange" with the addition of a third ball. Don't worry if you are confused -- I will explain. Get back up again, and now hold two balls in your right hand and one in your left. Make a perfect toss with one of the balls in your right hand and then an exchange with the one in your left hand. The ball coming from your left hand should now be exchanged with the, as of now, unused ball in your right hand. This process should be continued until you find yourself reaching under nearby chairs for bouncing tennis balls. It is true that many persons' backs and legs become sore when learning how to juggle because they've been picking up balls that they've inadvertently tossed around the room. Try practicing over a bed; you won't have to reach down so far. Don't get too upset if things aren't going well; you're probably keeping the same pace as everyone else at this stage. You're certainly doing better than I was because you've had me as a teacher.

6

Transitional paragraph

Don't worry, this teacher is not going to leave you stranded with hours of repetition of the basic steps. I am sure that you have already run into some basic problems. I will now try to relate some of my beginner's troubles and some of the best solutions you can try for them.

7

Problem one, you are getting nowhere after the simple toss. This requires a basic

Discussion of
problem one and
solutions

improvement of hand to eye coordination. Solution one is to just go back and practice
the simple toss again and again. Unfortunately, this becomes quite boring. Solution
two is not as tedious and involves quite a
bit of skill. Try juggling two balls in one
hand. Some people show me this when I ask
them if they can juggle -- they're not fooling anyone. Real juggling is what you're
here to learn. First try circular juggling
in one hand. This involves tosses similar to
"the perfect toss." They differ in that the
balls go half as far towards the opposite
hand, are tossed and grabbed by the same
hand, and end up making their own circles
(as opposed to going up and down in upside
down V's like exchanges). Then try juggling
the balls in the same line style. I think
this is harder. You have to keep two balls
traveling in their own vertical paths (the
balls should go as high as they do in a
"perfect toss") with only one hand. I think
this is harder than the circular style because my hands normally tend to make little
circles when I juggle.

Problem two, you can make exchanges but 8
you just can't accomplish step three. The

Discussion of
problem two and
solution

best solution to this is to just continue
practicing step two, but now add a twist. As
soon as the first ball is caught by the left
hand in our step two, throw it back up in
another perfect toss for another exchange.
Continue this and increase speed up to the
point where two balls just don't seem like
enough. You should now be ready to add the
third ball and accomplish what you couldn't
before -- real Michael Davis kind of juggling.

Problem three, you have become the 9
"runaway juggler." This means you can suc-

*Discussion of
problem three and
solutions*

cessfully achieve numerous exchanges but you're always chasing after balls tossed too far in front of you. The first solution is to stand in front of a wall. This causes you to end up catching a couple of balls bouncing off the wall or else you'll end up consciously keeping your tosses in closer to your body. The second solution is to put your back up against a wall. This will tend to make you toss in closer to yourself because you will be restricted to keeping your back up against the wall. This solution can work, but more often than not you'll find yourself watching balls fly across the room in front of you! I've told you about the back-on-the-wall method because some people find it effective. As you can tell, I don't.

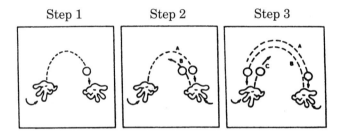

| Step 1 | Step 2 | Step 3 |

*Conclusion with
visual presentation
of three-step
process*

Juggling is a simple three-step process. Following my routine is the easiest way to get from being a spastic ball chaser to an accomplished juggler. Patience and coordination are really not required. The only requirements are a few tennis balls, the ability to follow some basic instructions, and the time to have some fun.

10

Analyzing William Peterson's Essay of Process Analysis:
Questions for Discussion

1. Peterson uses personal experience as a basis for his essay. How do his experiences learning to juggle help the reader, who is presumably playing the role of novice juggler?

2. Successful juggling depends on successfully tying together a series of basic steps, so the transitions in the above essay are extremely important. Identify what Peterson does to create smooth transitions between the steps, which are presented in a series of paragraphs.

3. Peterson presents the whole process of learning to juggle before presenting common problems. Why does he address the problems after the fact? How does the organization help his readers reach their goal?

SUGGESTIONS FOR WRITING A PROCESS ANALYSIS ESSAY

In a process analysis, always aim for precision and clarity. Few things are more frustrating to readers of directions than an unclear, misplaced, or omitted step that prevents them from achieving the results the writer has promised. The same sort of error in an informational process analysis will cause misunderstanding and confusion. Whatever your purpose, process analysis requires a systematic, logical approach.

Know the Process You Are Writing About

There's no substitute for thorough knowledge of your subject. Be sure that you have more than a vague or general grasp of the process you are writing about. Make sure you analyze it fully, from beginning to end. You can sometimes convince yourself that you understand an entire process when, in fact, your understanding is somewhat superficial. If you were analyzing the process by which children learn language, you wouldn't want to rely on only one expert's account. Instead, it would be a good idea to read explanations by several authorities on the subject. Turning to more than one account not only reinforces your understanding of key points in the process, but also points out various ways the process is performed; you may want to consider these alternatives in your writing.

Have a Clear Purpose

Giving directions for administering cardiopulmonary resuscitation and explaining how the El Niño phenomenon unfolds are worthy purposes for writing a process analysis paper. Many process analysis papers go beyond these fundamental purposes, however. They lay out processes to evaluate them, to suggest alternative steps, to point out shortcomings in our generally accepted practices, and to suggest improvements. Nikki Giovanni uses process analysis in "Campus Racism 101" to show how and why minority students should go about seizing the opportunity for a good education in predominantly white institutions. In short, process analysis papers are frequently persuasive or argumentative; they use an understanding and discussion of process analysis to achieve another goal: to persuade readers that there is a better way of doing or understanding a given process.

Divide the Process into Steps

As much as possible, make each step a simple and well-defined action, preferably a single action. To guide yourself in doing so, write a scratch outline listing the steps. Here, for example, is an outline of Bernard Gladstone's directions for building a fire.

Process Analysis of Building a Fire in a Fireplace
1. Put down crumpled newspaper.
2. Lay kindling.
3. Place back log near rear wall but not touching.
4. Place front log an inch forward.
5. Bridge logs with kindling.
6. Place third log on top of kindling bridge.

Next, check your outline to make sure that the steps are in the right order and that none have been omitted. Then analyze your outline more carefully. Are any steps so complex that they need to be described in some detail — or perhaps divided into more steps? Will you need to explain the purpose of a certain step because the reason for it is not obvious? Especially in an informational process analysis, two steps may take place at the same time; perhaps they are performed by different people or different parts of the body. Does your outline make this clear? (One solution is to assign both steps the same number but divide them into substeps by labeling one of them "A" and the other "B.") When you feel certain that the steps of the process are complete and correct, ask yourself two more questions. Will the reader need any other information to understand the process — definitions of unusual terms, for example, or descriptions of special equipment? Should you anticipate common mistakes or misunderstandings and discuss them, as Gladstone does? If so, be sure to add an appropriate note or two to your scratch outline as a reminder.

Use Transitions to Link the Steps

Transitional words and phrases like *then, next, after doing this,* and *during the summer months* can both emphasize and clarify the sequence of steps in your process analysis. The same is true of sequence markers like *first, second, third,* and so on. Devoe uses such words to make clear which stages in the hibernation process are simultaneous and which are not; Gladstone includes an occasional *first* or *then* to alert us to shifts from one step to the next. But both writers are careful not to overuse these words, and so should you be. Transitional words are a resource of language, but they should not be used arbitrarily.

Consider Your Audience, and Choose Appropriate Diction

The success of a process analysis essay depends heavily on how well you consider your audience. Are your readers very familiar, moderately familiar, or completely unfamiliar with the process you are trying to explain? If you are preparing a set of directions for processing film in the photo lab for a beginners' photography club, your readers will not know the meanings of technical terms and will not be able to accomplish the task without specific directions; thus you will need to include definitions and detailed explanations. If you are writing a process analysis of how tornadoes are formed for your classmates in a meteorology course, you will naturally have a fairly good sense of how much your audience already knows. Remember, in either case, that you should keep audience assessment and choice of diction — from concrete to abstract, from specific to general — in mind as you write.

Test the Effectiveness of Your Process Analysis

After finishing the first draft of your essay, have someone else read it. If you are writing a directional process analysis, ask your reader to follow the instructions and then to tell you whether he or she was able to understand each step and perform it satisfactorily. Was the desired result achieved? Did the fire burn well, the computer program run, the lasagna taste good? If not, examine your process analysis step-by-step, looking for errors and omissions that would explain the unsatisfactory result (no kindling wood, perhaps, or a loop in the program, or too much garlic).

In fact, William Peterson gave his essay on juggling to some friends to have them test his directions. "I gave it to people who had never tried juggling to see if there were any 'bugs' or unclear sections in my instructions. This helped me a lot as a writer because they told me where certain things were not clear or outright confusing. This enabled me to go back and revise, knowing exactly what the problem was." Peterson's readers had difficulty understanding his directions for the simple toss in his rough draft. Peterson agreed with their criticism: "I just couldn't get detailed enough in my rough draft. I had real trouble with paragraph 2, the explanation of the simple toss." Here is an early draft of that paragraph:

```
    Step one is the simple toss. Stand erect and hold
one object (we'll call it a ball from now on) in your
most adroit hand (we'll say the right). Toss the ball
into the air to approximately an inch above your head and
to about half an arm's length in front of you. The ball
should take an arched path traveling from your right hand
to your left. This step should now be repeated using your
left hand first and returning it to your right hand. Re-
peat this until completely proficient. We'll now call
this action the "perfect toss." Take a breather and then
move on.
```

"After several drafts," Peterson says, "I finally felt satisfied with my directions." To see what changes he made, compare the paragraph above with paragraph 2 in his final essay.

With an informational process analysis, it may be a bit trickier to ensure that your reader really understands. Test your reader's comprehension by asking a few questions. If there seems to be any confusion, try rereading what you have written with an objective eye. Sometimes an especially intricate or otherwise difficult step can be made clear by rewriting it in everyday language; sometimes a recognizable comparison or analogy will help, especially if you are analyzing a scientific or otherwise unfamiliar process. For example, American readers might better understand the British game of rugby if you compare it with American football; nonspecialists might grasp the circulation of blood more easily through an analogy between the cardiovascular system and domestic plumbing. (See the introduction to Chapter 9 for discussions of *comparison and contrast* and *analogy*.) Again, try to pin down the specific cause of any misunderstanding — the step or steps that are confusing your reader. Make sure the sequence is consistently clear. Keep on revising until your reader can demonstrate a thorough understanding of the process you've tried to explain.

► **Questions for Revision: Process Analysis**

1. Do I have a thorough knowledge of the process I chose to write about?

2. Have I clearly informed readers about how to perform the process (directional process analysis), or have I explained how a process occurs (informational process analysis)? Does my choice reflect the overall purpose of my process analysis paper?

3. Have I divided the process into clear, readily understandable steps?

4. Did I pay particular attention to transitional words to take readers from one step to the next?

5. Have I succeeded in tailoring my diction to my audience's familiarity with the subject?

6. How did my test reader respond to your essay? Did he or she find any confusing passages or any missing steps?

How to Mark a Book

Mortimer Adler

Writer, editor, and educator Mortimer Adler (1902–2001) was born in New York City. A high school dropout, Adler completed the undergraduate program at Columbia University in three years, but he did not graduate because he refused to take the mandatory swimming test. Adler is recognized for his editorial work on the Encyclopaedia Britannica *and for his leadership of the Great Books Program at the University of Chicago, where adults from all walks of life gathered twice a month to read and discuss the classics.*

In the following essay, which first appeared in the Saturday Review of Literature *in 1940, Adler offers a timeless lesson: He explains how to take full ownership of a book by marking it up, by making it "a part of yourself."*

BEFORE YOU READ

When you read a book that you must understand thoroughly and remember for a class or for your own purposes, what techniques do you use to help you understand what you are reading? What helps you remember important parts of the book and improve your understanding of what the author is saying?

You know you have to read "between the lines" to get the most out of anything. I want to persuade you to do something equally important in the course of your reading. I want to persuade you to "write between the lines." Unless you do, you are not likely to do the most efficient kind of reading. 1

I contend, quite bluntly, that marking up a book is not an act of mutilation but of love. 2

You shouldn't mark up a book which isn't yours. Librarians (or your friends) who lend you books expect you to keep them clean, and you should. If you decide that I am right about the usefulness of marking books, you will have to buy them. Most of the world's great books are available today, in reprint editions, at less than a dollar. 3

There are two ways in which one can own a book. The first is the property right you establish by paying for it, just as you pay for clothes and furniture. But this act of purchase is only the prelude to possession. Full ownership comes only when you have made it a part of yourself, and the best way to make yourself a part of it is by writing in it. An illustration may make the point clear. You buy a beefsteak and transfer it from the butcher's icebox to your own. But you do not 4 own the beefsteak in the most important sense until you consume it and get it into your bloodstream. I am arguing that books, too, must be absorbed in your bloodstream to do you any good.

Confusion about what it means to *own* a book leads people to a false reverence for paper, binding, and type — a respect for the physical thing — the craft of the printer rather than the genius of the author. They forget that it is possible for a man to acquire the idea, to possess the beauty, which a great book contains, without staking his claim by pasting his bookplate inside the cover. Having a fine library doesn't prove that its owner has a mind enriched by books; it proves nothing more than that he, his father, or his wife, was rich enough to buy them.

There are three kinds of book owners. The first has all the standard sets and best-sellers — unread, untouched. (This deluded individual owns woodpulp and ink, not books.) The second has a great many books — a few of them read through, most of them dipped into, but all of them as clean and shiny as the day they were bought. (This person would probably like to make books his own, but is restrained by a false respect for their physical appearance.) The third has a few books or many — every one of them dog-eared and dilapidated, shaken and loosened by continual use, marked and scribbled in from front to back. (This man owns books.)

Is it false respect, you may ask, to preserve intact and unblemished a beautifully printed book, an elegantly bound edition? Of course not. I'd no more scribble all over a first edition of *Paradise Lost* than I'd give my baby a set of crayons and an original Rembrandt! I wouldn't mark up a painting or a statue. Its soul, so to speak, is inseparable from its body. And the beauty of a rare edition or of a richly manufactured volume is like that of a painting or a statue.

But the soul of a book *can* be separated from its body. A book is more like the score of a piece of music than it is like a painting. No great musician confuses a symphony with the printed sheets of music. Arturo Toscanini reveres Brahms, but Toscanini's score of the C-minor Symphony is so thoroughly marked up that no one but the maestro himself can read it. The reason why a great conductor makes notations on his musical scores — marks them up again and again each time he returns to study them — is the reason why you should mark your books. If your respect for magnificent binding or typography gets in the way, buy yourself a cheap edition and pay your respects to the author.

Why is marking up a book indispensable to reading? First, it keeps you awake. (And I don't mean merely conscious; I mean wide awake.) In the second place, reading, if it is active, is thinking, and thinking tends to express itself in words, spoken or written. The marked book is usually the thought-through book. Finally, writing helps you remember the thoughts you had, or the thoughts the author expressed. Let me develop these three points.

If reading is to accomplish anything more than passing time, it   10
must be active. You can't let your eyes glide across the lines of a book and come up with an understanding of what you have read. Now an ordinary piece of light fiction, like say, *Gone with the Wind,* doesn't require the most active kind of reading. The books you read for pleasure can be read in a state of relaxation, and nothing is lost. But a great book, rich in ideas and beauty, a book that raises and tries to answer great fundamental questions, demands the most active reading of which you are capable. You don't absorb the ideas of John Dewey[1] the way you absorb the crooning of Mr. Vallee.[2] You have to reach for them. That you cannot do while you're asleep.

If, when you've finished reading a book, the pages are filled with   11
your notes, you know that you read actively. The most famous active reader of great books I know is President Hutchins, of the University of Chicago. He also has the hardest schedule of business activities of any man I know. He invariably reads with a pencil, and sometimes, when he picks up a book and pencil in the evening, he finds himself, instead of making intelligent notes, drawing what he calls "caviar factories" on the margins. When that happens, he puts the book down. He knows he's too tired to read, and he's just wasting time.

But, you may ask, why is writing necessary? Well, the physical act   12
of writing, with your own hand, brings words and sentences more sharply before your mind and preserves them better in your memory. To set down your reaction to important words and sentences you have read, and the questions they have raised in your mind, is to preserve those reactions and sharpen those questions.

Even if you wrote on a scratch pad, and threw the paper away   13
when you had finished writing, your grasp of the book would be surer. But you don't have to throw the paper away. The margins (top and bottom, as well as side), the end-papers, the very space between the lines, are all available. They aren't sacred. And, best of all, your marks and notes become an integral part of the book and stay there forever. You can pick up the book the following week or year, and there are all your points of agreement, disagreement, doubt, and inquiry. It's like resuming an interrupted conversation with the advantage of being able to pick up where you left off.

---

[1] John Dewey (1859–1952) was an educational philosopher who had a profound influence on learning through experimentation.

[2] Rudy Vallee (1901–1986) was a popular singer of the 1920s, famous for his crooning high notes.

And that is exactly what reading a book should be: a conversation 14
between you and the author. Presumably he knows more about the
subject than you do; naturally, you'll have the proper humility as you
approach him. But don't let anybody tell you that a reader is supposed
to be solely on the receiving end. Understanding is a two-way operation; learning doesn't consist in being an empty receptacle. The
learner has to question himself and question the teacher. He even has
to argue with the teacher, once he understands what the teacher is
saying. And marking a book is literally an expression of your differences, or agreements of opinion, with the author.

There are all kinds of devices for marking a book intelligently and 15
fruitfully. Here's the way I do it:

1. *Underlining:* of major points, of important or forceful state- 16
ments.

2. *Vertical lines at the margin:* to emphasize a statement already un- 17
derlined.

3. *Star, asterisk, or other doo-dad at the margin:* to be used sparingly, 18
to emphasize the ten or twenty most important statements in the
book. (You may want to fold the bottom corner of each page on
which you use such marks. It won't hurt the sturdy paper on which
most modern books are printed, and you will be able to take the book
off the shelf at any time and, by opening it at the folded-corner page,
refresh your recollection of the book.)

4. *Numbers in the margin:* to indicate the sequence of points the 19
author makes in developing a single argument.

5. *Numbers of other pages in the margin:* to indicate where else in the 20
book the author made points relevant to the point marked; to tie up
the ideas in a book, which, though they may be separated by many
pages, belong together.

6. *Circling:* of key words or phrases. 21

7. *Writing in the margin, or at the top or bottom of the page, for the* 22
sake of: recording questions (and perhaps answers) which a passage
raised in your mind; reducing a complicated discussion to a simple
statement; recording the sequence of major points right through the
book. I use the end-papers at the back of the book to make a personal
index of the author's points in the order of their appearance.

The front end-papers are, to me, the most important. Some people 23
reserve them for a fancy bookplate. I reserve them for fancy thinking.
After I have finished reading the book and making my personal index
on the back end-papers, I turn to the front and try to outline the book,
not page by page, or point by point (I've already done that at the back),
but as an integrated structure, with a basic unity and an order of parts.
This outline is, to me, the measure of my understanding of the work.

If you're a die-hard anti-book-marker, you may object that the 24
margins, the space between the lines, and the end-papers don't give

you room enough. All right. How about using a scratch pad slightly smaller than the page-size of the book — so that the edges of the sheets won't protrude? Make your index, outlines, and even your notes on the pad, and then insert these sheets permanently inside the front and back covers of the book.

Or, you may say that this business of marking books is going to slow up your reading. It probably will. That's one of the reasons for doing it. Most of us have been taken in by the notion that speed of reading is a measure of our intelligence. There is no such thing as the right speed for intelligent reading. Some things should be read quickly and effortlessly, and some should be read slowly and even laboriously. The sign of intelligence in reading is the ability to read different things differently according to their worth. In the case of good books, the point is not to see how many of them you can get through, but rather how many can get through you — how many you can make your own. A few friends are better than a thousand acquaintances. If this be your aim, as it should be, you will not be impatient if it takes more time and effort to read a great book than it does a newspaper. 25

You may have one final objection to marking books. You can't lend them to your friends because nobody else can read them without being distracted by your notes. Furthermore, you won't want to lend them because a marked copy is a kind of intellectual diary, and lending it is almost like giving your mind away. 26

If your friend wishes to read your *Plutarch's Lives, Shakespeare,* or *The Federalist Papers,* tell him gently but firmly to buy a copy. You will lend him your car or your coat — but your books are as much a part of you as your head or your heart. 27

RESPONDING TO READING

After you have read Adler's essay, compare your answer to the Before You Read prompt with Adler's guidelines for reading. What are the most significant differences between Adler's guidelines and your own? How can you better make the books you read part of yourself?

QUESTIONING THE TEXT

1. What are the three kinds of book owners Adler identifies? What are their differences?

2. According to Adler, why is marking up a book indispensable to reading? Do you agree with his three arguments? Why or why not?

3. Adler says that reading a book should be a conversation between the reader and the author. What characteristics does he say the conversation should have? How does marking a book assist in carrying on and preserving the conversation?

UNDERSTANDING THE WRITER'S CRAFT

1. In the first paragraph, Adler writes, "I want to persuade you to do something equally important in the course of your reading. I want to persuade you to 'write between the lines.'" What assumptions does Adler make about his audience when he chooses to use the parallel structure of "I want to persuade you . . ."? (Glossary: *Audience; Parallelism*) Is stating his intention so blatantly an effective way of presenting his argument? Why or why not?

2. Adler expresses himself very clearly throughout the essay and his topic sentences are carefully crafted. Reread the topic sentences for paragraphs 3–6, and identify how each introduces the main idea for the paragraph and unifies it. (Glossary: *Topic Sentence*)

3. Throughout the essay, Adler provides the reader with a number of verbal cues ("There are two ways," "Let me develop these three points"). What do these verbal cues indicate about the organizational connections of the essay? Explain how Adler's organization creates an essay that logically follows from sentence to sentence and from paragraph to paragraph. (Glossary: *Organization*)

4. Summarize in your own words Adler's process analysis about how one should mark a book. Explain how Adler's process analysis is also an argument for the correct way to read. (Glossary: *Argument*)

EXPLORING LANGUAGE

1. Adler makes an analogy that links reading books with the statement, "A few friends are better than a thousand acquaintances" (paragraph 25). Explain how this analogy works. (Glossary: *Analogy*) Why is this analogy important to Adler's overall argument?

2. Throughout the essay, Adler uses the personal pronoun *I* to describe his reading experience. How does this personalized voice help or hinder the explanation of the process of reading?

3. Refer to your desk dictionary to determine the meanings of the following words as Adler uses them in this selection: *deluded* (paragraph 6), *dilapidated* (6), *typography* (8), *integral* (13), *protrude* (24).

COMBINING RHETORICAL STRATEGIES

Adler's process analysis is also a description of an event or a sequence of events (how to read). Does he claim that his recommended reading process will aid the reader's understanding, increase the reader's interest, or both? (Glossary: *Cause and Effect Analysis*)

WRITING SUGGESTIONS

1. **(Process Analysis)** Write a directional process analysis in which you present your techniques for getting the most enjoyment out of a common

activity. For example, perhaps you have a set routine you follow for spending an evening watching TV — preparing popcorn, checking the program listings, clearing off the coffee table, finding the remote control, settling into your favorite chair, and so on. Choose from the following topics:

> How to listen to music
> How to eat an ice cream cone
> How to reduce stress
> How to wash a dog
> How to play a sport or game

2. **(Process Analysis)** Think about a process that you are familiar with that you think needs improvement. After choosing your topic, you might want to do a little background research in the library. Make sure that you are able to put the old process in your own words, and then write a process analysis in which you argue for a proposed revision to the old process.

3. **(Other Strategies)** Adler devotes a large portion of his essay to persuading his audience that marking books is a worthwhile task. Write an essay in which you instruct your audience about how to do something they do not necessarily wish to do or they do not think they need to do. For instance, before explaining how to buy the best renter's insurance, you may need to convince readers that they *should* buy renter's insurance. Write your directional process analysis after making a convincing argument for the validity of the process you wish to present.

4. **(Research)** In the library, and possibly on the Internet, research how federal income taxes are collected. Do further research into some alternative methods for tax collection, such as the flat tax. Write an essay in which you describe the current tax-collection process and compare and contrast this method with at least one alternative method.

- **TaxResources**
  <http://www.taxresources.com>

  This Web site offers a comprehensive index to tax information on the World Wide Web.

- **The *Digital Daily***
  <http://www.irs.ustreas.gov/prod/index.html>

  Read the Internal Revenue Service's daily online magazine at this site.

- **Taxpayers Revolution Home Page**
  <http://www.noirs.com/noirs>

  This Web site is devoted to the campaign for a 10 percent flat income tax.

- **Americans for Tax Reform Home Page**
  <http://www.atr.org>

  This site offers information on and links to tax reform resources on the Internet.

How to Say Nothing in 500 Words

Paul Roberts

Paul Roberts (1917–1967) was a linguist, a teacher, and a writer at San José State College from 1946 to 1960 and at Cornell University from 1962 to 1964. His books on writing, including English Syntax *(1954) and* Patterns of English *(1956), have helped generations of high school and college students become better writers.*

"How to Say Nothing in 500 Words" is taken from his best-known book, Understanding English *(1958). Although written over forty years ago, the essay is still relevant for student writers today. Good writing, Roberts tells us, is not simply a matter of filling up a page; rather, the words have to hold the reader's interest, and they must say something. In this essay, Roberts uses lively prose and a step-by-step process to guide the student from the blank page to the finished essay. His bag of writing strategies holds good advice to anyone who wants to write well.*

BEFORE YOU READ

How do you feel about writing? Do you find writing difficult? What are some of your most memorable experiences with writing in school or out? How have these experiences affected your current attitude toward writing? Explain.

NOTHING ABOUT SOMETHING

It's Friday afternoon, and you have almost survived another week of classes. You are just looking forward dreamily to the weekend when the English instructor says: "For Monday you will turn in a five-hundred word composition on college football." 1

Well, that puts a good big hole in the weekend. You don't have any strong views on college football one way or the other. You get rather excited during the season and go to all the home games and find it rather more fun than not. On the other hand, the class has been reading Robert Hutchins in the anthology and perhaps Shaw's "Eighty-Yard Run," and from the class discussion you have got the idea that the instructor thinks college football is for the birds. You are no fool, you. You can figure out what side to take. 2

After dinner you get out the portable typewriter that you got for high school graduation. You might as well get it over with and enjoy Saturday and Sunday. Five hundred words is about two double-spaced pages with normal margins. You put in a sheet of paper, think up a title, and you're off: 3

284

WHY COLLEGE FOOTBALL SHOULD
BE ABOLISHED

College football should be abolished because it's bad for the school and also bad for the players. The players are so busy practicing that they don't have any time for their studies.

This, you feel, is a mighty good start. The only trouble is that it's only thirty-two words. You still have four hundred and sixty-eight to go, and you've pretty well exhausted the subject. It comes to you that you do your best thinking in the morning, so you put away the type-writer and go to the movies. But the next morning you have to do your washing and some math problems, and in the afternoon you go to the game. The English instructor turns up too, and you wonder if you've taken the right side after all. Saturday night you have a date, and Sunday morning you have to go to church. (You shouldn't let English assignments interfere with your religion.) What with one thing and another, it's ten o'clock Sunday night before you get out the typewriter again. You make a pot of coffee and start to fill out your views on college football. Put a little meat on the bones.

4

WHY COLLEGE FOOTBALL SHOULD
BE ABOLISHED

In my opinion, it seems to me that college football should be abolished. The reason why I think this to be true is because I feel that football is bad for the colleges in nearly every respect. As Robert Hutchins says in his article in our anthology in which he discusses college football, it would be better if the colleges had race horses and had races with one another, because then the horses would not have to attend classes. I firmly agree with Mr. Hutchins on this point, and I am sure that many other students would agree too.

One reason why it seems to me that college football is bad is that it has become too commercial. In the olden times when people played football just for the fun of it, maybe college football was all right, but they do not play football just for the fun of it now as they used to in the old days. Nowadays college football is what you might call a big business. Maybe this is not true at all schools, and I don't think it is especially true here at State, but certainly this is the case at most colleges and universities in America nowadays, as Mr. Hutchins points out in his very interesting article. Actually the coaches and alumni go around to the high schools and offer the high school stars large salaries to come to their colleges and play football for them. There was one case where a high school star was offered a convertible if he would play football for a certain college.

Another reason for abolishing college football is that it is bad for the players. They do not have time to get a college education, because they are so busy playing football. A football player has to practice every afternoon from three to six, and then he is so tired that he can't concentrate on his studies. He just feels like dropping off to sleep after dinner, and then the next day he goes to his classes without having studied and maybe he fails the test.

(Good ripe stuff so far, but you're still a hundred and fifty-one words from home. One more push.)

Also I think college football is bad for the colleges and the universities because not very many students get to participate in it. Out of a college of ten thousand students only seventy-five or a hundred play football, if that many. Football is what you might call a spectator sport. That means that most people go to watch it but do not play it themselves.

(Four hundred and fifteen. Well, you still have the conclusion, and when you retype it, you can make the margins a little wider.)

These are the reasons why I agree with Mr. Hutchins that college football should be abolished in American colleges and universities.

On Monday you turn it in, moderately hopeful, and on Friday it comes back marked "weak in content" and sporting a big "D." 5

This essay is exaggerated a little, not much. The English instructor will recognize it as reasonably typical of what an assignment on college football will bring in. He knows that nearly half of the class will contrive in five hundred words to say that college football is too commercial and bad for the players. Most of the other half will inform him that college football builds character and prepares one for life and brings prestige to the school. As he reads paper after paper all saying the same thing in almost the same words, all bloodless, five hundred words dripping out of nothing, he wonders how he allowed himself to get trapped into teaching English when he might have had a happy and interesting life as an electrician or a confidence man. 6

Well, you may ask, what can you do about it? The subject is one on which you have few convictions and little information. Can you be expected to make a dull subject interesting? As a matter of fact, this is precisely what you are expected to do. This is the writer's essential task. All subjects, except sex, are dull until somebody makes them interesting. The writer's job is to find the argument, the approach, the angle, the wording that will take the reader with him. This is seldom easy, and it is particularly hard in subjects that have been much discussed: College Football, Fraternities, Popular Music, Is Chivalry Dead?, and the like. You will feel that there is nothing you can do with such subjects except repeat the old bromides. But there are some 7 things you can do which will make your papers, if not throbbingly alive, at least less insufferably tedious than they might otherwise be.

AVOID THE OBVIOUS CONTENT

Say the assignment is college football. Say that you've decided to be against it. Begin by putting down the arguments that come to your mind: it is too commercial, it takes the students' minds off their studies, it is hard on the players, it makes the university a kind of circus instead of an intellectual center, for most schools it is financially ruinous. Can you think of any more arguments just off hand? All right. Now when you write your paper, *make sure that you don't use any of the material on this list.* If these are the points that leap to your mind, they will leap to everyone else's too, and whether you get a "C" or a "D" may depend on whether the instructor reads your paper early when he is fresh and tolerant or late, when the sentence "In my opinion, college football has become too commercial," inexorably repeated, has brought him to the brink of lunacy.

Be against college football for some reason or reasons of your own. If they are keen and perceptive ones, that's splendid. But even if they are trivial or foolish or indefensible, you are still ahead so long as they are not everybody else's reasons too. Be against it because the colleges don't spend enough money on it to make it worthwhile, because it is bad for the characters of spectators, because the players are forced to attend classes, because the football stars hog all the beautiful women, because it competes with baseball and is therefore un-American and possibly Communist inspired. There are lots of more or less unused reasons for being against college football.

Sometimes it is a good idea to sum up and dispose of the trite and conventional points before going on to your own. This has the advantage of indicating to the reader that you are going to be neither trite nor conventional. Something like this:

> We are often told that college football should be abolished because it has become too commercial or because it is bad for the players. These arguments are no doubt very cogent, but they don't really go to the heart of the matter.

Then you go to the heart of the matter.

TAKE THE LESS USUAL SIDE

One rather simple way of getting interest into your paper is to take the side of the argument that most of the citizens will want to avoid. If the assignment is an essay on dogs, you can, if you choose, explain that dogs are faithful and lovable companions, intelligent, useful as guardians of the house and protectors of children, indispensable in police work — in short, when all is said and done, man's best friends. Or you can suggest that those big brown eyes conceal, more often than not, a vacuity of mind and an inconstancy of purpose; that the dogs you have known most intimately have been mangy, ill-tempered brutes, incapable of instruction; and that only your nobility of mind and fear of arrest prevent you from kicking the flea-ridden animals when you pass them on the street.

Naturally, personal convictions will sometimes dictate your approach. If the assigned subject is "Is Methodism Rewarding to the Individual?" and you are a pious Methodist, you have really no choice. But few assigned subjects, if any, will fall in this category. Most of them will lie in broad areas of discussion with much to be said on both sides. They are intellectual exercises and it is legitimate to argue now one way and now another, as debaters do in similar circumstances. Always take the side that looks to you hardest, least defensible. It will almost always turn out to be easier to write interestingly on that side. 12

This general advice applies where you have a choice of subjects. If you are to choose among "The Value of Fraternities" and "My Favorite High School Teacher" and "What I Think about Beetles," by all means plump for the beetles. By the time the instructor gets to your paper, he will be up to his ears in tedious tales about the French teacher at Bloombury High and assertions about how fraternities build character and prepare one for life. Your views on beetles, whatever they are, are bound to be a refreshing change. 13

Don't worry too much about figuring out what the instructor thinks about the subject so that you can cuddle up with him. Chances are his views are no stronger than yours. If he does have convictions and you oppose them, his problem is to keep from grading you higher than you deserve in order to show he is not biased. This doesn't mean that you should always cantankerously dissent from what the instructor says; that gets tiresome too. And if the subject assigned is "My Pet Peeve," do not begin, "My pet peeve is the English instructor who assigns papers on 'my pet peeve.'" This was still funny during the War of 1812, but it has sort of lost its edge since then. It is in general good manners to avoid personalities. 14

SLIP OUT OF ABSTRACTION

If you will study the essay on college football . . . you will perceive that one reason for its appalling dullness is that it never gets down to 15 particulars. It is just a series of not very glittering generalities: "football is bad for the colleges," "it has become too commercial," "football is a big business," "it is bad for the players," and so on. Such round phrases thudding against the reader's brain are unlikely to convince him, though they may well render him unconscious.

If you want the reader to believe that college football is bad for the players, you have to do more than say so. You have to display the evil. Take your roommate, Alfred Simkins, the second-string center. Picture poor old Alfy coming home from football practice every evening, bruised and aching, agonizingly tired, scarcely able to shovel the mashed potatoes into his mouth. Let us see him staggering up to the room, getting out his econ textbook, peering desperately at it with his good eye, falling asleep and failing the test in the morning. Let us share his unbearable tension as Saturday draws near. Will he fail, be demoted, lose his monthly allowance, be forced to return to the coal mines? And if he succeeds, what will be his reward? Perhaps a slight ripple of applause when the third-string center replaces him, a moment of elation in the locker room if the team wins, of despair if it loses. What will he look back on when he graduates from college? Toil and torn ligaments. And what will be his future? He is not good enough for pro football, and he is too obscure and weak in econ to succeed in stocks and bonds. College football is tearing the heart from Alfy Simkins and, when it finishes with him, will callously toss aside the shattered hulk. 16

This is no doubt a weak enough argument for the abolition of college football, but it is a sight better than saying, in three or four variations, that college football (in your opinion) is bad for the players. 17

Look at the work of any professional writer and notice how constantly he is moving from the generality, the abstract statement, to the concrete example, the facts and figures, the illustration. If he is writing on juvenile delinquency, he does not just tell you that juveniles are (it seems to him) delinquent and that (in his opinion) something should be done about it. He shows you juveniles being delinquent, tearing up movie theatres in Buffalo, stabbing high school principals in Dallas, smoking marijuana in Palo Alto. And more than likely he is moving toward some specific remedy, not just a general wringing of the hands. 18

It is no doubt possible to be *too* concrete, too illustrative or anecdotal, but few inexperienced writers err this way. For most the soundest advice is to be seeking always for the picture, to be always turning general remarks into seeable examples. Don't say, "Sororities teach girls the social graces." Say, "Sorority life teaches a girl how to carry on a conversation while pouring tea, without sloshing the tea into the saucer." Don't say, "I like certain kinds of popular music very much." Say, "Whenever I hear Gerber Spinklittle play 'Mississippi Man' on the trombone, my socks creep up my ankles." 19

GET RID OF OBVIOUS PADDING

The student toiling away at his weekly English theme is too often tor- 20
mented by a figure: five hundred words. How, he asks himself, is he to
achieve this staggering total? Obviously by never using one word
when he can somehow work in ten.

He is therefore seldom content with a plain statement like "Fast 21
driving is dangerous." This has only four words in it. He takes
thought, and the sentence becomes:

> In my opinion, fast driving is dangerous.

Better, but he can do better still:

> In my opinion, fast driving would seem to be rather dangerous.

If he is really adept, it may come out:

> In my humble opinion, though I do not claim to be an expert
> on this complicated subject, fast driving, in most circumstances,
> would seem to be rather dangerous in many respects, or at least so
> it would seem to me.

Thus four words have been turned into forty, and not an iota of content has been added.

Now this is a way to go about reaching five hundred words, and if 22
you are content with a "D" grade, it is as good a way as any. But if you
aim higher, you must work differently. Instead of stuffing your sentences with straw, you must try steadily to get rid of the padding, to
make your sentences lean and tough. If you are really working at it,
your first draft will greatly exceed the required total, and then you will
work it down, thus:

> It is thought in some quarters that fraternities do not con-
> tribute as much as might be expected to campus life.

> Some people think that fraternities contribute little to campus
> life.

> The average doctor who practices in small towns or in the
> country must toil night and day to heal the sick.

> Most country doctors work long hours.

> When I was a little girl, I suffered from shyness and embarrass-
> ment in the presence of others.

> I was a shy little girl.

> It is absolutely necessary for the person employed as a marine
> fireman to give the matter of steam pressure his undivided atten-
> tion at all times.

> The fireman has to keep his eye on the steam gauge.

You may ask how you can arrive at five hundred words at this rate. Simply. You dig up more real content. Instead of taking a couple of obvious points off the surface of the topic and then circling warily around them for six paragraphs, you work in and explore, figure out the details. You illustrate. You say that fast driving is dangerous, and then you prove it. How long does it take to stop a car at forty and at eighty? How far can you see at night? What happens when a tire blows? What happens in a head-on collision at fifty miles an hour? Pretty soon your paper will be full of broken glass and blood and headless torsos, and reaching five hundred words will not really be a problem.

CALL A FOOL A FOOL

Some of the padding in freshman themes is to be blamed not on anxiety about the word minimum but on excessive timidity. The student writes, "In my opinion, the principal of my high school acted in ways that I believe every unbiased person would have to call foolish." This isn't exactly what he means. What he means is, "My high school principal was a fool." If he was a fool, call him a fool. Hedging the thing about with "in-my-opinion's" and "it-seems-to-me's" and "as-I-see-it's" and "at-least-from-my-point-of-view's" gains you nothing. Delete these phrases whenever they creep into your paper.

The student's tendency to hedge stems from a modesty that in other circumstances would be commendable. He is, he realizes, young and inexperienced, and he half suspects that he is dopey and fuzzy-minded beyond the average. Probably only too true. But it doesn't help to announce your incompetence six times in every paragraph. Decide what you want to say and say it as vigorously as possible, without apology and in plain words.

Linguistic diffidence can take various forms. One is what we call *euphemism.* This is the tendency to call a spade "a certain garden implement" or women's underwear "unmentionables." It is stronger in some eras than others and in some people than others but it always operates more or less in subjects that are touchy or taboo: death, sex, madness, and so on. Thus we shrink from saying, "He died last night" but say instead, "passed away," "left us," "joined his Maker," "went to his reward." Or we try to take off the tension with a lighter cliché: "kicked the bucket," "cashed in his chips," "handed in his dinner pail." We have found all sorts of ways to avoid saying *mad:* "mentally ill," "touched," "not quite right upstairs," "feeble-minded," "innocent," "simple," "off his trolley," "not in his right mind." Even such a now plain word as *insane* began as a euphemism with the meaning "not healthy."

Modern science, particularly psychology, contributes many poly- 27
syllables in which we can wrap our thoughts and blunt their force. To
many writers there is no such thing as a bad schoolboy. Schoolboys
are maladjusted or unoriented or misunderstood or in need of guidance or lacking in continued success toward satisfactory integration of
the personality as a social unit, but they are never bad. Psychology no
doubt makes us better men or women, more sympathetic and tolerant,
but it doesn't make writing any easier. Had Shakespeare been con-
fronted with psychology, "To be or not to be" might have come out,
"To continue as a social unit or not to do so. That is the personality
problem. Whether 'tis a better sign of integration at the conscious
level to display a psychic tolerance toward the maladjustments and re-
pressions induced by one's lack of orientation in one's environment
or —" But Hamlet would never have finished the soliloquy.

Writing in the modern world, you cannot altogether avoid mod- 28
ern jargon. Nor, in an effort to get away from euphemism, should you
salt your paper with four-letter words. But you can do much if you will
mount guard against those roundabout phrases, those echoing polysyllables that tend to slip into your writing to rob it of its crispness
and force.

BEWARE OF THE PAT EXPRESSION

Other things being equal, avoid phrases like "other things being 29
equal." Those sentences that come to you whole, or in two or three
doughy lumps, are sure to be bad sentences. They are no creation of
yours but pieces of common thought floating in the community soup.

Pat expressions are hard, often impossible, to avoid, because they 30
come too easily to be noticed and seem too necessary to be dispensed
with. No writer avoids them altogether, but good writers avoid them
more often than poor writers.

By "pat expressions" we mean such tags as "to all practical intents 31
and purposes," "the pure and simple truth," "from where I sit," "the
time of his life," "to the ends of the earth," "in the twinkling of an
eye," "as sure as you're born," "over my dead body," "under cover of
darkness," "took the easy way out," "when all is said and done," "told
him time and time again," "parted the best of friends," "stand up and
be counted," "gave him the best years of her life," "worked her fingers
to the bone." Like other clichés, these expressions were once forceful.
Now we should use them only when we can't possibly think of anything else.

Some pat expressions stand like a wall between the writer and 32
thought. Such a one is "the American way of life." Many student writ-

ers feel that when they have said that something accords with the American way of life or does not they have exhausted the subject. Actually, they have stopped at the highest level of abstraction. The American way of life is the complicated set of bonds between a hundred and eighty million ways. All of us know this when we think about it, but the tag phrase too often keeps us from thinking about it.

So with many another phrase dear to the politician: "this great 33 land of ours," "the man in the street," "our national heritage." These may prove our patriotism or give a clue to our political beliefs, but otherwise they add nothing to the paper except words.

COLORFUL WORDS

The writer builds with words, and no builder uses a raw material more 34 slippery and elusive and treacherous. A writer's work is a constant struggle to get the right word in the right place, to find that particular word that will convey his meaning exactly, that will persuade the reader or soothe him or startle or amuse him. He never succeeds altogether — sometimes he feels that he scarcely succeeds at all — but such successes as he has are what make the thing worth doing.

There is no book of rules for this game. One progresses through 35 everlasting experiment on the basis of ever-widening experience. There are few useful generalizations that one can make about words as words, but there are perhaps a few.

Some words are what we call "colorful." By this we mean that they 36 are calculated to produce a picture or induce an emotion. They are dressy instead of plain, specific instead of general, loud instead of soft. Thus, in place of "Her heart beat," we may write "Her heart *pounded, throbbed, fluttered, danced.*" Instead of "He sat in his chair," we may say, "He *lounged, sprawled, coiled.*" Instead of "It was hot," we may say, "It was *blistering, sultry, muggy, suffocating, steamy, wilting.*"

However, it should not be supposed that the fancy word is always 37 better. Often it is as well to write "Her heart beat" or "It was hot" if that is all it did or all it was. Ages differ in how they like their prose. The nineteenth century liked it rich and smoky. The twentieth has usually preferred it lean and cool. The twentieth-century writer, like all writers, is forever seeking the exact word, but he is wary of sounding feverish. He tends to pitch it low, to understate it, to throw it away. He knows that if he gets too colorful, the audience is likely to giggle.

See how this strikes you: "As the rich, golden glow of the sunset 38 died away along the eternal western hills, Angela's limpid blue eyes looked softly and trustingly into Montague's flashing brown ones, and her heart pounded like a drum in time with the joyous song surging in her soul." Some people like that sort of thing, but most modern readers would say, "Good grief," and turn on the television.

COLORED WORDS

Some words we would call not so much colorful as colored — that is, loaded with associations, good or bad. All words — except perhaps structure words — have associations of some sort. We have said that the meaning of a word is the sum of the contexts in which it occurs. When we hear a word, we hear with it an echo of all the situations in which we have heard it before.   39

In some words, these echoes are obvious and discussable. The word *mother*, for example, has, for most people, agreeable associations. When you hear *mother* you probably think of home, safety, love, food, and various other pleasant things. If one writes, "She was like a mother to me," he gets an effect which he would not get in "She was like an aunt to me." The advertiser makes use of the associations of *mother* by working it in when he talks about his product. The politician works it in when he talks about himself.   40

So also with such words as *home, liberty, fireside, contentment, patriot, tenderness, sacrifice, childlike, manly, bluff, limpid.* All of these words are loaded with favorable associations that would be rather hard to indicate in a straightforward definition. There is more than a literal difference between "They sat around the fireside" and "They sat around the stove." They might have been equally warm and happy around the stove, but *fireside* suggests leisure, grace, quiet tradition, congenial company, and *stove* does not.   41

Conversely, some words have bad associations. *Mother* suggests pleasant things, but *mother-in-law* does not. Many mothers-in-law are heroically lovable and some mothers drink gin all day and beat their children insensible, but these facts of life are beside the point. The thing is that *mother* sounds good and *mother-in-law* does not.   42

Or consider the word *intellectual*. This would seem to be a complimentary term, but in point of fact it is not, for it has picked up associations of impracticality and ineffectuality and general dopiness. So also with such words as *liberal, reactionary, Communist, Socialist, capitalist, radical, schoolteacher, truck driver, undertaker, operator, salesman, huckster, speculator.* These convey meanings on the literal level, but beyond that — sometimes, in some places — they convey contempt on the part of the speaker.   43

The question of whether to use loaded words or not depends on what is being written. The scientist, the scholar, try to avoid them; for the poet, the advertising writer, the public speaker, they are standard   44 equipment. But every writer should take care that they do not substitute for thought. If you write, "Anyone who thinks that is nothing but a Socialist (or Communist or capitalist)" you have said nothing except that you don't like people who think that, and such remarks are effective only with the most naïve readers. It is always a bad mistake to think your readers more naïve than they really are.

COLORLESS WORDS

But probably most student writers come to grief not with words that   45
are colorful or those that are colored but with those that have no color at all. A pet example is *nice,* a word we would find it hard to dispense with in casual conversation but which is no longer capable of adding much to a description. Colorless words are those of such general meaning that in a particular sentence they mean nothing. Slang adjectives, like *cool* ("That's real cool.") tend to explode all over the language. They are applied to everything, lose their original force, and quickly die.

Beware also of nouns of very general meaning, like *circumstances,*   46
cases, instances, aspects, factors, relationships, attitudes, eventualities, etc. In most circumstances you will find that those cases of writing which contain too many instances of words like these will in this and other aspects have factors leading to unsatisfactory relationships with the reader resulting in unfavorable attitudes on his part and perhaps other eventualities, like a grade of "D." Notice also what "etc." means. It means "I'd like to make this list longer, but I can't think of any more examples."

RESPONDING TO READING

In this essay, Roberts points out certain features, positive and negative, found in the work of many writers. Does your writing exhibit any of these features, good or bad? How would you rate your writing with respect to each of these features?

QUESTIONING THE TEXT

1. According to Roberts, what is the job of the writer? Why, in particular, is it difficult for college students to do this job well? Discuss how your college experience leads you to agree or disagree with Roberts.

2. The author offers several "tricks" or techniques of good writing in his essay. What are they? Do you find them more useful than other techniques? Explain.

3. If, according to Roberts, a good writer never uses unnecessary words, what then are the legitimate ways a student can reach the goal of the five-hundred-word essay?

4. According to Roberts, how has modern psychology made it more difficult to write well?

UNDERSTANDING THE WRITER'S CRAFT

1. Make a scratch outline of Roberts's essay. What are the similarities between his organization of material and the process analysis he outlines for students? Explain. (Glossary: *Organization*)

2. What kind of information does the title of Roberts's essay lead you to expect? Does the author deliver what the title promises? Why do you think he chose this title?

3. What are Roberts's main points? How do his examples help him explain and clarify his main points? (Glossary: *Exemplification*)

EXPLORING LANGUAGE

1. Roberts wrote this essay more than forty years ago, and at some points the facts he cites indicate this; he gives the population of the United States as 180 million (paragraph 32), whereas today it is closer to 290 million. Is there anything in his diction or word choice that makes Roberts's writing seem dated, or does it sound contemporary? Choose examples from the text to support your answer. (Glossary: *Diction*)

2. What is Roberts's tone in this essay? What words does he use to create this tone? Explain how the tone affects you as a reader. (Glossary: *Tone*)

3. Refer to your desk dictionary to determine the meanings of the following words as Roberts uses them in this selection: *contrive* (paragraph 6), *bromides* (7), *cogent* (10), *cantankerously* (14), *diffidence* (26), *soliloquy* (27).

COMBINING RHETORICAL STRATEGIES

Roberts's writing style is well-suited to his student audience; he includes examples that would be familiar to many students. How would you describe his writing style? What are some of the ways he uses narration and exemplification to make the process analysis easy to follow? (Glossary: *Exemplification; Narration*)

WRITING SUGGESTIONS

1. **(Process Analysis)** In paragraph 16, Roberts explains how a brief but good essay on college football might be written. He obeys the first rule of good writing — show, don't tell. Thus, instead of a dry lump of words, his brief "essay" uses humor, exaggeration, and concrete details

to breathe life into the football player. Review Roberts's strategies for good writing. Then choose one of the dull topics he suggests or one of your own, and following the steps he lays out in his selection, write a five-hundred-word essay.

2. **(Process Analysis)** Pick and analyze a process. You might think of a process encountered in school or everyday life, such as dorm room assignments, class registration, how to cook a lobster, or how to pack for a camping trip. Write an analysis explaining how the process could be done more effectively, efficiently, or fairly.

3. **(Other Strategies)** Find a piece of your own writing or exchange papers with a classmate (you might want to use a Before You Read or a Responding to Reading exercise). Using an editor's eye (almost anyone can edit other people's writing), rewrite the piece, eliminating unnecessary words, substituting colorful action verbs for dull ones, and perhaps even shifting the focus of the piece to make it more interesting. After you have rewritten the piece, write an essay analyzing the role of the editor. To aid you in your editing, a number of useful editing-related Internet resources are listed below.

- **The Wordsmyth English Dictionary-Thesaurus**
  <http://www.wordsmyth.net>

  This site offers features that are particularly useful to editors.

- ***The Elements of Style* Online**
  <http://www.bartleby.com/141>

  Read William Strunk Jr.'s classic *The Elements of Style* online in its entirety at this Web site.

- **Copyediting Resources on the Internet**
  <http://www.towson.edu/~lieb/editlinx.html>

  Towson University's list of editing and copyediting resources is available here.

Campus Racism 101

Nikki Giovanni

Yolanda Cornelia "Nikki" Giovanni was born in Knoxville, Tennessee, in 1943 and was raised in Ohio. After graduating from Fisk University, she organized the Black Arts Festival in Cincinnati and then entered graduate school at the University of Pennsylvania. Her first book of poetry, Black Feeling, Black Talk, *was published in 1968 and began a lifetime of writing that reflects on the African American identity. Recent books of poetry include the anthologies* Selected Poems of Nikki Giovanni *(1996) and* Love Poems *(1997) and a new collection,* Blues for All the Changes: New Poems *(1999). Her honors include the NAACP Image Award for Literature in 1998, the Langston Hughes Award for Distinguished Contributions to Arts and Letters in 1996, and Woman of the Year awards from several magazines, including* Essence, Mademoiselle, *and* Ladies Home Journal. *She is currently professor of English and Gloria D. Smith Professor of Black Studies at Virginia Tech.*

The following selection, taken from her nonfiction work Racism 101, *instructs Black students about how to succeed at predominantly white colleges.*

BEFORE YOU READ

How would you characterize race relations at your school? How much do white and minority students interact, and what, in your experience, is the tone of those interactions? What is being done within the institution to address any problems or to foster greater respect and understanding?

There is a bumper sticker that reads: TOO BAD IGNORANCE ISN'T PAINFUL. I like that. But ignorance is. We just seldom attribute the pain to it or even recognize it when we see it. Like the postcard on my corkboard. It shows a young man in a very hip jacket smoking a cigarette. In the background is a high school with the American flag waving. The caption says: "Too cool for school. Yet too stupid for the real world." Out of the mouth of the young man is a bubble enclosing the words "Maybe I'll start a band." There could be a postcard showing a jock in a uniform saying, "I don't need school. I'm going to the NFL or NBA." Or one showing a young man or woman studying and a group of young people saying, "So you want to be white." Or something equally demeaning. We need to quit it.

I am a professor of English at Virginia Tech. I've been here for four years, though for only two years with academic rank. I am tenured, which means I have a teaching position for life, a rarity on a predominantly white campus. Whether from malice or ignorance, people who think I should be at a predominantly Black institution will ask, "Why are you at Tech?" Because it's here. And so are Black students. But even if Black students weren't here, it's painfully obvious that this nation and this world cannot allow white students to go through higher education without interacting with Blacks in authoritative positions. It is equally clear that predominantly Black colleges cannot accommodate the numbers of Black students who want and need an education.

Is it difficult to attend a predominantly white college? Compared with what? Being passed over for promotion because you lack credentials? Being turned down for jobs because you are not college-educated? Joining the armed forces or going to jail because you cannot find an alternative to the streets? Let's have a little perspective here. Where can you go and what can you do that frees you from interacting with the white American mentality? You're going to interact; the only question is, will you be in some control of yourself and your actions, or will you be controlled by others? I'm going to recommend self-control.

What's the difference between prison and college? They both prescribe your behavior for a given period of time. They both allow you to read books and develop your writing. They both give you time alone to think and time with your peers to talk about issues. But four years of prison doesn't give you a passport to greater opportunities. Most likely that time only gives you greater knowledge of how to get back in. Four years of college gives you an opportunity not only to lift yourself but to serve your people effectively. What's the difference when you are called nigger in college from when you are called nigger in prison? In college you can, though I admit with effort, follow procedures to have those students who called you nigger kicked out or suspended. You can bring issues to public attention without risking your life. But mostly, college is and always has been the future. We, neither less nor more than other people, need knowledge. There are discomforts attached to attending predominantly white colleges, though no more so than living in a racist world. Here are some rules to follow that may help:

Go to class. No matter how you feel. No matter how you think the professor feels about you. It's important to have a consistent presence in the classroom. If nothing else, the professor will know you care enough and are serious enough to be there.

Meet your professors. Extend your hand (give a firm handshake) and tell them your name. Ask them what you need to do to make an A. You may never make an A, but you have put them on notice that you are serious about getting good grades.

Do assignments on time. Typed or computer-generated. You have the syllabus. Follow it, and turn those papers in. If for some reason you can't complete an assignment on time, let your professor know before it is due and work out a new due date — then meet it.

Go back to see your professor. Tell him or her your name again. If an assignment received less than an A, ask why, and find out what you need to do to improve the next assignment.   8

Yes, your professor is busy. So are you. So are your parents who are working to pay or help with your tuition. Ask early what you need to do if you feel you are starting to get into academic trouble. Do not wait until you are failing.   9

Understand that there will be professors who do not like you; there may even be professors who are racist or sexist or both. You must discriminate among your professors to see who will give you the help you need. You may not simply say, "They are all against me." They aren't. They mostly don't care. Since you are the one who wants to be educated, find the people who want to help.   10

Don't defeat yourself. Cultivate your friends. Know your enemies. You cannot undo hundreds of years of prejudicial thinking. Think for yourself and speak up. Raise your hand in class. Say what you believe no matter how awkward you may think it sounds. You will improve in your articulation and confidence.   11

Participate in some campus activity. Join the newspaper staff. Run for office. Join a dorm council. Do something that involves you on campus. You are going to be there for four years, so let your presence be known, if not felt.   12

You will inevitably run into some white classmates who are troubling because they often say stupid things, ask stupid questions — and expect an answer. Here are some comebacks to some of the most common inquiries and comments: 13

Q: What's it like to grow up in a ghetto?   14
A: I don't know.   15

Q: (from the teacher) Can you give us the Black perspective on Toni Morrison, Huck Finn, slavery, Martin Luther King, Jr., and others?   16
A: I can give you *my* perspective. (Do not take the burden of 22 million people on your shoulders. Remind everyone that you are an individual, and don't speak for the race or any other individual within it.)   17

Q: Why do all the Black people sit together in the dining hall?   18
A: Why do all the white students sit together?   19

Q: Why should there be an African-American studies course?   20
A: Because white Americans have not adequately studied the contributions of Africans and African-Americans. Both Black and white students need to know our total common history.   21

Q: Why are there so many scholarships for "minority" students?   22
A: Because they wouldn't give my great-grandparents their forty acres   23
and the mule.

Q: How can whites understand Black history, culture, literature, and   24
so forth?
A: The same way we understand white history, culture, literature, and   25
so forth. That is why we're in school: to learn.

Q: Should whites take African-American studies courses?   26
A: Of course. We take white-studies courses, though the universities   27
don't call them that.

Comment: When I see groups of Black people on campus, it's really   28
intimidating.
Comeback: I understand what you mean. I'm frightened when I see   29
white students congregating.

Comment: It's not fair. It's easier for you guys to get into college   30
than for other people.
Comeback: If it's so easy, why aren't there more of us?   31

Comment: It's not our fault that America is the way it is.   32
Comeback: It's not our fault, either, but both of us have a responsi-   33
bility to make changes.

It's really very simple. Educational progress is a national concern;   34
education is a private one. Your job is not to educate white people; it
is to obtain an education. If you take the racial world on your shoulders, you will not get the job done. Deal with yourself as an individual
worthy of respect, and make everyone else deal with you the same
way. College is a little like playing grown-up. Practice what you want
to be. You have been telling your parents you are grown. Now is your
chance to act like it.

RESPONDING TO READING

Giovanni concludes her essay by pointing out the nature of the "job" black
students have undertaken, focusing on what it does *not* involve for them.
For you, does the "job" of being a student involve more than just getting an
education? If so, what other priorities do you have, and what additional
challenges do they present? If not, explain your situation. How well are you
able to put other things aside to achieve your educational goals?

QUESTIONING THE TEXT

1. Who is Giovanni's audience? Where does the intended audience first
   become clear? (Glossary: *Audience*)

2. Why does Giovanni dismiss the notion that it is difficult being a black student at a predominantly white college? What contexts does she use to support her contention?

3. The rules Giovanni presents to help black students succeed at white colleges offer a lot of sound advice for any student at any college. Why does Giovanni use what could be considered general information in her essay?

4. On what topic does Giovanni provide sample questions and answers for her readers? Why is the topic important to her readers?

UNDERSTANDING THE WRITER'S CRAFT

1. Giovanni begins her essay with staccato rhythm. Short sentences appear throughout the essay, but they are emphasized in the beginning. (Glossary: *Beginnings/Endings*) Reread paragraph 1. What does Giovanni accomplish with her rapid-fire delivery? Why is it appropriate for the subject matter?

2. What does Giovanni gain by including her short personal narrative in paragraph 2? (Glossary: *Narration*) Why is it necessary to know her personal history and current situation?

3. After beginning her essay with straight prose, Giovanni uses a list with full explanations and a series of Q&A examples to outline strategies to help black students cope at predominantly white colleges. Why did Giovanni use these techniques to convey her material? How might they add to the usefulness of the essay for the reader?

4. What does Giovanni mean when she says, "Educational progress is a national concern; education is a private one" (paragraph 34)? In what ways is this point important to her purpose? (Glossary: *Purpose*)

EXPLORING LANGUAGE

1. How did you first react to Giovanni's title, "Campus Racism 101"? What did it connote to you? (Glossary: *Connotation/Denotation*) After reading the essay, do you think the title is appropriate? Explain your answer.

2. Giovanni uses the word *stupid* on two occasions. The first use (paragraph 1), "too stupid for the real world," provides a context for how she views the word, while the second characterizes what white students sometimes ask or say to black students. The second use (paragraph 13) is a little jarring — often these days the characterization is softened to "insensitive" or "thoughtless." The use of *stupid* implies a more active ignorance on the part of the questioner. What does Giovanni gain by using the word? Do you think it is meant to be pejorative toward the white students? Explain your answer.

3. Refer to your desk dictionary to determine the meanings of the following words as Giovanni uses them in this selection: *predominantly* (paragraph 2), *syllabus* (7), *articulation* (11).

COMBINING RHETORICAL STRATEGIES

Giovanni states that the discomforts of attending a mostly white college are no greater than those encountered simply living in a racist world. Based on her essay, how do you think Giovanni defines "racist world"? Write a short definition, then discuss with your class the ways in which higher education can serve to reduce or end racism as well as the issues it cannot address effectively or at all.

WRITING SUGGESTIONS

1. **(Process Analysis)** What specific strategies do you employ to do well in your classes? Do you ask the professor what is needed for an A and make sure you attend every class, as Giovanni suggests in her essay? Do you take meticulous notes, study every day, just cram the night before exams, or have a lucky shirt for test days? Write a process analysis in which you present your method for success in school in a way that others could emulate — should they so choose.

2. **(Other Strategies)** In Giovanni's Q&A section, she answers the question, "Why are there so many scholarships for 'minority' students?" with the answer, "Because they wouldn't give my great-grandparents their forty acres and the mule" (paragraphs 22–23). Write an argumentative essay in which you react to both Giovanni's answer and the situation as a whole. Do you think qualified minority students should receive preferential treatment for admissions and financial aid? If you argue no, what other strategies would you support to address the current educational inequities between whites and blacks?

3. **(Research)** Giovanni's essay covers a subject — blacks attending predominantly white colleges — with a relatively short history in many areas of the country. Although blacks have a long history of success in higher education in the Northeast, where they were admitted to some schools as early as the 1820s, it has only been in the last four decades that the final barriers have been removed for them to attend colleges nationwide. The battle over education rights became one of the most important components of the civil rights movement and led to some of its most contentious showdowns. In the library or on the Internet, research the history of higher education for blacks over the past fifty years. What gains did they make during the civil rights movement? Has increased opportunity translated into increased percentages of blacks at various campuses? What roadblocks do blacks still face on the way to receiving higher education?

- **U.S. Civil Rights from Spartacus Encyclopedia**
  <http://www.spartacus.schoolnet.co.uk/USAcivilrights.htm>

  The Spartacus Encyclopedia lists civil rights history information from 1890 to 1980 by people and events, including James Meredith and the 1962 University of Mississippi Riot.

- **American Association of Higher Education's Diversity Initiatives**
  <http://www.aahe.org/diversityprogram.htm>

  American Association for Higher Education's Diversity Program page links to statistics on enrollment and retention for all ages and ethnicities since 1910.

- **ERIC Clearinghouse on Higher Education**
  <http://www.eriche.org>

  This site is a clearinghouse of information on higher education.

Inside the Engine

Tom and Ray Magliozzi

Tom Magliozzi was born in East Cambridge, Massachusetts, in 1938. He graduated from the Massachusetts Institute of Technology and earned a doctorate in marketing before opening the Good News Garage in Cambridge in 1973 with his younger brother Ray (b. 1947), who had been teaching junior high school. In 1977, Tom joined other mechanics on a WBUR-FM radio show to talk about car repair. When he was invited back, he brought Ray with him, and they were soon offered their own weekly program, Car Talk. *The Magliozzis called themselves Click and Clack, the Tappet Brothers, and dispensed easy-to-understand advice with heavy doses of humor and raucous laughter.* Car Talk *built a large local audience before premiering as a national program on National Public Radio in 1987. The Magliozzis earned a Peabody Award in 1992 and are now heard by more than 2.3 million listeners each week. The Magliozzis' newspaper column, "Click and Clack Talk Cars," appears in 250 newspapers, and they also produce a popular Web site.*

While almost all of their early work could only be heard on the radio, the Magliozzis assembled some of their best advice in the book Car Talk, *published in 1991. The following selection offers lots of information and sensible advice about car engines while conveying the brothers' irreverent style.*

BEFORE YOU READ

How comfortable are you working with machines? Do you like to tinker with car engines and lawn mowers, or do you scream for help if they malfunction? If you do not know much about mechanical devices, why is that? Is it that you find mechanical topics intimidating but would like to know more, or that you find them of little interest and are happy to get expert assistance when necessary?

A customer of ours had an old Thunderbird that he used to drive back and forth to New York to see a girlfriend every other weekend. And every time he made the trip he'd be in the shop the following Monday needing to get something fixed because the car was such a hopeless piece of trash. One Monday he failed to show up and Tom said, "Gee, that's kind of unusual." I said jokingly, "Maybe he blew the car up."

Well, what happened was that he was on the Merritt Parkway in Connecticut when he noticed that he had to keep the gas pedal all the way to the floor just to go 30 m.p.h., with this big V-8 engine, and he figured something was awry.

So he pulled into one of those filling stations where they sell gaso-   3
line and chocolate-chip cookies and milk. And he asked the attendant to look at the engine and, of course, the guy said, "I can't help you. All I know is cookies and milk." But the guy agreed to look anyway since our friend was really desperate. His girlfriend was waiting for him and he needed to know if he was going to make it. Anyway, the guy threw open the hood and jumped back in terror. The engine was glowing red. Somewhere along the line, probably around Hartford, he must have lost all of his motor oil. The engine kept getting hotter and hot-ter, but like a lot of other things in the car that didn't work, neither did his oil pressure warning light. As a result, the engine got so heated up that it fused itself together. All the pistons melted, and the cylinder heads deformed, and the pistons fused to the cylinder walls, and the bearings welded themselves to the crankshaft — oh, it was a terrible sight! When he tried to restart the engine, he just heard a *click, click, click* since the whole thing was seized up tighter than a drum.

That's what can happen in a case of extreme engine neglect. Most   4
of us wouldn't do that, or at least wouldn't do it knowingly. Our friend didn't do it knowingly either, but he learned a valuable lesson. He learned that his girlfriend wouldn't come and get him if his car broke down. Even if he offered her cookies and milk.

The oil is critical to keeping things running since it not only acts   5
as a lubricant, but it also helps to keep the engine cool. What happens is that the oil pump sucks the oil out of what's called the sump (or the crankcase or the oil pan), and it pushes that oil, under pressure, up to all of the parts that need lubrication.

The way the oil works is that it acts as a cushion. The molecules of   6
oil actually separate the moving metal parts from one another so that they don't directly touch; the crankshaft *journals,* or the hard parts of the crankshaft, never touch the soft connecting-rod *bearings* because there's a film of oil between them, forced in there under pressure. From the pump.

It's pretty high pressure too. When the engine is running at high-   7
way speed, the oil, at 50 or 60 pounds or more per square inch (or about 4 bars, if you're of the metric persuasion — but let's leave religion out of this), is coursing through the veins of the engine and keeping all these parts at safe, albeit microscopic, distances from each other.

But if there's a lot of dirt in the oil, the dirt particles get embedded   8
in these metal surfaces and gradually the dirt acts as an abrasive and wears away these metal surfaces. And pretty soon the engine is junk.

It's also important that the motor oil be present in sufficient   9
quantity. In nontechnical terms, that means there's got to be enough

of it in there. If you have too little oil in your engine, there's not going to be enough of it to go around, and it will get very hot, because four quarts will be doing the work of five, and so forth. When that happens, the oil gets overheated and begins to burn up at a greater than normal rate. Pretty soon, instead of having four quarts, you have three and a half quarts, then three quarts doing the work of five. And then, next thing you know, you're down to two quarts and your engine is glowing red, just like that guy driving to New York, and it's chocolate-chip cookie time.

In order to avoid this, some cars have gauges and some have warning lights; some people call them "idiot lights." Actually, we prefer to reverse it and call them "idiot gauges." I think gauges are bad. When you drive a car — maybe I'm weird about this — I think it's a good idea to look at the road most of the time. And you can't look at the road if you're busy looking at a bunch of gauges. It's the same objection we have to these stupid radios today that have so damn many buttons and slides and digital scanners and so forth that you need a copilot to change stations. Remember when you just turned a knob? 10

Not that gauges are bad in and of themselves. I think if you have your choice, what you want is idiot lights — or what we call "genius lights" — and gauges too. It's nice to have a gauge that you can kind of keep an eye on for an overview of what's going on. For example, if you know that your engine typically runs at 215 degrees and on this particular day, which is not abnormally hot, it's running at 220 or 225, you might suspect that something is wrong and get it looked at before your radiator boils over. 11

On the other hand, if that gauge was the only thing you had to rely on and you didn't have a light to alert you when something was going wrong, then you'd look at the thing all the time, especially if your engine had melted on you once. In that case, why don't you take the bus? Because you're not going to be a very good driver, spending most of your time looking at the gauges. 12

Incidentally, if that oil warning light ever comes on, shut the engine off! We don't mean that you should shut it off in rush-hour traffic when you're in the passing lane. Use all necessary caution and get the thing over to the breakdown lane. But don't think you can limp to the next exit, because you can't. Spend the money to get towed and you may save the engine. 13

It's a little-known fact that the oil light does *not* signify whether or not you have oil in the engine. The oil warning light is really monitoring the oil *pressure*. Of course, if you have no oil, you'll have no oil pressure, so the light will be on. But it's also possible to have plenty of oil and an oil pump that's not working for one reason or another. In 14 this event, a new pump would fix the problem, but if you were to drive the car (saying, "It must be a bad light, I just checked the oil!") you'd melt the motor.

So if the oil warning light comes on, even if you just had an oil 15 change and the oil is right up to the full mark on the dipstick and is nice and clean — don't drive the car!

Here's another piece of useful info. When you turn the key to the 16 "on" position, all the little warning lights *should light up:* the temperature light, the oil light, whatever other lights you may have. Because that is the *test mode* for these lights. If those lights *don't* light up when you turn the key to the "on" position (just before you turn it all the way to start the car), does that mean you're out of oil? No. It means that something is wrong with the warning light itself. If the light doesn't work then, it's not going to work at all. Like when you need it, for example.

One more thing about oil: overfilling is just as bad as underfilling. 17 Can you really have too much of a good thing? you ask. Yes. If you're half a quart or even a quart overfilled, it's not a big deal, and I wouldn't be afraid to drive the car under those circumstances. But if you're a quart and a half or two quarts or more overfilled, you could have so much oil in the crankcase that the spinning crankshaft is going to hit the oil and turn it into suds. It's impossible for the pump to pump suds, so you'll ruin the motor. It's kind of like a front-loading washing machine that goes berserk and spills suds all over the floor when you put too much detergent in. That's what happens to your motor oil when you overfill it.

With all this talk about things that can go wrong, let's not forget 18 that modern engines are pretty incredible. People always say, "You know, the cars of yesteryear were wonderful. They built cars rough and tough and durable in those days."

Horsefeathers. 19

The cars of yesteryear were nicer to look at because they were very 20 individualistic. They were all different, and some were even beautiful. In fact, when I was a kid, you could tell the year, make, and model of a car from a hundred paces just by looking at the taillights or the grille.

Nowadays, they all look the same. They're like jellybeans on 21 wheels. You can't tell one from the other. But the truth is, they've never made engines as good as they make them today. Think of the abuse they take! None of the cars of yesteryear was capable of going 60 or 70 miles per hour all day long and taking it for 100,000 miles.

Engines of today — and by today I mean from the late '60s on 22 up — are far superior. What makes them superior is not only the design and the metallurgy, but the lubricants. The oil they had thirty years ago was lousy compared to what we have today. There are magic additives and detergents and long-chain polymers and what-have-you that make them able to hold dirt in suspension and to neutralize acids and to lubricate better than oils of the old days.

There aren't too many things that will go wrong, because the en- 23
gines are made so well and the tolerances are closer. And aside from doing stupid things like running out of oil or failing to heed the warning lights or overfilling the thing, you shouldn't worry.

But here's one word of caution about cars that have timing belts: 24
Lots of cars these days are made with overhead camshafts. The camshaft, which opens the valves, is turned by a gear and gets its power from the crankshaft. Many cars today use a notched rubber *timing belt* to connect the two shafts instead of a chain because it's cheaper and easy to change. And here's the caveat: *if you don't change it and the belt breaks, it can mean swift ruin to the engine.* The pistons can hit the valves and you'll have bent valves and possibly broken pistons.

So you can do many hundreds of dollars' worth of damage by fail- 25
ing to heed the manufacturer's warning about changing the timing belt in a timely manner. No pun intended. For most cars, the timing belt replacement is somewhere between $100 and $200. It's not a big deal.

I might add that there are many cars that have rubber timing belts 26
that will *not* cause damage to the engine when they break. But even if you have one of those cars, make sure that you get the belt changed, at the very least, when the manufacturer suggests it. If there's no specific recommendation and you have a car with a rubber belt, we would recommend that you change it at 60,000 miles. Because even if you don't do damage to the motor when the belt breaks, you're still going to be stuck somewhere, maybe somewhere unpleasant. Maybe even Cleveland! So you want to make sure that you don't fall into that situation.

Many engines that have rubber timing belts also use the belt to 27
drive the water pump. On these, don't forget to change the water pump when you change the timing belt, because the leading cause of premature belt failure is that the water pump seizes. So if you have a timing belt that drives the water pump, get the water pump out of there at the same time. You don't want to put a belt in and then have the water pump go a month later, because it'll break the new belt and wreck the engine.

The best way to protect all the other pieces that you can't get to 28
without spending a lot of money is through frequent oil changes. The manufacturers recommend oil changes somewhere between seven and ten thousand miles, depending upon the car. We've always

recommended that you change your oil at 3,000 miles. We realize for some people that's a bit of an inconvenience, but look at it as cheap insurance. And change the filter every time too.

And last but not least, I want to repeat this because it's important: Make sure your warning lights work. The oil pressure and engine temperature warning lights are your engine's lifeline. Check them every day. You should make it as routine as checking to see if your zipper's up. You guys should do it at the same time. 29

What you do is, you get into the car, check to see that your zipper's up, and then turn the key on and check to see if your oil pressure and temperature warning lights come on. 30

I don't know what women do. 31

RESPONDING TO READING

The Magliozzis offer several direct instructions in their essay, some of which they present forcefully. How did you respond to the instructions? If you own a car, did the Magliozzis inspire you to follow their directions, or did you find the instructions less than convincing? Explain your answer.

QUESTIONING THE TEXT

1. What happened to the Magliozzis' customer on his drive down the Merritt Parkway? What did he learn from his experience?

2. Why is having too much oil in your engine just as bad as having too little in some cases?

3. What do the Magliozzis like about older cars compared to new ones? Why do they think the cars of today are better overall?

4. What dangers are inherent in the new rubber timing belts? Why is it so important to follow the recommendations for having them replaced?

UNDERSTANDING THE WRITER'S CRAFT

1. The Magliozzis begin their essay with a story about a customer of theirs that graphically demonstrates what happens when there is no oil in an engine. (Glossary: *Beginnings/Endings*) Why is the story an effective way to begin their discussion of the workings of an engine? Why didn't they begin with a more technical presentation?

2. The Magliozzis use several analogies to help explain the workings of the engine. (Glossary: *Analogy*) Identify two of the analogies they use, and explain how they help readers understand the material.

3. As anyone who has ever heard their radio show can attest, the Magliozzis are popular because of the way they combine sometimes out-

rageous humor with sound technical knowledge and advice. Do you find their humorous, rather rambling presentation effective or distracting? Explain your answer with specific examples from the essay.

4. What audience are the Magliozzis trying to reach? (Glossary: *Audience*) What techniques do they use to make the material understandable without being condescending?

EXPLORING LANGUAGE

1. Discuss the significance of the terms *idiot lights* and *idiot gauges* (paragraph 10). How are the Magliozzis able to use such terms without offending the reader?

2. Technical terms — whether used by scientists, technicians, or mechanics — can easily intimidate lay readers. Although the Magliozzis do not get overly technical, they must present some terms and processes that many of their readers have probably avoided learning. Evaluate how well they present the more technical material. How do they adapt their presentation and their diction to make the technical issues more accessible? (Glossary: *Diction*) In your opinion, how well do they succeed?

3. Refer to your desk dictionary to determine the meanings of the following words as the Magliozzis use them in this selection: *grille* (paragraph 20), *metallurgy* (22), *polymers* (22), *caveat* (24).

COMBINING RHETORICAL STRATEGIES

Following the model established by the Magliozzis, write an accessible, offbeat description of a car you know — your own, your parents', a friend's. Do you like it? Hate it? How well does it handle, and how durable is it? Make the description lively, but make sure to convey your dominant impression of the car.

WRITING SUGGESTIONS

1. **(Process Analysis)** Based on the Magliozzis' essay, your own knowledge, and another source about engines, write a straightforward process analysis of how to take care of a car engine. Include both the steps to take and the rationale behind those steps. Organize the steps chronologically, beginning with the purchase of a new car and going through 100,000 miles or so. Cars are different and some require steps that others do not, so be as comprehensive as you can, but not exhaustively so. Focus instead on clarity and making your essay understandable to nonmechanics.

2. **(Other Strategies)** Consider the following cartoon by Ed Koren. As the cartoon demonstrates, car and transportation issues can pervade every aspect of our lives. Even when we think we have everything under

"Is this a good time to bring up a car problem?"

control, a breakdown or a fender bender can turn any day into a bad day. The Magliozzis use humor to help explain the workings of the car; likewise, the cartoonist uses humor to introduce the ways in which cars insinuate themselves in our lives — even into our most intimate inter-actions. Write an essay in which you discuss the cartoon and the impli-cations of the Magliozzis' advice. Why are they both funny? What is-sues do both the essay and the cartoon point up regarding cars and the troubles they cause us?

3. **(Research)** Research the mechanical and performance specifications of your dream vehicle. It could be a car, but it could also be a motorcycle, an airplane, or even a space shuttle. Using the library or the Internet to do your research, write a paper in which you present a detailed report about the vehicle, including the workings of its engine, its capabilities, its intended use, and so on. Also explain why the vehicle appeals to you. Does it look good? Would it help you take care of day-to-day tasks? Would it be fun? How practical are you when it comes to vehicles?

• **Under the Hood**
<http://library.thinkquest.org/19199>

This site contains beginner and advanced tutorials in car maintenance, as well as interactive games and information about how to diagnose car problems.

- **A-Car.com**

  <http://www.a-car.com>

  This site contains the latest news and developments for cars today, including xenon headlights, global positioning systems, and alternative fuels.

- **Alternative Fuel Data Center**

  <http://www.afdc.nrel.gov>

  This guide from the Office of Transportation Technologies lists the benefits and general facts about using alternative fuels in automobiles.

- **Automotive Learning Online**

  <http://www.innerauto.com/innerauto/htm/auto.html>

  Click on one of ten pictures of automotive systems to learn everything about the inner workings of cars.

COMBINING SUBJECTS AND STRATEGIES

The photograph below depicts many of the same themes and strategies as the Combining Rhetorical Strategies essay that follows. Your observations about the photograph will help guide you to the key themes and strategies in the essay. After you've read the essay, you may use your observations about both the photograph and the essay to examine how the overlapping themes and strategies work in each medium.

One person's treasure is another person's trash. That statement is especially true around college campuses, when moving students often throw away their large — but often still quite useful — personal possessions. In the following photograph, "Dumpster Diving" by Christopher Johnson, taken in Cambridge, Massachusetts, the college Dumpsters have obviously become focal points of interest for others in the community. Perhaps this could be termed the purest form of recycling, and it underscores the transient nature of our material possessions.

© Christopher S. Johnson/Stock Boston

For Discussion

In the preceding photograph, focus on the goods that were thrown away, but are in the process of being salvaged by people diving into the dumpster. Are the items being sorted through things that you might use? Why or why not? You yourself may have thrown away items that have outlasted their usefulness. Did you have regrets about your decisions? Did it feel good to throw the items away? Were they shabby? Not attractive? Still good but not the latest in style or color? Explain.

On Dumpster Diving

Lars Eighner

Born in Texas in 1948, Lars Eighner attended the University of Texas at Austin. After graduation, he wrote essays and fiction, and several of his articles were published in magazines like Threepenny Review, *the* Guide, *and* Inches. *A volume of short stories,* Bayou Boy and Other Stories, *was published in 1985. Eighner became homeless in 1988 when he left his job as an attendant at a mental hospital. The following piece, which appeared in the* Utne Reader, *is an abridged version of an essay that first appeared in* Threepenny Review. *The piece eventually became part of Eighner's startling account of the three years he spent as a homeless person,* Travels with Lizbeth *(1993). His publications include the novels,* Pawn to Queen Four *(1995), and* Whispered in the Dark *(1996), and the nonfiction book* Gay Cosmos *(1995).*

Eighner uses a number of rhetorical strategies in "On Dumpster Diving," but pay particular attention to the importance of his delineation of the "stages that a person goes through in learning to scavenge" to the success of the essay as a whole.

BEFORE YOU READ

Are you a pack rat, or do you get rid of what is not immediately useful to you? Outside of the usual kitchen garbage and empty toothpaste tubes, how do you make the decision to throw something away?

I began Dumpster diving about a year before I became homeless. 1

I prefer the term *scavenging.* I have heard people, evidently meaning 2
to be polite, use the word *foraging,* but I prefer to reserve that word for gathering nuts and berries and such, which I also do, according to the season and opportunity.

I like the frankness of the word *scavenging*. I live from the refuse of   3
others. I am a scavenger. I think it a sound and honorable niche, although if I could I would naturally prefer to live the comfortable consumer life, perhaps — and only perhaps — as a slightly less wasteful
consumer owing to what I have learned as a scavenger.

Except for jeans, all my clothes come from Dumpsters. Boom   4
boxes, candles, bedding, toilet paper, medicine, books, a typewriter, a
virgin male love doll, coins sometimes amounting to many dollars: all
came from Dumpsters. And, yes, I eat from Dumpsters, too.

There is a predictable series of stages that a person goes through in   5
learning to scavenge. At first the new scavenger is filled with disgust
and self-loathing. He is ashamed of being seen.

This stage passes with experience. The scavenger finds a pair of run-   6
ning shoes that fit and look and smell brand-new. He finds a pocket calculator in perfect working order. He finds pristine ice cream, still frozen,
more than he can eat or keep. He begins to understand: people do throw
away perfectly good stuff, a lot of perfectly good stuff.

At this stage he may become lost and never recover: All the   7
Dumpster divers I have known come to the point of trying to acquire
everything they touch. Why not take it, they reason, it is all free. This
is, of course, hopeless, and most divers come to realize that they must
restrict themselves to items of relatively immediate utility.

The finding of objects is becoming something of an urban art.   8
Even respectable, employed people will sometimes find something
tempting sticking out of a Dumpster or standing beside one. Quite a
number of people, not all of them of the bohemian type, are willing to
brag that they found this or that piece in the trash.

But eating from Dumpsters is the thing that separates the dilet-   9
tanti from the professionals. Eating safely involves three principles:
using the senses and common sense to evaluate the condition of the
found materials; knowing the Dumpsters of a given area and checking
them regularly; and seeking always to answer the question "Why was
this discarded?"

Yet perfectly good food can be found in Dumpsters. Canned   10
goods, for example, turn up fairly often in the Dumpsters I frequent. I
also have few qualms about dry foods such as crackers, cookies, cereal,
chips, and pasta if they are free of visible contaminants and still dry
and crisp. Raw fruits and vegetables with intact skins seem perfectly
safe to me, excluding, of course, the obviously rotten. Many are discarded for minor imperfections that can be pared away.

A typical discard is a half jar of peanut butter — though nonor-   11
ganic peanut butter does not require refrigeration and is unlikely to
spoil in any reasonable time. One of my favorite finds is yogurt —
often discarded, still sealed, when the expiration date has passed —
because it will keep for several days, even in warm weather.

No matter how careful I am I still get dysentery at least once a 12 month, oftener in warm weather. I do not want to paint too romantic a picture. Dumpster diving has serious drawbacks as a way of life.

I find from the experience of scavenging two rather deep lessons. 13 The first is to take what I can use and let the rest go. I have come to think that there is no value in the abstract. A thing I cannot use or make useful, perhaps by trading, has no value, however fine or rare it may be.

The second lesson is the transience of material being. I do not sup- 14 pose that ideas are immortal, but certainly they are longer-lived than material objects.

The things I find in Dumpsters, the love letters and rag dolls of so 15 many lives, remind me of this lesson. Now I hardly pick up a thing without envisioning the time I will cast it away. This, I think, is a healthy state of mind. Almost everything I have now has already been cast out at least once, proving that what I own is valueless to someone.

I find that my desire to grab for the gaudy bauble has been largely 16 sated. I think this is an attitude I share with the very wealthy — we both know there is plenty more where whatever we have came from. Between us are the rat-race millions who have confounded their selves with the objects they grasp and who nightly scavenge the cable channels for they know not what.

I am sorry for them. 17

RESPONDING TO READING

In paragraph 15, Eighner writes, "I hardly pick up a thing without envisioning the time I will cast it away. This, I think, is a healthy state of mind." React to this statement. Do you think such an attitude is healthy or defeatist? If many people thought this way, what impact would it have on our consumer society?

QUESTIONING THE TEXT

1. What stages do beginning Dumpster divers go through before they become what Eighner terms "professionals" (paragraph 9)? What examples does Eighner use to illustrate the passage through these stages? (Glossary: *Exemplification*)

2. What three principles does one need to follow in order to eat safely from Dumpsters? What foods are best to eat from Dumpsters? What are the risks?

3. What two lessons has Eighner learned from his Dumpster diving experiences? Why are they significant to him?

UNDERSTANDING THE WRITER'S CRAFT

1. Eighner's essay deals with both the immediate, physical aspects of Dumpster diving, such as what can be found in a typical Dumpster and the physical price one pays for eating out of them, and the larger, abstract issues that Dumpster diving raises, such as materialism and the transience of material objects. (Glossary: *Concrete/Abstract*) Why does he describe the concrete things before he discusses the abstract issues raised by their presence in Dumpsters? What does he achieve by using both types of elements?

2. Eighner's account of Dumpster diving focuses primarily on the odd appeal and interest inherent in the activity. Paragraph 12 is his one disclaimer, in which he states, "I do not want to paint too romantic a picture." Why does Eighner include this disclaimer? How does it add to the effectiveness of his piece? Why do you think it is so brief and abrupt?

3. Eighner uses many rhetorical techniques in his essay, but its core is a fairly complete process analysis of how to Dumpster dive. Summarize this process analysis. Why do you think Eighner did not title the essay "How to Dumpster Dive"?

EXPLORING LANGUAGE

1. Eighner says he prefers the word *scavenging* to *Dumpster diving* or *foraging*. What do those three terms mean to him? Why do you think he finds the discussion of the terms important enough to discuss at the beginning of his essay? (Glossary: *Diction*)

2. According to Eighner, "eating from Dumpsters is the thing that separates the dilettanti from the professionals" (paragraph 9). What do the words *dilettante* and *professional* connote to you? (Glossary: *Connotation/Denotation*) Why does Eighner choose to use them instead of the more straightforward *casual* and *serious?*

3. Eighner says, "The finding of objects is becoming something of an urban art" (paragraph 8). What does this sentence mean to you? Based on the essay, do you find his use of the word *art* appropriate when discussing any aspect of Dumpster diving? Why or why not?

4. Refer to your desk dictionary to determine the meanings of the following words as Eighner uses them in this selection: *foraging* (paragraph 2), *pristine* (6), *bohemian* (8), *dilettanti* (9), *transience* (14), *sated* (16).

COMBINING RHETORICAL STRATEGIES

1. Dumpster diving has had a profound effect on Eighner and the way he lives. How do his explanations of choices he makes, such as deciding which items to keep, enhance his presentation of the practical art of Dumpster diving?

2. Discuss how Eighner uses exemplification to bring the world of Dumpster diving to life. What characterizes the examples he uses?

3. Writers often use process analysis in conjunction with other strategies, especially argument, to try to improve the way a process is carried out. In this essay, Eighner uses a full process analysis to lay out his views on American values and materialism. How is this an effective way to combine strategies? Think of other arguments that could be strengthened if they included elements of process analysis.

WRITING SUGGESTIONS

1. **(Process Analysis)** Write a process analysis in which you relate how you acquire a consumer item of some importance or expense to you. Do you compare brands, store prices, and so on? What are your priorities — must the item be stylish or durable, offer good overall value, give high performance? How do you decide to spend your money? In other words, what determines which items are worth the sacrifice?

2. **(Other Strategies)** Eighner's essay and Christopher Johnson's photo both suggest that what goes — or doesn't go — into our own trash reflects on who we are. Referring to both the selection and the photo, write an essay in which you explore how the ways we sort, judge, divide, and categorize material goods reflect on our priorities and values. What do you throw away? What do you keep? If you have ever moved from one home into another, how did you decide what to get rid of? What do these choices say about you? What do they say about our disposable, consumerist society?

3. **(Research)** Speak with someone in the department or company that handles garbage disposal on your campus or in your area. How much waste is produced in your dorm, campus, or town each day? Is there a problem with where to put all this garbage? What can you do to reduce your contributions to the garbage stream? Use the library and possibly the Internet to find out more about waste on your campus or in your area. Write a paper in which you present your findings. What suggestions do you have for improving the way waste is currently handled? Discuss the future of waste disposal and what people can do to be less wasteful.

- **Recycler's World**
  <http://www.recycle.net>

  This site was established as a worldwide trading site for information related to secondary or recyclable commodities, by-products, and used and surplus items or materials.

- **Welcome to Recycle City**
  <http://www.epa.gov/recyclecity>

  This recycling Web site is sponsored by the Environmental Protection Agency.

- **The U.S. Department of Energy Office of Environmental Management**
  <http://www.em.doe.gov/em30>

  This is the official Web site of the U.S. Department of Energy's Office of Environmental Management and offers information on waste management, treatment, storage, and disposal.

How to Become a Writer (FICTION)

Lorrie Moore

Lorrie Moore was born Marie Lorena Moore in 1957 in Glens Falls, New York. She attended St. Lawrence University on a Regents scholarship and, while there, won Seventeen *magazine's fiction contest. After graduation, she moved to New York City and worked as a paralegal for two years before entering Cornell University's M.F.A. program in writing in 1980. In 1983, she assembled a collection of stories — most from her master's thesis — into a collection entitled* Self-Help, *which found almost immediate acceptance from a publisher and rave reviews from critics when published in 1985. She has since published two novels,* Anagrams *(1986) and* Who Will Run the Frog Hospital? *(1994), and two more collections of short stories, most recently* Birds of America *(1998). Moore is currently a professor of English at the University of Wisconsin.*

In the following selection from Self-Help, *Moore constructs a story about an inspiring writer as a directional process analysis. The unusual presentation provides a unique perspective on both her subject matter and the "how-to" genre as a whole.*

BEFORE YOU READ

Do you have a plan regarding how to achieve your career goals? If so, what steps do you need to take? If not, or if your goals are still unclear, how do you plan to decide what you want to do and how to do it?

First, try to be something, anything, else. A movie star/astronaut. A movie star/missionary. A movie star/kindergarten teacher. President of the World. Fail miserably. It is best if you fail at an early age — say, fourteen. Early, critical disillusionment is necessary so that at fifteen you can write long haiku sequences about thwarted desire. It is a pond, a cherry blossom, a wind brushing against sparrow wing leaving for mountain. Count the syllables. Show it to your mom. She is tough and practical. She has a son in Vietnam and a husband who may be having an affair. She believes in wearing brown because it hides spots. She'll look briefly at your writing, then back up at you with a face blank as a donut. She'll say: "How about emptying the dishwasher?" Look away. Shove the forks in the fork drawer. Accidentally break one of the freebie gas station glasses. This is the required pain and suffering. This is only for starters.

In your high school English class look at Mr. Killian's face. Decide faces are important. Write a villanelle about pores. Struggle. Write a

321

sonnet. Count the syllables: nine, ten, eleven, thirteen. Decide to experiment with fiction. Here you don't have to count syllables. Write a short story about an elderly man and woman who accidentally shoot each other in the head, the result of an inexplicable malfunction of a shotgun which appears mysteriously in their living room one night. Give it to Mr. Killian as your final project. When you get it back, he has written on it: "Some of your images are quite nice, but you have no sense of plot." When you are home, in the privacy of your own room, faintly scrawl in pencil beneath his black-inked comments: "Plots are for dead people, pore-face."

Take all the babysitting jobs you can get. You are great with kids. They love you. You tell them stories about old people who die idiot deaths. You sing them songs like "Blue Bells of Scotland," which is their favorite. And when they are in their pajamas and have finally stopped pinching each other, when they are fast asleep, you read every sex manual in the house, and wonder how on earth anyone could ever do those things with someone they truly loved. Fall asleep in a chair reading Mr. McMurphy's *Playboy*. When the McMurphys come home, they will tap you on the shoulder, look at the magazine in your lap, and grin. You will want to die. They will ask you if Tracey took her medicine all right. Explain, yes, she did, that you promised her a story if she would take it like a big girl and that seemed to work out just fine. "Oh, marvelous," they will exclaim.

Try to smile proudly.

Apply to college as a child psychology major.

As a child psychology major, you have some electives. You've always liked birds. Sign up for something called "The Ornithological Field Trip." It meets Tuesdays and Thursdays at two. When you arrive at Room 134 on the first day of class, everyone is sitting around a seminar table talking about metaphors. You've heard of these. After a short, excruciating while, raise your hand and say diffidently, "Excuse me, isn't this Bird-watching One-oh-one?" The class stops and turns to look at you. They seem to all have one face — giant and blank as a vandalized clock. Someone with a beard booms out, "No, this is Creative Writing." Say: "Oh — right," as if perhaps you knew all along. Look down at your schedule. Wonder how the hell you ended up here. The computer, apparently, has made an error. You start to get up to leave and then don't. The lines at the registrar this week are huge. Perhaps you should stick with this mistake. Perhaps your creative writing isn't all that bad. Perhaps it is fate. Perhaps this is what your dad meant when he said, "It's the age of computers, Francie, it's the age of computers."

Decide that you like college life. In your dorm you meet many nice people. Some are smarter than you. And some, you notice, are dumber than you. You will continue, unfortunately, to view the world in exactly these terms for the rest of your life.

The assignment this week in creative writing is to narrate a violent happening. Turn in a story about driving with your Uncle Gordon and another one about two old people who are accidentally electrocuted when they go to turn on a badly wired desk lamp. The teacher will hand them back to you with comments: "Much of your writing is smooth and energetic. You have, however, a ludicrous notion of plot." Write another story about a man and a woman who, in the very first paragraph, have their lower torsos accidentally blitzed away by dynamite. In the second paragraph, with the insurance money, they buy a frozen yogurt stand together. There are six more paragraphs. You read the whole thing out loud in class. No one likes it. They say your sense of plot is outrageous and incompetent. After class someone asks you if you are crazy.

Decide that perhaps you should stick to comedies. Start dating someone who is funny, someone who has what in high school you called a "really great sense of humor" and what now your creative writing class calls "self-contempt giving rise to comic form." Write down all of his jokes, but don't tell him you are doing this. Make up anagrams of his old girlfriend's name and name all of your socially handicapped characters with them. Tell him his old girlfriend is in all of your stories and then watch how funny he can be, see what a really great sense of humor he can have.

Your child psychology advisor tells you you are neglecting courses in your major. What you spend the most time on should be what you're majoring in. Say yes, you understand.

In creative writing seminars over the next two years, everyone continues to smoke cigarettes and ask the same things: "But does it work?" "Why should we care about this character?" "Have you earned this cliché?" These seem like important questions.

On days when it is your turn, you look at the class hopefully as they scour your mimeographs for a plot. They look back up at you, drag deeply, and then smile in a sweet sort of way.

You spend too much time slouched and demoralized. Your boyfriend suggests bicycling. Your roommate suggests a new boyfriend. You are said to be self-mutilating and losing weight, but you continue writing. The only happiness you have is writing something new, in the middle of the night, armpits damp, heart pounding, something no one has yet seen. You have only those brief, fragile, untested moments of exhilaration when you know: you are a genius. Understand what you must do. Switch majors. The kids in your nursery project will be disappointed, but you have a calling, an urge, a delusion, an unfortunate habit. You have, as your mother would say, fallen in with a bad crowd.

Why write? Where does writing come from? These are questions to ask yourself. They are like: Where does dust come from? Or: Why is there war? Or: If there's a God, then why is my brother now a cripple? 14

These are questions that you keep in your wallet, like calling cards. These are questions, your creative writing teacher says, that are good to address in your journals but rarely in your fiction. 15

The writing professor this fall is stressing the Power of the Imagination. Which means he doesn't want long descriptive stories about your camping trip last July. He wants you to start in a realistic context but then to alter it. Like recombinant DNA. He wants you to let your imagination sail, to let it grow big-bellied in the wind. This is a quote from Shakespeare. 16

Tell your roommate your great idea, your great exercise of imaginative power: a transformation of Melville to contemporary life. It will be about monomania and the fish-eat-fish world of life insurance in Rochester, New York. The first line will be "Call me Fishmeal," and it will feature a menopausal suburban husband named Richard, who because he is so depressed all the time is called "Mopey Dick" by his witty wife Elaine. Say to your roommate: "Mopey Dick, get it?" Your roommate looks at you, her face blank as a large Kleenex. She comes up to you, like a buddy, and puts an arm around your burdened shoulders. "Listen, Francie," she says, slow as speech therapy. "Let's go out and get a big beer." 17

The seminar doesn't like this one either. You suspect they are beginning to feel sorry for you. They say: "You have to think about what is happening. Where is the story here?" 18

The next semester the writing professor is obsessed with writing from personal experience. You must write from what you know, from what has happened to you. He wants deaths, he wants camping trips. Think about what has happened to you. In three years there have been three things: you lost your virginity; your parents got divorced; and your brother came home from a forest ten miles from the Cambodian border with only half a thigh, a permanent smirk nestled into one corner of his mouth. 19

About the first you write: "It created a new space, which hurt and cried in a voice that wasn't mine, 'I'm not the same anymore, but I'll be okay.'" 20

About the second you write an elaborate story of an old married couple who stumble upon an unknown land mine in their kitchen and accidentally blow themselves up. You call it: "For Better or for Liverwurst."

About the last you write nothing. There are no words for this. 22
Your typewriter hums. You can find no words.

At undergraduate cocktail parties, people say, "Oh, you write? 23
What do you write about?" Your roommate, who has consumed too much wine, too little cheese, and no crackers at all, blurts: "Oh, my god, she always writes about her dumb boyfriend."

Later on in life you will learn that writers are merely open, help- 24
less texts with no real understanding of what they have written and therefore must half-believe anything and everything that is said of them. You, however, have not yet reached this stage of literary criticism. You stiffen and say, "I do not," the same way you said it when someone in the fourth grade accused you of really liking oboe lessons and your parents really weren't just making you take them.

Insist you are not very interested in any one subject at all, that 25
you are interested in the music of language, that you are interested in — in — syllables, because they are the atoms of poetry, the cells of the mind, the breath of the soul. Begin to feel woozy. Stare into your plastic wine cup.

"Syllables?" you will hear someone ask, voice trailing off, as they 26
glide slowly toward the reassuring white of the dip.

Begin to wonder what you do write about. Or if you have any- 27
thing to say. Or if there even is such a thing as a thing to say. Limit these thoughts to no more than ten minutes a day; like sit-ups, they can make you thin.

You will read somewhere that all writing has to do with one's gen- 28
itals. Don't dwell on this. It will make you nervous.

Your mother will come visit you. She will look at the circles under 29
your eyes and hand you a brown book with a brown briefcase on the cover. It is entitled: *How to Become a Business Executive.* She has also brought the *Names for Baby* encyclopedia you asked for; one of your characters, the aging clown–school teacher, needs a new name. Your mother will shake her head and say: "Francie, Francie, remember when you were going to be a child psychology major?"

Say: "Mom, I like to write." 30

She'll say: "Sure you like to write. Of course. Sure you like to 31
write."

Write a story about a confused music student and title it: 32
"Schubert Was the One with the Glasses, Right?" It's not a big hit,

although your roommate likes the part where the two violinists accidentally blow themselves up in a recital room. "I went out with a violinist once," she says, snapping her gum.

Thank god you are taking other courses. You can find sanctuary in nineteenth-century ontological snags and invertebrate courting rituals. Certain globular mollusks have what is called "Sex by the Arm." The male octopus, for instance, loses the end of one arm when placing it inside the female body during intercourse. Marine biologists call it "Seven Heaven." Be glad you know these things. Be glad you are not just a writer. Apply to law school. 33

From here on in, many things can happen. But the main one will be this: you decide not to go to law school after all, and, instead, you spend a good, big chunk of your adult life telling people how you decided not to go to law school after all. Somehow you end up writing again. Perhaps you go to graduate school. Perhaps you work odd jobs and take writing courses at night. Perhaps you are working on a novel and writing down all the clever remarks and intimate personal confessions you hear during the day. Perhaps you are losing your pals, your acquaintances, your balance. 34

You have broken up with your boyfriend. You now go out with men who, instead of whispering "I love you," shout: "Do it to me, baby." This is good for your writing. 35

Sooner or later you have a finished manuscript more or less. People look at it in a vaguely troubled sort of way and say, "I'll bet becoming a writer was always a fantasy of yours, wasn't it?" Your lips dry to salt. Say that of all the fantasies possible in the world, you can't imagine being a writer even making the top twenty. Tell them you were going to be a child psychology major. "I bet," they always sigh, "you'd be great with kids." Scowl fiercely. Tell them you're a walking blade. 36

Quit classes. Quit jobs. Cash in old savings bonds. Now you have time like warts on your hands. Slowly copy all of your friends' addresses into a new address book. 37

Vacuum. Chew cough drops. Keep a folder full of fragments. 38

An eyelid darkening sideways.
World as conspiracy.
Possible plot? A woman gets on a bus.
Suppose you threw a love affair and nobody came.

At home drink a lot of coffee. At Howard Johnson's order the cole slaw. Consider how it looks like the soggy confetti of a map: where 39 you've been, where you're going — "You Are Here," says the red star on the back of the menu.

Occasionally a date with a face blank as a sheet of paper asks you 40 whether writers often become discouraged. Say that sometimes they do and sometimes they do. Say it's a lot like having polio.

"Interesting," smiles your date, and then he looks down at his arm 41 hairs and starts to smooth them, all, always, in the same direction.

RESPONDING TO READING

Why does Moore's narrator ("you") find "sanctuary" in solid, prosaic subjects like biology? What do such classes offer the narrator that writing does not? Does such a balance affect your own class schedule? Are you able to focus almost entirely in one area, or does a mix of subjects and academic pressures help you cope?

QUESTIONING THE TEXT

1. What does the narrator's writing lack on a consistent basis? Why is it important?

2. Why is it necessary for Moore's narrator to switch majors? What does writing offer her that child psychology does not?

3. What is the story "For Better or for Liverwurst" (paragraph 21) about on the surface? What is it really about?

4. What can happen to the narrator after college? What is the main thing that "will" happen?

UNDERSTANDING THE WRITER'S CRAFT

1. It does not take long for the reader to realize that Moore is presenting a personal narrative in the form of a directional process analysis. (Glossary: *Narration*) What does she gain by using this technique? What does she lose? Did you find her unusual presentation to be effective? Explain your answer.

2. A recurring theme in the "plotless" stories presented by Moore is the simultaneous gruesome death or disfiguring of couples. What might the repetition of this theme represent? What might such a theme symbolize about Moore's own experiences? (Glossary: *Symbol*)

3. To Moore, the question "Why write?" is rhetorical, an association she strongly establishes in paragraph 14. (Glossary: *Rhetorical Question*) What does that association say about what it means to her to write?

4. Moore equates the discouragement inherent in being a writer with having polio. Do you find her metaphor effective? (Glossary: *Figures of Speech*) What is she implying about writing? What parallels might there be between writing and a terrible disease like polio?

EXPLORING LANGUAGE

1. The faces that confront the narrator in Moore's story are blank. Blank "as a vandalized clock" (paragraph 6) or "a sheet of paper" (40). What does her use of the word *blank* imply about the nature of the people around a writer? What does it imply about the nature of the writer herself?

2. Moore describes the compulsion to write as "a calling, an urge, a delusion, an unfortunate habit" (paragraph 13). What do each of these terms connote to you? (Glossary: *Connotation/Denotation*) As a group, what do they say about Moore's opinion about writing and writers?

3. Refer to your desk dictionary to determine the meanings of the following words as Moore uses them in this selection: *villanelle* (paragraph 2), *diffidently* (6), *anagrams* (9), *monomania* (17), *woozy* (25), *ontological* (33).

COMBINING RHETORICAL STRATEGIES

Write a short essay in which you reverse the way Moore uses rhetorical strategies by turning a process analysis into a personal narrative. Present how you did something or followed a process to the desired end. Include the steps of the process, but include your thoughts, emotions, and anything else that will help you turn a straightforward process analysis into an interesting personal narrative.

WRITING SUGGESTIONS

1. **(Process Analysis)** Speak with someone who is established in a career about how that person got to where he or she is now. It can be a friend, parent, sibling, or more distant relative. Write a process analysis essay in which you present the steps the person took in school, following graduation, and so on, to gain entry and succeed in his or her chosen field. Such processes are often not the result of planning or linear progression; try to integrate any setbacks and side steps into the process you present.

2. **(Other Strategies)** Write an essay in which you compare and contrast the experience Moore's narrator has in college and the experience you are actually having. What experiences are fairly common, almost universal? What experiences in the essay do you think are relatively unique? What unusual or unique experiences have you had? How has your college life helped shape your goals for the future?

3. **(Research)** Research the life of a well-known twentieth-century fiction writer in three ways: biography, writing, and literary interpretation of the writing. In other words, what was the writer's life like, what is his or her writing like, and what do scholars and critics think the writing expresses? Write an essay in which you present significant experiences in the writer's life and explain how those experiences may have influenced his or her writing. Although Moore's story is tongue-in-cheek, keep it in mind as you do your research. What roles do the themes in Moore's

story — early personal failure, critical failure, passion for writing, difficulties with relationships — play in your writer's life, if at all?

• **Authors on the Web**

<http://www.people.virginia.edu/~jbh/author.html>

Biographical sketches on a number of contemporary authors can be found at this site.

• **Catharton: Authors**

<http://www.catharton.com/authors/index.htm>

This site offers an alphabetical listing of authors with links to Web pages and complete listings of their works.

• **Central Booking**

<http://www.centralbooking.com>

This site includes biographies, reviews, useful links, and writings about contemporary authors.

WRITING SUGGESTIONS
FOR PROCESS ANALYSIS

1. Write a directional process analysis on one of the following topics:
   a. how to make chocolate-chip cookies
   b. how to adjust brakes on a bicycle
   c. how to change a tire
   d. how to throw a party
   e. how to use the memory function on a calculator
   f. how to add, drop, or change a course
   g. how to play a specific card game
   h. how to wash a sweater
   i. how to develop film
   j. how to make a pizza
   k. how to make a long-distance call from a phone booth and charge it to your home phone
   l. how to build a Web page
   m. how to select a major course of study
   n. how to winterize a car
   o. how to rent an apartment
   p. how to develop confidence
   q. how to start and operate a small business
   r. how to run for student government office
   s. how to do a magic trick

2. Write an informational process analysis on one of the following topics:
   a. how your heart functions
   b. how a U.S. president is elected
   c. how ice cream is made
   d. how a hurricane forms
   e. how hailstones form
   f. how a volcano erupts
   g. how the human circulatory system works
   h. how a camera works
   i. how photosynthesis takes place
   j. how an atomic bomb or reactor works
   k. how fertilizer is made
   l. how a refrigerator works
   m. how water evaporates
   n. how flowers bloom
   o. how a recession occurs
   p. how an automobile is made
   q. how a bill becomes law in your state
   r. how a caterpillar becomes a butterfly
   s. how the judicial appeals process works
   t. how a video camera works

3. Think about your favorite pastime or activity. Write an essay in which you explain one or more of the processes you follow in participating in that activity. For example, if golf is your hobby, how do you go about taking a tee shot or getting out of a sand trap? If you are a stamp collector, how do you mount a stamp? If you are a photographer, how do you develop and print a picture? If you are an amateur investor, how do you go about choosing and purchasing a stock? Do you follow standard procedures, or do you personalize the process in some way?

4. Although each of us hopes never to be in an automobile accident, many of us have been or will be. Accidents are unsettling, and it is important that people know what to do if they ever find themselves in a collision. Write an essay in which you explain the steps that a person should follow to protect life and property.

5. All college students have to register for courses each term. What is the registration process like at your college? Do you find any part of the process unnecessarily frustrating or annoying? In a letter to your campus newspaper or an appropriate administrator, evaluate your school's current registration procedure, offering suggestions for making the process more efficient and pleasurable.

6. Writing to a person who is a computer novice, explain how to do a Web search using popular Web search engines like Yahoo!, AltaVista, Lycos, and Infoseek. Be sure to define key terms and to illustrate the steps in your process with printouts of critical search directories and sites.

CHAPTER 9

Comparison and Contrast

WHAT ARE COMPARISON AND CONTRAST?

A comparison presents two or more subjects (people, ideas, or objects), considers them together, and shows in what ways they are alike; a contrast shows how they differ. These two perspectives, apparently in contradiction to each other, actually work so often in conjunction that they are commonly considered a single strategy, called comparison and contrast or simply comparison for short.

Comparison and contrast are so much a part of daily life that we are often not aware of using them. Whenever you make a choice — what to wear, where to eat, what college to attend, what career to pursue — you implicitly use comparison and contrast to evaluate your options and arrive at your decision. Consider a simple choice, like picking a shirt to wear for the day. You probably have at least a few to choose from, and all are comparable in certain ways — they fit you reasonably well, they are clean and ready to wear, and in some way each of them reflects your taste in clothes. To make a choice, you must reflect first on the situation in which the shirt will be worn: the weather, the people you will see, the work or play you will engage in, whether the occasion calls for casual or formal attire. Then you consider the shirts themselves and decide whether you want long sleeves or short; white, colored, or patterned fabric; a fastidious button-down collar, a sweatshirt, or a tee shirt with a sports logo. Even though you may not consciously realize it, you make your choice by comparing and contrasting the items in your wardrobe and the context that makes one item more suitable than the others.

The strategy of comparison and contrast is most commonly used in writing when the subjects under discussion belong to the same class or general category: four makes of car, for example, or two candidates for the Senate. (See Chapter 10, "Division and Classification," for a more complete discussion of classes.) Such subjects are said to be *comparable,* or to have a strong basis for comparison.

Point-by-Point and Block Comparison

There are two basic ways to organize an essay of comparison and contrast. In the first, *point-by-point comparison,* the author starts by comparing both subjects in terms of a particular point, then moves on to a second point and compares both subjects, then moves on to a third point, and so on. The other way to organize a comparison is called *block comparison.* In this pattern, the information about one subject is gathered into a block, which is followed by a block of comparable information about the second subject. Each pattern of comparison has its own advantages and disadvantages. Point-by-point comparison allows the reader to grasp fairly easily the specific points of comparison the author is making; it may be harder, though, to pull together the details and convey a distinct impression of what each subject is like. The block comparison guarantees that each subject will receive a more unified discussion; however, the points of comparison between them may be less clear.

The first of the following two annotated passages illustrates a point-by-point comparison. This selection, written before the dissolution of the Soviet Union, is from *Why They Behave Like Russians* by John Fischer.

Point-by-point comparison in second sentence (five points in one sentence)

The Ukrainians are the Texans of Russia. They believe they can fight, drink, ride, sing, and make love better than anybody else in the world, and if pressed will admit it. Their country, too, was a borderland — that's what "Ukraine" means — and like Texas it was originally settled by outlaws, horse thieves, land-hungry farmers, and people who hadn't made a go of it somewhere else. Some of these hard cases banded together, long ago, to raise hell and some livestock. They called themselves Cossacks, and they would have felt right at home in any Western movie. Even today the Ukrainians cherish a wistful tradition of horsemanship, although most of

The basis of comparison: subjects similar in class, attitude, and geographic region

them would feel as uncomfortable in a saddle as any Dallas banker. They still like to wear knee-high boots and big, furry hats, made of gray or black Persian lamb, which are the local equivalent of a Stetson.

Even the country looks a good deal like Texas — flat, dry prairie, shading off in the south to semidesert.

Explicit comparison between Texas and Ukraine in description of country

Through the middle runs a strip of dark, rich soil, the Chernozom Belt, which is almost identical with the black waxy soil of central Texas. It grows the best wheat in the Soviet Union. The Ukraine is also famous for its cattle, sheep, and cotton, and — again like Texas — it has been in the throes of an industrial boom for the last twenty years. On all other people the Ukrainians look with a sort of kindly pity. They might have thought up for their own use the old Western rule of etiquette: "Never ask a man where he comes from. If he's a Texan, he'll tell you; if he's not, don't embarrass him."

Implicit comparison: Ukrainians described in terms of familiar Texas mythology

In the following example from *Harper's* magazine, Otto Friedrich uses a block format to contrast a newspaper story with a newsmagazine story.

Subjects of comparison: newspaper story and magazine story. Each belongs to the same class.

There is an essential difference between a news story, as understood by a newspaperman or a wire-service writer, and a newsmagazine story. The chief purpose of the conventional news story is to tell what happened. It starts with the most important information and continues into increasingly inconsequential details, not only because the reader may not read beyond the first paragraph, but because an editor working on galley proofs a few minutes before press time likes to be able to cut freely from the end of the story.

Block comparison: each paragraph deals with one type of story.

A newsmagazine is very different. It is written to be read consecutively from beginning to end, and each of its stories is designed, following the critical theories of Edgar Allan Poe, to create one emotional effect. The news, what happened that week, may be told in the beginning, the middle, or the end; for the purpose is not to throw information at the reader but to seduce him into reading the whole story, and into accepting the dramatic (and often political) point being made.

In this selection, Friedrich has two purposes: to offer information that explains the differences between a newspaper story and a newsmagazine story, and to persuade readers that magazine stories tend to be more biased than newspaper stories.

Analogy: A Special Form of Comparison and Contrast

When the subject under discussion is unfamiliar, complex, or abstract, the resourceful writer may use a special form of comparison called *analogy* to help readers understand the difficult subject. An analogy compares two largely dissimilar subjects to look for illuminating similarities. Most comparisons analyze items within the same class. For example, an exploration of the similarities and differences between short stories and novels — two forms of fiction — would constitute a logical comparison. Short stories and novels belong to the same class, and your purpose would be to tell something about both. In contrast, analogy pairs things of different classes. In analogy, the only basis for comparison lies in the writer's imagination. In addition, while the typical comparison seeks to illuminate specific features of both subjects, the primary purpose of analogy is to clarify one subject that is complex or unfamiliar by pointing out its similarities to a more familiar or concrete subject. If, for example, your purpose were to explain the craft of fiction writing, you might note its similarities to the craft of carpentry. In this case, you would be drawing an analogy, because the two subjects clearly belong to different classes. Your imagination will suggest many ways in which the concrete work of the carpenter can be used to help readers understand the more abstract work of the novelist. You can use analogy in one or two paragraphs to clarify a particular aspect of the larger topic, or you can use it as the organizational strategy for an entire essay.

In the following example from *The Mysterious Sky* (1960), observe how Lester Del Rey explains the functions of the earth's atmosphere (a subject that people have difficulty with because they can't "see" it) by making an analogy with an ordinary window.

> The atmosphere of Earth acts like any window in serving two very important functions. It lets light in and it permits us to look out. It also serves as a shield to keep out dangerous or uncomfortable things. A normal glazed window lets us keep our houses warm by keeping out cold air, and it prevents rain, dirt, and unwelcome insects and animals from coming in. As we have already seen, Earth's atmospheric window also helps to keep our planet at a comfortable temperature by holding back radiated heat and protecting us from dangerous levels of ultraviolet light.
>
> Lately, we have discovered that space is full of a great many very dangerous things against which our atmosphere guards us. It is not a perfect shield, and sometimes one of these dangerous objects does get through. There is even some evidence that a few of these messengers from space contain life, though this has by no means been proved yet.

You'll notice that Del Rey's analogy establishes no direct relationship between the subjects under comparison. The analogy is effective precisely because it enables the reader to visualize the atmosphere, which is unobservable, by comparing it to something quite different — a window — that is familiar and concrete.

WHY DO WRITERS USE COMPARISON AND CONTRAST?

To compare one thing or idea with another, to discover the similarities and differences between them, is one of the most basic human strategies for learning, evaluating, and making decisions. Because it serves so many fundamental purposes, comparison and contrast is a particularly useful strategy for the writer. It may be the primary mode for essay writers who seek to educate or persuade the reader; to evaluate things, people, or events; and to differentiate between apparently similar subjects or to reconcile the differences between dissimilar ones.

The essays in this chapter illustrate a number of uses of comparison and contrast. For example, an author who wishes primarily to impart information about two related subjects can bring each into clear focus by comparing and contrasting them. In "Grant and Lee: A Study in Contrasts" (p. 377), Bruce Catton opens by describing the scene at Appomattox Court House in Virginia on April 9, 1865. He then contrasts the two generals who had come to represent the strengths of the North and the South in the Civil War.

Sometimes, instead of giving specifics about individuals, the author seeks to emphasize the particular qualities of two types of people. Such generalization may lead to evaluation, as in Suzanne Britt's essay entitled "Neat People vs. Sloppy People" (p. 351), in which she makes an unexpected argument for the virtues of sloppiness. Generalization of types may also lead to a better understanding of relationships. Gary Soto, in "Like Mexicans" (p. 361), explains how he grew up hearing of the virtues of Mexican girls but fell in love with a Japanese woman. He goes on to describe why he and his family were anxious about an intercultural marriage until he met his fiancée's family and discovered that "her people were like Mexicans, only different." In "Sex, Lies, and Conversation" (p. 368), a complex exploration of two types of people, Deborah Tannen compares and contrasts the ways in which men and women communicate, drawing an analogy between cross-cultural communication and communication between the sexes. Instead of arguing that one conversational style is superior, Tannen uses the strategy of comparison and contrast to educate the reader about how to reconcile the differences between the styles.

Writers may choose to compare objects or processes rather than people. Student author Barbara Bowman's primary goal (p. 337) is to persuade the reader that cameras are more desirable than guns in the hands of those who hunt animals. But Mark Twain has a more subtle purpose in "Two Ways of Seeing a River" (p. 346); Twain shows how the Mississippi River, and indeed many aspects of life, may appear different to two different observers, or to a single observer at different times in life. Finally, in "Polaroids" (p. 356), Anne Lamott uses the analogy of watching a Polaroid picture develop to explain what it is like to write a first draft of an article.

Comparison and contrast may be combined readily with other writing strategies and often serves to sharpen, clarify, and add interest to essays written in a different primary mode. For example, an essay of argumentation gains credibility when the writer contrasts desirable and undesirable reasons or examples. In the Declaration of Independence (p. 596), Thomas Jefferson effectively contrasts the actual behavior of the English king with the ideals of a democratic society. In "I Have a Dream" (p. 602), Martin Luther King Jr. compares 1960s America with the promise of what ought to be to argue that realization of the dream of freedom for all American citizens is long overdue. Likewise, Maya Angelou ("Living Well. Living Good.," p. 584) compares the lives of a wealthy couple to that of their live-in housekeeper to make a statement about the art of living well. Finally, in "The Men We Carry in Our Minds" (p. 439), Scott Russell Sanders discovers how different the images of men that he carries in his mind are from those that college women carry.

Many descriptive essays rely heavily on comparison and contrast; one of the most effective ways to describe any person, place, or thing is to show how it is like another model of the same class and how it differs. Robert Ramírez ("The Barrio," p. 195) describes his Hispanic neighborhood against "the harshness and the coldness of the Anglo world." Definition is also clarified and enriched by the use of comparison and contrast. Virtually all the essays in Chapter 11 employ this strategy to some degree.

AN ANNOTATED STUDENT ESSAY USING COMPARISON AND CONTRAST

A studio art major from Pittsburgh, Pennsylvania, Barbara Bowman has a special interest in photography. In her writing courses, Bowman has discovered many similarities between the writing process and the process that an artist follows. Her essay "Guns and Cameras," however, explores similarities of another kind: those between hunting with a gun and hunting with a camera.

Guns and Cameras

Barbara Bowman

Discussion of the objects of comparison

With a growing number of animals heading toward extinction, and with the idea of protecting such animals on game reserves

1

increasing in popularity, photographic safaris are replacing hunting safaris. This
may seem odd because of the obvious differences between guns and cameras. Shooting is
aggressive, photography is passive; shooting
eliminates, photography preserves. However,
some hunters are willing to trade their guns
for cameras because of similarities in the
way the equipment is used, as well as in the
relationship among equipment, user, and
"prey."

Block 1 (the
hunter) begins.

The hunter has a deep interest in the   2
apparatus he uses to kill his prey. He carries various types of guns, different kinds

Point A: equipment
of ammunition, and special sights and tele-
scopes to increase his chances of success.
He knows the mechanics of his guns and understands how and why they work. This fascination with the hardware of his sport is
practical -- it helps him achieve his
goal -- but it frequently becomes an end,
almost a hobby in itself.

Point B: stalking
Not until the very end of the long   3
process of stalking an animal does a game
hunter use his gun. First he enters into the
animal's world. He studies his prey, its
habitat, its daily habits, its watering
holes and feeding areas, its migration patterns, its enemies and allies, its diet and
food chain. Eventually the hunter himself
becomes animal-like, instinctively sensing
the habits and moves of his prey. Of course,
this instinct gives the hunter a better
chance of killing the animal; he knows where
and when he will get the best shot. But it
gives him more than that. Hunting is not
just pulling the trigger and killing the
prey. Much of it is a multifaceted and ritu-
alistic identification with nature.

Point C: the result
After the kill, the hunter can do a   4
number of things with his trophy. He can
sell the meat or eat it himself. He can hang

the animal's head on the wall or lay its hide on the floor or even sell these objects. But any of these uses is a luxury, and its cost is high. An animal has been destroyed; a life has been eliminated.

Block 2 (the photographer) begins.

Like the hunter, the photographer has a great interest in the tools he uses. He carries various types of cameras, lenses, and film to help him get the picture he wants. He understands the way cameras work, the uses of telephoto and micro lenses, and *Point A: equipment* often the technical procedures of printing and developing. Of course, the time and interest a photographer invests in these mechanical aspects of his art allow him to capture and produce the image he wants. But as with the hunter, these mechanics can and often do become fascinating in themselves.

Point B: stalking

The wildlife photographer also needs to stalk his "prey" with knowledge and skill in order to get an accurate "shot." Like the hunter, he has to understand the animal's patterns, characteristics, and habitat; he must become animal-like in order to succeed. And like the hunter's, his pursuit is much more prolonged and complicated than the shot itself. The stalking processes are almost identical and give many of the same satisfactions.

Point C: the result

The successful photographer also has something tangible to show for his efforts. A still picture of an animal can be displayed in a home, a gallery, a shop; it can be printed in a publication, as a postcard, or as a poster. In fact, a single photograph can be used in all these ways at once; it can be reproduced countless times. And despite all these ways of using his "trophies," the photographer continues to preserve his prey.

Photography is obviously the less violent and to me the more acceptable method for obtaining a trophy of a wild animal. We

5

6

7

8

Conclusion: The two activities are similar and give the same satisfaction, so why kill?

no longer need to hunt in order to feed or clothe ourselves, and hunting for "sport" seems to be barbaric. Luckily, the excitement of pursuing an animal, learning its habits and patterns, outsmarting it on its own level, and finally "getting" it can all be done with a camera. So why use guns?

Analyzing Barbara Bowman's Essay of Comparison and Contrast: Questions for Discussion

1. What is Bowman's thesis in this essay?
2. What are her main points of comparison between hunting with a gun and hunting with a camera?
3. How has Bowman organized her comparison? Why do you suppose she decided on this option? Explain.
4. How else could she have organized her essay? Would this alternative organization have been as effective as the one she used? Explain.
5. How does Bowman conclude her essay? In what ways is her conclusion a reflection of her thesis?

In discussing how she came to write about cameras and guns, Bowman said, "Photography is a big part of my life right now. I'm a studio art major, and this summer I'll be an intern with the local weekly newspaper, their only staff photographer. So you can see why my bias is toward cameras instead of guns." As to how she came up with the idea of comparing guns and cameras, she said, "I was reading a photography book and it mentioned a safari in Africa that used cameras instead of guns. I thought that was very interesting, so I thought I'd use it for a writing subject. I don't know that much about guns, but there's a guy in my English class who's a big hunter — he wrote a paper for the class about hunting — so I asked him about it. I could tell from what he said that he got the same gratification from it that a nature photographer would. Other people I know who hunt do it mostly for the meat and for the adventure of stalking prey. So that's how I got what I needed to know about hunting. Photography I knew lots about already, of course."

As to why she chose to use a block method of organization rather than a point-by-point method, Bowman explained, "Well, the first draft was a point-by-point comparison, and it was very bumpy, shifting back and forth between the hunter and the photographer, and I thought it was probably confusing. As I kept developing the paper, it just made more sense to switch to the block comparison. Unfortunately, this meant that I had to throw out some paragraphs in the first draft that I liked. That's hard for me — throw out some writing that seems different and new — but it wasn't fitting right, so I had to make the cuts."

Asked if she made any other large-scale changes as she revised, Bowman responded, "Nothing in particular, but each time I revised I threw things out that I didn't need, and now the essay is only half as long as it used to be. For example, here's a sentence from the next-to-last draft: 'Guns kill, cameras don't; guns use ammunition, cameras use film; shooting eliminates, photography preserves.' Everybody knows this, and the first and last parts say the same thing. I liked the last part, the way the words go together, so I kept that, but I cut out the rest. I did a lot of that."

Finally, in reflecting on the purpose of her writing, Bowman turned to her dislike of killing. "I don't like the idea of killing things for sport. I can see the hunter's argument that you've got to keep the animals' numbers under control, but I still would rather they weren't shot to death. That was the point of the comparison right from the first draft."

SUGGESTIONS FOR WRITING A COMPARISON AND CONTRAST ESSAY

Many assignments in college ask you to use the strategy of comparison and contrast. As you read an assignment, look for one or more of the words that suggest the use of this strategy. When you are asked to *compare* and *contrast* one item with another or to identify the *similarities* and *differences* between two items, you should use comparison and contrast. Other assignments might ask you to determine which of two options is *better* or to select the *best* solution to a particular problem. Again, the strategy of comparison and contrast will help you make this evaluation and arrive at a sound, logical conclusion. As you start planning and writing an essay of comparison and contrast, keep in mind the basic requirements of this writing strategy.

Ensure That Subjects Share Basic Characteristics

Remember that the subjects of your comparison should be in the same class or general category, so that you can establish a clear basis for comparison. (There are any number of possible classes, such as particular types of persons, places, and things, as well as occupations, activities, philosophies, points in history, and even concepts and ideas.) If your subject is difficult, complex, or unobservable, you may find that analogy is the most effective form of comparison. Remember, also, that if the similarities and differences between the subjects are obvious, your reader is certain to lose interest quickly.

Determine Your Purpose, and Focus on It

Suppose you choose to compare and contrast solar energy with wind energy. It is clear that both are members of the same class — energy — so there is a basis for comparing them; there also seem to be enough interesting differences to make a comparison and contrast possible. But before going any further, you must ask yourself why you want to compare and contrast these particular subjects. What audience do you seek to address? Do you want to inform, to emphasize, to explain, to evaluate, to persuade? Do you have more than one purpose? Whatever your purpose, it will influence the content and organization of your comparison.

In comparing and contrasting solar and wind energy, you will certainly provide factual information; yet you will probably also want to evaluate the two energy sources to determine whether either is a practical means of producing energy. You may also want to persuade your readers that one technology is superior to the other.

Formulate a Thesis Statement

Once you have your purpose clearly in mind, formulate a preliminary thesis statement. At this early stage in the writing process, the thesis statement is not cast in stone; you may well want to modify it later on, as a result of research and further consideration of your subject. A preliminary thesis statement has two functions: First, it fixes your purpose so that you will be less tempted to stray into byways while doing research and writing drafts; second, establishing the central point of the essay makes it easier for you to gather supporting material and to organize your essay.

Suppose, for example, that you live in the Champlain Valley of Vermont, one of the cloudiest areas of the country, where the wind whistles along the corridor between the Green Mountains and the Adirondacks. If you were exploring possible alternative energy sources for the area, your purpose might be to persuade readers of a local environmental journal that wind is preferable to sun as a source of energy for this region. The thesis statement for this essay will certainly differ from that of a writer for a national newsmagazine whose goal is to offer general information about alternative energy sources to a broad readership.

Choose the Points of Comparison

Points of comparison are the qualities and features of your subjects on which you base your comparison. For some comparisons, you will find the information you need in your own head; for others, you will have to search for that information in the library or on the Internet. At this stage, if you know only a little about the subjects of your comparison, you may have only a few hazy ideas for points of comparison. Perhaps wind energy means no more to you than an image of giant windmills lined up on a California ridge, and solar energy brings to mind only the reflective, glassy roof on a Colorado ski lodge. Even so, it is possible to list points of comparison that will be relevant to your subjects and your purpose. Here, for example, are important points of comparison in considering energy sources:

> Cost
> Convenience
> Efficiency
> Environmental impact

As you learn more about your subjects and think about what you are learning, you may want to change some of these points or add new ones. Meanwhile, a tentative list will help you by suggesting the kind of information you need to gather for your comparison and contrast. Let your tentative points of comparison be your guide, but remain alert for others you may not have thought of. For example, as you conduct research, you may find that maintenance requirements are another important factor in considering energy systems, and thus you might add that point to your list.

Organize the Points of Comparison

Once you have gathered the necessary information, you should decide which organizational pattern, block or point-by-point, will best serve your purpose. In deciding which pattern to use, you may find it helpful to jot down a scratch outline before beginning your draft.

Block organization works best when the two objects of comparison are relatively straightforward and when the points of comparison are rather general, are few in number, and can be stated succinctly. As a scratch outline illustrates, block organization makes for a unified discussion of each object, which can help your readers understand the information you have to give them.

Block Organization Outline
BLOCK ONE   **Solar Energy**
  Point 1. Cost
  Point 2. Efficiency

344 | COMPARISON AND CONTRAST

        Point 3. Convenience
        Point 4. Maintenance requirements
        Point 5. Environmental impact

    Block Two   **Wind Energy**
        Point 1. Cost
        Point 2. Efficiency
        Point 3. Convenience
        Point 4. Maintenance requirements
        Point 5. Environmental impact

If your essay will be more than two or three pages long, however, block organization may be a poor choice. By the time your readers come to your discussion of the costs of wind energy, they may well have forgotten what you had to say about solar energy costs several pages earlier and may have to flip back and forth to grasp the comparison. If such difficulties are a possibility, you would do better to use point-by-point organization, in which comparisons are made immediately as each point is raised.

Point-by-Point Outline

    Point One   **Maintenance Requirements**
        Subject 1. Solar energy
        Subject 2. Wind energy

    Point Two   **Environmental Impact**
        Subject 1. Solar energy
        Subject 2. Wind energy

    Point Three   **Cost**
        Subject 1. Solar energy
        Subject 2. Wind energy

    Point Four   **Efficiency**
        Subject 1. Solar energy
        Subject 2. Wind energy

    Point Five   **Convenience**
        Subject 1. Solar energy
        Subject 2. Wind energy

Draw a Conclusion from the Comparison

Only after you have gathered your information and made your comparisons will you be ready to decide on a conclusion. When drawing the conclusion to your essay, remember your purpose in writing, and keep in mind both your audience and your emphasis. Perhaps, having presented information about both technologies, your comparison shows that solar and wind energy are both feasible, with solar energy having a slight edge on most points. If your purpose has been evaluation for a general audience, you might conclude, "Both solar and wind energy are practical alternatives to conventional energy sources." If you wish to persuade your readers that one of the technologies is superior to the other, your comparison will support a more persuasive conclusion. For the general audience, you might say, "While both solar and wind energy are practical technologies, solar energy now seems the better investment." However, for a readership made up of residents of the cloudy Champlain Valley, you might conclude, "While both solar and wind energy are practical technologies, wind energy makes more sense for investors in northwest Vermont."

▶ *Questions for Revision: Comparison and Contrast*

1. Are the subjects of my comparison comparable; that is, do they belong to the same class of items (for example, two cars, two advertisements, two landscape paintings) so that there is a clear basis for comparison?

2. Are there any complex or abstract concepts that might be clarified by using an analogy, in which I convey what the concept has in common with a more familiar or concrete subject?

3. Is the purpose of my comparison clearly stated?

4. Have I presented a clear thesis statement?

5. Have I chosen my points of comparison well? Have I avoided obvious points of comparison, concentrating instead on similarities between obviously different items or differences between essentially similar items?

6. Have I developed my points of comparison in sufficient detail so that my readers can appreciate my thinking?

7. Have I chosen the best pattern — block or point-by-point — to organize my information?

8. Have I drawn a conclusion that is in line with my thesis and purpose?

Two Ways of Seeing a River

Mark Twain

Mark Twain, the pen name of Samuel L. Clemens (1835–1910), was born in Florida, Missouri, and raised in Hannibal, Missouri. He created Tom Sawyer *(1876),* The Prince and the Pauper *(1882),* Huckleberry Finn *(1884), and* A Connecticut Yankee in King Arthur's Court *(1889), among other classics. One of America's most popular writers, Twain is generally regarded as the most important practitioner of the realistic school of writing, a style that emphasizes observable details.*

The following passage is taken from Life on the Mississippi *(1883), Twain's study of the great river and his account of his early experiences learning to be a river steamboat pilot. As you read the passage, notice how Twain uses figurative language in describing two quite different ways of seeing the Mississippi River.*

BEFORE YOU READ

Our way of seeing an event or a place in our life often changes over time. Recall an important event or a place you visited in the past. Tell a story based on your memories. Has your view of this event or place changed over time? How?

N ow when I had mastered the language of this water and had come to know every trifling feature that bordered the great river as familiarly as I knew the letters of the alphabet, I had made a valuable acquisition. But I had lost something, too. I had lost something which could never be restored to me while I lived. All the grace, the beauty, the poetry, had gone out of the majestic river! I still kept in mind a certain wonderful sunset which I witnessed when steamboating was new to me. A broad expanse of the river was turned to blood; in the middle distance the red hue brightened into gold, through which a solitary log came floating, black and conspicuous; in one place a long, slanting mark lay sparkling upon the water; in another the surface was broken by boiling, tumbling rings that were as many-tinted as an opal; where the ruddy flush was faintest was a smooth spot that was covered with graceful circles and radiating lines, ever so delicately traced; the shore on our left was densely wooded, and the somber shadow that fell from this forest was broken in one place by a long, ruffled trail that shone like silver; and high above the forest wall a clean-stemmed dead tree waved a single leafy bough that glowed like a flame in the unobstructed splendor that was flowing from the sun. There were graceful curves, reflected images, woody heights, soft dis-

1

tances, and over the whole scene, far and near, the dissolving lights drifted steadily, enriching it every passing moment with new marvels of coloring.

I stood like one bewitched. I drank it in, in a speechless rapture. The world was new to me and I had never seen anything like this at home. But as I have said, a day came when I began to cease from noting the glories and the charms which the moon and the sun and the twilight wrought upon the river's face; another day came when I ceased altogether to note them. Then, if that sunset scene had been repeated, I should have looked upon it without rapture and should have commented upon it inwardly after this fashion: "This sun means that we are going to have wind tomorrow; that floating log means that the river is rising, small thanks to it; that slanting mark on the water refers to a bluff reef which is going to kill somebody's steamboat one of these nights, if it keeps on stretching out like that; those tumbling 'boils' show a dissolving bar and a changing channel there; the lines and circles in the slick water over yonder are a warning that that troublesome place is shoaling up dangerously; that silver streak in the shadow of the forest is the 'break' from a new snag and he has located himself in the very best place he could have found to fish for steamboats; that tall dead tree, with a single living branch, is not going to last long, and then how is a body ever going to get through this blind place at night without the friendly old landmark?"

No, the romance and beauty were all gone from the river. All the value any feature of it had for me now was the amount of usefulness it could furnish toward compassing the safe piloting of a steamboat. Since those days, I have pitied doctors from my heart. What does the lovely flush in a beauty's cheek mean to a doctor but a "break" that ripples above some deadly disease? Are not all her visible charms sown thick with what are to him the signs and symbols of hidden decay? Does he ever see her beauty at all, or doesn't he simply view her professionally and comment upon her unwholesome condition all to himself? And doesn't he sometimes wonder whether he has gained most or lost most by learning his trade?

RESPONDING TO READING

In the essay, Twain points to a change of attitude he underwent as a result of seeing the river from a new perspective, that of a steamboat pilot. Why and how do you think perspectives change? How would you characterize Twain's change of perspective?

QUESTIONING THE TEXT

1. What points of contrast does Twain refer to between his two ways of seeing the river?

2. What point does Twain make regarding the difference between appearance and reality, between romance and practicality? What role does knowledge play in Twain's inability to see the river as he once did?

3. Now that he has learned the trade of steamboating, does Twain feel he has "gained most or lost most" (paragraph 3)? What has he gained, and what has he lost?

UNDERSTANDING THE WRITER'S CRAFT

1. What method of organization does Twain use in this selection? What alternative methods might he have used? What would have been gained or lost? (Glossary: *Organization*)

2. Explain the analogy that Twain uses in paragraph 3. What is his purpose in using this analogy? (Glossary: *Analogy*)

3. Does Twain rely on subjective description, objective description, or a combination of both? Explain. (Glossary: *Description*)

4. Reread Twain's conclusion. How effective do you find it? Why does he switch the focus to a doctor's perspective? (Glossary: *Beginnings/ Endings*)

EXPLORING LANGUAGE

1. Twain uses a number of similes and metaphors in this selection. Identify three of each, and explain what is being compared in each case. What do these figures add to Twain's writing? (Glossary: *Figures of Speech*)

2. What effect do the italicized words have in each of the following quotations from this selection? What do these words contribute to Twain's description?
   a. "ever so *delicately* traced" (paragraph 1)
   b. "shadow that *fell* from this forest" (1)
   c. "*wrought* upon the river's face" (2)
   d. "show a *dissolving* bar" (2)
   e. "get through this *blind* place at night" (2)
   f. "lovely *flush* in a beauty's cheek" (3)

3. Refer to your desk dictionary to determine the meanings of the following words as Twain uses them in this selection: *acquisition* (paragraph 1), *hue* (1), *opal* (1), *rapture* (2), *romance* (3).

COMBINING RHETORICAL STRATEGIES

In reflecting on his two ways of seeing the river, Twain relies on a combination of subjective and objective descriptions. Identify places in the essay where Twain uses description. How does the inclusion of these descriptions enhance his overall comparison and contrast? (Glossary: *Description*)

WRITING SUGGESTIONS

1. **(Comparison and Contrast)** Consider the following cartoon from *The New Yorker*. What perspective does the cartoon give you on Twain's point about his different views of the Mississippi River? How does Twain's essay help you understand the cartoon? Is it possible for a person to have two different views of a single scene, event, or issue at the same time? How might experience or perspective change how we view something? Write an essay modeled on Twain's in which you offer two different views of a scene, an event, or an issue. You might consider a reporter's view compared with a victim's view, a teacher's view compared with a student's view, or a customer's view compared with a sales clerk's view.

"*By George, your'e right! I thought there was something familiar about it.*"

2. **(Other Strategies)** Write an essay in which you use comparison and contrast to help you describe one of the following places or another place of your choice. (Glossary: *Description*)
   a. a place of worship
   b. a fast-food restaurant
   c. your dormitory
   d. your college library

    e. your favorite place   g. your hometown
    f. your college student center

3. **(Research)** Think of a public event from the past, such as the Anita Hill–Clarence Thomas affair, the uproar over Salman Rushdie's *Satanic Verses,* the death of Princess Diana, or the impeachment of Bill Clinton. Go to the library and find commentary on the event that addresses the event at the time it happened. You might look in the newspaper or in newsmagazines like *U.S. News & World Report, Time,* or *Newsweek.* You might also want to check the Internet sites of major newsmagazines or newspapers or other electronic sources for news, such as Lexis/Nexis. Write an essay in which you compare and contrast the view that you read about from the past with your own view of the event today.

- *U.S. News* **Online**
  <http://www.usnews.com/usnews/home.htm>

  This online version of *U.S. News & World Report* offers a searchable archive of articles.

- **The** *New York Times* **Online**
  <http://nytimes.com>

  This site offers access to a searchable archive of *New York Times* articles from the past year.

- **My Virtual Reference Desk**
  <http://www.refdesk.com>

  This site provides numerous links to newspapers, magazines, and other information sources on almost every conceivable topic.

Neat People vs. Sloppy People

Suzanne Britt

Born in Winston-Salem, North Carolina, Suzanne Britt now makes her home in Raleigh. She graduated from Salem College and Washington University, where she received her M.A. in English. A freelance writer, Britt has a regular column in North Carolina Gardens and Homes. *Her work has appeared in the* New York Times, Newsweek, *and the* Boston Globe. *Her essays have been collected in two books,* Skinny People Are Dull and Crunchy Like Carrots *and* Show and Tell. *Currently, she teaches English at Meredith College in North Carolina and continues to write.*

In the following essay taken from Show and Tell, *Britt takes a humorous look at the differences between neat and sloppy people by giving us some insights about several important personality traits.*

BEFORE YOU READ

Many people in our society are fond of comparing people, places, and things. Often, these comparisons are premature and even damaging. Consider the ways people judge others based on clothes, appearance, or hearsay. Write about a time in your life when you made such a comparison about someone or something. Did your initial judgment hold up? If not, why did it change?

I've finally figured out the difference between neat people and sloppy people. The distinction is, as always, moral. Neat people are lazier and meaner than sloppy people.

Sloppy people, you see, are not really sloppy. Their sloppiness is merely the unfortunate consequence of their extreme moral rectitude. Sloppy people carry in their mind's eye a heavenly vision, a precise plan, that is so stupendous, so perfect, it can't be achieved in this world or the next.

Sloppy people live in Never-Never Land. Someday is their métier. Someday they are planning to alphabetize all their books and set up home catalogs. Someday they will go through their wardrobes and mark certain items for tentative mending and certain items for passing on to relatives of similar shape and size. Someday sloppy people will make family scrapbooks into which they will put newspaper clippings, postcards, locks of hair, and the dried corsage from their senior prom. Someday they will file everything on the surface of their desks, including the cash receipts from coffee purchases at the snack shop. Someday they will sit down and read all the back issues of *The New Yorker*.

For all these noble reasons and more, sloppy people never get   4
neat. They aim too high and wide. They save everything, planning
someday to file, order, and straighten out the world. But while these
ambitious plans take clearer and clearer shape in their heads, the
books spill from the shelves onto the floor, the clothes pile up in the
hamper and closet, the family mementos accumulate in every drawer,
the surface of the desk is buried under mounds of paper and the unread magazines threaten to reach the ceiling.

Sloppy people can't bear to part with anything. They give loving   5
attention to every detail. When sloppy people say they're going to
tackle the surface of the desk, they really mean it. Not a paper will go
unturned; not a rubber band will go unboxed. Four hours or two
weeks into the excavation, the desk looks exactly the same, primarily
because the sloppy person is meticulously creating new piles of papers
with new headings and scrupulously stopping to read all of the old
book catalogs before he throws them away. A neat person would just
bulldoze the desk.

Neat people are bums and clods at heart. They have cavalier atti-   6
tudes toward possessions, including family heirlooms. Everything is
just another dust-catcher to them. If anything collects dust, it's got to
go and that's that. Neat people will toy with the idea of throwing the
children out of the house just to cut down on the clutter.

Neat people don't care about process. They like results. What they   7
want to do is get the whole thing over with so they can sit down and
watch the rasslin' on TV. Neat people operate on two unvarying principles: never handle any item twice, and throw everything away.

The only thing messy in a neat person's house is the trash can.   8
The minute something comes to a neat person's hand, he will look at
it, try to decide if it has immediate use and, finding none, throw it in
the trash.

Neat people are especially vicious with mail. They never go   9
through their mail unless they are standing directly over a trash can. If
the trash can is beside the mailbox, even better. All ads, catalogs, pleas
for charitable contributions, church bulletins and money-saving
coupons go straight into the trash can without being opened. All letters from home, postcards from Europe, bills and paychecks are
opened, immediately responded to, then dropped in the trash can.
Neat people keep their receipts only for tax purposes. That's it. No sentimental salvaging of birthday cards or the last letter a dying relative
ever wrote. Into the trash it goes.

Neat people place neatness above everything, even economics.   10
They are incredibly wasteful. Neat people throw away several toys
every time they walk through the den. I knew a neat person once who
threw away a perfectly good dish drainer because it had mold on it.
The drainer was too much trouble to wash. And neat people sell their

furniture when they move. They will sell a La-Z-Boy recliner while you are reclining in it.

Neat people are no good to borrow from. Neat people buy every- 11
thing in expensive little single portions. They get their flour and sugar in two-pound bags. They wouldn't consider clipping a coupon, saving a leftover, reusing plastic nondairy whipped cream containers or rinsing off tin foil and draping it over the unmoldy dish drainer. You can never borrow a neat person's newspaper to see what's playing at the movies. Neat people have the paper all wadded up and in the trash by 7:05 A.M.

Neat people cut a clean swath through the organic as well as the 12
inorganic world. People, animals, and things are all one to them. They are so insensitive. After they've finished with the pantry, the medicine cabinet, and the attic, they will throw out the red geranium (too many leaves), sell the dog (too many fleas), and send the children off to boarding school (too many scuffmarks on the hardwood floors).

RESPONDING TO READING

Suzanne Britt reduces people to two types: sloppy and neat. What does she see as the defining characteristics of each type? Do you consider yourself a sloppy or a neat person? Perhaps you are neither. If this is the case, make up your own category, and explain why Britt's categories are not broad enough.

QUESTIONING THE TEXT

1. Why do you suppose Britt characterizes the distinction between sloppy and neat people as a "moral" one (paragraph 1)? What is she really poking fun at with this reference? (Glossary: *Irony*)

2. In your own words, what is the "heavenly vision," the "precise plan," Britt refers to in paragraph 2? How does Britt use this idea to explain why sloppy people can never be neat?

3. Exaggeration, as Britt uses it, is only effective if it departs from some shared idea of the truth. What commonly understood ideas about sloppy and neat people does Britt rely on? Do you agree with her? Why or why not?

UNDERSTANDING THE WRITER'S CRAFT

1. Note Britt's use of transitions as she moves from trait to trait. How well does she use transitions to achieve unity in her essay? Explain. (Glossary: *Transitions*)

2. One of the ways Britt achieves a sense of the ridiculous in her essay is to switch the commonly accepted attributes of sloppy and neat people. Cite examples of this technique, and discuss the ways in which it adds

to her essay. What does it reveal to the reader about her purpose in writing the essay? (Glossary: *Purpose*)

3. Britt uses block comparison to point out the differences between sloppy and neat people. Make a side-by-side list of the traits of sloppy and neat people. After reviewing your list, determine any ways in which sloppy and neat people may be similar. Why do you suppose Britt does not include any of the ways in which they are the same?

4. Why do you think Britt has chosen to use a block comparison? What would have been gained or lost had she used a point-by-point system of contrast?

EXPLORING LANGUAGE

1. Cite examples of Britt's diction that indicate her change of tone when she is talking about either sloppy or neat people. (Glossary: *Diction; Tone*)

2. How would you characterize Britt's vocabulary in the essay — easy or difficult? What does her choice of vocabulary say about her intended audience? In which places does Britt use precise word choice to particularly good effect?

3. Refer to your desk dictionary to determine the meanings of the following words as Britt uses them in this selection: *rectitude* (paragraph 2), *tentative* (3), *meticulously* (5), *heirlooms* (6), *salvaging* (9), *swath* (12).

COMBINING RHETORICAL STRATEGIES

Throughout the essay, Britt uses numerous examples to show the differences between sloppy and neat people. Cite five examples that Britt uses to exemplify the points she makes about people. How effective do you find Britt's use of examples? What do they add to her essay of comparison and contrast? (Glossary: *Exemplification*)

WRITING SUGGESTIONS

1. **(Comparison and Contrast)** Write an essay in which you describe yourself as either sloppy or neat. In what ways does your behavior compare or contrast with the traits Britt offers? You may follow Britt's definition of sloppy and neat, or you may come up with your own.

2. **(Other Strategies)** Take some time to reflect on a relationship in your life — perhaps one with a friend, a family member, or a teacher. Write an essay in which you discuss what it is about you and that other person that makes the relationship work. You may find it helpful to think of a relationship that doesn't work to better understand why the relationship you're writing about does work. What discoveries about yourself did you make while working on this paper? Explain. (Glossary: *Description*)

3. **(Research)** Despite what Britt claims, neat people are often considered to be well mannered, while sloppy people are considered to be rude or to have poor manners. In the library, and possibly on the Internet as well, do some research on the history or function of manners (manners are also known as *etiquette*). Write an essay on the topic of etiquette; you might want to argue that etiquette is important or that it is not as important as some people think. You might also consider writing an essay on the etiquette of cyberspace (often referred to as *netiquette*).

- **Netiquette Home Page**
  <http://www.albion.com/netiquette>

  This Web site offers information on protocols for interacting with others on the Internet.

- **The Net: User Guidelines and Netiquette**
  <http://www.fau.edu/netiquette/net/netiquette.html>

  This award-winning Web site, maintained at Florida Atlantic University, offers information, links, and more.

- **Emily Post's** *Etiquette*
  <http://www.bartleby.com/95>

  Here you will find etiquette maven Emily Post's 1922 opus, *Etiquette in Society, in Business, in Politics and at Home*, in its entirety. Post's definitive book on etiquette includes thousands of tips on how to write correspondence, plan weddings, throw parties, and act in a plethora of public and private settings.

Polaroids

Anne Lamott

Born in San Francisco in 1954, Anne Lamott is a graduate of Goucher College in Baltimore and is the author of four novels, including Rosie *(1983),* Crooked Little Heart *(1997), and* All New People *(2000). She has also been a food reviewer for* California *magazine, a book reviewer for* Mademoiselle, *and a regular contributor to* Salon's "Mothers Who Think." *Her nonfiction books include* Operating Instructions: A Journal of My Son's First Year *(1993), in which she describes her adventures as a single parent, and* Traveling Mercies: Some Thoughts on Faith *(1999), in which she charts her journey toward faith in God.*

The selection below is from Lamott's popular book about writing, Bird by Bird *(1994). The entire essay is built around the analogy of a developing Polaroid photograph. As you read, notice how effectively Lamott weaves in references to the familiar Polaroid to explain and clarify the key points she wishes to make about the process of writing.*

BEFORE YOU READ

Do you or does someone in your family enjoy taking photographs? Do the pictures always come out just the way you expected (or hoped) they would, or do they sometimes contain surprises? Perhaps the developed prints made you laugh or disappointed you or revealed something of value — some new insight into a familiar person, scene, or relationship. Describe a photograph or photographs that literally developed into something unexpected.

W riting a first draft is very much like watching a Polaroid develop. 1 You can't — and, in fact, you're not supposed to — know exactly what the picture is going to look like until it has finished developing. First you just point at what has your attention and take the picture. In the last chapter, for instance, what had my attention were the contents of my lunch bag. But as the picture developed, I found I had a really clear image of the boy against the fence. Or maybe *your* Polaroid was supposed to be a picture of that boy against the fence, and you didn't notice until the last minute that a family was standing a few feet away from him. Now, maybe it's his family, or the family of one of the kids in his class, but at any rate these people are going to be in the photograph, too. Then the film emerges from the camera with a grayish green murkiness that gradually becomes clearer and clearer; and finally you see the husband and wife holding their baby with two children standing beside them. And at first it all seems very sweet, but then the shadows begin to appear; and then you start to see the animal tragedy, the baboons baring their teeth. And then you see a flash of bright red flowers in the bottom left quadrant that you didn't even know were in the picture when you took it, and these flowers evoke a time or a memory that moves you mysteriously. And finally, as the portrait comes into focus, you begin to notice all the props surrounding these people, and you begin to understand how props define us and comfort us, and show us what we value and what we need, and who we think we are.

You couldn't have had any way of knowing what this piece of work 2
would look like when you first started. You just knew that there was something about these people that compelled you, and you stayed with that something long enough for it to show you what it was about.

Watch this Polaroid develop: 3

Six or seven years ago I was asked to write an article on the Special 4
Olympics. I had been going to the local event for years, partly because a couple of friends of mine compete. Also, I love sports, and I love to watch athletes, special or otherwise. So I showed up this time with a great deal of interest but no real sense of what the finished article might look like.

Things tend to go very, very slowly at the Special Olympics. It is 5
not like trying to cover the Preakness. Still, it has its own exhilaration, and I cheered and took notes all morning.

The last track-and-field event before lunch was a twenty-five-yard 6
race run by some unusually handicapped runners and walkers, many of whom seemed completely confused. They lumped and careened along, one man making a snail-slow break for the stands, one heading out toward the steps where the winners receive their medals; both of them were shepherded back. The race took just about forever. And here it was nearly noon and we were all so hungry. Finally, though, everyone crossed over the line, and those of us in the stands got up to go — when we noticed that way down the track, four or five yards from the starting line, was another runner.

She was a girl of about sixteen with a normal-looking face above a 7
wracked and emaciated body. She was on metal crutches, and she was just plugging along, one tiny step after another, moving one crutch forward two or three inches, then moving a leg, then moving the other crutch two or three inches, then moving the other leg. It was just excruciating. Plus, I was starving to death. Inside I was going, Come on, come on, come on, swabbing at my forehead with anxiety, while she kept taking these two- or three-inch steps forward. What felt like four hours later, she crossed the finish line, and you could see that she was absolutely stoked, in a shy, girlish way.

A tall African American man with no front teeth fell into step with 8
me as I left the bleachers to go look for some lunch. He tugged on the sleeve of my sweater, and I looked up at him, and he handed me a

Polaroid someone had taken of him and his friends that day. "Look at us," he said. His speech was difficult to understand, thick and slow as a warped record. His two friends in the picture had Down's syndrome. All three of them looked extremely pleased with themselves. I admired the picture and then handed it back to him. He stopped, so I stopped, too. He pointed to his own image. "That," he said, "is one cool man."

And this was the image from which an article began forming, although I could not have told you exactly what the piece would end up being about. I just knew that something had started to emerge.   9

After lunch I wandered over to the auditorium, where it turned out a men's basketball game was in progress. The African American man with no front teeth was the star of the game. You could tell that he was because even though no one had made a basket yet, his teammates almost always passed him the ball. Even the people on the *other* team passed him the ball a lot. In lieu of any scoring, the men stampeded in slow motion up and down the court, dribbling the ball thunderously. I had never heard such a loud game. It was all sort of crazily beautiful. I imagined describing the game for my article and then for my students: the loudness, the joy. I kept replaying the scene of the girl on crutches making her way up the track to the finish line — and all of a sudden my article began to appear out of the grayish green murk. And I could see that it was about tragedy transformed over the years into joy. It was about the beauty of sheer effort. I could see it almost as clearly as I could the photograph of that one cool man and his two friends.   10

The auditorium bleachers were packed. Then a few minutes later, still with no score on the board, the tall black man dribbled slowly from one end of the court to the other, and heaved the ball up into the air, and it dropped into the basket. The crowd roared, and all the men on both teams looked up wide-eyed at the hoop, as if it had just burst into flames.   11

You would have loved it, I tell my students. You would have felt like you could write all day.   12

RESPONDING TO READING

After reading Lamott's essay, what new understanding of writing, especially the writing of a first draft, do you have? In what ways, if at all, did her analogy of "watching a Polaroid develop" (paragraph 1) help you arrive at your new insights?

QUESTIONING THE TEXT

1. In paragraph 1, Lamott identifies four elements in *"your* Polaroid" that you didn't expect to find. What are the four surprises? What point do you think Lamott is making in bringing these aspects of the Polaroid picture to our attention?

2. In what way does the African American man's perception of himself in the Polaroid picture help Lamott with her writing assignment?

3. According to Lamott, what ultimately was the focus of her article about the Special Olympics? What was it that triggered this insight for her?

UNDERSTANDING THE WRITER'S CRAFT

1. This entire essay is based on one broad analogy, a special kind of comparison and contrast. (Glossary: *Analogy*) What is the analogy? How does it serve to explain Lamott's central idea?

2. Identify at least one metaphor and one simile that Lamott uses in her essay. (Glossary: *Figures of Speech*) How does each figure of speech work? What do they add to Lamott's discussion of writing?

3. How has Lamott organized her essay? Why do you suppose that she tells readers about taking a Polaroid picture and watching it develop before she narrates the story about writing an article on the Special Olympics? What would have happened had the order been reversed? How does the third paragraph function in the context of the essay?

EXPLORING LANGUAGE

1. How would you describe the diction of Lamott's essay? (Glossary: *Diction*) Point to words or phrases that clearly support your characterization.

2. Lamott uses the phrase "grayish green murkiness" in the first paragraph and refers again to "grayish green murk" near the end of the essay in paragraph 10. Why do you think she repeats these words? What does this phrase mean to a photographer? To a writer? For which of them does the phrase function as a metaphor?

3. Refer to your desk dictionary to determine the meanings of the following words as Lamott uses them in this selection: *quadrant* (paragraph 1), *props* (1), *wracked* (7), *emaciated* (7), *excruciating* (7).

COMBINING RHETORICAL STRATEGIES

Identify passages in Lamott's essay where she uses process analysis, narration, and description. Explain how each of these strategies supports the central comparison between writing a first draft and watching a Polaroid develop.

WRITING SUGGESTIONS

1. **(Comparison and Contrast)** When we think about our daily activities, we often clarify our understanding of some aspect of them by seeing one activity in terms of another. Not everyone's perceptions will be the same: A good horseback rider, for example, might come back from a relaxing day on the trail thinking, "Riding a horse is a form of meditation," while the novice bumping around in the saddle might think, "Riding a horse is a form of torture." A computer expert might find that

surfing the Web is like traveling on a magic carpet, while someone else might find it more like being lost in a labyrinth. Choose an activity in your daily life that suggests such a comparison. Using Lamott's piece as a model, write an essay about the activity that uses an analogy to clarify our understanding of it.

2. **(Other Strategies)** With sudden insight, Lamott understands what the Special Olympics meant to her: "It was about tragedy transformed over the years into joy. It was about the beauty of sheer effort" (paragraph 10). Everyone has experiences in life that take on special meaning. Look back on a significant event that you witnessed or in which you took part, one that has come to represent to you some important truth about life. Write a narrative essay describing the event. Wait until you are at or near the end of your story to reveal explicitly your insight into its meaning.

3. **(Research)** Write a paper in which you explore your own writing process — that is, the steps you go through in producing a piece of writing. In preparation for this essay, do some research in your library or on the Internet about the writing process. What do professional writers have to say about the way they tackle a writing assignment? How does your own process compare to that of other writers? What parts of the writing process do you find most challenging? Try to explain why you find these parts so difficult. In an essay explain how important it is for a writer to have an understanding of his or her own writing process.

- **University of Richmond's Writer's Web**
  <http://www.richmond.edu/~writing/wweb.html>

  Maintained by the University of Richmond, this site features a step-by-step breakdown and explanation of the writing process. It also includes useful information about using research in papers and about documenting sources.

- **Writing the Journey**
  <http://www.writingthejourney.com>

  Written for a general audience, this site features an online journal-writing workshop with exercises and resources to spark your own writing.

- **Paradigm Online Writing Assistant**
  <http://www.powa.org>

  This site is an online writer's guide and handbook covering many aspects of the writing process from finding a topic to editing a draft. Additional resources are also available for specific writing styles and topics.

- **The *New York Times* on the Web: Writers on Writing Series**
  <http://www.nytimes.com/books/specials/writers.html>

  This site contains the complete archive of the *New York Times* "Writers on Writing" column, in which such renowned writers as Russell Banks, Richard Ford, Jamaica Kincaid, Jane Smiley, Kurt Vonnegut, and Alice Walker discuss and explore literary themes.

Like Mexicans

Gary Soto

Born in Fresno, California, in 1952 to working-class Mexican American parents, Gary Soto currently teaches English and Chicano studies at the University of California at Berkeley. After laboring as a migrant farmworker in the San Joaquin Valley during the 1960s, he studied geography at California State University at Fresno and at the University of California at Irvine before turning his hand to poetry. In his first two collections of poetry — The Elements of San Joaquin (1977) and The Tale of Sunlight (1978) — Soto draws heavily on his childhood experiences as a Mexican American growing up in southern California. As critics have noted, his poetry captures the violent reality of city life and the backbreaking work of the migrant worker, together with the frustration of lost innocence. To date he has published four other volumes of poetry, a collection of short stories, and four works of nonfiction, including Living Up the Street: Narrative Recollections (1985) and A Summer Life (1991).

In the following selection, first published in Small Faces (1985), Soto recalls the day he went to meet his Japanese fiancée's family for the first time, contrasting the reality of the visit with the speculations he had had beforehand about how they would compare to his own Mexican family.

BEFORE YOU READ

Consider the racial and ethnic makeup of your hometown community. How aware were you of this diversity? Do you recall whether you and your friends were more interested in the differences among the various cultures or in the common ground that they shared? Explain.

My grandmother gave me bad advice and good advice when I was in my early teens. For the bad advice, she said that I should become a barber because they made good money and listened to the radio all day. "Honey, they don't work como burros," she would say every time I visited her. She made the sound of donkeys braying. "Like that, honey!" For the good advice, she said that I should marry a Mexican girl. "No Okies, hijo" — she would say — "Look, my son. He marry one and they fight every day about I don't know what and I don't know what." For her, everyone who wasn't Mexican, black, or Asian were Okies. The French were Okies, the Italians in suits were Okies. When I asked about Jews, whom I had read about, she asked for a picture. I rode home on my bicycle and returned with a calendar depicting the important races of the world. "Pues sí, son Okies tambien!"[1] she said, nodding her head. She waved the calendar away and we went to the living room where she lectured me on the virtues of the Mexican girl: first, she could cook and, second, she acted like a woman, not a man, in her husband's home. She said she would tell me about a third when I got a little older.

I asked my mother about it — becoming a barber and marrying Mexican. She was in the kitchen. Steam curled from a pot of boiling beans, the radio was on, looking as squat as a loaf of bread. "Well, if you want to be a barber — they say they make good money." She slapped a round steak with a knife, her glasses slipping down with each strike. She stopped and looked up. "If you find a good Mexican girl, marry her of course." She returned to slapping the meat and I went to the backyard where my brother and David King were sitting on the lawn feeling the inside of their cheeks.

"This is what girls feel like," my brother said, rubbing the inside of his cheek. David put three fingers inside his mouth and scratched. I ignored them and climbed the back fence to see my best friend, Scott, a second-generation Okie. I called him and his mother pointed to the side of the house where his bedroom was a small aluminum trailer, the kind you gawk at when they're flipped over on the freeway, wheels spinning in the air. I went around to find Scott pitching horseshoes.

I picked up a set of rusty ones and joined him. While we played, we talked about school and friends and record albums. The horseshoes scuffed up dirt, sometimes ringing the iron that threw out a meager shadow like a sundial. After three argued-over games, we pulled two oranges apiece from his tree and started down the alley still talking school and friends and record albums. We pulled more oranges from the alley and talked about who we would marry. "No offense, Scott," I said with an orange slice in my mouth, "but I would never marry an Okie." We walked in step, almost touching, with a sled of shadows dragging behind us. "No offense, Gary," Scott said, "but I would *never* marry a Mexican." I looked at him: a fang of orange slice showed from his munching mouth. I didn't think anything of it. He had his girl and I had mine. But our seventh-grade vision was the same: to marry, get jobs, buy cars and maybe a house if we had money left over.

We talked about our future lives until, to our surprise, we were on the downtown mall, two miles from home. We bought a bag of popcorn at Penneys and sat on a bench near the fountain watching Mexican and Okie girls pass. "That one's mine," I pointed with my chin when a girl with eyebrows arched into black rainbows ambled by. "She's cute," Scott said about a girl with yellow hair and a mouthful of gum. We dreamed aloud, our chins busy pointing out girls. We agreed that we couldn't wait to become men and lift them onto our laps.

---

[1] Well yes, they're Okies too.

But the woman I married was not Mexican but Japanese. It was a sur- 6
prise to me. For years, I went about wide-eyed in my search for the brown
girl in a white dress at a dance. I searched the playground at the baseball
diamond. When the girls raced for grounders, their hair bounced like
something that couldn't be caught. When they sat together in the lunch-
room, heads pressed together, I knew they were talking about us Mexican
guys. I saw them and dreamed them. I threw my face into my pillow,
making up sentences that were good as in the movies.

But when I was twenty, I fell in love with this other girl who wor- 7
ried my mother, who had my grandmother asking once again to see
the calendar of the Important Races of the World. I told her I had
thrown it away years before. I took a much-glanced-at snapshot from
my wallet. We looked at it together, in silence. Then grandma reclined
in her chair, lit a cigarette, and said, "Es pretty." She blew and asked
with all her worry pushed up to her forehead: "Chinese?"

I was in love and there was no looking back. She was the one. I told 8
my mother who was slapping hamburger into patties. "Well, sure if you
want to marry her," she said. But the more I talked, the more concerned
she became. Later I began to worry. Was it all a mistake? "Marry a Mexican girl," I heard my mother say in my mind. I heard it at breakfast. I
heard it over math problems, between Western Civilization and cultural
geography. But then one afternoon while I was hitchhiking home from
school, it struck me like a baseball in the back: my mother wanted me to
marry someone of my own social class — a poor girl. I considered my fiancée, Carolyn, and she didn't look poor, though I knew she came from
a family of farm workers and pull-yourself-up-by-your-bootstraps
ranchers. I asked my brother, who was marrying Mexican poor that fall,
if I should marry a poor girl. He screamed "Yeah" above his terrible gui-
tar playing in his bedroom. I considered my sister who had married
Mexican. Cousins were dating Mexican. Uncles were remarrying poor
women. I asked Scott, who was still my best friend, and he said, "She's
too good for you, so you better not."

I worried about it until Carolyn took me home to meet her par- 9
ents. We drove in her Plymouth until the houses gave way to farms
and ranches and finally her house fifty feet from the highway. When
we pulled into the drive, I panicked and begged Carolyn to make a
U-turn and go back so we could talk about it over a soda. She pinched
my cheek, calling me a "silly boy." I felt better, though, when I got
out of the car and saw the house: the chipped paint, a cracked window, boards for a walk to the back door. There were rusting cars near
the barn. A tractor with a net of spiderwebs under a mulberry. A field.
A bale of barbed wire like children's scribbling leaning against an
empty chicken coop. Carolyn took my hand and pulled me to my future mother-in-law who was coming out to greet us.

We had lunch: sandwiches, potato chips, and iced tea. Carolyn 10
and her mother talked mostly about neighbors and the congregation

at the Japanese Methodist Church in West Fresno. Her father, who was in khaki work clothes, excused himself with a wave that was almost a salute and went outside. I heard a truck start, a dog bark, and then the truck rattle away.

Carolyn's mother offered another sandwich, but I declined with a   11
shake of my head and a smile. I looked around when I could, when I was not saying over and over that I was a college student, hinting that I could take care of her daughter. I shifted my chair. I saw newspapers piled in corners, dusty cereal boxes and vinegar bottles in corners. The wallpaper was bubbled from rain that had come in from a bad roof. Dust. Dust lay on lamp shades and window sills. These people are just like Mexicans, I thought. Poor people.

Carolyn's mother asked me through Carolyn if I would like a   12
sushi. A plate of black and white things were held in front of me. I took one, wide-eyed, and turned it over like a foreign coin. I was biting into one when I saw a kitten crawl up the window screen over the sink. I chewed and the kitten opened its mouth of terror as she crawled higher, wanting in to paw the leftovers from our plates. I looked at Carolyn who said that the cat was just showing off. I looked up in time to see it fall. It crawled up, then fell again.

We talked for an hour and had apple pie and coffee, slowly.   13
Finally, we got up with Carolyn taking my hand. Slightly embarrassed, I tried to pull away but her grip held me. I let her have her way as she led me down the hallway with her mother right behind me. When I opened the door, I was startled by a kitten clinging to the screen door, its mouth screaming "cat food, dog biscuits, *sushi.* . . ." I opened the door and the kitten, still holding on, whined in the language of hungry animals. When I got into Carolyn's car, I looked back: the cat was still clinging. I asked Carolyn if it were possibly hungry, but she said the cat was being silly. She started the car, waved to her mother, and bounced us over the rain-poked drive, patting my thigh for being her lover baby. Carolyn waved again. I looked back, waving, then gawking at a window screen where there were now three kittens clawing and screaming to get in. Like Mexicans, I thought. I remembered the Molinas and how the cats clung to their screens — cats they shot down with squirt guns. On the highway, I felt happy, pleased by it all. I patted Carolyn's thigh. Her people were like Mexicans, only different.

RESPONDING TO READING

In paragraph 9, Soto confesses that he worried about marrying Carolyn because his best friend, Scott, had told him, "She's too good for you, so you better not." What do you think Scott, meant by "too good"? What do you think Soto understood him to mean? What does Soto need to determine before he can feel comfortable marrying Carolyn?

QUESTIONING THE TEXT

1. Why does Soto's grandmother advise him to become a barber? What other advice does she give him? How does his mother react when he asks for her opinion of the grandmother's advice?

2. How does Soto's mother react when he tells her that he wants to marry a Japanese woman? Why do you suppose he begins to doubt his decision to marry Carolyn? How does Soto finally quiet the words of his mother — "Marry a Mexican girl" (paragraph 8) — that he carries with him?

3. How does Soto feel about visiting Carolyn's parents in their home? Why do you suppose he panics when he and Carolyn pull into the driveway? As he gets out of the car, what elements of the scene begin to relieve his anxiety?

UNDERSTANDING THE WRITER'S CRAFT

1. In paragraphs 3 through 5, Soto recounts an afternoon he spent walking to the downtown mall with his best friend, Scott, and talking about whom they would marry when they got older. What do the two boys have in common? How do these paragraphs facilitate the transition between the first two paragraphs and the remainder of the essay? Explain.

2. How has Soto organized his essay? (Glossary: *Organization*) Does he use a point-by-point organization, a block organization, or a combination of both?

3. What similarities between Carolyn's family and his own people does Soto note? What for you is the most telling similarity? How is Carolyn's family different?

EXPLORING LANGUAGE

1. What effect does Soto create by having his grandmother speak English, sometimes interspersed with Spanish words?

2. Identify three or four of the many similes and metaphors Soto uses in his essay, and explain how each one enhances his description. (Glossary: *Figures of Speech*)

3. Refer to your desk dictionary to determine the meanings of the following words as Soto uses them in this selection: *gawk* (paragraph 3), *scuffed* (4), *ambled* (5), *bootstraps* (8), *sushi* (12), *embarrassed* (13).

COMBINING RHETORICAL STRATEGIES

Soto uses a great deal of description in this essay. For example, in paragraphs 9 through 13, he portrays his visit with Carolyn's parents using specific, concrete images. What are some of the most memorable details in this section of the essay? How does Soto's use of description enhance the central comparison of the essay? (Glossary: *Description*).

WRITING SUGGESTIONS

1. **(Comparison and Contrast)** Write a comparison and contrast essay about your relationship with your mother or father. In what ways are you similar? How do you differ? Do any of these similarities or differences surprise or intrigue you? What values do you share or disagree about? How have the different eras and circumstances of your respective childhoods shaped your relationship?

2. **(Other Strategies)** Everyone can be categorized or labeled according to such groupings as gender, race, religion, income, cultural background, and even appearance. Using these categories, how would you label yourself? What is your own image of the categories to which you belong? How do outsiders view these categories? Which categories do you think are most important in defining yourself? Do any of the categories to which you belong have a stigma or prejudice attached to them? To what degree are these categories inadequate in defining who you are? Write an essay in which you discuss the concept of self-image and the need to define oneself.

3. **(Research)** Soto's grandmother and mother advise him to marry a Mexican girl, yet he marries a Japanese woman. It wasn't that long ago that many parents strongly advised their children to marry within their own racial, ethnic, or religious group. People who did not heed this advice were often met with anger and prejudice from society at large. Today, even though some parents still offer this kind of advice, our society seems to be much more accepting of interracial marriages like the Sotos'. The biracial children of these marriages, however, are facing unanticipated problems of identity. Using the library and possibly the Internet to do your research, write an essay on the subject of biracial children. What are the problems that confront these children? What help is there for biracial children? What still needs to be done? What are your reactions to predicaments facing these children and young adults? Report your findings in an essay.

   • **Project Reclassify All Children Equally (RACE)**
   <http://www.projectrace.com>

   "Project RACE advocates for multiracial children and adults through education, community awareness and legislation," according to this site, which features news, legislative updates, health information, and links to similar sites.

- **You Don't Look Japanese**

  <http://www.angelfire.com/or/biracial>

  This site, devoted to "biracial/interracial issues," includes many links to related resources. Arranged topically, these links include news, arts, humor, political information, and book recommendations.

- *Interracial Voice*

  <http://www.webcom.com/~intvoice>

  Interracial Voice is an online magazine "serving the mixed-race/interracial community in cyberspace." This site features news, opinion articles, reviews, poetry, and discussion forums.

- *Mavin* Magazine

  <http://www.mavin.net/magazine.html>

  Founded by a nineteen-year-old student at Wesleyan University, the goal of *Mavin* magazine is to "celebrate the mixed race experience." Full-text articles, book recommendations, and links to related sources are included at this site.

- **Association of MultiEthnic Americans**

  <http://www.ameasite.org>

  The AMEA's "primary goal is to educate and advocate on behalf of multiethnic individuals and families." This site features legal and governmental news and information and links to resources for multiethnic and multiracial Americans.

Sex, Lies, and Conversation

Deborah Tannen

Deborah Tannen, professor of linguistics at Georgetown University, was born in 1945 in Brooklyn, New York. Tannen received her B.A. in English from the State University of New York at Binghamton in 1966 and taught English in Greece until 1968. She then earned an M.A. in English literature from Wayne State University in 1970. While pursuing her Ph.D. in linguistics at the University of California, Berkeley, she received several prizes for her poetry and short fiction. Her work has appeared in New York *magazine,* Vogue, *and the* New York Times Magazine. *In addition, she has authored three best-selling language books:* You Just Don't Understand *(1990),* That's Not What I Meant *(1991), and* Talking from Nine to Five *(1994). The success of these books attests to the public's interest in language, especially when it pertains to gender differences. Tannen's most recent book, in which she explores how family members communicate, is entitled* I Only Say This Because I Love You *(2000).*

In this essay, which first appeared in the Washington Post *in 1990, Tannen examines the differences between men's and women's public and private speech. Interestingly, she concludes that cross-gender conversation, when seen as cross-cultural communication, "allows us to understand the problem and forge solutions without blaming either party."*

BEFORE YOU READ

How important is it for people to be aware of gender and cultural differences when interacting with others? What are some of the potential benefits of such awareness?

I was addressing a small gathering in a suburban Virginia living room — a women's group that had invited men to join them. Throughout the evening, one man had been particularly talkative, frequently offering ideas and anecdotes, while his wife sat silently beside him on the couch. Toward the end of the evening, I commented that women frequently complain that their husbands don't talk to them. This man quickly concurred. He gestured toward his wife and said, "She's the talker in our family." The room burst into laughter; the man looked puzzled and hurt. "It's true," he explained. "When I come home from work I have nothing to say. If she didn't keep the conversation going, we'd spend the whole evening in silence."

This episode crystallizes the irony that although American men tend to talk more than women in public situations, they often talk less at home. And this pattern is wreaking havoc with marriage.

The pattern was observed by political scientist Andrew Hacker in the late '70s. Sociologist Catherine Kohler Riessman reports in her new book *Divorce Talk* that most of the women she interviewed — but only a few of the men — gave lack of communication as the reason for their divorces. Given the current divorce rate of nearly 50 percent, that amounts to millions of cases in the United States every year — a virtual epidemic of failed conversation.

In my own research, complaints from women about their husbands most often focused not on tangible inequities such as having given up the chance for a career to accompany a husband to his, or doing far more than their share of daily life-support work like cleaning, cooking, social arrangements, and errands. Instead, they focused on communication: "He doesn't listen to me," "He doesn't talk to me." I found, as Hacker observed years before, that most wives want their husbands to be, first and foremost, conversational partners, but few husbands share this expectation of their wives.

In short, the image that best represents the current crisis is the stereotypical cartoon scene of a man sitting at the breakfast table with a newspaper held up in front of his face, while a woman glares at the back of it, wanting to talk.

LINGUISTIC BATTLE OF THE SEXES

How can women and men have such different impressions of communication in marriage? Why the widespread imbalance in their interests and expectations?

In the April issue of *American Psychologist,* Stanford University's Eleanor Maccoby reports the results of her own and others' research showing that children's development is most influenced by the social structure of peer interactions. Boys and girls tend to play with children of their own gender, and their sex-separate groups have different organizational structures and interactive norms.

I believe these systematic differences in childhood socialization make talk between women and men like cross-cultural communication, heir to all the attraction and pitfalls of that enticing but difficult enterprise. My research on men's and women's conversations uncovered patterns similar to those described for children's groups.

For women, as for girls, intimacy is the fabric of relationships, and talk is the thread from which it is woven. Little girls create and maintain friendships by exchanging secrets; similarly, women regard conversation as the cornerstone of friendship. So a woman expects her husband to be a new and improved version of a best friend. What is important is not the individual subjects that are discussed but the sense of closeness, of a life shared, that emerges when people tell their thoughts, feelings, and impressions.

Bonds between boys can be as intense as girls', but they are based less on talking, more on doing things together. Since they don't assume talk is the cement that binds a relationship, men don't know what kind of talk women want, and they don't miss it when it isn't there. 10

Boys' groups are larger, more inclusive, and more hierarchical, so boys must struggle to avoid the subordinate position in the group. This may play a role in women's complaints that men don't listen to them. Some men really don't like to listen, because being the listener makes them feel one-down, like a child listening to adults or an employee to a boss. 11

But often when women tell men, "You aren't listening," and the men protest, "I am," the men are right. The impression of not listening results from misalignments in the mechanics of conversation. The misalignment begins as soon as a man and a woman take physical positions. This became clear when I studied videotapes made by psychologist Bruce Dorval of children and adults talking to their same-sex best friends. I found that at every age, the girls and women faced each other directly, their eyes anchored on each other's faces. At every age, the boys and men sat at angles to each other and looked elsewhere in the room, periodically glancing at each other. They were obviously attuned to each other, often mirroring each other's movements. But the tendency of men to face away can give women the impression they aren't listening even when they are. A young woman in college was frustrated: Whenever she told her boyfriend she wanted to talk to him, he would lie down on the floor, close his eyes, and put his arm over his face. This signaled to her, "He's taking a nap." But he insisted he was listening extra hard. Normally, he looks around the room, so he is easily distracted. Lying down and covering his eyes helped him concentrate on what she was saying. 12

Analogous to the physical alignment that women and men take in conversation is their topical alignment. The girls in my study tended to talk at length about one topic, but the boys tended to jump from topic to topic. The second-grade girls exchanged stories about people they knew. The second-grade boys teased, told jokes, noticed things in the room, and talked about finding games to play. The sixth-grade girls talked about problems with a mutual friend. The sixth-grade boys talked about 55 different topics, none of which extended over more than a few turns. 13

LISTENING TO BODY LANGUAGE

Switching topics is another habit that gives women the impression men aren't listening, especially if they switch to a topic about themselves. But the evidence of the 10th-grade boys in my study indicates 14 otherwise. The 10th-grade boys sprawled across their chairs with bodies parallel and eyes straight ahead, rarely looking at each other. They looked as if they were riding in a car, staring out the windshield. But they were talking about their feelings. One boy was upset because a girl had told him he had a drinking problem, and the other was feeling alienated from all his friends.

Now, when a girl told a friend about a problem, the friend responded by asking probing questions and expressing agreement and understanding. But the boys dismissed each other's problems. Todd assured Richard that his drinking was "no big problem" because "sometimes you're funny when you're off your butt." And when Todd said he felt left out, Richard responded, "Why should you? You know more people than me."

Women perceive such responses as belittling and unsupportive. But the boys seemed satisfied with them. Whereas women reassure each other by implying, "You shouldn't feel bad because I've had similar experiences," men do so by implying, "You shouldn't feel bad because your problems aren't so bad."

There are even simpler reasons for women's impression that men don't listen. Linguist Lynette Hirschman found that women make more listener-noise, such as "mhm," "uhuh," and "yeah," to show "I'm with you." Men, she found, more often give silent attention. Women who expect a stream of listener-noise interpret silent attention as no attention at all.

Women's conversational habits are as frustrating to men as men's are to women. Men who expect silent attention interpret a stream of listener-noise as overreaction or impatience. Also, when women talk to each other in a close, comfortable setting, they often overlap, finish each other's sentences, and anticipate what the other is about to say. This practice, which I call "participatory listenership," is often perceived by men as interruption, intrusion, and lack of attention.

A parallel difference caused a man to complain about his wife, "She just wants to talk about her own point of view. If I show her another view, she gets mad at me." When most women talk to each other, they assume a conversationalist's job is to express agreement and support. But many men see their conversational duty as pointing out the other side of an argument. This is heard as disloyalty by women, and refusal to offer the requisite support. It is not that women don't want to see other points of view, but that they prefer them phrased as suggestions and inquiries rather than as direct challenges.

In his book *Fighting for Life,* Walter Ong points out that men use "agonistic" or warlike, oppositional formats to do almost anything; thus discussion becomes debate, and conversation a competitive sport. In contrast, women see conversation as a ritual means of establishing rapport. If Jane tells a problem and June says she has a similar one, they walk away feeling closer to each other. But this attempt at establishing rapport can backfire when used with men. Men take too literally women's ritual "troubles talk," just as women mistake men's ritual challenges for real attack.

THE SOUNDS OF SILENCE

These differences begin to clarify why women and men have such different expectations about communication in marriage. For women, talk creates intimacy. Marriage is an orgy of closeness: you can tell your feelings and thoughts, and still be loved. Their greatest fear is being pushed away. But men live in a hierarchical world, where talk maintains independence and status. They are on guard to protect themselves from being put down and pushed around.

This explains the paradox of the talkative man who said of his silent wife, "She's the talker." In the public setting of a guest lecture, he felt challenged to show his intelligence and display his understanding of the lecture. But at home, where he has nothing to prove and no one to defend against, he is free to remain silent. For his wife, being home means she is free from the worry that something she says might offend someone, or spark disagreement, or appear to be showing off; at home she is free to talk.

The communication problems that endanger marriage can't be fixed by mechanical engineering. They require a new conceptual framework about the role of talk in human relationships. Many of the psychological explanations that have become second nature may not be helpful, because they tend to blame either women (for not being assertive enough) or men (for not being in touch with their feelings). A sociolinguistic approach by which male–female conversation is seen as cross-cultural communication allows us to understand the problem and forge solutions without blaming either party.

Once the problem is understood, improvement comes naturally, as it did to the young woman and her boyfriend who seemed to go to sleep when she wanted to talk. Previously, she had accused him of not listening, and he had refused to change his behavior, since that would be admitting fault. But then she learned about and explained to him the differences in women's and men's habitual ways of aligning themselves in conversation. The next time she told him she wanted to talk, he began, as usual, by lying down and covering his eyes. When the familiar negative reaction bubbled up, she reassured herself that he really was listening. But then he sat up and looked at her. Thrilled, she asked why. He said, "You like me to look at you when we talk, so I'll try to do it." Once he saw their differences as cross-cultural rather than right and wrong, he independently altered his behavior.

Women who feel abandoned and deprived when their husbands 25
won't listen to or report daily news may be happy to discover their
husbands trying to adapt once they understand the place of small talk
in women's relationships. But if their husbands don't adapt, the
women may still be comforted that for men, this is not a failure of intimacy. Accepting the difference, the wives may look to their friends
or family for that kind of talk. And husbands who can't provide it
shouldn't feel their wives have made unreasonable demands. Some
couples will still decide to divorce, but at least their decisions will be
based on realistic expectations.

In these times of resurgent ethnic conflicts, the world desperately 26
needs cross-cultural understanding. Like charity, successful cross-cultural communication should begin at home.

RESPONDING TO READING

Consider the times in your life when you have experienced problems in conversation. Do you think that these problems might have occurred as a result
of gender or cultural differences, as Tannen explains?

QUESTIONING THE TEXT

1. In paragraph 8, Tannen compares conversational problems between
   men and women to the problems of "cross-cultural communication."
   What does she mean by this comparison?

2. In paragraph 7, Tannen reports on a study that shows boys' and girls'
   conversational development follows different patterns. How does she
   think these patterns carry over into adult conversational patterns?

3. Throughout the essay, Tannen makes a conscious effort to treat both
   her male and female readers fairly. In what ways has she sought to encourage understanding rather than attach blame?

UNDERSTANDING THE WRITER'S CRAFT

1. Deciding on an organizational plan is important when writing a comparison and contrast essay. How does Tannen organize her essay —
   point-by-point or block organization? Why do you think she makes this
   choice, and is it effective?

2. In hopes of explaining conversational differences between men and
   women, Tannen employs the analogy of cross-cultural communication.
   How well does the analogy work? Did it help you gain a better understanding of her topic? Explain. (Glossary: *Analogy*)

3. In keeping with her role as a popularizer of linguistic research, Tannen
   assumes an informal, almost conversational tone in the essay. Why do
   you think she chose to keep her own experiences out of the essay?

What could she have gained or lost by including personal experience? (Glossary: *Tone*)

EXPLORING LANGUAGE

1. Tannen's essay appeals to a wide audience because of her informal, conversational diction. Is there anything in her choice of words that reveals her academic background? (Glossary: *Audience; Diction*)

2. In paragraph 18, Tannen introduces her term "participatory listenership." What does she mean by it? How does Tannen's use of this term point to the larger problem of gender miscommunication? (Glossary: *Definition*)

3. Refer to your desk dictionary to determine the meanings of the following words as Tannen uses them in this selection: *fabric* (paragraph 9), *hierarchical* (11), *mechanics* (12), *rapport* (20), *paradox* (22), *framework* (23).

COMBINING RHETORICAL STRATEGIES

In discussing speech differences, Tannen attempts to explain the causes of our different approaches to conversation. How does a knowledge of these causes help us better understand their effects on cross-gender conversations? Explain how Tannen's use of cause and effect strengthens her overall argument. (Glossary: *Cause and Effect Analysis*)

WRITING SUGGESTIONS

1. **(Comparison and Contrast)** Write an essay modeled on Tannen's in which you analyze the characteristics of conversation she has labeled as particularly "masculine" or particularly "feminine," using examples from your own experience. How does your own experience of what men and women do when they converse compare with Tannen's explanation?

2. **(Other Strategies)** Imagine that your college is considering the adoption of a course entitled "Language, Gender, and Communication." As a concerned student, position yourself to argue for or against such a course. Present your argument as an essay or as a letter to the editor of your school newspaper. (Glossary: *Argument*)

3. **(Research)** There are many ethnic newspapers and magazines that offer multicultural perspectives on contemporary issues. Research some of these publications; search in the library with *Ethnic Information Sources of the United States,* or look for periodicals on the Internet. Spend some time reading several of the periodicals that you find. What does the continuing popularity of these periodicals suggest about the status of cultural relations in society today? Do you think such periodicals create greater understanding or more divisions within society? Write an essay in which you explain your analysis of one or more of these periodicals.

- **The Afro-American Newspapers Home Page**
  <http://www.afroam.org/information/news/current/news.html>

  This site contains current as well as archived articles on topics of interest to the African American community.

- *Asian Week* **Online**
  <http://www.asianweek.com>

  This weekly Internet magazine for the Asian American community includes an archive of back issues.

- *Oklahoma Indian Times*
  <http://www.okit.com>

  This site is "an independent, online newspaper serving Oklahoma's federally recognized Indian Nations."

- *La Prensa* **San Diego**
  <http://www.laprensa-sandiego.org>

  La Prensa is a "Spanish/English newspaper covering the issues of the Hispanic/Chicano community on a local and national level."

- **Deborah Tannen's Official Web Site**
  <http://www.georgetown.edu/tannen>

  This site offers extensive information about the author and her language-related work.

COMBINING SUBJECTS AND STRATEGIES

The photographs below depict many of the same themes and strategies as the Combining Rhetorical Strategies essay that follows. Your observations about the photographs will help guide you to the key themes and strategies in the essay. After you've read the essay, you may use your observations about both the photographs and the essay to examine how the overlapping themes and strategies work in each medium.

During the Civil War (1861–1865), Northerners (from the anti-slavery states of the Union) and Southerners (from the eleven pro-slavery states of the Confederacy) fought fiercely over the future of slavery. The names of Civil War leaders Ulysses S. Grant and Robert E. Lee have become synonymous with the Union and the Confederacy. The photograph of Grant (left) was taken by Mathew Brady after the Battle of the Wilderness in 1864, during which the Union lost roughly 18,000 soldiers. Instead of retreating, Grant pushed his troops forward, forcing Lee's army back toward Richmond, Virginia. Lee didn't like to pose; the photograph by Minnis and Cowell (right) is one of the few that exists. Taken in early 1863 — when the South was still optimistic about winning the war — it was Lee's first formal portrait as a Confederate general.

For Discussion

How would you describe the appearance — both dress and posture — of these two generals? What details in the photographs are most telling for you? Explain why. In what ways can Grant and Lee be said to represent the way of life associated with the side each commanded? Explain.

Grant and Lee: A Study in Contrasts

Bruce Catton

Bruce Catton (1899–1978) was born in Petoskey, Michigan, and attended Oberlin College. Early in his career, Catton worked as a reporter for various newspapers, among them the Cleveland Plain Dealer. *Having an interest in history, Catton became a leading authority on the Civil War and wrote a number of books on the subject. These include* Mr. Lincoln's Army *(1951),* Glory Road *(1952),* A Stillness at Appomattox *(1977),* This Hallowed Ground *(1956),* The Coming Fury *(1980),* Never Call Retreat *(1965), and* Gettysburg: The Final Fury *(1974). Catton won both the Pulitzer Prize and the National Book Award in 1954.*

The following selection was included in The American Story, *a collection of historical essays edited by Earl Schenk Miers. In this essay, Catton considers "two great Americans, Grant and Lee — very different, yet under everything very much alike."*

BEFORE YOU READ

What do you know about America's Civil War and the roles played by Ulysses S. Grant and Robert E. Lee in that monumental struggle? For you, what does each of these men represent? Do you consider either of them to be an American hero? Explain.

When Ulysses S. Grant and Robert E. Lee met in the parlor of a   1
modest house at Appomattox Court House, Virginia, on April 9, 1865, to work out the terms for the surrender of Lee's Army of Northern Virginia, a great chapter in American life came to a close, and a great new chapter began.

These men were bringing the Civil War to its virtual finish. To be   2
sure, other armies had yet to surrender, and for a few days the fugitive Confederate government would struggle desperately and vainly, trying to find some way to go on living now that its chief support was gone. But in effect it was all over when Grant and Lee signed the papers. And the little room where they wrote out the terms was the scene of one of the poignant, dramatic contrasts in American history.

They were two strong men, these oddly different generals, and they   3
represented the strengths of two conflicting currents that, through them, had come into final collision.

Back of Robert E. Lee was the notion that the old aristocratic con-   4
cept might somehow survive and be dominant in American life.

Lee was tidewater Virginia, and in his background were family, 5
culture, and tradition . . . the age of chivalry transplanted to a New
World which was making its own legends and its own myths. He embodied a way of life that had come down through the age of knight-
hood and the English country squire. America was a land that was beginning all over again, dedicated to nothing much more complicated
than the rather hazy belief that all men had equal rights and should
have an equal chance in the world. In such a land Lee stood for the
feeling that it was somehow of advantage to human society to have a
pronounced inequality in the social structure. There should be a
leisure class, backed by ownership of land; in turn, society itself
should be keyed to the land as the chief source of wealth and influence. It would bring forth (according to this ideal) a class of men with
a strong sense of obligation to the community; men who lived not to
gain advantage for themselves, but to meet the solemn obligations
which had been laid on them by the very fact that they were privi-
leged. From them the country would get its leadership; to them it
could look for the higher values — of thought, of conduct, of personal
deportment — to give it strength and value.

Lee embodied the noblest elements of this aristocratic ideal. 6
Through him, the landed nobility justified itself. For four years, the
Southern states had fought a desperate war to uphold the ideals for
which Lee stood. In the end, it almost seemed as if the Confederacy
fought for Lee; as if he himself was the Confederacy . . . the best thing
that the way of life for which the Confederacy stood could ever have
to offer. He had passed into legend before Appomattox. Thousands of
tired, underfed, poorly clothed Confederate soldiers, long since past
the simple enthusiasm of the early days of the struggle, somehow considered Lee the symbol of everything for which they had been willing
to die. But they could not quite put this feeling into words. If the Lost
Cause, sanctified by so much heroism and so many deaths, had a living justification, its justification was General Lee.

Grant, the son of a tanner on the Western frontier, was everything 7
Lee was not. He had come up the hard way and embodied nothing in
particular except the eternal toughness and sinewy fiber of the men
who grew up beyond the mountains. He was one of a body of men
who owed reverence and obeisance to no one, who were self-reliant to
a fault, who cared hardly anything for the past but who had a sharp
eye for the future.

These frontier men were the precise opposite of the tidewater aris- 8
tocrats. Back of them, in the great surge that had taken people over
the Alleghenies and into the opening Western country, there was a
deep, implicit dissatisfaction with a past that had settled into grooves.
They stood for democracy, not from any reasoned conclusion about
the proper ordering of human society, but simply because they had

grown up in the middle of democracy and knew how it worked. Their society might have privileges, but they would be privileges each man had won for himself. Forms and patterns meant nothing. No man was born to anything, except perhaps to a chance to show how far he could rise. Life was competition.

Yet along with this feeling had come a deep sense of belonging to a national community. The Westerner who developed a farm, opened a shop, or set up in business as a trader, could hope to prosper only as his own community prospered — and his community ran from the Atlantic to the Pacific and from Canada down to Mexico. If the land was settled, with towns and highways and accessible markets, he could better himself. He saw his fate in terms of the nation's own destiny. As its horizons expanded, so did his. He had, in other words, an acute dollars-and-cents stake in the continued growth and development of his country.

And that, perhaps, is where the contrast between Grant and Lee becomes most striking. The Virginia aristocrat, inevitably, saw himself in relation to his own region. He lived in a static society which could endure almost anything except change. Instinctively, his first loyalty would go to the locality in which that society existed. He would fight to the limit of endurance to defend it, because in defending it he was defending everything that gave his own life its deepest meaning.

The Westerner, on the other hand, would fight with an equal tenacity for the broader concept of society. He fought so because everything he lived by was tied to growth, expansion and a constantly widening horizon. What he lived by would survive or fall with the nation itself. He could not possibly stand by unmoved in the face of an attempt to destroy the Union. He would combat it with everything he had, because he could only see it as an effort to cut the ground out from under his feet.

So Grant and Lee were in complete contrast, representing two diametrically opposed elements in American life. Grant was the modern man emerging; beyond him, ready to come on the stage, was the great age of steel and machinery, of crowded cities and a restless burgeoning vitality. Lee might have ridden down from the old age of chivalry, lance in hand, silken banner fluttering over his head. Each man was the perfect champion of his cause, drawing both his strengths and his weaknesses from the people he led.

Yet it was not all contrast, after all. Different as they were — in background, in personality, in underlying aspiration — these two great soldiers had much in common. Under everything else, they were marvelous fighters. Furthermore, their fighting qualities were really very much alike.

Each man had, to begin with, the great virtue of utter tenacity and fidelity. Grant fought his way down the Mississippi Valley in spite of acute personal discouragement and profound military handicaps. Lee hung on in the trenches at Petersburg after hope itself had died. In each man there was an indomitable quality . . . the born fighter's refusal to give up as long as he can still remain on his feet and lift his two fists.

Daring and resourcefulness they had, too; the ability to think faster and move faster than the enemy. These were the qualities which gave Lee the dazzling campaigns of Second Manassas and Chancellorsville and won Vicksburg for Grant.

Lastly, and perhaps greatest of all, there was the ability, at the end, to turn quickly from war to peace once the fighting was over. Out of the way these two men behaved at Appomattox came the possibility of a peace of reconciliation. It was a possibility not wholly realized, in the years to come, but which did, in the end, help the two sections to become one nation again . . . after a war whose bitterness might have seemed to make such a reunion wholly impossible. No part of either man's life became him more than the part he played in their brief meeting in the McLean house at Appomattox. Their behavior there put all succeeding generations of Americans in their debt. Two great Americans, Grant and Lee — very different, yet under everything very much alike. Their encounter at Appomattox was one of the great moments of American history.

RESPONDING TO READING

Catton concludes with the claim that Grant and Lee's "encounter at Appomattox was one of the great moments of American history" (paragraph 16). How does Catton prepare readers for this claim? What, for Catton, do these two Civil War generals represent, and what does he see as the implications of Lee's surrender for the country?

QUESTIONING THE TEXT

1. In paragraphs 10 through 12, Catton discusses what he considers to be the most striking contrast between Grant and Lee. What is that difference?

2. List the similarities that Catton sees between Grant and Lee. Which similarity does Catton believe is most important? Why?

3. What attitudes and ideas does Catton describe to support his view that the culture of tidewater Virginia was a throwback to the "age of chivalry" (paragraph 5)?

4. Catton says that Grant was "the modern man emerging" (paragraph 12). How does he support that statement? Do you agree?

UNDERSTANDING THE WRITER'S CRAFT

1. What would have been lost had Catton looked at the similarities between Grant and Lee before looking at the differences? Would anything have been gained?

2. How does Catton organize the body of his essay (paragraphs 3 to 16)? When answering this question, you may find it helpful to summarize the point of comparison in each paragraph and to label whether the paragraph concerns Lee, Grant, or both. (Glossary: *Organization*)

3. Catton makes clear transitions between paragraphs. Identify the transitional devices he uses to lead readers from one paragraph to the next throughout the essay. As a reader, how do these transitions help you? (Glossary: *Transitions*) Explain.

EXPLORING LANGUAGE

1. Identify at least two metaphors that Catton uses, and explain what each contributes to his comparison. (Glossary: *Figures of Speech*)

2. Refer to your desk dictionary to determine the meanings of the following words as Catton uses them in this selection: *poignant* (paragraph 2), *chivalry* (5), *sanctified* (6), *sinewy* (7), *obeisance* (7), *tidewater* (8), *tenacity* (11), *aspiration* (13).

COMBINING RHETORICAL STRATEGIES

How does Catton use both description and cause and effect analysis to enhance his comparison and contrast of Grant and Lee? In what ways does description serve to sharpen the differences between these generals? How does Catton use cause and effect analysis to explain their respective natures? Cite several examples of Catton's use of each strategy to illustrate your answer.

WRITING SUGGESTIONS

1. **(Comparison and Contrast)** Catton gives readers few details of the physical appearance of Grant and Lee, but the portraits preceding this essay do show us what these men looked like. Write a brief essay in which you compare and contrast the men you see in the portraits. How closely does your assessment of each general match the "picture" Catton presents in his essay?

2. **(Other Strategies)** In the persons of Grant and Lee, Catton sees the "final collision" (paragraph 3) between two ways of living and thinking — the "age of steel and machinery" (12) conquering the "age of chivalry" (5). What do you see as the dominant ways of living and thinking in the current "age of information"? Do today's lifestyles appear to be on a collision course with one another, or do you think they can all coexist? Write an essay in which you present your position and defend it using appropriate examples.

3. **(Research)** Write an essay in which you compare and contrast two world leaders, sports figures, or celebrities whose careers — like those of Grant and Lee — have at some point crossed in a dramatic or decisive way: John F. Kennedy and Richard Nixon, for example, or Venus Williams and Lindsay Davenport, or Sir Thomas More and Henry VIII, or Marilyn Monroe and Joe DiMaggio, or George W. Bush and Al Gore,

or two people of your choosing. Research your two famous people in the library and on the Internet.

- **The Biographical Dictionary**
  <http://www.s9.com/biography>

  This dictionary, searchable by date, name, or keyword, "covers more than 28,000 notable men and women who have shaped our world from ancient times to the present day" and features links to biographical information on almost everyone of historical significance, from prominent astronauts to Shakespeare.

- **Biography.com**
  <http://biography.com>

  This site from the A&E television show offers profiles of 25,000 personalities.

- **The History Channel Online**
  <http://historychannel.com>

  This companion site to the popular cable network allows you to search for information on any historical topic by keyword or time line.

- **Lives**
  <http://amillionlives.com>

  This site, searchable by keyword and directory, features an exhaustive catalog of annotated Web links "to thousands of biographies, autobiographies, memoirs, diaries, letters, narratives, oral histories and more."

- **Infoplease Biography**
  <http://www.infoplease.com/people.html>

  This online database features biographies of more than 30,000 notable people. You can search this site by keyword or by directory.

WRITING SUGGESTIONS FOR COMPARISON AND CONTRAST

1. Write an essay in which you compare and contrast two objects, people, or events to show at least one of the following.

    a. their important differences
    b. their significant similarities
    c. their relative value
    d. their distinctive qualities

2. Select a topic from the list that follows. Write an essay using comparison and contrast as your primary means of development. Be sure that your essay has a definite purpose and a clear direction.

    a. two methods of dieting
    b. two television situation comedies
    c. two types of summer employment
    d. two people who display different attitudes toward responsibility
    e. two restaurants
    f. two courses in the same subject area
    g. two friends who exemplify different lifestyles
    h. two network television or local news programs
    i. two professional quarterbacks
    j. two ways of studying for an exam
    k. two rooms in which you have classes
    l. two of your favorite magazines
    m. two attitudes toward death
    n. two ways to heat a home

3. Use one of the following "before and after" situations as the basis for an essay of comparison and contrast.

    a. before and after an examination
    b. before and after seeing a movie
    c. before and after reading an important book
    d. before and after dieting
    e. before and after a long trip

4. Most of us have seen something important in our lives — a person, place, or thing — undergo a significant change, either in the subject itself or in our own perception of it. Write an essay comparing and contrasting the person, place, or thing before and after the change. First, reread Mark Twain's "Two Ways of Seeing a River" in this chapter (p. 222) and Malcolm X's "Coming to an Awareness of Language" in Chapter 7 (p. 346), and then consider your topic. There are many possibilities to consider. Perhaps a bucolic vista of open fields has become a shopping mall; perhaps a favorite athletic team has gone from glory to shame; perhaps a loved one has been altered by decisions, events, or illness.

5. Interview a professor who has taught for many years at your college or university. Ask the professor to compare and contrast the college as it was when he or she first taught there with the way it is now; encourage reminiscence and evaluation. Combine strategies of description, comparison and contrast, and possibly definition as you write your essay.

6. Seven of the essays in this book deal, more or less directly, with issues related to the definition, achievement, or nature of manhood in America. The essays are "How to Give Orders Like a Man" (p. 117) and "Sex, Lies, and Conversation" (p. 368), both by Deborah Tannen; "Like Mexicans" by Gary Soto (p. 361); "Grant and Lee: A Study in Contrasts" by Bruce Catton (p. 377); "The Men We Carry in Our Minds" by Scott Russell Sanders (p. 439); "The Company Man" by Ellen Goodman (p. 462); and "How Boys Become Men" by Jon Katz (p. 521). Read these essays, and discuss with classmates the broad issues they raise. Choose one topic of particular interest to you, and study the three or four essays that seem to bear most directly on this topic. Write a paper in which you compare, contrast, and evaluate the assertions in these essays.

CHAPTER 10

Division and Classification

WHAT ARE DIVISION AND CLASSIFICATION?

Like comparison and contrast, division and classification are separate yet closely related operations. Division involves breaking down a single large unit into smaller subunits or separating a group of items into discrete categories. For example, a state government can be divided into its three main branches and even further into departments or agencies within those branches; the whole pool of registered voters in the United States can be divided among political affiliations: Democrat, Republican, independent, and so forth. Classification, on the other hand, entails placing individual items into established categories: a boxer is classified with other boxers according to weight, a movie is placed in a rating category according to content, a library book is shelved according to an elaborate system of subject codes, and a voter can be categorized according to his or her political party. Division, then, takes apart, whereas classification groups together. But even though the two processes can operate separately, writers tend to use them together.

Division can be the most effective method for making sense of one large, complex, or multifaceted entity. Consider, for example, the following passage from E. B. White's *Here Is New York*, in which he discusses New Yorkers and their city.

Division into categories occurs in the opening sentence.   There are roughly three New Yorks. There is, first, the New York of the man or woman who was born here, who takes the city for granted and accepts its size and its turbulence as natural and inevitable. Second, there is the

385

New York of the commuter — the city that is devoured by locusts each day and spat out each night. Third, there is the New York of the person who was born somewhere else and came to New York in quest of something. Of these three trembling cities the greatest is the last — the city of final destination, the city that is a goal. It is this third city that accounts for New York's highstrung disposition, its poetical deportment, its dedication to the arts, and its incomparable achievements. Commuters give the city its tidal restlessness; natives give it solidarity and continuity; but the settlers give it passion. And whether it is a farmer arriving from Italy to set up a small grocery store in a slum, or a young girl arriving from a small town in Mississippi to escape the indignity of being observed by her neighbors, or a boy arriving from the Corn Belt with a manuscript in his suitcase and a pain in his heart, it makes no difference: each embraces New York with the intense excitement of first love, each absorbs New York with the fresh eyes of an adventurer, each generates heat and light to dwarf the Consolidated Edison Company.

Author explains the nature of people in each category.

In his opening sentences, White suggests a principle for dividing the population of New York, establishing his three categories on the basis of a person's relation to the city. There is the New York of the native, the New York of the commuter, and the New York of the immigrant. Although White gives specific examples for only his third grouping, it is easy to see where any individual would be classified. The purpose and result of White's divisions are clear and effective. They help him make a point about the character of New York City, depicting its restlessness, its solidarity, and its passion.

In contrast to breaking a large idea into parts, classification can be used to draw connections between disparate elements based on a common category — price, for example. Often, classification is used in conjunction with another rhetorical strategy, such as comparison and contrast. Consider, for example, how the following passage from Toni Cade Bambara's "The Lesson" classifies a toy in F.A.O. Schwarz and other items in the $35 category to compare the relative value of things in the life of two girls, Sylvia and Sugar.

Same thing in the store. We all walkin on tiptoe and hardly touchin the games and puzzles and things. And I watched Miss Moore who is steady watchin us like she waitin for a sign. Like Mama Drewery watches the sky and sniffs the air and takes note of just how much slant is in the bird formation. Then me and Sugar bump smack into each other, so busy gazing at the toys, 'specially the

First mention of price

sailboat. But we don't laugh and go into our fat-lady bump-stomach routine. We just stare at that price tag. Then Sugar run a finger over the whole boat. And I'm jealous and want to hit her. Maybe not her, but I sure want to punch somebody in the mouth.

"Whatcha bring us here for, Miss Moore?"

"You sound angry, Sylvia. Are you mad about something?" Givin me one of them grins like she tellin a grown-up joke that never turns out to be funny. And she's lookin very closely at me like maybe she plannin to do my portrait from memory. I'm mad, but I won't give her that satisfaction. So I slouch around the store being very bored and say, "Let's go."

Me and Sugar at the back of the train watchin the tracks whizzin by large then small then getting gobbled up in the dark. I'm thinkin about this tricky toy I saw in the store. A clown that somersaults on a bar then does chin-ups just cause you yank lightly at his leg. Cost $35. I could see me askin my mother for a $35 birthday clown. "You wanna who that costs what?" she'd say, cocking her head to the side to get a better view of the hole in my head.

Classification used along with comparison and contrast

Thirty-five dollars could buy new bunk beds for Junior and Gretchen's boy. Thirty-five dollars and the whole household could go visit Grand-daddy Nelson in the country. Thirty-five dollars would pay for the rent and the piano bill too. Who are these people that spend that much for performing clowns and $1000 for toy sailboats? What kinda work they do and how they live and how come we ain't in on it?

Another example may help clarify how division and classification work hand in hand. Suppose a sociologist wants to determine whether the socioeconomic status of the people in a particular neighborhood has any influence on their voting behavior. Having decided on her purpose, the sociologist chooses as her subject the fifteen families living on Maple Street. Her goal then becomes to group these families in a way that will be relevant to her purpose. She immediately knows that she wants to divide the neighborhood in two ways: (1) according to socioeconomic status (low-income earners, middle-income earners, and high-income earners) and (2) according to voting behavior (voters and nonvoters). However, her process of division won't be complete until she can classify individual families into her various groupings.

In confidential interviews with each family, the sociologist learns first its income and then whether any member of the household has voted in a state or federal election during the last four years. Based on this information, she begins to classify each family according to her established categories and at the same time to divide the neighborhood into the subclasses crucial to her study. Her work leads her to construct the following diagram of her divisions/classifications. This diagram allows the sociologist to visualize her division and classification system and its essential components: subject, basis or principle of division, subclasses or categories, and conclusion. It is clear that her ultimate conclusion depends on her ability to work back and forth between the potential divisions or subclasses and the actual families to be classified.

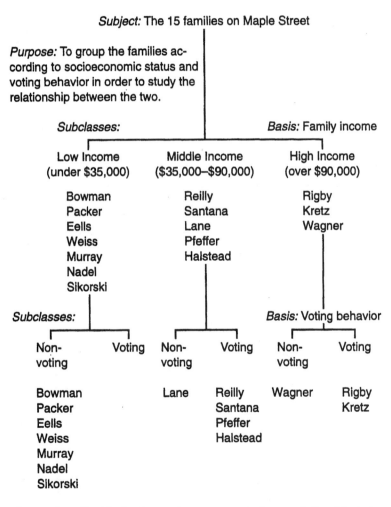

Subject: The 15 families on Maple Street

Purpose: To group the families according to socioeconomic status and voting behavior in order to study the relationship between the two.

Subclasses:

Basis: Family income

Low Income (under $35,000)	Middle Income ($35,000–$90,000)	High Income (over $90,000)
Bowman Packer Eells Weiss Murray Nadel Sikorski	Reilly Santana Lane Pfeffer Halstead	Rigby Kretz Wagner

Subclasses:

Basis: Voting behavior

Non-voting	Voting	Non-voting	Voting	Non-voting	Voting
Bowman Packer Eells Weiss Murray Nadel Sikorski		Lane	Reilly Santana Pfeffer Halstead	Wagner	Rigby Kretz

Conclusion: On Maple Street there seems to be a relationship between socioeconomic status and voting behavior: The low-income families are nonvoters.

WHY DO WRITERS USE DIVISION AND CLASSIFICATION?

As the work of the Maple Street sociologist shows, division and classification are used primarily to demonstrate a particular point about the subject under discussion. In a paper about the emphasis a television network places on reaching various audiences, you could begin by dividing prime-time programming into suitable subclasses: shows primarily for adults, shows for families, shows for children, and so forth. You could then classify each of that network's individual programs into one of these categories. Ultimately, you would want to analyze how the programs are divided among the various categories; in this way you could make a point about which audiences the network tries hardest to reach.

Classification and division can also help to explain a broadly complicated subject by reducing it to its more manageable parts. In her essay "Propaganda: How Not To Be Bamboozled" later in this chapter, for example, Donna Woolfolk Cross identifies and classifies the many different propaganda techniques that are used to shape our opinions.

Another purpose of division and classification is to help writers and readers make choices. A voter may classify politicians on the basis of their attitudes toward nuclear energy or abortion; *Consumer Reports* classifies laptop computers on the basis of available memory, screen size, processor speed, repair record, and warranty; high school seniors classify colleges and universities on the basis of selectivity, geographic location, programs available, and tuition fees. In such cases, division and classification have an absolutely practical end: making a decision about whom to vote for, which laptop to buy, and where to apply for admission to college.

Finally, writers use division and classification as a basic organizational strategy, one that brings a sense of order to a large amorphous whole. As you'll see later in this chapter, for example, Russell Baker's system of classification in "The Plot against People" establishes three categories of inanimate objects (those that break down, those that get lost, and those that don't work), thus creating a clear and logical structure for his tongue-in-cheek musings.

AN ANNOTATED STUDENT ESSAY USING DIVISION AND CLASSIFICATION

Gerald Cleary studied mathematics as an undergraduate and later attended law school at Cornell University. He spent his last two years of high school in West Germany as a military dependent. During that time, Cleary sold stereo equipment at a large post exchange. In this essay, Cleary has fun dividing and classifying the different types of customers he dealt with during his time on the job.

How Loud? How Good? How Much?
How Pretty?

Gerald Cleary

Introduction: Division of stereo buyers into four categories. Labels make for ease of reference.

As stereo equipment gets better and prices go down, stereo systems are becoming household necessities rather than luxuries. People are buying stereos by the thousands. During my year as a stereo salesman, I witnessed this boom firsthand. I dealt with hundreds of customers, and it didn't take long for me to learn that people buy stereos for different reasons. Eventually, though, I was able to divide all the stereo buyers into four basic categories: the looks buyer, the wattage buyer, the price buyer, and the quality buyer.

1

Organization: Least appealing buyer to salesperson is discussed.

The looks buyer cannot be bothered with the question of how her stereo will sound. Her only concern is how the stereo looks, making her the buyer least respected by the stereo salesperson. The looks buyer has an irresistible attraction to flashing lights, knobs, switches, and frivolous features. Even the loudspeakers are chosen on the basis of appearance -- the looks buyer always removes the grille to make sure a couple of knobs are present. Enjoyment for her is watching the output meters flash on her amplifier, or playing with her cassette deck's remote control. No matter what component she is shopping for, the looks buyer

2

Typical statement used as example

always decides on the flashiest, exclaiming, "Wait 'til my friends see this!"

Organization: Second, more appealing, buyer is discussed.

Slightly more respected is the wattage buyer, who is most easily identified by his trademark question: "How many watts does it put out?" He will not settle for less than 100 watts from his amp, and his speakers

3

must be able to handle all this power. He is
interested only in the volume level his
stereo can produce, for the wattage buyer
always turns it up loud -- so loud that most
would find it painful. The wattage buyer
genuinely enjoys his music -- either soul or
heavy metal -- at this volume. He is actually proud of his stereo's ability to put
out deafening noise. As a result, the
wattage buyer becomes as well-known to his
neighbors as he is to the salesperson. His
competitive nature makes him especially obvious as he pays for his new system, telling
Typical statement his friend, "Man, this is gonna blow Jones's
used as example stereo away!"

Organization: In this money-conscious world, the   4
Third, still more price buyer has the understanding, if not
appealing, buyer is the respect, of the salesperson. Often,
discussed. she is ashamed of her budget limitations
and will try to disguise herself as one of
the other types of buyers, asking, "What's
the loudest receiver I can buy for $200?"
Or, "What's the best turntable for under
$150?" It is always obvious that price is
this buyer's greatest worry -- she doesn't
really want the "loudest" or the "best."
The price buyer can be spotted looking
over the sale items or staring open-
mouthed at the price tag of an expensive
unit. After asking the salesperson where
the best deal in the store can be found,
she cringes at the standard reply: "You
Dialogue usually get what you pay for." But the
price buyer still picks the cheapest
model, telling her friends, "You won't believe the deal I got on this!"

Organization: Only one category remains: the quality   5
Fourth, and most buyer. He is the buyer most respected by the
appealing, buyer is salesperson, although he is often not even
discussed. in the store to buy -- he may simply want to
listen to the new compact-disc player tested

in his latest issue of <u>High Fidelity.</u> The quality buyer never buys on impulse; he has already read about and listened to any piece of equipment he finally buys. But along with high quality comes high price. The quality buyer can often be seen fingering the price tag of that noise-reduction unit he just has to own but can't yet afford. He never considers a cheaper model, preferring to wait until he can afford the high standard of quality he demands. The quality buyer shuns salespeople, believing that he knows more than they do anyway. Asking him "May I help you?" is the greatest insult of all.

Conclusion: How classifying buyers helped the author do his job

Recognizing the kind of buyer I was dealing with helped me steer her to the right corner of the store. I took looks buyers to the visually dazzling working displays, and wattage buyers into the soundproof speaker rooms. I directed price buyers to the sale items and left quality buyers alone. By the end of the year, I was able to identify the type of buyer almost instantly. My expertise paid off, making me the most successful salesperson in the store.

6

Analyzing Gerald Cleary's Essay of Division and Classification: Questions for Discussion

1. What categories does Gerald Cleary use to classify his subject? Brainstorm about other categories of stereo shoppers that might exist. Could these alternate categories be used to make a similar point?

2. How did Cleary organize the categories in his essay? Is his organization effective, or could he have chosen a better way to arrange his categories?

3. What other strategies might Cleary have used to strengthen his essay? Be specific about the benefits of each strategy.

SUGGESTIONS FOR WRITING A DIVISION AND CLASSIFICATION ESSAY

Begin by making certain that your subject represents a single, coherent entity. To do so, you will have to set definite limits for yourself and then stick to them. For example, the sociologist whose purpose was to survey relationships between family income and voting patterns limited her study to residents of Maple Street. Including a family from Oak Street would introduce new variables: a different neighborhood, possibly different socioeconomic conditions, and so on. Not abiding by a strict set of limits upsets the established system and, consequently, suggests the need to set new limits. Similarly, if you take as your subject for classification the student body at your school, you obviously cannot include students who are visiting from somewhere else unless you first redefine your subject.

As you define your classification essay, pay particular attention to your purpose, the divisions of your subject, your organization, and your conclusion. The later processes of planning and writing will depend on your purpose and on how that purpose leads you to divide your subject.

Determine Your Purpose, and Focus on It

The principle you use to divide your subject into categories depends on your larger purpose. It is crucial, then, that you determine a clear purpose for your division and classification before you begin to examine your subject in detail. For example, in studying the student body at your school, you might have any number of purposes: to discover how much time your classmates spend in the library during the week, to explain how financial aid is distributed, to discuss the most popular movies or music on campus, to describe styles of dorm-room decor. The categories into which you divide the student body will vary according to your chosen purpose.

Let's say, for example, that you are in charge of writing an editorial for your school newspaper that will make people aware of how they might reduce the amount of trash going to the landfill. How might you approach such a task using division and classification? Having established your purpose, your next task might be to identify the different ways objects can be handled to avoid sending them to the landfill. For instance, you might decide that there are four basic ways to prevent things from ending up in the trash. Then you could establish a sequence or order of importance in which they should be addressed. Your first draft might start something like the following.

Over the course of the last semester, more trash was removed from our campus than in any semester in history. But was it all trash that had to go to the landfill? For example, many of us love to wear fleece vests, but did you know that they are made from recycled plastic bottles? Much of what is considered trash need not go to the landfill at all. There are four ways we can prevent trash from being sent to the landfill. I call them the four R's. First, we can all either reduce the amount of individually packaged goods that we send to the landfill by buying frequently used items in family-size or bulk containers. Next, we can reuse those containers, as well as other items, either for their original purpose or for another. Be creative. After a while, though, things will wear out after repeated use. Then it's a good time to try and restore them. If that, too, can no longer be done, then they should be recycled. Only after these options have failed should items be considered "real" trash and removed to the landfill. Using the four R's -- Reduce, Reuse, Restore, Recycle -- we can reduce the amount of trash our campus sends to the landfill every semester.

This introduction should make the purpose of the editorial clear. In her editorial the author attempts to change her readers' behavior and to reduce the amount of trash they throw out. Once items have been divided or classified, the classification can be used to persuade readers toward or away from certain types of actions. As we will see in the essay "The Ways of Meeting Oppression" later in this chapter, Martin Luther King Jr., by identifying three categories of protest, is able to cite historical precedents to argue against violent forms of protest and in favor of nonviolent ones. Argumentation, especially in conjunction with other strategies, can be one of the most powerful rhetorical modes and will be explained in detail in Chapter 13.

Formulate a Thesis Statement

When writing a division and classification essay, be sure that your thesis statement presents clearly both the type and the number of categories that you will be using to make your point. Here are a few examples from this chapter.

- "There are roughly three New Yorks." E. B. White's thesis statement asserts that there are three different ways of interpreting New York City.

- "Eventually, though, I was able to divide all the stereo buyers into four basic categories: the looks buyer, the wattage buyer, the price buyer, and the quality buyer." This thesis statement, from the annotated student essay by Gerald Cleary, presents the subject — stereo buyers — and the four different categories into which they fall. This makes it clear to the reader what the essay will be about and the points that the author will make.

- "Inanimate objects are classified scientifically into three major categories — those that break down, those that get lost, and those that don't work." This thesis statement, from Russell Baker's "The Plot against People" later in the chapter, also clearly defines both the type and the number of categories. From this opening sentence, the reader knows exactly what Baker intends to discuss and how.

When you begin to formulate your thesis statement, keep these examples in mind. You could also look for other examples of thesis statements in the essays throughout this book. As you begin to develop your thesis statement, ask yourself, "What is my point?" Next ask yourself, "What categories will be most useful in making my point?" If you can't answer these questions, write some ideas down, and try to determine your main point from these ideas.

Once you have settled on an idea, go back to the two questions above, and write down your answers to them. Then combine the answers into a single thesis statement like the examples above. Your thesis statement does not necessarily have to be one sentence; making it one sentence, though, can be an effective way of focusing both your point and your categories.

By answering these two questions you should be well on your way to writing a clear and effective thesis statement. Use this thesis statement to guide readers through your essay and to help them understand your point and purpose.

Establish Appropriate Characteristics

Once you have decided on a subject and determined a purpose, your principle of division will usually be obvious. The sociologist studying voting patterns on Maple Street immediately divided her topic into three socioeconomic classes and into voters and nonvoters. Her important task was then to classify families according to these categories. In a study of how much time students spend in the library, you might just as readily divide your subject into categories: for example, those who spend less than five hours a week, those who spend between five and twenty hours, and those who spend more than twenty hours. You would then use these categories as your basis for classifying various individuals.

When establishing categories, make sure that they meet three criteria:

- *The categories must be appropriate to your purpose.* In determining the factors affecting financial aid distribution, you might consider family income, academic major, and athletic participation, but obviously you would not consider style of dress or preferred brand of toothpaste.
- *The categories must be consistent and mutually exclusive.* For example, dividing the student body into the classes men, women, and athletes would be illogical because athletes can be either male or female. Instead, you could divide the student body into male athletes, female athletes, male nonathletes, and female nonathletes.
- *The categories must be complete, and they must account for all the members or aspects of your subject.* In dividing the student body according to place of birth, it would be inaccurate to consider only states in the United States; such a division would not account for foreign students or citizens born outside the country.

You may often find that a diagram (such as the one of families on Maple Street), a chart, or a table can help you visualize your organization and help you make sure that your categories meet the three criteria. It can help you determine whether your classes are appropriate, mutually exclusive, and complete.

For some subjects and purposes, appropriate divisions will not be immediately apparent. In fact, your most challenging task will often be the creation of interesting and accurate classes based on careful observation. Dividing dorm rooms according to style of decor, for example, will require some canvassing before a system of classification becomes clear. Once you have developed a system, though, you can easily classify individual rooms: homey, bare, youthful, contemporary, cluttered, and so on. The effect of many informal essays depends on the writer's ability to establish clever yet useful divisions and classifications that the reader might not otherwise notice.

Organize the Points of Your Essay

Essays of division and classification, when sensibly planned, can generally be organized with little trouble; the essay's chief divisions will reflect the classes into which the subject itself has been divided. A scratch outline can help you see those divisions and plan your order of presentation. For example, here is an outline of student Gerald Cleary's essay "How Loud? How Good? How Much? How Pretty!"

Four Types of Stereo Shoppers
1. The Looks Buyer
   a. Least respected by salespeople
   b. Appearance of stereo paramount
2. The Wattage Buyer
   a. More respected
   b. Volume level capability paramount
3. The Price Buyer
   a. Not respected but understood
   b. Cost concerns paramount
4. The Quality Buyer
   a. Most respected
   b. Quality and sound reproduction paramount

Such an outline clearly reveals the essay's overall structure.

State Your Conclusion

Your essay's purpose will determine the kinds of conclusions you reach. For example, a study of the student body of your college might show that 67 percent of all male athletes receive financial aid, compared with 46 percent of all female athletes, 45 percent of all male nonathletes, and 44 percent of all female nonathletes. These facts could provide a conclusion in themselves, or they might be the basis for a more controversial assertion about your school's athletic program. A study of dorm-room decor might conclude with the observation that juniors and seniors tend to have more elaborate rooms than first-year students. Your conclusion will depend on the way you work back and forth between the various classes you establish and the individual items available for you to classify.

Use Other Rhetorical Strategies

Although division and classification can be used effectively as a separate writing strategy, writers more commonly use it in combination with other strategies. For an essay about waste disposal, for example, it would be logical to add excerpts from interviews or dialogue between people discussing the subject. By combining narration (see Chapter 7) with division and classification, the writer could make her categories clearer and more powerful. Additionally, she could incorporate argumentation (see Chapter 13) to try to persuade the reader to act in a certain manner or to take a specific position on the issue of waste disposal.

When you are writing a division and classification essay, ask yourself how you might use other strategies. Consider, for example, Gerald Cleary's essay on stereo buyers. How might adding narration have changed or strengthened Cleary's essay? What other strategies might he have used? Comparison and contrast? Description? Exemplification? By using multiple strategies, you will make your writing more effective and evocative.

▶ *Questions for Revision: Division and Classification*

1. Is my subject a coherent entity that readily lends itself to analysis by division and classification?
2. Does the manner in which I divide my subject into categories help me achieve my purpose in writing the essay?
3. Does my thesis statement clearly identify the number and type of categories I will be using in my essay?
4. Do I stay focused on my subject and stay within the limits of my categories throughout my essay?
5. Do my categories meet the following three criteria: Are they appropriate to my purpose, consistent and mutually exclusive, and complete?
6. Have I organized my essay in a way that makes it easy for the reader to understand my categories and how they relate to my purpose?
7. Are there other rhetorical strategies that I can use to help me achieve my purpose?

The Plot against People

Russell Baker

Born in Virginia in 1925, Russell Baker graduated from Johns Hopkins University in 1947 and began his career as a newspaper reporter with the Baltimore Sun. He joined the New York Times *in 1954; after eight years with its Washington bureau covering national politics, he began writing his syndicated "Observer" column, which is now published once a week. In 1979, he was awarded the Pulitzer Prize, journalism's highest award, for his column. Baker's books include* An American in Washington *(1961),* Poor Russell's Almanac *(1972),* So This Is Depravity *(1980), and the autobiographical works* Growing Up *(1982), which won a Pulitzer, and* The Good Times *(1989). An anthology entitled* Russell Baker's Book of American Humor *was published in 1993.*

In the following essay, which first appeared in the New York Times *in 1968, Baker humorously classifies inanimate objects according to the method they use "to resist man and ultimately to defeat him."*

BEFORE YOU READ

Why do you think people feel the need to speak about inanimate objects as if they were alive? Have you ever spoken in these terms? If so, what was the reaction of those who heard you?

Inanimate objects are classified scientifically into three major categories — those that break down, those that get lost, and those that don't work.

The goal of all inanimate objects is to resist man and ultimately to defeat him, and the three major classifications are based on the method each object uses to achieve its purpose. As a general rule, any object capable of breaking down at the moment when it is most needed will do so. The automobile is typical of the category.

With the cunning peculiar to its breed, the automobile never breaks down while entering a filling station which has a large staff of idle mechanics. It waits until it reaches a downtown intersection in the middle of the rush hour, or until it is fully loaded with family and luggage on the Ohio Turnpike. Thus it creates maximum inconvenience, frustration, and irritability, thereby reducing its owner's lifespan.

Washing machines, garbage disposals, lawn mowers, furnaces, TV sets, tape recorders, slide projectors — all are in league with the automobile to take their turn at breaking down whenever life threatens to flow smoothly for their enemies.

Many inanimate objects, of course, find it extremely difficult to break down. Pliers, for example, and gloves and keys are almost totally incapable of breaking down. Therefore, they have had to evolve a different technique for resisting man.

They get lost. Science has still not solved the mystery of how they 6 do it, and no man has ever caught one of them in the act. The most plausible theory is that they have developed a secret method of locomotion which they are able to conceal from human eyes.

It is not uncommon for a pair of pliers to climb all the way from 7 the cellar to the attic in its single-minded determination to raise its owner's blood pressure. Keys have been known to burrow three feet under mattresses. Women's purses, despite their great weight, frequently travel through six or seven rooms to find hiding space under a couch.

Scientists have been struck by the fact that things that break down 8 virtually never get lost, while things that get lost hardly ever break down. A furnace, for example, will invariably break down at the depth of the first winter cold wave, but it will never get lost. A woman's purse hardly ever breaks down; it almost invariably chooses to get lost.

Some persons believe this constitutes evidence that inanimate ob- 9 jects are not entirely hostile to man. After all, they point out, a furnace could infuriate a man even more thoroughly by getting lost than by breaking down, just as a glove could upset him far more by breaking down than by getting lost.

Not everyone agrees, however, that this indicates a conciliatory at- 10 titude. Many say it merely proves that furnaces, gloves and pliers are incredibly stupid.

The third class of objects — those that don't work — is the most 11 curious of all. These include such objects as barometers, car clocks, cigarette lighters, flashlights and toy-train locomotives. It is inaccurate, of course, to say that they *never* work. They work once, usually for the first few hours after being brought home, and then quit. Thereafter, they never work again.

In fact, it is widely assumed that they are built for the purpose of 12 not working. Some people have reached advanced ages without ever seeing some of these objects — barometers, for example — in working order.

Science is utterly baffled by the entire category. There are many 13 theories about it. The most interesting holds that the things that don't work have attained the highest state possible for an inanimate object, the state to which things that break down and things that get lost can still only aspire.

They have truly defeated man by conditioning him never to ex- 14 pect anything of them. When his cigarette lighter won't light or his flashlight fails to illuminate, it does not raise his blood pressure. Objects that don't work have given man the only peace he receives from inanimate society.

RESPONDING TO READING

Baker's essay was written in 1968. How well do his examples hold up more than thirty years later? Have we moved away from his type of thinking about inanimate objects? What types of explanations do we use to rationalize mysterious objects in the present?

QUESTIONING THE TEXT

1. Into what three broad categories does Baker classify inanimate objects? How do you suppose he arrived at these particular categories? In what other ways might inanimate objects be classified?

2. According to Baker, what is the relationship between objects that break down and objects that get lost?

3. According to Baker, what is the highest possible state an inanimate object can reach? What does he mean when he says, "Objects that don't work have given man the only peace he receives from inanimate society" (paragraph 14)?

4. Explain the meaning of Baker's title. Why does he use the word *plot?*

UNDERSTANDING THE WRITER'S CRAFT

1. How does Baker make it clear at the beginning of the essay that his approach to the subject is humorous? How does he succeed in being more than simply silly? Point to several passages to illustrate your answer.

2. How does Baker organize his essay? Why do you think he waits until the conclusion to discuss "objects that don't work"? (Glossary: *Organization*)

3. How does paragraph 5 act as a transition? How does Baker use this transition to strengthen his classification? (Glossary: *Transitions*)

4. Throughout his essay, Baker personifies inanimate objects. What is the effect of his doing so? Identify several specific examples of personification. (Glossary: *Figures of Speech*)

EXPLORING LANGUAGE

1. How would you describe Baker's tone? Point to specific words and phrases to explain your answer. (Glossary: *Tone*)

2. How would you describe Baker's attitude toward inanimate objects? How does his diction help reveal his attitude? (Glossary: *Diction*)

3. Refer to your desk dictionary to determine the meanings of the following words as Baker uses them in this selection: *cunning* (paragraph 3), *league* (4), *plausible* (6), *conciliatory* (10), *baffled* (13).

COMBINING RHETORICAL STRATEGIES

How does Baker use exemplification in paragraphs 7 and 8? Besides these paragraphs, where else does Baker offer examples? For what purposes does he use them? (Glossary: *Exemplification*)

WRITING SUGGESTIONS

1. **(Division and Classification)** Using Baker's essay as a model, create a system of classification for one of the following topics. Then write an essay like Baker's classifying objects within that system.
   a. cars
   b. friends
   c. recreational activities
   d. sports
   e. drivers
   f. students
   g. music
   h. pet peeves

2. **(Other Strategies)** Most of us have had frustrating experiences with mechanical objects that seem to have perverse minds of their own. Write a narrative recounting one such experience — with a vending machine, a television set, an automobile, a computer, a pay telephone, or any other such object. Be sure to establish a clear context for your essay. (Glossary: *Narration*)

3. **(Research)** Throughout the essay, Baker looks to science to provide an explanation for the mysterious actions of inanimate objects. Why do you think he places science in such a position of authority? Go to your library, and do some research on how people have come to rely on science to explain the way our world works. You might begin your search in history books and then move on to current periodicals like *Wired* and *Scientific American;* you might also search the Internet, starting with the Web sites listed here. After your research, write an essay arguing for or against the human reliance on science.

   • **History of Science, Medicine, and Technology**
   <http://www.polyglot.lss.wisc.edu/histsci/histsci.html>

   This extensive site, maintained at the University of Wisconsin—Madison, offers numerous links to history-of-science topics.

   • **Technology History Web Site**
   <http://www.refstar.com/techhist>

   This site offers links to resources on the history of technology.

   • **The WWW Virtual Library: Philosophy**
   <http://www.bris.ac.uk/Depts/Philosophy/VL>

   Go to this philosophy-oriented Web site for links to resources on the philosophy of science.

The Truth about Lying

Judith Viorst

Judith Viorst, poet, journalist, author of children's books, and novelist,
was born in 1931. She has chronicled her life in such books as It's Hard
to Be Hip Over Thirty and Other Tragedies of Married Life *(1968),*
How Did I Get to Be Forty and Other Atrocities *(1976), and* When
Did I Stop Being Twenty and Other Injustices: Selected Prose from
Single to Mid-Life *(1987). In 1981, she went back to school, taking*
courses at the Washington Psychoanalytic Institute. This study, along
with her personal experience of psychoanalysis, helped to inspire Necessary Losses *(1986), a popular and critical success. Combining theory,*
poetry, interviews, and anecdotes, Viorst approaches personal growth as a
shedding of illusions. Her recent work includes Imperfect Control: Our
Lifelong Struggles with Power and Surrender *(1998) and* Suddenly
Sixty: And Other Shocks of Later Life *(2000).*

In this essay, first published in the March 1981 issue of Redbook,
the author approaches lying with delicacy and candor as she carefully
classifies the different types of lies we all encounter.

BEFORE YOU READ

Lying happens every day in our society, whether it is a politician
hiding behind a subtly worded statement or a guest fibbing to a
host about the quality of a meal. What, for you, constitutes lying?
Are all lies the same? In other words, are there different degrees or
types of lying?

I've been wanting to write on a subject that intrigues and challenges 1
me: the subject of lying. I've found it very difficult to do. Everyone
I've talked to has a quite intense and personal but often rather intoler-
ant point of view about what we can — and can never *never* — tell lies
about. I've finally reached the conclusion that I can't present any ultimate conclusions, for too many people would promptly disagree. Instead, I'd like to present a series of moral puzzles, all concerned with
lying. I'll tell you what I think about them. Do you agree?

SOCIAL LIES

Most of the people I've talked with say that they find social lying ac- 2
ceptable and necessary. They think it's the civilized way for folks to
behave. Without these little white lies, they say, our relationships
would be short and brutish and nasty. It's arrogant, they say, to insist
on being so incorruptible and so brave that you cause other people

unnecessary embarrassment or pain by compulsively assailing them with your honesty. I basically agree. What about you?

Will you say to people, when it simply isn't true, "I like your new 3
hairdo," "You're looking much better," "It's so nice to see you," "I had a wonderful time"?

Will you praise hideous presents and homely kids? 4

Will you decline invitations with "We're busy that night — so 5
sorry we can't come," when the truth is you'd rather stay home than dine with the So-and-sos?

And even though, as I do, you may prefer the polite evasion of 6
"You really cooked up a storm" instead of "The soup" — which tastes like warmed-over coffee — "is wonderful," will you, if you must, proclaim it wonderful?

There's one man I know who absolutely refuses to tell social lies. 7
"I can't play that game," he says; "I'm simply not made that way." And his answer to the argument that saying nice things to someone doesn't cost anything is, "Yes, it does — it destroys your credibility." Now, he won't, unsolicited, offer his views on the painting you just bought, but you don't ask his frank opinion unless you want *frank,* and his silence at those moments when the rest of us liars are muttering, "Isn't it lovely?" is, for the most part, eloquent enough. My friend does not indulge in what he calls "flattery, false praise and mellifluous comments." When others tell fibs he will not go along. He says that social lying is lying, that little white lies are still lies. And he feels that telling lies is morally wrong. What about you?

PEACE-KEEPING LIES

Many people tell peace-keeping lies; lies designed to avoid irritation or 8
argument; lies designed to shelter the liar from possible blame or pain; lies (or so it is rationalized) designed to keep trouble at bay without hurting anyone.

I tell these lies at times, and yet I always feel they're wrong. I un- 9
derstand why we tell them, but still they feel wrong. And whenever I lie so that someone won't disapprove of me or think less of me or holler at me, I feel I'm a bit of a coward, I feel I'm dodging responsibility, I feel . . . guilty. What about you?

Do you, when you're late for a date because you overslept, say that 10
you're late because you got caught in a traffic jam?

Do you, when you forget to call a friend, say that you called sev- 11
eral times but the line was busy?

Do you, when you didn't remember that it was your father's birth- 12
day, say that his present must be delayed in the mail?

And when you're planning a weekend in New York City and you're not in the mood to visit your mother, who lives there, do you conceal — with a lie, if you must — the fact that you'll be in New York? Or do you have the courage — or is it the cruelty? — to say, "I'll be in New York, but sorry — I don't plan on seeing you"? 13

(Dave and his wife Elaine have two quite different points of view on this very subject. He calls her a coward. She says she's being wise. He says she must assert her right to visit New York sometimes and not see her mother. To which she always patiently replies: "Why should we have useless fights? My mother's too old to change. We get along much better when I lie to her.") 14

Finally, do you keep the peace by telling your husband lies on the subject of money? Do you reduce what you really paid for your shoes? And in general do you find yourself ready, willing and able to lie to him when you make absurd mistakes or lose or break things? 15

"I used to have a romantic idea that part of intimacy was confessing every dumb thing that you did to your husband. But after a couple of years of that," says Laura, "have I changed my mind!" 16

And having changed her mind, she finds herself telling peace-keeping lies. And yes, I tell them too. What about you? 17

PROTECTIVE LIES

Protective lies are lies folks tell — often quite serious lies — because they're convinced that the truth would be too damaging. They lie because they feel there are certain human values that supersede the wrong of having lied. They lie, not for personal gain, but because they believe it's for the good of the person they're lying to. They lie to those they love, to those who trust them most of all, on the grounds that breaking this trust is justified. 18

They may lie to their children on money or marital matters. 19

They may lie to the dying about the state of their health. 20

They may lie about adultery, and not — or so they insist — to save their own hide, but to save the heart and the pride of the men they are married to. 21

They may lie to their closest friend because the truth about her talents or son or psyche would be — or so they insist — utterly devastating. 22

I sometimes tell such lies, but I'm aware that it's quite presumptuous to claim I know what's best for others to know. That's called playing God. That's called manipulation and control. And we never can be sure, once we start to juggle lies, just where they'll land, exactly where they'll roll. 23

And furthermore, we may find ourselves lying in order to back up   24
the lies that are backing up the lie we initially told.

And furthermore — let's be honest — if conditions were reversed,   25
we certainly wouldn't want anyone lying to us.

Yet, having said all that, I still believe that there are times when   26
protective lies must nonetheless be told. What about you?

If your Dad had a very bad heart and you had to tell him some   27
bad family news, which would you choose: to tell him the truth or lie?

If your former husband failed to send his monthly child-support   28
check and in other ways behaved like a total rat, would you allow your
children — who believed he was simply wonderful — to continue to
believe that he was wonderful?

If your dearly beloved brother selected a wife whom you deeply   29
disliked, would you reveal your feelings or would you fake it?

And if you were asked, after making love, "And how was that for   30
you?" would you reply, if it wasn't too good, "Not too good"?

Now, some would call a sex lie unimportant, little more than so-   31
cial lying, a simple act of courtesy that makes all human intercourse
run smoothly. And some would say all sex lies are bad news and unac-
ceptably protective. Because, says Ruth, "a man with an ego that
fragile doesn't need your lies — he needs a psychiatrist." Still others
feel that sex lies are indeed protective lies, more serious than simple
social lying, and yet at times they tell them on the grounds that when
it comes to matters sexual, everybody's ego is somewhat fragile.

"If most of the time things go well in sex," says Sue, "I think   32
you're allowed to dissemble when they don't. I can't believe it's good
to say, 'Last night was four stars, darling, but tonight's performance
rates only a half.'"

I'm inclined to agree with Sue. What about you?   33

TRUST-KEEPING LIES

Another group of lies are trust-keeping lies, lies that involve triangula-   34
tion, with *A* (that's you) telling lies to *B* on behalf of *C* (whose trust
you'd promised to keep). Most people concede that once you've
agreed not to betray a friend's confidence, you can't betray it, even if
you must lie. But I've talked with people who don't want you telling
them anything that they might be called on to lie about.

"I don't tell lies for myself," says Fran, "and I don't want to have to   35
tell them for other people." Which means, she agrees, that if her best
friend is having an affair, she absolutely doesn't want to know about it.

"Are you saying," her best friend asks, "that if I went off with a   36
lover and I asked you to tell my husband I'd been with you, that you
wouldn't lie for me, that you'd betray me?"

Fran is very pained but very adamant. "I wouldn't want to betray you, so . . . don't ask me." 37

Fran's best friend is shocked. What about you? 38

Do you believe you can have close friends if you're not prepared to receive their deepest secrets? 39

Do you believe you must always lie for your friends? 40

Do you believe, if your friend tells a secret that turns out to be quite immoral or illegal, that once you've promised to keep it, you must keep it? 41

And what if your friend were your boss — if you were perhaps one of the President's men — would you betray or lie for him over, say, Watergate? 42

As you can see, these issues get terribly sticky. 43

It's my belief that once we've promised to keep a trust, we must tell lies to keep it. I also believe that we can't tell Watergate lies. And if these two statements strike you as quite contradictory, you're right — they're quite contradictory. But for now they're the best I can do. What about you? 44

Some say that truth will out and thus you might as well tell the truth. Some say you can't regain the trust that lies lose. Some say that even though the truth may never be revealed, our lies pervert and damage our relationships. Some say . . . well, here's what some of them have to say. 45

"I'm a coward," says Grace, "about telling close people important, difficult truths. I find that I'm unable to carry it off. And so if something is bothering me, it keeps building up inside till I end up just not seeing them any more." 46

"I lie to my husband on sexual things, but I'm furious," says Joyce, "that he's too insensitive to know I'm lying." 47

"I suffer most from the misconception that children can't take the truth," says Emily. "But I'm starting to see that what's harder and more damaging for them is being told lies, is *not* being told the truth." 48

"I'm afraid," says Joan, "that we often wind up feeling a bit of contempt for the people we lie to." 49

And then there are those who have no talent for lying. 50

"Over the years, I tried to lie," a friend of mine explained, "but I always got found out and I always got punished. I guess I gave myself away because I feel guilty about any kind of lying. It looks as if I'm stuck with telling the truth." 51

For those of us, however, who are good at telling lies, for those of us who lie and don't get caught, the question of whether or not to lie can be a hard and serious moral problem. I liked the remark of a friend of mine who said, "I'm willing to lie. But just as a last resort — the truth's always better." 52

"Because," he explained, "though others may completely accept   53
the lie I'm telling, I don't."

I tend to feel that way too.   54

What about you?   55

RESPONDING TO READING

The title of the essay plays with the relationship between lies and the truth. Viorst discusses lies that help to conceal the truth, but she's quick to point out that not all lies are malicious. Look at her subsections about "protective lies" (paragraphs 18–33) and "trust-keeping lies" (34–44). Do you think that these lies are necessary? Or would it be easier to tell the truth? Explain.

QUESTIONING THE TEXT

1. Why is Viorst wary of giving advice on the subject of lying?

2. Viorst admits to contradicting herself in her section on "trust-keeping lies." Where else do you see her contradicting herself?

3. In telling a "protective lie," what assumption about the person hearing the lie does Viorst make? Would you make the same assumption? Why or why not?

4. What's the difference between a "peace-keeping lie" and a "protective lie"?

UNDERSTANDING THE WRITER'S CRAFT

1. Into what main categories does Viorst divide lying? Do you agree with her division or do some of her categories seem to overlap? Explain.

2. Viorst recognizes that many people have steadfast views on lying. What accommodations does she make for this audience? How does she challenge this audience? (Glossary: *Audience*)

3. There are at least two parties involved in a lie — the liar and the listener. How much significance does the author give to each of these parties? How does she make the distinction?

4. Viorst presents the reader with a series of examples or moral puzzles. How do these puzzles encourage further thought on the subject of lying? Are they successful? Why or why not?

5. Viorst chooses an unconventional way to conclude her essay by showing different people's opinions of lying. What do you think she's doing in this last section, beginning in paragraph 45? Does this ending intensify any of the points she has made? Explain. (Glossary: *Beginnings/ Endings*)

EXPLORING LANGUAGE

1. How would you characterize Viorst's diction in this essay? Consider the essay's subject and audience. Cite specific examples of her word choice to support your conclusions. (Glossary: *Diction*)

2. Refer to your desk dictionary to determine the meaning of the following words as Viorst uses them in this selection: *mellifluous* (paragraph 7), *supersede* (18), *dissemble* (32).

COMBINING RHETORICAL STRATEGIES

Viorst wants us to see that a lie is not a lie is not a lie is not a lie (i.e., that not all lies are the same). To clarify the various types of lies, she uses division and classification. She also uses exemplification to illustrate the ways in which people lie. Using several of the examples that work best for you, discuss how Viorst's use of exemplification strengthens and enhances her classification. (Glossary: *Exemplification*)

WRITING SUGGESTIONS

1. **(Division and Classification)** The popular comic strip *Dilbert* derives humor from workplace situations that are absurd but nevertheless come too close to the truth for many readers. Examine the cartoon on page 410, which appears with the heading "Translating Marketing Talk." Although the cartoon character's statement might be considered a euphemism rather than an outright lie, what it communicates is certainly not true. How do you think Viorst would classify such a statement? How would she react to it? Write an essay in which you discuss Viorst's attitude toward such statements in relation to your own. Do you find such "business-speak" amusing or infuriating? Are there any categories of lying that Viorst has failed to consider? What are they?

2. **(Other Strategies)** Viorst wrote this essay for *Redbook,* which is usually considered a women's magazine. If you were writing this essay for a male audience, would you change the examples? If so, how would you change them? If not, why not? Do you think men are more likely to tell lies of a certain category? Explain. Write an essay in which you discuss whether men and women share similar perspectives about lying. (Glossary: *Comparison and Contrast*)

3. **(Research)** It is often difficult to discern the truths in advertising or news reporting. Select a current print advertisement or news story for analysis. Analyze the ad or story to determine just how much factual material is included; you may find it helpful to read Sarah Federman's article, "What's Natural about Our Natural Products?" (p. 473), as you analyze the language of your advertisement or news story. Based on your analysis, write an essay in which you argue for more consumer education in the area of advertising or news reporting. For help with

selecting a print advertisement or news story and with analyzing it, you may wish to consult the following Web sites.

- *Adweek* **Online Magazine**
  <http://www.adweek.com>

  This Web site covers current trends in the advertising industry.

- **The Truth in Advertising Web Site**
  <http://www.chickenhead.com/truth/index.html>

  Here you will find an archive of "vintage" print and photo cigarette ads.

- *Consumer Reports* **Online Magazine**
  <http://www.consumerreports.org>

  This is a good place to find information about a product's actual performance as compared with claims made in advertisements.

- **CNN Online**
  <http://www.cnn.com>

  This searchable news Web site is updated hourly.

- **ABC News Online**
  <http://www.abcnews.go.com>

  This site offers coverage of current news stories.

The Ways of Meeting Oppression

Martin Luther King Jr.

Martin Luther King Jr. (1929–1968) was the son of a Baptist minister. Ordained at the age of eighteen, King went on to study at Morehouse College, Crozer Theological Seminary, Boston University, and Chicago Theological Seminary. He came to prominence in 1955 in Montgomery, Alabama, when he led a successful boycott against the city's segregated bus system. A powerful orator and writer, King went on to become the leading spokesman for the civil rights movement during the 1950s and 1960s. In 1964, he was awarded the Nobel Peace Prize for his policy of nonviolent resistance to racial injustice, a policy that he explains in the following selection. King was assassinated in April 1968 after speaking at a rally in Memphis, Tennessee.

This selection is excerpted from the book Stride Toward Freedom *(1958).*

BEFORE YOU READ

Summarize what you know about the civil rights movement of the late 1950s and early 1960s. What tactics did its leaders use? How successful were these tactics? What is your impression of the movement as part of American history? How did this movement change American society?

Oppressed people deal with their oppression in three characteristic ways. One way is acquiescence: the oppressed resign themselves to their doom. They tacitly adjust themselves to oppression, and thereby become conditioned to it. In every movement toward freedom some of the oppressed prefer to remain oppressed. Almost 2800 years ago Moses set out to lead the children of Israel from the slavery of Egypt to the freedom of the promised land. He soon discovered that slaves do not always welcome their deliverers. They become accustomed to being slaves. They would rather bear those ills they have, as Shakespeare pointed out, than flee to others that they know not of. They prefer the "fleshpots of Egypt" to the ordeals of emancipation.

There is such a thing as the freedom of exhaustion. Some people are so worn down by the yoke of oppression that they give up. A few years ago in the slum areas of Atlanta, a Negro guitarist used to sing almost daily: "Been down so long that down don't bother me." This is the type of negative freedom and resignation that often engulfs the life of the oppressed.

But this is not the way out. To accept passively an unjust system is to cooperate with that system; thereby the oppressed become as evil as

411

the oppressor. Noncooperation with evil is as much a moral obligation as is cooperation with good. The oppressed must never allow the conscience of the oppressor to slumber. Religion reminds every man that he is his brother's keeper. To accept injustice or segregation passively is to say to the oppressor that his actions are morally right. It is a way of allowing his conscience to fall asleep. At this moment the oppressed fails to be his brother's keeper. So acquiescence — while often the easier way — is not the moral way. It is the way of the coward. The Negro cannot win the respect of his oppressor by acquiescing; he merely increases the oppressor's arrogance and contempt. Acquiescence is interpreted as proof of the Negro's inferiority. The Negro cannot win the respect of the white people of the south or the peoples of the world if he is willing to sell the future of his children for his personal and immediate comfort and safety.

A second way that oppressed people sometimes deal with oppression is to resort to physical violence and corroding hatred. Violence often brings about momentary results. Nations have frequently won their independence in battle. But in spite of temporary victories, violence never brings permanent peace. It solves no social problem; it merely creates new and more complicated ones. 4

Violence as a way of achieving racial justice is both impractical and immoral. It is impractical because it is a descending spiral ending in destruction for all. The old law of an eye for an eye leaves everybody blind. It is immoral because it seeks to humiliate the opponent rather than win his understanding; it seeks to annihilate rather than to convert. Violence is immoral because it thrives on hatred rather than love. It destroys community and makes brotherhood impossible. It leaves society in monologue rather than dialogue. Violence ends by defeating itself. It creates bitterness in the survivors and brutality in the destroyers. A voice echoes through time saying to every potential Peter, "Put up your sword." History is cluttered with the wreckage of nations that failed to follow this command. 5

If the American Negro and other victims of oppression succumb to the temptation of using violence in the struggle for freedom, future generations will be the recipients of a desolate night of bitterness, and our chief legacy to them will be an endless reign of meaningless chaos. Violence is not the way. 6

The third way open to oppressed people in their quest for freedom is the way of nonviolent resistance. Like the synthesis in Hegelian philosophy, the principle of nonviolent resistance seeks to reconcile the truths of two opposites — the acquiescence and violence — while avoiding the extremes and immoralities of both. The nonviolent resister agrees with the person who acquiesces that one should not be physically aggressive toward his opponent; but he balances the equation by agreeing with the person of violence that evil must be resisted. 7

He avoids the nonresistance of the former and the violent resistance of the latter. With nonviolent resistance, no individual or group need submit to any wrong, nor need anyone resort to violence in order to right a wrong.

It seems to me that this is the method that must guide the actions of the Negro in the present crisis in race relations. Through nonviolent resistance the Negro will be able to rise to the noble height of opposing the unjust system while loving the perpetrators of the system. The Negro must work passionately and unrelentingly for full stature as a citizen, but he must not use inferior methods to gain it. He must never come to terms with falsehood, malice, hate, or destruction. 8

Nonviolent resistance makes it possible for the Negro to remain in the South and struggle for his rights. The Negro's problem will not be solved by running away. He cannot listen to the glib suggestion of those who would urge him to migrate en masse to other sections of the country. By grasping his great opportunity in the South he can make a lasting contribution to the moral strength of the nation and set a sublime example of courage for generations yet unborn. 9

By nonviolent resistance, the Negro can also enlist all men of good will in his struggle for equality. The problem is not a purely racial one, with Negroes set against whites. In the end, it is not a struggle between people at all, but a tension between justice and injustice. Nonviolent resistance is not aimed against oppressors but against oppression. Under its banner consciences, not racial groups, are enlisted. 10

RESPONDING TO READING

Find the definition of *oppress* or *oppression* in the dictionary. Exactly what does Martin Luther King Jr. mean when he speaks of people being "oppressed" in the South in twentieth-century America? Do you think that people are still being oppressed in America today? Explain.

QUESTIONING THE TEXT

1. What does King mean by the term "freedom of exhaustion" (paragraph 2)? Why is he scathing in his assessment of people who succumb to such a condition in response to oppression?

2. According to King, what is the role of religion in the battle against oppression?

3. Why does King advocate the avoidance of violence in fighting oppression, despite the short-term success violence often achieves for the victors? How do such victories affect the future?

4. According to King, how does nonviolent resistance transform a racial issue into one of conscience?

UNDERSTANDING THE WRITER'S CRAFT

1. King's essay is easy to read and understand, and everything in it relates to his purpose. (Glossary: *Purpose*) What is that purpose? Summarize how each paragraph supports his purpose. How does the essay's organization help King achieve his purpose?

2. King says that "nonviolent resistance is not aimed against oppressors but against oppression" (paragraph 10). What does he mean by this? Why does he deflect anger and resentment away from a concrete example, the oppressors, to an abstract concept, oppression? (Glossary: *Concrete/Abstract*) How does this choice support his purpose? (Glossary: *Purpose*)

3. King evokes the names of Moses, Shakespeare, and Hegel in his essay. What does this tell you about his intended audience? (Glossary: *Audience*) Why does King address the audience in this way?

EXPLORING LANGUAGE

1. In his discussion about overcoming oppression with violence, King says that "future generations will be the recipients of a desolate night of bitterness" (paragraph 6). What image do his words evoke for you? Why do you think he chooses to use a striking metaphor here, instead of a less poetic statement? (Glossary: *Figures of Speech*)

2. King urges Negroes to avoid "falsehood, malice, hate, or destruction" (paragraph 8) in their quest to gain full stature as citizens. How does each of these terms relate to his earlier argument about avoiding violence? How does each enhance or add new meaning to his earlier argument?

3. Refer to your desk dictionary to determine the meanings of the following words as King uses them in this selection: *acquiescence* (paragraph 1), *tacitly* (1), *yoke* (2), *perpetrators* (8), *glib* (9), *sublime* (9).

COMBINING RHETORICAL STRATEGIES

King uses division and classification to help him argue his point in this essay. What other rhetorical strategies does King use? How does each strategy, including division and classification and argument, contribute to the effectiveness of the essay?

WRITING SUGGESTIONS

1. **(Division and Classification)** Write a division and classification essay in which you follow King's model by arguing for or advocating one of the categories. Identify three methods that you can use to achieve a goal — study for a test, apply to graduate school, or interview for a job, for example. Choose one method to advocate, then frame your essay so that the division and classification strategy helps you make your point.

2. **(Other Strategies)** Toward the end of his essay, King states, "By grasping his great opportunity in the South [the Negro] can make a lasting contribution to the moral strength of the nation and set a sublime example of courage for generations yet unborn" (paragraph 9). With your classmates, discuss whether the movement that King led achieved its goal of solving many of the underlying racial tensions and inequities in the United States. In terms of equality, what has happened in the United States since King's famous "I Have a Dream" speech (p. 602)? Write a paper in which you argue for or against the idea that King's "dream" is still intact. (Glossary: *Argument*)

3. **(Research)** Research the situation of African Americans in the southern United States in the 1940s and 1950s. In general, describe the living conditions there at that time. How pervasive were Jim Crow laws? How restricted were African Americans in the political arena? Why did the conditions make it so important for King to argue against both despair and violence before advocating nonviolent resistance? Write a paper in which you present the conditions and use the information to provide a context for King's essay. You may find it helpful to consult the following Web sites.

- **W. E. B. Du Bois Institute for Afro-American Research**
  <http://web-dubois.fas.harvard.edu>

  This Web site, maintained by Harvard University, offers links to African American history and culture sites.

- **Georgia African-American History and Culture**
  <http://www.cviog.uga.edu/Projects/gainfo/blackga.htm>

  This site, maintained by the University of Georgia, offers numerous links to African American resources nationally and in the state of Georgia.

- **Online Timeline of the American Civil Rights Movement**
  <http://www.wmich.edu/politics/mlk>

  This timeline, maintained by Western Michigan University, provides photographs and short historical essays outlining key events in the civil rights movement.

The Myth of the Latin Woman

Judith Ortiz Cofer

Author and educator Judith Ortiz Cofer was born in Hormigueros, Puerto Rico, in 1952, but her family immigrated to the United States in 1954. She grew up in New Jersey but moved south to continue her education — she received her M.A. in English from Florida Atlantic University in 1977 — and is now Franklin Professor of English and Creative Writing at the University of Georgia. Her published works include a novel, The Line of the Sun, *two collections of poetry, and several other titles that collect and combine her essays, stories, and poetry. One of these,* Silent Dancing, *a collection of essays and poetry, was awarded the Pushcart Prize for nonfiction in 1990; Cofer received an O. Henry Prize for short stories in 1994. Her most recent collection of short stories,* An Island Like You: Stories of the Barrio *(1995), was named a Best Book of the Year by the American Library Association.*

Much of Cofer's writing focuses on Hispanic issues and the culture clashes that occur between the Anglo and Hispanic communities. As she says in the following selection, which first appeared in the January 1992 issue of Glamour, *and which was later included in her book* The Latin Deli *(1993), "You can leave the island [Puerto Rico]. . . , [but] the island travels with you."*

BEFORE YOU READ

In what ways has your ethnicity played a part in your life? What advantages, disadvantages, and special circumstances have you experienced because of your appearance and your cultural upbringing? Have you encountered any cultural tensions between your own heritage and what you consider to be modern American culture?

On a bus trip to London from Oxford University where I was earning 1 some graduate credits one summer, a young man, obviously fresh from a pub, spotted me and as if struck by inspiration went down on his knees in the aisle. With both hands over his heart he broke into an Irish tenor's rendition of "Maria" from *West Side Story.* My politely amused fellow passengers gave his lovely voice the round of gentle applause it deserved. Though I was not quite as amused, I managed my version of an English smile: no show of teeth, no extreme contortions of the facial muscles — I was at this time of my life practicing reserve and cool. Oh, that British control, how I coveted it. But "Maria" had followed me to London, reminding me of a prime fact of my life: you can leave the island, master the English language, and travel as far as you can, but if you are a Latina, especially one like me who so obviously belongs to Rita Moreno's gene pool, the island travels with you.

This is sometimes a very good thing — it may win you that extra   2
minute of someone's attention. But with some people, the same
things can make *you* an island — not a tropical paradise but an Alca-
traz, a place nobody wants to visit. As a Puerto Rican girl living in the
United States and wanting like most children to "belong," I resented
the stereotype that my Hispanic appearance called forth from many
people I met.

Growing up in a large urban center in New Jersey during the   3
1960s, I suffered from what I think of as "cultural schizophrenia." Our
life was designed by my parents as a microcosm of their *casas* on the
island. We spoke in Spanish, ate Puerto Rican food bought at the
bodega, and practiced strict Catholicism at a church that allotted us a
one-hour slot each week for mass, performed in Spanish by a Chinese
priest trained as a missionary for Latin America.

As a girl I was kept under strict surveillance by my parents, since   4
my virtue and modesty were, by their cultural equation, the same as
their honor. As a teenager I was lectured constantly on how to behave
as a proper *señorita.* But it was a conflicting message I received, since
the Puerto Rican mothers also encouraged their daughters to look and
act like women and to dress in clothes our Anglo friends and their
mothers found too "mature" and flashy. The difference was, and is,
cultural; yet I often felt humiliated when I appeared at an American
friend's party wearing a dress more suitable to a semi-formal than to a
playroom birthday celebration. At Puerto Rican festivities, neither the
music nor the colors we wore could be too loud.

I remember Career Day in our high school, when teachers told us   5
to come dressed as if for a job interview. It quickly became obvious
that to the Puerto Rican girls "dressing up" meant wearing their
mother's ornate jewelry and clothing, more appropriate (by mainstream standards) for the company Christmas party than as daily office attire. That morning I had agonized in front of my closet, trying
to figure out what a "career girl" would wear. I knew how to dress for
school (at the Catholic school I attended, we all wore uniforms), I
knew how to dress for Sunday mass, and I knew what dresses to wear
for parties at my relatives' homes. Though I do not recall the precise
details of my Career Day outfit, it must have been a composite of
these choices. But I remember a comment my friend (an Italian American) made in later years that coalesced my impressions of that day.
She said that at the business school she was attending, the Puerto
Rican girls always stood out for wearing "everything at once." She
meant, of course, too much jewelry, too many accessories. On that
day at school we were simply made the negative models by the nuns,
who were themselves not credible fashion experts to any of us. But it
was painfully obvious to me that to the others, in their tailored skirts
and silk blouses, we must have seemed "hopeless" and "vulgar."

Though I now know that most adolescents feel out of step much of the time, I also know that for the Puerto Rican girls of my generation that sense was intensified. The way our teachers and classmates looked at us that day in school was just a taste of the cultural clash that awaited us in the real world, where prospective employers and men on the street would often misinterpret our tight skirts and jingling bracelets as a "come-on."

Mixed cultural signals have perpetuated certain stereotypes — for example, that of the Hispanic woman as the "hot tamale" or sexual firebrand. It is a one-dimensional view that the media have found easy to promote. In their special vocabulary, advertisers have designated "sizzling" and "smoldering" as the adjectives of choice for describing not only the foods but also the women of Latin America. From conversations in my house I recall hearing about the harassment that Puerto Rican women endured in factories where the "boss-men" talked to them as if sexual innuendo was all they understood, and worse, often gave them the choice of submitting to their advances or being fired. 6

It is custom, however, not chromosomes, that leads us to choose scarlet over pale pink. As young girls, it was our mothers who influenced our decisions about clothes and colors — mothers who had grown up on a tropical island where the natural environment was a riot of primary colors, where showing your skin was one way to keep cool as well as to look sexy. Most important of all, on the island, women perhaps felt freer to dress and move more provocatively since, in most cases, they were protected by the traditions, mores, and laws of a Spanish/Catholic system of morality and machismo whose main rule was: *You may look at my sister, but if you touch her I will kill you.* The extended family and church structure could provide a young woman with a circle of safety in her small pueblo on the island; if a man "wronged" a girl, everyone would close in to save her family honor. 7

My mother has told me about dressing in her best party clothes on Saturday nights and going to the town's plaza to promenade with her girlfriends in front of the boys they liked. The males were thus given an opportunity to admire the women and to express their admiration in the form of *piropos:* erotically charged street poems they composed on the spot. (I have myself been subjected to a few *piropos* while visiting the island, and they can be outrageous, although custom dictates that they must never cross into obscenity.) This ritual, as I understand it, also entails a show of studied indifference on the woman's part; if she is "decent," she must not acknowledge the man's impassioned words. So I do understand how things can be lost in translation. When a Puerto Rican girl dressed in her idea of what is attractive meets a man from the mainstream culture who has been 8 trained to react to certain types of clothing as a sexual signal, a clash is likely to take place. I remember the boy who took me to my first formal dance leaning over to plant a sloppy, over-eager kiss painfully on my mouth; when I didn't respond with sufficient passion, he remarked resentfully: "I thought you Latin girls were supposed to mature early," as if I were expected to *ripen* like a fruit or vegetable, not just grow into womanhood like other girls.

It is surprising to my professional friends that even today some 9 people, including those who should know better, still put others "in their place." It happened to me most recently during a stay at a classy metropolitan hotel favored by young professional couples for weddings. Late one evening after the theater, as I walked toward my room with a colleague (a woman with whom I was coordinating an arts program), a middle-aged man in a tuxedo, with a young girl in satin and lace on his arm, stepped directly into our path. With his champagne glass extended toward me, he exclaimed "Evita!"

Our way blocked, my companion and I listened as the man half- 10 recited, half-bellowed "Don't Cry for Me, Argentina." When he finished, the young girl said: "How about a round of applause for my daddy?" We complied, hoping this would bring the silly spectacle to a close. I was becoming aware that our little group was attracting the attention of the other guests. "Daddy" must have perceived this too, and he once more barred the way as we tried to walk past him. He began to shout-sing a ditty to the tune of "La Bamba" — except the lyrics were about a girl named Maria whose exploits rhymed with her name and gonorrhea. The girl kept saying "Oh, Daddy" and looking at me with pleading eyes. She wanted me to laugh along with the others. My companion and I stood silently waiting for the man to end his offensive song. When he finished, I looked not at him but at his daughter. I advised her calmly never to ask her father what he had done in the army. Then I walked between them and to my room. My friend complimented me on my cool handling of the situation, but I confessed that I had really wanted to push the jerk into the swimming pool. This same man — probably a corporate executive, well-educated, even worldly by most standards — would not have been likely to regale an Anglo woman with a dirty song in public. He might have checked his impulse by assuming that she could be somebody's wife or mother, or at least *somebody* who might take offense. But, to him, I was just an Evita or a Maria: merely a character in his cartoon-populated universe.

Another facet of the myth of the Latin woman in the United 11 States is the menial, the domestic — Maria the housemaid or counter-girl. It's true that work as domestics, as waitresses, and in factories is all that's available to women with little English and few skills. But the myth of the Hispanic menial — the funny maid, mispronouncing words and cooking up a spicy storm in a shiny California kitchen — has been perpetuated by the media in the same way that "Mammy" from *Gone with the Wind* became America's idea of the black woman for generations. Since I do not wear my diplomas around my neck for all to see, I have on occasion been sent to that "kitchen" where some think I obviously belong.

One incident has stayed with me, though I recognize it as a minor 12 offense. My first public poetry reading took place in Miami, at a restaurant where a luncheon was being held before the event. I was nervous and excited as I walked in with notebook in hand. An older woman motioned me to her table, and thinking (foolish me) that she wanted me to autograph a copy of my newly published slender volume of verse, I went over. She ordered a cup of coffee from me, assuming that I was the waitress. (Easy enough to mistake my poems for menus, I suppose.) I know it wasn't an intentional act of cruelty. Yet of all the good things that happened later, I remember that scene most clearly, because it reminded me of what I had to overcome before anyone would take me seriously. In retrospect I understand that my anger gave my reading fire. In fact, I have almost always taken any doubt in my abilities as a challenge, the result most often being the satisfaction of winning a convert, of seeing the cold, appraising eyes warm to my words, the body language change, the smile that indicates I have opened some avenue for communication. So that day as I read, I looked directly at that woman. Her lowered eyes told me she was embarrassed at her faux pas, and when I willed her to look up at me, she graciously allowed me to punish her with my full attention. We shook hands at the end of the reading and I never saw her again. She has probably forgotten the entire incident, but maybe not.

Yet I am one of the lucky ones. There are thousands of Latinas 13 without the privilege of an education or the entrees into society that I have. For them life is a constant struggle against the misconceptions perpetuated by the myth of the Latina. My goal is to try to replace the old stereotypes with a much more interesting set of realities. Every time I give a reading, I hope the stories I tell, the dreams and fears I examine in my work, can achieve some universal truth that will get my audience past the particulars of my skin color, my accent, or my clothes.

I once wrote a poem in which I called all Latinas "God's brown 14 daughters." This poem is really a prayer of sorts, offered upward, but also, through the human-to-human channel of art, outward. It is a prayer for communication and for respect. In it, Latin women pray "in Spanish to an Anglo God/ with a Jewish heritage," and they are "fervently hoping/ that if not omnipotent,/ at least He be bilingual."

RESPONDING TO READING

The way in which Latinas dress — and why they do so — establishes one of the primary culture clashes presented in Cofer's essay. The strict Catholic culture of Puerto Rico by and large denies young women the possibility of promiscuity, so an eye-catching outfit highlights only the beauty of the wearer without connoting a direct sexual invitation. Ironically, American culture effectively denies women the ability to wear eye-catching clothing without also sending a message to some men that the wearer expects and perhaps welcomes sexual advances. Discuss the paradox presented by the culture clash and how it relates to our society. How might American society be able to modify or separate the ties between one's appearance and the message that it sends to others?

QUESTIONING THE TEXT

1. Why does Cofer say that "the island travels with you" (paragraph 1)? In what ways is that a good thing? How can it be negative?

2. How does Cofer's experience at Career Day capture the clash of American and Puerto Rican cultures with which she has struggled her entire life?

3. Advertisers have fed the stereotype of the "sizzling" Latin American woman. What gave rise to the stereotype, and how does it affect Latinas themselves?

4. What are *piropos*? What is their place in Puerto Rican society?

5. What happens at Cofer's first public poetry reading that illustrates another stereotype that Hispanic women must confront? Despite her difficulties, why does Cofer consider herself "one of the lucky ones" (paragraph 13)?

UNDERSTANDING THE WRITER'S CRAFT

1. How does Cofer define "cultural schizophrenia" in her essay? (Glossary: *Definition*) Why is the term so important to her overall purpose? (Glossary: *Purpose*)

2. Cofer uses personal experiences to illustrate the Latina stereotypes she identifies in her essay. (Glossary: *Examples*) Do you find her examples effective? Does she lose any credibility by not quoting or referring to Hispanic women outside of her immediate family? Explain your answer.

3. Cofer ends her essay by discussing and quoting from one of her poems, which she calls "a prayer for communication and for respect" (paragraph 14). (Glossary: *Beginnings/Endings*) Why does she introduce poetry at the end of an otherwise prosaic essay based on personal narrative? (Glossary: *Narration*) What does the poetry communicate that the prose perhaps does not?

EXPLORING LANGUAGE

1. Cofer states that "'Maria' had followed me to London" (paragraph 1). For Cofer and for other Latinas, what does the name Maria connote? (Glossary: *Connotation/Denotation*) How does Cofer's use of the name foreshadow the issues she presents in her essay?

2. List the adjectives Cofer uses to describe how Latinas tend to dress. What is the overall impression she gives of their style of dress? How does this impression explain the sexual stereotyping that Latinas often endure?

3. Refer to your desk dictionary to determine the meanings of the following words as Cofer uses them in this selection: *microcosm* (paragraph 3), *coalesced* (5), *innuendo* (6), *mores* (7), *menial* (11), *faux pas* (12).

COMBINING RHETORICAL STRATEGIES

Cofer's personal narratives demonstrate how others have classified her by her appearance alone. In other words, others conclude that because she belongs, as Cofer states, "to Rita Moreno's gene pool" (paragraph 1), she must be of a certain type or must occupy a certain position in society. Write a short personal narrative in which you present a situation in which you were "classified" in some way based on appearance, position, or occupation alone, not on knowledge of who you are and what you can do. It does not have to be based on ethnicity or race. For example, a tall person may face the assumption that he or she is skilled at basketball, or an artist may be assumed to be impractical. Discuss the basis of the classification. Was it based on a stereotype or on a bias particular to the other person? How did the "classification" make you feel?

WRITING SUGGESTIONS

1. **(Division and Classification)** Cofer's essay reveals that she categorizes herself in several ways that have nothing to do with her ethnicity. She is a poet. She is highly educated. In London, she was an expatriate. Think about the "classification" of this kind that you most aspire to represent. Do you wish to be considered a star athlete? A scholar? A person of religious faith? A premedical student with a great future ahead as a doctor? What is it about that classification that appeals to you? What potential disadvantages does it carry, such as the implied separation from others who do not share the classification? What negative stereotypes (dumb jock, for example) might be applied to you? Do you like whatever exclusivity such a classification entails, or do you try to downplay it as much as possible so as not to set yourself apart? Explain.

2. **(Other Strategies)** Cofer blames the mass media for the perpetuation of Latina stereotypes. Few of us can claim that we do not carry with us stereotypes or assumptions that are based on preconceived notions rather than direct experience. What are some of the "myths" you have believed — and perhaps still believe — about others? How did you

acquire them? Based on your experience, write a paper in which you argue for or against Cofer's contention that ethnic stereotypes are harmfully perpetuated by the media. Does the media create our values and biases, or does it merely provide us with depictions that agree with our own preconceived notions of what is true?

3. **(Research)** Psychologists, in trying to understand what makes people function and think the way they do, have developed new ways in which to classify people by personality typing. Research this topic at the library or perhaps on the Internet. Books like *Please Understand Me* (1978) by David Kiersey and Marilyn Bates include tests that help determine your personality type. Take one of these tests with two friends you know well. Write a paper in which you discuss the results. How well does your "type" describe you? How accurate do you think the results were for your friends? What benefits can be realized from "typing" people? What possible dangers, if any, do you see from applying this kind of typing to large numbers of people?

• **Personality Tests**

<http://www.universityoflife.com/serious.htm>

This site features free online personality tests of every stripe.

• **LegalMetrics: Psychometrics and the Law**

<http://www.legalmetrics.com>

Here you will find links and information on the legal and educational ramifications of using personality and intelligence testing. There are also links to professional psychometric organizations and standards groups.

• **ERIC Clearinghouse on Assessment and Evaluation**

<http://ericae.net>

The Educational Resources Information Center (ERIC) claims to be "one of the major bibliographic databases in the world." At this site, you can search full-text articles on every aspect of psychology and psychological research, including personality testing and psychometrics. You can also access online journals and books on the topic of assessment.

Propaganda: How Not to Be Bamboozled

Donna Woolfolk Cross

*Donna Woolfolk Cross is a professor of English at Onondaga Commu-
nity College in Syracuse, New York. She graduated from the University of
Pennsylvania in 1969 and received her M.A. from the University of California, Los Angeles. Her books include* Mediaspeak: How Television
Makes Up Your Mind *(1981) and* Word Abuse: How the Words We
Use Use Us *(1979), which won an award from the National Council of
Teachers of English. Her early work as an advertising copywriter influences her teaching and writing. In an interview she said, "We tend to
think of language as something we use; we are much less often aware of
the way we are used by language. The only defense is to become wise to
the ways of words."*

In the following essay, which first appeared in Speaking of Words:
A Language Reader *(1978), Cross takes the mystery out of propaganda.
She classifies the "tricks" of the propagandist into thirteen major cate-
gories and discusses each thoroughly.*

BEFORE YOU READ

What do you think of when you hear the word *propaganda?* What
kinds of people do you associate with it? Why do you think these
people use propaganda?

Propaganda. If an opinion poll were taken tomorrow, we can be sure 1
that nearly everyone would be against it because it *sounds* so bad.
When we say, "Oh, that's just propaganda," it means, to most people,
"That's a pack of lies." But really, propaganda is simply a means of
persuasion and so it can be put to work for good causes as well as
bad — to persuade people to give to charity, for example, or to love
their neighbors, or to stop polluting the environment.

For good or evil, propaganda pervades our daily lives, helping to 2
shape our attitudes on a thousand subjects. Propaganda probably determines the brand of toothpaste you use, the movies you see, the
candidates you elect when you get to the polls. Propaganda works by
tricking us, by momentarily distracting the eye while the rabbit pops
out from beneath the cloth. Propaganda works best with an uncritical
audience. Joseph Goebbels, propaganda minister in Nazi Germany,
once defined his work as "the conquest of the masses." The masses
would not have been conquered, however, if they had known how to
challenge and to question, how to make distinctions between propaganda and reasonable argument.

People are bamboozled mainly because they don't recognize propaganda when they see it. They need to be informed about the various devices that can be used to mislead and deceive — about the propagandist's overflowing bag of tricks. The following, then, are some common pitfalls for the unwary.

1. NAME-CALLING

As its title suggests, this device consists of labeling people or ideas with words of bad connotation, literally, "calling them names." Here the propagandist tries to arouse our contempt so we will dismiss the "bad name" person or idea without examining its merits.

Bad names have played a tremendously important role in the history of the world. They have ruined reputations and ended lives, sent people to prison and to war, and just generally made us mad at each other for centuries.

Name-calling can be used against policies, practices, beliefs and ideals, as well as against individuals, groups, races, nations. Name-calling is at work when we hear a candidate for office described as a "foolish idealist" or a "two-faced liar" or when an incumbent's policies are denounced as "reckless," "reactionary," or just plain "stupid." Some of the most effective names a public figure can be called are ones that may not denote anything specific: "Congresswoman Jane Doe is a *bleeding heart!*" (Did she vote for funds to help paraplegics?) or "The senator is a *tool of Washington!*" (Did he happen to agree with the president?) Senator Yakalot uses name-calling when he denounces his opponent's "radical policies" and calls them (and him) "socialist," "pinko," and part of a "heartless plot." He also uses it when he calls cars "puddle-jumpers," "can openers," and "motorized baby buggies."

The point here is that when the propagandist uses name-calling, he doesn't want us to think — merely to react, blindly, unquestioningly. So the best defense against being taken in by name-calling is to stop and ask, "Forgetting the bad name attached to it, what are the merits of the idea itself? What does this name really mean, anyway?"

2. GLITTERING GENERALITIES

Glittering generalities are really name-calling in reverse. Name-calling uses words with bad connotations; glittering generalities are words with good connotations — "virtue words," as the Institute for Propaganda Analysis has called them. The Institute explains that while name-calling tries to get us to *reject* and *condemn* someone or something without examining the evidence, glittering generalities try to get us to *accept* and *agree* without examining the evidence.

We believe in, fight for, live by "virtue words" which we feel 9
deeply about: "justice," "motherhood," "the American way," "our
Constitutional rights," "our Christian heritage." These sound good,
but when we examine them closely, they turn out to have no specific,
definable meaning. They just make us feel good. Senator Yakalot uses
glittering generalities when he says, "I stand for all that is good in
America, for our American way and our American birthright." But
what exactly *is* "good for America"? How can we define our "American birthright"? Just what parts of the American society and culture
does "our American way" refer to?

We often make the mistake of assuming we are personally unaf- 10
fected by glittering generalities. The next time you find yourself assuming that, listen to a political candidate's speech on TV and see
how often the use of glittering generalities elicits cheers and applause.
That's the danger of propaganda; it *works.* Once again, our defense
against it is to ask questions: Forgetting the virtue words attached to
it, what are the merits of the idea itself? What does "Americanism" (or
"freedom" or "truth") really *mean* here? [. . .]

Both name-calling and glittering generalities work by stirring our 11
emotions in the hope that this will cloud our thinking. Another approach that propaganda uses is to create a distraction, a "red herring,"
that will make people forget or ignore the real issues. There are several
different kinds of "red herrings" that can be used to distract attention.

3. PLAIN-FOLKS APPEAL

"Plain folks" is the device by which a speaker tries to win our confi- 12
dence and support by appearing to be a person like ourselves — "just
one of the plain folks." The plain-folks appeal is at work when candidates go around shaking hands with factory workers, kissing babies in
supermarkets, and sampling pasta with Italians, fried chicken with
Southerners, bagels and blintzes with Jews. "Now I'm a businessman
like yourselves" is a plain-folks appeal, as is "I've been a farm boy all
my life." Senator Yakalot tries the plain-folks appeal when he says,
"I'm just a small-town boy like you fine people." The use of such expressions once prompted Lyndon Johnson to quip, "Whenever I hear
someone say, 'I'm just an old country lawyer,' the first thing I reach
for is my wallet to make sure it's still there."

The irrelevancy of the plain-folks appeal is obvious: even if the 13
man *is* "one of us" (which may not be true at all), that doesn't mean
that his ideas and programs are sound — or even that he honestly has
our best interests at heart. As with glittering generalities, the danger
here is that we may mistakenly assume we are immune to this appeal.

But propagandists wouldn't use it unless it had been proved to work. You can protect yourself by asking, "Aside from his 'nice guy next door' image, what does this man stand for? Are his ideas and his past record really supportive of my best interests?"

4. *ARGUMENTUM AD POPULUM* (STROKING)

Argumentum ad populum means "argument to the people" or "telling the people what they want to hear." The colloquial term from the Watergate era is "stroking," which conjures up pictures of small animals or children being stroked or soothed with compliments until they come to like the person doing the complimenting — and, by extension, his or her ideas. 14

We all like to hear nice things about ourselves and the group we belong to — we like to be liked — so it stands to reason that we will respond warmly to a person who tells us we are "hard-working taxpayers" or "the most generous, free-spirited nation in the world." Politicians tell farmers they are the "backbone of the American economy" and college students that they are the "leaders and policy makers of tomorrow." Commercial advertisers use stroking more insidiously by asking a question which invites a flattering answer: "What kind of a man reads *Playboy?*" (Does he really drive a Porsche and own $10,000 worth of sound equipment?) Senator Yakalot is stroking his audience when he calls them the "decent law-abiding citizens that are the great pulsing heart and the life blood of this, our beloved country," and when he repeatedly refers to them as "you fine people," "you wonderful folks." 15

Obviously, the intent here is to sidetrack us from thinking critically about the man and his ideas. Our own good qualities have nothing to do with the issue at hand. Ask yourself, "Apart from the nice things he has to say about me (and my church, my nation, my ethnic group, my neighbors), what does the candidate stand for? Are his or her ideas in my best interests?" 16

5. *ARGUMENTUM AD HOMINEM*

Argumentum ad hominem means "argument to the man" and that's exactly what it is. When a propagandist uses *argumentum ad hominem,* he wants to distract our attention from the issue under consideration with personal attacks on the people involved. For example, when Lincoln issued the Emancipation Proclamation, some people responded by calling him the "baboon." But Lincoln's long arms and 17 awkward carriage had nothing to do with the merits of the Proclamation or the question of whether or not slavery should be abolished.

Today *argumentum ad hominem* is still widely used and very effective. You may or may not support the Equal Rights Amendment, but you should be sure your judgment is based on the merits of the idea itself, and not the result of someone's denunciation of the people who support the ERA as "fanatics" or "lesbians" or "frustrated old maids." Senator Yakalot is using *argumentum ad hominem* when he dismisses the idea of using smaller automobiles with a reference to the personal appearance of one of its supporters, Congresswoman Doris Schlepp. Refuse to be waylaid by *argumentum ad hominem* and ask, "Do the personal qualities of the person being discussed have anything to do with the issue at hand? Leaving him or her aside, how good is the idea itself?"

6. TRANSFER (GUILT OR GLORY BY ASSOCIATION)

In *argumentum ad hominem,* an attempt is made to associate negative aspects of a person's character or personal appearance with an issue or idea he supports. The transfer device uses this same process of association to make us accept or condemn a given person or idea.

A better name for the transfer device is guilt (or glory) by association. In glory by association, the propagandist tries to transfer the positive feelings of something we love and respect to the group or idea he wants us to accept. "This bill for a new dam is in the best tradition of this country, the land of Lincoln, Jefferson, and Washington," is glory by association at work. Lincoln, Jefferson, and Washington were great leaders that most of us revere and respect, but they have no logical connection to the proposal under consideration — the bill to build a new dam. Senator Yakalot uses glory by association when he says full-sized cars "have always been as American as Mom's apple pie or a Sunday drive in the country."

The process works equally well in reverse, when guilt by association is used to transfer our dislike or disapproval of one idea or group to some other idea or group that the propagandist wants us to reject and condemn. "John Doe says we need to make some changes in the way our government operates; well, that's exactly what the Ku Klux Klan has said, so there's a meeting of great minds!" That's guilt by association for you; there's no logical connection between John Doe and the Ku Klux Klan apart from the one the propagandist is trying to create in our minds. He wants to distract our attention from John Doe and get us thinking (and worrying) about the Ku Klux Klan and its politics of violence. (Of course, there are sometimes legitimate associations between the two things; if John Doe had been a *member* of the Ku Klux Klan, it would be reasonable and fair to draw a connection between the man and his group.) Senator Yakalot tries to trick his audience with guilt by association when he remarks that "the words 'community' and 'communism' look an awful lot alike!" He does it again when he mentions that Mr. Stu Pott "sports a Fidel Castro beard."

How can we learn to spot the transfer device and distinguish between fair and unfair associations? We can teach ourselves to *suspend judgment* until we have answered these questions: "Is there any legitimate connection between the idea under discussion and the thing it is associated with? Leaving the transfer device out of the picture, what are the merits of the idea by itself?" 22

7. BANDWAGON

Ever hear of the small, ratlike animal called the lemming? Lemmings are arctic rodents with a very odd habit: periodically, for reasons no one entirely knows, they mass together in a large herd and commit suicide by rushing into deep water and drowning themselves. They all run in together, blindly, and not one of them ever seems to stop and ask, "*Why* am I doing this? Is this really what I want to do?" and thus save itself from destruction. Obviously, lemmings are driven to perform their strange mass suicide rites by common instinct. People choose to "follow the herd" for more complex reasons, yet we are still all too often the unwitting victims of the bandwagon appeal. 23

Essentially, the bandwagon urges us to support an action or an opinion because it is popular — because "everyone else is doing it." This call to "get on the bandwagon" appeals to the strong desire in most of us to be one of the crowd, not to be left out or alone. Advertising makes extensive use of the bandwagon appeal ("join the Pepsi people"), but so do politicians ("Let us join together in this great cause"). Senator Yakalot uses the bandwagon appeal when he says that "More and more citizens are rallying to my cause every day," and asks his audience to "join them — and me — in our fight for America." 24

One of the ways we can see the bandwagon appeal at work is in the overwhelming success of various fashions and trends which capture the interest (and the money) of thousands of people for a short time, then disappear suddenly and completely. For a year or two in the fifties, every child in North America wanted a coonskin cap so they could be like Davy Crockett; no one wanted to be left out. After that there was the hula-hoop craze that helped to dislocate the hips of thousands of Americans. More recently, what made millions of people rush out to buy their very own "pet rocks"? 25

The problem here is obvious: just because everyone's doing it 26
doesn't mean that *we* should too. Group approval does not prove that
something is true or is worth doing. Large numbers of people have
supported actions we now condemn. Just a generation ago, Hitler and
Mussolini rose to absolute and catastrophically repressive rule in two
of the most sophisticated and cultured countries of Europe. When
they came into power they were welled up by massive popular support
from millions of people who didn't want to be "left out" at a great historical moment.

Once the mass begins to move — on the bandwagon — it be- 27
comes harder and harder to perceive the leader *riding* the bandwagon.
So don't be a lemming, rushing blindly on to destruction because
"everyone else is doing it." Stop and ask, "Where is this bandwagon
headed? Never mind about everybody else, is this what is best for
me?" [. . .]

As we have seen, propaganda can appeal to us by arousing our 28
emotions or distracting our attention from the real issues at hand. But
there's a third way that propaganda can be put to work against us —
by the use of faulty logic. This approach is really more insidious than
the other two because it gives the appearance of reasonable, fair argument. It is only when we look more closely that the holes in the logical fiber show up. The following are some of the devices that make use
of faulty logic to distort and mislead.

8. FAULTY CAUSE AND EFFECT

As the name suggests, this device sets up a cause-and-effect relation- 29
ship that may not be true. The Latin name for this logical fallacy is
post hoc ergo propter hoc, which means "after this, therefore because of
this." But just because one thing happened after another doesn't mean
that one *caused* the other.

An example of false cause-and-effect reasoning is offered by the 30
story (probably invented) of the woman aboard the ship *Titanic*. She
woke up from a nap and, feeling seasick, looked around for a call button to summon the steward to bring her some medication. She finally
located a small button on one of the walls of her cabin and pushed it.
A split second later, the *Titanic* grazed an iceberg in the terrible crash
that was to send the entire ship to its destruction. The woman
screamed and said, "Oh, God, what have I done? What have I done?"
The humor of that anecdote comes from the absurdity of the woman's
assumption that pushing the small red button resulted in the destruction of a ship weighing several hundred tons: "It happened after I
pushed it, therefore it must be *because* I pushed it" — *post hoc ergo*

propter hoc reasoning. There is, of course, no cause-and-effect relationship there.

The false cause-and-effect fallacy is used very often by political candidates. "After I came to office, the rate of inflation dropped to 6 percent." But did the person do anything to cause the lower rate of inflation or was it the result of other conditions? Would the rate of inflation have dropped anyway, even if he hadn't come to office? Senator Yakalot uses false cause and effect when he says "our forefathers who made this country great never had free hot meal handouts! And look what they did for our country!" He does it again when he concludes that "driving full-sized cars means a better car safety record on our American roads today."

False cause-and-effect reasoning is terribly persuasive because it seems so logical. Its appeal is apparently to experience. We swallowed X product — and the headache went away. We elected Y official and unemployment went down. Many people think, "There *must* be a connection." But causality is an immensely complex phenomenon; you need a good deal of evidence to prove that an event that follows another in time was "therefore" caused by the first event.

Don't be taken in by false cause and effect; be sure to ask, "Is there enough evidence to prove that this cause led to that effect? Could there have been any *other* causes?"

9. FALSE ANALOGY

An analogy is a comparison between two ideas, events, or things. But comparisons can be fairly made only when the things being compared are alike in significant ways. When they are not, false analogy is the result.

A famous example of this is the old proverb "Don't change horses in the middle of a stream," often used as an analogy to convince voters not to change administrations in the middle of a war or other crisis. But the analogy is misleading because there are so many differences between the things compared. In what ways is a war or political crisis like a stream? Is the president or head of state really very much like a horse? And is a nation of millions of people comparable to a man trying to get across a stream? Analogy is false and unfair when it compares two things that have little in common and assumes that they are identical. Senator Yakalot tries to hoodwink his listeners with false analogy when he says, "Trying to take Americans out of the kind of cars they love is as undemocratic as trying to deprive them of the right to vote."

Of course, analogies can be drawn that are reasonable and fair. It would be reasonable, for example, to compare the results of busing in one small Southern city with the possible results in another, *if* the towns have the same kind of history, population, and school policy. We can decide for ourselves whether an analogy is false or fair by asking, "Are the things being compared truly alike in significant ways? Do the differences between them affect the comparison?"

10. BEGGING THE QUESTION

Actually, the name of this device is rather misleading, because it does   37
not appear in the form of a question. Begging the question occurs when, in discussing a questionable or debatable point, a person assumes as already established the very point that he is trying to prove. For example, "No thinking citizen could approve such a completely unacceptable policy as this one." But isn't the question of whether or not the policy *is* acceptable the very point to be established? Senator Yakalot begs the question when he announces that his opponent's plan won't work "because it is unworkable."

We can protect ourselves against this kind of faulty logic by ask-   38
ing, "What is assumed in this statement? Is the assumption reasonable, or does it need more proof?"

11. THE TWO-EXTREMES FALLACY (FALSE DILEMMA)

Linguists have long noted that the English language tends to view re-   39
ality in sets of two extremes or polar opposites. In English, things are either black or white, tall or short, up or down, front or back, left or right, good or bad, guilty or not guilty. We can ask for a "straightforward yes-or-no answer" to a question, the understanding being that we will not accept or consider anything in between. In fact, reality cannot always be dissected along such strict lines. There may be (usually are) *more* than just two possibilities or extremes to consider. We are often told to "listen to both sides of the argument." But who's to say that every argument has only two sides? Can't there be a third — even a fourth or fifth — point of view?

The two-extremes fallacy is at work in this statement by Lenin, the   40
great Marxist leader: "You cannot eliminate *one* basic assumption, one substantial part of this philosophy of Marxism (it is as if it were a block of steel), without abandoning truth, without falling into the arms of bourgeois-reactionary falsehood." In other words, if we don't agree 100 percent with every premise of Marxism, we must be placed at the opposite end of the political-economic spectrum — for Lenin,

"bourgeois-reactionary falsehood." If we are not entirely *with* him, we must be against him; those are the only two possibilities open to us. Of course, this is a logical fallacy; in real life there are any number of political positions one can maintain *between* the two extremes of Marxism and capitalism. Senator Yakalot uses the two-extremes fallacy in the same way as Lenin when he tells his audience that "in this world a man's either for private enterprise or he's for socialism."

One of the most famous examples of the two-extremes fallacy in re- 41
cent history is the slogan, "America: Love it or leave it," with its implicit suggestion that we either accept everything just as it is in America today without complaint — or get out. Again, it should be obvious that there is a whole range of action and belief between those two extremes.

Don't be duped; stop and ask, "Are those really the only two op- 42
tions I can choose from? Are there other alternatives not mentioned that deserve consideration?"

12. CARD STACKING

Some questions are so multifaceted and complex that no one can 43
make an intelligent decision about them without considering a wide variety of evidence. One selection of facts could make us feel one way and another selection could make us feel just the opposite. Card stack-ing is a device of propaganda which selects only the facts that support the propagandist's point of view, and ignores all the others. For ex-ample, a candidate could be made to look like a legislative dynamo if you say, "Representative McNerd introduced more new bills than any other member of the Congress," and neglect to mention that most of them were so preposterous that they were laughed off the floor.

Senator Yakalot engages in card stacking when he talks about the 44
proposal to use smaller cars. He talks only about jobs without mentioning the cost to the taxpayers or the very real — though still denied — threat of depletion of resources. He says he wants to help his countrymen keep their jobs, but doesn't mention that the corpora-tions that offer the jobs will also make large profits. He praises the "American chrome industry," overlooking the fact that most chrome is imported. And so on.

The best protection against card stacking is to take the "Yes, 45
but . . ." attitude. This device of propaganda is not untrue, but then again it is not the *whole* truth. So ask yourself, "Is this person leaving something out that I should know about? Is there some other infor-mation that should be brought to bear on this question?" [. . .]

So far, we have considered three approaches that the propagandist 46
can use to influence our thinking: appealing to our emotions, distract-ing our attention, and misleading us with logic that may appear to be

reasonable but is in fact faulty and deceiving. But there is a fourth approach that is probably the most common propaganda trick of them all.

13. TESTIMONIAL

The testimonial device consists in having some loved or respected person give a statement of support (testimonial) for a given product or idea. The problem is that the person being quoted may *not* be an expert in the field; in fact, he may know nothing at all about it. Using the name of a man who is skilled and famous in one field to give a testimonial for something in another field is unfair and unreasonable.   47

Senator Yakalot tries to mislead his audience with testimonial when he tells them that "full-sized cars have been praised by great Americans like John Wayne and Jack Jones, as well as by leading experts on car safety and comfort."   48

Testimonial is used extensively in TV ads, where it often appears in such bizarre forms as Joe Namath's endorsement of a pantyhose brand. Here, of course, the "authority" giving the testimonial not only is no expert about pantyhose, but obviously stands to gain something (money!) by making the testimonial.   49

When celebrities endorse a political candidate, they may not be making money by doing so, but we should still question whether they are in any better position to judge than we ourselves. Too often we are willing to let others we like or respect make our decisions *for us,* while we follow along acquiescently. And this is the purpose of testimonial — to get us to agree and accept *without* stopping to think. Be sure to ask, "Is there any reason to believe that this person (or organization or publication or whatever) has any more knowledge or information than I do on this subject? What does the idea amount to on its own merits, without the benefit of testimonial?"   50

The cornerstone of democratic society is reliance upon an informed and educated electorate. To be fully effective citizens we need to be able to challenge and to question wisely. A dangerous feeling of indifference toward our political processes exists today. We often abandon our right, our duty, to criticize and evaluate by dismissing *all* politicians as "crooked," *all* new bills and proposals as "just more government bureaucracy." But there are important distinctions to be made, and this kind of apathy can be fatal to democracy.   51

If we are to be led, let us not be led blindly, but critically, intelligently, with our eyes open. If we are to continue to be a government   52 "by the people," let us become informed about the methods and purposes of propaganda, so we can be the masters, not the slaves of our destiny.

RESPONDING TO READING

Think about your last significant purchase in light of Cross's essay. What did you buy? Why did you buy it? Think about the advertisements for the product and what the salesperson said to you as you were considering the product. How much of a role do you think these things played in your decision to buy? Did they appeal to your emotions, your logic, or both? Would you make the same purchase again? Why or why not?

QUESTIONING THE TEXT

1. Why does Cross believe that it is necessary for people in a democratic society to become informed about the methods and practices of propaganda? What is her advice for dealing with it?

2. In what ways are name-calling and glittering generalities two sides of the same propaganda technique?

3. What is "begging the question"? Why is it a useful technique for propagandists?

4. What, according to Cross, is the most common propaganda trick of them all? Provide an example of it from your own experience.

5. Presumably, Joe Namath does not wear panty hose. What does the panty hose manufacturer gain, then, by hiring him to endorse its product? What does this example indicate about testimonials in general?

UNDERSTANDING THE WRITER'S CRAFT

1. Cross frequently quotes Senator Yakalot to provide examples for her types of propaganda, even though she uses real examples as well. (Glossary: *Examples*) What does she gain by creating this fictitious politician for her essay? What, if anything, does she lose? Do you find the examples effective? Explain.

2. In addition to classifying the different types of propaganda, Cross organizes the discussion of each propaganda device in a particular way. (Glossary: *Organization*) How does she do this? How does the consistent organization contribute to the readability of the essay?

3. In her discussion of the bandwagon appeal, Cross uses the analogy of the lemmings. (Glossary: *Analogy*) How does the analogy work? Is it a "false analogy"? Why or why not? How do analogies help you, as a writer, to explain your subject for readers?

EXPLORING LANGUAGE

1. Based on your reading of Cross's essay, define the word *propaganda*. (Glossary: *Definition*) Does this definition differ from any connotations it might have had for you before reading the essay? (Glossary: *Connotation/ Denotation*) Explain.

2. Some words are particularly effective at provoking certain reactions by their mere mention, regardless of the context. Cross mentions several such words in her essay. Other current ones include *refreshing,* which communicates positive pleasure and ease, and *stress,* which communicates negative tension. Develop a list of five or six such words that you have observed being used effectively in advertising, by the news media, or in politics. What is your immediate reaction to each word? How might their skillful use lead you to accept an advertiser's or politician's message without careful thought?

3. Refer to your desk dictionary to determine the meanings of the following words as Cross uses them in this selection: *bamboozled* (paragraph 3), *irrelevancy* (13), *colloquial* (14), *insidiously* (15), *denunciation* (18), *fallacy* (29), *causality* (32), *bourgeois* (40), *implicit* (41), *acquiescently* (50).

COMBINING RHETORICAL STRATEGIES

Choose an issue that you know fairly well. It is best if you have followed it in the news, studied it in a class, or researched it for a paper. Write a short argument piece in which you use one or more of Cross's propaganda techniques, rather than information or logic, to present your side of the issue. Do what you can to engage your readers' emotions, distract them from dissenting arguments, and otherwise impel them to agree with you. Share your essay with your classmates.

WRITING SUGGESTIONS

1. **(Division and Classification)** As is readily apparent in Cross's essay, advertisers depend on several different kinds of propaganda to win you over to their products. Yet they use other techniques as well, including simple dissemination of information, side-by-side comparisons, logical argumentation, and so on. Watch a couple of hours of television, and note the techniques used in each commercial. Then write a division and classification essay in which you present the different techniques and describe how the advertisers use them. What techniques, other than Cross's kinds of propaganda, are the most popular?

2. **(Other Strategies)** Propaganda and argumentation share a basic attribute — trying to persuade others to a certain way of thinking — but they have many differences as well. Write an essay in which you discuss how propaganda differs from argumentation. You will probably want to set it up as a comparison and contrast essay (see Chapter 9) to effectively relate the two ways of communicating.

3. **(Research)** Cross invokes several societies in which propaganda became a frighteningly effective political technique and was used to lead millions of people to conclusions and actions they never would have considered independently. Research a prominent society in which the leaders were able to use propaganda as a way to "conquer the masses," to paraphrase Goebbels' chilling phrase. Nazi Germany is an excellent example. Others from the twentieth century include the Soviet Union, imperial Japan, and Italy under Mussolini. Using the library and perhaps the Internet to do your research, write a paper in which you present the phrases, rhetoric, and labels chosen by the leader to shape the thinking of the "masses." What propaganda techniques did the leader rely on? How effective were these campaigns? What questions might have caused the propaganda to fail, had enough people had the thoughtfulness and courage to ask them?

• **German Propaganda Archive**

<http://www.calvin.edu/academic/cas/gpa>

Maintained by Professor Randall Bytwerk from Calvin College, this site catalogs visual and written propaganda from Nazi Germany as well as from the German Democratic Republic. The site also features "Material for Propagandists" — full-text articles that Nazi propagandists were reading.

• **The Institute for Propaganda Analysis**

<http://carmen.artsci.washington.edu/propaganda/contents.htm>

This site features an archive of written, visual, and video propaganda from the twentieth century, from World War I to the Democratic National Committee. There are also explanations and examples of the different propaganda techniques.

• **World War II Poster Collection**

<http://www.library.nwu.edu/govpub/collections/wwii-posters>

This site, maintained by the Government Publications Department at Northwestern University Library, features an online collection of more than three hundred posters issued by U.S. federal agencies during World War II.

• **The PolitProp Library**

<http://www.mcad.edu/classrooms/POLITPROP/palace/central/library.html>

Minneapolis College of Art and Design's PolitProp library features propaganda research and resources and texts on propaganda history, theory, and development. This site features links to modern propaganda art and evaluation sources.

COMBINING SUBJECTS AND STRATEGIES

The photograph below depicts many of the same themes and strategies as the Combining Rhetorical Strategies essay that follows. Your observations about the photograph will help guide you to the key themes and strategies in the essay. After you've read the essay, you may use your observations about both the photograph and the essay to examine how the overlapping themes and strategies work in each medium.

Imagine working long hours every day underground, with only the light of a headlamp to see by, coal dust settling in your lungs, and the pounding din of machinery echoing in the enclosed space. Danger lurks in the short term from cave-ins and other potential disasters and in the long term from disease and disability. There are few more difficult ways to make a living than coal mining, yet it is a way of life for thousands of men — the kind of men Scott Russell Sanders grew up with and discusses in the essay that follows.

Pittsburgh Courier Archives/Archive Photos

For Discussion

Examine the photograph of the miner, paying particular attention to his expression, possessions, and surroundings. What does the photograph communicate to you about both the mine and the man who works in it? What kind of life do you think the man has outside of his work? Explain your answer.

The Men We Carry in Our Minds

Scott Russell Sanders

Born in 1945 to a poor midwestern farm family, Scott Russell Sanders has achieved a successful career as an author and academic while remaining true to his roots. In an interview he said, "Much of my writing deals with the lives of rural people, with children, with the elderly, with outcasts, with figures who are neither literary nor intellectual; and I would like the real-life counterparts of those people to be engaged and moved by my fiction." Like many of the contemporary authors whose essays appear in this book, Sanders has a strong background in both scientific and literary studies, and his knowledge of science plays a significant role in much of his work. He has written in an unusually wide variety of forms: realistic, historical, and science fiction; folk tales; children's stories; personal essays; and literary criticism. Several of his books have won awards, including Hear the Wind Blow: American Folksongs Retold *(1985),* Stone Country *(1985),* Bad Man Ballad *(1986), and* The Paradise of Bombs *(1987). A professor for many years at the University of Indiana, Sanders has written a regular newspaper column ("One Man's Fiction,"* Chicago Sun-Times*) and has contributed widely to books, anthologies, and literary magazines.*

The following selection, taken from Paradise of Bombs *(1984), examines the world of "warriors and toilers," as Sanders classifies the men he knew in his childhood.*

BEFORE YOU READ

When you were a child, did you expect that when you grew up you would lead a life similar to the lives your parents led? Did you want this to happen? In what ways is your life similar to your parents' lives, and in what ways is it different?

When I was a boy, the men I knew labored with their bodies. They were marginal farmers, just scraping by, or welders, steelworkers, carpenters; they swept floors, dug ditches, mined coal, or drove trucks, their forearms ropy with muscle; they trained horses, stoked furnaces, built tires, stood on assembly lines wrestling parts onto cars and refrigerators. They got up before light, worked all day long whatever the weather, and when they came home at night they looked as though somebody had been whipping them. In the evenings and on weekends they worked on their own places, tilling gardens that were lumpy with clay, fixing broken-down cars, hammering on houses that were always too drafty, too leaky, too small.

The bodies of the men I knew were twisted and maimed in ways visible and invisible. The nails of their hands were black and split, the

439

hands tattooed with scars. Some had lost fingers. Heavy lifting had given many of them finicky backs and guts weak from hernias. Racing against conveyor belts had given them ulcers. Their ankles and knees ached from years of standing on concrete. Anyone who had worked for long around machines was hard of hearing. They squinted, and the skin of their faces was creased like the leather of old work gloves. There were times, studying them, when I dreaded growing up. Most of them coughed, from dust or cigarettes, and most of them drank cheap wine or whiskey, so their eyes looked bloodshot and bruised. The fathers of my friends always seemed older than the mothers. Men wore out sooner. Only women lived into old age.

As a boy I also knew another sort of men, who did not sweat and   3
break down like mules. They were soldiers, and so far as I could tell they scarcely worked at all. During my early school years we lived on a military base, an arsenal in Ohio, and every day I saw GIs in the guardshacks, on the stoops of barracks, at the wheels of olive drab Chevrolets. The chief fact of their lives was boredom. Long after I left the Arsenal I came to recognize the sour smell the soldiers gave off as that of souls in limbo. They were all waiting — for wars, for transfers, for leaves, for promotions, for the end of their hitch — like so many braves waiting for the hunt to begin. Unlike the warriors of older tribes, however, they would have no say about when the battle would start or how it would be waged. Their waiting was broken only when they practiced for war. They fired guns at targets, drove tanks across the churned-up fields of the military reservation, set off bombs in the wrecks of old fighter planes. I knew this was all play. But I also felt certain that when the hour for killing arrived, they would kill. When the real shooting started, many of them would die. This was what soldiers were *for*, just as a hammer was for driving nails.

Warriors and toilers: those seemed, in my boyhood vision, to be   4
the chief destinies for men. They weren't the only destinies, as I learned from having a few male teachers, from reading books, and from watching television. But the men on television — the politicians, the astronauts, the generals, the savvy lawyers, the philosophical doctors, the bosses who gave orders to both soldiers and laborers — seemed as removed and unreal to me as the figures in tapestries. I could no more imagine growing up to become one of these cool, potent creatures than I could imagine becoming a prince.

A nearer and more hopeful example was that of my father, who   5
had escaped from a red-dirt farm to a tire factory, and from the assembly line to the front office. Eventually he dressed in a white shirt and tie. He carried himself as if he had been born to work with his mind. But his body, remembering the earlier years of slogging work, began to give out on him in his fifties, and it quit on him entirely before he turned sixty-five. Even such a partial escape from man's fate as he had

accomplished did not seem possible for most of the boys I knew. They joined the Army, stood in line for jobs in the smoky plants, helped build highways. They were bound to work as their fathers had worked, killing themselves or preparing to kill others.

A scholarship enabled me not only to attend college, a rare enough feat in my circle, but even to study in a university meant for the children of the rich. Here I met for the first time young men who had assumed from birth that they would lead lives of comfort and power. And for the first time I met women who told me that men were guilty of having kept all the joys and privileges of the earth for themselves. I was baffled. What privileges? What joys? I thought about the maimed, dismal lives of most of the men back home. What had they stolen from their wives and daughters? The right to go five days a week, twelve months a year, for thirty or forty years to a steel mill or a coal mine? The right to drop bombs and die in war? The right to feel every leak in the roof, every gap in the fence, every cough in the engine, as a wound they must mend? The right to feel, when the lay-off comes or the plant shuts down, not only afraid but ashamed? 6

I was slow to understand the deep grievances of women. This was because, as a boy, I had envied them. Before college, the only people I had ever known who were interested in art or music or literature, the only ones who read books, the only ones who ever seemed to enjoy a sense of ease and grace were the mothers and daughters. Like the menfolk, they fretted about money, they scrimped and made-do. But, when the pay stopped coming in, they were not the ones who had failed. Nor did they have to go to war, and that seemed to me a blessed fact. By comparison with the narrow, ironclad days of fathers, there was an expansiveness, I thought, in the days of mothers. They went to see neighbors, to shop in town, to run errands at school, at the library, at church. No doubt, had I looked harder at their lives, I would have envied them less. It was not my fate to become a woman, so it was easier for me to see the graces. Few of them held jobs outside the home, and those who did filled thankless roles as clerks and waitresses. I didn't see, then, what a prison a house could be, since houses seemed to me brighter, handsomer places than any factory. I did not realize — because such things were never spoken of — how often women suffered from men's bullying. I did learn about the wretchedness of abandoned wives, single mothers, widows; but I also learned about the wretchedness of lone men. Even then I could see how exhausting it was for a mother to cater all day to the needs of young children. But if I had been asked, as a boy, to choose between tending a baby and tending a machine, I think I would have chosen the baby. (Having now tended both, I know I would choose the baby.) 7

So I was baffled when the women at college accused me and my sex of having cornered the world's pleasures. I think something like my bafflement has been felt by other boys (and by girls as well) who 8 grew up in dirt-poor farm country, in mining country, in black ghettos, in Hispanic barrios, in the shadows of factories, in Third World nations — any place where the fate of men is as grim and bleak as the fate of women. Toilers and warriors. I realize now how ancient these identities are, how deep the tug they exert on men, the undertow of a thousand generations. The miseries I saw, as a boy, in the lives of nearly all men I continue to see in the lives of many — the body-breaking toil, the tedium, the call to be tough, the humiliating powerlessness, the battle for a living and for territory.

When the women I met at college thought about the joys and privileges of men, they did not carry in their minds the sort of men I had known in my childhood. They thought of their fathers, who were bankers, physicians, architects, stockbrokers, the big wheels of the big cities. These fathers rode the train to work or drove cars that cost more than any of my childhood houses. They were attended from morning to night by female helpers, wives and nurses and secretaries. They were never laid off, never short of cash at month's end, never lined up for welfare. These fathers made decisions that mattered. They ran the world. 9

The daughters of such men wanted to share in this power, this glory. So did I. They yearned for a say over their future, for jobs worthy of their abilities, for the right to live at peace, unmolested, whole. Yes, I thought, yes yes. The difference between me and these daughters was that they saw me, because of my sex, as destined from birth to become like their fathers, and therefore as an enemy to their desires. But I knew better. I wasn't an enemy, in fact or in feeling. I was an ally. If I had known, then, how to tell them so, would they have believed me? Would they now? 10

RESPONDING TO READING

Sanders escaped what he calls "man's fate" (paragraph 5) through education. What assumptions does he make about the purposes of education? Are they valid? For what purposes are you pursuing an education? How do these purposes agree with, differ from, or go beyond his?

QUESTIONING THE TEXT

1. Note the title of the essay. In what sense does Sanders carry with him the men he knew as a child? How does the title affect the way you read the essay?

2. Why did Sanders at times dread growing up? What did time do to the men and women of his hometown?

3. In what way did Sanders, as a college student, identify with the women of his generation? Why?

UNDERSTANDING THE WRITER'S CRAFT

1. Sanders uses several startling similes. (Glossary: *Figures of Speech*) In paragraph 3, for example, he likens soldiers to souls in limbo; in paragraph 4, he draws a simile between the men he sees on television and figures in tapestries. Find other similes in the essay. What does each of them mean? What effect do they have on the reader?

2. Why do you think Sanders ends his essay with a pair of questions?

3. How would you describe the tone of this essay? (Glossary: *Tone*) How does Sanders use vocabulary and paragraph structure to sustain this tone?

EXPLORING LANGUAGE

1. Twice (paragraphs 2 and 6) Sanders uses the word *maimed* in respect to the men he knew as a child. Analyze his use of this word in each context; does he use it in the same way or differently? Explain.

2. The vocabulary in this essay appears simple, but Sanders is finely attuned to the nuances of words. (Glossary: *Connotation/Denotation*) Be sure you know the denotative meaning of each of the following words, then explore their connotations in context: *marginal* (paragraph 1), *arsenal* (3), *limbo* (3), *potent* (4), *baffled* (6), *grievances* (7), *expansiveness* (7), *barrios* (8).

COMBINING RHETORICAL STRATEGIES

1. In a very short essay (only ten paragraphs), Sanders divides and classifies men and women into a number of distinct subcategories. Identify the various classifications into which he places people. Is it valid to pigeonhole people so precisely? Do you agree with his classifications, or would you draw others — or would you resist the temptation to try? Explain your reasoning.

2. In classifying the various groups of men and women he has encountered in his youth, in academe, and on TV, Sanders also draws several clear comparisons and contrasts. (Glossary: *Comparison and Contrast*) Identify them, and show how each is related to the others and to the essay's purpose.

3. Each of the first two paragraphs of this essay is composed of one brief introductory sentence followed by a list of examples. What is the purpose of cramming so many illustrations into so small a space? How does this affect the reader? (Glossary: *Exemplification*)

WRITING SUGGESTIONS

1. **(Division and Classification)** How do you view your childhood role models of your own sex? Do they fit neatly into one or more culturally defined categories? Write an essay in which you divide and classify the

lifestyles, goals, and ideals of the men or women most familiar to you with the norms and ideals of mainstream America, both then (during your childhood) and now.

2. **(Other Strategies)** As a child, Sanders believed that the chief destinies of men were to become toilers or warriors, "killing themselves or preparing to kill others" (paragraph 5). Sanders would describe the miner whose photograph appears before the essay as a toiler, killing himself little by little doing his job. Study the photograph again. Basing your answer on the photograph and on your own experience, what words would you use to define and describe such toilers? What words would you use to describe the chief destinies of women, and how would you define their "ancient . . . identities" (8)? Write an essay exploring the lives of men and women who were not born to privilege.

3. **(Research)** Refer to your Responding to Reading answers, and ask yourself a question: What are the purposes of a college education? Interview a variety of people connected with your college or university: several students from different backgrounds, alumni, faculty members, and administrators. Make sure you interview both men and women. Write an essay in which you define the purposes of an education, classifying the answers of your sources and illustrating your points with their quotes. You may also want to do research in the library and on the Internet to find out what others think about education.

- **The National Endowment for the Humanities Home Page**
  <http://www.neh.fed.us>

  This is the official site of the NEH, "a federal agency that supports learning in history, literature, philosophy, and other areas of the humanities."

- **The *Chronicle of Higher Education* Online**
  <http://chronicle.com>

  This is the official Web site of the *Chronicle of Higher Education,* a widely read news source for college and university faculty members and administrators.

- **Voice of the Shuttle Web Page for Humanities Research**
  <http://vos.ucsb.edu>

  This extensive site, maintained by the University of California, Santa Barbara, offers numerous education and humanities links.

WRITING SUGGESTIONS
FOR DIVISION AND CLASSIFICATION

1. To write a meaningful paper of classification, you must analyze a body of unorganized material, arranging it for a particular purpose. For example, to identify for a buyer the most economical cars currently on the market, you might initially determine which cars can be purchased for under $20,000 and which cost between $20,000 and $30,000. Then, using a second basis of selection — fuel economy — you could determine which cars have the best gas mileage within each price range.

   Select one of the following subjects, and write a paper of classification. Be sure that your purpose is clearly explained and that your bases of selection are chosen and ordered in accordance with your purpose.

   a. attitudes toward physical fitness
   b. contemporary American music
   c. reading materials
   d. reasons for going to college
   e. attitudes toward the religious or spiritual side of life
   f. choosing a hobby
   g. television comedies
   h. college professors
   i. local restaurants
   j. choosing a career
   k. college courses
   l. recreational activities
   m. ways of financing a college education
   n. parties or other social events

2. We sometimes resist classifying other people because it can seem like "pigeonholing" or stereotyping individuals unfairly. In an essay, compare and contrast two or more ways of classifying people, including at least one that you would call legitimate and one that you would call misleading. What conclusions can you draw about the difference between useful classifications and damaging stereotypes?

3. Both E. B. White (p. 385) and Toni Cade Bambara (p. 386) used division and classification to help explain their understanding of New York City. Bambara, however, uses other strategies, including comparison and contrast, to create a stronger image of the division between the rich, who can spend $35 on a toy clown at F.A.O. Schwartz, and the poor, who would use $35 very differently. She also uses narration to develop the characters of Sylvia and Miss Moore and their reaction to the prices at the toy store.

   Use division and classification to explain your school or town. What categories might you use? Would you divide your subject into different types of people the way E. B. White did? Would you classify people by their spending habits as Toni Cade Bambara did? What are the other ways in which you might explain your school or town? What other rhetorical strategies might you incorporate to strengthen your presentation? You might want to look at the Web site of your school or town to find out what categories it uses to present itself.

4. Let's say that you are given an assignment in your American government class to write an essay about the types of presidents that have been elected since the invention of television. How would you organize the different presidents and elections? Would you divide the presidents by political party? By age? By their geographic origins? By their political programs — domestic, international, military, economic, and so forth? What other rhetorical strategies might you use to develop and explain your categories? Considering that the assignment covers presidents elected since television appeared, would narration be an effective strategy to add to your analysis?

CHAPTER 11

Definition

WHAT IS DEFINITION?

A definition explains the meaning of a word or phrase; if you have ever used a dictionary, you will be familiar with the concept of definition. Words need to be defined because their sounds and spelling hardly ever indicate exactly what they are intended to mean and because sometimes a single word can have more than one meaning. A word like *draft* can refer to a current of air, conscription, a ship's depth in the water, a bank check, the official recruiting of an athlete, or the first attempt at a piece of writing. It's amazing that this jumble of meanings can all belong to one word; but after all, words are abstract symbols and represent large and complex worlds of objects, actions, and ideas.

We can only communicate with one another properly when all of us define the words we use in the same way — and that is not always easy. What one person believes he or she is saying might be construed differently by the listener. For example, if someone told you to be *discriminatory*, you might understand the word in a manner not intended by the speaker. Let's look at how Robert Keith Miller attempts to define *discrimination* in his essay called "Discrimination Is a Virtue," which first appeared in *Newsweek* in 1980.

> We have a word in English which means "the ability to tell differences." That word is *discrimination*. But within the last twenty years, this word has been so frequently misused that an entire generation has grown up believing that "discrimination" means "racism." People are always proclaiming that "discrimina-

tion" is something that should be done away with. Should that ever happen, it would prove to be our undoing.

Discrimination means discernment; it means the ability to perceive the truth, to use good judgment and to profit accordingly. The *Oxford English Dictionary* traces this meaning of the word back to 1648 and demonstrates that for the next 300 years, "discrimination" was a virtue, not a vice. Thus, when a character in a nineteenth-century novel makes a happy marriage, Dickens has another character remark, "It does credit to your discrimination that you should have found such a very excellent young woman."

Of course, "the ability to tell differences" assumes that differences exist, and this is unsettling for a culture obsessed with the notion of equality. The contemporary belief that discrimination is a vice stems from the compound "discriminate against." What we need to remember, however, is that some things deserve to be judged harshly: We should not leave our kingdoms to the selfish and the wicked.

Discrimination is wrong only when someone or something is discriminated against because of prejudice. But to use the word in that sense, as so many people do, is to destroy its true meaning. If you discriminate against something because of general preconceptions rather than particular insights, then you are not discriminating — bias has clouded the clarity of vision that discrimination demands.

How does Miller define *discrimination?* He mainly uses a technique called *extended definition,* a definition that requires a full discussion. This is only one of many types of definition that you could use to explain what a word or an idea means to you. The following paragraphs identify and explain several types of definition. While learning the various kinds of definition, see if you can find examples of them in Miller's article.

A *formal definition* — a definition such as that found in a dictionary — explains the meaning of a word by assigning it to a class and then differentiating it from other members of that class.

Term		Class	Differentiation
Music	is	sound	made by voices or instruments and characterized by melody, harmony, or rhythm.

Note how crucial the differentiation is here: There are many sounds — from the roar of a passing jet airplane to the fizz of soda in a glass — that must be excluded for the definition to be precise and useful. Dictionary entries often follow the class-differentiation pattern of the formal definition.

A *synonymous definition* explains a word by pairing it with another word of similar but perhaps more limited meaning.

> Music is melody.

Synonymous definition is almost never as precise as formal definition because few words share exactly the same meaning. But particularly when the word being defined is reasonably familiar and somewhat broad, a well-chosen synonym can provide readers with a surer sense of its meaning in context.

A *negative definition* explains a word by saying what it does not mean.

> Music is not silence, and it is not noise.

Such a definition must obviously be incomplete: There are sounds that are neither silence nor noise and yet are not music — quiet conversation, for example. But specifying what something is not often helps to clarify other statements about what it is.

An *etymological definition* also seldom stands alone, but by tracing a word's origins it helps readers understand its meaning. *Etymology* itself is defined as the study of the history of a linguistic form — the history of words.

> Music is descended from the Greek word *mousikē,* meaning literally "the art of the Muse."

The Muses, according to Greek mythology, were deities and the sources of inspiration in the arts. Thus the etymology suggests why we think of music as an art and as the product of inspiration. Etymological definitions often reveal surprising sources that suggest new ways of looking at ideas or objects.

A *stipulative definition* is a definition invented by a writer to convey a special or unexpected sense of an existing and often familiar word.

> Music is a language, but a language of the intangible, a kind of soul-language.
>
> — Edward MacDowell

> Music is the arithmetic of sounds.
>
> — Claude Debussy

Although these two examples seem to disagree with each other, and perhaps also with your idea of what music is, note that neither is arbitrary. (That is, neither assigns to the word *music* a completely foreign meaning, as Humpty Dumpty did in *Through the Looking-Glass* when he defined *glory* as "a nice knock-down argument.") The stipulative definitions by MacDowell and Debussy help explain each composer's conception of the subject and can lead, of course, to further elaboration. Stipulative definitions almost always provide the basis for a more complex discussion. These definitions are often the subjects of an extended definition.

Sometimes a word, or the idea it stands for, requires more than a sentence of explanation. Such a longer definition — called, naturally enough, *extended definition* — may go on for a paragraph, a page, an essay, or even an entire book. It may employ any of the techniques already mentioned in this chapter, as well as the various strategies discussed throughout the text. An extended definition tends to differ greatly from a formal definition; writers use extended definition to make a specific, and often unusual, point about an idea. An extended definition of music might provide *examples,* ranging from African drumming to a Bach fugue to a Bruce Springsteen song, to develop a fuller and more vivid sense of what music is. A writer might *describe* music in detail by showing its characteristic features, or explain the *process* of composing music, or *compare and contrast* music with language (according to MacDowell's stipulative definition) or arithmetic (according to Debussy's). Each of these strategies, and others too, helps make the meaning of a writer's words and ideas clear.

Robert Keith Miller primarily used an extended definition to explain his understanding of the word *discrimination.* What other types did you find in his article? Let's go through the essay again to see the various definitions that he used. To begin with, Miller used a very brief formal definition of *discrimination* [term]: "the ability [class] to tell differences" [differentiation]. He then offered a negative definition (discrimination is not racism) and a synonymous definition (discrimination is discernment). Next he cited the entry in a great historical dictionary of English to support his claim, and he quoted an example to illustrate his definition. He concluded by contrasting the word *discrimination* with the compound "discriminate against." Each of these techniques helped make the case that the most precise meaning of discrimination is in direct opposition to its common usage today.

For an analysis of another extended definition, consult the discussion of Laurence Perrine's "Paradox" in Chapter 1 (p. 6).

WHY DO WRITERS USE DEFINITION?

Since most readers have dictionaries, it might seem that writers would hardly ever have to define their terms with formal definitions. In fact, writers don't necessarily do so all the time, even when using an un-usual word like *tergiversation,* which few readers have in their active vocabularies; if readers don't know it, the reasoning goes, let them look it up. But there are times when a definition is quite necessary. One of these times is when a writer uses a word so specialized or so new that it simply won't be in dictionaries; another is when a writer must use a number of unfamiliar technical terms within only a few sentences. Also, when a word has several different meanings or may mean different things to different people, writers will often state ex-actly the sense in which they are using the word. In each of these cases, definition serves the purpose of achieving clarity.

But writers also sometimes use definition, particularly extended definition, to explain the essential nature of the things and ideas they write about. For example, consider E. B. White's definition of *democracy,* which first appeared in *The New Yorker* on July 3, 1943.

> We received a letter from the Writers' War Board the other day asking for a statement on "The Meaning of Democracy." It presumably is our duty to comply with such a request, and it is certainly our pleasure.
>
> Surely the Board knows what democracy is. It is the line that forms on the right. It is the don't in don't shove. It is the hole in the stuffed shirt through which the sawdust slowly trickles; it is the dent in the high hat. Democracy is the recurrent suspicion that more than half of the people are right more than half of the time. It is the feeling of privacy in the voting booths, the feeling of com-munion in the libraries, the feeling of vitality everywhere. Democracy is a letter to the editor. Democracy is the score at the begin-ning of the ninth. It is an idea which hasn't been disproved yet, a song the words of which have not gone bad. It's the mustard on the hot dog and the cream in the rationed coffee. Democracy is a re-quest from a War Board, in the middle of a morning in the middle of a war, wanting to know what democracy is.

Such writing goes beyond answering the question, "What does _____ mean exactly?" to tackle the much broader and deeper ques-tion "What is _____, and what does it represent?" In fact, every selec-tion in this chapter is written as an extended definition.

Although exploring a term and what it represents is often the pri-mary object of such a definition, sometimes writers go beyond giving a formal definition; they also use extended definitions to make persua-sive points. Take the Miller essay, for example (p. 447). The subject of Miller's extended definition is clearly the word *discrimination*. His pur-pose, however, is less immediately obvious. At first it appears that he wants only to explain what the word means. But by the third sentence he is distinguishing what it does not mean, and at the end it's clear he's trying to persuade readers to use the word correctly and thus to discriminate more sharply and more justly themselves. Ellen Goodman in "The Company Man" (p. 462) and Jo Goodwin Parker in "What Is Poverty?" (p. 467) later in this chapter also use extended definitions to make persuasive points.

AN ANNOTATED STUDENT ESSAY USING DEFINITION

Originally a native of New York City, Howard Solomon studied in France as part of the American Field Services Intercultural Program in high school, and he majored in French at the University of Vermont. Solomon's other interests include foreign affairs, languages, photography, and cycling; in his wildest dreams, he imagines becoming an international lawyer. For the following essay, Solomon began by interviewing students in his dormitory, collecting information and opinions that he eventually brought together with his own experiences to develop a definition of *best friends*.

Best Friends

Howard Solomon Jr.

Introduction: brief definition of best friend

Best friends, even when they are not a part of our day-to-day lives, are essential to our well-being. They supply the companionship, help, security, and love that we all need. It is not easy to put into words exactly what a best friend is, because the matter is so personal. From time to time, however, we may think about our best friends -- who they are, what characteristics they share, and why they are so important to us -- in order to gain a better understanding of ourselves and our relationships.

Purpose: In defining best friend, writer comes to new understanding of self and relationships.

Organization: Writer uses sequence of interview questions for structure.

I recently asked several people for their opinions on the subject, beginning with the qualities they valued in their own best friends. They all agreed on three traits: reciprocity, honesty, and love. Reciprocity means that one can always rely on a best friend in times of need. A favor

1

2

Three-part answer to question 1: What qualities do you value in a best friend?

doesn't necessarily have to be returned; but best friends will return it anyway, because they want to. Best friends are willing to help each other for the sake of helping and not just for personal gain. One woman said that life seemed more secure because she knew her best friend was there if she ever needed help.

Honesty in a best friendship is the   3
sharing of feelings openly and without re-
serve. The people I interviewed said they
could rely on their best friends as confi-
dants: They could share problems with their
best friends and ask for advice. They also
felt that, even if best friends were critical of each other, they would never be hurt-
ful or spiteful.

Love is probably the most important   4
quality of a best friend relationship, ac-
cording to the people I interviewed. They
very much prized the affection and enjoyment
they felt in the company of their best
friends. One man described it as a "gut reaction," and all said it was a different
feeling from being with other friends. Private jokes, looks, and gestures create personal communication between best friends
that is at a very high level -- many times
one person knows what the other is thinking
without anything being said. The specifics
differ, but almost everyone I talked to
agreed that a special feeling exists, which
is best described as love.

Answers to question 2: Who can be a best friend?

I next asked who could be a best friend   5
and who could not. My sources all felt it
was impossible for parents, other relatives,
and people of the opposite sex (especially
husbands or wives) to be best friends. One
woman said such people were "too inhibi-
tive." Personally, I disagree -- I have two
best friends who are women. However, I may
be an exception, and most best friends may

fit the above requirements. There could be a good reason for this, too: Most of the people I interviewed felt that their best friends were not demanding, while relatives and partners of the opposite sex can be very demanding.

Answers to question 3: How many best friends can a person have?

To the question of how many best friends one can have, some in my sample responded that it is possible to have several best friends, although very few people can do so; others said it was possible to have only a very few best friends; and still others felt they could have just one -- that single friend who is most outstanding. It was interesting to see how ideas varied on this question. Although best friends may be no less special for one person than another, people do define the concept differently.

6

Answers to question 4: How long does it take to become a best friend?

Regarding how long it takes to become best friends and how long the relationship lasts, all were in agreement. "It is a long hard process which takes a lot of time," one woman explained. "It isn't something that can happen overnight," suggested another. One man said, "You usually know the person very well before you consider him your best friend. In fact you know everything about him, his bad points as well as his good points, so there is little likelihood that you can come into conflict with him." In addition, everyone thought that once a person has become a best friend, he or she remains so for the rest of one's life.

7

Difference in responses from men and women

During the course of the interviews I discovered one important and unexpected difference between men and women regarding the qualities of their best friends. The men all said that a best friend usually possessed one quality that stood out above all others -- an easygoing manner or humor or

8

sympathy, for example. One of them told me that he looked not for loyalty but for honesty, for someone who was truthful, because it was so rare to find this quality in anyone. The women I surveyed, however, all responded that they looked for a well-rounded person who had many good qualities. One said that a person who had just one good quality and not several would be "too boring to associate with." Does this difference hold true beyond my sample? If so, it means that men and women have quite different definitions of their best friends.

Personal example: what the writer learned about best friends at the time of his father's death

    I have always wondered why my own best friends were so important to me; but it wasn't until recently that something happened to make me really understand my relationship with my best friends. My father died, and this was a crisis for me. Most of my friends gave me their condolences. But my best friends did more than that: they actually supported me. They called long distance to see how I was and what I needed, to try and help me work out my problems or simply to talk. Two of my best friends even took time from their spring break and, along with two other best friends, attended my father's memorial service; none of my other friends came. Since then, these are the only people who have continued to worry about me and talk to me about my father. I know that whenever I need someone they will be there and willing to help me. I know also that whenever they need help I will be ready to do the same for them.

9

Conclusion: personal definition of best friend

    Yet, I don't value my best friends so much just for what they do for me. I simply enjoy their company more than anyone else's. We talk, joke, play sports, and do all kinds of things when we are together. I never feel ill at ease, even after we've been apart for

10

Thesis a while. However, the most important thing
for me about best friends is the knowledge
that I am never alone, that there are others
in the world who care about my well-being as
much as I do about theirs. Surely this is a
comforting feeling for everyone.

Analyzing Howard Solomon Jr.'s Essay of Definition: Questions for Discussion

1. How does Solomon define *best friend* in his opening paragraph?
2. According to the people Solomon surveyed, what three qualities are valued most in a best friend?
3. Which of these qualities is considered the most important? Why?
4. How do men's and women's definitions of a best friend differ? Do you agree with Solomon's informants?
5. In what ways do Solomon's interviews enhance his own definition of best friend?
6. In the final analysis, why does Solomon think people value their best friends so much?

SUGGESTIONS FOR WRITING A DEFINITION ESSAY

Whatever your subject, make sure you have a clear sense of your purpose. Why are you writing a definition? If it's only to explain what a word or phrase means, you'll probably run out of things to say in a few sentences, or you'll find that a good dictionary has already said them for you. An effective extended definition should attempt to explain the essential nature of a thing or an idea, whether it be *photosynthesis* or *spring fever* or *Republicanism* or *prison* or *common sense*.

Often the challenge of writing a paper using the rhetorical strategy of definition is in getting your audience to understand your particular perception of the term or idea you are trying to define and explain. Take, for example, the selection on page 457 from a student essay. For many years, the citizens of Quebec, one of Canada's ten provinces, have been debating and voting on the issue of secession from Canada. At the core of this volatile issue is the essential question of Canadian identity. As you will see from the student's introduction, the Quebecois define themselves very differently from other Canadians.

Quebecois Are Canadians

The peaceful formation of Canada as an independent
nation has led to the current identity crisis in Quebec.
The Quebecois perceive themselves to be different from all
other Canadians because of their French ancestry and their
unique history as both rulers and minorities in Canada. In
an attempt to create a unified Canada the government has
tried to establish a common Canadian culture through the
building of a transcontinental railroad, a nationalized
medical system, a national arts program, a national
agenda, and the required use of both French and English in
all publications and on all signs. As the twenty-first century begins, however, Canadians, especially the Quebecois,
continue to grapple with the issue of what it means to be a
Canadian, and unless some consensus can be reached on the
definition of the Canadian identity, Quebec's attempt to
secede from Canada may succeed.

The essay introduction establishes the need to define the terms
Canadians and *Quebecois*. Implicit in any discussion of the meanings
for these two terms is another rhetorical strategy: comparison and
contrast. The writer might go on to use other strategies, such as description or illustration, to highlight common characteristics or differences of the Canadians and Quebecois. Judging from the title, it is
clear that an argument (see Chapter 13) will be made that, based on
the definitions, Quebecois are Canadians.

When you decide on your topic, consider an idea or term that you
would like to clarify or explain to someone. For example, Howard
Solomon hit on the idea of defining what a best friend is. He recalls
that "a friend of mine had become a best friend, and I was trying to
figure out what had happened, what was different. So I decided to explore what was on my mind." At the beginning, you should have at
least a general idea of what your subject means to you, as well as a
sense of the audience you are writing your definition for and the impact you want your definition to achieve. The following advice will
guide you as you plan and draft your essay.

Choose a Sufficiently Broad Subject

Certain subjects, like Republicanism and discrimination, lend themselves to different interpretations, depending on the writer's point of
view. While readers may agree in general about what such subjects

mean, there will be much disagreement over particulars and therefore room for you to propose and defend your own definitions. Photosynthesis, on the other hand, is a specific natural process, so all definitions of it must agree very closely on particulars, even though your delivery of the definition may be quite original. For example, even though you are conveying factual information, you could present your definition of *photosynthesis* from the point of view of a plant or tree or in question-and-answer format. In defining a specific subject like photosynthesis, your preparation will include some reading and note taking to make sure that you've got your facts right. If your subject is more general or subjective, there may be fewer facts to look for, but it is still wise to take your readers' views into account, and possibly the views of other writers on the subject — not necessarily to change your own definition, but to present it more effectively to your audience.

Howard Solomon remembers the difficulties he had getting started with his essay on best friends. "The first draft I wrote was nothing. I tried to get a start with the dictionary definition, but it didn't help — it just put into two words what really needs hundreds of words to explain, and the words it used had to be defined, too. My teacher suggested I might get going better if I talked about my topic with other people. I decided to make it semiformal, so I made up a list of a few specific questions — five questions — and went to about a dozen people I knew and asked them. Questions like, 'What qualities do your best friends have?' and 'What are some of the things they've done for you?' And I took notes on the answers. I was surprised when so many of them agreed. It isn't a scientific sampling, but the results helped me get started."

Formulate a Thesis Statement

A strong, clear thesis statement is critical in any essay. When writing an essay using extended definition, you should formulate a thesis statement that states clearly both the word or idea that you want to define or explain and the way in which you are going to present your thoughts. Here are two examples from this chapter.

- "We have a word in English which means 'the ability to tell differences.' That word is *discrimination*. But within the last twenty years, this word has been so frequently misused that an entire generation has grown up believing that 'discrimination' means 'racism.'" Robert Keith Miller's thesis statement tells us that he will be discussing the word *discrimination* and how it is not the same as racism.

- "As the twenty-first century begins, however, Canadians, especially the Quebecois, continue to grapple with the issue of what it means to be a Canadian, and unless some consensus can be reached on the definition of the Canadian identity, Quebec's attempt to secede from Canada may succeed." Here, the writer makes it clear that the identity of both the Canadians and the Quebecois will be defined. This thesis statement also conveys a sense of the urgency of discussing these definitions.

As you begin to develop your thesis statement, ask yourself, "What is my point?" Next ask yourself, "What types of definitions will be most useful in making my point?" If you can't answer these questions yet, write some ideas down and try to determine your main point from these ideas.

Once you have settled on an idea, go back to the two questions above and write down your answers to them. Then combine the answers into a single-sentence thesis statement. Your eventual thesis statement does not have to be one sentence, but this exercise can be an effective way of focusing your point.

Consider Your Audience

What do your readers know? If you're an economics major in an undergraduate writing course, you can safely assume that you know your subject better than most of your readers do, and so you will have to explain even very basic terms and ideas. If, however, you're writing a paper for your course in econometrics, your most important reader — the one who grades your paper — won't even slow down at your references to *monetary aggregates* and *Philips Curves* — provided, of course, that you obviously know what they mean.

Choose a Technique of Definition

How you choose to develop your definition depends on your subject, your purpose, and your readers. Many inexperienced writers believe that any extended definition, no matter what the subject, should begin with a formal "dictionary" definition or should at least introduce one before the essay has proceeded very far. This is not necessarily so; you will find that most of the essays in this chapter include no such formal definition. Assume that your readers have dictionaries and know how to use them. If, however, you think your readers do require a short, formal definition at some point, don't simply quote from a dictionary. Unless you have some very good reason for doing otherwise, put the definition into your own words — words that suit your approach and the probable readers of your essay. (Certainly, in an essay about photosynthesis, nonscientists would be baffled by an opening such as this: "The dictionary defines *photosynthesis* as 'the process by which chlorophyll-containing cells in green plants convert incident light to chemical energy and synthesize organic compounds from inorganic compounds, especially carbohydrates from carbon dioxide and water, with the simultaneous release of oxygen.'") There's another advantage to using your own words: You won't have to write "The dictionary defines..." or "According to *Webster's*..."; stock phrases like these almost immediately put the reader's mind to sleep.

Develop Your Organizational Plan

Once you have gathered all the information that you will need for your essay of extended definition, you will want to settle on an organizational plan that suits your purpose and your materials. If you want to show that one definition of *family* is better than others, for example, you might want to lead with the definitions that you plan to discard and end with the one that you want your readers to accept.

Howard Solomon can trace several distinct stages that his paper went through before he settled on the plan of organizing his examples around the items on his interview questionnaire. "Doing this paper showed me that writing isn't all that easy. Boy, I went through so many copies — adding some things, taking out some things, reorganizing. At one point half the paper was a definition of friends, so I could contrast them with best friends. That wasn't necessary. Then the personal stuff came in late. In fact, my father died after I'd begun writing the paper, so that paragraph came in almost last of all. On the next-to-last draft everything was there, but it was put together in a sort of random way — not completely random, one idea would lead to the next and then the next — but there was a lot of circling around. My teacher pointed this out and suggested I outline what I'd written and work on the outline. So I tried it, and I saw what the problem was and what I had to do. It was just a matter of getting my examples into the right order, and finally everything clicked into place."

Use Other Rhetorical Strategies

Although definition can be used effectively as a separate rhetorical strategy, it is generally used alongside other writing strategies. Photosynthesis, for example, is a natural process, so one logical strategy for defining it would be *process analysis;* readers who know little about biology may better understand photosynthesis if you draw an *analogy* with the eating and breathing of human beings. Common sense is an abstract concept, so its meaning could certainly be *illustrated* with concrete *examples;* in addition, its special nature might emerge more sharply through *comparison and contrast* with other ways of thinking. To define a salt marsh, you might choose a typical marsh and *describe* it. To define economic inflation or a particular disease, you might discuss its *causes and effects.* Howard Solomon builds his essay of definition around the many examples he garnered from his interviews with other students and from his own personal experiences. Before you combine strategies, however, consider the purpose of your essay and the tone that you wish to adopt. Only two requirements limit your choice of rhetorical strategy: The strategy must be appropriate to your subject, and it must help you explain your subject's essential nature.

As you read the essays in this chapter, consider all of the writing strategies that the authors have used to support their definitions. How do you think these other strategies have added to or changed the style of the essay? Are there strategies that you might have added or taken out? What strategies, if any, do you think you might use to strengthen your definition essay?

▶ *Questions for Revision: Definition*

1. Have I selected a subject in which there is some controversy or at least a difference of opinion about the definitions of key words?
2. Is the purpose of my definition clearly stated?
3. Have I presented a clear thesis statement?
4. Have I considered my audience? Do I oversimplify material for knowledgeable people or complicate material for beginners?
5. Have I used the types of definitions (*formal definition, synonymous definition, negative definition, etymological definition, stipulative definition,* and *extended definition*) that are most useful in making my point?
6. Is my essay of definition easy to follow? That is, is there a clear organizational principle (chronological or logical, for example)?
7. Have I used other rhetorical strategies — such as illustration, comparison and contrast, and cause and effect analysis — as needed and appropriate to enhance my definition?
8. Does my conclusion stem logically from my thesis statement and purpose?

The Company Man

Ellen Goodman

Ellen Goodman was born in Boston in 1941. After graduating cum laude from Radcliffe College in 1963, she worked as a reporter and researcher for Newsweek. *In 1967, she began working at the* Boston Globe *and, since 1974, has been a full-time columnist. Her regular column, "At Large," is syndicated by the* Washington Post *Writer's Group and appears in nearly four hundred newspapers across the country. In addition, her writing has appeared in* McCall's, Harper's Bazaar, *and* Family Circle, *and her commentaries have been broadcast on radio and television. In 1979, Goodman published* Close to Home, *a collection of her columns; several other collections have appeared since then, including* At Large *(1981),* Keeping in Touch *(1985),* Making Sense *(1989), and* Value Judgments *(1993).*

In "The Company Man," taken from Close to Home, *Goodman defines the* workaholic *by offering a poignant case-in-point example.*

BEFORE YOU READ

Have you ever known a workaholic, someone who is overinvolved with his or her schooling or career? What are the defining personality traits of that person? If you don't know a workaholic, what does this word mean to you?

He worked himself to death, finally and precisely, at 3:00 A.M. Sunday morning.

The obituary didn't say that, of course. It said that he died of a coronary thrombosis — I think that was it — but everyone among his friends and acquaintances knew it instantly. He was a perfect Type A, a workaholic, a classic, they said to each other and shook their heads — and thought for five or ten minutes about the way they lived.

This man who worked himself to death finally and precisely at 3:00 A.M. Sunday morning — on his day off — was fifty-one years old and a vice-president. He was, however, one of six vice-presidents, and one of three who might conceivably — if the president died or retired soon enough — have moved to the top spot. Phil knew that.

He worked six days a week, five of them until eight or nine at night, during a time when his own company had begun the four-day week for everyone but the executives. He worked like the Important People. He had no outside "extracurricular interests," unless, of course, you think about a monthly golf game that way. To Phil, it was work. He always ate egg salad sandwiches at his desk. He was, of course, overweight, by 20 or 25 pounds. He thought it was okay, though, because he didn't smoke.

462

On Saturdays, Phil wore a sports jacket to the office instead of a suit, because it was the weekend.

He had a lot of people working for him, maybe sixty, and most of them liked him most of the time. Three of them will be seriously considered for his job. The obituary didn't mention that.

But it did list his "survivors" quite accurately. He is survived by his wife, Helen, forty-eight years old, a good woman of no particular marketable skills, who worked in an office before marrying and mothering. She had, according to her daughter, given up trying to compete with his work years ago, when the children were small. A company friend said, "I know how much you will miss him." And she answered, "I already have."

"Missing him all these years," she must have given up part of herself which had cared too much for the man. She would be "well taken care of."

His "dearly beloved" eldest of the "dearly beloved" children is a hard-working executive in a manufacturing firm down South. In the day and a half before the funeral, he went around the neighborhood researching his father, asking the neighbors what he was like. They were embarrassed.

His second child is a girl, who is twenty-four and newly married. She lives near her mother and they are close, but whenever she was alone with her father, in a car driving somewhere, they had nothing to say to each other.

The youngest is twenty, a boy, a high-school graduate who has spent the last couple of years, like a lot of his friends, doing enough odd jobs to stay in grass and food. He was the one who tried to grab at his father, and tried to mean enough to him to keep the man at home. He was his father's favorite. Over the last two years, Phil stayed up nights worrying about the boy.

The boy once said, "My father and I only board here."

At the funeral, the sixty-year-old company president told the forty-eight-year-old widow that the fifty-one-year-old deceased had meant much to the company and would be missed and would be hard to replace. The widow didn't look him in the eye. She was afraid he would read her bitterness and, after all, she would need him to straighten out the finances — the stock options and all that.

Phil was overweight and nervous and worked too hard. If he wasn't at the office, he was worried about it. Phil was a Type A, a heart-attack natural. You could have picked him out in a minute from a lineup.

So when he finally worked himself to death, at precisely 3:00 A.M. Sunday morning, no one was really surprised.

By 5:00 P.M. the afternoon of the funeral, the company president had begun, discreetly of course, with care and taste, to make inquiries about his replacement. One of three men. He asked around: "Who's been working the hardest?"

RESPONDING TO READING

It is clear why Goodman refers to Phil as a "company man." To what extent would you call Phil a "family man"? How do you think Phil's survivors would view him as a husband and a father? How do you think Phil's fellow workers viewed him as a family man?

QUESTIONING THE TEXT

1. In your own words, give a brief definition of *workaholic* based on the information that Goodman provides in this essay. What information, if any, has the author failed to provide? How does Goodman's workaholic compare to your Before You Read workaholic?

2. In paragraph 4, Goodman says that Phil "worked like the Important People." What does she mean? (Glossary: *Connotation/Denotation*)

3. Why did Phil's son go around the neighborhood researching his father? What is ironic about this? What significance do you see in the fact that Phil's son is "a hardworking executive in a manufacturing firm down South" (paragraph 9)? (Glossary: *Irony*)

4. In your own words, explain the meaning of paragraph 11. What did the youngest son mean to Phil?

5. Do you think Phil's problems were all his own? Does Goodman suggest that the "system" may, in part, also be responsible for Phil's untimely end? Explain.

UNDERSTANDING THE WRITER'S CRAFT

1. What is Goodman's purpose in this essay? Explain why Goodman's unemotional tone is especially fitting for her purpose. (Glossary: *Purpose; Tone*)

2. What significance do you see in the statement, "I think that was it" in describing Phil's cause of death (paragraph 2)? Why does Goodman bother to include this statement at all?

3. In paragraphs 1, 3, and 15, Goodman tells us the precise time of Phil's death. Why do you suppose this is an important fact for Goodman? Why does she repeat the information? What does the time of death tell the reader about Phil's life?

4. Comment on the effectiveness of Goodman's final paragraph, then on the last sentence. Why does Goodman shift the focus of the ending? In what ways is the ending ironic? (Glossary: *Beginnings/Endings*)

EXPLORING LANGUAGE

1. Why does the author place the phrase "dearly beloved" in quotation marks in paragraph 9?

2. How does Goodman use her diction to achieve an ironic or sarcastic tone in the essay? (Glossary: *Diction*)

3. Refer to your desk dictionary to determine the meanings of the following words as Goodman uses them in this selection: *obituary* (paragraph 2), *coronary thrombosis* (2), *workaholic* (2), *conceivably* (3), *marketable* (7), *deceased* (13), *discreetly* (16).

COMBINING RHETORICAL STRATEGIES

What dominant impression of the company man does Goodman create in this essay? (Glossary: *Dominant Impression*) Just how much do we know about this man named Phil? What details does Goodman use to describe him? In what ways does the description of the company man help to define Phil? (Glossary: *Description*)

WRITING SUGGESTIONS

1. **(Definition)** The procrastinator — the type of person who continually puts off responsibilities and jobs — is very different from the workaholic. Write an essay modeled on Goodman's that attempts to use an extended example to define this interesting personality type.

2. **(Other Strategies)** One issue that Goodman does not raise is how a person becomes a workaholic. Write an essay in which you speculate about some reasons for such an addiction. How might workaholism be avoided? Or should it be? You may want to do some library reading or interview a psychologist on his or her opinions on workaholism. (Glossary: *Cause and Effect Analysis*)

3. **(Research)** Construct a brief study of the work habits of people you know who work full time and have families; consider acquaintances or the parents of peers. Devise a brief questionnaire or interview questions suggested by Goodman's definition of Phil's workaholism. What conclusions can you draw about these working people? What are the implications of the patterns of the working habits that you discover? You might also want to do research in the library and possibly on the Internet on American working practices. Support your conclusions in a paper.

- **The U.S. Department of Labor's Bureau of Labor Statistics Web Site**
  <http://stats.bls.gov>

  This Web site offers information on American labor trends.

- **The Department of Labor Home Page**
  <http://www.dol.gov>

  This searchable site offers links to labor-related information.

- **The Current Population Survey**
  <http://www.bls.census.gov/cps/cpsmain.htm>

  Here you will find information from the Bureau of the Census, including estimates on employment, unemployment, earnings, and hours of work.

- **Work-Related Links**
  <http://www.directory.google.com/Top/Society/Work>

  The Google.com work directory offers many useful links.

What Is Poverty?

Jo Goodwin Parker

All we know about Jo Goodwin Parker is that when George Henderson, a professor at the University of Oklahoma, was preparing his 1971 book America's Other Children: Public Schools Outside Suburbia, *the following essay was mailed to him from West Virginia under Parker's name. Henderson included Parker's essay in his book, and according to him, the piece was an unpublished speech given in De Land, Florida, on December 27, 1965. Perhaps Parker is, as her essay says, one of the rural poor who eke out a difficult living just beyond view of America's middle-class majority; or perhaps she is a spokesperson for them, writing not from her own experience but from long and sympathetic observation. In either case, her definition of poverty is so detailed and forceful that it conveys, even to those who have never known it, the nature of poverty.*

BEFORE YOU READ

What does it mean to you to be poor? What do you see as some of the effects of poverty on people?

Y ou ask me what is poverty? Listen to me. Here I am, dirty, smelly, and with no "proper" underwear on and with the stench of my rotting teeth near you. I will tell you. Listen to me. Listen without pity. I cannot use your pity. Listen with understanding. Put yourself in my dirty, worn out, ill-fitting shoes, and hear me. 1

Poverty is getting up every morning from a dirt- and illness-stained mattress. The sheets have long since been used for diapers. Poverty is living in a smell that never leaves. This is a smell of urine, sour milk, and spoiling food sometimes joined with the strong smell of long-cooked onions. Onions are cheap. If you have smelled this smell, you did not know how it came. It is the smell of the outdoor privy. It is the smell of young children who cannot walk the long dark way in the night. It is the smell of the mattresses where years of "accidents" have happened. It is the smell of the milk which has gone sour because the refrigerator long has not worked, and it costs money to get it fixed. It is the smell of rotting garbage. I could bury it, but where is the shovel? Shovels cost money. 2

Poverty is being tired. I have always been tired. They told me at the hospital when the last baby came that I had chronic anemia caused from poor diet, a bad case of worms, and that I needed a corrective operation. I listened politely — the poor are always polite. The poor always listen. They don't say that there is no money for iron pills, or better food, or worm medicine. The idea of an operation is frightening and costs so much that, if I had dared, I would have 3 laughed. Who takes care of my children? Recovery from an operation takes a long time. I have three children. When I left them with "Granny" the last time I had a job, I came home to find the baby covered with fly specks, and a diaper that had not been changed since I left. When the dried diaper came off, bits of my baby's flesh came with it. My other child was playing with a sharp bit of broken glass, and my oldest was playing alone at the edge of a lake. I made twenty-two dollars a week, and a good nursery school costs twenty dollars a week for three children. I quit my job.

Poverty is dirt. You say in your clean clothes coming from your clean house, "Anybody can be clean." Let me explain about housekeeping with no money. For breakfast I give my children grits with no oleo or cornbread without eggs and oleo. This does not use up many dishes. What dishes there are, I wash in cold water and with no soap. Even the cheapest soap has to be saved for the baby's diapers. Look at my hands, so cracked and red. Once I saved for two months to buy a jar of Vaseline for my hands and the baby's diaper rash. When I had saved enough, I went to buy it and the price had gone up two cents. The baby and I suffered on. I have to decide every day if I can bear to put my cracked, sore hands into the cold water and strong soap. But you ask, why not hot water? Fuel costs money. If you have a wood fire it costs money. If you burn electricity, it costs money. Hot water is a luxury. I do not have luxuries. I know you will be surprised when I tell you how young I am. I look so much older. My back has been bent over the wash tubs for so long, I cannot remember when I ever did anything else. Every night I wash every stitch my school age child has on and just hope her clothes will be dry by morning.

Poverty is staying up all night on cold nights to watch the fire, knowing one spark on the newspaper covering the walls means your sleeping children die in flames. In summer poverty is watching gnats and flies devour your baby's tears when he cries. The screens are torn and you pay so little rent you know they will never be fixed. Poverty means insects in your food, in your nose, in your eyes, and crawling over you when you sleep. Poverty is hoping it never rains because diapers won't dry when it rains and soon you are using newspapers. Poverty is seeing your children forever with runny noses. Paper handkerchiefs cost money and all your rags you need for other things. Even more costly are antihistamines. Poverty is cooking without food and cleaning without soap.

Poverty is asking for help. Have you ever had to ask for help, knowing your children will suffer unless you get it? Think about asking for a loan from a relative, if this is the only way you can imagine asking for help. I will tell you how it feels. You find out where the office is that you are supposed to visit. You circle that block four or five times. Thinking of your children, you go in. Everyone is very busy. Finally, someone comes out and you tell her that you need help. That never is the person you need to see. You go see another person, and after spilling the whole shame of your poverty all over the desk between you, you find that this isn't the right office after all — you must repeat the whole process, and it never is any easier at the next place.

You have asked for help, and after all it has a cost. You are again told to wait. You are told why, but you don't really hear because of the red cloud of shame and the rising black cloud of despair. 7

Poverty is remembering. It is remembering quitting school in junior high because "nice" children had been so cruel about my clothes and my smell. The attendance officer came. My mother told him I was pregnant. I wasn't but she thought that I could get a job and help out. I had jobs off and on, but never long enough to learn anything. Mostly I remember being married. I was so young then. I am still young. For a time, we had all the things you have. There was a little house in another town, with hot water and everything. Then my husband lost his job. There was unemployment insurance for a while and what few jobs I could get. Soon, all our nice things were repossessed and we moved back here. I was pregnant then. This house didn't look so bad when we first moved in. Every week it gets worse. Nothing is ever fixed. We now had no money. There were a few odd jobs for my husband, but everything went for food then, as it does now. I don't know how we lived through three years and three babies, but we did. I'll tell you something, after the last baby I destroyed my marriage. It had been a good one, but could you keep on bringing children in this dirt? Did you ever think how much it costs for any kind of birth control? I knew my husband was leaving the day he left, but there were no good-byes between us. I hope he has been able to climb out of this mess somewhere. He never could hope with us to drag him down. 8

That's when I asked for help. When I got it, you know how much it was? It was, and is, seventy-eight dollars a month for the four of us; that is all I ever can get. Now you know why there is no soap, no needles and thread, no hot water, no aspirin, no worm medicine, no hand cream, no shampoo. None of these things forever and ever and ever. So that you can see clearly, I pay twenty dollars a month rent, and most of the rest goes for food. For grits and cornmeal, and rice and milk and beans. I try my best to use only the minimum electricity. If I use more, there is that much less for food. 9

Poverty is looking into a black future. Your children won't play with my boys. They will turn to other boys who steal to get what they want. I can already see them behind the bars of their prison instead of behind the bars of my poverty. Or they will turn to the freedom of alcohol or drugs, and find themselves enslaved. And my daughter? At best, there is for her a life like mine. 10

But you say to me, there are schools. Yes, there are schools. My children have no extra books, no magazines, no extra pencils, or crayons, or paper and the most important of all, they do not have health. They have 11 worms, they have infections, they have pinkeye all summer. They do not sleep well on the floor, or with me in my one bed. They do not suffer from hunger, my seventy-eight dollars keeps us alive, but they do suffer from malnutrition. Oh yes, I do remember what I was taught about health in school. It doesn't do much good. In some places there is a surplus commodities program. Not here. The county said it cost too much. There is a school lunch program. But I have two children who will already be damaged by the time they get to school.

But, you say to me, there are health clinics. Yes, there are health 12 clinics and they are in the towns. I live out here eight miles from town. I can walk that far (even if it is sixteen miles both ways), but can my little children? My neighbor will take me when he goes; but he expects to get paid, *one way or another*. I bet you know my neighbor. He is that large man who spends his time at the gas station, the barbershop, and the corner store complaining about the government spending money on the immoral mothers of illegitimate children.

Poverty is an acid that drips on pride until all pride is worn away. 13 Poverty is a chisel that chips on honor until honor is worn away. Some of you say that you would do *something* in my situation, and maybe you would, for the first week or the first month, but for year after year after year?

Even the poor can dream. A dream of a time when there is money. 14 Money for the right kinds of food, for worm medicine, for iron pills, for toothbrushes, for hand cream, for a hammer and nails and a bit of screening, for a shovel, for a bit of paint, for some sheeting, for needles and thread. Money to pay *in money* for a trip to town. And, oh, money for hot water and money for soap. A dream of when asking for help does not eat away the last bit of pride. When the office you visit is as nice as the offices of other governmental agencies, when there are enough workers to help you quickly, when workers do not quit in defeat and despair. When you have to tell your story to only one person, and that person can send you for other help and you don't have to prove your poverty over and over and over again.

I have come out of my despair to tell you this. Remember I did not 15 come from another place or another time. Others like me are all around you. Look at us with an angry heart, anger that will help you help me. Anger that will let you tell of me. The poor are always silent. Can you be silent too?

RESPONDING TO READING

Throughout the essay, Parker describes the feelings and emotions associated with her poverty. Have you ever witnessed or observed people in Parker's situation? What was your reaction?

QUESTIONING THE TEXT

1. Why didn't Parker have the operation that was recommended for her? Why did she quit her job?

2. In Parker's view, what makes asking for help such a difficult and painful experience? What compels her to do so anyway?

3. Why did Parker's husband leave her? How does she justify her attitude toward his leaving? (Glossary: *Attitude*)

4. In paragraph 12, Parker says the following about a neighbor giving her a ride to the nearest health clinic: "My neighbor will take me when he goes; but he expects to get paid, *one way or another*. I bet you know my neighbor." What is she implying in these sentences and in the rest of the paragraph?

5. What are the chances that the dreams described in paragraph 14 will come true? What do you think Parker would say?

UNDERSTANDING THE WRITER'S CRAFT

1. What is Parker's purpose in defining poverty as she does? (Glossary: *Purpose*) Why has she cast her essay in the form of an extended definition? What effect does this have on the reader?

2. What techniques of definition does Parker use? What is missing that you would expect to find in a more general and impersonal definition of poverty? Why does Parker leave such information out?

3. How would you characterize Parker's tone and her style? How do you respond to her use of the pronoun *you*? Point to specific examples of her diction and descriptions as support for your view. (Glossary: *Style; Tone*)

4. Parker repeats words and phrases throughout this essay. Choose several examples, and explain their impact on you. (Glossary: *Coherence*)

EXPLORING LANGUAGE

1. Although her essay is written for the most part in simple, straightforward language, Parker does make use of an occasional striking figure of speech. Identify at least three such figures — you might begin with those in paragraph 13 (for example, "Poverty is an acid") — and explain their effect on the reader. (Glossary: *Figures of Speech*)

2. In paragraph 10, Parker states that "poverty is looking into a black future." How does she use language to characterize her children's future?

3. Refer to your desk dictionary to determine the meanings of the following words as Parker uses them in this selection: *chronic* (paragraph 3), *anemia* (3), *grits* (4), *oleo* (4), *antihistamines* (5).

COMBINING RHETORICAL STRATEGIES

In depicting poverty, Parker uses description to create vivid verbal pictures, and she illustrates the various aspects of poverty with examples drawn from her experience. What are the most striking details she uses? How do you account for the emotional impact of the details and images she has selected? (Glossary: *Description; Exemplification*) In what ways do description and exemplification enhance her definition of poverty?

WRITING SUGGESTIONS

1. **(Definition)** Using Parker's essay as a model, write an extended definition of a topic about which you have some expertise. Choose as your subject a particular environment (suburbia, the inner city, a dormitory, a shared living area), a way of living (the child of divorce, the physically handicapped, the working student), or a topic of your own choosing. If you prefer, you can adopt a persona instead of writing from your own perspective.

2. **(Other Strategies)** Write a proposal or a plan of action that would make people aware of poverty or some other social problem in your community. What is the problem? What needs to be done to increase awareness? What practical steps would you propose be undertaken once the public is made aware of the situation?

3. **(Research)** Write an essay of your own defining poverty. In your library and possibly on the Internet, research and gather statistical data on the problem as it exists today in the United States or in your state or city. Another alternative is to focus exclusively on a particular family or neighborhood as a case study.

- **U.S. Department of Health and Human Services Home Page**
  <http://aspe.os.dhhs.gov/poverty/poverty.htm>

  This Web site offers information and statistics on poverty from the U.S. government.

- **Institute for Research on Poverty at the University of Wisconsin–Madison**
  <http://www.ssc.wisc.edu/irp>

  Here you will find information and links to other poverty-related Internet resources.

- **Future of Children Web Site**
  <http://www.futureofchildren.org/cap/index.htm>

  This page, maintained by the David and Lucile Packard Foundation, is devoted to the study of children living in poverty.

What's Natural about Our Natural Products?

Sarah Federman

Sarah Federman was born in New York City in 1976. She graduated from the University of Pennsylvania in 1998, where she majored in history. A strong interest in medicine led her to her current work at the Institute for Health and Healing at California Pacific Medical Center in San Francisco, where she researches alternative therapies for patients to complement their traditional medical treatments.

Federman's essay "What's Natural About Our Natural Products?" was first published in Language Awareness *(2000), an anthology of articles about contemporary language usage. She first became curious about the word* natural *as an undergraduate, when she defended its use as a meaningful word on food labels in a class debate. Since that time, Federman has had a change of heart. As she reports in her essay, the meaning of* natural *is elusive and extremely difficult to pin down.*

BEFORE YOU READ

Do you think "natural" products are better for you than other products? What natural products do you use? What do you think you're buying when you purchase a product with the word *natural* on its label? Are you willing to pay more for a natural product?

Whether you grab a bottle of Nature's Energy Supplements in the vitamin department or a box of Quaker 100% Natural Granola in the cereal aisle, you might find yourself with more hype than product. The use of the word "natural" often serves as more of a marketing ploy than a heartfelt attempt to convey something meaningful about a product or service. Variations of the words "nature" and "natural" are used as slogans and names for everything from blue jeans to toothpaste, and while they may be especially prevalent in San Francisco, the hype has spread everywhere. In a recent issue of *Delicious* magazine, for example, these words were used 85 times in the first 40 pages, with advertisements using them 8 times! Now pet owners can even skim through a copy of *Natural Dog* or *Natural Cat* while waiting at the vet.

Nowhere is the buzzword "natural" more prevalent than at the local grocery store where Fantastic Soups, Enrico's Pizza Sauce, Health Valley Cereals, and Celestial Seasonings tea, among others, brag unabashedly about the "naturalness" of their products. Before a psychology professor challenged my definition of "natural," I would throw Tom's Natural Toothpaste, Pop-Secret Natural Flavored Popcorn, and Grape-Nuts Natural Wheat and Barley Cereal into my shopping cart with the utmost confidence that these natural varieties prove far superior to their "unnatural" or "less natural" counterparts. Recently, I took a closer look at the labels of my revered products only to discover the widespread abuse of the word "natural."

But this is not news. More than a decade ago the Consumers Union   3
first sounded the alarm about "natural." The report alerted consumers to the fact that their beloved Quaker 100% Natural Cereal contained 24 percent sugar, not to mention the nine grams of fat which, according to the March 1999 *Nutrition Action Health Newsletter,* is the same as a small McDonald's hamburger. But despite the best efforts of the Union, nothing has changed. In fact, things have gotten worse, *especially* in the cereal aisle where 22 varieties, including Froot Loops, proclaim their commitment to "natural" ingredients. Berry Berry Kix, a brightly colored kids' cereal, promises "natural Fruit Flavors." While Berry Berry Kix contains some grape and strawberry juices, it also has sugar, partially hydrogenated oils, corn syrup, dicalcium and trisodium phosphates. That's it for the fruits, the rest is corn meal and starch.

The Consumer Union's report also explained how companies pur-   4
posely use "natural" as an "indeterminate modifier," rather than as an adjective to convey some meaningful information about their product. In other words, placing the word "natural" in a slogan or product description without having it refer to anything in particular. For example, most major U.S. supermarkets sell Kraft's Natural Shredded Non-Fat Cheese, Natural Reduced Fat Swiss, and Natural Cheese Cubes. But don't dare to ask, What does that mean? Kraft has done nothing special with the cheese itself; "natural" in this case presumably relates to the shredding, reducing, and cubing process. What is natural cubing?

To me, a "natural" product or service suggests any or all of the fol-   5
lowing: a healthy alternative, an environmentally friendly product, vegetarian, and/or produced without synthetic chemicals. Friends and family have also taken natural to mean wholesome, pure, low-fat, healthy, organic, and, simply, better. The meanings given in one popular dictionary, however, prove less specific: 1) determined by nature, 2) of or relating to nature, 3) having normal or usual character, 4) grown without human care, 5) not artificial, 6) present in or produced by nature. Interestingly, these definitions make no value judgments. There is nothing in the dictionary meaning to suggest, for instance, that a natural banana (one grown in the wild) is healthier than one raised by banana farmers. This positive spin we add ourselves.

Unlike using low-fat, organic, and vegetarian, food manufacturers   6
can use "natural" any way they choose. The Nutrition Labeling and Education Act of 1990 (NLEA) restricted the use of the following terms on food labels: low fat, low sodium, low cholesterol, low calorie, lean, extra lean, reduced, good source, less, fewer, light, and more. A calorie-free product, for example, must have fewer than 5 calories per serving, while a cholesterol-free product must have 2 milligrams or

less of cholesterol per serving. *Mother Earth News* reports that products labeled "organic" must align themselves with one of the 40 sets of organic standards, most often the California Organic Foods Act of 1990. This leaves "natural" as one of the few unregulated words.

Health-food companies and mainstream producers use the word to create an aura around the product. Actually, they use the word and "we" create the aura, allowing them to get away with higher prices or simply to take up more shelf space at the supermarket. For example, every month thousands of bags of Lays "Naturally Baked" Potato Chips travel through desert and farmland to enable us to "Ohh, ahh" and purchase these natural wonders. When first seeing this name, I had visions of organic farms and rugged, healthy farmers cultivating a much-loved product. Unfortunately, a closer look at the label served to shatter rather than support my countryside fantasy. While the ingredients reveal less fat per serving than the standard chip (1.5 grams versus 9 grams), I found nothing that explained the meaning of "naturally baked." Do you think this means they leave the chips out in the sun to crispen up? Probably not, so why does this natural process cost more per ounce (5.5 ounces for $1.99 versus 7.5 ounces) when it uses less fat?

Motts and Delmonte use "natural" to promote a new line without knocking their standard product. Motts applesauce has three products on the shelf of my local San Francisco market — "Apple Sauce," "Natural Apple Sauce," and "Chunky Apple Sauce." A comparison of the labels reveals that the "natural" version has no corn syrup added. Now, if they just wrote "no corn syrup added" on the label, we consumers would immediately become aware that there is, indeed, sweetener added to their standard version. Delmonte Fruit Cocktail has a two-product line-up with "Fruit Naturals" right next to "Fruit Cocktail." The natural variety costs 6 cents more and actually has *fewer* ingredients, presumably requiring less manufacturing. The natural version has no sugar and preservatives; the standard version has added corn syrup and sugar.

Fantastic, maker of dried soups and instant mixes, uses "natural" to connote something about the food and the type of person who may buy it. Under the heading Instant Black Beans, Fantastic writes "All Natural. Vegetarian." A vegetarian product, we know, means without meat. But what does "all natural" mean? Adding this phrase right before Vegetarian suggested to me that this product should appeal to vegetarians and self-proclaimed naturals. Mildly health-conscious people surely would prefer to ally themselves with natural rather than unnatural foods. Whether or not this product serves as a healthy alternative to other brands is irrelevant because the point is that Fantastic could sell you artery-clogging lard and still use the word.

Next to vitamins, bottled beverages probably use the word more than any other product. Every Snapple bottle promises an "all natural" treat, although the most natural iced tea is quite simply brewed tea with ice. In Snapple's case, you end up paying more for tasty sugar water, but with Hansen's Natural soda you are outright deceived. Hansen's soda has exactly the same ingredients as Sprite and 7-Up minus the sodium citrate. Blue Sky Natural Soda has fructose sweetener, caramel color, and something called tartaric acid. Doesn't Blue Sky Natural Soda sound refreshing? Too bad your intestines can't distinguish it from Coca-Cola.

At least we have natural bottled water as an alternative. Or do we? 11 The Natural Resources Defense Council, a national environmental group, found dangerous amounts of arsenic in Crystal Geyser's "Natural" Spring water. A four-year study revealed that one-third of the 103 bottled waters tested contained contaminants beyond safe federal limits. Odwalla "Natural" Spring Water, another popular beverage company, especially among health-food lovers, had high bacteria counts in a number of bottles. Hey, bacteria are natural so what's the problem? The problem is that natural or not, some bacteria make us sick. So it seems you cannot win with beverages. "Natural" serves as a meaningless label, a deceptive marketing tool, or means "contains natural critters and natural toxins that may make you sick." Best to just purchase a "Pur" (pronounced "pure") water filter; just don't ask what they mean by pure.

Some products come closer to meeting my expectations. The Hain 12 Food Group, a "natural-food producer" whose projected 1999 annual sales are $300 million, manufactures soup called "Healthy Naturals." Although the split peas are not certified organic, Hain uses no preservatives or MSG. The ingredients are listed as water, split green peas, carrots, celery, onion powder, and spices. This product lives up to my notion of natural. But even Hain veers from their presumed commitment to health food. The 14 product "Hain Kidz" line, introduced early in 1999, includes marshmallow crisp cereal and snack bars, gummybear-like candy, and animal cookies. It appears that as major brands (Kraft, Motts, Quaker) increasingly tout their new-found "naturalness," health-food companies such as Hain have started going toward more "unnatural" products.

So as the line between specialty health-food company and stan- 13 dard food producer becomes more elusive, I begin to wonder why the extra cost? Why do plain peas and carrots cost *more* than highly refined and processed soups? And how did we get to a point where we need a special label to tell us that the product is what it says it is? Before I infuse one more dollar into this industry, I will assuredly read the list of ingredients more carefully and do some research at <http://www.naturalinvestor.com>.

RESPONDING TO READING

According to Federman, what is the literal meaning of the word *natural?* Do you agree with her definition, or would you define *natural* differently? Explain.

QUESTIONING THE TEXT

1. What restrictions does the Nutrition Labeling and Education Act of 1990 place on what manufacturers can say on food labels? How is the word *organic* regulated? What restrictions, if any, are imposed on the use of the term *natural?*

2. According to Federman, what are the two main reasons that companies use the word *natural?* What does she mean when she says that companies "use the word and 'we' create the aura" (paragraph 7)?

3. What point does Federman make by discussing Kraft's Natural Shredded Non-Fat Cheese and Lays "Naturally Baked" Potato Chips? Discuss other products whose labels use the words *natural* or *naturally* in an unclear or ambiguous manner.

4. Why do you suppose that manufacturers charge more for their "natural" products when, in fact, these products may cost less to produce?

UNDERSTANDING THE WRITER'S CRAFT

1. What is Federman's thesis? (Glossary: *Thesis*)

2. Federman carefully illustrates her points with a variety of examples of different food products from her local grocery store. (Glossary: *Examples*) These examples not only give her authority on her subject, but also serve to support her thesis. Which examples did you find most interesting and effective, and why?

3. What do you think Federman would like her readers to do as a result of reading her essay? What, in the essay itself, led you to this conclusion? (Glossary: *Audience; Purpose*)

4. Federman ends paragraph 7 with a rhetorical question. How does it function in the context of her essay? What other questions does Federman ask? Do these questions engage you to think about her subject and how it affects you?

EXPLORING LANGUAGE

1. What connotations does Federman claim customers bring to the word *natural?* (Glossary: *Connotation/Denotation*) What connotations does the word have for you?

2. Identify at least a dozen strong action verbs that Federman uses. What do these verbs add to her prose? Explain by discussing several specific verbs. What other verbs could she have used?

3. Refer to your desk dictionary to determine the meanings of the following words as Federman uses them in this selection: *ploy* (paragraph 1), *slogans* (1), *unabashedly* (2), *counterparts* (2), *aura* (7), *contaminants* (11), *tout* (12), *elusive* (13), *infuse* (13).

COMBINING RHETORICAL STRATEGIES

Federman points out that the Consumer Union first blew the whistle on the word *natural* by showing that manufacturers were using the word as "an 'indeterminate modifier,' rather than as an adjective to convey some meaningful information about the product" (paragraph 4). What exactly is an indeterminate modifier? Discuss how Federman uses examples to demonstrate the ways manufacturers render *natural* virtually meaningless while they play on consumers' positive associations with the word.

Michael Newman/PhotoEdit

WRITING SUGGESTIONS

1. **(Definition)** What, for you, are the connotations of the terms *Health Valley, organic, natural, fresher tasting,* and *stay fresh fruit pack,* which appear on the cereal boxes in the photograph above? Do you believe, as some have claimed, that these words are inherently deceptive? Write an essay in which you argue for or against the regulation of these words in advertising. Before starting to write, you may find it helpful to review your response to the Before You Read exercise for this selection.

2. **(Other Strategies)** Federman claims that "the word 'natural' has become more a marketing ploy than a way to communicate meaningful information about a product" (paragraph 2). Do you agree? What exactly are the economics of natural products? When consumers pay more for a natural product, are they in fact getting more? Spend some time at your local supermarket comparing the pricing and ingredients of natural products and their regular counterparts. Do price differences correlate with ingredient differences? Write an essay in which you present your conclusions about the pricing of natural products.

3. **(Research)** Using materials in your college library and on the Internet, research the Nutrition Labeling and Education Act of 1990 and food labeling in general. Why are people so concerned about the language used on our food labels? What issues did the NLEA solve? What food labeling issues still need to be addressed? Write an essay in which you summarize your findings and state your position on the importance of food labels for today's consumers.

- **The Food Label**
  <http://www.fda.gov/opacom/backgrounders/foodlabel/newlabel.html>

  This site, maintained by the Food and Drug Administration, features a full-text guide to reading and understanding the food labels mandated by the Nutrition Labeling and Education Act of 1990. The site also outlines the criteria food products must meet before certain health claims can be printed on their packaging.

- **What Do Food Labels Really Say?**
  <http://kidshealth.org/teen/nutrition/menu/food_labels.html>

  Here you will find a history of the food label and a guide to reading the new food labels. Among other information, this site includes links to nutrition-related sites and a checklist for comparing the nutritional value of snacks and other foods.

- **Mothers for Natural Law**
  <http://www.safe-food.org>

  Mothers for Natural Law is a public-interest group dedicated to the consumer's right to know about genetically engineered (GE) foods. This site explains what genetically engineered food is and outlines the argument against it. Links to like-minded organizations' Web sites, lists of non-GE foods, and guidelines for growing your own organic produce are also included.

- **Campaign to Label Genetically Engineered Foods**
  <http://www.thecampaign.org>

  The Campaign's mission is to lobby Congress and the president "to pass legislation that will require the labeling of genetically engineered foods in the United States." This site includes an online newsletter, a petition, and information on how you can become involved with the movement to label genetically engineered food.

Take Me Out to the Counterfactual Present Tense

David Carkeet

David Carkeet was born in Sonora, California, in 1946. He graduated from the University of California at Davis and earned graduate degrees at the University of Wisconsin and Indiana University. Currently, he is a professor of English at the University of Missouri in St. Louis, where he directs the M.F.A. program. Carkeet is the author of five novels for adults, including I Been There Before *(1985),* The Full Catastrophe *(1990), and* The Error of Our Ways *(1997). He has also written two novels for young adults,* The Silent Treatment *(1988) and* Quiver River *(1991). His short stories and essays have appeared in numerous literary magazines and periodicals, including* American Literature, *the* North American Review, *the* San Francisco Review of Books, New York Stories, *the* New York Times Magazine, *and the* Village Voice. *Carkeet received an Edgar nomination by the Mystery Writers of America in the first-novel category for* Double Negative *(1980), an O. Henry Award, and a National Endowment for the Arts Fellowship.*

In "Take Me Out to the Counterfactual Present Tense," an essay that first appeared in the New York Times Magazine *in July 2000, Carkeet examines a new use of the all-purpose English present tense that has sneaked into widespread usage in the sports world.*

BEFORE YOU READ

What were your thoughts after reading the title to this selection? Did you think of grammar? What memories, if any, did the title bring back for you? What do you think the counterfactual present tense is?

> For of all sad words of tongue or pen,
> The saddest are these: "It might have been!"
>
> — JOHN GREENLEAF WHITTIER

In sports, there is a great deal of talk about what might have been. 1
Players point to if-then turning points: "If the ball had cleared the fence, we would have won." But they don't always say it like that. Sometimes they say it this way: "If the ball clears the fence, we win."

Let me hasten to point out that the moment in question is over. 2
The events that happened — and did not happen — are in the past. The ball did not clear the fence; "we" did not win. Although the speaker is describing a *past* incident that did not come about (a counterfactual), the speaker is using the *present* tense to narrate the non-event.

The construction is common in sports and goes back at least as far   3
as a 1984 *San Diego Union-Tribune* story, in which a losing ballplayer
recalls a bases-loaded, shoe-top catch by the Chicago Cubs outfielder
Keith Moreland: "To me, that was the turning point. If that ball gets
by Moreland, we've got three runs and we're back in the game." Note
the shift from the first sentence, an ordinary assertion about the past
("that was the turning point"), to the second sentence, where the
present tense undoes a past-time fact.

Baseball pitchers live regret-filled lives, and their postgame com-   4
ments provide many examples. The San Francisco Giants pitcher Robb
Nen rues an August 1998 homer that he gave up: "I left the ball over
the middle, and he did what he wanted to do with it. If I get it a little
inside or a little outside, maybe he gets a hit, but probably not a home
run." The St. Louis Cardinal Rick Croushore laments his failure to field
a ball cleanly in a game against the Arizona Diamondbacks: "If I make
that play, maybe it's a different game." Another Cardinal pitcher,
Lance Painter, bemoans an umpire's call that proved decisive in a loss
to the Cubs: "But if that call goes our way, it's a 1-1 game going into
the fifth."

To a historian of the language, the emergence of a new meaning   5
for an old tense is an earth-shaking event, and yet the counterfactual
present tense has sneaked into usage without notice. It is to be found
in many sports; I have culled examples from football, basketball, soccer and golf. Tiger Woods used it wistfully about his fifth-place finish
in the Masters: "If those putts go in at 10 and 11. . . ." But it occurs
most often in baseball, a game that habitually offers from its hum-
drum rhythm a pivotal moment for our contemplation, a crisis in
which a single player stands alone as hero or goat. It is this characteristic that breeds the old what-might-have-been.

How the new construction came about is not at all obvious. Lin-   6
guistic change usually involves a gradual mechanism. "Smug" used to
mean "neat," but it took on negative meaning by virtue of a slow
shift, year by year, from a preponderance of positive uses to a preponderance of negative ones until the scale finally tipped. But it is hard to
imagine a comparable step-wise process that takes us gradually from
(a) to (b) below, from the conventional past-perfect expression for a
past event that did not happen to the new present-tense way of saying
it: (a) "If the ball had cleared the fence, we would have won"; (b) "If
the ball clears the fence, we win."

Of course, (b) has existed all along with a different meaning — to   7
express a future possibility. Even today, although it would be decidedly uncool, an eager rookie could shout (b) from the dugout in the
bottom of the ninth inning, while the ball is in flight and its destination is yet to be determined. Note the time reference — the rookie is
looking ahead, into the future, yet he is using the present tense.

Therein lies the probable explanation for the form of the construction. The English present is an all-purpose tense, used for definitions ("a triangle has three sides"), general facts ("the towhee sings 'drink-your-tea'"), recurring actions ("I fish in Vermont"), future possibilities (our eager rookie's shout) and even, in the historical present, past facts ("At this point, Hermann the German annihilates the Roman legions"). The hard-working present tense has taken on one more job, a blend of the last two functions above, now referring to a past possibility that was not realized.

The sports counterfactual is an oral, short, peppery construction that feels inappropriate to the analysis of complex events. Try this, for example: "If the Californian responds to the Titanic's distress signals, not a soul is lost." Or this: "If Nixon shaves before the debate, there is no Camelot." These retrospective sentences are offensively glib. They sound like something John Madden would cry out from the broadcast booth, waving his arms as he rewrites the historical record.   8

Thus, for negative reasons, the sports counterfactual, unlike a smash by Sosa or McGwire, will probably never leave the ballpark. But there is a positive sense in which the new construction suits the world of athletics. To play sports is to fail, sometimes agonizingly, and declaring that the outcome could have been different gives one solace. Using the present tense to express this alternative — that is, using the same tense you would use if you were really looking ahead at an outcome still to be determined — casts these events into a land of perpetual potential. "If the ball clears the fence, we win." The ax has not yet fallen; the opposing players' fists are not yet raised in celebration. The thwarted outcome, preserved in an eternal present, exists robustly in the imagination of those who live and die by the vicissitudes of the game.   9

RESPONDING TO READING

Why do you suppose Carkeet starts his essay with an epigraph from John Greenleaf Whittier? In what ways does it relate to the point of his article? Did you find it appropriate and effective? Explain.

QUESTIONING THE TEXT

1. According to Carkeet, what is the counterfactual present tense? How does it differ from the present tense used to express a future possibility? Why is this grammatical construction of interest to the language historian?

2. What is it about the sports world, baseball in particular, that seems to invite the use of the counterfactual present tense? In Carkeet's view,

what positive contribution does this new construction have on the world of athletics?

3. Why does Carkeet think that the counterfactual present tense will be limited to sports talk? On what grounds does he feel that its usage with complex national or international events is inappropriate? Do you agree with his assessment?

4. What does Carkeet mean when he says, "The English present is an all-purpose tense" (paragraph 7)?

UNDERSTANDING THE WRITER'S CRAFT

1. What is Carkeet's purpose in writing this essay? (Glossary: *Purpose*) How does he establish his authority for writing on this subject?

2. In paragraph 6, Carkeet tells us of the transformation that the word *smug* has undergone. Why do you suppose he thought he needed to describe this linguistic change in order to explain how the counterfactual present tense came about?

3. What devices does Carkeet use to make his transitions from one paragraph to the next? (Glossary: *Transitions*) Which of his transitions work particularly for you? Why?

EXPLORING LANGUAGE

1. Carkeet's subject in this essay is a linguistic phenomenon that occurs in the sports world. In what ways does his diction show his interest in both language study and sports, especially baseball? Did his vocabulary ever get too technical for you, or did you find it appropriate given his subject and audience? (Glossary: *Technical Language*)

2. Refer to your desk dictionary to determine the meanings of the following words as Carkeet uses them in this selection: *construction* (paragraph 3), *assertion* (3), *rues* (4), *laments* (4), *culled* (5), *wistfully* (5), *preponderance* (6), *peppery* (8), *retrospective* (8), *glib* (8), *solace* (9), *thwarted* (9), *vicissitudes* (9).

COMBINING RHETORICAL STRATEGIES

How does Carkeet use exemplification to develop his definition of the counterfactual present tense? Point to instances where he uses comparison and contrast to sharpen or clarify examples.

WRITING SUGGESTIONS

1. **(Definition)** Think for a while about the slang of students at school. Is the language of high school students different from that of college students? How does their language allow students to distance themselves from their teachers or parents? In an essay, identify some current buzzwords or catchphrases that you and other students use, explain what each means, and speculate how each word or phrase evolved.

2. **(Other Strategies)** The sports world is filled with terminology that often mystifies people who don't follow sports. Select a sport that you know something about, and list current jargon used by participants and spectators of that game. Write an essay in which you define the words you have chosen, and explain why you think players and fans like to use such language.

3. **(Research)** Although we are not aware of linguistic change on a day-to-day or even a year-to-year basis, language does change. Some words become obsolete, and new ones are coined or enter English from other languages. Pronunciation changes, and even grammatical constructions like the counterfactual present tense, come into being. During its relatively brief four-hundred-year history, American English has consistently been characterized by change. Can you identify any ways in which American English is changing today? After doing some research in your college library or on the Internet, write an essay about the effects a particular event or thing has had on American English. Possibilities include the disputed 2000 presidential election, the NASA space program, global warming and other climatic changes, the drug culture, professional sports, computers and other new technologies, the women's movement, the global economy, and recent waves of immigration.

- **Mencken's American Language**
  <http://www.bartleby.com/185>

  Here you will find the full text of H. L. Mencken's book *The American Language: An Inquiry into the Development of English in the United States.* This site is also a wonderful source of reference material and other on-line texts in the public domain.

- **American Dialect Society**
  <http://www.americandialect.org>

  The American Dialect Society is "dedicated to the study of the English language in North America." This site features downloadable versions of the society's newsletters, links to resources on new words and usages, information on the history of the English language, and an insightful list of the best new words for each year of the twentieth century.

- **New Words in English**
  <http://www.owlnet.rice.edu/~ling215/NewWords/index.html>

  This site, maintained by the Linguistics Department at Rice University, features a searchable index of new words in the American English language. This site also features links to similar resources on the Internet.

- **The Word Spy**
  <http://www.logophilia.com/WordSpy>

  Word Spy is "devoted to recently coined words, existing words that have enjoyed a recent renaissance, and older words that are now being used in new ways." This site features a searchable index of links to other new-word sites.

Ain't I a Woman?

Sojourner Truth

Sojourner Truth was born a slave named Isabella in Ulster County, New York, in 1797. After her escape from slavery in 1827, she went to New York City and underwent a profound religious transformation. She worked as a domestic servant, and as an evangelist, she tried to reform prostitutes. Adopting the name Sojourner Truth in 1843, she became a traveling preacher and abolitionist, frequently appearing with Frederick Douglass. Although she never learned to write, Truth's compelling presence gripped her audience as she spoke eloquently about emancipation and women's rights. After the Civil War and until her death in 1883, she worked to provide education and employment for emancipated slaves.

At the Women's Rights Convention in Akron, Ohio, in May 1851, Truth extemporaneously delivered the following speech, as transcribed by Elizabeth Cady Stanton, to a nearly all-white audience.

BEFORE YOU READ

What comes to mind when you hear the word *speech?* Have you ever attended a rally or convention and heard speeches given on behalf of a social cause or political issue? What were your impressions of the speakers and their speeches?

Well, children, where there is so much racket there must be something out of kilter. I think that 'twixt the Negroes of the South and the women of the North, all talking about rights, the white men will be in a fix pretty soon. But what's all this here talking about?

That man over there says that women need to be helped into carriages, and lifted over ditches, and to have the best place everywhere. Nobody ever helps me into carriages, or over mud-puddles, or gives me any best place! And ain't I a woman? Look at me! Look at my arm! I have ploughed and planted, and gathered into barns, and no man could head me! And ain't I a woman? I could work as much and eat as much as a man — when I could get it — and bear the lash as well! And ain't I a woman? I have borne thirteen children, and seen them most all sold off to slavery, and when I cried out with my mother's grief, none but Jesus heard me! And ain't I a woman?

Then they talk about this thing in the head; what's this they call it? [Intellect, someone whispers.] That's it, honey. What's that got to do with women's rights or negro's rights? If my cup won't hold but a pint, and yours holds a quart, wouldn't you be mean not to let me have my little half-measure full?

Then that little man in black there, he says women can't have as much rights as men, 'cause Christ wasn't a woman! Where did your

Christ come from? Where did your Christ come from? From God and a woman! Man had nothing to do with Him.

If the first woman God ever made was strong enough to turn the world upside down all alone, these women together ought to be able to turn it back, and get it right side up again! And now they is asking to do it, the men better let them. 5

Obliged to you for hearing me, and now old Sojourner ain't got nothing more to say. 6

RESPONDING TO READING

What are your immediate impressions of Truth's speech? Now take a minute to read her speech again, this time aloud. What are your impressions now? Are they different, and if so, how and why? What aspects of her speech are memorable?

QUESTIONING THE TEXT

1. What does Truth mean when she says, "Where there is so much racket there must be something out of kilter" (paragraph 1)? Why does Truth believe that white men are going to find themselves in a "fix" (1)?

2. What does Truth put forth as her "credentials" as a woman?

3. How does Truth counter the argument that "women can't have as much rights as men, 'cause Christ wasn't a woman" (4)?

UNDERSTANDING THE WRITER'S CRAFT

1. What is Truth's purpose in this essay? (Glossary: *Purpose*) Why is it important for her to define what a woman is for her audience?

2. How does Truth use the comments of "that man over there" (paragraph 2) and "that little man in black" (4) to help her establish her definition of *woman*?

3. What, for you, is the effect of Truth's repetition of the question "And ain't I a woman?" four times? What other questions does she ask? Why do you suppose Truth doesn't provide answers to the questions in paragraph 3, but does for the question in paragraph 4?

4. How would you characterize Truth's tone in this speech? What phrases in the speech suggest that tone to you? (Glossary: *Tone*)

EXPLORING LANGUAGE

1. How would you describe Truth's diction in this speech? What does her diction reveal about her character and background? (Glossary: *Diction*)

2. Refer to your desk dictionary to determine the meanings of the following words as Truth uses them in this selection: *kilter* (paragraph 1), *ditches* (2), *intellect* (3), *obliged* (6).

COMBINING RHETORICAL STRATEGIES

Explain how Truth uses comparison and contrast to help establish her definition of *woman*, especially in paragraph 2.

WRITING SUGGESTIONS

1. **(Definition)** Sojourner Truth spoke out against the injustice she saw around her. In arguing for the rights of women, she found it helpful to define *woman* in order to make her point. What social cause do you find most compelling today? Human rights? AIDS awareness? Domestic abuse? Alcoholism? Gay marriage? Racism? Select an issue about which you have strong feelings. Now carefully identify all key terms that you must define before arguing your position. Write an essay in which you use definition to make your point convincingly.

2. **(Other Strategies)** Sojourner Truth's speech holds out hope for the future. She envisioned a future in which women join together to take charge and "turn [the world] back, and get it right side up again" (paragraph 5). What she envisioned has, to some extent, come to pass. Write an essay in which you speculate about how Truth would react to the world as we know it. What do you think would please her? What would disappoint her? What do you think she would want to change about our society? Explain your reasoning.

3. **(Research)** Sojourner Truth's journey from slave to activist, to speaker, and posthumously, to cultural icon was an arduous and circuitous one. Research her life at the library and perhaps on the Internet. There are several biographies about her, including Nell Irvin Painter's acclaimed *Sojourner Truth: A Life, a Symbol* (1996), which offer a foundation for your research. Write an essay in which you assess her strengths and weaknesses. How was she able to overcome and transcend the deprivations and indignities of her early years? What role did religion play in her life and accomplishments? Consider what she might have done had she lived during the era of Martin Luther King Jr. Do you think her abilities and beliefs would have been effective in the age of mass media? Why or why not?

- **Sojourner Truth Institute**
  <http://www.sojournertruth.org>

  The Sojourner Truth Institute's home page documents Truth's life from her birth into slavery through a long career as an antislavery spokeswoman.

- ***The Narrative of Sojourner Truth***
  <http://digital.library.upenn.edu/women/truth/1850/1850.html>

  Browse the complete text of Sojourner Truth's autobiography, as dictated to Olive Gilbert in 1850.

- *World Book Encyclopedia* **Presents: The African American Journey**
  <http://www.worldbook.com/fun/aajourny/html/index.html>

  Sojourner Truth's biography is presented here within the larger context of the African American journey from slavery through the abolitionist campaign to the modern civil rights movement.

COMBINING SUBJECTS AND STRATEGIES

The photograph below depicts many of the same themes and strategies as the Combining Rhetorical Strategies essay that follows. Your observations about the photograph will help guide you to the key themes and strategies in the essay. After you've read the essay, you may use your observations about both the photograph and the essay to examine how the overlapping themes and strategies work in each medium.

Lydia Gans captured the image below of Ruthanne Shpiner in Berkeley, California, in 1995. More than fifteen years ago, Shpiner, once an avid sportswoman, became a paraplegic as a result of an accident. She is now an attorney and a part-time tennis player.

Lydia Gans/Impact Visuals

For Discussion

Is it fair to call this photograph an "action shot"? What strikes you most about the woman in the wheelchair? What feelings do you have about her playing tennis in a wheelchair? Does this photograph give you reason to re-think words like *handicapped* or *crippled?* How would you define these words now?

On Being a Cripple

Nancy Mairs

Nancy Mairs, a poet and writer, was born in Long Beach, California, in 1943. She attended Wheaton College in Massachusetts, where she earned a B.A. in English in 1964. From 1964 until 1972, Mairs took a number of teaching and writing jobs around Boston, and it was during this period that she learned she had multiple sclerosis and experienced major depression. In 1972, Mairs decided to pursue a career in writing and entered the creative writing program at the University of Arizona, where she earned an M.F.A. in poetry (1975) and then a Ph.D. in English (1984). In works like Plaintext *(1986),* Carnal Acts *(1990), and* Waist High in the World *(1997), which consist mostly of autobiographical essays, Mairs has refused to deny or cover up the specificities of her life as a woman. In fact, Mairs has often used the most intimate details of her inner life as the essential material of her art. Through her writing, Mairs has called into question what can and cannot be revealed about one's life in writing for a public audience.*

"On Being a Cripple" is an essay from her critically acclaimed Plaintext. *In this essay, she writes poignantly about living with MS and about the strategies she has developed to cope with it. But, more important, she has written of the ways in which "being a cripple" has intensified and even enhanced her artistic vision.*

BEFORE YOU READ

The word *cripple* carries powerful connotations. What visual and emotional responses does it arouse in you? Do you object to the word? Why or why not?

To escape is nothing. Not to escape is nothing.

— Louise Bogan

The other day I was thinking of writing an essay on being a cripple. I was thinking hard in one of the stalls of the women's room in my office building, as I was shoving my shirt into my jeans and tugging up my zipper. Preoccupied, I flushed, picked up my book bag, took my cane down from the hook, and unlatched the door. So many movements unbalanced me, and as I pulled the door open I fell over backward, landing fully clothed on the toilet seat with my legs splayed in front of me: the old beetle-on-its-back routine. Saturday afternoon, the building deserted, I was free to laugh aloud as I wriggled back to my feet, my voice bouncing off the yellowish tiles from all directions. Had anyone been there with me, I'd have been still and faint and hot with chagrin. I decided that it was high time to write the essay.

490

First, the matter of semantics. I am a cripple. I choose this word to name me. I choose from among several possibilities, the most common of which are "handicapped" and "disabled." I made the choice a number of years ago, without thinking, unaware of my motives for doing so. Even now, I'm not sure what those motives are, but I recognize that they are complex and not entirely flattering. People — crippled or not — wince at the word "cripple," as they do not at "handicapped" or "disabled." Perhaps I want them to wince. I want them to see me as a tough customer, one to whom the fates/gods/viruses have not been kind, but who can face the brutal truth of her existence squarely. As a cripple, I swagger.

But, to be fair to myself, a certain amount of honesty underlies my choice. "Cripple" seems to me a clean word, straightforward and precise. It has an honorable history, having made its first appearance in the Lindisfarne Gospel in the tenth century. As a lover of words, I like the accuracy with which it describes my condition: I have lost the full use of my limbs. "Disabled," by contrast, suggests an incapacity, physical or mental. And I certainly don't like "handicapped," which implies that I have deliberately been put at a disadvantage, by whom I can't imagine (my God is not a Handicapper General), in order to equalize chances in the great race of life. These words seem to me to be moving away from my condition, to be widening the gap between word and reality. Most remote is the recently coined euphemism "differently abled," which partakes of the same semantic hopefulness that transformed countries from "undeveloped" to "underdeveloped," then to "less developed," and finally to "developing" nations. People have continued to starve in those countries during the shift. Some realities do not obey the dictates of language.

Mine is one of them. Whatever you call me, I remain crippled. But I don't care what you call me, so long as it isn't "differently abled," which strikes me as pure verbal garbage designed, by its ability to describe anyone, to describe no one. I subscribe to George Orwell's thesis that "the slovenliness of our language makes it easier for us to have foolish thoughts." And I refuse to participate in the degeneration of the language to the extent that I deny that I have lost anything in the course of this calamitous disease; I refuse to pretend that the only differences between you and me are the various ordinary ones that distinguish any one person from another. But call me "disabled" or "handicapped" if you like. I have long since grown accustomed to them; and if they are vague, at least they hint at the truth. Moreover, I use them myself. Society is no readier to accept crippledness than to accept death, war, sex, sweat, or wrinkles. I would never refer to another person as a cripple. It is the word I used to name only myself.

I haven't always been crippled, a fact for which I am soundly grateful. To be whole of limb is, I know from experience, infinitely more pleasant and useful than to be crippled; and if that knowledge leaves me open to bitterness at my loss, the physical soundness I once enjoyed (though I did not enjoy it half enough) is well worth the occasional stab of regret. Though never any good at sports, I was a normally active child and young adult. I climbed trees, played hopscotch, jumped rope, skated, swam, rode my bicycle, sailed. I despised team sports, spending some of the wretchedest afternoons of my life sweaty and humiliated, behind a field-hockey stick and under a basketball hoop. I tramped alone for miles along the bridle paths that webbed the woods behind the house I grew up in. I swayed through countless dim hours in the arms of one man or another under the scattered shot of light from mirrored balls, and gyrated through countless more as Tab Hunter and Johnny Mathis gave way to the Rolling Stones, Creedence Clearwater Revival, Cream. I walked down the aisle. I pushed baby carriages, changed tires in the rain, marched for peace.

When I was twenty-eight I started to trip and drop things. What at first seemed my natural clumsiness soon became too pronounced to shrug off. I consulted a neurologist, who told me that I had a brain tumor. A battery of tests, increasingly disagreeable, revealed no tumor. About a year and a half later I developed a blurred spot in one eye. I had, at last, the episodes "disseminated in space and time" requisite for a diagnosis: multiple sclerosis. I have never been sorry for the doctor's initial misdiagnosis, however. For almost a week, until the negative results of the tests were in, I thought that I was going to die right away. Every day for the past nearly ten years, then, has been a kind of gift. I accept all gifts. 6

Multiple sclerosis is a chronic degenerative disease of the central nervous system, in which the myelin that sheathes the nerves is somehow eaten away and scar tissue forms in its place, interrupting the nerves' signals. During its course, which is unpredictable and uncontrollable, one may lose vision, hearing, speech, the ability to walk, control of bladder and/or bowels, strength in any or all extremities, sensitivity to touch, vibration, and/or pain, potency, coordination of movements — the list of possibilities is lengthy and yes, horrifying. One may also lose one's sense of humor. That's the easiest to lose and the hardest to survive without. 7

In the past ten years, I have sustained some of these losses. Characteristic of MS are sudden attacks, called exacerbations, followed by remissions, and these I have not had. Instead, my disease has been slowly progressive. My left leg is now so weak that I walk with the aid of a brace and a cane; and for distances I use an Amigo, a variation on the electric wheelchair that looks rather like an electrified kiddie car. I no longer have much use of my left hand. Now my right side is weakening as well. I still have the blurred spot in my right eye. Overall, though, I've been lucky so far. My world has, of necessity, been 8 circumscribed by my losses, but the terrain left me has been ample enough for me to continue many of the activities that absorb me: writing, teaching, raising children and cats and plants and snakes, reading, speaking publicly about MS and depression, even playing bridge with people patient and honorable enough to let me scatter cards every which way without sneaking a peek.

Lest I begin to sound like Pollyanna, however, let me say that I 9
don't like having MS. I hate it. My life holds realities — harsh ones, some of them — that no right-minded human being ought to accept without grumbling. One of them is fatigue. I know of no one with MS who does not complain of bone-weariness; in a disease that presents an astonishing variety of symptoms, fatigue seems to be a common factor. I wake up in the morning feeling the way most people do at the end of a bad day, and I take it from there. As a result, I spend a lot of time *in extremis* and, impatient with limitation, I tend to ignore my fatigue until my body breaks down in some way and forces rest. Then I miss picnics, dinner parties, poetry readings, the brief visits of old friends from out of town. The offspring of a puritanical tradition of exceptional venerability, I cannot view these lapses without shame. My life often seems a series of small failures to do as I ought.

I lead, on the whole, an ordinary life, probably rather like the one 10
I would have led had I not had MS. I am lucky that my predilections were already solitary, sedentary, and bookish — unlike the world-famous French cellist I have read about, or the young woman I talked with one long afternoon who wanted only to be a jockey. I had just begun graduate school when I found out something was wrong with me, and I have remained, interminably, a graduate student. Perhaps I would not have if I'd thought I had the stamina to return to a full-time job as a technical editor; but I've enjoyed my studies.

In addition to studying, I teach writing courses. I also teach med- 11
ical students how to give neurological examinations. I pick up free-lance editing jobs here and there. I have raised a foster son and sent him into the world, where he has made me two grandbabies, and I am still escorting my daughter and son through adolescence. I go to Mass every Saturday. I am a superb, if messy, cook. I am also an enthusiastic laundress, capable of sorting a hamper full of clothes into five subtly differentiated piles, but a terrible housekeeper. I can do italic writing and, in an emergency, bathe an oil-soaked cat. I play a fiendish game of Scrabble. When I have the time and the money, I like to sit on my front steps with my husband, drinking Amaretto and smoking a cigar, as we imagine our counterparts in Leningrad and make sure that the sun gets down once more behind the sharp childish scrawl of the Tucson Mountains.

This lively plenty has its bleak complement, of course, in all the 12
things I can no longer do. I will never run again, except in dreams,

and one day I may have to write that I will never walk again. I like to go camping, but I can't follow George and the children along the trails that wander out of a campsite through the desert or into the mountains. In fact, even on the level I've learned never to check the weather or try to hold a coherent conversation: I need all my attention for my wayward feet. Of late, I have begun to catch myself wondering how people can propel themselves without canes. With only one usable hand, I have to select my clothing with care not so much for style as for ease of ingress and egress, and even so, dressing can be laborious. I can no longer do fine stitchery, pick up babies, play the piano, braid my hair. I am immobilized by acute attacks of depression, which may or may not be physiologically related to MS but are certainly its logical concomitant.

These two elements, the plenty and the privation, are never pure, nor are the delight and wretchedness that accompany them. Almost every pickle that I get into as a result of my weakness and clumsiness — and I get into plenty — is funny as well as maddening and sometimes painful. I recall one May afternoon when a friend and I were going out for a drink after finishing up at school. As we were climbing into opposite sides of my car, chatting, I tripped and fell, flat and hard, onto the asphalt parking lot, my abrupt departure interrupting him in mid-sentence. "Where'd you go?" he called as he came around the back of the car to find me hauling myself up by the door frame. "Are you all right?" Yes, I told him, I was fine, just a bit rattly, and we drove off to find a shady patio and some beer. When I got home an hour or so later, my daughter greeted me with "What have you done to yourself?" I looked down. One elbow of my white turtleneck with the green froggies, one knee of my white trousers, one white kneesock were blood-soaked. We peeled off the clothes and inspected the damage, which was nasty enough but not alarming. That part wasn't funny: The abrasions took a long time to heal, and one got a little infected. Even so, when I think of my friend talking earnestly, suddenly, to the hot thin air while I dropped from his view as though through a trap door, I find the image as silly as something from a Marx Brothers movie. 13

I may find it easier than other cripples to amuse myself because I live propped by the acceptance and the assistance and, sometimes, the amusement of those around me. Grocery clerks tear my checks out of my checkbook for me, and sales clerks find chairs to put into dressing rooms when I want to try on clothes. The people I work with make sure I teach at times when I am least likely to be fatigued, in places I can get to, with the materials I need. My students, with one anonymous exception (in an end-of-the-semester evaluation) have been unperturbed by my disability. Some even like it. One was immensely cheered by the information that I paint my own fingernails; she 14 decided, she told me, that if I could go to such trouble over fine details, she could keep on writing essays. I suppose I became some sort of bright-fingered muse. She wrote good essays, too.

The most important struts in the framework of my existence, of course, are my husband and children. Dismayingly few marriages survive the MS test, and why should they? Most twenty-two- and nineteen-year-olds, like George and me, can vow in clear conscience, after a childhood of chickenpox and summer colds, to keep one another in sickness and in health so long as they both shall live. Not many are equipped for catastrophe: the dismay, the depression, the extra work, the boredom that a degenerative disease can insinuate into a relationship. And our society, with its emphasis on fun and its association of fun with physical performance, offers little encouragement for a whole spouse to stay with a crippled partner. Children experience similar stresses when faced with a crippled parent, and they are more helpless, since parents and children can't usually get divorced. They hate, of course, to be different from their peers, and the child whose mother is tacking down the aisle of a school auditorium packed with proud parents like a Cape Cod dinghy in a stiff breeze jolly well stands out in a crowd. Deprived of legal divorce, the child can at least deny the mother's disability, even her existence, forgetting to tell her about recitals and PTA meetings, refusing to accompany her to stores or church or the movies, never inviting friends to the house. Many do.

But I've been limping along for ten years now, and so far George and the children are still at my left elbow, holding tight. Anne and Matthew vacuum floors and dust furniture and haul trash and rake up dog droppings and button my cuffs and bake lasagne and Toll House cookies with just enough grumbling so I know that they don't have brain fever. And far from hiding me, they're forever dragging me by racks of fancy clothes or through teeming school corridors, or welcoming gaggles of friends while I'm wandering through the house in Anne's filmy pink babydoll pajamas. George generally calls before he brings someone home, but he does just as many dumb thankless chores as the children. And they all yell at me, laugh at some of my jokes, write me funny letters when we're apart — in short, treat me as an ordinary human being for whom they have some use. I think they like me. Unless they're faking. . . .

Faking. There's the rub. Tugging at the fringes of my consciousness always is the terror that people are kind to me only because I'm a cripple. My mother almost shattered me once, with that instinct mothers have — blind, I think, in this case, but unerring nonetheless — for striking blows along the fault-lines of their children's hearts, by telling me, in an attack on my selfishness, "We all have to make allowances for you, of course, because of the way you are." From the distance of a couple of years, I have to admit that I haven't any idea just what she meant, and I'm not sure that she knew either. She was awfully angry. But at the time, as the words thudded home, I felt my worst fear, suddenly realized. I could bear being called selfish: I am. But I couldn't bear the corroboration that those around me were doing in fact what I'd always suspected them of doing, professing fondness while silently putting up with me because of the way I am. A cripple. I've been a little cracked ever since.

Along with this fear that people are secretly accepting shoddy goods comes a relentless pressure to please — to prove myself worth the burdens I impose, I guess, or to build a substantial account of goodwill against which I may write drafts in times of need. Part of the pressure arises from social expectations. In our society, anyone who deviates from the norm had better find some way to compensate. Like fat people, who are expected to be jolly, cripples must bear their lot meekly and cheerfully. A grumpy cripple isn't playing by the rules. And much of the pressure is self-generated. Early on I vowed that, if I had to have MS, by God I was going to do it well. This is a class act, ladies and gentlemen. No tears, no recriminations, no faintheartedness. 18

One way and another, then, I wind up feeling like Tiny Tim, peering over the edge of the table at the Christmas goose, waving my crutch, piping down God's blessing on us all. Only sometimes I don't want to play Tiny Tim. I'd rather be Caliban, a most scurvy monster. Fortunately, at home no one much cares whether I'm a good cripple or a bad cripple as long as I make vichyssoise with fair regularity. One evening several years ago, Anne was reading at the dining-room table while I cooked dinner. As I opened a can of tomatoes, the can slipped in my left hand and juice spattered me and the counter with bloody spots. Fatigued and infuriated, I bellowed, "I'm so sick of being crippled!" Anne glanced at me over the top of her book. "There now," she said, "do you feel better?" "Yes," I said, "yes, I do." She went back to her reading. I felt better. That's about all the attention my scurviness ever gets. 19

Because I hate being crippled, I sometimes hate myself for being a cripple. Over the years I have come to expect — even accept — attacks of violent self-loathing. Luckily, in general our society no longer connects deformity and disease directly with evil (though a charismatic once told me that I have MS because a devil is in me) and so I'm allowed to move largely at will, even among small children. But I'm not sure that this revision of attitude has been particularly helpful. Physical imperfection, even freed of moral disapprobation, still defies and violates the ideal, especially for women, whose confinement in their bodies as objects of desire is far from over. Each age, of course, has its ideal, and I doubt that ours is any better or worse than any other. Today's ideal woman, who lives on the glossy pages of dozens of magazines, seems to be between the ages of eighteen and twenty-five; her 20 hair has body, her teeth flash white, her breath smells minty, her underarms are dry; she has a career but is still a fabulous cook, especially of meals that take less than twenty minutes to prepare; she does not ordinarily appear to have a husband or children; she is trim and deeply tanned; she jogs, swims, plays tennis, rides a bicycle, sails, but does not bowl; she travels widely, even to out-of-the-way places like Finland and Samoa, always in the company of the ideal man, who possesses a nearly identical set of characteristics. There are a few exceptions. Though usually white and often blonde, she may be black, Hispanic, Asian, or Native American, so long as she is unusually sleek. She may be old, provided she is selling a laxative or is Lauren Bacall. If she is selling a detergent, she may be married and have a flock of strikingly messy children. But she is never a cripple.

Like many women I know, I have always had an uneasy relationship   21
with my body. I was not a popular child, largely, I think now, because I was peculiar: intelligent, intense, moody, shy, given to unexpected actions and inexplicable notions and emotions. But as I entered adolescence, I believed myself unpopular because I was homely: my breasts too flat, my mouth too wide, my hips too narrow, my clothing never quite right in fit or style. I was not, in fact, particularly ugly, old photographs inform me, though I was well off the ideal; but I carried this sense of self-alienation with me into adulthood, where it regenerated in response to the depredations of MS. Even with my brace I walk with a limp so pronounced that, seeing myself on the videotape of a television program on the disabled, I couldn't believe that anything but an inchworm could make progress humping along like that. My shoulders droop and my pelvis thrusts forward as I try to balance myself upright, throwing my frame into a bony S. As a result of contractures, one shoulder is higher than the other and I carry one arm bent in front of me, the fingers curled into a claw. My left arm and leg have wasted into pipe-stems, and I try always to keep them covered. When I think about how my body must look to others, especially to men, to whom I have been trained to display myself, I feel ludicrous, even loathsome.

At my age, however, I don't spend much time thinking about my   22
appearance. The burning egocentricity of adolescence, which assures one that all the world is looking all the time, has passed, thank God, and I'm generally too caught up in what I'm doing to step back, as I used to, and watch myself as though upon a stage. I'm also too old to believe in the accuracy of self-image. I know that I'm not a hideous crone, that in fact, when I'm rested, well dressed, and well made up, I look fine. The self-loathing I feel is neither physically nor intellectually substantial. What I hate is not me but a disease.

I am not a disease.   23

And a disease is not — at least not singlehandedly — going to de-   24
termine who I am, though at first it seemed to be going to. Adjusting

to a chronic incurable illness, I have moved through a process similar to that outlined by Elizabeth Kübler-Ross in *On Death and Dying*. The major difference — and it is far more significant than most people recognize — is that I can't be sure of the outcome, as the terminally ill cancer patient can. Research studies indicate that, with proper medical care, I may achieve a "normal" life span. And in our society, with its vision of death as the ultimate evil, worse even than decrepitude, the response to such news is, "Oh well, at least you're not going to *die*." Are there worse things than dying? I think that there may be.

I think of two women I know, both with MS, both enough older than I to have served as models. One took to her bed several years ago and has been there ever since. Although she can sit in a high-backed wheelchair, because she is incontinent she refuses to go out at all, even though incontinence pants, which are readily available at any pharmacy, could protect her from embarrassment. Instead, she stays at home and insists that her husband, a small quiet man, a retired civil servant, stay there with her except for a quick weekly foray to the supermarket. The other woman, whose illness was diagnosed when she was eighteen, a nursing student engaged to a young doctor, finished her training, married her doctor, accompanied him to Germany when he was in the service, bore three sons and a daughter, now grown and gone. When she can, she travels with her husband; she plays bridge, embroiders, swims regularly; she works, like me, as a symptomatic-patient instructor of medical students in neurology. Guess which woman I hope to be.

At the beginning, I thought about having MS almost incessantly. And because of the unpredictable course of the disease, my thoughts were always terrified. Each night I'd get into bed wondering whether I'd get out again the next morning, whether I'd be able to see, to speak, to hold a pen between my fingers. Knowing that the day might come when I'd be physically incapable of killing myself, I thought perhaps I ought to do so right away, while I still had the strength. Gradually I came to understand that the Nancy who might one day lie inert under a bedsheet, arms and legs paralyzed, unable to feed or bathe herself, unable to reach out for a gun, a bottle of pills, was not the Nancy I was at present, and that I could not presume to make decisions for that future Nancy, who might well not want in the least to die. Now the only provision I've made for the future Nancy is that when the time comes — and it is likely to come in the form of pneumonia, friend to the weak and the old — I am not to be treated with machines and medications. If she is unable to communicate by then, I hope she will be satisfied with these terms.

Thinking all the time about having MS grew tiresome and intrusive, especially in the large and tragic mode in which I was accustomed to considering my plight. Months and even years went by without catastrophe (at least without one related to MS), and really I was awfully busy, what with George and children and snakes and students and poems, and I hadn't the time, let alone the inclination, to devote myself to being a disease. Too, the richer my life became, the funnier it seemed, as though there were some connection between largesse and laughter, and so my tragic stance began to waver until, even with the aid of a brace and cane, I couldn't hold it for very long at a time.

After several years I was satisfied with my adjustment. I had suffered my grief and fury and terror, I thought, but now I was at ease with my lot. Then one summer day I set out with George and the children across the desert for a vacation in California. Part way to Yuma I became aware that my right leg felt funny. "I think I've had an exacerbation," I told George. "What shall we do?" he asked. "I think we'd better get the hell to California," I said, "because I don't know whether I'll ever make it again." So we went on to San Diego and then to Orange, and up the Pacific Coast Highway to Santa Cruz, across to Yosemite, down to Sequoia and Joshua Tree, and so back over the desert to home. It was a fine two-week trip, filled with friends and fair weather, and I wouldn't have missed it for the world, though I did in fact make it back to California two years later. Nor would there have been any point in missing it, since in MS, once the symptoms have appeared, the neurological damage has been done, and there's no way to predict or prevent that damage. 28

The incident spoiled my self-satisfaction, however. It renewed my grief and fury and terror, and I learned that one never finishes adjusting to MS. I don't know now why I thought one would. One does not, after all, finish adjusting to life, and MS is simply a fact of my life — not my favorite fact, of course — but as ordinary as my nose and my tropical fish and my yellow Mazda station wagon. It may at any time get worse, but no amount of worry or anticipation can prepare me for a new loss. My life is a lesson in losses. I learn one at a time. 29

And I had best be patient in the learning, since I'll have to do it like it or not. As any rock fan knows, you can't always get what you want. Particularly when you have MS. You can't, for example, get cured. In recent years researchers and the organizations that fund research have started to pay MS some attention even though it isn't fatal; perhaps they have begun to see that life is something other than a quantitative phenomenon, that one may be very much alive for a very long time in a life that isn't worth living. The researchers have made some progress toward understanding the mechanism of the disease: It may well be an autoimmune reaction triggered by a slow-acting virus. But they are nowhere near its prevention, control, or cure. And most of us want to be cured. Some, unable to accept incurability, grasp at one treatment after another, no matter how bizarre: 30

megavitamin therapy, gluten-free diet, injections of cobra venom, hypothermal suits, lymphocytopharesis, hyperbaric chambers. Many treatments are probably harmless enough, but none are curative.

The absence of a cure often makes MS patients bitter toward their 31 doctors. Doctors are, after all, the priests of modern society, the new shamans, whose business is to heal, and many an MS patient roves from one to another, searching for the "good" doctor who will make him well. Doctors too think of themselves as healers, and for this reason many have trouble dealing with MS patients, whose disease in its intransigence defeats their aims and mocks their skills. Too few doctors, it is true, treat their patients as whole human beings, but the reverse is also true. I have always tried to be gentle with my doctors, who often have more at stake in terms of ego than I do. I may be frustrated, maddened, depressed by the incurability of my disease, but I am not diminished by it, and they are. When I push myself up from my seat in the waiting room and stumble toward them, I incarnate the limitation of their powers. The least I can do is refuse to press on their tenderest spots.

This gentleness is part of the reason that I'm not sorry to be a 32 cripple. I didn't have it before. Perhaps I'd have developed it anyway — how could I know such a thing? — and I wish I had more of it, but I'm glad of what I have. It has opened and enriched my life enormously, this sense that my frailty and need must be mirrored in others, that in searching for and shaping a stable core in a life wrenched by change and loss, change and loss, I must recognize the same process, under individual conditions, in the lives around me. I do not deprecate such knowledge, however I've come by it.

All the same, if a cure were found, would I take it? In a minute. I 33 may be a cripple, but I'm only occasionally a loony and never a saint. Anyway, in my brand of theology God doesn't give bonus points for a limp. I'd take a cure; I just don't need one. A friend who also has MS startled me once by asking, "Do you ever say to yourself, 'Why me, Lord?'" "No, Michael, I don't," I told him, "because whenever I try, the only response I can think of is 'Why not?'" If I could make a cosmic deal, who would I put in my place? What in my life would I give up in exchange for sound limbs and a thrilling rush of energy? No one. Nothing. I might as well do the job myself. Now that I'm getting the hang of it.

RESPONDING TO READING

According to the old saying, every cloud has a silver lining. Mairs weighs both the positive and negative sides of dealing with a difficult illness. Why and how does adversity bring out the good in people? Consider her responses as well as your own.

QUESTIONING THE TEXT

1. Why does Mairs choose to identify herself by the term *cripple?* What objections does she have to terms more generally accepted in American culture today (i.e., *disabled, handicapped*)? How do you think she would respond to the more current phrase, *physically challenged?*

2. Mairs says she had been planning to write this essay for some time. What incident finally prompted her to do it? What is noteworthy about her response to this incident?

3. In paragraph 5, review the normal activities Mairs engaged in as a child and young adult. Why do you think she chooses to list these particular activities?

UNDERSTANDING THE WRITER'S CRAFT

1. For what purpose does Mairs introduce her essay with the quote from Louise Bogan? How does this quote bear on her topic? (Glossary: *Purpose*)

2. Although this long essay covers many years and numerous ideas, it flows seamlessly for the reader. In large measure, this unity is brought about by the use of careful transitions from paragraph to paragraph. (Glossary: *Unity*) Find several examples of transitions that move the piece forward effectively even though the paragraphs they connect are quite different in form or content.

3. Mairs says that an MS sufferer may lose many things in life, including a sense of humor, "the easiest to lose and the hardest to survive without" (paragraph 7). What are some of the many ways she shows in the essay that she has not lost hers? Is humor appropriate in a piece of writing about such a dire topic?

EXPLORING LANGUAGE

1. What does Mairs mean when she says, at the end of paragraph 3, "Some realities do not obey the dictates of language"? By what example does she illustrate this assertion? (Glossary: *Exemplification*)

2. Why does Mairs describe herself as a "bright-fingered muse" at the end of paragraph 14? Beyond the incident she describes here, what is the significance of the phrase? In what ways do you think this phrase reflects the way Mairs views herself?

3. Much of the challenging vocabulary in this essay is directly related to MS and its effects, direct or indirect, on the victim. Look up these words, noting the best definitions for the context in which they are used: *splayed* (paragraph 1), *chagrin* (1), *euphemism* (3), *calamitous* (4), *disseminated* (6), *requisite* (6), *degenerative* (7), *circumscribed* (8), *venerability* (9), *predilections* (10), *concomitant* (12), *muse* (14), *corroboration* (17), *recriminations* (18), *charismatic* (20), *disapprobation* (20), *depredations* (21), *decrepitude* (24), *largesse* (27), *intransigence* (31).

COMBINING RHETORICAL STRATEGIES

1. Mairs does not recount her struggles with MS as a strict narrative in chronological order. Why do you think she chooses to structure her essay largely on the contrast between past and present? (Glossary: *Comparison and Contrast*)

2. Throughout this essay, Mairs uses brief narrative vignettes, such as her dropping a can of tomatoes or her family trip to California, to exemplify her points about living with multiple sclerosis. Explain how these two strategies together support Mairs's purpose. (Glossary: *Exemplification; Narration*)

3. Mairs's extended definition makes a point about how events in life often lead to choices and varying results — for example, her description of two different women with multiple sclerosis in paragraph 25. Point out some places where Mairs uses cause and effect to support her extended definition and her main point.

WRITING SUGGESTIONS

1. **(Definition)** Mairs says, "I lead, on the whole, an ordinary life" (paragraph 10). Many of her readers could be excused for considering it quite extraordinary. Examine the photograph that accompanies this essay on page 489. How "ordinary" do you consider Ruthanne Shpiner's life of playing tennis in a wheelchair? What is an ordinary life? How much of what one considers ordinary depends upon one's perspective? Write an essay in which you define an ordinary life, including examples of how you follow and fail to follow your own definition.

2. **(Other Strategies)** Interview a student or faculty member at your college or university who would meet Mairs's definition of a "cripple." How does this person's experience of academic life compare with hers? With what particular difficulties and successes has your interviewee been faced? Write an essay illustrating the life led in an academic institution by the person you interviewed. (Glossary: *Exemplification*)

3. **(Research)** Many laws have been enacted at both the national and the state levels to provide equal access and opportunities for people with disabilities. Acquaint yourself with the major laws in your area, with the effects of these laws, and with the cost of implementing them. Do the research in your library and possibly on the Internet. How much responsibility — in terms of money, time, and adaptive technology — should a society assume for people who need special accommodations? Write an essay in which you examine the role you feel society should play in the lives of the disabled.

- **The President's Committee on Employment of People with Disabilities**
  <http://www.pcepd.gov>

  Here you will find information on the Americans with Disabilities Act.

- **Cornucopia of Disability Information**
  <http://codi.buffalo.edu>

  Maintained by the State University of New York at Buffalo, this site contains "resources for consumers and professionals by providing disability information in a wide variety of areas."

- **Disability Discussion Forum**
  <http://www.tell-us-your-story.com>

  This site offers a "disability discussion forum for stories about awareness, rights, and inspiration."

WRITING SUGGESTIONS
FOR DEFINITION

1. Some of the most pressing social issues in American life today are further complicated by imprecise definitions of critical terms. Various
   medical cases, for example, have brought worldwide attention to the
   legal and medical definitions of the word *death*. Debates continue about
   the meanings of other controversial words, such as these:

   a. morality
   b. minority (ethnic)
   c. alcoholism
   d. cheating
   e. pornography
   f. kidnapping
   g. lying
   h. censorship
   i. remedial
   j. insanity
   k. monopoly (business)
   l. sex
   m. success
   n. happiness
   o. life
   p. equality

   Select one of these words, and write an essay in which you discuss not
   only the definition of the term but also the problems associated with
   defining it.

2. Write an essay in which you define one of the words listed below by
   telling not only what it is, but also what it is *not*. (For example, one
   could say that "poetry is that which cannot be expressed in any other
   way.") Remember, however, that defining by negation does not relieve
   you of the responsibility of defining the term in other ways as well.

   a. intelligence
   b. leadership
   c. fear
   d. patriotism
   e. wealth
   f. failure
   g. family
   h. style
   i. loyalty
   j. selflessness
   k. creativity
   l. humor

3. Since the fall of the Berlin Wall in 1989 and the collapse of the Soviet
   Union, a number of democracies have appeared in Eastern Europe.

Write an essay presenting your definition of *democracy*. You may wish to consider using some or all six types of definition. You also may want to think about presenting specific examples or using comparison and contrast to differentiate between different types of democracies.

4. Karl Marx defined *capitalism* as an economic system in which the bourgeois owners of the means of production exploit the proletariat, who lack the means of production, for their own selfish gain. How would you define *capitalism?* Write an essay defining *capitalism* that includes all six types of definition: formal, synonymous, negative, etymological, stipulative, and extended.

5. *Marriage* is a word that often means different things to different people. What does *marriage* mean to you? How would you define it? Write a definition essay to explain your understanding of marriage and what it means to be married. To make your definition clearer to your reader, you might consider describing a marriage with which you are personally familiar. Perhaps it would be helpful to compare and contrast two or more different marriages. You could also incorporate some narration or exemplification to make your definition more powerful.

6. Consider the sample introduction to the essay defining Quebecois and Canadian identity. Think about your school, town, or country's identity. How would you define its essential character? Choose a place that is important in your life, and write an essay defining its character and its significance to you. You may choose to integrate other rhetorical strategies, such as division and classification, to strengthen your essay, or use narration or description to help clarify your essay.

CHAPTER 12

Cause and Effect Analysis

WHAT IS CAUSE AND EFFECT ANALYSIS?

People exhibit their natural curiosity about the world by asking questions. These questions represent a fundamental human need to find out how things work. Questioning the world around us is among the most common of human activities: "Why are babies born?" "Why do people cheat?" "What are the environmental causes of cancer?" "Why are there homeless and hungry people in America?" "What would happen if grades were abolished in colleges and universities?" "What if the stock market crashed again?" "What would happen if drunk drivers were given mandatory jail sentences?" "What would happen if the U.S. space program were expanded?" Answering questions like these means engaging in the process of *cause and effect analysis.* Whenever a question asks *why*, answering it will require discovering a *cause* or a series of causes for a particular *effect*; whenever a question asks *what if*, its answer will point out the effect or effects that can result from a particular cause. Cause and effect analysis, then, explores the relationship between events or circumstances and the outcomes that result from them.

You will have frequent opportunity to use cause and effect analysis in your college writing. For example, a history instructor might ask you to explain the causes of the Seven-Day War between Egypt and Israel. In a paper for an American literature course, you might try to determine why *Huckleberry Finn* has sparked so much controversy in a number of schools and communities. On an environmental studies exam, you might have to speculate about the long-term effects acid rain will have on the ecology of northeastern Canada and the United States. Demonstrating an understanding of cause and effect is crucial to the process of learning.

One common use of the strategy is for the writer to identify a particular causal agent or circumstance and then discuss the consequences or effects it has had or may have. In the following passage from *The Telephone* by John Brooks, it is clear from the first sentence that the author is primarily concerned with the effects that the telephone has had or may have had on modern life.

First sentence establishes purpose in the form of a question.

A series of effects with the telephone as cause

What has the telephone done to us, or for us, in the hundred years of its existence? A few effects suggest themselves at once. It has saved lives by getting rapid word of illness, injury, or famine from remote places. By joining with the elevator to make possible the multistory residence or office building, it has made possible — for better or worse — the modern city. By bringing about a quantum leap in the speed and ease with which information moves from place to place, it has greatly accelerated the rate of scientific and technological change and growth in industry. Beyond doubt it has crippled if not killed the ancient art of letter writing. It has made living alone possible for persons with normal social impulses; by so doing, it has played a role in one of the greatest social changes of this century, the breakup of the multigenerational household. It has made the waging of war chillingly more efficient than formerly. Perhaps (though not provably) it has prevented wars that might have arisen out of international misunderstanding caused by written communication. Or perhaps — again not provably — by magnifying and extending irrational personal conflicts based on voice contact, it has caused wars. Certainly it has extended the scope of human conflicts, since it impartially disseminates the useful knowledge of scientists and the babble of bores, the affection of the affectionate and the malice of the malicious.

The bulk of Brooks's paragraph is devoted to answering the very question he poses in his opening sentence: "What has the telephone done to us, or for us, in the hundred years of its existence?" Notice that even though many of the effects Brooks discusses are verifiable or probable, he is willing to admit that he is speculating about those effects that he cannot prove.

A second common use of the strategy is to reverse the forms by first examining the effect; the writer describes an important event or problem (effect) and then examines the possible reasons (causes) for it.

For example, experts might trace the causes of poverty to any or all of the following: poor education, a nonprogressive tax system, declining commitment to social services, inflation, discrimination, or even, perhaps, the welfare system that is designed to help those most in need.

A third use of the strategy is for the writer to explore a complex causal chain. In this selection from his book *The Politics of Energy*, Barry Commoner examines the series of malfunctions that led to the near disaster at the Three Mile Island nuclear facility in Harrisburg, Pennsylvania.

On March 28, 1979, at 3:53 A.M., a pump at the Harrisburg plant failed. Because the pump failed, the reactor's heat was not drawn off in the heat exchanger and the very hot water in the primary loop overheated. The pressure in the loop increased, opening a release valve that was supposed to counteract such an event. But the valve stuck open and the primary loop system lost so much water (which ended up as a highly radioactive pool, six feet deep, on the floor of the reactor building) that it was unable to carry off all the heat generated within the reactor core. Under these circumstances, the intense heat held within the reactor could, in theory, melt its fuel rods, and the resulting "meltdown" could then carry a hugely radioactive mass through the floor of the reactor. The reactor's emergency cooling system, which is designed to prevent this disaster, was then automatically activated, but when it was, apparently, turned off too soon, some of the fuel rods overheated. This produced a bubble of hydrogen gas at the top of the reactor. (The hydrogen is dissolved in the water in order to react with oxygen that is produced when the intense reactor radiation splits water molecules into their atomic constituents. When heated, the dissolved hydrogen bubbles out of the solution.) This bubble blocked the flow of cooling water so that despite the action of the emergency cooling system the reactor core was again in danger of melting down. Another danger was that the gas might contain enough oxygen to cause an explosion that could rupture the huge containers that surround the reactor and release a deadly cloud of radioactive material into the surrounding countryside. Working desperately, technicians were able to gradually reduce the size of the gas bubble using a special apparatus brought in from the atomic laboratory at Oak Ridge, Tennessee, and the danger of a catastrophic release of radioactive materials subsided. But the sealed-off plant was now so radioactive that no one could enter it for many months — or, according to some observers, for years — without being exposed to a lethal dose of radiation.

Tracing a causal chain, as Commoner does here, is similar to narration. The writer must organize the events sequentially to show clearly how each event leads to the next.

In a causal chain, an initial cause brings about a particular effect, which in turn becomes the immediate cause of a further effect, and so on, bringing about a series of effects that also act as new causes. The so-called domino effect is a good illustration of the idea of a causal chain; the simple tipping over of a domino (initial cause) can result in the toppling of any number of dominoes down the line (series of effects). For example, before a computer salesperson approaches an important client about a big sale, she prepares extensively for the meeting (initial cause). Her preparation causes her to impress the client (effect A), which guarantees her the big sale (effect B), which in turn results in her promotion to district sales manager (effect C). The sale she made is the most immediate and the most obvious cause of her promotion, but it is possible to trace the chain back to its more essential cause: her hard work preparing for the meeting.

While the ultimate purpose of cause and effect analysis may seem simple — to know or to understand why something happens — determining causes and effects is often a thought-provoking and complex strategy. One reason for this complexity is that some causes are less obvious than others. *Immediate causes* are readily apparent because they are closest in time to the effect; the immediate cause of a flood, for example, may be the collapse of a dam. However, *remote causes* may be just as important, even though they are not as apparent and are perhaps even hidden. The remote (and, in fact, primary) cause of the flood might have been an engineering error or the use of substandard building materials or the failure of personnel to relieve the pressure on the dam caused by unseasonably heavy rains. In many cases, it is necessary to look beyond the most immediate causes to discover the true underlying sources of an event.

A second reason for the complexity of this strategy is the difficulty of distinguishing between possible and actual causes, as well as between possible and actual effects. An upset stomach may be caused by spoiled food, but it may also be caused by overeating, by flu, by nervousness, by pregnancy, or by a combination of factors. Similarly, an increase in the cost of electricity may have multiple effects: higher profits for utility companies, fewer sales of electrical appliances, higher prices for other products that depend on electricity in their manufacture, even the development of alternative sources of energy. Making reasonable choices among the various possibilities requires thought and care.

WHY DO WRITERS USE CAUSE AND EFFECT ANALYSIS?

Writers may use cause and effect analysis for three essential purposes: to inform, to speculate, and to argue. Most commonly, they will want to inform — to help their readers understand some identifiable fact. A state wildlife biologist, for example, might wish to tell the public about the effects severe winter weather has had on the state's deer herds. Similarly, in a newsletter, a member of Congress might explain to his or her constituency the reasons changes are being made in the Social Security system. In an essay later in this chapter ("The Great Kern County Mouse War," p. 532), Kennedy P. Maize uses cause and effect analysis to inform, by exploring how disrupting the balance of nature can have disastrous effects.

Cause and effect analysis may also allow writers to speculate — to consider what might be or what might have been. To satisfy the board of trustees, for example, a university treasurer might discuss the impact an increase in tuition will have on the school's budget. A columnist for *People* magazine might speculate about the reasons for a new singer's sudden popularity. Similarly, pollsters estimate the effects that various voter groups will have on future elections, and historians evaluate how the current presidency will continue to influence American government in the coming decades.

Finally, cause and effect analysis provides an excellent basis from which to argue a given position or point of view. An editorial writer, for example, could argue that bringing a professional ball club into the area would have many positive effects on the local economy and on the community as a whole. Educators who think that video games are a cause of delinquency and poor school performance have argued in newspapers and professional journals against the widespread acceptance of such games. Kennedy P. Maize's essay "The Great Kern County Mouse War" (p. 532) makes an absorbing and effective argument against humankind's interference with natural processes. This essay provides an example of how cause and effect analysis can provide the basis for an effective argument.

AN ANNOTATED STUDENT ESSAY
USING CAUSE AND EFFECT ANALYSIS

Born in Brooklyn, New York, Kevin Cunningham spent most of his life in Flemington, New Jersey. While enrolled in the mechanical engineering program at the University of Vermont, Cunningham shared an apartment near the Burlington waterfront with several other students. There he became interested in the effects that private real estate development — or gentrification — would have on his neighborhood. Such development is not unique to Burlington; it is happening in the older sections of cities across the country. After gathering information for his essay by talking with the various people who live in the neighborhood, Cunningham found it useful to discuss both the causes and the effects of gentrification.

Gentrification

Kevin Cunningham

> I went back to Ohio, and my city
> was gone....
> -- Chrissie Hynde, of the Pretenders

Thesis

My city is in Vermont, not Ohio, but soon my neighborhood will probably be gone, too. Or maybe it's I who will be gone. My street, Lakeview Terrace, lies unobtrusively in the old northwest part of Burlington and is notable, as its name suggests, for spectacular views of Lake Champlain framed by the Adirondacks. It's not that the neighborhood is going to seed -- no, quite the contrary. Recently it has been Discovered, and now it is on the verge of being Gentrified. For some of us who live here, that's bad.

Description of life cycle of city neighborhoods

Cities are often assigned human characteristics, one of which is a life cycle: they have a birth, a youth, a middle age, and an old age. A neighborhood is built and settled by young, vibrant people, proud of their sturdy new homes. Together, residents and houses mature, as families grow larger and extensions get built on. Eventually, though, the neighborhood begins to show its age. Buildings sag a little, houses aren't repainted as quickly, and maintenance slips. The neighborhood may grow poorer, as the young and upwardly mobile find new jobs and move away, while the older and less successful inhabitants remain.

Decay, renewal, or redevelopment awaits aging neighborhoods.

One of three fates awaits the aging neighborhood. Decay may continue until the neighborhood becomes a slum. It may face

1

2

3

urban renewal, with old buildings being razed, and ugly, new apartment houses taking their place. Or it may undergo redevelopment, in which government encourages the upgrading of existing housing stock by offering low-interest loans or outright grants; thus, the original character of the neighborhood may be retained or restored, allowing the city to keep part of its identity.

Example of Hoboken, New Jersey

An example of redevelopment at its best   4
is Hoboken, New Jersey. In the early 1970s Hoboken was a dying city, with rundown housing and many abandoned buildings. However, low-interest loans enabled some younger residents to begin to refurbish their homes, and soon the area began to show signs of re-

Effects of redevelopment on Hoboken

newed vigor. Even outsiders moved in and rebuilt some of the abandoned houses. Today, whole blocks have been restored, and neighborhood life is active again. The city does well too, because property values are higher

Transition: Writer moves from example of Hoboken to his Lakeview Terrace neighborhood.

and so are property taxes. And there, at least for my neighborhood, is the rub.

Lakeview Terrace is a demographic pot-   5
pourri of students and families, young professionals and elderly retirees, homeowners and renters. It's a quiet street where kids can play safely and the neighbors know each other. Most of the houses are fairly old and look it, but already some redevelopment has

Describes "gentrification" to date

begun. Recently, several old houses were bought by a real estate company, rebuilt, and sold as condominiums; the new residents drive BMWs and keep to themselves. The house where I live is owned by a Young Urban Professional couple -- he's an architect -- and they have renovated the place to what it must have looked like when it was new. They did a nice job, too. These two kinds of development are the main forms of gentrification, and so far they have done no real harm.

Redevelopment causes property values to increase, which will cause property taxes to rise.

But the city is about to start a major property tax reappraisal. Because of the renovations, the houses on Lakeview Terrace are currently worth more than they used to be; soon there will be a big jump in property taxes. And then a lot of people will be hurt -- even dispossessed from their own neighborhood.

6

Effects of gentrification on local property owners

Clem is a retired General Electric employee who has lived on Lakeview for over thirty years and who owns his home. About three years ago some condos were built on the lot next door, which didn't please Clem -- he says they just don't fit in. But with higher property taxes, it may be Clem who no longer fits in. At the very least, since he's on a fixed income, he will have to make sacrifices in order to stay. Ryan works as a mailman and also owns his Lakeview Terrace home, which is across the street from the houses that were converted into condos: same cause, same effect.

7

Effects of gentrification on renters

Then there are those of us who rent. As our landlords have to pay higher property taxes, they will naturally raise rents at least as much (and maybe more, if they've spent money on renovations of their own). Some of us won't be able to afford the increase and will have to leave. "Some of us" almost certainly includes me, as well as others who have lived on Lakeview Terrace much longer than I have. In fact, the exodus has already begun, with the people who were displaced by the condo conversions.

8

Conclusion

Of course, many people would consider what's happening on Lakeview Terrace a genuine improvement in every way, resulting not only in better-looking houses but also in a better class of people. I dispute that. The

9

new people may be more affluent than those they displace, but certainly not "better," not by any standard that counts with me. Gentrification may do wonders for a neighborhood's aesthetics, but it certainly can be hard on its soul.

Restatement of thesis

Analyzing Kevin Cunningham's Essay of Cause and Effect Analysis: Questions for Discussion

1. According to Cunningham, in what way are cities like humans? What does he describe as the three possible outcomes for aging neighborhoods?

2. Cunningham presents this causal chain: Redevelopment (cause) increases property values (effect), which in turn increases property taxes upon reassessment by the city (effect), which leads to the displacement of poorer residents. What other effects can you think of for redevelopment?

3. Cunningham decries the gentrification of the neighborhood, but a neighborhood descending into disrepair is not a desirable alternative outcome. What do you think Cunningham would like to see happen on Lakeview Terrace? How can a neighborhood fend off decay while still maintaining its "soul"?

4. Would the essay have benefited if Cunningham had proposed and speculated about a viable alternative to gentrification? Explain.

SUGGESTIONS FOR WRITING A CAUSE AND EFFECT ANALYSIS

Begin by selecting a manageable topic for your essay. In making your decision, you will need to consider both the amount of information available to you and the time you have to complete your research and writing. For a short essay due in two weeks, for example, you might concentrate on a narrowly defined topic, such as what is causing increasing numbers of students in your community to seek part-time jobs. You probably should not try to examine the reasons for the decline of American labor unions. The second topic would clearly require a significant amount of research and a more elaborate presentation; it is more suitable for a term paper. What is necessary for a successful cause and effect analysis is a clear sense of purpose as well as a careful and objective examination of the topic.

One way to approach writing a cause and effect essay would be to choose a subject, such as the Internet, to view it as a cause, and to write about the effects it has had or will have. The following sample essay introduction sets up the question of whether the effects of the Internet have been positive or negative.

The Internet: Boon or Bane?

Although the Internet has created a wonderful way to access vast amounts of timely information, it has done little to protect the veracity and credibility of the information itself, prompting educators and some government officials to consider establishing a separate Internet with more tightly controlled access. The benefits of the Internet, however, far outweigh the adverse consequences. The Internet can provide free access to product, news, travel, sports, and other timely information. It also allows primary and secondary sources to be easily available to students and researchers around the world. The problem remains, however, that the truth and reliability of the information cannot be determined from the Internet itself. This has raised tremendous concerns among the academic and governmental communities, leading to discussions about starting a more closely watched system of information. Despite this concern, however, the Internet has changed the way information is distributed to the world and has had, as a result, a tremendously positive impact on the world.

While the cause and effect strategy in the preceding essay could be the sole rhetorical approach, the writer has chosen to incorporate the strategy of argument (see Chapter 13). The writer not only sets out to explain the various effects of the Internet, but also to defend it against those who criticize the system for its openness. What other strategies might you add to help explain the cause and effect of the Internet? Would you, for example, compare and contrast life before the arrival of the Internet with life today?

The sample essay introduction illustrates only one approach to writing a cause and effect essay. Another approach would be to choose an effect and to explain its cause or causes. For example, you might decide to write about the women's soccer team at your school to explain why, after two losses, they have won five matches in a row. To do this, you could consult the coach or team members, speak to opponents, check game statistics, or watch a video of the last five matches — if you didn't happen to see them yourself. Once you have gathered and examined the relevant information, you should be ready to determine your thesis statement and to write your cause and effect essay. A possible introduction for this essay follows:

> Transition Game Key to Victories
>
> The women's soccer team has won five straight matches against their toughest opponents. The coach, the players, and even their opponents have ascribed their success to the powerful transition game of the team's halfbacks. Although each victory is won by the efforts of the whole team, the recent victories can be attributed to the halfbacks' gaining control and possession of the ball and dominating play in the quick transitions from defense to offense and their ability to prevent their opponents from doing the same. Clearly, in the last five matches, the transition game has been responsible for the team's victories.

The purpose of the essay is to explain the success of the women's soccer team in its last five matches. Through research, the writer ascertained that the cause of the victories was the strong play of the halfbacks in controlling the transition game.

Establish Your Focus

Decide whether your essay will propose causes, talk about effects, or analyze both causes and effects. Any research you do and any questions you ask will depend on how you wish to concentrate your attention. For example, let's say that as a reporter for the school paper, you are writing a story about a fire that destroyed a high-rise apartment building in the neighborhood, killing four people. In planning your story, you might focus on the cause of the fire: Was there more than one cause? Was carelessness to blame? Was the fire of suspicious origin? You might focus on the effects of the fire: How much damage was done to the building? How many people were left homeless? What was the impact on the families of the four victims? Or you might cover both the reasons for this tragic event and its ultimate effects, setting up a sort of causal chain. Such a focus is crucial as you gather information. For example, student Kevin Cunningham decided early on that he wanted to explore what would happen (the effects) if gentrification continued on his street.

Determine Your Purpose

Once you begin to draft your essay and as you continue to refine it, make sure your purpose is clear. Do you wish your cause and effect analysis to be primarily informative, speculative, or argumentative? An informative essay allows readers to say, "I learned something from this. I didn't know that the fire was caused by faulty wiring." A speculative essay suggests to readers new possibilities: "That never occurred to me before. The high-rise apartment house could indeed be replaced by an office building." An argumentative essay convinces readers that some sort of action should be taken: "I have to agree — fire inspections should occur more regularly in our neighborhood." In his essay on gentrification, Cunningham uses cause and effect analysis to question the value of redevelopment by examining what it does to the heart and soul of a neighborhood. Whatever your purpose, be sure to provide the information necessary to carry it through.

Formulate a Thesis Statement

All essays need a strong, clear thesis statement. When writing an essay using cause and effect, a thesis statement should present clearly either a cause and its effect(s) or an effect and its cause(s). As a third approach, your essay could focus on a complex causal chain of events. Here are a few examples from this chapter.

- "What has the telephone done to us, or for us, in the hundred years of its existence?" John Brooks's opening sentence makes it very easy for the reader to know that he has chosen the telephone as his cause and that he will be exploring its effects in the essay.
- "On March 28, 1979, at 3:53 A.M., a pump at the Harrisburg plant failed." Here, Barry Commoner has chosen the failure of the pump to introduce the causal chain of events that led to the near nuclear disaster at Three Mile Island.
- "Clearly, in the last five matches, the transition game has been responsible for the team's victories." From this sentence, the reader knows that the effect was a series of victories and that the cause was the transition game.

When you begin to formulate your thesis statement, keep these examples in mind. You can find other examples of thesis statements in the essays throughout this book. As you begin to develop your thesis statement, ask yourself, "What is my point?" Next, ask yourself, "What approach to a cause and effect essay will be most useful in making my point?" If you can't answer these questions yet, write some ideas down and try to determine your main point from these ideas.

Avoid Oversimplification and Errors of Logic

Sound and thoughtful reasoning, while present in all good writing, is central to any analysis of cause and effect. Writers of convincing cause and effect analysis must examine their material objectively and develop their essays carefully, taking into account any potential objections that readers might raise. Therefore, do not jump to conclusions or let your prejudices interfere with the logic of your interpretation or the completeness of your presentation. In gathering information for his essay, Kevin Cunningham discovered that he had to watch himself — that he had to distinguish between cause and effect and mere coincidence. "You have to know your subject, and you have to be honest. For example, my downstairs neighbors moved out last month because the rent was raised. Somebody who didn't know the situation might say, 'See? Gentrification.' But that wasn't the reason — it's that heating costs went up. This is New England, and we had a cold winter; gentrification had nothing to do with it. It's something that is just beginning to happen, and it's going to have a big effect, but we haven't actually felt many of the effects here yet."

Be sure that you do not oversimplify the cause and effect relationship you are writing about. A good working assumption is that most important matters cannot be traced to a single verifiable cause; similarly, a cause or set of causes rarely produces a single isolated effect. To be believable, your analysis of your topic must demonstrate a thorough understanding of the surrounding circumstances; there is nothing less convincing than the single-minded determination to show one particular connection. For example, someone writing about how the passage of a tough new crime bill (cause) has led to a decrease in arrests in a particular area (effect) will have little credibility unless other possible causes — socioeconomic conditions, seasonal fluctuations in crime, the size and budget of the police force, and so on — are also examined and taken into account. Of course, to achieve coherence, you will want to emphasize the important causes or the most significant effects. But be careful not to lose your reader's trust by insisting on an oversimplified "X leads to Y" relationship.

The other common problem in cause and effect analysis is lack of evidence in establishing a cause or effect. This error is known as the "after this, therefore because of this" fallacy (in Latin, *post hoc, ergo propter hoc*). In attempting to discover an explanation for a particular event or circumstance, a writer may point to something that merely preceded it in time, assuming a causal connection where none has in fact been proven. If you have dinner out one evening and the next day come down with stomach cramps, you may blame your illness on the restaurant where you ate the night before; but you do so without justification if your only proof is the fact that you ate there beforehand. More evidence would be required to establish a causal relationship. The *post hoc, ergo propter hoc* fallacy is often harmlessly foolish ("I failed the exam because I lost my lucky key chain"). It can, however, lead writers into serious errors of judgment and blind them to more reasonable explanations of cause and effect. And, like oversimplification, such mistakes in logic can undercut a reader's confidence. Make sure that the causal relationships you cite are, in fact, based on demonstrable evidence and not merely on a temporal connection.

Strike a Balanced Tone

Be careful to neither overstate nor understate your position. Avoid exaggerations like "there can be no question" and "the evidence speaks for itself." Such diction is usually annoying and undermines your interpretation. Instead, allow your analysis of the facts to convince readers of the cause and effect relationship you wish to suggest. Do not be afraid to admit the possibility of other viewpoints. At the same time, no analytical writer convinces by understating or qualifying information with words and phrases such as *it seems that, perhaps, maybe, I think, sometimes, most often, nearly always,* or *in my opinion.* While it may be your intention to appear reasonable, overusing such qualifying words can make you sound unclear or indecisive, and it renders your analysis less convincing. Present your case forcefully, but do so honestly and sensibly.

Use Other Rhetorical Strategies

Although cause and effect analysis can be used effectively as a separate writing strategy, it is more common for essays to combine different strategies. For example, the sample essay introduction about the soccer team's victories could have added comparison and contrast to highlight the differences between the team's play in the two losses and in the five victories. Narration from interviews could also have been added to make the piece more colorful and more effective. The essay on the Internet could have incorporated the strategy of argument (see Chapter 13) as well as definition to defend the openness and effectiveness of the Internet. The argument could analyze exactly how the benefits outweigh the drawbacks, while definition could be used to focus the subject matter to better achieve the author's purpose. By combining strategies, the author could have made his point more clearly and more forcefully.

You must always keep the purpose of your essay and the tone you wish to adopt in the front of your mind when combining strategies. Without careful planning, using more than one rhetorical strategy can alter both the direction and the tone of your essay in ways that detract from, rather than contribute to, your ability to achieve your purpose.

As you read the essays in this chapter, consider all of the writing strategies that the authors have used to support their cause and effect analysis. How have these other strategies added to or changed the style of the essay? Are there strategies that you might have added or taken out? What strategies, if any, do you think you might use to strengthen your cause and effect essay? Although some essays are developed using a single rhetorical strategy, more often good writing takes advantage of several strategies to develop the writer's purpose and thesis to produce a stronger essay that is more informative, persuasive, and entertaining.

▶ **Questions for Revision: Cause and Effect Analysis**

1. Why do I want to use cause and effect: to inform, to speculate, or to argue? Does my analysis help me achieve my purpose?

2. Is my topic manageable for the essay I wish to write? Have I effectively established my focus?

3. Does my thesis statement clearly state either the cause and its effects or the effect and its causes?

4. Have I identified the nature of my cause and effect scenario? Is there a causal chain? Have I identified immediate and remote causes? Have I distinguished between possible and actual causes and effects?

5. Have I been able to avoid oversimplifying the cause and effect relationship I am writing about? Are there any errors in my logic?

6. Is my tone balanced, neither overstating nor understating my position?

7. Is there another rhetorical strategy that I can use with cause and effect to assist me in achieving my purpose? If so, have I been able to implement it with care so that I have not altered either the direction or the tone of my essay?

How Boys Become Men

Jon Katz

Journalist and novelist Jon Katz was born in 1947. He writes with a keen understanding of life in contemporary suburban America. Each of his four mystery novels is a volume in the Suburban Detective Mystery series: The Family Stalker *(1994),* Death by Station Wagon *(1994),* The Father's Club *(1996), and* The Last Housewife *(1996). The best known of these novels,* The Last Housewife, *won critical praise for its insights into the pressures and conflicts experienced by young professional couples in their efforts to achieve the American dream. It has been made into a popular film. Katz is also the author of* Media Rants: Postpolitics in the Digital Nation *(1997), a collection of his newspaper columns dealing primarily with the role and influence of the media in the public life of modern America;* Virtuous Reality: How Americans Surrendered Discussion of Moral Values to Opportunists, Nitwits, and Blockheads Like William Bennett *(1998); and* Geeks: How Two Lost Boys Rode the Internet Out of Idaho *(2000).*

In the following essay, first published in January 1993 in Glamour, *Katz explains why many men appear insensitive.*

BEFORE YOU READ

How important are childhood experiences to the development of identity? How do the rituals of the playground, the slumber party, and the neighborhood gang help mold us as men and women? Can you think of examples from your own experience?

Two nine-year-old boys, neighbors and friends, were walking home from school. The one in the bright blue windbreaker was laughing and swinging a heavy-looking book bag toward the head of his friend, who kept ducking and stepping back. "What's the matter?" asked the kid with the bag, whooshing it over his head. "You chicken?"

His friend stopped, stood still and braced himself. The bag slammed into the side of his face, the thump audible all the way across the street where I stood watching. The impact knocked him to the ground, where he lay mildly stunned for a second. Then he struggled up, rubbing the side of his head. "See?" he said proudly. "I'm no chicken."

No. A chicken would probably have had the sense to get out of the way. This boy was already well on the road to becoming a *man,* having learned one of the central ethics of his gender: Experience pain rather than show fear.

Women tend to see men as a giant problem in need of solution. They tell us that we're remote and uncommunicative, that we need to demonstrate less machismo and more commitment, more humanity. But if you don't understand something about boys, you can't understand why men are the way we are, why we find it so difficult to make friends or to acknowledge our fears and problems.

Boys live in a world with its own Code of Conduct, a set of ruthless, unspoken, and unyielding rules: 5

> Don't be a goody-goody.
> Never rat. If your parents ask about bruises, shrug.
> Never admit fear. Ride the roller coaster, join the fistfight, do what you have to do. Asking for help is for sissies.
> Empathy is for nerds. You can help your best buddy, under certain circumstances. Everyone else is on his own.
> Never discuss anything of substance with anybody. Grunt, shrug, dump on teachers, laugh at wimps, talk about comic books. Anything else is risky.

Boys are rewarded for throwing hard. Most other activities — reading, befriending girls, or just thinking — are considered weird. And if there's one thing boys don't want to be, it's weird.   6

More than anything else, boys are supposed to learn how to handle themselves. I remember the bitter fifth-grade conflict I touched off by elbowing aside a bigger boy named Barry and seizing the cafeteria's last carton of chocolate milk. Teased for getting aced out by a wimp, he had to reclaim his place in the pack. Our fistfight, at recess, ended with my knees buckling and my lip bleeding while my friends, sympathetic but out of range, watched resignedly.   7

When I got home, my mother took one look at my swollen face and screamed. I wouldn't tell her anything, but when my father got home I cracked and confessed, pleading with them to do nothing. Instead, they called Barry's parents, who restricted his television for a week.   8

The following morning, Barry and six of his pals stepped out from behind a stand of trees. "It's the rat," said Barry.   9

I bled a little more. *Rat* was scrawled in crayon across my desk.   10

They were waiting for me after school for a number of afternoons to follow. I tried varying my routes and avoiding bushes and hedges. It usually didn't work.   11

I was as ashamed for telling as I was frightened. "You did ask for it," said my best friend. Frontier Justice has nothing on Boy Justice.   12

In panic, I appealed to a cousin who was several years older. He followed me home from school, and when Barry's gang surrounded me, he came barreling toward us. "Stay away from my cousin," he shouted, "or I'll kill you."   13

After they were gone, however, my cousin could barely stop laughing. "You were afraid of *them?*" he howled. "They barely came up to my waist."   14

Men remember receiving little mercy as boys; maybe that's why 15
it's sometimes difficult for them to show any.

"I know lots of men who had happy childhoods, but none who 16
have happy memories of the way other boys treated them," says a
friend. "It's a macho marathon from third grade up, when you start
butting each other in the stomach."

"The thing is," adds another friend, "you learn early on to hide 17
what you feel. It's never safe to say, 'I'm scared.' My girlfriend asks me
why I don't talk more about what I'm feeling. I've gotten better at it,
but it will *never* come naturally."

You don't need to be a shrink to see how the lessons boys learn af- 18
fect their behavior as men. Men are being asked, more and more, to
show sensitivity, but they dread the very word. They struggle to build
their increasingly uncertain work lives but will deny they're in trouble.
They want love, affection, and support but don't know how to ask for
them. They hide their weaknesses and fears from all, even those they
care for. They've learned to be wary of intervening when they see others
in trouble. They often still balk at being stigmatized as weird.

Some men get shocked into sensitivity — when they lose their 19
jobs, their wives, or their lovers. Others learn it through a strong marriage, or through their own children.

It may be a long while, however, before male culture evolves to 20
the point that boys can learn more from one another than how to hit
curve balls. Last month, walking my dog past the playground near my
house, I saw three boys encircling a fourth, laughing and pushing
him. He was skinny and rumpled, and he looked frightened. One boy
knelt behind him while another pushed him from the front, a trick familiar to any former boy. He fell backward.

When the others ran off, he brushed the dirt off his elbows and 21
walked toward the swings. His eyes were moist and he was struggling
for control.

"Hi," I said through the chain-link fence. "How ya doing?" 22

"Fine," he said quickly, kicking his legs out and beginning his 23
swing.

RESPONDING TO READING

Do you agree with Katz that men in general are less communicative, less
sensitive, and less sympathetic in their behavior than women? Why or why
not? Where does "Boy Justice" originate?

QUESTIONING THE TEXT

1. In paragraph 12, what does Katz mean when he says, "Frontier Justice
   has nothing on Boy Justice"?

2. What is it that boys are supposed to learn "more than anything else" (paragraph 7)? What do you think girls are supposed to learn more than anything else?

3. How, according to Katz, do some men finally achieve sensitivity? Can you think of other softening influences on adult males?

UNDERSTANDING THE WRITER'S CRAFT

1. This essay was originally published in *Glamour* magazine. Can you find any places where Katz addresses himself specifically to an audience of young women? Where are these places? (Glossary: *Audience*)

2. Early in the essay, Katz refers to men as "we," but later he refers to men as "they." What is the purpose of this change?

3. Notice that in paragraphs 16 and 17, Katz quotes two friends on the nature of male development. Why is the location of these quotes crucial to the structure of the essay?

EXPLORING LANGUAGE

1. In paragraph 3, Katz identifies what he describes as "one of the central ethics" of his gender. Why does he call it an ethic rather than a rule?

2. Be sure you know the meanings of these words within the context of the essay: *remote* (paragraph 4), *machismo* (4), *empathy* (5), *resignedly* (7), *barreling* (13), *balk* (18), *stigmatized* (18).

COMBINING RHETORICAL STRATEGIES

Katz illustrates his thesis with three anecdotes. Identify each of them. Where in the essay is each located? How do they differ? How does each serve to enhance the author's message? (Glossary: *Narration*)

WRITING SUGGESTIONS

1. **(Cause and Effect)** Discuss with classmates the expectations that shape women; in your discussion you might find it helpful to share anecdotes from your own experience. (It may be helpful to review your response to the Before You Read questions.) Write an essay patterned on "How Boys Become Men," showing the causes and effects surrounding females growing up in American culture. You might come to the conclusion that women do not have a standard way of growing up; you could also write a cause and effect essay supporting this idea. Either way, be sure to include forceful examples.

2. **(Other Strategies)** The differences between men and women have always been food for controversy — and humor, as *The New Yorker* cartoon on page 525 by Ed Fisher demonstrates. What gender stereotypes does the cartoon use in its humor? What does it say about male-female

relations in general? The subject perpetually spawns a lot of discussion and debate, and a spate of recently published and widely read books have commented seriously on relationship issues. Read one of these books. (*Men Are from Mars, Women Are from Venus* by John Gray and *You Just Don't Understand* by Deborah Tannen are good examples.) Write a review presenting and evaluating the major thesis of the book you have chosen. Other than evolution, what issues make male-female relations so problematic so much of the time? What can be done to bridge what the cartoon communicates is a huge "gender gap" that many of us seem to need experts, books, and teaching to understand?

"It isn't that I don't love you. It's just that I've evolved and you haven't."

3. **(Research)** With classmates, brainstorm a list of professions in which the character and behavior of the practitioners are sharply affected by cultural expectations (physician and professional athlete are obvious examples). Choose from this list a profession that interests you. Interview two or three people involved in the profession to discover their views about how they are expected to act, the means by which they learned to behave appropriately, and how they feel about the pressures to meet cultural expectations. Write an essay examining the causes and effects of particular professional behaviors. You may wish to support your essay with research from the library and possibly the Internet. The following Web sites will help you get started on your research.

- **Association for Women in Science**
  <http://www.serve.com/awis>

  This Web site's goal is "achieving equity and full participation for women in science, technology, and engineering."

- **Job Listings**

<http://directory.google.com/Top/Business/Employment>

The Google.com employment Web directory includes links to job databases and recruiting and career consultant services for a huge spectrum of employment fields ranging from agriculture and forestry to translation services.

Changing My Name after Sixty Years

Tom Rosenberg

Tom Rosenberg was born in Berlin, Germany, but in 1938 his family fled Nazi persecution, settling in New York City when Rosenberg was six years old. In an attempt to downplay their Jewish heritage, the Rosenbergs changed their surname to Ross upon arriving in the United States. As Tom Ross, Rosenberg grew up in New York, graduated from the University of Pittsburgh, then joined the Marines and served in Korea. He moved to the West Coast upon returning to the United States and served as a political consultant for nearly thirty years, spearheading environmental and outdoor recreation initiatives. He recently published his first novel, Phantom on His Wheel *(2000), which draws upon his interests in journalism, environmentalism, and politics.*

The following essay, which appeared in the July 17, 2000, issue of Newsweek, *shows how Rosenberg spent most of his life denying his heritage and explains why he has chosen to embrace it now.*

BEFORE YOU READ

Surnames mean a lot in our culture; whether or not we like it, they tell others something about our ethnicity, our heritage, and our possible cultural influences. Not long ago, having a surname that was readily identifiable as "foreign" could be a liability. For the most part, attitudes about names have changed for the better. What do you think your surname says about you? Is it relatively common or unusual? Have you ever felt hindered or discriminated against because of it? If you could change it, would you? Why or why not?

My parents left Nazi Germany in 1938, when I was 6 and my mother was pregnant with my sister. They arrived in America with a lot of baggage — guilt over deserting loved ones, anger over losing their home and business, and a lifelong fear of anti-Semitism. 1

Shortly thereafter, whether out of fear, a desire to assimilate or a combination of both, they changed our family name from Rosenberg to Ross. My parents were different from the immigrants who landed on Ellis Island and had their names changed by an immigration bureaucrat. My mother and father voluntarily gave up their identity and a measure of pride for an Anglicized name. 2

Growing up a German-Jewish kid in the Bronx in the 1940s, a time when Americans were dying in a war fought in part to save Jews from the hated Nazis, was difficult. Even my new name failed to protect me from bigotry; the neighborhood bullies knew a "sheenie" when they saw one. 3

The bullying only intensified the shame I felt about my family's religious and ethnic background. I spent much of my youth denying 4 my roots and vying for my peers' acceptance as "Tom Ross." Today I look back and wonder what kind of life I might have led if my parents had kept our family name.

In the '50s, I doubt Tom Rosenberg would have been accepted as a pledge by Theta Chi, a predominantly Christian fraternity at my college. He probably would have pledged a Jewish fraternity or had the self-confidence and conviction to ignore the Greek system altogether. Tom Rosenberg might have married a Jewish woman, stayed in the East and maintained closer ties to his Jewish family.

As it was, I moved west to San Francisco. Only after I married and became a father did I begin to acknowledge my Jewish heritage.

My first wife, a liberal Methodist, insisted that I stop running from Judaism. For years we attended both a Unitarian church and a Jewish temple. Her open-minded attitude set the tone in our household and was passed on to our three kids. As a family, we celebrated Christmas and went to temple on the High Holidays. But even though my wife and I were careful to teach our kids tolerance, their exposure to either religion was minimal. Most weekends, we took the kids on ski trips, rationalizing that the majesty of the Sierra was enough of a spiritual experience.

So last year, when I decided to tell my children that I was legally changing my name back to Rosenberg, I wondered how they would react. We were in a restaurant celebrating the publication of my first novel. After they toasted my tenacity for staying with fiction for some 30 years, I made my announcement: "I want to be remembered by the name I was born with."

I explained that the kind of discrimination and stereotyping still evident today had made me rethink the years I'd spent denying my family's history, years that I'd been ashamed to talk about with them. The present political climate — the initiatives attacking social services for immigrants, bilingual education, affirmative action — made me want to shout "I'm an immigrant!" My children were silent for a moment before they smiled, leaned over and hugged me.

The memories of my years of denial continued to dog me as I told friends and family that I planned to change my name. The rabbi at the Reform temple that I belong to with my second wife suggested I go a step further. "Have you thought of taking a Hebrew first name?" he asked.

He must have seen the shocked look on my face. I wondered, is he suggesting I become more religious, more Jewish?" "What's involved?" I asked hesitatingly.

The rabbi explained that the ceremony would be simple and private, just for family and friends. I would make a few remarks about why I had selected my name, and then he would say a blessing.

It took me a moment to grasp the significance of what the rabbi 13 was proposing. He saw my name change as a chance to do more than reclaim a piece of my family's history; it was an opportunity to renew my commitment to Jewish ideals. I realized it was also a way to give my kids the sense of pride in their heritage that they had missed out on as children.

A few months later I stood at the pulpit in front of an open, 14 lighted ark, flanked by my wife and the rabbi. Before me stood my children, holding their children. I had scribbled a few notes for my talk, but felt too emotional to use them. I held on to the lectern for support and winged it.

"Every time I step into a temple, I'm reminded that Judaism has 15 survived for 4,000 years. It's survived because it's a positive religion. My parents, your grandparents, changed their name out of fear. I'm changing it back out of pride. I chose the name Tikvah because it means hope."

RESPONDING TO READING

Why does Rosenberg frame his name change in terms of the present political climate? Do you think his action is an appropriate response to what he terms "the kind of discrimination and stereotyping still evident today" (paragraph 9)? Explain.

QUESTIONING THE TEXT

1. Why did Rosenberg's parents change their name to Ross soon after arriving in the United States?

2. What advantages did Rosenberg enjoy as Tom Ross? How might his life have been different if he had grown up as a Rosenberg?

3. When and why did Rosenberg stop denying his Jewish heritage? When and why did he decide to change his name?

4. What is the significance of Rosenberg's not only changing his last name but also taking a Hebrew first name? Why does he do it?

UNDERSTANDING THE WRITER'S CRAFT

1. Rosenberg's title, along with his name, grab the reader's attention. (Glossary: *Title*) What are some of the questions that his title raises? How effectively does his essay answer them?

2. Trace the causal chain that begins with the primary cause of Rosenberg's parents' changing their surname to Ross. What are the effects on their lives and on the life of their son?

3. Rosenberg uses a mostly chronological organization for his essay. (Glossary: *Organization*) Why is this organization effective? How does he foreshadow his conclusion?

EXPLORING LANGUAGE

1. Rosenberg uses the epithet "sheenie" (paragraph 3) to describe how he was viewed by other kids in the Bronx. What does his use of the slang of the day add to his essay?

2. Identify the words Rosenberg uses to describe himself in the essay. What do they say about the self-image he had as Tom Ross?

3. Discuss Rosenberg's choice of a Hebrew name, Tikvah. Why is it appropriate? By adopting it, what does he wish to say to his family and, through his essay, to his readers?

COMBINING STRATEGIES

Rosenberg says that for years he rationalized that a ski trip to the Sierras offered "enough of a spiritual experience" for his children (paragraph 7). In the context of his essay, define what he means by "spiritual." Why do the secular experiences prove to be inadequate to him in the end?

WRITING SUGGESTIONS

1. **(Cause and Effect)** Write a personal cause and effect essay, using your name, heritage, religion, or some form of inner identification as the primary cause. What effects has it had on your life? How has it enhanced your life? What adverse effects, if any, has it had for you? Without it, how might you be different as a person?

2. **(Other Strategies)** Choose a grandparent from either your maternal or paternal lineage. Write a narrative history of his or her life. What challenges did your grandparent face? How did ethnic and cultural heritage affect the way he or she lived? What has this grandparent passed along to you that you are proud of and wish to pass along to your children? What would you just as soon forget?

3. **(Research)** Select a major religion with which you have little familiarity. It could be Judaism, Islam, Buddhism, Hinduism, or even Christianity. Research the core beliefs, teachings, ethical guidelines, major events and holidays, and basic history of the religion, and write a paper in which you present your findings. How long has the religion prospered? Through what medium are its teachings passed from one generation to the next? How has it been shaped through the years? Why is it of importance today?

- **BeliefNet**
  <http://www.beliefnet.com>

  From the Baha'i faith to Zoroastrianism, this site is an exhaustive resource for information on world religions. It also contains news articles and helpful tools, like a religion question-and-answer section, a dictionary, and advice on finding a house of worship.

- **Religion/Religions/Religious Studies**
  <http://www.clas.ufl.edu/users/gthursby/rel>

  This site, maintained by Professor Gene Thursby of the University of Florida, is a useful source for finding "information and links for study and interpretation of religions." Not only does this site cover most world religions, it also features information and links on "alternative" or "new religions."

- *Religion and Ethics* Newsweekly
  <http://www.pbs.org/wnet/religionandethics>

  This online companion to the popular PBS television series features articles that address "America's growing religious diversity, spiritual practices, and difficult ethical issues."

- **Internet Sacred Text Archive**
  <http://www.sacred-texts.com/index.htm>

  This very thorough site features the full texts of the world's religions. Topics include Eastern, Western, traditional, and esoteric religions.

The Great Kern County Mouse War

Kennedy P. Maize

An environmental journalist, Kennedy P. Maize was born in Pittsburgh, Pennsylvania, in 1944. A 1966 graduate of Penn State University, Maize is a freelance writer whose articles on environmental and energy issues have appeared in Environmental Action, *the* New Republic, Analog, *and* Harper's. *In the early 1990s, Maize's interests in corporate structures and how they interact with environmental concerns led him to start his own newsletter, the* Electricity Daily. *Maize lives in Knoxville, Maryland, where he also maintains a small sheep farm.*

A letter to the editor of the local newspaper about the misguided practice of shooting vultures led Maize to research the events chronicled in the following essay. The essay, which appeared in Audubon *magazine in 1977, explores the war against the rodents of Kern County, California, in the 1920s. Maize's story serves as a lesson for today's readers about just what can happen when humans interfere with the balance of nature.*

BEFORE YOU READ

What sorts of animal pests would you love to get rid of? The cockroaches overrunning your apartment, the skunks that spray your dog, the mosquitoes that make a misery of early summer, the feral cats or raccoons raiding neighborhood garbage cans? How might you go about eliminating them? How would your life be improved as a result? What other consequences might occur?

O nce upon a time, some 75 years ago, the good people of Kern County, California, had an idea. They thought they were very smart. They would rid themselves of all the evil predators that killed their domestic animals, frightened their children, and made life unpleasant. 1

So in the early years of this century, the good citizens of Kern County oiled their shotguns, cleaned their traps, and brewed batches of strychnine. For 20 years they killed the evil predators — the skunk, the fox, the badger, the weasel, the snake, the owl, the hawk. Killed them all, every one they could find. The good folk of Kern County were very pleased. 2

In 1924 the good sheepmen of Kern County concocted a final solution to the "coyote problem." They hired a U.S. Biological Survey team (then part of the Department of Agriculture) to exterminate the entire coyote population. Soon there were no more coyotes in Kern County. 3

The good folk of Kern County were filled with satisfaction by 4
what they had accomplished. They supposed they had created a pleasant paradise where their chickens would have no natural enemies,
their children would never be frightened by talon or fang, and their
dogs would never return stinking of skunk. Providence, they were
sure, would bless their work with healthy animals, happy children,
and bountiful harvests.

Most of the good people of Kern County were either farmers or 5
townsmen in Taft, Tupman, McKittrick, Ford City, and other small vil-
lages. There was one city, Bakersfield, a market center with a population of under 10,000 people. Most of the good people of Kern County
rarely got to Bakersfield. Despite oil derricks that dotted the landscape,
Kern County in the 1920s was rural, agricultural.

Farming in Kern County was risky. Every year farmers planted 6
grain in the fertile 25,000 acres of the dry bed of Buena Vista Lake.
Three years out of every four the lake bed flooded in the fall, destroying the crop. But the fourth year — what a harvest for the good people
of Kern County.

Such a year was 1926. There was kafir corn and barley in such 7
bounty that all California took notice of Kern County's good fortune.
The good merchants of Kern County rubbed their hands together as
they thought about the dresses and cars and fencing and paint and
other things the good farmers would buy with their grain receipts. So
the good farmers reaped their grain, leaving behind 25,000 acres of
stubble and scattered seed. The farmers took their grain to market and
felt secure in their good fortune.

By October the good people of Kern County had begun to notice a 8
minor annoyance. A farmer came to town one Saturday to buy supplies and a new shotgun, and he told the other farmers and the merchants about his little problem, "I killed nearly 500 mice in my barn
last evening," he said. "You'd better sell me some poison, George."

Just as the storekeeper was reaching for the rat poison, his wife 9
was telling a neighbor, "I just don't know about this cat of mine. She's
getting so lazy. Seems like everywhere I look there's a mouse."

And there were mice. Everywhere the good people of Kern County 10
looked, there were mice. The mice had bred in the Buena Vista Lake,
unmolested by predators and well fed on residue from the harvest,
until there were many millions of them. So many, in fact, that the
food supply began to run out. Most were still in the dry lake bed,
which looked as if it had just been cultivated, the result of mice burrowing in the ground. Mice were feeding on the grain residue, and
continuing to breed.

A few mice, maybe a hundred thousand or so, had ventured out of 11
the lake bed by November. The foraging vanguard increased in December. They were invading barns, granaries, and houses looking for

food. In some places near the lake the mice were ankle-deep. People killed them by the thousands. "The way we're slaughtering mice," one farmer said, "they'll soon be as scarce as coyotes. Now, if you'll excuse me, I have to shoot some owls I found in my silo."

If the farmer was wrong about the effect of killing thousands of mice, he can be excused his error. So far the good citizens of Kern County had fought only skirmishes in what would quickly become the Great Kern County Mouse War. But the good people of Kern County thought they had taken heroic measures and that they had won. After all, hadn't the West Side Businessmen's Club in Taft donated $50 for poisoned wheat after the county's deputy horticultural commissioner, C. H. Bowen, described the problem? Taft Mayor Clarence Williams said he would hand out the poison to the good farmers. That ought to do the trick.   12

The effort seemed to work. By Christmas of 1926 Commissioner Bowen, whom the press was calling "General" for his leadership of the war against the mice, told reporters, "By the first of the week I expect our work to be finished." The *Los Angeles Times* of December 29th reported, "Field mouse infestations at Taft and Tupman have been brought under control through the use of poisoned grain, the horticultural commissioner's office announced today."   13

But Kern County didn't understand the dimensions of its mouse problem. All the few hundred pounds of poisoned grain had accomplished was to delay hordes of mice that were marching out of the lake toward new food supplies. A cold snap at Christmas probably did as much to cause the delay as did the poisoned grain.   14

The new year of 1927 opened cold and clear, and the good people of Kern County faced the future with confidence. The mice seemed under control, and there would be prosperity ahead if they continued their eternal vigilance against the hawks, owls, coyotes, and other varmints.   15

Those good people who subscribed to the *Los Angeles Times* may have noticed a small feature article on New Year's Day. A park naturalist pointed out that the hated coyote is a very good mouser. But, of course, the article didn't mean much to the good people of Kern County. There were no coyotes in Kern County.   16

The cold snap broke on January 6th, and the mice emerged from the lake bed in a squirming, furry wave, driven by starvation. The mice had consumed every edible item in the lake bed. Scrambling up the barren, 100-foot Buena Vista Hills, the mice headed for Ford City, McKittrick, and Taft. Millions of mice were on the march toward food. U.S. Highway 399, which ran along the lake bed, became slippery with squashed mice, and cars slid into the ditches. Warning signs reading "Slow: slippery conditions" were posted.   17

Superintendent Bob Maguire of the Honolulu Oil Company put 18 men from the derricks on mouse detail. They dug trenches and spread poisoned barley. Maguire's mouse-control crew killed 50,000 mice in one day on one small piece of company property.

By January 16th, the U.S. Biological Survey was calling the affair 19 in Kern County the greatest rodent infestation in U.S. history. The only other comparable incident was a mouse migration in 1908 in Nevada. But the Biological Survey said the Nevada episode was minuscule compared with the problem in Kern County. Observers reported a "moving landscape" as mice poured over the earth in ankle-deep waves.

One January morning during the mouse invasion, a teacher at 20 Conley School near the lake, opened her desk for the day's lesson plan. A dozen mice leaped out, and she leaped out the school door, shrieking. Mice were in every wastebasket. Mice occupied the principal's office. Mice darted from classroom to classroom. Mice were everywhere.

On January 15th, a headline appeared in the *Los Angeles Times:* 21 "Army of Field Mice Kill and Eat Sheep at Taft." The article reported, "A skirmishing force of the second army of field mice reported to be invading Taft attacked, killed, and ate a sheep at the San Emidio Ranch." The unlucky ewe was kept in a small pen at the head of a canyon and was unable to escape. The article concluded dryly, "The mice have become a distinct annoyance to golfers on the Petroleum Club links on the Maricopa Road."

By January 19th, the mouse war was the *Times'* lead story on the 22 front page. The headlines said:

Pied Pipers
Lure Mice

Poison Stemming
Vast Hegira

Thousands of Rodents Prey
of Own Appetites During
Kern County Trek

"Gen." Bowen Thinks Peril
to Centers of Population
Has Been Overcome

The story was a full description of what was occurring in Kern   23
County, telling of "roads carpeted with mice" and concluding with
the apt observation, "The plague has been aggravated by the fact that
for many years past an unceasing warfare has been waged on the natural enemies of the invaders, such as coyotes, hawks, wildcats, and
other predatory beasts and birds." The reference to the Pied Piper was
a piece of a headline writer's fancy.

Folks around the country offered various ways to redress the nat-   24
ural balance. The northern California town of Merced offered hundreds of hungry cats to the good citizens of Kern County. But cats, it
turned out, weren't much of a solution. There were just too many
mice. A cat, after killing and eating a dozen or so mice, becomes sated
and bored.

Lewis Gingery of Rushville, Missouri, told the good folks of Kern   25
County that a couple of hundred skunks could take care of the problem. He was surprised that local skunks hadn't prevented the population increase in the first place.

But the good citizens of Kern County had killed all the skunks,   26
and they still didn't understand what they had done. Mice surging up
from the lake bed attracted flocks of hawks, owls, ravens, crows, vultures, and even a couple thousand seagulls which flew in from the
coast. As the birds swooped down on the mice, the good people of
Kern County shot-gunned them. They hung the carcasses on fence-
posts to deter other feathered predators.

The good citizens of Kern County were losing the war against the   27
invaders. The mice had multiplied freely over the years. The bumper
crop of food in 1926 had produced a bumper crop of mice. The population spurted until the food ran out. Then tens of millions of mice
found they had to migrate or starve. The mice moved inexorably. By
mid-January they occupied a sector twelve by eight miles.

Then the war escalated. On January 19th, it was announced that   28
the chief poison specialist and exterminator for the U.S. Biological
Survey — the man who had conquered the 1908 Nevada migration —
was being sent from Washington, D.C. The headline writer for the
Times had been prescient. Stanley E. Piper was the exterminator's reassuring name.

Piper arrived in Kern County on Saturday, January 22nd, to exam-   29
ine the area and map his battle plan. On Monday he announced his
intentions. Working with a full-time crew of 25 men, Piper would
stage a counterattack at Buena Vista Lake.

Federal forces set up camp on a high spot in the middle of the dry   30
lake, a place called Pelican Island. The crew then attempted to determine the size of the enemy forces. They dug up an acre of lake bottom
and counted the mouse burrows. They counted 4,000 burrows and
were stunned. They were facing an army of 100 million mice.

Piper quickly hauled in 40 tons of chopped alfalfa, generously   31
laced with strychnine. Piper asked the oil companies to work harder at
controlling the spread of the mice outward, and he concentrated on
the lake bed.

By the end of February, Piper had won. But it had been a costly   32
war. The good farmers of Kern County had lost more than a half-
million dollars in damaged crops, buildings, and fences. The good
townsfolk had lost a similar amount in property damage and unreal-
ized business revenues. Piper's efforts cost $5,000 for grain and sup-
plies, paid for by the good citizens of Kern County. The great Kern
County Mouse War lasted over three months, and mouse deaths
amounted to unknown millions. The sweet prosperity of 1926 had
turned sour.

If one pair of adult mice produces offspring, who in turn produce   33
offspring, who in turn produce offspring, and so on for one year, the
result will be over one million mice — unless there are predators. It is
a lesson that the good people of Kern County should have learned
well. It is a lesson that we all should learn well.

Build a better mousetrap, the old saying has it, and the world will   34
beat a path to your door. The Great Kern County Mouse War proves
that no one builds better mousetraps than nature. Let us beat a path to
her door.

RESPONDING TO READING

How could the people of Kern County have dealt with the problem of local
predators in other ways than systematically killing them off?

QUESTIONING THE TEXT

1. Why was it during a year of bountiful harvest that the mouse population exploded? Why were the people of Kern County initially unable to
   control the explosion?

2. What connection between causes and effects did the people of Kern
   County fail to make?

3. Why were cats not an effective solution to the mouse problem? How
   was the mouse war eventually won?

4. What conflicting roles did the U.S. Biological Survey play in the Mouse
   War?

UNDERSTANDING THE WRITER'S CRAFT

1. What is Maize's thesis? Where in the article is it located? How does its
   location strengthen the impact of the essay?

2. How does Maize inject humor into his factual account? Point out a number of examples. Considering that the subject is a serious one, do you think that humor is appropriate? Why or why not?

3. Four times Maize cites the *Los Angeles Times* (paragraphs 13, 16, 21, 22). What are his purposes in doing so?

EXPLORING LANGUAGE

1. Maize uses the adjective "good" two dozen times to describe the people of Kern County. What is his purpose? Is he being ironic? (Glossary: *Irony*)

2. Precise word usage is important in this tale of an actual environmental disaster. Be sure you know the meaning of each of the following words: *strychnine* (paragraph 2), *kafir corn* (7), *residue* (10), *foraging* (11), *vanguard* (11), *horticultural* (12), *infestations* (13), *vigilance* (15), *varmints* (15), *minuscule* (19), *hegira* (22), *sated* (24), *inexorably* (27), *prescient* (28).

COMBINING RHETORICAL STRATEGIES

Except for the last two brief paragraphs, "The Great Kern County Mouse War" is a single extended illustration of Maize's thesis, written in the form of a historical narrative. Is one long example sufficient to prove a point? How does he succeed or fail to succeed in turning a story into an argument? (Glossary: *Argument; Exemplification*)

WRITING SUGGESTIONS

1. **(Cause and Effect)** Many other attempts to kill "destructive" animals — not just predators, but also creatures that destroy crops or become household pests — have gone awry. Many people are familiar, for example, with the story of how the insecticide DDT was first hailed but finally banned because it was extremely harmful to many forms of life, including humans. Working with classmates and using library resources, compile a list of instances in which human efforts to eliminate a pest have precipitated a dangerous environmental imbalance. Using Maize's essay as a model, choose, research, and write the story of one of these events.

2. **(Other Strategies)** Some environmental crises have been precipitated not by human attempts to destroy pests, but by the introduction, either intentional or inadvertent, of a new species to a particular area. Think, for example, of the huge flocks of starlings that descend from time to time on unsuspecting midwestern towns or of the beautiful purple loosestrife that is taking over the fields of New England. What is being done to combat harmful nonnative species? Following the procedures suggested in the previous assignment, write the story of one introduced species.

3. **(Research)** In his book *Never Cry Wolf,* Canadian author Farley Mowat decries systematic efforts by the Canadian government to eliminate this native animal. Using the library and possibly the Internet, learn and write about the history of the wolf during the last fifty years on the North American continent: the reasons for attempting to eliminate wolf populations in the United States and Canada, the effects of these efforts, and the conflicts resulting from more recent efforts to reintroduce the species. The following Web sites will help you get started on your research.

- **Yellowstone Wolf Report**

  <http://www.yellowstone-natl-park.com/wolf.htm>

  This site, part of the Total Yellowstone Page, offers information about wolves in Yellowstone National Park and beyond.

- **NOVA Online**

  <http://www.pbs.org/wgbh/nova/wolves>

  This site offers articles, resources, and links to information about wolves in North America.

- **Reintroduction of the Wolf into the Southwestern U.S.**

  <http://www.ems.psu.edu/Wolf>

  This Web site, maintained at Penn State University, gives information on both sides of the wolf reintroduction debate.

- **North American Wolf Association**

  <http://www.nawa.org>

  This site is maintained by "a non-profit organization dedicated to the reintroduction and preservation of wolves."

The Face of Beauty

Diane Ackerman

Diane Ackerman was born in 1948 in Waukegan, Illinois, and received degrees from Pennsylvania State University and Cornell University. A prolific writer, Ackerman is admired by readers and critics alike for her poetic skill combined with a wide knowledge of science and natural history. She is best known for several nonfiction works that showcase this combination: A Natural History of the Senses *(1990);* The Moon by Whale Light, and Other Adventures among Bats, Penguins, Crocodilians, and Whales *(1991);* A Natural History of Love *(1994); and* The Rarest of the Rare: Vanishing Animals, Timeless Worlds *(1995). Ackerman has been a staff writer for* The New Yorker, *a writer-in-residence at several major universities, and the host of the Public Broadcasting System series* Mystery of the Senses. *She has also published two volumes of memoirs and a number of books of poetry, the most recent of which is* I Praise My Destroyer *(1998).*

The following essay, which originally appeared in A Natural History of the Senses, *offers a good example of Ackerman's fine eye for detail and her adventurousness, qualities that have won her a wide following.*

BEFORE YOU READ

What physical characteristics do you find particularly attractive in other people? What are the chief physical qualities that make one person appear beautiful to others? Do these ideas of attractiveness and beauty change over time?

In a study in which men were asked to look at photographs of pretty women, it was found they greatly preferred pictures of women whose pupils were dilated. Such pictures caused the pupils of the men's eyes to dilate as much as 30 percent. Of course, this is old news to women of the Italian Renaissance and Victorian England alike, who used to drop belladonna (a poisonous plant in the nightshade family, whose name means "beautiful woman") into their eyes to enlarge their pupils before they went out with gentlemen. Our pupils expand involuntarily when we're aroused or excited; thus, just seeing a pretty woman with dilated pupils signaled the men that she found them attractive, and that made their pupils begin a body-language tango in reply. When I was on shipboard recently, traveling through the ferocious winds and waves of Drake Passage and the sometimes bouncy waters around the Antarctic peninsula, the South Orkneys, South Georgia, and the Falklands, I noticed that many passengers wore a scopolamine patch behind one ear to combat seasickness. Greatly dilated pupils, a side effect of the patch, began to appear a few days into the trip; everybody one met had large, welcoming eyes, which no

doubt encouraged the feeling of immediate friendship and camaraderie. Some people grew to look quite zombielike, as they drank in
wide gulps of light, but most seemed especially open and warm. Had
they checked, the women would have discovered that their cervixes
were dilated, too. In professions where emotion or sincere interests
need to be hidden, such as gambling or jade-dealing, people often
wear dark glasses to hide intentions visible in their telltale pupils.

We may pretend that beauty is only skin deep, but Aristotle was   2
right when he observed that "beauty is a far greater recommendation
than any letter of introduction." The sad truth is that attractive people
do better in school, where they receive more help, better grades, and
less punishment; at work, where they are rewarded with higher pay,
more prestigious jobs, and faster promotions; in finding mates, where
they tend to be in control of the relationships and make most of the
decisions; and among total strangers, who assume them to be interesting, honest, virtuous, and successful. After all, in fairy tales, the first
stories most of us hear, the heroes are handsome, the heroines are
beautiful, and the wicked sots are ugly. Children learn implicitly that
good people are beautiful and bad people are ugly, and society restates
that message in many subtle ways as they grow older. So perhaps it's
not surprising that handsome cadets at West Point achieve a higher
rank by the time they graduate, or that a judge is more likely to give
an attractive criminal a shorter sentence. In a 1968 study conducted in
the New York City prison system, men with scars, deformities, and
other physical defects were divided into three groups. The first group
received cosmetic surgery, the second intensive counseling and therapy, and the third no treatment at all. A year later, when the researchers checked to see how the men were doing, they discovered
that those who had received cosmetic surgery had adjusted the best
and were less likely to return to prison. In experiments conducted by
corporations, when different photos were attached to the same ré-
sumé, the more attractive person was hired. Prettier babies are treated
better than homelier ones, not just by strangers but by the baby's parents as well. Mothers snuggle, kiss, talk to, play more with their baby
if it's cute; and fathers of cute babies are also more involved with
them. Attractive children get higher grades on their achievement tests,
probably because their good looks win praise, attention, and encouragement from adults. In a 1975 study, teachers were asked to evaluate
the records of an eight-year-old who had a low IQ and poor grades.
Every teacher saw the same records, but to some the photo of a pretty
child was attached, and to others that of a homely one. The teachers
were more likely to recommend that the homely child be sent to a
class for retarded children. The beauty of another can be a valuable ac-
cessory. One particularly interesting study asked people to look at a
photo of a man and a woman, and to evaluate only the man. As it

turned out, if the woman on the man's arm was pretty, the man was thought to be more intelligent and successful than if the woman was unattractive.

Shocking as the results of these and similar experiments might be, they confirm what we've known for ages: Like it or not, a woman's face has always been to some extent a commodity. A beautiful woman is often able to marry her way out of a lower class and poverty. We remember legendary beauties like Cleopatra and Helen of Troy as symbols of how beauty can be powerful enough to cause the downfall of great leaders and change the career of empires. American women spend millions on makeup each year; in addition, there are the hairdressers, the exercise classes, the diets, the clothes. Handsome men do better as well, but for a man the real commodity is height. One study followed the professional lives of 17,000 men. Those who were at least six feet tall did much better — received more money, were promoted faster, rose to more prestigious positions. Perhaps tall men trigger childhood memories of looking up to authority — only our parents and other adults were tall, and they had all the power to punish or protect, to give absolute love, set our wishes in motion, or block our hopes.

The human ideal of a pretty face varies from culture to culture, of course, and over time, as Abraham Cowley noted in the seventeenth century:

> Beauty, thou wild fantastic ape
> Who dost in every country change thy shape!

But in general what we are probably looking for is a combination of mature and immature looks — the big eyes of a child, which make us feel protective, the high cheekbones and other features of a fully developed woman or man, which make us feel sexy. In an effort to look sexy, we pierce our noses, elongate our earlobes or necks, tattoo our skin, bind our feet, corset our ribs, dye our hair, have the fat liposuctioned from our thighs, and alter our bodies in countless other ways. Throughout most of western history, women were expected to be curvy, soft, and voluptuous, real earth mothers radiant with sensuous fertility. It was a preference with a strong evolutionary basis: A plump woman had a greater store of body fat and the nutrients needed for pregnancy, was more likely to survive during times of hunger, and would be able to protect her growing fetus and breast-feed it once it was born. In many areas of Africa and India, fat is considered not only beautiful but prestigious for both men and women. In the United States, in the Roaring Twenties and also in the Soaring Seventies and Eighties, when ultrathin was in, men wanted women to have the figures of teenage boys, and much psychological hay could be made from how this reflected the changing role of women in society and the work place. These days, most men I know prefer women to have a curvier, reasonably fit body, although most women I know would still prefer to be "too" thin.

But the face has always attracted an admirer's first glances, especially the eyes, which can be so smoldery and eloquent, and throughout the ages people have emphasized their facial features with makeup. Archaeologists have found evidence of Egyptian perfumeries and beauty parlors dating to 4,000 B.C., and makeup paraphernalia going back to 6,000 B.C. The ancient Egyptians preferred green eye shadow topped with a glitter made from crushing the iridescent carapaces of certain beetles; kohl eye liner and mascara; blue-black lipstick; red rouge; and fingers and feet stained with henna. They shaved their eyebrows and drew in false ones. A fashionable Egyptian woman of those days outlined the veins on her breasts in blue and coated her nipples with gold. Her nail polish signaled social status, red indicating the highest. Men also indulged in elaborate potions and beautifiers; and not only for a night out: Tutankhamen's tomb included jars of makeup and beauty creams for his use in the afterlife. Roman men adored cosmetics, and commanders had their hair coiffed and perfumed and their nails lacquered before they went into battle. Cosmetics appealed even more to Roman women, to one of whom Martial wrote in the first century A.D., "While you remain at home, Galla, your hair is at the hairdresser's; you take out your teeth at night and sleep tucked away in a hundred cosmetic boxes — even your face does not sleep with you. Then you wink at men under an eyebrow you took out of a drawer that same morning." A second-century Roman physician invented cold cream, the formula for which has changed little since then. We may remember from the Old Testament that Queen Jezebel painted her face before embarking on her wicked ways, a fashion she learned from the high-toned Phoenicians in about 850 B.C. In the eighteenth century, European women were willing to eat Arsenic Complexion Wafers to make their skin whiter; it poisoned the hemoglobin in the blood so that they developed a fragile, lunar whiteness. Rouges often contained such dangerous metals as lead and mercury, and when used as lip-stain they went straight into the bloodstream. Seventeenth-century European women and men sometimes wore beauty patches in the shape of hearts, suns, moons, and stars, applying them to their breasts and face, to draw an admirer's eye away from any imperfections, which, in that era, too often included smallpox scars.

Studies conducted recently at the University of Louisville asked college men what they considered to be the ideal components in a woman's face, and fed the results into a computer. They discovered that their ideal woman had wide cheekbones; eyes set high and wide apart; a smallish nose; high eyebrows; a small neat chin; and a smile that could fill half of the face. On faces deemed "pretty," each eye was one-fourteenth as high as the face, and three-tenths its width; the nose didn't occupy more than five percent of the face; the distance from the bottom lip to the chin was one-fifth the height of the face, and the distance from the middle of the eye to the eyebrow was one-tenth the height of the face. Superimpose the faces of many beautiful women onto these computer ratios, and none will match up. What this geometry of beauty boils down to is a portrait of an ideal mother — a young, healthy woman. A mother had to be fertile, healthy, and energetic to protect her young and continue to bear lots of children, many of whom might die in infancy. Men drawn to such women had a stronger chance of their genes surviving. Capitalizing on the continuing subtleties of that appeal, plastic surgeons sometimes advertise with extraordinary bluntness. A California surgeon, Dr. Vincent Forshan, once ran an eight-page color ad in *Los Angeles* magazine showing a gorgeous young woman with a large, high bosom, flat stomach, high, tight buttocks, and long sleek legs posing beside a red Ferrari. The headline over the photo ran: "Automobile by Ferrari . . . *body by Forshan*." Question: What do those of us who aren't tall, flawlessly sculpted adolescents do? Answer: Console ourselves with how relative beauty can be. Although it wins our first praise and the helpless gift of our attention, it can curdle before our eyes in a matter of moments. I remember seeing Omar Sharif in *Doctor Zhivago* and *Lawrence of Arabia,* and thinking him astoundingly handsome. When I saw him being interviewed on television some months later, and heard him declare that his only interest in life was playing bridge, which is how he spent most of his spare time, to my great amazement he was transformed before my eyes into an unappealing man. Suddenly his eyes seemed rheumy and his chin stuck out too much and none of the pieces of his anatomy fell together in the right proportions. I've watched this alchemy work in reverse, too, when a not-particularly-attractive stranger opened his mouth to speak and became ravishing. Thank heavens for the arousing qualities of zest, intelligence, wit, curiosity, sweetness, passion, talent, and grace. Thank heavens that, though good looks may rally one's attention, a lasting sense of a person's beauty reveals itself in stages. Thank heavens, as Shakespeare puts it in *A Midsummer Night's Dream:* "Love looks not with the eyes, but with the mind."

RESPONDING TO READING

Ackerman lists in some detail certain social advantages of being physically attractive. Are all these advantages completely desirable, or do these advantages also have their downside? What are the disadvantages of being beautiful?

QUESTIONING THE TEXT

1. Historically, what are some dangerous practices in which people have been willing to indulge to appear beautiful? Can you think of any current examples?

2. Ackerman calls it a "sad truth" (paragraph 2) that attractive people often have advantages. Why does she make this claim? Do you agree?

3. What does Ackerman mean when she refers to a woman's face and a man's height as "commodities"?

4. According to Ackerman, what qualities other than physical characteristics may cause a person to appear beautiful? What further characteristics might you add to her list?

UNDERSTANDING THE WRITER'S CRAFT

1. This essay consists of only six long paragraphs. What is the purpose of each paragraph? Find the topic sentence of each. (Glossary: *Purpose; Topic Sentence*)

2. Define the audience for which this essay was apparently intended. (Glossary: *Audience*) What individuals or groups might respond negatively to the piece? Why?

3. Throughout her essay, Ackerman moves between historical and contemporary examples of beauty. What is her purpose in structuring the essay in this way? (Glossary: *Organization*)

EXPLORING LANGUAGE

1. Ackerman uses a number of vivid or unusual words and phrases — for example, *body-language tango* (paragraph 1), *wicked sots* (2), *psychological hay* (4), *smoldery* (5), *high-toned* (5). What is the meaning, both explicit and implicit, of each? What is the impact on the reader of such unexpected language? Can you find other examples?

2. Determine the meaning of each of these words: *involuntarily* (paragraph 1), *camaraderie* (1), *prestigious* (2), *implicitly* (2), *commodity* (3), *iridescent* (5), *carapaces* (5), *kohl* (5), *henna* (5), *superimpose* (6), *rheumy* (6), *zest* (6).

COMBINING RHETORICAL STRATEGIES

In this essay, Diane Ackerman argues that physical beauty holds many advantages for those who possess it. What is the chief means by which she supports her argument? Do you find that her technique makes the essay convincing? Why or why not? (Glossary: *Argument*)

WRITING SUGGESTIONS

1. **(Cause and Effect)** The quote from Martial in paragraph 5 brings to mind the Beatles' description of Eleanor Rigby, who "sits by her window, wearing a face that she keeps in a jar by the door." Many people, men and women both, define themselves in part through makeup and accessories, but it would seem that not all are necessarily seeking to beautify themselves. Who chooses to wear outrageous makeup, hairdos, and accessories, and for what purposes? Write an essay in which you explore the causes behind highly unconventional body adornments and the effects desired or achieved by the wearers.

2. **(Other Strategies)** In her essay "Yellow Woman and a Beauty of the Spirit" (p. 142), Leslie Marmon Silko presents a completely different view from Ackerman's of what it means to be beautiful. Write a paper in which you analyze, contrast, and evaluate the concepts of beauty presented in these two essays.

3. **(Research)** Different cultures define physical beauty differently. Choose a culture, such as classical Greece or Renaissance Italy, from which many realistic artistic representations of human beauty still exist. Study a variety of examples, and generalize the characteristics of beauty you find represented by this culture's artists. As an alternative, you might choose a non-Western or pre-Hellenic culture in which the artists represent human beauty in a highly stylized form. Write an essay comparing and contrasting their ideals of beauty with those of modern America; be sure to cite examples. You may choose to illustrate your essay with reproductions of paintings, sculpture, and photographs. The following Web sites will help you get started on your research.

- **The Smithsonian**
  <http://www.si.edu>

  The official Web site of the Smithsonian offers information on all Smithsonian museums and links to other museums.

- **ArtNet Worldwide**
  <http://www.artnet.com>

  This Web site offers information and links regarding contemporary and ancient art.

- **Arts on the Web**
  <http://www.bc.edu/bc_org/avp/cas/fnart/Artweb.html>

  This Web site, maintained at Boston College, offers numerous links to art resources.

- **Web Museum Network**
  <http://watt.emf.net>

  At this collaborative Web site, you will find an index of Internet art resources and museums from around the globe.

- **American Society for Aesthetics**
  <http://aesthetics-online.org>

  This searchable Web site offers links to resources dealing with the philosophical and theoretical aspects of art.

COMBINING SUBJECTS AND STRATEGIES

The photograph below depicts many of the same themes and strategies as the Combining Rhetorical Strategies essay that follows. Your observations about the photograph will help guide you to the key themes and strategies in the essay. After you've read the essay, you may use your observations about both the photograph and the essay to examine how the overlapping themes and strategies work in each medium.

As the photo below, "Ballet Class" by Gale Zucker, suggests, the teaching of dance involves a paradox. As an art form, dance is not natural — it must be taught. At the same time, however, successful teaching gives dancers a sense of control over both their bodies and their lives. The teacher must therefore catalyze the learning process while at the same time allowing the students to discover what they can do for themselves.

Gale Zucker/Stock, Boston

For Discussion

The teacher in the photograph on page 548 is obviously taking a direct approach to teaching correct foot placement to his pupil. Examine the posture and expressions of the two primary figures. What do you notice about them? What is the interaction between them? Does the girl enjoy her dance class? Explain your answer.

I Show a Child
What Is Possible

Jacques d'Amboise

Jacques d'Amboise (b. 1934) is better known as a dancer than as a writer. As a small child growing up in a dangerous section of New York City, he was required to accompany his sister to her ballet lessons, primarily as a means to keep him off the streets. A wise teacher enticed the bored child into participating in class. Within a year he was studying under the great George Balanchine, and by the time he was twelve, d'Amboise was dancing professionally. He enjoyed a long, distinguished career as principal dancer with the New York City Ballet Company. He has also appeared in films, Broadway productions, and television specials. Upon retiring from the stage, d'Amboise decided to return to the tough neighborhoods of New York City and teach children as he had been taught. He founded the National Dance Institute for this purpose in 1976 and has since taught dance to thousands of children. With Hope Cooke and his wife, Carolyn George, d'Amboise has coauthored a book, Teaching the Magic of Dance *(1983).*

In the following deceptively simple essay, which first appeared in Parade *in 1989, d'Amboise uses a variety of rhetorical strategies to invite the reader into the world of a great artist and charismatic teacher.*

BEFORE YOU READ

Do you suspect you may have a talent that hasn't been explored or developed? Why is it still lying dormant? What could you do to bring it out?

When I was 7 years old, I was forced to watch my sister's ballet classes. This was to keep me off the street and away from my pals, who ran with gangs like the ones in *West Side Story*. The class was taught by Madame Seda, a Georgian-Armenian who had a school at 181st Street and St. Nicholas Avenue in New York City. As she taught the little girls, I would sit, fidget and diabolically try to disrupt the class by making irritating little noises.

But she was very wise, Madame Seda. She let me get away with it, ignoring me until the end of the class, when everybody did the big jumps, a series of leaps in place, called *changements*.   2

At that point, Madame Seda turned and, stabbing a finger at me, said, "All right, little brother, if you've got so much energy, get up and do these jumps. See if you can jump as high as the girls." So I jumped. And loved it. I felt like I was flying. And she said, "Oh, that was wonderful! From now on, if you are quiet during the class, I'll let you join in the *changements*."   3

After that, I'd sit quietly in the class and wait for the jumps. A few classes later, she said, "You've got to learn how to jump and not make any noise when you come down. You should learn to do the *pliés* [graceful knee bends] that come at the beginning of the class." So I would do *pliés*, then wait respectfully for the end of class to do the jumps.   4

Finally she said, "You jump high, and you are landing beautifully, but you look awful in the air, flaying your arms about. You've got to take the rest of the class and learn how to do beautiful hands and arms."   5

I was hooked.   6

An exceptional teacher got a bored little kid, me, interested in ballet. How? She challenged me to a test, complimented me on my effort and then immediately gave me a new challenge. She set up an environment for the achievement of excellence and cared enough to invite me to be part of it. And, without realizing it fully at the time, I made an important discovery.   7

Dance is the most immediate and accessible of the arts because it involves your own body. When you learn to move your body on a note of music, it's exciting. You have taken control of your body and, by learning to do that, you discover that you can take control of your life.   8

I took classes with Madame Seda for six months, once a week, but at the end of spring, in June 1942, she called over my mother, my sister and me and did an unbelievably modest and generous thing. She said, "You and your sister are very talented. You should go to a better teacher." She sent us to George Balanchine's school — the School of American Ballet.   9

Within a few years, I was performing children's roles. At 15, I became part of a classical ballet company. What an extraordinary thing for a street boy from Washington Heights, with friends in gangs. Half grew up to become policemen and the other half gangsters — and I became a ballet dancer!   10

I had dreamed of being a doctor or an archaeologist or a priest. But by the time I was 17, I was a principal dancer performing major roles in the ballets, and by the time I was 21, I was doing movies,   11

Broadway shows and choreography. I then married a ballerina from New York City Ballet, Carolyn George, and we were (and still are) blessed with two boys and twin daughters.

It was a joyful career that lasted four decades. That's a long time to be dancing and, inevitably, a time came when I realized that there were not many years left for me as a performer. I wasn't sure what to do next, but then I thought about how I had become a dancer, and the teachers who had graced my life. Perhaps I could engage young children, especially boys, in the magic of the arts — in dance in particular. Not necessarily to prepare them to be professional performers, but to create an awareness by giving them a chance to experience the arts. So I started the National Dance Institute. 12

That was 13 years ago. Since then, with the help of fellow teachers and staff at NDI, I have taught dance to thousands of inner-city children. And in each class, I rediscover why teaching dance to children is so important. 13

Each time I can use dance to help a child discover that he can control the way he moves, I am filled with joy. At a class I recently taught at P.S. 59 in Brooklyn, there was one boy who couldn't get from his right foot to his left. He was terrified. Everyone was watching. And what he had to do was so simple: take a step with his left foot on a note of music. All his classmates could do it, but he couldn't. 14

He kept trying, but he kept doing it wrong until finally he was frozen, unable to move at all. I put my arm around him and said, "Let's do it together. We'll do it in slow motion." We did it. I stepped back and said, "Now do it alone, and fast." With his face twisted in concentration, he slammed his left foot down correctly on the note. He did it! 15

The whole class applauded. He was so excited. But I think I was even happier, because I knew what had taken place. He had discovered he could take control of his body, and from that he can learn to take control of his life. If I can open the door to show a child that that is possible, it is wonderful. 16

Dance is the art to express time and space. That is what our universe is about. We can hardly make a sentence without signifying some expression of distance, place or time: "See you later." "Meet you at the corner in five minutes." 17

Dance is the art that human beings have developed to express that we live, right now, in a world of movement and varying tempos. 18

Dance, as an art, has to be taught. However, when teaching, it's important to set up an environment where both the student and teacher can discover together. Never teach something you don't love and believe in. But how to set up that environment? 19

When I have a new group of young students and I'm starting a class, I use Madame Seda's technique. I say, "Can you do this test? I'm 20 going to give all 100 of you exactly 10 seconds to get off your seats and be standing and spread out all over the stage floor. And do it silently. Go!" And I start a countdown. Naturally, they run, yelling and screaming, and somehow arrive with several seconds to spare. I say, "Freeze. You all failed. You made noise, and you got there too soon. I said 'exactly 10 seconds' — not 6 or 8 or 11. Go back to your seats, and we'll do it again. And if you don't get it, we'll go back and do it again until you do. And if, at the end of the hour, you still haven't gotten it, I'm not going to teach you."

They usually get it the second time. Never have I had to do it   21
more than three.

Demand precision, be clear and absolutely truthful. When they re-   22
spond — and they will — congratulate them on the extraordinary control they have just exhibited. Why is that important? Because it's the beginning of knowing yourself, knowing that you can manage yourself if you want. And it's the beginning of dance. Once the children see that we are having a class of precision, order and respect, they are relieved, and we have a great class.

I've taught dance to Russian children, Australian children, Indian   23
children, Chinese children, fat children, skinny children, handicapped children, groups of Australian triathletes, New York City police, senior citizens and 3-year-olds. The technique is the same everywhere, although there are cultural differences.

For example, when I was in China, I would say to the children, "I   24
want everybody to come close and watch what I am going to do." But in China they have had to deal with following a teacher when there are masses of them. And they discovered that the way to see what the teacher does is not to move close but to move away. So 100 people moved back to watch the one — me.

I realized they were right. How did they learn that? Thousands of   25
years of masses of people having to follow one teacher.

There are cultural differences and there are differences among   26
people. In any group of dancers, there are some who are ready and excel more than others. There are many reasons — genetic, environment, the teachers they had. People blossom at different times.

But whatever the differences, someone admiring you, encouraging   27
you, works so much better than the reverse. "You can do it, you are wonderful," works so much better than, "You're no good, the others are better than you, you've got to try harder." That never works.

I don't think there are any untalented children. But I think there   28
are those whose talents never get the chance to flower. Perhaps they were never encouraged. Perhaps no one took the time to find out how to teach them. That is a tragedy.

However, the single most terrible thing we are doing to our chil-   29
dren, I believe, is polluting them. I don't mean just with smog and

crack, but by not teaching them the civilizing things we have taken millions of years to develop. But you cannot have a dance class without having good manners, without having respect. Dance can teach those things.

I think of each person as a trunk that's up in the attic. What are you going to put in the trunk? Are you going to put in machine guns, loud noises, foul language, dirty books and ignorance? Because, if you do, that's what is going to be left after you, that's what your children are going to have, and that will determine the world of the future. Or are you going to fill that trunk with music, dance, poetry, literature, good manners and loving friends? 30

I say, fill your trunk with the best that is available to you from the wealth of human culture. Those things will nourish you and your children. You can clean up your own environment and pass it on to the next generation. That's why I teach dance. 31

RESPONDING TO READING

Recall a teacher who inspired you to become interested in a subject that might not have caught your attention otherwise. How did this teacher engage you? What qualities did this teacher have in common with d'Amboise, and in what ways was he or she different? In your opinion, what are the most important characteristics of a great teacher?

QUESTIONING THE TEXT

1. According to d'Amboise, what makes dance such an ideal artistic discipline for children? How does it empower them?

2. How does he create a classroom environment of "precision, order and respect" (paragraph 22)? Specifically, how does he organize his students? How do they respond?

3. What does d'Amboise mean when he talks about a person's trunk (paragraphs 30 and 31)? Reread the lists of things he would leave out and put into the trunk. Do you agree with his choices? What else might you choose to leave out? To put in?

UNDERSTANDING THE WRITER'S CRAFT

1. Most of the paragraphs in "I Show a Child What Is Possible" are very short. How does d'Amboise support his arguments even though he does not use traditional paragraph structures to do so?

2. Note especially paragraph 6, which consists of one three-word sentence. What is the rhetorical function of this paragraph? How does it affect you as a reader?

3. Paragraph 12 is one of the longer paragraphs in the essay. Show how its structure and purpose differ from those of all the other paragraphs. (Glossary: *Transitions*)

EXPLORING LANGUAGE

1. In paragraph 29, d'Amboise says the worst thing we are doing to our children is "polluting" them. What does he mean? What makes this unexpected word choice effective?

2. Why do you suppose Madame Seda uses the technical dance terms *changements* (paragraph 3) and *pliés* (4) with the child instead of just saying "jumps" and "knee bends"? Does her use of these words relate to d'Amboise's advice to be "absolutely truthful" (22)?

3. Most of the language in this essay is simple and familiar. Be sure you know the meanings of *diabolically* (paragraph 1) and *accessible* (8).

COMBINING RHETORICAL STRATEGIES

1. The language of this essay is easy to read, and its message is clear, but it is a complex piece of writing in structure and purpose. For example, d'Amboise examines not just one but multiple cause and effect relationships. Identify the causes and effects that lie at the heart of the essay.

2. This essay is built in two sections, each of which is introduced by a narrative. (Glossary: *Narration*) What is the purpose of these narratives? In what way are they parallel? How does d'Amboise use personal narrative to make his essay more accessible and immediate?

3. D'Amboise tells the reader very clearly how to teach a discipline effectively. (Glossary: *Process Analysis*) How does he integrate these instructions into the essay, making them relevant and interesting rather than preachy or peripheral?

WRITING SUGGESTIONS

1. **(Cause and Effect)** Review your Responding to Reading answer. Interview a teacher who has been a particular inspiration to you. Following the pattern set by d'Amboise, show what you have learned from your teacher and present in an essay his or her views on (a) the importance and value of the subject matter, both for the teacher and for the students (i.e., what does the subject matter "make possible"?); (b) ways to bring about a desire for learning in students; (c) the relative importance of encouragement and criticism in teaching; (d) things of importance that the teacher has learned from students.

2. **(Other Strategies)** D'Amboise says, "I don't think there are any untalented children" (paragraph 28). Do you agree with him? What do you think he means by *talent?* Examine again "Ballet Class," the photograph of the dancer and teacher by Gale Zucker. If the student is, by

d'Amboise's definition, talented, what is the teacher doing? What is the relationship between talent and teaching or coaching? Write an essay in which you develop your own definition of talent and use it to support or disagree with d'Amboise's statement. (Glossary: *Definition*) In your essay, discuss the role teaching plays in nurturing and developing inherent talent.

3. **(Research)** When the school budget becomes a problem, programs in the arts are often the first to be cut by the school board. Why is this true? How important are the arts in a school program? Write a letter to a school board (theoretical or actual) supporting either the retention of a school program in a particular artistic field or the board's proposal to cut such a program, giving the reasons for your opinion. Make sure you use research in supporting your position. The following Web sites will help you get started on your research.

- **National Endowment for the Arts**
  <http://arts.endow.gov>

  This Web site offers information on grants, endowments, sponsorships, and school-based arts programs.

- **Association for the Advancement of Arts Education**
  <http://www.aaae.org>

  Here you will find links, resources, and information about arts programs in schools.

- **Visual and Performing Arts INFOMINE**
  <http://lib-www.ucr.edu/vpainfo.html>

  This searchable Web site offers a comprehensive index to art-related Internet resources.

Hands *(FICTION)*

Sherwood Anderson

Sherwood Anderson (1876–1941) grew up in Clyde, Ohio, a small town like those he was later to picture in his novels and short stories. He had little formal education and at first drifted from job to job, soon achieving some success as an advertising copywriter and later as the president of a paint factory. He found emptiness in his success, however, and quite suddenly, at the age of thirty-six, he went to Chicago and began a career as a writer of fiction. He wrote several novels, including Windy McPherson's Son *(1916) and* Dark Laughter *(1925), but is best known for his short stories, especially those in the collection* Winesburg, Ohio *(1919), from which "Hands" is taken. Anderson's works all touch upon two themes: the loneliness and frustrations of life in a small town and the alienation felt by people living and working in industrial society.*

BEFORE YOU READ

Have you known a person whom you considered to be eccentric or odd in a benign way? What characteristics set him or her apart? Did the person care about how others thought of him or her? Do you know anything of the person's history that either forced or allowed him or her to behave or live in unusual ways?

U pon the half decayed veranda of a small frame house that stood   1
near the edge of a ravine near the town of Winesburg, Ohio, a fat little old man walked nervously up and down. Across a long field that had been seeded for clover but that had produced only a dense crop of yellow mustard weeds, he could see the public highway along which went a wagon filled with berry pickers returning from the fields. The berry pickers, youths and maidens, laughed and shouted boisterously. A boy clad in a blue shirt leaped from the wagon and attempted to drag after him one of the maidens who screamed and protested shrilly. The feet of the boy in the road kicked up a cloud of dust that floated across the face of the departing sun. Over the long field came a thin girlish voice. "Oh, you Wing Biddlebaum, comb your hair, it's falling into your eyes," commanded the voice to the man, who was bald and whose nervous little hands fiddled about the bare white forehead as though arranging a mass of tangled locks.

Wing Biddlebaum, forever frightened and beset by a ghostly band   2
of doubts, did not think of himself as in any way a part of the life of the town where he had lived for twenty years. Among all the people of Winesburg but one had come close to him. With George Willard, son of Tom Willard, the proprietor of the new Willard House, he had formed something like a friendship. George Willard was the reporter

on the *Winesburg Eagle* and sometimes in the evenings he walked out along the highway to Wing Biddlebaum's house. Now as the old man walked up and down on the veranda, his hands moving nervously about, he was hoping that George Willard would come and spend the evening with him. After the wagon containing the berry pickers had passed, he went across the field through the tall mustard weeds and climbing a rail fence peered anxiously along the road to the town. For a moment he stood thus, rubbing his hands together and looking up and down the road, and then, fear overcoming him, ran back to walk again upon the porch of his own house.

In the presence of George Willard, Wing Biddlebaum, who for twenty years had been the town mystery, lost something of his timidity, and his shadowy personality, submerged in a sea of doubts, came forth to look at the world. With the young reporter at his side, he ventured in the light of day into Main Street or strode up and down on the rickety front porch of his own house, talking excitedly. The voice that had been low and trembling became shrill and loud. The bent figure straightened. With a kind of wriggle, like a fish returned to the brook by the fisherman, Biddlebaum the silent began to talk, striving to put into words the ideas that had been accumulated by his mind during long years of silence.

Wing Biddlebaum talked much with his hands. The slender expressive fingers, forever active, forever striving to conceal themselves in his pockets or behind his back, came forth and became the piston rods of his machinery of expression.

The story of Wing Biddlebaum is a story of hands. Their restless activity, like unto the beating of the wings of an imprisoned bird, had given him his name. Some obscure poet of the town had thought of it. The hands alarmed their owner. He wanted to keep them hidden away and looked with amazement at the quiet inexpressive hands of other men who worked beside him in the fields, or passed, driving sleepy teams on country roads.

When he talked to George Willard, Wing Biddlebaum closed his fists and beat with them upon a table or on the walls of his house. The action made him more comfortable. If the desire to talk came to him when the two were walking in the fields, he sought out a stump or the top board of a fence and with his hands pounding busily talked with renewed ease.

The story of Wing Biddlebaum's hands is worth a book itself. Sympathetically set forth it would tap many strange, beautiful qualities in obscure men. It is a job for a poet. In Winesburg the hands had attracted attention merely because of their activity. With them Wing Biddlebaum had picked as high as a hundred and forty quarts of strawberries in a day. They became his distinguishing feature, the source of his fame. Also they made more grotesque an already grotesque and elusive individuality. Winesburg was proud of the hands of Wing Biddlebaum in the same spirit in which it was proud of Banker White's new stone house and Wesley Moyer's bay stallion, Tony Tip, that had won the two-fifteen trot at the fall races in Cleveland.

As for George Willard, he had many times wanted to ask about the hands. At times an almost overwhelming curiosity had taken hold of him. He felt that there must be a reason for their strange activity and their inclination to keep hidden away and only a growing respect for Wing Biddlebaum kept him from blurting out the questions that were often in his mind.   8

Once he had been on the point of asking. The two were walking in the fields on a summer afternoon and had stopped to sit upon a grassy bank. All afternoon Wing Biddlebaum had talked as one inspired. By a fence he had stopped and beating like a giant woodpecker upon the top board had shouted at George Willard, condemning his tendency to be too much influenced by the people about him. "You are destroying yourself," he cried.   9

"You have the inclination to be alone and to dream and you are afraid of dreams. You want to be like others in town here. You hear them talk and you try to imitate them."   10

On the grassy bank Wing Biddlebaum had tried again to drive his point home. His voice became soft and reminiscent, and with a sigh of contentment he launched into a long rambling talk, speaking as one lost in a dream.   11

Out of the dream Wing Biddlebaum made a picture for George Willard. In the picture men lived again in a kind of pastoral golden age. Across a green open country came clean-limbed young men, some afoot, some mounted upon horses. In crowds the young men came to gather about the feet of an old man who sat beneath a tree in a tiny garden and who talked to them.   12

Wing Biddlebaum became wholly inspired. For once he forgot the hands. Slowly they stole forth and lay upon George Willard's shoulders. Something new and bold came into the voice that talked. "You must try to forget all you have learned," said the old man. "You must begin to dream. From this time on you must shut your ears to the roaring of the voices."   13

Pausing in his speech, Wing Biddlebaum looked long and earnestly at George Willard. His eyes glowed. Again he raised the hands to caress the boy and then a look of horror swept over his face.   14

With a convulsive movement of his body, Wing Biddlebaum sprang to his feet and thrust his hands deep into his trousers pockets. Tears came to his eyes. "I must be getting along home. I can talk no more with you," he said nervously.   15

Without looking back, the old man had hurried down the hillside   16
and across a meadow, leaving George Willard perplexed and frightened upon the grassy slope. With a shiver of dread the boy arose and
went along the road toward town. "I'll not ask him about his hands,"
he thought, touched by the memory of the terror he had seen in the
man's eyes. "There's something wrong, but I don't want to know what
it is. His hands have something to do with his fear of me and of everyone."

And George Willard was right. Let us look briefly into the story of   17
the hands. Perhaps our talking of them will arouse the poet who will
tell the hidden wonder story of the influence for which the hands
were but fluttering pennants of promise.

In his youth Wing Biddlebaum had been a school teacher in a   18
town in Pennsylvania. He was not then known as Wing Biddlebaum,
but went by the less euphonic name of Adolph Myers. As Adolph
Myers he was much loved by the boys of his school.

Adolph Myers was meant by nature to be a rare teacher of youth.   19
He was one of those rare, little-understood men who rule by a power
so gentle that it passes as a lovable weakness. In their feeling for the
boys under their charge such men are not unlike the finer sort of
women in their love of men.

And yet that is but crudely stated. It needs the poet there. With   20
the boys of his school, Adolph Myers had walked in the evening or
had sat talking until dusk upon the schoolhouse steps lost in a kind of
dream. Here and there went his hands, caressing the shoulders of the
boys, playing about the tousled heads. As he talked his voice became
soft and musical. There was a caress in that also. In a way the voice
and the hands, the stroking of the shoulders and the touching of the
hair was a part of the schoolmaster's effort to carry a dream into the
young minds. By the caress that was in his fingers he expressed himself. He was one of those men in whom the force that creates life is
diffused, not centralized. Under the caress of his hands doubt and dis-
belief went out of the minds of the boys and they began also to
dream.

And then the tragedy. A half-witted boy of the school became en-   21
amored of the young master. In his bed at night he imagined unspeakable things and in the morning went forth to tell his dreams as facts.
Strange, hideous accusations fell from his loose-hung lips. Through
the Pennsylvania town went a shiver. Hidden, shadowy doubts that
had been in men's minds concerning Adolph Myers were galvanized
into beliefs.

The tragedy did not linger. Trembling lads were jerked out of bed   22
and questioned. "He put his arms about me," said one. "His fingers
were always playing in my hair," said another.

One afternoon a man of the town, Henry Bradford, who kept a sa- ²³
loon, came to the schoolhouse door. Calling Adolph Myers into the
school yard he began to beat him with his fists. As his hard knuckles
beat down into the frightened face of the schoolmaster, his wrath became more and more terrible. Screaming with dismay, the children
ran here and there like disturbed insects. "I'll teach you to put your
hands on my boy, you beast," roared the saloon keeper, who, tired of
beating the master, had begun to kick him about the yard.

Adolph Myers was driven from the Pennsylvania town in the ²⁴
night. With lanterns in their hands a dozen men came to the door of
the house where he lived alone and commanded that he dress and
come forth. It was raining and one of the men had a rope in his
hands. They had intended to hang the schoolmaster, but something
in his figure, so small, white, and pitiful, touched their hearts and
they let him escape. As he ran away into the darkness they repented of
their weakness and ran after him, swearing and throwing sticks and
great balls of soft mud at the figure that screamed and ran faster and
faster into the darkness.

For twenty years Adolph Myers had lived alone in Winesburg. He ²⁵
was but forty but looked sixty-five. The name Biddlebaum he got from
a box of goods seen at a freight station as he hurried through an eastern Ohio town. He had an aunt in Winesburg, a black-toothed old
woman who raised chickens, and with her he lived until she died. He
had been ill for a year after the experience in Pennsylvania, and after
his recovery worked as a day laborer in the fields, going timidly about
and striving to conceal his hands. Although he did not understand
what had happened he felt that the hands must be to blame. Again
and again the fathers of the boys had talked of the hands. "Keep your
hands to yourself," the saloon keeper had roared, dancing with fury in
the schoolhouse yard.

Upon the veranda of his house by the ravine, Wing Biddlebaum ²⁶
continued to walk up and down until the sun had disappeared and
the road beyond the field was lost in the grey shadows. Going into his
house he cut slices of bread and spread honey upon them. When the
rumble of the evening train that took away the express cars loaded
with the day's harvest of berries had passed and restored the silence of
the summer night, he went again to walk upon the veranda. In the
darkness he could not see the hands and they became quiet. Although
he still hungered for the presence of the boy, who was the medium
through which he expressed his love of man, the hunger became
again a part of his loneliness and his waiting. Lighting a lamp, Wing
Biddlebaum washed the few dishes soiled by his simple meal and, setting up a folding cot by the screen door that led to the porch, prepared to undress for the night. A few stray white bread crumbs lay on
the cleanly washed floor by the table; putting the lamp upon a low

stool he began to pick up the crumbs, carrying them to his mouth one by one with unbelievable rapidity. In the dense blotch of light beneath the table, the kneeling figure looked like a priest engaged in some service of his church. The nervous expressive fingers, flashing in and out of the light, might well have been mistaken for the fingers of the devotee going swiftly through decade after decade of his rosary.

RESPONDING TO READING

"Hands" is a disturbing story, told in an unusual manner. What would you say is the tone of the story? (Glossary: *Tone*) How well do you think it fits with the subject matter? Explain your answers.

QUESTIONING THE TEXT

1. What is remarkable about Wing Biddlebaum's hands? How are they associated with the name he has acquired?

2. What is Wing's relationship with George Willard? Why does Willard refrain from asking about his friend's hands?

3. What was Wing's name in his former life? What was his gift?

4. How did Wing come to be persecuted? Why did he flee?

UNDERSTANDING THE WRITER'S CRAFT

1. What does George Willard symbolize to Wing Biddlebaum and to the reader? (Glossary: *Symbol*) Why does Wing like George and allow him to get closer to him than the others? Why does George also cause Wing to feel such pain?

2. Anderson allows the reader to get to "know" the Wing Biddlebaum that Winesburg, Ohio, knows before revealing his history and the causal chain behind his eccentric, frightened character. What does he gain by beginning with the end of the story, so to speak? How effective is his cause and effect presentation as a result? Explain your answer.

3. At the end of the story, Anderson uses an analogy regarding Biddlebaum's posture and movements. (Glossary: *Analogy*) What is the analogy? What does it connote about Biddlebaum, his life, and his predicament?

EXPLORING LANGUAGE

1. Hands, as Anderson states, are an integral part of Wing's story. What words does Anderson use to describe them? To what does he compare them? (Glossary: *Figures of Speech*) Why are Biddlebaum's hands so compelling?

2. In describing the teaching style of Adolph Myers, Anderson says he tried to "carry a dream into the young minds" (paragraph 20). What does that statement mean? In what way might this sort of teaching be better than a more prosaic passing of information? In what way does his teaching method later get Myers into trouble?

3. Anderson characterizes Wing Biddlebaum's hands as making "more grotesque an already grotesque and elusive individuality" (paragraph 7). Yet he also states that Winesburg is "proud" of those hands (7). What does the use of *grotesque* in this context connote to you? (Glossary: *Connotation/Denotation*)

4. Refer to your desk dictionary to determine the meanings of the following words as Anderson uses them in this selection: *veranda* (paragraph 2), *pastoral* (12), *pennants* (17), *euphonic* (18), *galvanized* (21), *devotee* (26).

COMBINING RHETORICAL STRATEGIES

Write a short description of a middle school or high school teacher who, as you look back, was able to connect with you and teach you better than your other teachers. Be sure to include in your description exactly how he or she was able to reach you so effectively.

WRITING SUGGESTIONS

1. **(Cause and Effect)** Write a cause and effect essay in which you present the causal chain beginning with the teacher you described in your Combining Rhetorical Strategies answer. Use what you learned from this teacher as the primary cause, and trace the effects, in terms of how you think, what you have done, and what you are doing now. How did that teacher influence the person you are today? What other effects may be possible in the future?

2. **(Other Strategies)** Consider the statement "No matter where you go, there you are." Wing Biddlebaum escapes lynching in Pennsylvania, but he takes himself — his hands, his gift of teaching, his torment — with him. Write an essay using personal narrative and definition to present the characteristics that define you. If you had to leave your current life behind and start anew elsewhere — if you had to try to re-create yourself — what about yourself would you be unable to leave behind? Is there anything about yourself that you would like to be able to cast aside, if it were only possible?

3. **(Research)** Recent headlines have included several stories about the controversy surrounding suppressed memories. It is a clinical fact that the mind can suppress traumatic or horrible events so effectively that they do not exist in memory, but instead must be revealed through therapy and hypnosis. On the other hand, many contend that therapists, if not reputable or not careful, can lead their patients to create "memories" that are not based on fact. At the library or perhaps on the Internet, research this issue. Write a paper in which you present your

research and assess how valid the therapy is. Given the possibility of mistakes and abuse — with horrific consequences — is the benefit of the therapy worth the risk of "creating" memories that are not, in fact, real?

- **Questions and Answers about Memories of Childhood Abuse**
<http://www.apa.org/pubinfo/mem.html>

This question-and-answer page on the American Psychological Association Web site provides some basic information about suppressed memories and the controversy surrounding this topic.

- **Memory and Reality**
<http://www.fmsonline.com>

The False Memory Syndrome Foundation's Web site features an online newsletter, FAQs, and information about preventing false memory syndrome (FMS) and healing individuals affected by it. This site also explains the foundation's theories about the validity and causes of FMS.

- **Recovered Memory Project**
<http://www.brown.edu/Departments/Taubman_Center/Recovmem/Archive.html>

Maintained by Professor Ross E. Cheit of the Taubman Center for Public Policy and American Institutions at Brown University, this site is an online archive of corroborated cases of recovered memories.

- **Recovered Memories and "False Memory Syndrome"**
<http://www.hollandcrosspsych.com/recoverd.htm>

This site features useful lists of Web and print resources on the debate over suppressed memories.

WRITING SUGGESTIONS FOR CAUSE AND EFFECT ANALYSIS

1. Write an essay in which you analyze the most significant reasons why you went to college. You may wish to discuss such matters as your family background, your high school experience, people and events that influenced your decision, and your goals in college as well as in later life.

2. It is interesting to think of ourselves in terms of the influences that have caused us to be who we are. Write an essay in which you discuss two or three of what you consider the most important influences on your life. Following are some areas you may wish to consider in planning and writing your paper.

   a. a parent
   b. a book or movie
   c. a member of the clergy
   d. a teacher
   e. a friend
   f. a hero
   g. a youth organization
   h. a coach
   i. your neighborhood
   j. your ethnic background

3. Decisions often involve cause and effect relationships; that is, a person usually weighs the possible results of an action before deciding to act. Write an essay in which you consider the possible effects that would result from one decision or another in one of the following controversies.

   a. taxing cars on the basis of fuel consumption
   b. reinstituting the military draft
   c. legalizing marijuana
   d. mandatory licensing of handguns
   e. raising the mandatory fuel efficiency rating of cars
   f. cloning humans
   g. abolishing grades for college courses
   h. raising the minimum wage
   i. mandatory community service (one year) for all eighteen-year-olds
   j. banning the use of pesticides on produce
   k. requiring an ethics course in college

4. Write an essay about a recent achievement of yours or about an important achievement in your community. Explain the causes of this success. Look at all of the underlying elements involved in the accomplishment, and explain how you selected the one main cause or the causal chain that led to the achievement. To do this, you will probably want to use the rhetorical strategy of comparison and contrast. You might also use exemplification and process analysis to explain the connection between your cause and its effect.

CHAPTER 13

Argumentation

WHAT IS ARGUMENT?

The word *argument* probably brings to mind verbal disagreements we have all witnessed, if not participated in directly. Occasionally, such disputes are satisfying; you can take pleasure in knowing that you have converted someone to your point of view. More often, though, arguments like these are inconclusive and result only in anger over your opponent's stubbornness or in the frustration of realizing that you have failed to make your position understood. Such dissatisfaction is inevitable because verbal arguments usually arise spontaneously and cannot be thoughtfully planned or researched. Indeed, often it is not until later, in retrospect, that the convincing piece of evidence or the forcefully phrased assertion comes to mind.

Written arguments have much in common with verbal ones: They attempt to convince readers to agree with a particular point of view, to make a particular decision, or to pursue a particular course of action; they involve the presentation of well-chosen evidence and the artful control of language. However, writers of argument have no one around to dispute their words directly, so they must imagine their probable audience to predict the sorts of objections that may be raised. This requires that written arguments be carefully planned. The writer must settle in advance on a specific thesis or proposition, rather than grope toward one, as in a verbal argument. There is a greater need for organization, for choosing the most effective types of evidence from all that is available, for determining the strategies of rhetoric, language, and style that will best suit the argument's subject, its purpose, its thesis, and its effect on the intended audience.

Most strong arguments are concentrated around an effective thesis statement. Take, for example, the following opening to the essay "The Case for Short Words" by Richard Lederer (p. 590).

Thesis statement	When you speak and write, there is no law that says you have to use big words. Short words are as good as long ones, and short, old words — like *sun* and *grass* and *home* — are best of all. A lot of small words, more than you might think, can meet your needs with a strength, grace, and charm that large words do not have.
Several examples support the thesis.	Big words can make the way dark for those who read what you write and hear what you say. Small words cast their clear light on big things — night and day, love and hate, war and peace, and life and death. Big words at times seem strange to the eye and the ear and the mind and the heart. Small words are the ones we seem to have known from the time we were born, like the hearth fire that warms the home.

Note how Lederer uses examples to support his thesis statement. When you read the whole essay, you will want to check whether Lederer's argument is well reasoned and carefully organized. You will also want to check that his argument is logical and persuasive. A strong argument will have all of these qualities.

Most people who specialize in the study of argument identify two essential categories: persuasion and logic.

Persuasive argument relies primarily on appeals to emotion, to the subconscious, even to bias and prejudice. These appeals involve diction, slanting, figurative language, analogy, rhythmic patterns of speech, and a tone that encourages a positive, active response. Examples of persuasive argument are found in the exaggerated claims of advertisers and in the speech making of politicians and social activists.

Logical argument, on the other hand, appeals primarily to the mind — to the audience's intellectual faculties, understanding, and knowledge. Such appeals depend on the reasoned movement from assertion to evidence to conclusion and on an almost mathematical system of proof and counterproof. Logical argument, unlike persuasion, does not normally impel its audience to action. Logical argument is commonly found in scientific or philosophical articles, in legal decisions, and in technical proposals.

Most arguments, however, are neither purely persuasive nor purely logical in nature. A well-written newspaper editorial that supports a controversial piece of legislation or that proposes a solution to a local problem, for example, will rest on a logical arrangement of assertions and evidence but will employ striking diction and other persuasive patterns of language to make it more effective. Thus the kinds of appeals a writer emphasizes depend on the nature of the topic, the thesis or proposition of the argument, the various kinds of support (e.g., evidence, opinions, examples, facts, statistics) offered, and a thoughtful consideration of the audience. Knowing the differences between persuasive and logical arguments is, then, essential in learning both to read and to write arguments.

Some additional types of argument that are helpful in expanding your understanding are described below.

Informational, or Exploratory, Argument

It is often useful to provide a comprehensive review of the various facets of an issue. This is done to inform an audience, especially one that may not understand why the issue is controversial in the first place, and to help that audience take a position. An example of this kind of argument is Ernest van den Haag's "For the Death Penalty" (p. 639). The writer of this type of argument does not take a position but aims, instead, to render the positions taken by the various sides in accurate and clear language. Your instructors may occasionally call for this kind of argumentative writing as a way of teaching you to explore the complexity of a particular issue.

Focused Argument

This kind of argument has only one objective: to change the audience's mind about a controversial issue. Sherwin B. Nuland, in "Cruel and Unusual" (p. 646), focuses on a specific type of legal execution, which raises very specific moral and medical ethics issues. Being comprehensive or taking the broad view is not the objective here. If opposing viewpoints are considered, it is usually to show their inadequacies and thereby to strengthen the writer's own position. This is the kind that we usually think of as the traditional argument.

Action-Oriented Argument

This type of argument is highly persuasive and attempts to accomplish a specific task. This is the loud car salesman on your TV, the over-the-top subscription solicitation in your mail, the vote-for-me-because-I-am-the-only-candidate-who-can-lower-your-taxes type of argument. The language is emotionally charged, and buzzwords designed to arouse the emotions of the audience may even be used, along with such propaganda devices as glittering generalities (broad, sweeping statements) and bandwagonism ("Everyone else is voting for me — don't be left out").

Quiet, or Subtle, Argument

Some arguments do not immediately appear to the audience to be arguments at all. They set out to be informative and objective, but when closely examined, they reveal that the author has consciously, or perhaps subconsciously, shaped and slanted the evidence in such a manner as to favor a particular position. Such shaping may be the result of choices in diction that bend the audience to the writer's perspective, or they may be the result of decisions not to include certain types of evidence while admitting others. Such arguments can, of course, be quite convincing, as there are always those who distrust obvious efforts to convince them, preferring to make their own decisions on the issues. Kennedy P. Maize's cause and effect essay, "The Great Kern County Mouse War" (p. 532), contains a powerful argument against upsetting the balance of nature.

Reconciliation Argument

Increasingly popular today is a form of argument in which the writer attempts to explore all facets of an issue to find common ground or areas of agreement. Of course, one way of viewing that common ground is to see it as a new argumentative thrust, a new assertion, about which there may yet be more debate. The object, nevertheless, is to lessen stridency and the hardening of positions and to mediate opposing views into a rational and, where appropriate, even practical outcome. Martin Luther King Jr.'s speech "I Have a Dream" (p. 602) is perhaps the greatest example of a reconciliation argument of the past century.

WHY DO WRITERS USE ARGUMENT?

True arguments are limited to assertions about which there is a legitimate and recognized difference of opinion. It is unlikely that anyone will ever need to convince a reader that falling in love is a rare and intense experience, that crime rates should be reduced, or that computers are changing the world. Not everyone would agree, however, that women experience love more intensely than men, that the death penalty reduces the incidence of crime, or that computers are changing the world for the worse; these assertions are arguable and admit of differing perspectives. Similarly, a leading heart specialist might argue in a popular magazine that too many doctors are advising patients to have pacemakers implanted when they are not necessary; the editorial writer for a small-town newspaper could urge that a local agency supplying food to poor families be given a larger percentage of the town's budget; and in a lengthy and complex book, a foreign policy specialist might attempt to prove that the current administration exhibits no consistent policy in its relationship with other countries and that the State Department is in need of overhauling. No matter what forum it uses and no matter what its structure, an argument has as its chief purpose the detailed setting forth of a particular point of view and the rebuttal of any opposing views.

Classical thinkers believed that there are three key components in all rhetorical situations or attempts to communicate: the *speaker* (and for us the *writer*) who comments about a *subject* to an *audience*. For purposes of discussion we can isolate each of these three entities, but in actual rhetorical situations they are inseparable, each inextricably tied to and influencing the other two. The ancients also recognized the importance of qualities attached to each of these components that are especially significant in the case of argumentation: *ethos*, which is related to the speaker; *logos,* which is related to the subject; and *pathos,* which is related to the audience. Let's look a little closer at each of these.

Ethos (Greek for "character") has to do with the authority, the credibility, and, to a certain extent, the morals of the speaker or writer. Aristotle and Cicero, classical rhetoricians, believed that it was important for the speaker to be credible and to argue for a worthwhile cause. Putting one's argumentative skills in the service of a questionable cause was simply not acceptable. But how did one establish credibility? Sometimes it was gained through achievements outside the rhetorical arena. That is, the speaker had experience with an issue, had argued the subject before, and had been judged to be sincere and honest.

In the case of your own writing, establishing such credentials is not always possible, so you will need to be more concerned than usual with presenting your argument reasonably, sincerely, and in language untainted by excessive emotionalism. Finally, it is well worth remembering that you should always show respect for your audience in your writing.

Logos (Greek for "word"), related as it is to the subject, is the effective presentation of the argument itself. Is the thesis or claim a worthwhile one? Is it logical, consistent, and well buttressed by supporting evidence? Is the evidence itself factual, reliable, and convincing? Finally, is the argument so thoughtfully organized and so clearly presented that it has an impact on the audience and could change opinions? Indeed, this aspect of argumentation is the most difficult to accomplish but is, at the same time, the most rewarding.

Pathos (Greek for "emotion") has the most to do with the audience. The essential question is, How does the speaker or writer present an argument or a persuasive essay to maximize its appeal for a given audience? One way, of course, is through the artful and strategic use of well-crafted language. Certain buzzwords, slanted diction, or loaded language may become either rallying cries or causes of resentment in an argument.

It is worth remembering at this point that you can never be certain who your audience is; readers range along a spectrum from extremely friendly and sympathetic to extremely hostile and resistant, with a myriad of possibilities in between. The friendly audience will welcome new information and will support the writer's position; the hostile audience will look for just the opposite: flaws in logic and examples of dishonest manipulation by the writer. With many arguments, there is the potential for a considerable audience of interested parties who are uncommitted. If the targeted audience is judged to be friendly, then the writer need not be as concerned with *logos* and can be less cautious and more freewheeling. If the audience is thought to be hostile, the *logos* must be the writer's immediate concern, and the language should be straightforward and objective. The greatest caution, subtlety, and critical thinking must be applied to the attempt to win over an uncommitted audience.

In general, writers of argument are interested in explaining aspects of a subject as well as in advocating a particular view. Consequently, they frequently use the other rhetorical strategies. In your efforts to argue convincingly, you may find it necessary to define, to compare and contrast, to analyze causes and effects, to classify, to describe, to narrate. (For more information on the use of other strategies in argumentation, see the "Use Other Rhetorical Strategies" section at the end of this chapter introduction.) Nevertheless, it is the writer's attempt to convince, not explain, that is of primary importance in an argumentative essay. In this respect, it is helpful to know that there are two basic patterns of thinking and of presenting our thoughts that are followed in argumentation: *induction* and *deduction.*

Inductive reasoning moves from a set of specific examples to a general statement or principle. As long as the evidence is accurate, pertinent, complete, and sufficient to represent the assertion, the conclusion of an inductive argument can be regarded as valid; if, however, you can spot inaccuracies in the evidence or can point to contrary evidence, you have good reason to doubt the assertion as it stands. Inductive reasoning is the most common of argumentative structures.

Deductive reasoning, more formal and complex than inductive reasoning, moves from an overall premise, rule, or generalization to a more specific conclusion. Deductive logic follows the pattern of the *syllogism,* a simple three-part argument consisting of a major premise, a minor premise, and a conclusion. For example, notice how the following syllogism works.

a. All humans are mortal. *(Major premise)*
b. Catalina is a human. *(Minor premise)*
c. Catalina is mortal. *(Conclusion)*

The conclusion here is true because both premises are true and the logic of the syllogism is valid.

Obviously, a syllogism will fail to work if either of the premises is untrue.

a. All living creatures are mammals. *(Major premise)*
b. A lobster is a living creature. *(Minor premise)*
c. A lobster is a mammal. *(Conclusion)*

The problem is immediately apparent. The major premise is obviously false: There are many living creatures that are not mammals, and a lobster happens to be one of them. Consequently, the conclusion is invalid.

Syllogisms, however, can fail in other ways, even if both premises are objectively true. Such failures occur most often when the arguer jumps to a conclusion without taking obvious exceptions into account.

a. All college students read books. *(Major premise)*
b. Larry reads books. *(Minor premise)*
c. Larry is a college student. *(Conclusion)*

Both the premises in this syllogism are true, but the syllogism is still invalid because it does not take into account that other people besides college students read books. The problem is in the way the major premise has been interpreted: If the minor premise were instead "Larry is a college student," then the valid conclusion "Larry reads books" would logically follow.

It is fairly easy to see the problems in a deductive argument when its premises and conclusion are rendered in the form of a syllogism. It is often more difficult to see errors in logic when the argument is presented discursively, or within the context of a long essay. If you can reduce the argument to its syllogistic form, however, you will have much less difficulty testing its validity. Similarly, if you can isolate and examine out of context the evidence provided to support an inductive assertion, you can more readily evaluate the written inductive argument.

Consider the following excerpt from "The Draft: Why the Country Needs It," an article by James Fallows that first appeared in the *Atlantic* magazine in 1980.

The Vietnam draft was unfair racially, economically, educationally. By every one of those measures, the volunteer Army is less representative still. Libertarians argue that military service should be a matter of choice, but the plain fact is that service in the volunteer force is too frequently dictated by economics. Army enlisted ranks E1 through E4, the privates and corporals, the cannon fodder, the ones who will fight and die, are 36 percent black now. By the Army's own projections, they will be 42 percent black in three years. When other "minorities" are taken into account, we will have, for the first time, an army whose fighting members are mainly "non-majority," or more bluntly, a black and brown army defending a mainly white nation. The military has been an avenue of opportunity of many young blacks. They may well be first-class fighting men. They do not represent the nation.

Such a selective sharing of the burden has destructive spiritual effects in a nation based on the democratic creed. But its practical implications can be quite as grave. The effect of a fair, representative draft is to hold the public hostage to the consequences of its decisions, much as the children's presence in the public schools focuses parents' attention on the quality of the schools. If the citizens are willing to countenance a decision that means that someone's child may die, they may contemplate more deeply if there is the possibility that the child will be theirs. Indeed, I would like to extend this principle even further. Young men of nineteen are rightly suspicious of the congressmen and columnists who urge them to the fore. I wish there were a practical way to resurrect provisions of the amended Selective Service Act of 1940, which raised the draft age to forty-four. Such a gesture might symbolize the desire to offset the historic injustice of the Vietnam draft, as well as suggest the possibility that, when a bellicose columnist recommends dispatching the American forces to Pakistan, he might also realize that he could end up as a gunner in a tank.

Here Fallows presents an inductive argument against the volunteer army and in favor of reinstating a draft. His argument can be summarized as follows.

Assertion: The volunteer army is racially and economically unfair.

Evidence: He points to the disproportionate percentage of blacks in the army, as well as to projections indicating that, within three years of the article's publication, more than half of the army's fighting members will be nonwhite.

Conclusion: "Such a selective sharing of the burden has destructive spiritual effects in a nation based on the democratic creed." Not until there is a fair, representative draft will the powerful majority be held accountable for any decision to go to war.

Fallows's inductive scheme here is, in fact, very effective. The evidence is convincing, and the conclusion is strong. But his argument also depends on a more complicated deductive syllogism.

a. The democratic ideal requires equal representation in the responsibilities of citizenship. *(Major premise)*

b. Military service is a responsibility of citizenship. *(Minor premise)*

c. The democratic ideal requires equal representation in military service. *(Conclusion)*

To attack Fallows's argument, it would be necessary to deny one of his premises.

Fallows also employs a number of other persuasive techniques, including an analogy: "The effect of a fair, representative draft is to hold the public hostage to the consequences of its decisions, much as the children's presence in the public schools focuses parents' attention on the quality of the schools." The use of such an analogy proves nothing, but it can force readers to reconsider their viewpoint and can make them more open-minded. The same is true of Fallows's almost entirely unserious suggestion about raising the draft age to forty-four. Like most writers, Fallows uses persuasive arguments to complement his more important logical ones.

AN ANNOTATED STUDENT ESSAY USING ARGUMENT

Mark Jackson wrote the following essay while a student at the University of Cincinnati. Jackson's essay explores a number of arguments made in favor of a liberal arts education. In the course of the essay, Jackson rejects some of these arguments, such as the idea that a liberal arts education makes students well-rounded. He does, however, support the argument that a liberal arts education fosters critical thinking skills, and he comes to the conclusion that the ideal education would balance practical or vocational training and a grounding in the liberal arts.

The Liberal Arts:

A Practical View

Mark Jackson

Many students question the reasoning behind a liberal arts education. But even though they may have been forced to swallow liberal arts propaganda since junior high, students seldom receive a good explanation for why they should strive to be "well-rounded." They are told that they should

Writer introduces problem: liberal arts inadequately explained.

1

value the accumulation of knowledge for its own sake, yet this argument does not convince those, like myself, who believe that knowledge must have some practical value or material benefit to be worth seeking.

In "What Is an Idea?" Wayne Booth and 2 Marshall Gregory argue convincingly that "a liberal education is an education in ideas -- not merely memorizing them, but learning to move among them, balancing one against the other, negotiating relationships, accommodating new arguments, and returning for a closer look" (17). These writers propose that a liberal arts education is valuable to students because it helps to develop their analytical-thinking skills and writing skills. This is, perhaps, one of the best arguments for taking a broad range of classes in many different subjects.

First argument for liberal arts education

Other, more radical arguments in favor 3 of the liberal arts are less appealing. Lewis Thomas, a prominent scientist and physician, believes that classical Greek should form the backbone of a college student's education. This suggestion seems extreme. It is more reasonable to concentrate on the English language, since many students do not have a firm grasp of basic reading and writing skills. Freshman English and other English courses serve as a better foundation for higher education than classical Greek could.

Another, less convincing argument

The opposition to a liberal arts cur- 4 riculum grows out of the values that college-bound students learn from their parents and peers: They place an immeasurable value on success and disregard anything that is not pertinent to material achievements. Students often have trouble seeing what practical value studying a particular discipline can have for them. Teenagers who are headed for the world of nine-to-five employment tend to ignore certain studies in their haste to succeed.

Writer links personal experience to his attitude toward liberal arts.

My parents started discussing the pos- 5
sibility of college with me when I was in the sixth grade. They didn't think that it was important for me to go to college to become a more fulfilled human being. My mom and dad wanted me to go to college so that I might not have to live from paycheck to paycheck as they do. Their reason for wanting me to go to college has become my primary motivation for pursuing a college degree.

Personal examples used to illustrate inadequacy of some pro–liberal arts arguments.

I remember getting into an argument 6
with my high school counselor because I didn't want to take a third year of Spanish. I was an A student in Spanish II, but I hated every minute of the class. My counselor noticed that I didn't sign up for Spanish III, so he called me into his office to hassle me. I told him that I took two years of a foreign language so that I would be accepted to college, but that I did not want to take a third year. Mr. Gallivan told me that I needed a third year of a foreign language to be a "well-rounded" student. My immediate response was "So what?!" I hated foreign languages, and no counselor was going to make me take something that I didn't want or need. I felt Spanish was a waste of time.

I frequently asked my high school coun- 7
selor why I needed to take subjects like foreign languages and art. He never really gave me an answer (except for the lame idea about being "well-rounded"). Instead, Mr. Gallivan always directed my attention to a sign on the wall of his office which read, "THERE'S NO REASON FOR IT. IT'S JUST OUR POLICY!" I never found that a satisfactory explanation.

Writer cites authority to explain value of humanities for career-minded people.

Norman Cousins, however, does offer a more reasonable explanation for the necessity of a liberal education. In his essay "How to Make People Smaller Than They Are," Cousins points out how valuable the humanities are for career-minded people. He says, "The irony of the emphasis being placed on careers is that nothing is more valuable for anyone who has had a professional or vocational education than to be able to deal with abstractions or complexities, or to feel comfortable with subtleties of thought or language, or to think sequentially" (15). Cousins reminds us that technical or vocational knowledge alone will not make one successful in a chosen profession: Unique problems and situations may arise daily in the context of one's job, so an employee must be able to think creatively and deal with events that no textbook ever discussed. The workers who get the promotions and advance to high positions are the ones who can "think on their feet" when they are faced with a complex problem.

Writer points to communication skills learned through liberal arts.

9

Cousins also suggests that the liberal arts teach students communication skills that are critical for success. A shy, introverted person who was a straight A student in college would not make a very good public relations consultant, no matter how keen his or her intellectual abilities. Employees who cannot adequately articulate their ideas to a client or an employer will soon find themselves unemployed, even if they have brilliant ideas. Social integration into a particular work environment would be difficult without good communication skills and a wide range of interests and general knowledge. The broader a person's interests, the more compatible he or she will be with other workers.

Thesis

Though it is obvious that liberal arts courses do have considerable practical value, a college education would not be complete without some job training. The liberal arts should be given equal billing in the college curriculum, but by no means should they become the focal point of higher education. If specialization is outlawed in our institutions of higher learning, then college students might lose their competitive edge. Maxim Gorky has written that "any kind of knowledge is useful" (22), and, of course, most knowledge is useful; but it would be insane to structure the college curriculum around an overview of all disciplines instead of allowing a student to master one subject or profession. Universities must seek to maintain an equilibrium between liberal and specialized education. A liberal arts degree without specialization or intended future specialization (such as a master's degree in a specific field) is useless unless one wants to be a professional game show contestant.

10

Plan of action for college students

Students who want to make the most of their college years should pursue a major course of study while choosing electives or a few minor courses of study from the liberal arts. In this way, scholars can become experts in a profession and still have a broad enough background to ensure versatility, both within and outside the field. In a university's quest to produce "well-rounded" students, specialization must not come to be viewed as an evil practice.

11

Writer states that practical aspects of the liberal arts should be emphasized.

If educators really want to increase the number of liberal arts courses that each student takes, they must first increase the popularity of such studies. It is futile to try to get students to learn something just for the sake of knowing it. They must be

12

given examples, such as those already mentioned, of how a liberal education will further their own interests. Instead of telling students that they need to be "well-rounded" and feeding them meaningless propaganda, counselors and professors should point out the practical value and applications of a broad education in the liberal arts. It is difficult to persuade some college students that becoming a better person is an important goal of higher education. Many students want a college education so that they can make more money and have more power. This is the perceived value of a higher education in their world.

Works Cited

Booth, Wayne, and Marshall Gregory. "What Is an Idea?" The Harper and Row Reader. 2nd ed. New York: Harper, 1988.

Cousins, Norman. "How to Make People Smaller Than They Are." The Saturday Review. Dec. 1978: 15.

Gorky, Maxim. "How I Studied." On Literature. Trans. Julius Katzer. Seattle: University of Washington Press, 1973. 9–22.

Thomas, Lewis. "Debating the Unknowable." Atlantic Monthly. July 1981: 49–52.

Analyzing Mark Jackson's Essay of Argumentation: Questions for Discussion

1. Why did Jackson refuse to take Spanish III? How does his personal experience with Spanish and with his guidance counselor relate to his argument regarding liberal arts education?

2. What is Jackson's thesis? Where and how does he present it?

3. Jackson employs several arguments in favor of liberal arts education. How does he classify them? What does he accomplish by including a variety of rationales regarding the validity of a "well-rounded" education?

SUGGESTIONS FOR WRITING AN ARGUMENTATION ESSAY

Writing an argument can be very rewarding. By its nature, an argument must be carefully reasoned and thoughtfully structured to have maximum effect. In other words, the *logos* of the argument must be carefully tended. Allow yourself, therefore, enough time to think about your thesis, to gather the evidence you need, and to draft, revise, edit, and proofread your essay. Sloppy thinking, confused expression, and poor organization will be immediately evident to your reader and will make for weaker arguments.

For example, you might be given an assignment in your history class to write a paper explaining what you think was the main cause of the Civil War. How would you approach this topic? First, it would help to assemble a number of possible interpretations of the causes of the Civil War and to examine them closely. Once you have determined what you consider to be the main cause, you will need to develop points that support your position. Then you will need to explain why you did not choose other possibilities, and you will have to assemble reasons that refute them. For example, you might write an opening something like the following.

```
The Fugitive Slave Act Forced the North to Go to War
     While the start of the Civil War can be attributed to
many factors -- states' rights, slavery, a clash between
antithetical economic systems, and westward expansion --
the final straw for the North was the Fugitive Slave Act.
This act, more than any other single element of disagree-
ment between the North and the South, forced the North into
a position where the only option was to fight.
     Certainly, slavery and the clash over open lands in
the West contributed to the growing tensions between the
two sides, as did the economically incompatible systems
of production -- plantation and manufacture -- but the
Fugitive Slave Act required the North either to actively
support slavery or to run the risk of becoming a criminal
in defiance of it. The North chose not to support the
Fugitive Slave Act and was openly angered by the idea
that it should be required to do so by law. This anger
and open defiance led directly to the Civil War.
```

In these opening paragraphs, the author states the main argument for the cause of the Civil War and sets up, in addition, the possible alternatives to this view. The points outlined in the introduction would lead, one by one, to a logical argument asserting that the Fugitive Slave Act was responsible for the onset of the Civil War and refuting the other interpretations.

This introduction is mainly a *logical* argument. As was mentioned before, writers often use *persuasive,* or *emotional,* arguments along with logical ones. Persuasive arguments focus on issues that appeal to people's subconscious or emotional nature, along with their logical powers and intellectual understanding. Such arguments rely on powerful and charged language, and they appeal to the emotions. Persuasive arguments can be especially effective but should not be used without a strong logical backing. Indeed, this is the only way to use emotional persuasion ethically. Emotional persuasion, when not in support of a logical point, can be dangerous in that it can make an illogical point sound appealing to a listener or reader.

Determine Your Thesis or Proposition

Begin by determining a topic that interests you and about which there is some significant difference of opinion or about which you have a number of questions. Find out what's in the news, what people are talking about, what authors and instructors are emphasizing as important intellectual arguments. As you pursue your research, consider what assertion or assertions you can make about the topic you chose. The more specific this thesis or proposition, the more directed your research can become and the more focused your ultimate argument will be. While researching your topic, however, be aware that the information may point you in new directions. Don't hesitate at any point to modify or even reject an initial thesis as continued research warrants.

A thesis can be placed anywhere in an argument, but it is probably best while learning to write arguments to place the statement of your controlling idea somewhere near the beginning of your composition. Explain the importance of the thesis, and make clear to your reader that you share a common concern or interest in this issue. You may wish to state your central assertion directly in your first or second paragraph so that there is no possibility for your reader to be confused about your position. You may also wish to lead off with a particularly striking piece of evidence to capture your reader's interest.

Consider Your Audience

It is well worth remembering that in no other type of writing is the question of audience more important than in argumentation. Here, again, the *ethos* and *pathos* aspects of argumentation come into play. The tone you establish, the type of diction you choose, the kinds of evidence you select to buttress your assertions, and indeed the organizational pattern you design and follow will all influence your audience's perception of your trustworthiness and believability. If you make good judgments about the nature of your audience, respect its knowledge of the subject, and correctly envision whether it is likely to be hostile, neutral, complacent, or receptive, you will be able to tailor the various aspects of your argument appropriately.

Gather Supporting Evidence

For each point of your argument, be sure to provide appropriate and sufficient supporting evidence: verifiable facts and statistics, illustrative examples and narratives, or quotations from authorities. Don't overwhelm your reader with evidence, but don't skimp either; it is important to demonstrate your command of the topic and your control of the thesis by choosing carefully among all the evidence at your disposal. If there are strong arguments on both sides of the issue, you will need to take this into account while making your choices. (See "Consider Refutations to Your Argument" below.)

Choose an Organizational Pattern

Once you think that you have sufficient evidence to make your assertion convincing, consider how best to organize your argument. To some extent, your organization will depend on your method of reasoning: inductive, deductive, or a combination of the two. For example, is it necessary to establish a major premise before moving on to discuss a minor premise? Should most of your evidence precede or follow your direct statement of an assertion? Will induction work better with the particular audience you have targeted? As you present your primary points, you may find it effective to move from those that are least important to those that are most important or from those that are least familiar to those that are most familiar. A scratch outline can help, but it is often the case that a writer's most crucial revisions in an argument involve rearranging its components into a sharper, more coherent order. It is often difficult to tell what that order should be until the revision stage of the writing process.

Consider Refutations to Your Argument

As you proceed with your argument, you may wish to take into account well-known and significant opposing arguments. To ignore them would be to suggest to your readers any one of the following: You don't know about them, you know about them and are obviously and unfairly weighting the argument in your favor, or you know about them and have no reasonable answers to them. Grant the validity of the opposing argument or refute it, but respect your reader's intelligence by addressing the problems. Your readers will in turn respect you for doing so.

To avoid weakening your thesis, you must be very clear in your thinking and presentation. It must remain apparent to your readers why your argument is superior to the opposing points of view. If you feel that you cannot introduce opposing arguments because they will weaken rather than strengthen your thesis, you should probably reassess your thesis and the supporting evidence.

Avoid Faulty Reasoning

Have someone read your argument for errors in judgment and reasoning. Sometimes others can see easily what you can't because you are so intimately tied to your assertion. Review the following list of errors in reasoning, making sure that you have not committed any of them.

> ***Oversimplification*** — a foolishly simple solution to what is clearly a complex problem. *The reason we have a balance-of-trade deficit is that foreigners make better products than we do.*
>
> ***Hasty generalization*** — in inductive reasoning, a generalization that is based on too little evidence or on evidence that is not representative. *It was the best movie I saw this year, and so it should get an Academy Award.*
>
> ***Post hoc ergo propter hoc*** ("after this, therefore because of this") — confusing chance or coincidence with causation. The fact that one event comes after another does not necessarily mean that the first event caused the second. *Every time I wear my orange Syracuse sweater to a game, we win.*
>
> ***Begging the question*** — assuming in a premise something that needs to be proven. *Parking fines work because they keep people from parking illegally.*
>
> ***False analogy*** — making a misleading analogy between logically connected ideas. *Of course he'll make a fine coach. He was an all-star basketball player.*
>
> ***Either/or thinking*** — seeing only two alternatives when there may in fact be other possibilities. *Either you love your job or you hate it.*
>
> ***Non sequitur*** — ("It does not follow.") — an inference or conclusion that is not clearly related to the established premises or evidence. *She is very sincere; she must know what she is talking about.*

Conclude Forcefully

In the conclusion of your essay, be sure to restate your position in different language, at least briefly. Besides persuading your reader to accept your point of view, you may also want to encourage some specific course of action. Above all, your conclusion should not introduce new information that may surprise your reader; it should seem to follow naturally, almost seamlessly, from the series of points that have been carefully established in the body of the essay. Don't overstate your case, but at the same time don't qualify your conclusion with the use of too many words or phrases like *I think, in my opinion, maybe, sometimes,* and *probably*. Rather than making you seem rational and sensible, these words can often make you sound indecisive and muddled.

Use Other Rhetorical Strategies

Although argument is one of the most powerful single rhetorical strategies, it is almost always strengthened by incorporating other writing strategies. In every professional selection in this chapter, you will find a number of rhetorical strategies at work.

As you read the essays in this chapter, consider all of the writing strategies that the authors have used to support their arguments. How have these other strategies added to or changed the style of the essay? Are there strategies that you would have added or omitted? What strategies, if any, might you use to strengthen your argument?

▶ *Questions for Revision: Argumentation*

1. Is my thesis or proposition focused? Do I state my thesis well?
2. Assess the different kinds of arguments. Am I using the right technique to argue my thesis? Does my strategy fit my subject matter and audience?
3. Does my presentation include enough evidence to support my thesis? Do I acknowledge opposing points of view in a way that strengthens, rather than weakens, my argument?
4. Have I chosen an appropriate organizational pattern that makes it easy to support my thesis?
5. Have I avoided faulty reasoning within my essay? Have I had a friend read the essay to help me find problems in my logic?
6. Is my conclusion forceful and effective?
7. Have I thought about or attempted to combine rhetorical strategies to strengthen my argument? If so, is the combination of strategies effective? If not, what strategy or strategies would help my argument?

Living Well. Living Good.

Maya Angelou

Maya Angelou was born April 4, 1928, as Marguerite Johnson in Saint Louis, Missouri. When she was about three years old, her parents divorced, and she and her brother were sent to live with their grandmother in Stamps, Arkansas, a segregated, rural town. When she was visiting her mother in Saint Louis at the age of eight, Angelou was raped by her mother's boyfriend and, as a result, became mute for nearly five years. By the time she turned sixteen, she was a single mother. Angelou's first book, I Know Why The Caged Bird Sings *(1970), an autobiography that reflects her struggles to overcome the hardships of her youth, received widespread acclaim and became a best-seller. Now a renowned writer and speaker, Angelou has worked as a Broadway performer, poet, historian, author, actress, playwright, civil rights activist, journalist for foreign publications, teacher, producer, and director. She has received numerous awards and honors and currently holds a lifetime chair as the Z. Smith Reynolds Professor of American Studies at Wake Forest University. At the request of President Clinton, she wrote and recited a poem, "On the Pulse of the Morning," at the 1993 presidential inauguration.*

The following selection, taken from her memoir Wouldn't Take Nothing for My Journey Now *(1993), provides a glimpse at Angelou's outlook on life and offers thoughts on how others can apply it to their own situations.*

BEFORE YOU READ

The cliché "living the good life" can mean very different things to different people. For some, it means wealth; for others, prestige or achievement; and for still others, it simply means freedom to do what they wish, regardless of financial or social standing. What does "the good life" mean to you? What steps, if any, are you taking now to achieve it?

Aunt Tee was a Los Angeles member of our extended family. She   1
was seventy-nine when I met her, sinewy, strong, and the color of old lemons. She wore her coarse, straight hair, which was slightly streaked with gray, in a long braided rope across the top of her head. With her high cheekbones, old gold skin, and almond eyes, she looked more like an Indian chief than an old black woman. (Aunt Tee described herself and any favored member of her race as Negroes. *Black* was saved for those who had incurred her disapproval.)

She had retired and lived alone in a dead, neat ground-floor apart-   2
ment. Wax flowers and china figurines sat on elaborately embroidered and heavily starched doilies. Sofas and chairs were tautly upholstered. The only thing at ease in Aunt Tee's apartment was Aunt Tee.

I used to visit her often and perch on her uncomfortable sofa just 3
to hear her stories. She was proud that after working thirty years as a
maid, she spent the next thirty years as a live-in housekeeper, carrying
the keys to rich houses and keeping meticulous accounts.

"Living in lets the white folks know Negroes are as neat and clean as 4
they are, sometimes more so. And it gives the Negro maid a chance to see
white folks ain't no smarter than Negroes. Just luckier. Sometimes."

Aunt Tee told me that once she was housekeeper for a couple in 5
Bel Air, California, lived with them in a fourteen-room ranch house.
There was a day maid who cleaned, and a gardener who daily tended
the lush gardens. Aunt Tee oversaw the workers. When she had begun
the job, she had cooked and served a light breakfast, a good lunch,
and a full three- or four-course dinner to her employers and their
guests. Aunt Tee said she watched them grow older and leaner. After a
few years they stopped entertaining and ate dinner hardly seeing each
other at the table. Finally, they sat in a dry silence as they ate evening
meals of soft scrambled eggs, melba toast, and weak tea. Aunt Tee said
she saw them growing old but didn't see herself aging at all.

She became the social maven. She started "keeping company" (her 6
phrase) with a chauffeur down the street. Her best friend and her
friend's husband worked in service only a few blocks away.

On Saturdays Aunt Tee would cook a pot of pigs' feet, a pot of 7
greens, fry chicken, make potato salad, and bake a banana pudding.
Then, that evening, her friends — the chauffeur, the other housekeeper, and her husband — would come to Aunt Tee's commodious
live-in quarters. There the four would eat and drink, play records and
dance. As the evening wore on, they would settle down to a serious
game of bid whist.

Naturally, during this revelry jokes were told, fingers snapped, feet 8
were patted, and there was a great deal of laughter.

Aunt Tee said that what occurred during every Saturday party star- 9
tled her and her friends the first time it happened. They had been
playing cards, and Aunt Tee, who had just won the bid, held a handful
of trumps. She felt a cool breeze on her back and sat upright and
turned around. Her employers had cracked her door open and beck-
oned to her. Aunt Tee, a little peeved, laid down her cards and went to
the door. The couple backed away and asked her to come into the
hall, and there they both spoke and won Aunt Tee's sympathy forever.

"Theresa, we don't mean to disturb you. . ." the man whispered, 10
"but you all seem to be having such a good time . . ."

The woman added, "We hear you and your friends laughing every 11
Saturday night, and we'd just like to watch you. We don't want to
bother you. We'll be quiet and just watch."

The man said, "If you'll just leave your door ajar, your friends 12
don't need to know. We'll never make a sound." Aunt Tee said she

saw no harm in agreeing, and she talked it over with her company. They said it was OK with them, but it was sad that the employers owned the gracious house, the swimming pool, three cars, and numberless palm trees, but had no joy. Aunt Tee told me that laughter and relaxation had left the house; she agreed it was sad.

That story has stayed with me for nearly thirty years, and when a 13 tale remains fresh in my mind, it almost always contains a lesson which will benefit me.

My dears, I draw the picture of the wealthy couple standing in a 14 darkened hallway, peering into a lighted room where black servants were lifting their voices in merriment and comradery, and I realize that living well is an art which can be developed. Of course, you will need the basic talents to build upon: They are a love of life and ability to take great pleasure from small offerings, an assurance that the world owes you nothing and that every gift is exactly that, a gift. That people who may differ from you in political stance, sexual persuasion, and racial inheritance can be founts of fun, and if you are lucky, they can become even convivial comrades.

Living life as art requires a readiness to forgive. I do not mean that 15 you should suffer fools gladly, but rather remember your own shortcomings, and when you encounter another with flaws, don't be eager to righteously seal yourself away from the offender forever. Take a few breaths and imagine yourself having just committed the action which has set you at odds.

Because of the routines we follow, we often forget that life is an on- 16 going adventure. We leave our homes for work, acting and even believing that we will reach our destinations with no unusual event startling us out of our set expectations. The truth is we know nothing, not where our cars will fail or when our buses will stall, whether our places of employment will be there when we arrive, or whether, in fact, we ourselves will arrive whole and alive at the end of our journeys. Life is pure adventure, and the sooner we realize that, the quicker we will be able to treat life as art: to bring all our energies to each encounter, to remain flexible enough to notice and admit when what we expected to happen did not happen. We need to remember that we are created creative and can invent new scenarios as frequently as they are needed.

Life seems to love the liver of it. Money and power can liberate 17 only if they are used to do so. They can imprison and inhibit more finally than barred windows and iron chains.

RESPONDING TO READING

When your life falls into a routine or becomes full of stress, how easy is it to remember that life, as Angelou says, is "an ongoing adventure" (paragraph 16)?

Angelou's lesson is a familiar one in many ways, but it bears repeating. Why do you think it is a challenge to live life "as art" (16)?

QUESTIONING THE TEXT

1. Why is Aunt Tee's appearance important to the subsequent discussion of her life and outlook?

2. What is the difference between a maid and a live-in housekeeper? Why is the difference so profound to Aunt Tee?

3. Why do Aunt Tee's employers want to watch her Saturday parties with her friends? Why does their request win her sympathy?

4. Why does Aunt Tee's story have such an impact on Angelou? What lessons has she learned from it?

UNDERSTANDING THE WRITER'S CRAFT

1. For the most part, Angelou introduces Aunt Tee through description and narrative, but she allows the reader to "hear" Aunt Tee's voice by using a single direct quote. What does she accomplish by using this quote? How does it help the reader get to know Aunt Tee just a little better?

2. Angelou takes care to describe Aunt Tee's Saturday night parties at some length, instead of simply stating that she had some friends over each week. (Glossary: *Description*) Why is it important to know details about the food, the games, the company, and so on? How does the specificity of the description contribute to Angelou's purpose? (Glossary: *Purpose*)

3. Many essays communicate their lessons or messages by simply presenting a meaningful event or story, but Angelou segues from her story into a direct explanation of what it means to her — and, presumably, what it *should* mean to the reader. Angelou paints the image of the wealthy couple in the dark hallway, then comments on it at some length. What about the subject matter makes it important to discuss directly? Do you find Angelou's clarification effective? Why or why not?

EXPLORING LANGUAGE

1. What is the difference between living well and living good? Why is the difference profound enough to make the juxtaposition of the two terms a good title? (Glossary: *Title*)

2. Angelou describes living well as "living life as art" (paragraph 15). Define the word *art* in this context. (Glossary: *Definition*) How is living well analogous to an artistic endeavor? (Glossary: *Analogy*)

3. Refer to your desk dictionary to determine the meanings of the following words as Angelou uses them in this selection: *sinewy* (paragraph 1), *incurred* (1), *maven* (6), *commodious* (7), *founts* (14).

COMBINING RHETORICAL STRATEGIES

Write a short description of a person who taught you an important lesson or whose conduct made a difference to you during your life. Present the lesson in the context of the description. What was it about the person you chose that helped him or her teach you or lead you by example? Why was the lesson important to you?

WRITING SUGGESTIONS

1. **(Argumentation)** "The American dream" is a phrase widely used to describe a living arrangement that is increasingly difficult to achieve: a home (owned, not rented), two cars, a nuclear family, and the means to take care of everything and everyone and "get away from it all" during vacation time. During the 1950s and 1960s, these acquisitions were held up as the ideal on TV shows like *Donna Reed* and *Leave It to Beaver*. At that time, the American dream was within the reach of a large percentage of American families. These days, achieving that same dream is not as simple. Except for a select few, it takes two full-time wage earners to support such a lifestyle. Child care falls to strangers. Divorce, the loss of a job, and other misfortunes can put the ideal out of reach. Write an essay in which you assess the traditional American dream and the role it plays in today's society. Is it still a valid ideal, worth the struggle to achieve, or does it lead to unrealistic expectations and disappointment? Should there be a new American dream that accommodates the challenges faced by young adults today that affected their parents little, if at all? What would it be? Base your argument on personal experience and knowledge.

2. **(Other Strategies)** *The New Yorker* cartoon on page 589 by Bruce Eric Kaplan illustrates the underlying point of Angelou's essay. As Angelou and Kaplan suggest, there is a persistent drive in our society to acquire wealth and material goods, not for any specific purpose or pleasure, but simply to have them. Indeed, Angelou's "art of living" idea has nothing to do with things — it has to do with attitude and relationships. Still, there are products and services on the market that seem to offer us a chance to make our lives easier, more fun, or simply "better." With the cartoon and Angelou's essay in mind, write a personal definition of what it means to you to be "rich." Can one be rich without happiness? Can one achieve happiness without being materially rich? How could one achieve a balance? What would it entail?

3. **(Research)** Like Beverly Hills before it, the community of Bel Air, California, has become synonymous with great affluence. (Incidentally, both communities were celebrated in popular television shows: *The Beverly Hillbillies* and *The Fresh Prince of Bel Air*.) Research the history and demographics of these communities. Why have they attracted such wealth? How justified is the stereotype of wealth? What other lesser-known communities are like Beverly Hills and Bel Air? Write a paper in which you present your information.

"See? Isn't this better than being happy?"

- **City of Beverly Hills**
  <http://www.ci.beverly-hills.ca.us>

  On this Web page, you can read a short history of the city, browse demographics data, and follow links to the Visitor's Bureau and the Chamber of Commerce.

- **Official Guide to the Town of Palm Beach, Florida**
  <http://www.palmbeachchamber.com>

  From tourist information to town history, this guide to Palm Beach gives an overview of one of the most exclusive communities in the country.

- **America's Richest Towns: 2001**
  <http://www.worth.com/content_articles/0601_rich_towns.html>

  From Jupiter Island, Florida, to Mount Kisco, New York, browse *Worth* magazine's annual ranking of America's richest communities.

The Case for Short Words

Richard Lederer

A teacher at St. Paul's School in Concord, New Hampshire, Richard Lederer, born in 1938, is a lifelong student of language. Anyone who has read one of his many books will understand why he has been referred to as "America's wittiest verbalist." Lederer loves language and enjoys writing about its marvelous richness. Lederer's books include Anguished English *(1987),* Crazy English *(1989),* The Play of Words *(1990),* Adventures of a Verbivore *(1994),* Nothing Risque, Nothing Gained *(1995), and* The Bride of Anguished English *(2000). He holds a doctorate in linguistics from the University of New Hampshire, is a language commentator on New Hampshire public radio, and writes a weekly column called "Looking at Language" for the* Concord Monitor.

In the following selection, a chapter from The Miracle of Language *(1990), Lederer sings the praises of short words and reminds us that well-chosen monosyllabic words can be a writer's best friends because they are functional and often pack a powerful punch. Note the clever way in which he uses short words throughout the essay itself to support his argument.*

BEFORE YOU READ

Find a paragraph you like in a book that you enjoyed reading. What is it that appeals to you? What did the author do to make the writing so appealing? Do you like the vocabulary, the flow of the words, the imagery it presents, or something else?

When you speak and write, there is no law that says you have to use 1
big words. Short words are as good as long ones, and short, old words — like *sun* and *grass* and *home* — are best of all. A lot of small words, more than you might think, can meet your needs with a strength, grace, and charm that large words do not have.

Big words can make the way dark for those who read what you 2
write and hear what you say. Small words cast their clear light on big things — night and day, love and hate, war and peace, and life and death. Big words at times seem strange to the eye and the ear and the mind and the heart. Small words are the ones we seem to have known from the time we were born, like the hearth fire that warms the home.

Short words are bright like sparks that glow in the night, prompt 3
like the dawn that greets the day, sharp like the blade of a knife, hot like salt tears that scald the cheek, quick like moths that flit from flame to flame, and terse like the dart and sting of a bee.

Here is a sound rule: Use small, old words where you can. If a long 4
word says just what you want to say, do not fear to use it. But know that our tongue is rich in crisp, brisk, swift, short words. Make them

the spine and the heart of what you speak and write. Short words are like fast friends. They will not let you down.

The title of this chapter and the four paragraphs that you have just read are wrought entirely of words of one syllable. In setting myself this task, I did not feel especially cabined, cribbed, or confined. In fact, the structure helped me to focus on the power of the message I was trying to put across.

One study shows that twenty words account for twenty-five percent of all spoken English words, and all twenty are monosyllabic. In order of frequency they are: *I, you, the, a, to, is, it, that, of, and, in, what, he, this, have, do, she, not, on,* and *they.* Other studies indicate that the fifty most common words in written English are each made of a single syllable.

For centuries our finest poets and orators have recognized and employed the power of small words to make a straight point between two minds. A great many of our proverbs punch home their points with pithy monosyllables: "Where there's a will, there's a way," "A stitch in time saves nine," "Spare the rod and spoil the child," "A bird in the hand is worth two in the bush."

Nobody used the short word more skillfully than William Shakespeare, whose dying King Lear laments:

> And my poor fool is hang'd! No, no, no life!
> Why should a dog, a horse, a rat have life,
> And thou no breath at all? . . .
> Do you see this? Look on her; look, her lips.
> Look there, look there!

Shakespeare's contemporaries made the King James Bible a centerpiece of short words — "And God said, Let there be light: and there was light. And God saw the light, that it was good." The descendants of such mighty lines live on in the twentieth century. When asked to explain his policy to Parliament, Winston Churchill responded with these ringing monosyllables: "I will say: it is to wage war, by sea, land, and air, with all our might and with all the strength that God can give us." In his "Death of the Hired Man" Robert Frost observes that "Home is the place where, when you have to go there,/They have to take you in." And William H. Johnson uses ten two-letter words to explain his secret of success: "If it is to be,/It is up to me."

You don't have to be a great author, statesman, or philosopher to tap the energy and eloquence of small words. Each winter I ask my ninth graders at St. Paul's School to write a composition composed entirely of one-syllable words. My students greet my request with obligatory moans and groans, but, when they return to class with their essays, most feel that, with the pressure to produce high-sounding polysyllables relieved, they have created some of their most powerful and luminous prose. Here are submissions from two of my ninth graders:

> What can you say to a boy who has left home? You can say that he has done wrong, but he does not care. He has left home so that he will not have to deal with what you say. He wants to go as far as he can. He will do what he wants to do.
>
> This boy does not want to be forced to go to church, to comb his hair, or to be on time. A good time for this boy does not lie in your reach, for what you have he does not want. He dreams of ripped jeans, shorts with no starch, and old socks.
>
> So now this boy is on a bus to a place he dreams of, a place with no rules. This boy now walks a strange street, his long hair blown back by the wind. He wears no coat or tie, just jeans and an old shirt. He hates your world, and he has left it.
>
> — CHARLES SHAFFER

> For a long time we cruised by the coast and at last came to a wide bay past the curve of a hill, at the end of which lay a small town. Our long boat ride at an end, we all stretched and stood up to watch as the boat nosed its way in.
>
> The town climbed up the hill that rose from the shore, a space in front of it left bare for the port. Each house was a clean white with sky blue or grey trim; in front of each one was a small yard, edged by a white stone wall strewn with green vines.
>
> As the town basked in the heat of noon, not a thing stirred in the streets or by the shore. The sun beat down on the sea, the land, and the back of our necks, so that, in spite of the breeze that made the vines sway, we all wished we could hide from the glare in a cool, white house. But, as there was no one to help dock the boat, we had to stand and wait.
>
> At last the head of the crew leaped from the side and strode to a large house on the right. He shoved the door wide, poked his head through the gloom, and roared with a fierce voice. Five or six men came out, and soon the port was loud with the clank of chains and creak of planks as the men caught ropes thrown by the crew, pulled them taut, and tied them to posts. Then they set up a rough plank so we could cross from the deck to the shore. We all made for the large house while the crew watched, glad to be rid of us.
>
> — CELIA WREN

You too can tap into the vitality and vigor of compact expression. 11 Take a suggestion from the highway department. At the boundaries of your speech and prose place a sign that reads "Caution: Small Words at Work."

RESPONDING TO READING

Reread a piece of writing you turned in earlier this year — it doesn't matter for which class. Analyze your choice of words, and describe your writing vocabulary. Did you follow Lederer's admonition to use short words whenever they are appropriate, or did you tend to use longer, more important-sounding words in your writing? Is Lederer's essay likely to change the way you write papers in the future? Why or why not?

QUESTIONING THE TEXT

1. What rule does Lederer present for writing? What does he do to demonstrate the feasibility of this rule?

2. Lederer states that the twenty words that account for a quarter of all spoken English words are monosyllabic. So are the fifty most common written words. Why, then, do you think Lederer felt it was necessary to argue that people should use them? Who is his audience? (Glossary: *Audience*)

3. How do his students react to the assignment he gives them requiring short words? How do their essays turn out? What does the assignment teach them?

UNDERSTANDING THE WRITER'S CRAFT

1. As you read Lederer's essay for the first time, were you surprised by his announcement in paragraph 5 that the preceding four paragraphs contained only single-syllable words? If not, when were you first aware of what he was doing? What does Lederer's strategy tell you about small words?

2. Lederer starts using multisyllabic words when discussing the process of writing with single-syllable words. Why do you think he abandons his single-syllable presentation? Does it diminish the strength of his argument? Explain.

3. Lederer provides two long examples of writing by his own students. What does he accomplish by using these examples along with ones from famous authors? (Glossary: *Exemplification*)

EXPLORING LANGUAGE

1. Lederer uses similes to help the reader form associations and images with short words. (Glossary: *Figures of Speech*) What are some of these similes? Do you find the similes effective in the context of Lederer's argument? Explain.

2. In paragraph 9, Lederer uses such terms as *mighty* and *ringing monosyllables* to describe the passages he gives as examples. Do you think such descriptions are appropriate? Why do you think he includes them?

3. Carefully analyze the two student essays that Lederer presents. In particular, circle all the main verbs that each student uses. What, if anything, do these verbs have in common? What conclusions can you draw about verbs and strong, powerful writing?

4. Refer to your desk dictionary to define the following words as Lederer uses them in this selection: *cabined* (paragraph 5), *cribbed* (5), *monosyllabic* (6), *proverbs* (7), *eloquence* (10), *obligatory* (10), *vitality* (11).

COMBINING RHETORICAL STRATEGIES

Lederer illustrates his argument with examples from several prominent authors as well as from students. (Glossary: *Exemplification*) Which of these examples did you find the most effective? Why? Provide an example from your own reading that you think is effective in illustrating Lederer's argument.

WRITING SUGGESTIONS

1. **(Argumentation)** People tend to avoid single-syllable words because they are afraid they will look stupid and that their writing will lack sophistication. Are there situations in which demonstrating command of a large vocabulary is desirable? If you answer yes, present one situation, and argue that the overuse of short words in that situation is potentially detrimental. If you answer no, defend your reasoning. How can the use of short words convey the necessary style and sophistication in all situations?

2. **(Other Strategies)** Reread your Before You Read response. How many multisyllable words did you use? Try rewriting the entry using only single-syllable words. Share your results with your class, and discuss the exercise. How easy is it to use only single-syllable words for an assignment? How effective do you think the new "short-word" entries are?

3. **(Research)** Advertising is an industry that depends on efficient, high-impact words. Choose ten advertising slogans and three jingles that you find effective. For example, "Just Do It" and "Think Different" are two prominent slogans. Analyze the ratio of short to long words in the slogans and jingles, and write a paper in which you present your findings. What is the percentage of short words? Does this percentage support or contradict Lederer's contention that short words are often best for high-impact communicating? The following Web sites will help you get started on your research.

   - *Adweek* **Online**
     <http://www.adweek.com>

     This site features articles and news about consumer trends and the advertising industry.

- *Advertising Age* **Online**

  <http://www.adage.com>

  This Web site is "an online magazine covering marketing and media."

- **The Clio Awards**

  <http://www.clioawards.com>

  This site, which aims to honor "advertising excellence worldwide," includes an index of past winners of Clio Awards for print, television, and radio ads.

The Declaration of Independence

Thomas Jefferson

President, governor, statesman, diplomat, lawyer, architect, philosopher, thinker, and writer, Thomas Jefferson is one of the most important figures in U.S. history. He was born in Albemarle County, Virginia, in 1743 and attended the College of William and Mary. After being admitted to law practice in 1767, he began a long and illustrious career of public service to the colonies and, later, the new republic.

Jefferson drafted the Declaration of Independence in 1776. Although it was revised by Benjamin Franklin and his colleagues in the Continental Congress, in its sound logic and forceful, direct style the document retains the unmistakable qualities of Jefferson's prose.

BEFORE YOU READ

In your mind, what is the meaning of democracy? Where do your ideas about democracy come from?

When in the course of human events, it becomes necessary for one people to dissolve the political bands which have connected them with another, and to assume among the Powers of the earth, the separate and equal station to which the Laws of Nature and of Nature's God entitle them, a decent respect to the opinions of mankind requires that they should declare the causes which impel them to the separation.

We hold these truths to be self-evident, that all men are created equal, that they are endowed by their Creator with certain unalienable Rights, that among these are Life, Liberty and the pursuit of Happiness. That to secure these rights, Governments are instituted among Men deriving their just powers from the consent of the governed. That whenever any Form of Government becomes destructive of these ends, it is the Right of the People to alter or to abolish it, and to institute new Government, laying its foundation on such principles and organizing its powers in such form, as to them shall seem most likely to effect their Safety and Happiness. Prudence, indeed, will dictate that Governments long established should not be changed for light and transient causes; and accordingly all experience hath shown, that mankind are more disposed to suffer, while evils are sufferable, than to right themselves by abolishing the forms to which they are accustomed. But when a long train of abuses and usurpations pursuing invariably the same Object evinces a design to reduce them under absolute Despotism, it is their right, it is their duty, to throw off such government, and to provide new Guards for their future security. Such has been the patient sufferance of these Colonies; and such is now the necessity which constrains them to alter their former Systems of Government. The history of the present King of Great Britain is a history of repeated injuries and usurpations, all having in direct object the establishment of an absolute Tyranny over these States. To prove this, let Facts be submitted to a candid world.

He has refused his Assent to Laws, the most wholesome and necessary for the public good. 3

He has forbidden his Governors to pass Laws of immediate and pressing importance, unless suspended in their operation till his Assent should be obtained; and when so suspended, he has utterly neglected to attend to them. 4

He has refused to pass other Laws for the accommodation of large districts of people, unless those people would relinquish the right of Representation in the Legislature, a right inestimable to them and formidable to tyrants only. 5

He has called together legislative bodies at places unusual, uncomfortable, and distant from the depository of their Public Records, for the sole purpose of fatiguing them into compliance with his measures. 6

He has dissolved Representative Houses repeatedly, for opposing with manly firmness his invasions on the rights of the people. 7

He has refused for a long time, after such dissolutions, to cause others to be elected; whereby the Legislative Powers, incapable of Annihilation, have returned to the People at large for their exercise; the State remaining in the mean time exposed to all the dangers of invasion from without, and convulsions within. 8

He has endeavoured to prevent the population of these States; for that purpose obstructing the Laws of Naturalization of Foreigners; refusing to pass others to encourage their migration hither, and raising the conditions of new Appropriations of Lands. 9

He has obstructed the Administration of Justice, by refusing his Assent to Laws for establishing Judiciary Powers. 10

He has made Judges dependent on his Will alone, for the tenure of their offices, and the amount and payment of their salaries. 11

He has erected a multitude of New Offices, and sent hither swarms of Officers to harass our People, and eat out their substance. 12

He has kept among us, in time of peace, Standing Armies without the Consent of our Legislature. 13

He has affected to render the Military independent of and superior to the Civil Power. 14

He has combined with others to subject us to jurisdictions foreign to our constitution, and unacknowledged by our laws; giving his Assent to their acts of pretended Legislation: 15

For quartering large bodies of armed troops among us: 16

For protecting them, by a mock Trial, from Punishment for any Murders which they should commit on the Inhabitants of these States: 17

For cutting off our Trade with all parts of the world: 18

For imposing Taxes on us without our Consent: 19

For depriving us in many cases, of the benefits of Trial by Jury: 20

For transporting us beyond Seas to be tried for pretended offenses: 21

For abolishing the free System of English Laws in a Neighbouring 22 Province, establishing therein an Arbitrary government, and enlarging its boundaries so as to render it at once an example and fit instrument for introducing the same absolute rule into these Colonies:

For taking away our Charters, abolishing our most valuable Laws, 23 and altering fundamentally the Forms of our Governments:

For suspending our own Legislatures, and declaring themselves in- 24 vested with Power to legislate for us in all cases whatsoever.

He has abdicated Government here, by declaring us out of his Pro- 25 tection and waging War against us.

He has plundered our seas, ravaged our Coasts, burnt our towns 26 and destroyed the Lives of our people.

He is at this time transporting large Armies of foreign Mercenaries to 27 compleat works of death, desolation and tyranny already begun with circumstances of Cruelty & perfidy scarcely paralleled in the most bar- barous ages, and totally unworthy the Head of a civilized nation.

He has constrained our fellow Citizens taken Captive on the high 28 Seas to bear Arms against their Country, to become the executioners of their friends and Brethren, or to fall themselves by their Hands.

He has excited domestic insurrections amongst us, and has en- 29 deavoured to bring on the inhabitants of our frontiers, the merciless Indian Savages, whose known rule of warfare is an undistinguished de- struction of all ages, sexes and conditions.

In every stage of these Oppressions We Have Petitioned for Re- 30 dress in the most humble terms: Our repeated petitions have been an- swered only by repeated injury. A Prince, whose character is thus marked by every act which may define a Tyrant, is unfit to be the ruler of a free People.

Not have We been wanting in attention to our British brethren. 31 We have warned them from time to time of attempts by their legisla- ture to extend an unwarrantable jurisdiction over us. We have re- minded them of the circumstances of our emigration and settlement here. We have appealed to their native justice and magnanimity and we have conjured them by the ties of our common kindred to disavow these usurpations, which would inevitably interrupt our connections and correspondence. They too have been deaf to the voice of justice and of consanguinity. We must, therefore acquiesce in the necessity, which denounces our Separation, and hold them, as we hold the rest of mankind, Enemies in War, in Peace Friends.

We, therefore, the Representatives of the United States of America, 32 in General Congress, Assembled, appealing to the Supreme Judge of the world for the rectitude of our intentions, do, in the Name, and by Authority of the good People of these Colonies, solemnly publish and declare, That these United Colonies are, and of Right ought to be Free and Independent States; that they are Absolved from all Allegiance to the British Crown, and that all political connection between them and the State of Great Britain, is and ought to be totally dissolved; and that as Free and Independent States, they have full power to levy War, conclude Peace, contract Alliances, establish Commerce, and to do all other Acts and Things which Independent States may of right do. And for the support of this Declaration, with a firm reliance on the protection of Divine Providence, we mutually pledge to each other our lives, our Fortunes and our sacred Honor.

RESPONDING TO READING

Why do you think the Declaration is still such a powerful and important document more than two hundred years after it was written? Do any parts of the Declaration seem more memorable than others? Did any part of the Declaration surprise you in this reading?

QUESTIONING THE TEXT

1. Where, according to Jefferson, do rulers get their authority? What does Jefferson believe is the purpose of government?

2. What argument does the Declaration make for overthrowing any unacceptable government? What assumptions underlie this argument?

3. In paragraphs 3 through 29, Jefferson lists the many ways King George has wronged the colonists. Which of these "injuries and usurpations" (2) do you feel are just cause for the colonists to declare their independence?

4. According to the Declaration, how did the colonists try to persuade the English king to rule more justly?

5. What are the specific declarations that Jefferson makes in his final paragraph?

UNDERSTANDING THE WRITER'S CRAFT

1. The Declaration of Independence is a deductive argument; it is therefore possible to present it in the form of a syllogism. What is the major premise, the minor premise, and the conclusion of Jefferson's argument? (Glossary: *Syllogism*)

2. In paragraph 2, Jefferson presents certain "self-evident" truths. What are these truths, and how are they related to the intent of his argument?

3. The list of charges against the King is given as evidence in support of Jefferson's minor premise. Does he offer any evidence in support of his major premise? Why or why not? (Glossary: *Evidence*)

4. What pattern do you see to the list of grievances in paragraphs 3 through 29? Try to group them into categories. Describe the cumulative effect of this list on you as a reader.

EXPLORING LANGUAGE

1. Who is Jefferson's audience, and in what tone does he address this audience? Discuss why this tone is or isn't appropriate for this document. (Glossary: *Audience*)

2. Is the language of the Declaration of Independence coolly reasonable or emotional, or does it change from one to the other? Give examples to support your answer.

3. Paraphrase the following excerpt, and comment on Jefferson's diction and syntax: "They too have been deaf to the voice of justice and of consanguinity. We must, therefore acquiesce in the necessity, which denounces our Separation, and hold them, as we hold the rest of mankind, Enemies in War, in Peace Friends" (paragraph 31). Describe the author's tone in these two sentences.

4. Refer to your desk dictionary to determine the meanings of the following words as Jefferson uses them in this selection: *effect* (paragraph 2), *prudence* (2), *transient* (2), *usurpations* (2 and 31), *evinces* (2), *despotism* (2), *candid* (2), *affected* (14), *perfidy* (27), *excited* (29), *redress* (30), *magnanimity* (31), *conjured* (31), *disavow* (31), *too* (31), *consanguinity* (31), *acquiesce* (31), *rectitude* (32), *levy* (32).

COMBINING RHETORICAL STRATEGIES

Explain how Jefferson uses cause and effect thinking to justify the colonists' argument in declaring their independence. (Glossary: *Cause and Effect Analysis*)

WRITING SUGGESTIONS

1. **(Argumentation)** To some people, the Declaration of Independence still accurately reflects America's political philosophy and way of life; to others, it does not. What is your position on this issue? Discuss your analysis of the Declaration's contemporary relevance, and try to persuade others to your position.

2. **(Other Strategies)** How does a monarchy differ from American democracy? Write an essay in which you compare and contrast a particular monarchy and the presidency. How are they similar? You might also consider comparing the presidency with the British monarchy of 1776.

3. **(Research)** The adoption of the Declaration of Independence was, among other things, a matter of practical politics. Using library sources

and possibly the Internet, research the deliberations of the Continental Congress, and explain how and why the final version of the Declaration evolved. For example, you might examine why the final draft differs from Jefferson's first draft. The following Web sites will help you get started on your research.

- **American Memory: Documents from the Continental Congress and the Constitutional Convention, 1774–1789**
  <http://memory.loc.gov/ammem/ndlpedu/bdsd/bdsdfile.html>

  This searchable site, maintained by the Library of Congress, provides access to historical documents.

- **Declaring Independence: Drafting the Documents**
  <http://lcweb.loc.gov/exhibits/declara/declara1.html>

  This Library of Congress site includes facsimiles of various drafts of the Declaration of Independence.

- **The Declaration of Independence**
  <http://www.nara.gov/exhall/charters/declaration/decmain.html>

  This National Archives and Records Administration site provides historical information, images, and many links to other resources.

I Have a Dream

Martin Luther King Jr.

Civil rights leader Martin Luther King Jr. (1929–1968) was the son of a Baptist minister in Atlanta, Georgia. Ordained at the age of eighteen, King went on to earn academic degrees from Morehouse College, Crozer Theological Seminary, Boston University, and Chicago Theological Seminary. He came to prominence in 1955 in Montgomery, Alabama, when he led a successful boycott against the city's segregated bus system. The first president of the Southern Christian Leadership Conference, King became the leading spokesman for the civil rights movement during the 1950s and 1960s, espousing a consistent philosophy of nonviolent resistance to racial injustice. He also championed women's rights and protested the Vietnam War. Named Time *magazine's Man of the Year in 1963, King was awarded the Nobel Peace Prize in 1964. King was assassinated in April 1968 after speaking at a rally in Memphis, Tennessee.*

"I Have a Dream," the keynote address for the "March on Washington" in 1963, has become one of the most renowned and recognized speeches of the past century. Delivered from the steps of the Lincoln Memorial to commemorate the centennial of the Emancipation Proclamation, King's speech resonates with hope even as it condemns racial oppression.

BEFORE YOU READ

Most Americans have seen film clips of King delivering the "I Have a Dream" speech. What do you know of the speech? What do you know of the events and conditions under which King presented it?

Five score years ago, a great American, in whose symbolic shadow we stand, signed the Emancipation Proclamation. This momentous decree came as a great beacon light of hope to millions of Negro slaves who had been seared in the flames of withering injustice. It came as a joyous daybreak to end the long night of captivity.

But one hundred years later, we must face the tragic fact that the Negro is still not free. One hundred years later, the life of the Negro is still sadly crippled by the manacles of segregation and the chains of discrimination. One hundred years later, the Negro lives on a lonely island of poverty in the midst of a vast ocean of material prosperity. One hundred years later, the Negro is still languishing in the corners of American society and finds himself an exile in his own land. So we have come here today to dramatize an appalling condition.

In a sense we have come to our nation's Capitol to cash a check. When the architects of our republic wrote the magnificent words of the Constitution and the Declaration of Independence, they were signing a promissory note to which every American was to fall heir.

This note was a promise that all men would be guaranteed the unalienable rights of life, liberty, and the pursuit of happiness.

It is obvious today that America has defaulted on this promissory note insofar as her citizens of color are concerned. Instead of honoring this sacred obligation, America has given the Negro people a bad check; a check which has come back marked "insufficient funds." But we refuse to believe that the bank of justice is bankrupt. We refuse to believe that there are insufficient funds in the great vaults of opportunity of this nation. So we have come to cash this check — a check that will give us upon demand the riches of freedom and the security of justice. We have also come to this hallowed spot to remind America of the fierce urgency of *now*. This is no time to engage in the luxury of cooling off or to take the tranquilizing drug of gradualism. *Now* is the time to make real the promises of Democracy. *Now* is the time to rise from the dark and desolate valley of segregation to the sunlit path of racial justice. *Now* is the time to open the doors of opportunity to all of God's children. *Now* is the time to lift our nation from the quicksands of racial injustice to the solid rock of brotherhood.

It would be fatal for the nation to overlook the urgency of the moment and to underestimate the determination of the Negro. This sweltering summer of the Negro's legitimate discontent will not pass until there is an invigorating autumn of freedom and equality. 1963 is not an end, but a beginning. Those who hope that the Negro needed to blow off steam and will now be content will have a rude awakening if the nation returns to business as usual. There will be neither rest nor tranquility in America until the Negro is granted his citizenship rights. The whirlwinds of revolt will continue to shake the foundations of our nation until the bright day of justice emerges.

But there is something I must say to my people who stand on the warm threshold which leads into the palace of justice. In the process of gaining our rightful place we must not be guilty of wrongful deeds. Let us not seek to satisfy our thirst for freedom by drinking from the cup of bitterness and hatred. We must forever conduct our struggle on the high plane of dignity and discipline. We must not allow our creative protest to degenerate into physical violence. Again and again we must rise to the majestic heights of meeting physical force with soul force. The marvelous new militancy which has engulfed the Negro community must not lead us to a distrust of all white people, for many of our white brothers, as evidenced by their presence here today, have come to realize that their destiny is tied up with our destiny and their freedom is inextricably bound to our freedom. We cannot walk alone.

And as we walk, we must make the pledge that we shall march ahead. We cannot turn back. There are those who are asking the devotees of civil rights, "When will you be satisfied?" We can never be satisfied as long as the Negro is the victim of the unspeakable horrors of police brutality. We can never be satisfied as long as our bodies, heavy with the fatigue of travel, cannot gain lodging in the motels of the highways and the hotels of the cities. We cannot be satisfied as long as the Negro's basic mobility is from a smaller ghetto to a larger one. We can never be satisfied as long as a Negro in Mississippi cannot vote and a Negro in New York believes he has nothing for which to vote. No, no, we are not satisfied, and we will not be satisfied until justice rolls down like waters and righteousness like a mighty stream.

I am not unmindful that some of you have come here out of great 8 trials and tribulations. Some of you have come fresh from narrow jail cells. Some of you have come from areas where your quest for freedom left you battered by the storms of persecution and staggered by the winds of police brutality. You have been the veterans of creative suffering. Continue to work with the faith that unearned suffering is redemptive.

Go back to Mississippi, go back to Alabama, go back to South Carolina, go back to Georgia, go back to Louisiana, go back to the slums and ghettoes of our northern cities, knowing that somehow this situation can and will be changed. Let us not wallow in the valley of despair. 9

I say to you today, my friends, that in spite of the difficulties and 10 frustrations of the moment I still have a dream. It is a dream deeply rooted in the American dream.

I have a dream that one day this nation will rise up and live out 11 the true meaning of its creed: "We hold these truths to be self-evident; that all men are created equal."

I have a dream that one day on the red hills of Georgia the sons of 12 former slaves and the sons of former slaveowners will be able to sit down together at the table of brotherhood.

I have a dream that the state of Mississippi, a desert state sweltering 13 with the heat of injustice and oppression, will be transformed into an oasis of freedom and justice.

I have a dream that my four little children will one day live in a 14 nation where they will not be judged by the color of their skin but by the content of their character.

I have a dream today. 15

I have a dream that the state of Alabama, whose governor's lips 16 are presently dripping with the words of interposition and nullification, will be transformed into a situation where little black boys and black girls will be able to join hands with little white boys and white girls and walk together as sisters and brothers.

I have a dream today. 17

I have a dream that one day every valley shall be exalted, every 18 hill and mountain shall be made low, the rough places will be made plain, and the crooked places will be made straight, and the glory of the Lord shall be revealed, and all flesh shall see it together.

This is our hope. This is the faith with which I return to the 19
South. With this faith we will be able to hew out of the mountain of
despair a stone of hope. With this faith we will be able to transform
the jangling discords of our nation into a beautiful symphony of
brotherhood. With this faith we will be able to work together, to pray
together, to struggle together, to go to jail together, to stand up for
freedom together, knowing that we will be free one day.

This will be the day when all of God's children will be able to sing 20
with new meaning.

My country, 'tis of thee
Sweet land of liberty,
  Of thee I sing:
Land where my fathers died,
Land of the pilgrims' pride,
From every mountainside
  Let freedom ring.

And if America is to be a great nation this must become true. So 21
let freedom ring from the prodigious hilltops of New Hampshire. Let
freedom ring from the mighty mountains of New York. Let freedom
ring from the heightening Alleghenies of Pennsylvania!

Let freedom ring from the snowcapped Rockies of Colorado! 22

Let freedom ring from the curvaceous peaks of California! 23

But not only that; let freedom ring from Stone Mountain of 24
Georgia!

Let freedom ring from Lookout Mountain of Tennessee! 25

Let freedom ring from every hill and molehill of Mississippi. From 26
every mountainside, let freedom ring.

When we let freedom ring, when we let it ring from every village 27
and every hamlet, from every state and every city, we will be able to
speed up that day when all of God's children, black men and white
men, Jews and Gentiles, Protestants and Catholics, will be able to join
hands and sing in the words of the old Negro spiritual, "Free at last!
free at last! thank God almighty, we are free at last!"

RESPONDING TO READING

What speech or public presentation has had the most impact on you? Did
you find it informative and interesting, or did it actually inspire you to action or to a new way of thinking? What was it about the speaker and the
content of the message that caught your attention and made the event
memorable?

QUESTIONING THE TEXT

1. Why does King say that the Constitution and the Declaration of Independence act as a "promissory note" (paragraph 3) to the American people? In what way has America "defaulted" (4) on its promise?

2. What does King mean when he says that in gaining a rightful place in society "we must not be guilty of wrongful deeds" (paragraph 6)? Why is the issue so important to him?

3. When *will* King be satisfied in his quest for civil rights?

4. What, in a nutshell, is King's dream? What vision does he have for the future?

UNDERSTANDING THE WRITER'S CRAFT

1. King delivered his address to two audiences: the huge audience that listened to him in person, and another, even larger audience. (Glossary: *Audience*) What is that larger audience? What did King do in his speech to catch its attention and to deliver his point?

2. Explain King's choice of a title. (Glossary: *Title*) Why is the title particularly appropriate given the context in which the speech was delivered? What other titles might he have used?

3. Examine the speech, and determine how King organized his presentation. (Glossary: *Organization*) What are the main sections of the speech and what is the purpose of each? How does the organization serve King's overall purpose? (Glossary: *Purpose*)

EXPLORING LANGUAGE

1. King uses parallel constructions and repetition throughout his speech. Identify the phrases and words that he particularly emphasizes. Explain what these techniques add to the persuasiveness of his argument.

2. King makes liberal use of metaphor — and metaphorical imagery — in his speech. (Glossary: *Figures of Speech*) Choose a few examples, and examine what they add to the speech. How do they help King engage his listeners' feelings of injustice and give them hope for a better future?

3. Refer to your desk dictionary to determine the meanings of the following words as King uses them in this selection: *manacles* (paragraph 2), *languishing* (2), *gradualism* (4), *inextricably* (6), *tribulations* (8), *redemptive* (8), *nullification* (16), *prodigious* (21), *curvaceous* (23).

COMBINING RHETORICAL STRATEGIES

King portrayed an America in 1963 in which there was still systematic oppression of African Americans. What is oppression? Define the term, and then write a short essay that assesses its existence in America today. Have you ever felt yourself — or have you known others — to be oppressed or part of a group that is oppressed? Who are the oppressors? How can oppression be overcome?

WRITING SUGGESTIONS

1. **(Argumentation)** King's language is powerful and his imagery is vivid, but the effectiveness of any speech depends partially upon its delivery. If read in monotone, King's use of repetition and parallel language would sound almost redundant rather than inspiring. Keeping presentation in mind, write a short speech that argues a point of view about which you feel strongly. Use King's speech as a model, and incorporate imagery, repetition, and metaphor to communicate your point. Read your speech aloud to a friend to see how it flows and how effective your use of language is. Refine your presentation — both your text and how you deliver it — then present your speech to your class.

2. **(Other Strategies)** King uses a variety of metaphors in his speech, but a single encompassing metaphor can be useful to establish the tone and purpose of an essay. Write a description based on a metaphor that conveys an overall impression from the beginning. Try to avoid clichés ("My dorm is a beehive," "My life is an empty glass"), but make your metaphor readily understandable. For example, you could say, "A police siren is a lullaby in my neighborhood," or "My town is a car that has gone 15,000 miles since its last oil change." Carry the metaphor through the entire description.

3. **(Research)** Using King's assessment of the condition of African Americans in 1963 as a foundation, research the changes that have occurred in the years following King's speech. How have laws changed? How have demographics changed? Present your information in an essay that assesses what still needs to be done to fulfill King's dream for America. Where do we still fall short of the racial equality envisioned by King? What are the prospects for the future?

- **National Association for the Advancement of Colored People (NAACP)**
  <http://www.naacp.org>

  Throughout its ninety-one-year history, this organization of multiracial activists has been on the forefront of the civil rights movement.

- *Frontline:* **The Two Nations of Black America**
  <http://www.pbs.org/wgbh/pages/frontline/shows/race>

  PBS's *Frontline* series answers the question of how, more than thirty years after Martin Luther King Jr.'s death, such a large split has grown between the black upper and lower classes.

- **ACLU — Racial Equality**
  <http://www.aclu.org/issues/racial/hmre.html>

  On the ACLU's Racial Equality page, you can read about ACLU news, civil rights hearings in Congress, and recent discussions about racial profiling, affirmative action, race and the death penalty, and educational equity.

COMBINING SUBJECTS AND STRATEGIES

VIOLENCE IN THE MOVIES AND ON TELEVISION

The photograph below depicts many of the same themes as the essay that follows. Your observations about the photograph will help guide you to the key themes in the essay. After you've read the essay, you may use your observations about both the photograph and the essay to examine how the overlapping themes work in each medium.

The movie still below comes from *The Matrix* (1999), an action sci-fi thriller starring Keanu Reeves and Laurence Fishburne that quickly became a box-office hit. The film was so successful that two sequels have been planned. Directed by the Wachowski Brothers, the movie was noted for both its special effects and its highly stylized, violent fight scenes. In the photograph below, actress Carrie-Anne Moss, in her role as Trinity, totes an oversize automatic weapon and confronts the agent who is pursuing her on a skyscraper rooftop.

© Photofest

For Discussion

How would you describe Carrie-Anne Moss's stance, the look on her face, and the way she is pointing her weapon? What dominant impression do you get from this movie still? How does the setting itself contribute to this impression? What have the directors done in this shot to make violence look aesthetically cool and beautiful? If you saw the film, what message, if any, does it still contain for you?

Violence Is Us

Robert Scheer

Robert Scheer, a contributing editor with the Los Angeles Times *and a non-fiction writer, was born in 1936 in New York City. He received his B.A. from City College of New York in 1958 and did graduate work at Syracuse University and then at the University of California, Berkeley. After a four-year stint as managing editor of* Ramparts, *he became the editor in chief of that radical journal in 1969. His second book,* How the U.S. Got Involved in Vietnam, *was adapted for the magazine's first exposé. A Marxist, Scheer ran for a seat in the House of Representatives as an antiwar candidate in 1965 and for the Senate as a Peace and Freedom candidate in 1970. He has authored* America after Nixon: The Age of Multinationals *(1974),* With Enough Shovels: Reagan, Bush and Nuclear War *(1982), and* Thinking Tuna Fish, Talking Death: Essays on the Pornography of Power *(1988), a book of essays on the Vietnam War.*

In the following selection, first published in the November 15, 1994, issue of The Nation, *Scheer hints at the complications of a legal attack on television violence. He asks his readers to consider simply eschewing violent programming and supporting quality television.*

BEFORE YOU READ

Can you remember you or any of your friends ever acting out violence you saw on television as a child? Do you think television has the power to influence people's actions? Explain.

O nce again Congressional committees are holding hearings on TV violence, and network executives, sincere visages firmly in place, are promising to clean up their act. Attorney General Janet Reno testified that if they don't, "government should respond."

There is something so beside the point about this handwringing, which has gone on since 1952, when the first Congressional hearing on TV violence was held. In 1968 a national commission headed by Milton Eisenhower warned: "We are deeply troubled by the television's constant portrayal of violence . . . in pandering to a public preoccupation with violence that television itself has helped to generate."

Of course, violence and base stupidity on TV and in the movies is excessive and getting worse. With the proliferation of cable channels, the market has become much more competitive, and violence sells. Hardly a night of channel-flipping goes by when my cable service doesn't offer up several truly grotesque chainsaw massacre–type films complete with dismembered parts and spurting blood.

Then, too, there are the cleaner assassinations presented on the networks both in their entertainment and local news hours. Remember the orgy of voyeurism, with three separate network movies devoted to the Amy Fisher–Joey Buttafuoco story? So-called news shows featuring real-life crime represent a major segment of entertainment scheduling. The fatal graveside shooting of a woman by her ex-spouse, captured by a television news camera, was gratuitously "teased" during the evening in many markets to get people to watch the news that night.

Nor do I deny the claims of most experts that viewing violence 5 desensitizes people, particularly children, to the actual effects of violence, leaving them more likely to act out in antisocial ways. As the American Psychological Association reported to Congress in 1988, "Virtually all independent scholars agree that there is evidence that television can cause aggressive behavior."

More than 200 major studies support the common-sense suspi- 6 cion that watching endless hours of violence is a public health menace. Those same studies demonstrate, although the pro-censorship prudes will never accept it, that the violent R-rated movies — not the sexually explicit X-rated ones — desensitize men to sexual violence. (As an example of this weirdly skewed double standard, wannabe censor Rev. Donald Wildmon took out full-page ads attacking *NYPD Blue,* not for its explicit violence — six homicides in the first episode — but rather because of a nude lovemaking scene, calling it "soft-core pornography.")

Another thing those studies show is that the poorer a family 7 is, meaning the more vulnerable and desperate, the more hours they will spend in front of the television set. Children in poverty are most often left alone with the TV as the only available babysitter.

It can hardly be a good thing that children's shows two years ago 8 reached an all-time high of thirty-two violent incidents per hour and that nine in ten children's programs involve violence. An authoritative study by George Gerbner of the University of Pennsylvania indicated that the average 16-year-old has witnessed 200,000 violent acts on TV, including 33,000 murders. Given the ease with which children can get guns in this society, there has to be some connection between the ease with which citizens are blown away by teenagers on television and in what passes for real life. And when they do it in real life they can be assured of their fifteen minutes of fame with top billing on the nightly local news.

Wayne LaPierre, vice president of the National Rifle Association, 9 had a good point when he complained recently, "It galls us that every night we get lectured by ABC, NBC and CBS News, and then they go to their entertainment programming and show all kinds of gratuitous violence." Hypocrites they are, and the voluntary labeling code that the network executives recently adopted in an effort to head off Congressional prohibitions on violent programming will change nothing. Although 72 percent of Americans polled by *Times-Mirror* say that we have too much violence on TV and it leads to higher crime rates, many of them must be tuning in, or the television moguls wouldn't be scheduling such fare.

Maybe it is time to face the fact that we have all this mayhem in 10 our art and our lives because we like violence. Or if we don't actually like it, we need it. Why else would we favor local news programs that stress ambulance-chasing "action news"? Whether it's local or foreign news, our attention is grabbed completely only when death and destruction are at hand. That's what the endless focus groups conducted by news organizations report. It is true, as Steven Bochco, creator of *NYPD Blue,* has stated, that the violence issue on prime time is a "bogus issue," because "there's more violence on the 5 o'clock news than anything you'll see on the networks during prime time."

Anyway, how can you control it without putting decision-making 11 into the hands of small-minded censors? What are the guidelines? Some reasonable ones, to cut the harmful effects on children, were suggested by University of Michigan psychology professor Leonard Eron, who is the dean of research in this area. "Gratuitous violence that is not necessary to the plot should be reduced or eliminated," is one that the networks say they accept. Another we can all agree on is that the "devastating effects of violence, the permanence of its consequences . . . should be made clear," meaning you hurt or die from gunshot wounds. So far so good, but what about when he tells us, "Perpetrators of violence should not be rewarded for their violent acts," and that "those who act aggressively should be punished"? Those last two, while admirable goals, would distort a reality in which many criminals do get away with their crimes. Do we want television writers to lie to us? Don't we adults need to face up to the truth that crime is out of control?

Maybe adults should watch what they want, but should children, 12 who are by definition impressionable, be exposed to a steady diet of mind-numbing violence laced with general stupidity? No, they shouldn't, but is this an issue the government or other would-be censors ought to get involved with?

The answer is, they are already involved, but despite endless 13 guidelines for children's television, the fare is nastier than ever. The reason is that every regulation produces just that much more ingenuity on the part of the so-called creative people who make this junk. They are a crafty bunch and will always find some way of getting to the kids with the most primitive jolt.

Take the much-discussed *Beavis and Butt-Head* show, which now 14 leads the race for the lowest common denominator. When a 5-year-old in Ohio burned the family trailer to the ground, his mother blamed the show, her son's favorite, which had shown the two idiot characters setting fire to all sorts of objects. Hey, no problem, arson was taken out of the show in response to public outrage. There were the expected calls to ban *Beavis,* but no one stopped to ask the obvious question: Why had that mother let her 5-year-old watch endless hours of this repulsive show?

I asked the same question after reading a story in the *Los Angeles* 15 *Times* about firefighters having to visit the schools of Orange County, California, to warn the kids that setting fires at home is a no-no. In one class, almost all the 12-year-olds said they watched *Beavis and Butt-Head* regularly and then began chanting the call of the show's lead, "Burn, burn, burn." That was in the conservative white upper-middle-class community of Mission Viejo, one of those planned paradises. Again, why did all those parents allow their kids to watch the show? It is absurd to suggest that the government step in to censor viewing that parents have acquiesced in.

The more important question is, Why do the children of paradise 16 delight in this and other stupidities? I don't really know the full answer but it can't be, as Dan Quayle charged in the last election, that the cultural elite of Hollywood has seized their minds. Orange County voted overwhelmingly for Quayle and his running mate, the parents have thrown up the strongest defenses against Satan and his permissiveness, and church, Little League and Boy Scout attendance is very high.

One answer provided by the creators of this stuff is that it doesn't 17 mean a thing. Kids have always tuned in to cartoons and movies in which characters are splattered or blown away. They concede that things are a bit wilder now, with far more blood and gore and nastier images, but that's modern technology for you. The demand is there and the supply will follow, but no harm is done — it's just a picture.

I don't buy this argument, because the impact of television and 18 movies is too pervasive to be so easily dismissed. For many kids the electronic picture is their world, the result of an ever more technically effective medium having drowned out all other avenues of learning and stimulation.

It does desensitize and, yes, I don't think young kids should be 19 watching *Beavis and Butt-Head* scenes featuring a poke in the eye with a pencil with blood spurting out, or a dog thrown into a washing machine followed by an insane giggle of approval. I doubt very much that *Beavis* creator Mike Judge will allow his little girls to watch the show.

But "we," collectively, can't and should not do anything about it. 20 We can't because we live in a market economy in which blood lust and other primitive needs of people will be met one way or another, and trying to ban something just makes it more attractive and marketable. We shouldn't because it is the adults' right to flick on whatever they want on the increasingly responsive cable smorgasbord. And it is parents' responsibility to monitor what kids watch. The "we" as represented by the state should do nothing.

The alternative is for the public, or rather some segment of it, to 21
demand something better on at least a few of the many channels that
are opening up. There are plenty of good television programs and
movies that aim higher and do well at the box office. Since the market
is master, people need not be passive about expressing their tastes.
Where I live, for example, people have demanded successfully that the
cable company carry the excellent Bravo channel, which it was threatening to drop.

"In the final analysis, it is still the law of supply and demand on 22
all this stuff," says Norman Lear, whose *All in the Family* series first
upped the ante for thoughtful prime-time programming. "It goes back
to the advertisers; they are the people who pay for this stuff. If they
didn't want it, it wouldn't be there. They are just dealing with product. They know from experience that something hard and outrageous
will sell faster than something soft.

"It's no secret that there's a lot of baseness to human nature, but 23
we don't always pander to it, and reasonable people don't wish to
pander to it. But there is nothing reasonable about the bottom line
and about needing to please Wall Street by the quarter — to find the
instant rating successes that satisfy the bottom line.

"The network goes to someone to make a pilot, then they take it 24
to Madison Avenue, and people look at it and say, 'That's a fucking
hit.' They're the first people to look at it and say, 'I want in. I will
spend my millions of dollars here because I think it will rate.'"

He adds that because no single sponsor is identified with a show, as 25
was the case in the "Golden Age" of the *Philco Playhouse* and the *Alcoa
Hour,* "no sponsor is seriously associated with the quality of the show."

That's what happened with *Beavis and Butt-Head* — its creator, 26
Judge, had originally prepared it as a one-time entry for a festival of
"sick and twisted" cartoons. He had no intention of turning his one-
liner into a series, but MTV execs saw it and ordered up thirty-five
episodes, and soon it was a multinational operation with teams of ani-
mators in New York and Korea frantically turning the stuff out.

The MTV execs were right. The demand was there. It's MTV's hottest 27
show, and sixty-five more episodes are on the way for 1994 and worldwide distribution. If you don't like that because you think it represents
the dumbing-down of American and world culture, then vote — by just
turning the damn thing off. Don't beg Big Brother to do it for you.

RESPONDING TO READING

Scheer argues that we must fight the free market economy of commercial
television with our free choice. Do you find this a plausible solution to
avoiding the influence of television violence? Why or why not?

QUESTIONING THE TEXT

1. How does Scheer observe "action news" chasing higher ratings? In Scheer's opinion, what image of reality do these programs create?

2. What is the "weirdly skewed double standard" (paragraph 6) of R and X ratings?

3. What relationship have studies shown between poverty and television? What implications do you see in this conclusion?

4. Why does Scheer call the three major networks hypocrites?

5. Why doesn't the author think that the networks' decision to impose labeling on themselves will have an impact on TV violence?

6. Which recommendations for reducing TV violence does the author endorse? Why? Which ones does he criticize?

7. How do advertisers escape accountability for the content of programming?

UNDERSTANDING THE WRITER'S CRAFT

1. What is the author's thesis, and where does he state it? (Glossary: *Thesis*)

2. What use does the author make of the information from hundreds of studies that link television violence and real-life violence? How is this material related to his thesis?

3. Scheer encourages his reader to reevaluate his or her relationship to television. Does this essay make you think? Does it make you uncomfortable? Comment on the author's level of success in creating interest in this subject and persuading you to his point of view. Point to specific parts of his argument that had an impact on you.

4. In paragraph 20, Scheer uses a food metaphor when he calls television a "cable smorgasbord." What does the image lend to his argument? (Glossary: *Figures of Speech*)

5. Reread paragraphs 22 through 25, in which the author quotes Norman Lear. Do you think that this quotation justifies despair on this issue or encourages a realistic course of action? Explain.

EXPLORING LANGUAGE

1. Scheer plays with the language of problem solving on an issue that, as he demonstrates in a quotation from an early commission on TV violence, seems locked in its own dialectic. Using examples from the text, comment on his use of irony. (Glossary: *Irony*)

2. How would you characterize Scheer's diction in this essay — formal or informal? Did you find his diction appropriate in terms of his subject and audience? Explain.

3. Comment on Scheer's use of the pronoun *we* in paragraph 20.

4. Refer to your desk dictionary to determine the meanings of the following words as Scheer uses them in this selection: *visages* (paragraph 1), *pander* (2 and 23), *base* (3), *voyeurism* (4), *gratuitous* (4, 9, and 11), *galls* (9), *moguls* (9), *fare* (13), *acquiesced* (15).

COMBINING RHETORICAL STRATEGIES

Scheer makes extensive use of the *Beavis and Butt-Head* example in his essay. How does this example serve to further his argument? (Glossary: *Exemplification*) Would Scheer's argument have been even stronger had he used examples from other shows aimed at children? Explain.

WRITING SUGGESTIONS

1. **(Argumentation)** Do you believe that the goal of providing clear, pertinent information has been sacrificed by the "action news" programs the author writes about? How do you decide what news is pertinent? What would you consider an ideal news program? Write an essay in which you address these questions.

2. **(Other Strategies)** Scheer raises many of the same problems about violence on television and in the movies that Barbara Hattemer raises in her essay "Cause and Violent Effect: Media and Our Youth" (p. 616). Both authors stress the cardinal importance of individual adults to take action, but they disagree when it comes to censoring violence. Using one or both of these articles and the movie still from *The Matrix* on page 608, write an essay in which you present your position on television and movie censorship. How are Americans to deal with what seems like the ever-increasing amount of violence in the media?

3. **(Research)** What is it about television that makes it our primary media source? Do some research at the library about television's beginnings and its introduction into America's cultural mainstream. How long did it take for television to saturate most households? Think of some alternative forms of media besides television — periodicals, film, radio, the Internet. Why do you think these forms remain alternative? Do you think that any of these forms can compete with television, or do you think that television will continue to dominate the media scene? Write an essay in which you argue for your position. Be sure to use examples to illustrate your claims.

   • **Television History**
   <http://www.mediahistory.com/teevee.html>

   From the Media History Project Connection Pages, this Web site offers links, resources, and articles on television history and theory.

   • **Media and Culture: An Introduction to Mass Communication**
   <http://www.mediaculture.com>

   This Web site, maintained by Bedford/St. Martin's, offers information on the history of television as well as links to related resources.

Cause and Violent Effect: Media and Our Youth

Barbara Hattemer

A nonfiction writer and the founder and president of the National Family Foundation, Barbara Hattemer studies the effects of the media on individuals and families. Her articles have appeared in Yankee *magazine,* Guideposts, *and* Parents *magazine.*

In the following selection, first published in the July 1994 issue of The World and I, *Hattemer draws heavily from her book,* Don't Touch That Dial: The Impact of the Media on Children and the Family *(1993). She points to several studies demonstrating the link between television violence and real-life violence, and she argues that the vigilance of individuals will always have more effect than labeling.*

BEFORE YOU READ

What was your first encounter with violence in the media? What can you remember about that incident? What impact do you think it had on you?

Recent headlines proclaim increasing youth violence: "Four 1 Teenagers Charged in Murder of Tourist," "Pupils Told to Run for Their Lives — Teacher Describes Terror in Classroom," "FSU Student Murdered, Sister Raped — Eighteen-year-old Beaten to Death, Sister Tied to Tree in Ocala National Forest."

Youth crime is on everyone's mind. It is the focus of virtually 2 every political campaign of 1994. There is talk of boot camps, stricter laws, trying children as adults for committing serious crimes, larger prisons, harsher sentences, gun control, curfews. Take the kids off the streets so we can feel safe again! Keep them home! Why? So they can watch more murder and rape on television and video?

How weary we have grown of the statistics on how many murders 3 every high school graduate has seen. According to the American Psychological Association, even before leaving elementary school, the average child has seen eight thousand murders and one hundred thousand acts of violence on television.

Social science, clinical concepts, and common sense all agree that 4 what children watch affects who they become, what they believe, what they value, and how they behave.

EARLY INFLUENCE OF TV

Television's influence on our children starts earlier than most of us re- 5 alize. Andrew Meltzoff found that fourteen-month-old infants can

616

watch an unfamiliar toy being dismantled and reassembled on television and repeat the actions twenty-four hours later. Even at this early age, television acts as a guide to real-life behavior. Throughout childhood, children learn by imitating what they see others doing.

Two- to six-year-old children cannot evaluate the messages they receive from the media they watch. They simply accept what they see as normal behavior. Children cannot tell the difference between reality and fantasy until the fifth or sixth grade. Six- to twelve-year-olds imitate what they see and hear without fully understanding the consequences of what they are doing. Most adolescents do not have a fully developed, internal set of morals and values. They accept the conduct they see in the media as the social norm and integrate it into their own behavior patterns.

What are the predominant messages of television, movies, and other media that our children are accepting and imitating? That violence is an everyday occurrence and an acceptable way of solving problems and that promiscuous sex is normal and expected of everyone, including younger and younger children. These two messages merge as the philosophy of pornography, once thought to be limited to sleazy adult bookstores and out-of-the-way art cinemas, has been mainstreamed. The rape myth — that women secretly want to be raped and that they enjoy forced sex — has so permeated our children's minds that 65 percent of boys and 47 percent of girls agreed with a survey question that "it was acceptable for a man to force sex with a woman if he had been dating her more than six months."

While television has unlimited potential for good, at the present time its influence on children's lives is largely negative. Television programming, according to Dr. Paul Howard, prominent Boston psychiatrist, is so hostile and aggressive it produces tremendous anxiety in young watchers. "One weekend of children watching television," he declared, "undoes a whole week of psychotherapy for my young patients."

Television and violence have been almost synonymous since television became a part of nearly every home. As far back as 1977, 9 of every 10 TV programs contained violence. Today, while there is more variety, there are more sources of violence than ever before. In addition to violent action-adventure movies and television dramas, violence pervades music videos, rap songs, documentaries, commercials, and news broadcasts. The networks provide up to 10 violent acts per hour; cable, up to 18 violent acts per hour; and children's cartoons, 32 violent acts per hour. Movies like *Teenage Mutant Ninja Turtles* raise the count to 133 violent acts per hour. The body count is rising, too: *Total Recall,* 74 dead; *Robocop 2,* 81 dead; *Rambo III,* 106 dead; and *Die Hard 2,* 264 dead.

Mass-produced, cheap industrial violence is something quite new in our culture. The new heroes glamorize violence for its own sake.

The violence is the story, not an element necessary to the telling of a story. Add to this the influence of violent video games and fantasy games that encourage children to spend hours planning how to kill or maim more successfully. Mix in violent comic books and serial-killer trading cards, and you have a culture that gives its children a steady diet of violent role models but very little old-fashioned nurture and direction from parents.

VIOLENT YOUTH

For nearly a decade, judges and police officers have been exclaiming 11 that they have never before seen rapists and murderers who are so young. The news, in its promotion of the sensation, keeps the tragic headlines ever before us. What some feared might one day happen is indeed happening. The subculture that has long been singing about beating up women, killing parents, and murdering for fun has surfaced.

One-half of the sex offenders in this country are now under the 12 age of eighteen! A 1988 Michigan crime report stated that 681 juveniles who averaged fourteen years of age were convicted of sexually assaulting children who averaged seven years of age. These are not always violent or deeply troubled children; they are children who have been exposed too early to material they cannot process without imitating. They see it on cable in their own homes, they hear it on the telephone. Dial-a-porn companies have admitted that 75 to 85 percent of their customers are children. Overstimulated by what they see and hear, they act it out on younger siblings or playmates.

Violent crime is up 560 percent since 1960 and is rising. There are 13 three million incidents of school crime every year. In 1993 alone, the rate of violent encounters in schools rose 34 percent in the state of Florida. Rape, assault, and murder have replaced chewing gum, talking in class, and throwing wads of paper, the greatest school problems in the forties. From 1987 to 1991, teenagers arrested for murder increased 85 percent. In 1990, 4,200 teenagers were killed by guns. In New York City, one in five teenagers carries a weapon to school, and one in twenty, a gun. On any one day, 135,000 children carry guns to school across the nation.

It is said that we have always been a violent society, but there is a 14 new callousness among our young people. Many studies have found that using pornography increases men's callousness toward and distrust of women, as well as their inclination to rape. Research also has revealed that 100 percent of our high schoolers have seen soft-core pornography, and 90 percent of high school boys and 80 percent of girls have seen hard-core pornography. The younger they are when they see it, the more likely they are to want to imitate it.

Horror movies aimed at young teens desensitize them to violence 15 and create an ever-increasing appetite for it. If the camera angle allows the child to see the action through the eyes of the madman, a subtle shift takes place. He identifies not with the passive victim but with the active perpetrator. In his imagination, it is the child himself who wields the knife, the ax, or the deadly weapon. Identifying with the aggressor, he senses the thrill of momentary power over another and learns to enjoy committing a crime.

Park Dietz declares that exposing boys to films showing women 16 being mutilated in the midst of sex scenes is the best way to raise a generation of sexual sadists. One study found that Freddy of *Nightmare on Elm Street* and Jason of *Friday the 13th* are better known to ten- to thirteen-year-olds than Abraham Lincoln and George Washington. Seven- to twelve-year-olds name horror movies as their favorites and say they like seeing people killed and enjoy watching pain and torture. Freddy is the star of not only a series of movies, but a television series, comic book, 900 number, toys, and trading cards. The mayor of Los Angeles named a holiday for him. We are teaching our children to look to mass murderers as their role models.

Film critic Roger Ebert sees a basic change taking place in society 17 regarding women in danger. The sympathy of the audience has moved from the woman to the killer. As the camera takes the killer's point of view, the lust to kill is placed, not in the character of the killer, but in the audience.

Too often, that audience is full of impressionable children. They 18 can buy a ticket to any G or PG film and often slip into R-rated films in a mall complex. (They laugh when asked if they have trouble getting to see R-rated movies, and producers boast that if they make the movies, children will find a way to see them.) At video stores and libraries, even the pretense of restricting children from R-rated movies is gone. With the notable exception of Blockbuster video stores, there is no age restriction for obtaining violent movies.

REAL-LIFE AGGRESSION

No one today doubts that our children are seeing massive amounts of 19 violence in a wide variety of media presentations. Moreover, a vast amount of scientific research proves that watching violence on the screen is causally related to real-life aggression. Since the 1968 National Commission on the Causes and Prevention of Violence, a series of government commissions and reports and a consensus of medical associations have all found a link between screen violence and violent behavior.

The television and motion picture industries have been successful   20
in casting doubt on such findings by saying that some studies show an effect and others do not, but the studies that show the fewest effects have been sponsored by the industry. We now have over three thousand studies telling us that watching violent films increases violent behavior. Research has found that preschool children who frequently watch violent cartoons behave aggressively. First-graders who watch aggressive cartoons exhibit more hostile behavior in school than first-graders who watch neutral programming or even a football game. Because the impact is greater the more realistic the violent scenes are, researchers fear the more realistic human characters in today's cartoons may have an even greater influence on children.

Leonard Eron and Rowell Huesman conducted an important lon-   21
gitudinal study, following eight-year-olds for twenty-two years. They found that children who watched large amounts of violent television at age eight were more likely to be engaged in criminal behavior at age thirty. Not only did they commit serious crimes, they also punished their children more harshly and were much more aggressive when drinking.

Studies before and after the introduction of television in an area   22
reveal an increase in aggressive behavior after the arrival of television. Two years after television was introduced into Notel, Canada, physical aggression among children increased 160 percent.

A study by Brandon Centerwall focused on the effects of child-   23
hood exposure to television violence on adult criminal behavior in larger populations, comparing the effect of television on the roughly comparable white populations of the United States, Canada, and South Africa. Fifteen years after television was introduced into the United States and Canada, white homicide deaths had risen 93 percent and 92 percent, respectively. At the same time, in South Africa, where there was no TV, the white homicide rate had dropped 7 percent. Yet, eight years after South Africa received TV, the rate had already increased 56 percent, indicating that, in fifteen years, it would be close to that of the United States and Canada. In fact, by 1987, twelve years after television had been introduced into South Africa, the white homicide rate had risen by 130 percent.

Centerwall looked for every possible alternative explanation,   24
completing another eleven studies on factors such as the baby boom, urbanization, economic trends, alcohol consumption, capital punishment, civil unrest, and the availability of firearms, but he could find none. He ruled out such factors as the U.S. civil rights movement and the Vietnam War because these did not affect Canada. He concluded

that exposure to violent programming on television is causally related to roughly one-half the twenty thousand yearly homicides in the United States and one-half the rapes and assaults as well.

His conclusions held up when he looked at populations within the United States that acquired television at different times. When television appeared in the early 1950s, it was an expensive luxury. Since blacks tended to lag behind whites by about five years in acquiring television sets, he predicted that the white homicide rate would rise before the black homicide rate in the United States. In fact, the white homicide rate began to rise in 1958, while the black homicide rate dropped consistently throughout the next four years. Similarly, those regions of the United States like New York and New Jersey that acquired television before other sections of the country were also found to have an earlier increase in the homicide rate.

Centerwall believes that the lag of ten to fifteen years between the introduction of television and the rise in the homicide rate indicates that the greatest effect is on children under the age of twelve. In the past, it took these children ten to fifteen years to grow up before they were old enough to commit homicide. Today, however, children are not waiting to become adults to begin committing adult crimes. Youth crime is growing at a much faster rate than adult crime. The past ten years have seen an increase of 55 percent in the number of children arrested for murder. Centerwall explains this as the snowballing effect. The first generation raised on television learned values from the adults in their lives as well as from the TV set. With the increasing dominance of the media in society, the passing on of values from the older generation has diminished, while the second and third generations raised on TV have increasingly taken their values from the media culture.

LETHAL VIOLENCE

The increase in the seriousness of juvenile crime may be explained further by the fact that violence has become increasingly graphic and gory. According to journalist David Barry, the juvenile delinquency portrayed in 1950s movies "consisted almost entirely of assaults with fists and weapons which left victims injured, but alive. It was nonlethal violence. The notion of American teenagers as killers was beyond the threshold of credibility."

Since then, he says, the level of criminal violence reported in everyday news stories has become almost unrecognizable. He offers the following statistics as evidence of the effect of the first twenty-nine years of television on crime in the United States. In 1951, there were 6,820 murders, 16,800 rapes, and 52,090 robberies. By 1980, these had increased to 23,000 murders, 78,920 rapes, and 548,220 robberies — vastly more than the 47 percent population increase from 150 million to 220 million. The murder rate is increasing six times faster than the rate of population growth. It is now the leading cause of death for black youths and the second leading cause of death of all fifteen- to twenty-four-year-olds. Violence is the leading cause of injury to fifteen- to forty-four-year-old women. The U.S. Centers for Disease Control calls it both a leading public health issue and an epidemic.

Researchers offer numerous explanations of how and why media   29
violence translates into real-life violence. They theorize that when a child observes violence used as a means of solving conflicts, the event is recorded in his brain and stored in his memory bank. This scene can be reinforced by subsequent violent scenes, which eventually blend into a general script of how to react to conflict. The more graphic the violence, the more likely it will catch the child's attention and become part of a script stored in his memory, waiting to be retrieved when he faces a similar conflict situation in real life.

Older children are particularly responsive to violence that is realis-   30
tic or close to their personal experience and thus seems likely to happen in real life. Younger children are more likely to identify with and imitate violent behavior if the character is attractively portrayed. The more that children of all ages identify with a violent character, the more likely they are to be aggressive themselves.

Watching violence primes the pump and starts a network of asso-   31
ciations. As media violence is absorbed into a person's thoughts, it activates related aggressive ideas and emotions that eventually lead to aggressive behavior. What a child observes as the associative networks in his brain are developing is of paramount importance.

Violence that is rewarded or left unpunished appears to be sanc-   32
tioned in a child's mind. It is, therefore, much more likely to be imitated. Violence that appears to be justified or portrayed as necessary for a good cause is even more likely to be imitated. One reason the large amount of violence in Japanese films does not produce as much real-life violence as in the United States is the way that Japanese films portray violence, highlighting the pain, suffering, and tragic consequences that follow. They teach an altogether different lesson than America's glamorized violence.

Not everyone reacts the same way to violence. Poorly nurtured   33
children with few inner strengths and without internalized boundaries are more susceptible to its influence than well-nurtured children who have received a strong value system from their parents. Children who are undersupplied with parental love are often angry and chaotic

inside. They are drawn to violent films, heavy metal music, and gang-ster rap because it reflects their inner turmoil. It both reinforces and offers approval for their negative attitudes. The combination of being undersupplied with parental nurture and overstimulated by violent media can be deadly.

VIOLENCE IN MUSIC

In 1989, the American Medical Association concluded that music is an 34
even greater influence on teens than television. This is because they have more exposure to heavy metal music than to either pornography or horror films. MTV has introduced a whole generation of children to songs that glorify pleasure seeking and irresponsibility. Its videos con-tain thirteen violent acts per hour, and four out of five of them mix vi-olence with sex.

Rock stars are always available to young people starving for atten- 35
tion and understanding. They offer children unqualified acceptance. They appear to meet their needs and understand their chaotic emo-tions better than their parents. Prolonged listening to hard-rock music correlates with many negatives, from the mildly troubling to the very serious: increasing discomfort in family situations, a preference for friends over family, poor academic performance, increased chemical dependency, violence, stealing, and sexual activity. It makes disturbed adolescents feel powerful and in charge.

There is a strong relationship between antisocial or destructive 36
behavior and listening to rock music with destructive themes. The pref-erence for heavy metal music among juvenile delinquents is almost three times as high as among the general population of high schoolers. This music is filling our children's heads with rebellion, raw sex, violence, and a hatred and abuse of women of a degree never seen before. . . .

Newsweek speaks of the ability of rap music to alienate, of its im- 37
agery and lyrics as "pure confrontation." It educates our children on the crime and rage of inner-city life and fills their heads with rebel-lion, hate, and more raw sex. While the courts rule in favor of hateful speech, our culture struggles with how to deal with entertainment that spews hatred into children's minds.

THE FAMILY ANTIDOTE

Research has found that the best defense against the media is a strong 38
family that makes an effort to impart values and gives children clear boundaries. Youths from families with well-defined value systems use

them to interpret what they observe. Teenagers from homes in which family members communicate openly and engage in an active viewing style, discussing programs with their children, are less influenced by what they see.

Violent programming has a greater impact on boys than on girls, a greater impact on young men who are already callous than on those who are sensitive, and a greater impact on those from the inner city who experience violence in their daily lives. The latter, by their own admission, are more aroused by filmed violence, give it higher approval ratings, and watch more of it. With thousands of violent models stored in their memories and more aggressive associations implanted in their minds, why are we surprised when they react violently to real-life situations? 39

The entertainment industry could help our troubled children by cutting back on the number of violent portrayals, by making them less graphic and attention-getting, and by emphasizing the sorrowful consequences of violence rather than glamorizing and making heroes of violent men. 40

A possible solution is granting the Federal Communications Commission the power to include excessive violence in the broadcasting standard that limits indecency and obscenity on radio and television. Government censorship cannot raise the moral tone of the nation. A better answer is the return to standards and voluntary limits. Nothing shows so clearly how far we have fallen as a nation from the values we once agreed upon than a look at the old Motion Picture Production Code, in force from 1930 to 1966, which stated: 41

> Motion picture producers recognize the high trust and confidence which have been placed in them by the people of the world. . . . They recognize their responsibility to the public because of this trust and because entertainment and art are important influences in the life of the nation.

But a code should apply to television, cable, and satellite as well. Government hearings and citizen complaints could serve to pressure the industry to consider an updated and revised code for all its products.

For this to become a reality, citizens must demand a better balance between creative freedom and social responsibility, between anything for a profit and serving the public interest. The industry must stop the "Can you top this!" mentality, which makes each sequel more graphic and gory than the one before. We must become more discriminating viewers and stop watching violent programs. We must enter into dialogue with the industry, thanking studios and networks for every good offering and supporting them at the box office and in the ratings 42 races. We must support the sponsors of good programs and protest irresponsible companies at stockholders' meetings.

A return to standards is a better solution than labels. Parental advisories give permission to label and then go ahead and produce even more violent material. We need to recapture the essence of the old motion picture code, which declared that "there is no real substitute for successful self-government in industry" and that "self-regulation is wholly consonant with freedom of expression." 43

RESPONDING TO READING

Throughout her essay, Hattemer continually points to the influence television has on the developing child. Does she ever concede that television loses its influence after a certain age? What is her claim? Do you agree with her position? Why or why not?

QUESTIONING THE TEXT

1. What relationship does Hattemer delineate between television and the cognitive abilities of children?

2. According to the author, what characterizes the violence and heroes children see on television and in the movies?

3. In Hattemer's opinion, how have horror movies encouraged children to identify with the aggressor?

4. Hattemer writes, "Not everyone reacts the same way to violence" (paragraph 33). What explanation does she offer for this fact?

5. How does the study by Brandon Centerwall account for the rise in children arrested for murder in the past ten years?

6. What action does the author advocate to combat violence in the media, and why does she find parental advisory labeling futile?

UNDERSTANDING THE WRITER'S CRAFT

1. What is Hattemer's thesis, and where is it stated? (Glossary: *Thesis*)

2. How has Hattemer organized her essay? What function do her headings serve within this organizational pattern? (Glossary: *Organization*)

3. Consider the various ways in which Hattemer makes transitions from one paragraph to the next. (Glossary: *Transitions*) What do these transitions add to her essay?

4. Who is Hattemer addressing in this essay? (Glossary: *Audience*) Do you see the author's examples as aimed at this audience? Explain.

5. Which of the author's examples do you find most convincing in this essay? What do you think makes these examples so persuasive? (Glossary: *Exemplification*)

EXPLORING LANGUAGE

1. What is Hattemer's attitude toward violence in the media, and how is this attitude reflected in her diction? Cite specific examples to support your answer.

2. How would you characterize Hattemer's tone in this essay? (Glossary: *Tone*)

3. Refer to your desk dictionary to determine the meanings of the following words as Hattemer uses them in this selection: *permeated* (paragraph 7), *pervades* (9), *callousness* (14), *perpetrator* (15), *moreover* (19), *causally* (19 and 24), *longitudinal* (21), *paramount* (31), *sanctioned* (32), *spews* (37), *discriminating* (42), *consonant* (43).

COMBINING RHETORICAL STRATEGIES

Explain how the author uses cause and effect analysis to enhance her argumentative essay. (Glossary: *Cause and Effect Analysis*) Does her use of cause and effect thinking make her argument more convincing to you? Explain.

WRITING SUGGESTIONS

1. **(Argumentation)** According to Hattemer, television and popular music send the message "that violence is an everyday occurrence and an acceptable way of solving problems and that promiscuous sex is normal and expected of everyone, including younger and younger children" (paragraph 7). Write an essay in which you argue for or against Hattemer's position. Be sure to document your position with examples from today's television programs and popular music.

2. **(Other Strategies)** Hattemer believes that television has unlimited potential for good, although nothing in her examples seems to suggest this potential. What potential do you see for television? Given that so much of the criticism of television centers around children imitating bad examples shown on TV, do you think that television can, at its best, encourage critical analysis, or do you find that it encourages passivity regardless of the programming? Write an essay addressing these questions. Use examples to illustrate your points.

3. **(Research)** Hattemer writes, "MTV has introduced a whole generation of children to songs that glorify pleasure seeking and irresponsibility" (paragraph 34). Write an essay in which you compare Hattemer's views of MTV with those of Robert Scheer in "Violence Is Us" (p. 609). What is your position on MTV? Do research by watching MTV, using the library, and possibly using the Internet.

- **MTV Online**
  <http://www.mtv.com>

  The MTV Web site offers news, reviews, and information on music and popular culture.

- **Viacom**
  <http://www.viacom.com>

  This is the Web site of MTV's parent company.

COMBINING SUBJECTS AND STRATEGIES

COMPUTER TECHNOLOGY AND EDUCATION

The photograph below depicts many of the same themes as the essay that follows. Your observations about the photograph will help guide you to the key themes in the essay. After you've read the essay, you may use your observations about both the photograph and the essay to examine how the overlapping themes work in each medium.

Cyber cafés attract people who want to retrieve their e-mail, send messages, or just explore the Internet while grabbing a bite to eat or having a cup of coffee. The photograph below by Mathieu Polak was taken at an Internet café in London.

© Mathieu Polak/CORBIS/Sygma

For Discussion

Have you ever been to a cyber café? If so, what was it like? How would you describe the scene in this London cyber café? Which people in the photograph interest you most? What specific expressions or behaviors attracted your attention? Is there any human interaction in this crowded café, or is most of the interaction between individuals and their computers?

Needed: Techies Who Know Shakespeare

Ellen Ullman

Ellen Ullman is a programmer and author who writes extensively about technology, gender, and culture. She became fascinated by the world of computers while studying for a B.A. in English at Cornell University in the early 1970s. After creating business-to-business software for insurance companies, she worked with relational databases, interactive programs, and the design and implementation of a graphical user interface. In 1995, Ullman started to write about her experiences as a programmer. Her articles have appeared in such print and online publications as Wired, Harper's, Salon, *and the* New York Times. *Her critically acclaimed book* Close to the Machine: Technophilia and Its Discontents *(1997) chronicles Ullman's experiences on the front lines of the digital revolution. Ullman lives in San Francisco and is currently at work on a novel.*

The following essay first appeared in the New York Times *on July 8, 1998, just as technology stocks and dot-com businesses were about to take off on Wall Street. Ullman warns prospective programmers not to be lured by the promise of instant riches but to stay focused on the essence of well-rounded education.*

BEFORE YOU READ

How did you learn to use a personal computer and to access the Internet? Did you take a course in high school or college, or did you just pick it up along the way from friends or relatives? How confident are you in your computer skills and ability to use the Internet productively?

High-technology companies are so desperate for programmers, according to recent reports, that they are luring students out of the classroom with well-paying jobs. It's the schools' fault, say people in the industry and some computer-science professors. Students aren't being taught the skills they need and therefore don't see the point of getting a degree. 1

But critics are forgetting that the very idea of the computer science degree is a relatively recent point on the short time line of the computer industry. Historically, most programmers had plenty of education, but little of it came from computer science departments. The problem is not the technical curriculum, but the undergraduate computer-science degree itself. 2

Computer programming has always been a self-taught, maverick occupation. Except for a brief moment in the late 1980s and early 3

1990s — what I think of as the Dilbert era — no one thought that programming was something you should learn in college.

Prospective programmers spent a great deal of time in school, but   4
they typically studied something other than computers. Aside from a few famous dropouts — like Bill Gates, Steven Jobs and Stephen Wozniak — the profession has always attracted the very well-schooled.

Physicists and mathematicians created the industry just after   5
World War II and became the first programmers. As the need for such skills grew in the 1970s, business and government had to look beyond people with doctorates.

Fortunately, that demand coincided with the end of the 1960s,   6
when all sorts of overeducated people were on the loose, looking for a way to earn a living.

That's where I came in: I'm a member of the generation that came   7
to computing as a second, third or fourth vocation. My first boss had two master's degrees in social science and had spent years as a Sufi dancing disciple. My next boss, a former bartender, had a master's degree in library science. The head of technical services at the same company had a Ph.D. in anthropology, and she hired people who had completed all but their dissertations in linguistics, archeology and classics. In this crowd, I felt like the dunce with my undergraduate degree in English.

We had all taught ourselves computing. For us, it was just one   8
more difficult subject to learn. No one was intimidated by learning another computer language — or anything else for that matter. What we knew was how to learn, which is all that one can hang on to in a profession in which change is relentless.

The generation of programmers who followed us were, well, disap-   9
pointing. They had engineering and computer science degrees, and none of them seemed to have read anything but technical textbooks. They stood mute among us when we said the occasional phrase in French. They looked confused when we alluded to Shakespeare or Proust. If today's would-be programmers are fleeing the sort of education that these people received, well, that's wonderful.

A good friend of mine finished engineering school in the late   10
1980s. He managed to get his degree without having studied much of what some still call Western civilization.

Poignantly, he knows he's missed something. He is now a princi-   11
pal of a startup company developing E-mail services for the World Wide Web. My friend is building connections around the planet, and he is ashamed that he has never even studied a foreign language.

I don't mean for these stories to persuade aspiring programmers to   12
drop out of school. Quite the contrary, I hope it might make students and professors realize that programming instruction can take place in a few classes, and students can spend the rest of their time studying

foreign language, literature, linguistics, philosophy and history of science.

Schools might as well give up on teaching the latest skills, since   13
those skills will soon become obsolete anyway. Instead, they might
stress subjects that foster a flexible and open mind. Programmers seem
to be changing the world. It would be a relief, for them and for all of
us, if they knew something about it.

RESPONDING TO READING

What, according to Ullman, is the place of programming instruction and
other computer science courses in today's college curriculum? Do you agree
with her reasoning? Why or why not?

QUESTIONING THE TEXT

1. Whose fault is it that students are being lured away from school with
   the promise of high-paying jobs? What do you think Ullman means
   when she says, "The problem is not the technical curriculum, but the
   undergraduate computer-science degree itself" (paragraph 2)?

2. Why is it important to understand the history of computer programming?

3. Who is Ullman's audience for this essay? (Glossary: *Audience*) What do
   you think she wants her readers to believe or to do after reading and
   reflecting on her words?

UNDERSTANDING THE WRITER'S CRAFT

1. How has Ullman organized her essay? (Glossary: *Organization*) In what
   ways does this organizational plan prepare readers for her conclusion?

2. With what authority does Ullman speak on the subject of computer
   programming? Does her authority make her argument more or less convincing? Explain.

3. Ullman enhances the coherence of her essay by making smooth transitions between paragraphs. (Glossary: *Transitions*) Identify the various
   ways — transitional expression, pronoun reference, repeated key word
   or idea — that she moves from one paragraph to another. Which transitions strike you as being particularly effective?

EXPLORING LANGUAGE

1. Ullman seems to have consciously avoided the technical language of
   computers and computer programming in writing this essay about that
   subject. (Glossary: *Technical Language*) Why do you suppose she adopted

this strategy? How would you characterize her diction or word choice? (Glossary: *Diction*)

2. Refer to your desk dictionary to find the meanings of the following words as Ullman uses them in this selection: *maverick* (paragraph 3), *vocation* (7), *intimidated* (8), *relentless* (8), *poignantly* (11), *foster* (13).

COMBINING RHETORICAL STRATEGIES

Ullman draws heavily from her own personal experience in writing her argument. What do these examples add to her essay? How do the stories from Ullman's personal experience help her make her points?

WRITING SUGGESTIONS

1. **(Argumentation)** Ullman believes that she and others of her generation received a sound education. She claims, "What we knew was how to learn, which is all that one can hang on to in a profession in which change is relentless" (paragraph 8). Why are you in college? What do you see as the purpose of education: to learn information, to learn how to learn, some combination of these, or something else? Write an essay in which you explain and argue for your choice.

2. **(Other Strategies)** What role do computers play in your day-to-day life? Do you take class notes on a computer? Do you e-mail your family and friends? How often do you access the Internet for nonacademic purposes? Do you access the Internet from a computer other than your own, such as one in a school computer lab or a cyber café? Using examples from your own experience or observations as well as thoughts triggered by Mathieu Polak's photograph on page 628, write an essay in which you argue for or against the proposition that computers are indispensable tools for today's college students. Consider comparing and contrasting student life before computers with student life after computers, or classifying the various ways that today's college students use computers as you develop your argument.

3. **(Research)** Ullman mentions three giants in the computer world — Bill Gates, Steven Jobs, and Stephen Wozniak — who also happen to be college dropouts. What do you know about these three men? In preparation for writing a paper about the contributions of one of the three to the computer technology explosion in this country, conduct some research in your college library and on the Internet. How did the person you chose first get into the computer business? What achievements enabled him to climb to the top of the industry? What is he most likely to be remembered for?

- **Bill Gates's Web Site**

  <http://www.microsoft.com/billgates>

  Bill Gates's Web page at Microsoft.com features his writing, autobiography, and recent speeches, as well as news from his philanthropic organization.

- **Steve Jobs**
  <http://ei.cs.vt.edu/~history/Jobs.html>

  A Virginia Tech computer science student wrote this extensive biography of Steve Jobs and his work in the computer industry.

- **The Tech: Revolutionaries**
  <http://www.thetech.org/revolutionaries/wozniak>

  The Tech Museum of Innovation and the *San José Mercury News* collaborated on this 1997 project to interview nineteen of Silicon Valley's most innovative figures.

I Surf, Therefore I Am

Judith Levine

A media and communications professor, Judith Levine was born in 1952 in Queens, New York. She did her undergraduate work at City College of the City University and earned a graduate degree from the Columbia School of Journalism. Her articles on women's issues have appeared in the New York Times, the Village Voice, and Mother Jones, but she is best known for her books My Enemy, My Love: Man Hating and Ambivalence in Women's Lives (1992) and Harmful to Minors: How We Are Hurting Children by Protecting Them from Sex (1999).

In the following article, which first appeared in the online magazine Salon in July 1997, Levine questions the assumption that technology — and more specifically, the Internet — is the key to success.

BEFORE YOU READ

What has been your experience with the Internet? Are you comfortable "surfing" the Net and accessing information that you need? What kinds of information do you regularly seek on the Internet? And what problems, if any, have you encountered on the Net?

"Obviously, I'm somebody who believes that personal computers 1 are empowering tools," Bill Gates said after he bestowed a $200 million gift to America's public libraries so they could hook up to the Internet.

"People are entitled to disagree," Gates said. "But I would invite 2 them to visit some of these libraries and see the impact on kids using this technology."

Well, I have seen the impact, and I disagree. Many of my students — 3 undergraduate media and communications majors at a New York university — have access to the endless information bubbling through cyberspace, and *it is not* empowering.

Most of the data my students Net is like trash fish — and it is hard 4 for them to tell a dead one-legged crab from a healthy sea bass. Scant on world knowledge and critical thinking skills, they are ill-equipped to interpret or judge the so-called facts, which they insert into their papers confidently but in no discernible order.

Their writing often "clicks" from info-bit to info-bit, their argu- 5 ments free of that gluey, old-fashioned encumbrance — the transitional sentence. When I try to help them corral their impressions into coherent stories, I keep hearing the same complaint: "I can't concentrate." I've diagnosed this phenomenon as epidemic attention deficit disorder. And I can't help but trace its etiology, at least in part, to the promiscuous pointing and clicking that has come to stand in for intellectual inquiry.

These students surf; therefore, they do not read. They do not read 6 scholarly articles — which can be trusted because they are juried or challenged because they are footnoted. They do not read books — which tell stories and sustain arguments by placing idea and metaphor one on top of the other, so as to hold weight, like a stone wall. Even the journalism students read few magazines and even fewer newspapers, which are edited by people with recognizable and sometimes even admitted cultural and political biases and checked by fact-checkers using other edited sources.

On the Net, nobody knows if any particular "fact" is a dog. One 7 student handed in a paper about tobacco companies' liability for smokers' health, which she had gleaned almost entirely from the Web pages of the Tobacco Institute. Did she know what the Tobacco Institute is? Apparently not, because she had done her research on the Net, and was deprived of the modifying clause, "a research organization supported by the tobacco industry," obligatory in any edited news article.

Another young woman, writing about teen pregnancy, used data 8 generated by the Family Research Council, which, along with other right-wing Christian think tanks, dominates the links on many subjects related to family and sexuality and offers a decidedly one-sided view.

A teacher at another school told me one of her students had written a paper quoting a person who had a name but no identifying characteristics. "Who's this?" the professor asked. "Someone with a Web page," the young man said.

If there is no context on the Net, neither is there history. My 10 friend who teaches biology told me her students propose research that was completed, and often discredited, 50 years ago. "They go online," she said, "where nothing has been indexed before 1980."

A San Francisco librarian interviewed on National Public Radio 11 worried that, space and resources strained as they are, more computers will inevitably mean fewer books. Another commentator on the Gates gift suggested that the computers would not be very valuable without commensurate human resources — that is, trained workers to help people use them.

At New York's gleaming new Science, Industry, & Business Library 12 (SIBL), you can sit in an ergonomically correct chair at one of several hundred lovely color computer terminals and call up, among hundreds of other databases, the powerful journalistic and legal service Nexis/Lexis. But since Nexis/Lexis is in great demand, you have about 45 minutes at the screen, half of which the inexperienced user will blow figuring out the system, because there is only one harassed staff person to assist all the computer-users. Then you'll learn that the library cannot afford the stratospheric fees for downloading the articles. So most users, I imagine, will manage to copy out quotes from a couple of articles before relinquishing the seat to the next person waiting for the cyber-kiosk.

Unlike a paper or microfilm version of the same pieces, which 13 could be photocopied or copied at leisure onto a pad or laptop, the zillion articles available on the library's Nexis/Lexis are more or less unavailable — that is, to no avail. Useless.

Technology may empower, but how and to what end will that 14 power be used? What else is necessary to use it well and wisely? I'd suggest, for a start, reading books — literature and history, poetry and politics — and listening to people who know what they're talking about. Otherwise, the brains of those kids in Gates' libraries will be glutted with "information" but bereft of ideas, rich in tools but clueless about what to build or how to build it. Like the search engines that retrieve more than 100,000 links or none at all, they will be awkward at discerning meaning, or discerning at all.

RESPONDING TO READING

In your experience using the Internet for research, have you encountered any of the problems that Levine cites? In your estimation, are her criticisms of current technology and the Internet fair?

QUESTIONING THE TEXT

1. In paragraph 4, Levine says, "Most of the data my students Net is like trash fish." What point about her students and the information they collect is Levine making with this simile?

2. Levine is obviously disturbed by the writing that her students do. What faults does she find with their writing, and to what cause does she attribute these difficulties?

3. Why does Levine believe it is important for students to read scholarly articles, books, magazines, and newspapers?

4. What do you think Levine fears if we accept without question Bill Gates's claim that "personal computers are empowering tools" (paragraph 1)? According to Levine, what do students need in their educational program in order to use the power of technology wisely?

UNDERSTANDING THE WRITER'S CRAFT

1. What is Levine's thesis, and where does she state it? (Glossary: *Thesis*)

2. What do you suppose is Levine's purpose for writing the article? (Glossary: *Purpose*) What in the article led you to this conclusion?

3. Why do you suppose Levine began her essay by quoting Bill Gates on the power of technology and telling the story of his $200 million grant to America's public libraries so that they could access the Internet? Did you find it an effective beginning? Explain. (Glossary: *Beginnings/ Endings*)

4. Levine boldly states that "on the Net, nobody knows if any particular 'fact' is a dog" (paragraph 7). What evidence does she use to illustrate this claim? Which evidence did you find most convincing? Explain why.

5. Levine starts her concluding paragraph by asking two questions. What effect, if any, do these questions have on you as a reader? Do they effectively introduce Levine's concluding thoughts or solutions for the issues at hand? Explain.

EXPLORING LANGUAGE

1. Who is Levine's audience for this essay — computer experts, students, teachers, Internet users, businesspeople, or the general public? Point to specific words or phrases that she uses that led you to your conclusion.

2. Refer to your desk dictionary to define the following words as Levine uses them in this selection: *empowering* (paragraph 1), *coherent* (5), *etiology* (5), *promiscuous* (5), *juried* (6), *commensurate* (11), *ergonomically* (12), *stratospheric* (12).

COMBINING RHETORICAL STRATEGIES

Levine relies heavily on examples to develop her argument and to support her claims about the problems with technology and the Internet when students are ill-prepared to use them. Based on your own experience, how "real" are the problems that she presents? How representative are they? What does she gain by presenting a wide range of examples from different disciplines and geographic areas?

WRITING SUGGESTIONS

1. **(Argumentation)** Many educators, like Judith Levine, believe that Americans have been too quick to jump on the technology bandwagon. They question whether computers, the Internet, and dot-com businesses do, in fact, spell a better education, quicker access to accurate information, success, and quick riches. As Thomas L. Friedman reminds us in "My Favorite Teacher" (p. 7), "The real secret of success in the information age is what it always was: fundamentals — reading, writing and arithmetic, church, synagogue and mosque, the rule of law and good governance." Write an essay in which you argue for an educational program that will allow today's students to harness the power of the Internet and not be overwhelmed by information.

2. **(Other Strategies)** Carefully read Ellen Ullman's essay, "Needed: Techies Who Know Shakespeare" (p. 629). How does Levine's argument

compare to Ullman's? What in particular would she find attractive about Ullman's argument? Using examples from both of these essays and from your own personal experience, write an argument in favor of a broad-based liberal arts education for people considering a career in the computer world.

3. **(Research)** What is the computer science program like at your college or university? What courses are required? What electives are encouraged? How do you think Levine would evaluate your school's computer science program? Discuss the philosophy and requirements of the program with a professor, if possible, and with several computer science majors. Then, using resources in your library and on the Internet, research computer science programs at other schools. How do these programs differ from the one on your campus? Write an essay in which you evaluate your school's computer science program in light of your research. What facets of the program should remain intact? What changes or innovations would you recommend?

- **University of Washington Computer Science and Engineering**
  <http://www.cs.washington.edu>

- **Rose Hulman Institute of Technology Computer Science Department**
  <http://www.cs.rose-hulman.edu>

- **Carleton College Department of Mathematics and Computer Science**
  <http://www.mathcs.carleton.edu>

At these sites you can compare three computer science departments, the first at a large state university, the second at a technology school, and the third at a small liberal arts college, by reading about their undergraduate degree programs and course requirements.

For the Death Penalty

Ernest van den Haag

Ernest van den Haag was born in the Netherlands in 1914 and came to the United States in 1940. For years he taught sociology and criminal justice at Yale, Harvard, the New School for Social Research, and Fordham University Law School, where he is the retired John M. Olin Professor of Jurisprudence and Public Policy. As a writer, van den Haag has established a reputation as a conservative through his many articles and books. His many books include Passion and Social Restraint *(1963),* Political Violence and Civil Disobedience *(1972), and* Punishing Criminals: Concerning a Very Old and Painful Question *(1975). He is currently a practicing psychoanalyst.*

The following essay is taken from The Death Penalty Pro and Con: A Debate *(1983). In this essay, van den Haag argues articulately in favor of the death penalty as a deterrent. John P. Conrad, former chief of the U.S. Bureau of Prisons, defended the negative side in this debate.*

BEFORE YOU READ

Do you favor capital punishment or life imprisonment for those convicted of capital crimes? Explain why.

There are two basic arguments for the death penalty; they are inde- 1
pendent of, yet consistent with, one another.

The first argument is moral: The death penalty is just; it is de- 2
served for certain crimes. One can explain why one feels that certain crimes deserve the death penalty. But as usual with moral arguments, one cannot show this conviction to be *factually* correct (or, for that matter, incorrect) since moral arguments rest not on facts but on our evaluation of them. My evaluation leads me to believe that, e.g., premeditated murder or treason (a fact) is so grave and horrible a crime (an evaluation) as to deserve nothing less than the death penalty, that only the death penalty (a fact) is proportionate to the gravity of the crime (an evaluation).

My widely shared view is opposed by abolitionists, who claim that 3
the death penalty is unjust for any crime, and inconsistent with human dignity. Professor Conrad's arguments in favor of this position seem unconvincing to me. Since most abolitionists believe, as I do, that punishments should be proportionate to the perceived gravity of crimes, the abolitionist claim seems to me logically precarious. It implies either that murder is not so horrible after all — not horrible

639

enough, at any rate to deserve death — or that the death penalty is too harsh a punishment for it, and indeed for any conceivable crime. I find it hard to believe that one can hold either view seriously, let alone both. But I am wrong: Professor Conrad does, and he is by no means alone in the academic world.

I must confess that I have never understood the assorted arguments claiming that the death penalty is inconsistent with human dignity or that, somehow, society has no right to impose it. One might as well claim that death generally, or at least death from illness, is inconsistent with human dignity, or that birth is, or any suffering or any undesirable social condition. Most of these are unavoidable. At least death by execution can be avoided by not killing someone else, by not committing murder. One can preserve one's dignity in this respect if one values it. Incidentally, execution may be physically less humiliating and painful than death in a hospital. It is, however, morally more humiliating and meant to be: It indicates the extreme blame we attach to the crime of murder by deliberately expelling the murderer from among the living.

As for the dignity of society, it seems to me that by executing murderers it tries to keep its promise to secure the lives of innocents, to vindicate the law, and to impose retribution on those who so horribly violate it. To do anything less would be inconsistent with the dignity of society.

I see no evidence for society somehow not having "the right" to execute murderers. It has always done so. Traditional laws and Scriptures have always supported the death penalty. I know of no reasoning, even in a religious (theocratic) state, that denies the right of secular courts to impose it. We in America have a secular republic, of course, and therefore, the suggestion that the right to punish belongs only to God, or that the right to impose capital punishment does, is clearly out of place. It is not a religious but a secular task to put murderers to death. Our Constitution does provide for it (Amendments V and XIV). However much we believe in divine justice, it is to occur after, not in, this life. As for justice here and now, it is done by the courts, which are authorized in certain cases to impose the death penalty. A secular state cannot leave it to God. And incidentally, no theocratic state ever has. If they make mistakes, one can hope that God will correct the courts hereafter — but this is no ground for depriving courts of their duty to impose the penalties provided by law where required, nor is it a ground for depriving the law of the ability to prescribe the punishments felt to be just, including the death penalty.

The second argument in favor of capital punishment is material, grounded on empirical facts. They are contested, as readers of this book know, but no one would deny that what is contested are facts.

The factual question is: Does the death penalty deter murder more than life imprisonment, or does it make no difference?

I do not agree with Professor Conrad's wishful idea that the work 8 of Professor Isaac Ehrlich has been discredited. I believe that Ehrlich's findings — that the death penalty does indeed deter more than any other penalty currently inflicted, so that each execution saves between seven and nine innocent lives, the lives of victims who will not be murdered in the year of execution because of the deterrent effects of executions — have been confirmed by subsequent studies and have stood up sturdily under criticism competent and incompetent, which Ehrlich has convincingly refuted. However, Ehrlich's work is controversial. Anything is, if a sufficient number of people attack it. It is fair, therefore, to say that although the preponderance of evidence is now supporting the hypothesis that capital punishment deters more than any other punishment, the statistical demonstration has not been conclusive enough to convince everybody. Certainly not Professor Conrad and his friends. They have not changed their pre-Ehrlich convictions, and indeed tend to dismiss his work.

But Conrad's fellow abolitionists have admitted that they would 9 want to abolish the death penalty even if it were shown statistically that each execution does reduce the homicide rate by 500 murders per year. Why then worry about statistical proof? And why take seriously people so irrational that they would sacrifice the lives of 500 innocents to preserve the life of one convicted murderer?

Statistics have their place. But here I think they scarcely are 10 needed. Harsher penalties are more deterrent than milder ones. Not only does our whole criminal justice system accept this view; we all do to the extent to which deterrence is aimed at in our everyday life. All other things equal, we penalize our children, our friends, or our business partners the more harshly the more we feel we must deter them and others in the future from a wrong they have done. Social life would not be possible if we did not believe that we can attract people to actions we desire by giving them incentives, and deter them from actions we do not desire by disincentives. The incentives and disincentives are usually proportionate to the felt desirability or undesirability of what we want to attract to or deter from. Why should murder be an exception? Why should we not believe that the greatest disincentive — the threat of death — is most likely to be the greatest deterrent?

Where there is life there is hope. This certainly is one major argu- 11 ment in favor of the death penalty. The murderer who premeditates his crime — and crimes of passion are not subject to capital punishment — if he contemplates the risk of life imprisonment is not likely to believe that, if convicted, he will remain in prison for life. He knows, however inchoately, about parole, pardons, commutations —

he believes above all that he, a smart and superior fellow, will find a way to escape. Few prisoners actually do escape. But practically all "lifers" believe that they will, at least when they start their sentence. So believing, they do not greatly fear a sentence of life imprisonment and are not deterred by it. This is why the rate of stranger-murders — murders in which victim and murderer do not know one another and to which the threat of the death penalty should apply — as a proportion of all murders has steadily climbed in the last twenty years. The murderers knew that in practice they would get away with life imprisonment, from which they would be paroled after a few years. Or they hoped they would escape. After all, we executed all of five prisoners in 1981, only one of whom was executed against his wishes. (All of them were white, to the great disappointment of the civil liberties lobby.) At this rate no murderer can foresee execution or be deterred by it.

I find it hard to believe, as Professor Conrad does, that most men 12 are incapable of murder. I admire his optimism. But I find it hard to share. I do not see how he can cling to his faith after Stalin and Hitler, in the presence of assorted tyrants and murderers in power from Albania to Iran to China. But faith obviously is not subject to empirical verification. I am optimistic, however, in my own way, which seems more realistic to me: I believe that most men can be deterred from murder by the threat of the death penalty.

Even if Conrad were right, even if his claim that only a few men 13 would ever become murderers in the absence of the threat of punishment were correct, I should continue to advocate the death penalty to deter these few men. And even if only some of these men need the threat of capital punishment to be deterred, while others would be deterred by the threat of life imprisonment, I should advocate the death penalty to deter the very few who, according to Conrad, do, or even just may, require it to be deterred. The lives of the innocents that will or may be spared because of the death penalty are more valuable to me, and to any civilized society, than the lives of murderers. I do not want to risk their lives for the sake of the lives of murderers.

The reader will have to decide for himself on which side he wants 14 to be.

RESPONDING TO READING

Do you take issue with any of van den Haag's points in his defense of the death penalty? What counterarguments or evidence would you marshall to support your views?

QUESTIONING THE TEXT

1. According to van den Haag, what are the two basic arguments for the death penalty?

2. In paragraph 3, van den Haag admits that his opposition claims that "the death penalty is unjust for any crime, and inconsistent with human dignity." On what grounds does he counter each of these claims?

3. According to van den Haag, why doesn't a sentence of life imprisonment work as a deterrent? How does he use the statement "Where there is life there is hope" (paragraph 11) to argue in favor of the death penalty?

UNDERSTANDING THE WRITER'S CRAFT

1. According to van den Haag, how does a moral argument differ from a material one? Why is it important for you as a writer to be aware of these differences?

2. How has van den Haag organized his essay? (Glossary: *Organization*) Why do you suppose he presents his "moral argument" first and his "material argument" second?

3. How does van den Haag defend the work of Professor Isaac Ehrlich in paragraph 8? What evidence does he present? Do you find his line of argument convincing? Why or why not?

4. In paragraph 12, van den Haag admits that while he admires Conrad's "optimism" in his belief that "most men are incapable of murder," he finds this optimism difficult to share. Later in the same paragraph he states that he too is optimistic, but in a way that "seems more realistic to me." Is van den Haag simply playing with words, or is he making a legitimate point persuasively? Explain.

EXPLORING LANGUAGE

1. Examine the language that van den Haag uses in paragraphs 3, 4, 8, 9, 12, and 13 to discuss Professor Conrad and his allies and their arguments against capital punishment. How would you characterize his diction — objective, biased, politely critical, loaded, or condescending? Identify specific words or phrases that led you to your conclusion.

2. Refer to your desk dictionary to determine the meanings of the following words as van den Haag uses them in this selection: *proportionate* (paragraph 2), *abolitionists* (3), *humiliating* (4), *vindicate* (5), *retribution* (5), *empirical* (7), *preponderance* (8), *hypothesis* (8), *irrational* (9), *inchoately* (11), *advocate* (13).

COMBINING RHETORICAL STRATEGIES

To help readers understand how moral arguments "rest not on facts but on our evaluation of them," van den Haag shows readers step-by-step how he arrived at his belief that "the death penalty is just; it is deserved for certain crimes" (paragraph 2). In what ways does this example help readers follow and understand his reasoning in paragraphs 3 through 6? Explain.

WRITING SUGGESTIONS

1. **(Argumentation)** Write an argument in favor of life imprisonment over the death penalty for premeditated murder, treason, or other grave crimes. Be careful to address each of van den Haag's objections to life imprisonment as an appropriate punishment. As you start, you may find it helpful to review your response to the Before You Read question for this selection.

2. **(Other Strategies)** Some critics of the death penalty believe that it is a barbaric punishment and that it reflects negatively on American society. For them, capital punishment is nothing more than legal murder. On the other hand, supporters of capital punishment believe that it affirms life. As van den Haag argues, capital punishment "tries to keep its promise to secure the lives of innocents, to vindicate the law, and to impose retribution on those who so horribly violate it. To do anything less would be inconsistent with the dignity of society" (paragraph 5). Where do you stand? Write an essay in which you compare and contrast the strongest arguments on both sides of this controversial moral issue.

3. **(Research)** The question of whether the death penalty deters murder more than life imprisonment does is difficult to answer. How does one determine the deterrent effect of a particular punishment? That is, how does one identify murders that could have happened but didn't? Is it enough to simply assume that "harsher penalties are more deterrent than milder ones" (paragraph 10)? To discover how criminologists and sociologists calculate the deterrent effects of various punishments, research the work of Professor Isaac Ehrlich. Find as many recent studies as you can. What new methodologies have researchers experimented with? Do these studies tend to affirm Ehrlich's work or to contradict it? Write an essay in which you discuss the current thinking about the deterrent effect of capital punishment. What, if anything, has changed since van den Haag first presented his arguments in 1983 in his book *The Death Penalty Pro and Con: A Debate*?

- **Professor Isaac Ehrlich's Home Page**
  <http://wings.buffalo.edu/economics/ehrlich.htm>

  Professor Ehrlich's University of Buffalo home page contains his vitae and links to four pages in his areas of research, including crime and justice.

- **Isaac Ehrlich's Crime and Justice Page**

<http://wings.buffalo.edu/economics/IEcrime.html>

This site, maintained by Dr. Isaac Ehrlich, features a full-text, PDF version of his essay "The Deterrent Effect of Capital Punishment — A Question of Life and Death." Also included are citation information, abstracts, and full-text files for his other essays about crime and justice.

Cruel and Unusual

Sherwin B. Nuland

Surgeon and medical ethicist Sherwin B. Nuland was born in New York City in 1948 and graduated from Bronx High School. He went on to do undergraduate work at New York University, then obtained his M.D. at Yale Medical School. He has taught at Yale since 1962 and has published widely. His book How We Die: Reflections on Life's Final Chapter *(1994) received the National Book Award and was a finalist for the Pulitzer Prize. His other published works include* The Wisdom of the Body *(1997),* The Mysteries Within: A Surgeon Reflects on Medical Myths *(2000), and articles for* The New Yorker, National Geographic, Time, Life, *and other magazines.*

In the following selection, first published as an op-ed piece in the New York Times *in the fall of 1999, Nuland examines the medical and ethical consequences of using the electric chair as a tool for execution. After demonstrating the barbarity of electrocution, he argues that "the electric chair should be forbidden."*

BEFORE YOU READ

How do you view death, or do you try not to think about it at all? Does the reality that you will die someday cause you discomfort or anxiety? Does death frighten you? If so, how? If not, from what source do you find reassurance and comfort?

A swift and painless death is a mercy that few of us will be granted. Disease and aging do not often complete their lethal work without laying down lengthy and devastating barrages. Even the so-called "sudden death" of major injury is all too commonly accompanied by seconds or even minutes of anguish. But of all trauma victims, the murdered are most likely to end their lives in some form of agony and terror.

And so, some find it paradoxical that when murderers are to be executed, our society often tries to provide them with the painless death that only a small number of us will have been granted by nature or fortune. This paradox stands out anew with the announcement that the Supreme Court will soon decide whether Florida's use of the electric chair constitutes cruel and unusual punishment. Electrocution is the only method of capital punishment in Florida, Alabama, Georgia and Nebraska. It is a choice given to the condemned in Ohio, South Carolina and Virginia. What is specifically feared by those on death row, according to court papers, is that they will undergo "physical violence, disfigurement and torment" during the process of dying.

If the court decides that murderers deserve a quietus of which   3
they have deprived others, then the electric chair should unquestion-
ably be abolished as a method of execution.

Even when it functions exactly as it should, the electric chair is a   4
brutal killer. It depends on three jolts of electricity — some 2,000 volts
each, traveling from head to foot for anywhere from 8 seconds to 20
seconds. When performance is optimal, a very small circumference of
burnt skin will be produced at points of entrance and exit, but not
much else will be visible. For this to happen, the electrodes and their
attachments must be perfectly placed, resistance must be minimal and
all parts of the electrical apparatus — like the generator, switches and
wiring — must be in excellent working order.

Technical failures in any part of this complex apparatus can result   5
in a failure of the entire system. This explains the botched executions
we occasionally read about: the sparking, the smoke and flame and
the need for repeated shocks in a subject who may still be at least partially conscious.

If the electrical system does work perfectly, what then? What is   6
the mechanism of death? Ideally, passage of current through the head
and into the trunk should instantly cause unconsciousness, although
it simultaneously stimulates acute contractions of virtually every
muscle in the body. If the condemned is at all conscious, such contractions are exquisitely painful.

Death may be caused in any of several ways. By passing through   7
the cardiac center in the brain's medulla, the current arrests the heart.
By passing through the respiratory center, it stops breathing and asphyxiates the subject. By passing through the heart, it distorts normal
ventricular rhythm into an ineffective wormlike wriggling called fib-
rillation, which has the same effect as cardiac arrest.

All of these mechanisms take more than two minutes to cause   8
brain death, the legal definition of the end of life. Should the initial
shock not render the subject fully unconscious, he remains aware of
what is happening, particularly if he is being asphyxiated, a situation
appallingly obvious at autopsy.

Compared to the effectiveness and ease of executions carried out   9
by lethal injection, electrocution is a barbaric way to kill someone.
Unless revenge is what our society wants — and some would indeed
say that such a goal is justifiable — the court's path is clear: the electric chair should be forbidden. The answer is as simple as that.

RESPONDING TO READING

Nuland's conclusion is concise, but the caveat "Unless revenge is what our
society wants — and some would indeed say that such a goal is justifiable"

(paragraph 9) strengthens the impression that Nuland himself is unclear as to whether society should seek revenge. Based on your reading of the essay, where do you think Nuland stands on capital punishment? Defend your answer with references to the text.

QUESTIONING THE TEXT

1. In what ways is society's insistence that we provide murderers with a painless death "paradoxical" (paragraph 2)?

2. How does the electric chair cause death? Why might these various causes of death constitute "cruel and unusual punishment" (paragraph 2)?

3. Nuland describes the electric chair as a "brutal killer" (paragraph 4). Do you agree with his assessment? Why or why not?

UNDERSTANDING THE WRITER'S CRAFT

1. What is Nuland's thesis, and where is it stated? (Glossary: *Thesis*)

2. What is the purpose of Nuland's graphic description of death in the electric chair? In what ways does it support his argument?

3. Who is Nuland's audience — the general public or the justices of the Supreme Court? (Glossary: *Audience*) How do you know?

EXPLORING LANGUAGE

1. Analyze Nuland's choice of words in paragraphs 4 to 8. (Glossary: *Diction*) What words does he use to strengthen his portrayal of the condemned person's experience in the electric chair?

2. Refer to your desk dictionary to define the following words as Nuland uses them in this essay: *trauma* (paragraph 1), *paradoxical* (2), *quietus* (3), *botched* (5), *asphyxiates* (7), *ventricular* (7).

COMBINING RHETORICAL STRATEGIES

Nuland uses process analysis to describe in gruesome detail what happens step-by-step when a person is put to death in the electric chair. He only briefly mentions lethal injection, but he asks readers to accept that it is a far more "effective" alternative without providing any information to support his claim. Would his argument against the electric chair have been strengthened had he provided a more detailed contrast with lethal injection? Why or why not?

WRITING SUGGESTIONS

1. **(Argumentation)** The revenge mentality regarding punishment for criminals, often summarized as "an eye for an eye," is not generally advocated in today's society. Nonetheless, that criminals must be pun-

ished in some way for their crimes is seldom questioned, and candidates for political office often run on platforms that depict them as tough on crime. What, then, is the happy medium for capital crimes? What is your position on the death penalty? Did you find yourself agreeing or disagreeing with Nuland's argument against the use of the electric chair? Write an argument paper in which you present what you consider the best way to punish people convicted of capital crimes.

2. **(Other Strategies)** Coretta Scott King, a civil rights activist and the wife of the late Martin Luther King Jr., has argued that there has been an increase in support of the death penalty among Americans because there has been an increase in violent crime in our society. Do you agree that there is a causal relationship between violent crime and support for the death penalty? Is the death penalty the solution to this problem? Does capital punishment act as a deterrent to violent crime? Write an essay in which you argue that we must find ways to reduce violent crime rather than change our system of justice and punishment.

3. **(Research)** Research the role that the U.S. Supreme Court has played with regard to the death penalty since 1950. What were the major or landmark rulings? What is the current Court's attitude toward the death penalty? How have Supreme Court decisions shaped public opinion about capital punishment, if at all, and conversely, how has public opinion influenced the Court? After finishing your research in the library and on the Internet, formulate a thesis about the Supreme Court and the death penalty, and write an essay in which you support your claim.

- **Legal Information Institute: Supreme Court Collection**
  <http://www.cs.washington.edu>

  The Legal Information Institute has collected information on all Supreme Court cases since 1990 and maintains a comprehensive listing of historic cases.

- **History of the Death Penalty and Recent Developments**
  <http://www.uaa.alaska.edu/just/death/history.html#supremecourt>

  The University of Alaska's Death Penalty site highlights key Supreme Court cases from the last twenty years.

- **Supreme Court of the United States**
  <http://www.supremecourtus.gov>

  The U.S. Supreme Court's official Web page allows you to search current decisions and speeches on many subjects.

Sexism and the Death Chamber

Cathy Young

A columnist for the Detroit News, *Cathy Young was born in Moscow, in the former Soviet Union, in 1963. After graduating from Rutgers University in 1988, she launched her writing career with her book* Growing Up in Moscow: Memoirs of a Soviet Girlhood *(1989), as well as articles in publications like the* New York Times *and* American Spectator. *She is the author of* Cease-fire: Why Women and Men Must Join Forces to Achieve True Equality *(2000) and is currently writing* The Virgin of Terror: A Biography of Charlotte Corday, *a book about women's political activism in Russia. As a Fellow of the Cato Institute and vice president of the Women's Freedom Network, Young writes and speaks widely on women's issues in the workplace, domestic violence, and Russia.*

In the following essay, which first appeared in the online magazine Salon *on May 4, 2000, Young uses the execution of Christina Marie Riggs in Arkansas to raise the issue of gender discrimination and capital punishment in the United States.*

BEFORE YOU READ

What are your thoughts about executing a woman convicted of murder? Should women be treated any differently than men when it comes to imposing capital punishment? Why or why not?

On Tuesday night in Varner, Ark., 28-year-old Christina Marie Riggs was executed for the 1997 murders of her two small children. She was given a lethal injection of potassium chloride, the drug she had originally planned to use to kill her children. (She suffocated them after a botched attempt of the drugging plan.) 1

Riggs, a former nurse, was put to death despite pleas for her life from anti-death-penalty groups including Amnesty International and the American Civil Liberties Union. In fact, there was little difference between the execution of Riggs and the other 28 executions carried out in the United States so far this year, except that Riggs, who said she wanted to die to be with her "babies," had refused to appeal her sentence or to seek clemency from Arkansas Gov. Mike Huckabee. 2

And yet her death was much bigger news. 3

The cause for intense public soul-searching and beating of breasts was not the nature of Riggs' crime or her wish to die. It was her gender. It was, for all intents and purposes, a demonstration of garden-variety sexism. And this isn't the first time our hypocrisy has been blatantly displayed. 4

Riggs was the first woman to be executed in Arkansas in 150 years, and only the fifth executed in the nation since the U.S. Supreme Court lifted the ban on capital punishment in 1976. Obviously, the 5 very rarity of women's executions makes them newsworthy. But this is only the statistical manifestation of the stubborn gender discrimination that taints our attitude about capital punishment in this country.

Whether one sees the death penalty as justice or barbarism (and, 6 for the record, I have no moral objection to imposing it for premeditated murder, though the risk of the state taking an innocent life is troubling enough to warrant opposition to the practice), surely the perpetrator's gender should be irrelevant.

But that is not the way it works in the real world. We are consis- 7 tently more likely to seek mitigating circumstances for women's heinous deeds, to see female criminals as disturbed or victimized rather than evil. The thought of a woman in the death chamber makes people cringe — even those who have no problem with sending a man to his death for his crimes.

It appears that chivalry still lives when a woman must die. 8

Two years ago, there were many more headlines and much more de- 9 bate as Karla Faye Tucker awaited execution in Texas for a brutal double murder. Tucker had become a born-again Christian and her clemency petition was backed by such unusual suspects as Christian Coalition leader Pat Robertson, Moral Majority founder Jerry Falwell and right-wing hero Oliver North — all generally pro–capital punishment.

While most of Tucker's champions insisted that redemption and 10 not womanhood was the issue, none had intervened on behalf of male murderers who had experienced similar death-row conversions. And there was ample evidence to suggest that the support for "this sweet woman of God," as Robertson put it, was not entirely gender-neutral.

On CNN's "Crossfire," when asked if the crusade to save Tucker was 11 an instance of "misplaced chivalry," North gallantly replied, "I don't think chivalry can ever be misplaced" — though he went on to insist that "gender is not a factor." Meanwhile, on the left, the chivalrous Geraldo Rivera dispensed with any pretense of neutrality and issued a bizarre plea to Texas Gov. George W. Bush on his CNBC show: "Please, don't let this happen. This is — it's very unseemly, Texas, manhood, macho swagger . . . What are ya, going to kill a lady? Oh, jeez. Why?"

The lady in question, by the way, had used a pickax to dispatch 12 two sleeping people (one of whom had made her angry by parking his motorbike in her living room) and later bragged that she experienced an orgasm with every swing.

RESPONDING TO READING

What do you think Young means when she states, "It appears that chivalry still lives when a woman must die" (paragraph 8)? Is this a reasonable conclusion to reach based on the evidence Young presents?

QUESTIONING THE TEXT

1. What is Young's position on the death penalty? Why do you think Young included this information?

2. Why, according to Young, was Christina Marie Riggs's execution "much bigger news" (paragraph 3) than the other executions carried out earlier that same year?

3. Who backed Karla Faye Tucker's clemency petition? On what grounds did they lend her their support? How do you think Young herself feels about Tucker's execution?

UNDERSTANDING THE WRITER'S CRAFT

1. What is Young's thesis, and where does she present it? (Glossary: *Thesis*)

2. How does Young support her claim that the "intense public soul-searching and beating of breasts" leading up to the execution of Riggs was "a demonstration of garden-variety sexism" (paragraph 4)?

3. How does paragraph 8 function in the context of Young's essay? What, if anything, would have been lost or gained had she combined it with paragraph 7? Explain.

4. Why do you suppose Young chose to quote Pat Robertson, Oliver North, and Geraldo Rivera directly? What would she have lost had she chosen instead to summarize or to paraphrase their words?

EXPLORING LANGUAGE

1. What is Young's attitude toward Christina Marie Riggs and Karla Faye Tucker? How does she feel about those who championed both Riggs's and Tucker's causes? What in Young's diction led you to your conclusions?

2. Refer to your desk dictionary to determine the meanings of the following words as Young uses them in this selection: *botched* (paragraph 1), *clemency* (2), *blatantly* (4), *manifestation* (5), *mitigating* (7), *chivalry* (8), *intervened* (10), *pretense* (11).

COMBINING RHETORICAL STRATEGIES

Young's argument that a "stubborn gender discrimination" (paragraph 5) exists in the United States suggests the comparison of how men and women are treated differently when it comes to capital punishment. To illustrate what she means, Young presents two extended examples of women who became causes célèbres for anti-death-penalty groups and organizations. She does not, however, present contrasting examples of men convicted of capital crimes. In your opinion, could her argument have benefited from such examples? Why or why not?

WRITING SUGGESTIONS

1. **(Argumentation)** Write an essay in support of Young's claim that "the perpetrator's gender should be irrelevant" (paragraph 6) in capital cases. Where does Lance Morrow (p. 654) stand on the issue of gender and capital punishment?

2. **(Other Strategies)** Does the thought of a woman's execution make you "cringe" (paragraph 7)? Do you count yourself among those Americans who are "more likely to seek mitigating circumstances for women's heinous deeds" (7) than they are for men's crimes? What cultural values or traditions might help explain the causes of our attitudes toward gender and capital punishment? Write an essay in which you attempt to explain why, historically, Americans have been reluctant to execute women.

3. **(Research)** Research the issue of gender and punishment in America's criminal justice system. Is there gender equity in the way courts handle sentences? Is there any indication that one sex receives harsher sentences than the other for certain crimes? Have there been any public outcries against any forms of punishment for women other than the death penalty? What reasons, if any, did you discover in your research that might help explain any inequities you have uncovered? Write an essay in which you report your findings and make a proposal to correct any egregious inequities that exist.

- **Death Penalty Information Center: Women on Death Row**
  <http://www.deathpenaltyinfo.org/womenstats.html>

  This site features facts and figures about women on death row from the Death Penalty Information Center.

- **Why Women Aren't Executed**
  <http://www.abanet.org/irr/hr/genderbias.html>

  This article on gender bias and the death penalty from the American Bar Association explores the reasons women often escape harsher sentencing.

- **Prison Activist Resource Center: Women**
  <http://www.prisonactivist.org/women>

  This site features links to sites of interest to those concerned with the rights of women, especially mothers, in prison.

Why I Changed My Mind on the Death Penalty

Lance Morrow

*Lance Morrow was born in 1935 in Lewisburg, Pennsylvania, and gradu-
ated from Harvard. He began his writing career as a reporter for the*
Washington Star, *and then in 1965 he moved to* Time *magazine where
he was at one time a senior writer. His essays for* Time *earned him a National Magazine Award in 1981 and have been collected and published
as* Fishing in the Tiber *(1988). He has also published a number of other
books, including* The Chief *(1984), a memoir of his father, Hugh
Morrow, who was also a journalist, and* America: A Rediscovery
(1987).

*In the following "Web-only essay" from Time.com, which first ap-
peared on May 3, 2000, Morrow uses the execution of Christina Marie
Riggs, an Arkansas nurse who murdered her two children, to explain why
he has done an about-face on the issue of the death penalty.*

BEFORE YOU READ

Where do you stand on the death penalty? Have you always felt
this way? What beliefs or experiences contributed to the formation
of your position?

Christina Marie Riggs, a nurse in Arkansas and a single mother, 1
killed her two children — Justin, 5, and Shelby Alexis, 2 — by giving them injections of potassium chloride and then smothering them
with a pillow. She wrote a suicide note, and apparently tried to kill
herself with an overdose of 28 antidepressant tablets. She survived.

Or she did until last night, when the state of Arkansas put Riggs to 2
death by lethal injection at the state prison in Varner. She was the first
woman to be executed in Arkansas since 1845.

The state of Arkansas played the part of Jack Kevorkian in a case of 3
assisted suicide. Christina Riggs said she wanted to die. She had
dropped all legal appeals. She wanted to be with her children in
heaven. Just before Riggs died, she said, "I love you, my babies." Some
people said she had killed them because she was severely depressed.
The prosecutor, on the other hand, called her "a self-centered, selfish,
premeditated killer who did the unspeakable act of taking her own
children's lives."

So where do we stand on capital punishment now? (And, inciden- 4
tally, isn't it grand that we seem to be overcoming, at the speed of
light, our reluctance to execute women? Bless you, Gloria Steinem.)

Review the state of play: 5

- Deterrence is an unreliable argument for the death penalty, I think, because deterrence is unprovable.
- The fear of executing the wrong man (a more popular line of demurral these days) is an unreliable argument against all capital punishment. What if there are many witnesses to a murder? What if it's Hitler? Is capital punishment OK in cases of unmistakable guilt? George W. Bush says that he reviews each case to make sure he is absolutely certain a person did it before he allows a Texas execution to go ahead.

I have argued in the past that the death penalty was justified, in   6
certain brutal cases, on the basis of the social contract. That is: Some
hideous crimes demand the ultimate punishment in order to satisfy
the essentially civilizing deal that we make with one another as citizens. We forgo individual revenge, deferring to the law, but depend
upon a certainty that the law will give us a justice that must include
appropriate harshness. I favored the Texas folk wisdom: "He needs
killing." If the law fails in that task, I said, and people see that evil is
fecklessly tolerated, then the social contract disintegrates. Society
needs a measure of homeopathic revenge.

But I have changed my mind about capital punishment.   7

I think the American atmosphere, the American imagination   8
(news, movies, books, music, fact, fiction, entertainment, culture, life
in the streets, zeitgeist) is now so filled with murder and violence
(gang wars, random shootings not just in housing projects but in offices and malls and schools) that violence of any kind — including
solemn execution — has become merely a part of our cultural routine
and joins, in our minds, the passing parade of stupidity/psychosis/
chaos/entertainment that Americans seem to like, or have come to deserve. In Freudian terms, the once forceful (and patriarchal) American
Superego (arguably including the authority of law, of the presidency,
of the military, etc.) has collapsed into a great dismal swamp of Id.

And in the Swamp, I have come to think, capital punishment has   9
lost whatever cautionary social force it had — its exemplary meaning,
its power to proclaim, as it once arguably did, that some deeds are, in
our fine and virtuous company, intolerable.

I think those arguing in favor of capital punishment now are in-   10
dulging in a form of nostalgia. Capital punishment no longer works as
a morality play. Each execution (divorced from its moral meaning, including its capacity to shock and to warn the young) simply becomes
part of the great messy pageant, the vast and voracious stupidity, the
Jerry Springer show of American life.

Maybe most of our moral opinions are formed by emotions and   11
aesthetic reactions. My opinion is this: Capital punishment has lost its
moral meaning. Having lost its moral meaning, it has become as immoral as any other expression of violence. And therefore we should
stop doing it.

RESPONDING TO READING

What is the connection between the story of Christina Marie Riggs and
Morrow's about-face regarding the death penalty? Do you agree with him
when he likens Riggs's execution to "a case of assisted suicide" (paragraph 3)?
Explain.

QUESTIONING THE TEXT

1. According to Morrow, what is the current status of the death penalty argument? What other prominent arguments either for or against the
   death penalty have you heard?

2. On what grounds did Morrow previously argue that the death penalty
   was justified? How does the Texas folk saying "He needs killing" help
   explain Morrow's former position?

3. What do you think Morrow means when he says, "Capital punishment
   has lost its moral meaning" (paragraph 11)?

UNDERSTANDING THE WRITER'S CRAFT

1. Morrow begins his essay with the story of Christina Marie Riggs. How effective a beginning did you find this story? Why do you suppose Morrow
   includes the fact that Christina Marie Riggs was "the first woman to be executed in Arkansas since 1845" (paragraph 2)? (Glossary: *Beginnings/End-
   ings*) What does he gain by having Riggs and the prosecutor speak for
   themselves? How else might he have started the essay?

2. Paragraph 7 is a one-sentence paragraph. How does it function in the
   context of the essay? What would have been lost had Morrow combined it with either paragraph 6 or paragraph 8? Explain.

3. What counterarguments does Morrow put forth to meet the pro–capital
   punishment arguments?

4. Does Morrow explain why he has changed his mind on the death
   penalty issue in enough detail to satisfy your curiosity and to persuade
   you to his position? What else might he have included?

EXPLORING LANGUAGE

1. What is Morrow's tone in this essay? (Glossary: *Tone*) How does his
   choice of words help create this tone?

2. Refer to your desk dictionary to determine the meanings of the following words as Morrow uses them in this selection: *unspeakable* (paragraph 3), *demurral* (5), *fecklessly* (6), *homeopathic* (6), *zeitgeist* (8), *nostalgia* (10), *voracious* (10), *aesthetic* (11).

COMBINING RHETORICAL STRATEGIES

Morrow's change of heart is closely tied to a shift in American society and culture with regard to violence. How does he use comparison and contrast to sharpen his description of the difference between what once was and what now is? Has capital punishment indeed been reduced to being "part of the great messy pageant, the vast and voracious stupidity, the Jerry Springer show of American life" (paragraph 10)?

WRITING SUGGESTIONS

1. **(Argumentation)** In the end, Morrow calls for an end to capital punishment: "We should stop doing it" (paragraph 11). Where do you stand on the issue after reading Morrow's essay? Write an essay in which you argue either for or against Morrow's position. You may find it helpful to review what you wrote in response to the Before You Read questions for this selection.

2. **(Other Strategies)** What does capital punishment say about Americans as a people? Why is it that we have the highest number of executions of any modern industrialized country? Does capital punishment in any way mirror our violent American culture, as Morrow claims? What will be the possible outcome for our society if executions continue to escalate? Write an essay in which you discuss the relationship between capital punishment and the culture of America.

3. **(Research)** Morrow claims that "deterrence is an unreliable argument for the death penalty" (paragraph 5). Conduct some research in your college library or on the Internet about the effects of the death penalty on crime rates. Is there any evidence that capital punishment serves as a deterrent, or is deterrence "unprovable" (paragraph 5), as Morrow believes? What are the strongest arguments that you found for each side of the deterrence issue? On the basis of your research, where do you stand on deterrence? Write an essay in which you argue your position using the evidence you uncovered in your research.

- **Deterrence and the Death Penalty**
  <http://www.deathpenaltyinfo.org/deter.html>

  The Death Penalty Information Center (DPIC) contains crime statistics comparing states with and without the death penalty.

- **Study: Homicides Up during Time of Executions**
  <http://prisonactivist.org/death-penalty/dpstudy.html>

  This study by the Center on Juvenile and Criminal Justice examines how the death penalty has affected California's murder rate.

- **Sourcebook of Criminal Justice Statistics: Capital Punishment**
  <http://www.albany.edu/sourcebook/1995/ind/CAPITAL_
  PUNISHMENT.ind.html>

  This site contains information gleaned from the U.S. Department of Justice's *Sourcebook of Criminal Justice Statistics* on capital punishment and deterrence.

- **The Case Against the Death Penalty**
  <http://www.aclu.org/library/case_against_death.html>

  The American Civil Liberties Union (ACLU) maintains this site, which features eight objections to the death penalty, among which is the argument that capital punishment does not deter crime.

COMBINING SUBJECTS AND STRATEGIES

The photograph below depicts many of the same themes and strategies as the essay that follows. Your observations about the photograph will help guide you to the key themes and strategies in the essay. After you've read the essay, you may use your observations about both the photograph and the essay to examine how the overlapping themes and strategies work in each medium.

The photograph below by Joel Gordon, of an African American inmate in lockdown, was taken at a medium-security prison in Putnam County, Florida.

© Joel Gordon 2000

For Discussion

What attracted your attention when you first looked at this photograph? What do you see in the eyes and the hands of the African American inmate? In the hands of the inmate in the next cell? What feelings does the setting — the cell's steel bars and the cinder-block walls — arouse in you? In a word or phrase, what dominant impression does the photograph give you? What specific details help create this impression for you? What does this photograph seem to be arguing for?

When Justice Lets Us Down

Jim Dwyer, Peter Neufeld, and Barry Scheck

*Two-time Pulitzer Prize–winning journalist Jim Dwyer graduated from
the Columbia Graduate School of Journalism in 1980. After working for
three different newspapers in New Jersey, he joined* Newsday *in New
York City in 1984. He is currently a columnist for the* New York Daily
News. *Dwyer met defense lawyers Peter Neufeld and Barry Scheck while
covering a trial for his column. Neufeld and Scheck were public defenders
in the South Bronx in 1988 when they worked on a case in which they
concluded that DNA testing would easily have established the innocence
of an accused man but had been ignored as a tool for justice. That experience led them to found the Innocence Project in 1992, which has since
used DNA evidence to exonerate thirty-seven people convicted of crimes
they did not commit. Neufeld, who has a private practice in Manhattan,
and Scheck, currently a professor at the Benjamin N. Cardozo Law
School, teamed with Dwyer to write* Actual Innocence *(2000), a book
that details the work of the Innocence Project and calls for increased use
of DNA testing to establish guilt or innocence.*

In the following selection, adapted from Actual Innocence *and
published in* Newsweek *on February 14, 2000, the authors call for a
careful examination of our justice system, especially those cases in which
a person was wrongly convicted.*

BEFORE YOU READ

What have you heard about advances in DNA research? Do you
think DNA evidence should be allowed in court? Should our justice
system routinely use DNA testing when it can establish the innocence or guilt of a person? Should Americans have a record of their
DNA, just as they have fingerprints recorded? Why do you think
there is so much controversy surrounding DNA testing?

The warden was seated at the head of a long table when Ron   1
Williamson was led into the office and told to sit down. Once,
Williamson had been a professional baseball player, the hero jock who
married the beauty queen in his small Oklahoma town. Now, on an
August morning in 1994, at 41, the athlete had passed directly from
his prime to a state beyond age. His hair had gone stringy and white;
his face had shrunk to a skeletal mask wrapped in pasty, toneless skin.

The warden said he had a duty to carry out, and he read from a   2
piece of paper: You have been sentenced to die by lethal injection,
and such sentence will be carried out at 12:30 A.M., the 24th of September, 1994. The prison had received no stay of execution, the warden said, so Williamson would be brought to the holding area next to
the death chamber until the 24th.

He was led back to a cell, screaming from that moment on, night   3
and day, even after they moved him into another unit with double
doors to muffle the noise. On Sept. 17, Williamson was shifted into
the special cell for prisoners with less than a week to live. By then, the
screaming had torn his throat to ribbons, but everyone knew his
raspy, desperate litany: "I did not rape or kill Debra Sue Carter! I am
an innocent man!" In Norman, Okla., a public defender named Janet
Chesley frantically scrambled a team to move the case into federal
court, assembling a mass of papers and fresh arguments. With just five
days to go, they won a stay.

One year later, U.S. district court Judge Frank Seay would rule that   4
Williamson's trial had been a constitutional shambles. His conviction
and death sentence — ratified by every state court in Oklahoma —
had been plagued by unreliable informants, prosecutorial misconduct,
an inept defense lawyer, bogus scientific evidence and a witness who
himself was a likely suspect, the federal judge said. He vacated the
conviction.

Last April, before Williamson could be tried again, DNA tests   5
arranged by the Innocence Project at the Benjamin N. Cardozo Law
School in New York proved that he was actually innocent. Across the
country, the Ron Williamson story has happened over and over. Since
1976, Illinois has executed 12 people — and freed 13 from death row
as innocent. Last week Illinois Governor George Ryan declared a
moratorium on executions. The next day a California judge threw out
the convictions of nine people after prosecutors said they were among
at least 32 framed by a group of corrupt police officers within the Los
Angeles Police Department. New innocence cases, based on DNA tests,
are on the horizon in California, Texas, Florida and Louisiana.

A rare moment of enlightenment is at hand. In the last decade,   6
DNA tests have provided stone-cold proof that 69 people were sent to
prison and death row in North America for crimes they did not commit. The number has been rising at a rate of more than one a month.
What matters most is not how the wrongly convicted got out of jail,
but how they got into it. "How do you prevent another innocent man
or woman from paying the ultimate penalty for a crime he or she did
not commit?" asked Governor Ryan, a Republican and death-penalty
supporter. "Today I cannot answer that question."

In 22 states, the fabric of false guilt has been laid bare, and the   7
same vivid threads bind a wealthy Oklahoma businessman and a
Maryland fisherman; a Marine corporal in California and a boiler re-
pairman in Virginia; a Chicago drifter and a Louisiana construction
worker; a Missouri schoolteacher and the Oklahoma ballplayer. Sometimes, it turns out, eyewitnesses make mistakes. Snitches tell lies. Confessions are coerced or fabricated. Racism trumps the truth. Lab tests
are rigged. Defense lawyers sleep. Cops lie.

DNA testing can't solve these problems but it reveals their exis- 8
tence. Many can be fixed with simple reforms. To simply ignore them
means that more criminals go free, and the innocent will suffer. Clyde
Charles learned the crushing weight of the status quo: he was freed
just before Christmas, after 19 years of his life were squandered in
Louisiana's Angola prison. The last nine years were spent fighting for
the DNA lab work that cleared him in a matter of hours. In 48 states,
prisoners don't have statutory rights to tests that could prove their innocence, and too often authorities stubbornly resist. In more than
half its exonerations, the Innocence Project was forced into fierce liti-
gation simply to get the DNA tests.

"Our procedure," wrote Justice Learned Hand in 1923, "has always 9
been haunted by the ghost of the innocent man convicted. It is an unreal dream." Nearly 75 years later, Judge Seay in Oklahoma wrote an
epilogue to the writ of habeas corpus for Ron Williamson: "God help
us, if ever in this great country we turn our heads while people who
have not had fair trials are executed. That almost happened in this
case." For all the gigabytes of crime statistics kept in the United States,
no account is taken of the innocent person, wrongly convicted, ultimately exonerated. No one has the job of figuring out what went
wrong, or who did wrong. The moment has come to do so.

RESPONDING TO READING

According to Dwyer, Neufeld, and Scheck, DNA testing provides our justice
system with a powerful new tool to ensure that justice is served. Why do
you think it is so difficult to obtain DNA testing when it can so quickly provide clear-cut evidence of a convicted person's innocence?

QUESTIONING THE TEXT

1. On what grounds did Judge Frank Seay vacate Ron Williamson's conviction? How was Williamson's innocence later established?

2. According to the authors, "A rare moment of enlightenment is at hand"
   (paragraph 6). Who is being "enlightened," and about what?

3. What problems with the justice system can DNA testing reveal? What
   happens when we ignore these problems?

UNDERSTANDING THE WRITER'S CRAFT

1. The authors begin their argument with an anecdote rather than data or
   a preliminary statement of their point of view. Why do you think the
   anecdote is an effective way to introduce their argument? (Glossary:
   Beginnings/Endings) What does the Williamson case illustrate about the
   death penalty?

2. Reread the quotation from Governor George Ryan in paragraph 6. In what ways does this quotation strengthen the authors' argument?

3. Examine the last seven sentences in paragraph 7. What would have been lost or gained had the authors combined them into a single sentence? Explain.

4. What are the authors arguing for in this essay? What do you think they want their readers to do after hearing their argument?

EXPLORING LANGUAGE

1. Identify the figurative language used in paragraph 7. (Glossary: *Figures of Speech*) Why do you suppose the authors include this figure in what is otherwise a prosaic piece of writing? What image does the figure bring to mind?

2. Refer to your desk dictionary to define the following words as Dwyer, Neufeld, and Scheck use them in this selection: *stay* (paragraph 2), *litany* (3), *inept* (4), *moratorium* (5), *vivid* (7), *coerced* (7), *statutory* (8), *exonerations* (8).

COMBINING RHETORICAL STRATEGIES

Identify the different types of examples that Dwyer, Neufeld, and Scheck use in their argument. (Glossary: *Examples*) Are some examples more emotionally charged than others? Which ones could be described as objective? In what ways do these examples make their argument more convincing to you? Explain.

WRITING SUGGESTIONS

1. **(Argumentation)** Write an argument in favor of the proposition that a person charged with a crime has the right to request DNA testing to establish his or her innocence whenever DNA evidence is available at the crime scene.

2. **(Other Strategies)** Years can pass between a person's conviction for a capital crime and his or her execution. What happens during this time to ensure that the trial was fair and that justice was served? Write an essay in which you describe step-by-step the process that our justice system follows in handling a condemned person. Why does the process take so long? Does the process serve the best interests of the convicted person or the state? How do you think the system could be improved? Before you start writing, you may find it helpful to review your response to the Before You Read questions for this selection, Joel Gordon's photograph of an inmate in a prison cell on page 659, and other essays in this mini-casebook on the death penalty.

3. **(Research)** Investigate the issue of DNA testing. In addition to criminal prosecutions like the ones Dwyer, Neufeld, and Scheck discuss, how else

is DNA testing being used? What possible uses are being proposed? What kinds of information does DNA testing provide? Proponents of DNA testing point to the obvious advantages. How cautious should the public be before approving widespread DNA testing? What are some of the potential disadvantages or abuses that critics claim? Present your findings in a report on DNA testing.

- **National Commission on the Future of DNA Evidence**
  <http://www.ojp.usdoj.gov/nij/dna>

  This division of the National Institute of Justice features articles on such topics as the future of DNA evidence, what law enforcement should know about DNA forensics, and postconviction DNA testing.

- *Frontline:* **The Case for Innocence**
  <http://www.pbs.org/wgbh/pages/frontline/shows/case>

  Frontline's program on DNA and criminal prosecution highlights four cases, explains the legal community's resistance to DNA evidence, and explores where the future of DNA technology may take us.

- **Basics of DNA Fingerprinting**
  <http://www.biology.washington.edu/fingerprint/dnaintro.html>

  A class project from the University of Washington examines the basics, limitations, and innovations of DNA fingerprinting.

- **Forensics: DNA Evidence**
  <http://crime.about.com/newsissues/crime/msub3a.htm>

  This site contains links to sites explaining how DNA analysis is used in criminal cases.

WRITING SUGGESTIONS
FOR ARGUMENTATION

1. Think of a product that you like and want to use even though it has an annoying feature. Write a letter of complaint in which you attempt to persuade the manufacturer to improve the product. Your letter should include the following points:

   a. A statement concerning the nature of the problem
   b. Evidence supporting or explaining your complaint
   c. Suggestions for improving the product

2. Select one of the position statements that follow, and write an argumentative essay in which you defend that statement.

   a. Living in a dormitory is (*or* is not) as attractive as living off-campus.
   b. Student government shows (*or* does not show) that the democratic process is effective.
   c. America should (*or* should not) be a refuge for the oppressed.
   d. School spirit is (*or* is not) as important as it ever was.
   e. Interest in religion is (*or* is not) increasing in the United States.
   f. We have (*or* have not) brought air pollution under control in the United States.
   g. The need to develop alternative energy sources is (*or* is not) serious.
   h. America's great cities are (*or* are not) thriving.
   i. Fraternities and sororities do (*or* do not) build character.
   j. We have (*or* have not) found effective means to dispose of nuclear or chemical wastes.
   k. Fair play is (*or* is not) a thing of the past.
   l. Human life is (*or* is not) valued in a technological society.
   m. The consumer does (*or* does not) need to be protected.
   n. The family farm in America is (*or* is not) in danger of extinction.
   o. Grades do (*or* do not) encourage learning.
   p. America is (*or* is not) a violent society.
   q. Television is (*or* is not) a positive cultural force in America.
   r. America should (*or* should not) feel a commitment to the starving peoples of the world.
   s. The federal government should (*or* should not) regulate all utilities.
   t. Money is (*or* is not) the path to happiness.
   u. Animals do (*or* do not) have rights.
   v. Competition is (*or* is not) killing us.
   w. America is (*or* is not) becoming a society with deteriorating values.

3. Think of something on your campus or in your community that you would like to see changed. Write a persuasive argument that explains what is wrong and how you think it ought to be changed. Make sure you incorporate other writing strategies into your essay — for example, description, narration, or exemplification — to increase the effectiveness of your persuasive argument.

4. Read some articles in the editorial section of today's paper, and pick one with which you agree or disagree. Write a letter to the editor that presents your point of view. Use a logical argument to support or refute the editorial's assertions. Depending on the editorial, you might choose to use different rhetorical strategies to reach your audience. You might use cause and effect, for example, to show the correct (or incorrect) connections made by the editorial.

5. Working with a partner, choose a controversial topic like the legalization of marijuana or any of the topics in writing suggestion 2. Each partner should argue one side of the issue. Decide who is going to write on which side of the issue, and keep in mind that there are often more than two sides to an issue. Then each of you should write an essay trying to convince your partner that your position is the most logical and correct.

Glossary of Rhetorical Terms

Abstract See *Concrete/Abstract*.

Allusion An allusion is a passing reference to a familiar person, place, or thing drawn from history, the Bible, mythology, or literature. An allusion is an economical way for a writer to capture the essence of an idea, atmosphere, emotion, or historical era, as in "The scandal was his Watergate," or "He saw himself as a modern Job," or "Everyone there held those truths to be self-evident." An allusion should be familiar to the reader; if it is not, it will add nothing to the meaning.

Analogy Analogy is a special form of comparison in which the writer explains something unfamiliar by comparing it to something familiar: "A transmission line is simply a pipeline for electricity. In the case of a water pipeline, more water will flow through the pipe as water pressure increases. The same is true of a transmission line for electricity." See also the discussion of analogy on pages 334–36.

Analytical Reading Reading analytically means reading actively, paying close attention to both the content and the structure of the text. Analytical reading often involves answering several basic questions about the piece of writing under consideration:

1. What does the author want to say? What is his or her main point?

2. Why does the author want to say it? What is his or her purpose?

3. What strategy or strategies does the author use?

4. Why and how does the author's writing strategy suit both the subject and the purpose?

5. What is special about the way the author uses the strategy?

6. How effective is the essay? Why?

For a detailed example of analytical reading, see pages 7–10 in Chapter 1.

Appropriateness See *Diction*.

Argument Argument is one of the four basic types of prose. (Narration, description, and exposition are the other three.) To argue is to attempt to convince the reader to agree with a point of view, to make a given decision, or to pursue a particular course of action. Logical argument is based on reasonable explanations and appeals to the reader's intelligence. See Chapter 13 for further discussion of argumentation. See also *Logical Fallacies; Persuasion.*

Assertion   The thesis or proposition that a writer puts forward in argument.

Assumption   A belief or principle, stated or implied, that is taken for granted.

Attitude   A writer's attitude reflects his or her opinion of a subject. For example, a writer can think very positively or very negatively about a subject. In most cases, the writer's attitude falls somewhere between these two extremes. See also *Tone.*

Audience   An audience is the intended readership for a piece of writing. For example, the readers of a national weekly newsmagazine come from all walks of life and have diverse opinions, attitudes, and educational experiences. In contrast, the readership for an organic chemistry journal is made up of people whose interests and educational backgrounds are quite similar. The essays in this book are intended for general readers—intelligent people who may lack specific information about the subject being discussed.

Beginnings/Endings   A *beginning* is the sentence, group of sentences, or section that introduces an essay. Good beginnings usually identify the thesis or controlling idea, attempt to interest the reader, and establish a tone. Some effective ways in which writers begin essays include (1) telling an anecdote that illustrates the thesis, (2) providing a controversial statement or opinion that engages the reader's interest, (3) presenting startling statistics or facts, (4) defining a term that is central to the discussion that follows, (5) asking thought-provoking questions, (6) providing a quotation that illustrates the thesis, (7) referring to a current event that helps establish the thesis, or (8) showing the significance of the subject or stressing its importance to the reader.

An *ending* is the sentence or group of sentences that brings an essay to closure. Good endings are purposeful and well planned. Endings satisfy readers when they are the natural outgrowths of the essays themselves and convey a sense of finality or completion. Good essays do not simply stop; they conclude.

Cause and Effect Analysis   Cause and effect analysis is one of the types of exposition. (Process analysis, definition, division and classification, exemplification, and comparison and contrast are the others.) Cause and effect analysis answers the question *why?* It explains the reasons for an occurrence or the consequences of an action. See Chapter 12 for a detailed discussion of cause and effect analysis. See also *Exposition.*

Claim   The thesis or proposition put forth in argument.

Classification   Classification, along with division, is one of the types of exposition. (Process analysis, definition, comparison and contrast, exemplification, and cause and effect analysis are the others.) When classifying, the writer arranges and sorts people, places, or things into categories according to their differing characteristics, thus making them more manageable for the writer and more understandable for the reader. See Chapter 10 for a detailed discussion of classification. See also *Division; Exposition.*

Cliché   A cliché is an expression that has become ineffective through overuse. Expressions such as *quick as a flash, dry as dust, jump for joy,* and *slow as molasses* are all clichés. Good writers normally avoid such trite expressions and seek instead to express themselves in fresh and forceful language.

Coherence   Coherence is a quality of good writing that results when all sentences, paragraphs, and longer divisions of an essay are naturally connected. Coherent writing is achieved through (1) a logical sequence of ideas (arranged in chronological order, spatial order, order of importance, or some other appropriate order), (2) the thoughtful repetition of key words and ideas, (3) a pace suitable for your topic and your reader, and (4) the use of transitional words and expressions. Coherence should not be confused with unity. (See *Unity.*) Also see *Transitions.*

Colloquial Expressions   A colloquial expression is characteristic of or appropriate to spoken language or to writing that seeks its effect. Colloquial expressions are informal, as *chem, gym, come up with, be at loose ends, won't,* and *photo* illustrate. Thus, colloquial expressions are acceptable in formal writing only if they are used purposefully.

Comparison and Contrast   Comparison and contrast is one of the types of exposition. (Process analysis, definition, division and classification, exemplification, and cause and effect analysis are the others.) In comparison and contrast, the writer points out the similarities and differences between two or more subjects in the same class or category. The function of any comparison and contrast is to clarify—to reach some conclusion about the items being compared and contrasted. See Chapter 9 for a detailed discussion of comparison and contrast. See also *Exposition.*

Conclusions   See *Beginnings/Endings.*

Concrete/Abstract   A *concrete word* names a specific object, person, place, or action that can be directly perceived by the senses: *car, bread, building, book, Abraham Lincoln, Chicago,* or *hiking.* An *abstract word,* in contrast, refers to general qualities, conditions, ideas, actions, or relationships that cannot be directly perceived by the senses: *bravery, dedication, excellence, anxiety, stress, thinking,* or *hatred.*

 Although writers must use both concrete and abstract language, good writers avoid using too many abstract words. Instead, they rely on concrete words to define and illustrate abstractions. Because concrete words affect the senses, they are easily comprehended by the reader.

Connotation/Denotation   Both connotation and denotation refer to the meanings of words. *Denotation* is the dictionary meaning of a word, the literal meaning. *Connotation,* on the other hand, is the implied or suggested meaning of a word. For example, the denotation of *lamb* is "a young sheep." The connotations of lamb are numerous: *gentle, docile, weak, peaceful, blessed, sacrificial, blood, spring, frisky, pure, innocent,* and so on. Good writers are sensitive to both the denotations and the connotations of words, and they use these meanings to advantage in their writing. See also *Slanting.*

Controlling Idea   See *Thesis.*

Deduction   Deduction is the process of reasoning from a stated premise to a necessary conclusion. This form of reasoning moves from the general to the specific. See Chapter 13 for a discussion of deductive reasoning and its relation to argumentative writing. See also *Induction; Syllogism.*

Definition   Definition is one of the types of exposition. (Process analysis, division and classification, comparison and contrast, exemplification, and cause and effect analysis are the others.) Definition is a statement of the meaning of a word. A definition may be either brief or extended, part of an essay or an entire essay itself. See Chapter 11 for a detailed discussion of definition. See also *Exposition.*

Denotation   See *Connotation/Denotation.*

Description   Description is one of the four basic types of prose. (Narration, exposition, and argument are the other three.) Description tells how a person, place, or thing is perceived by the five senses. Objective description reports these sensory qualities factually, whereas subjective description gives the writer's interpretation of them. See Chapter 6 for a detailed discussion of description.

Dialogue Dialogue is conversation that is recorded in a piece of writing. Through dialogue writers reveal important aspects of characters' personalities as well as events in the narrative.

Diction Diction refers to a writer's choice and use of words. Good diction is precise and appropriate—the words mean exactly what the writer intends, and the words are well suited to the writer's subject, intended audience, and purpose in writing. The word-conscious writer knows that there are differences among *aged, old,* and *elderly; blue, navy,* and *azure;* and *disturbed, angry,* and *irritated.* Furthermore, this writer knows in which situation to use each word. See also *Connotation/Denotation.*

Division Like comparison and contrast, division and classification are separate yet closely related mental operations. Division involves breaking down a single large unit into smaller subunits or breaking down a large group of items into discrete categories. For example, the student body at your college or university can be divided into categories according to different criteria (by class, by home state or country, by sex, and so on).

Dominant Impression A dominant impression is the single mood, atmosphere, or quality a writer emphasizes in a piece of descriptive writing. The dominant impression is created through the careful selection of details and is, of course, influenced by the writer's subject, audience, and purpose. See also the discussion on pages 161–63 in Chapter 6.

Draft A draft is a version of a piece of writing at a particular stage in the writing process. The first version produced is usually called the *rough draft* or *first draft* and is a writer's beginning attempt to give overall shape to his or her ideas. Subsequent versions are called *revised drafts.* The copy presented for publication is the *final draft.*

Editing During the editing stage of the writing process, the writer makes his or her prose conform to the conventions of the language. This includes making final improvements in sentence structure and diction, and proofreading for wordiness and errors in grammar, usage, spelling, and punctuation. After editing, the writer is ready to prepare a final copy.

Emphasis Emphasis is the placement of important ideas and words within sentences and longer units of writing so that they have the greatest impact. In general, the end has the most impact, and the beginning nearly as much; the middle has the least. See also *Organization.*

Endings See *Beginnings/Endings.*

Essay An essay is a relatively short piece of nonfiction in which the writer attempts to make one or more closely related points. A good essay is purposeful, informative, and well organized.

Ethos A type of argumentative proof having to do with the ethics of the arguer: honesty, trustworthiness, even morals.

Evaluation An evaluation of a piece of writing is an assessment of its effectiveness or merit. In evaluating a piece of writing, you should ask the following questions: What is the writer's purpose? Is it a worthwhile purpose? Does the writer achieve the purpose? Is the writer's information sufficient and accurate? What are the strengths of the essay? What are its weaknesses? Depending on the type of writing and the purpose, more specific questions can also be asked. For example, with an argument you could ask: Does the writer follow the principles of logical thinking? Is the writer's evidence convincing?

Evidence Evidence is the data on which a judgment or argument is based or by which proof or probability is established. Evidence usually takes the form of statistics, facts, names, examples or illustrations, and opinions of authorities.

Examples   Examples illustrate a larger idea or represent something of which they are a part. An example is a basic means of developing or clarifying an idea. Furthermore, examples enable writers to show and not simply tell readers what they mean. The terms *example* and *illustration* are sometimes used interchangeably. See also the discussion of exemplification on pages 88–90 in Chapter 5.

Exemplification   Exemplification is a type of exposition. (Definition, division and classification, comparison and contrast, cause and effect analysis, and process analysis are the others.) With exemplification the writer uses examples —specific facts, opinions, samples, and anecdotes or stories — to support a generalization, and to make it more vivid, understandable, and persuasive. See Chapter 5 for a detailed discussion of exemplification. See also *Examples*.

Exposition   Exposition is one of the four basic types of prose. (Narration, description, and argument are the other three.) The purpose of exposition is to clarify, explain, and inform. The methods of exposition presented in this text are process analysis, definition, division and classification, comparison and contrast, exemplification, and cause and effect analysis. For a detailed discussion of each of these methods of exposition, see the appropriate chapter.

Fact   A piece of information presented as having a verifiable certainty or reality.

Fallacy   See *Logical Fallacies*.

Figures of Speech   Figures of speech are brief, imaginative comparisons that highlight the similarities between things that are basically dissimilar. They make writing vivid and interesting and therefore more memorable. The most common figures of speech are these:

Simile — An implicit comparison introduced by *like* or *as:* "The fighter's hands were *like* stone."

Metaphor — An implied comparison that uses one thing as the equivalent of another: "All the world's a stage."

Personification — A special kind of simile or metaphor in which human traits are assigned to an inanimate object: "The engine coughed and then stopped."

Focus   Focus is the limitation that a writer gives his or her subject. The writer's task is to select a manageable topic given the constraints of time, space, and purpose. For example, within the general subject of sports, a writer could focus on government support of amateur athletes or narrow the focus further to government support of Olympic athletes.

General   See *Specific/General*.

Idiom   An idiom is a word or phrase that is used habitually with a particular meaning in a language. The meaning of an idiom is not always readily apparent to nonnative speakers of that language. For example, *catch cold, hold a job, make up your mind,* and *give them a hand* are all idioms in English.

Illustration   See *Examples*. Also see Chapter 5.

Induction   Induction is the process of reasoning to a conclusion about all members of a class through an examination of only a few members of the class. This form of reasoning moves from the particular to the general. See Chapter 13 for a discussion of inductive reasoning and its relation to argumentative writing. Also see *Deduction*.

Introductions   See *Beginnings/Endings*.

Irony   Irony is the use of words to suggest something different from their literal meaning. For example, when Jonathan Swift proposes in "A Modest Proposal" that Ireland's problems could be solved if the people of Ireland fattened their babies and sold them to the English landlords for food, he meant that almost any other solution would be preferable. A writer can use irony to establish a special relationship with the reader and to add an extra dimension or twist to the meaning.

Jargon   See *Technical Language.*

Logical Fallacies   A logical fallacy is an error in reasoning that renders an argument invalid. Some of the more common logical fallacies are these:

Oversimplification — The tendency to provide simple solutions to complex problems: "The reason we have inflation today is that OPEC has unreasonably raised the price of oil."

Non sequitur ("It does not follow") — An inference or conclusion that does not follow from established premises or evidence: "It was the best movie I saw this year, and it should get an Academy Award."

Post hoc, ergo propter hoc ("After this, therefore because of this") — Confusing chance or coincidence with causation. Because one event comes after another one, it does not necessarily mean that the first event caused the second: "I won't say I caught cold at the hockey game, but I certainly didn't have it before I went there."

Begging the question — Assuming in a premise that which needs to be proven: "If American autoworkers built a better product, foreign auto sales would not be so high."

False analogy — Making a misleading analogy between logically unconnected ideas: "He was a brilliant basketball player; therefore, there's no question in my mind that he will be a fine coach."

Either/or thinking — The tendency to see an issue as having only two sides: "Used car salespeople are either honest or crooked."

See also Chapter 13.

Logical Reasoning   See *Deduction; Induction.*

Logos   A type of argumentative proof having to do with the logical qualities of an argument: data, evidence, factual information.

Metaphor   See *Figures of Speech.*

Narration   Narration is one of the four basic types of prose. (Description, exposition, and argument are the other three.) To narrate is to tell a story, to tell what happened. Although narration is most often used in fiction, it is also important in nonfiction, either by itself or in conjunction with other types of prose. See Chapter 7 for a detailed discussion of narration.

Objective/Subjective   *Objective* writing is factual and impersonal, whereas *subjective* writing, sometimes called *impressionistic* writing, relies heavily on personal interpretation. For a discussion of objective description and subjective description, see Chapter 6.

Opinion   An opinion is a belief or conclusion not substantiated by positive knowledge or proof. An opinion reveals personal feelings or attitudes or states a position. Opinion should not be confused with argument.

Organization   In writing, organization is the thoughtful arrangement and presentation of one's points or ideas. Narration is often organized chronologically. Exposition may be organized from simplest to most complex or from most familiar to least familiar. Argument may be organized from least important to most important. There is no single correct pattern of organization for a given piece of writing, but good writers are careful to discover an order of presentation suitable for their audience and their purpose.

Paradox   A paradox is a seemingly contradictory statement that may nonetheless be true. For example, "We little know what we have until we lose it" is a paradoxical statement. For a detailed discussion of paradox that includes additional examples, see Laurence Perrine's "Paradox" on page 6.

Paragraph The paragraph, the single most important unit of thought in an essay, is a series of closely related sentences. These sentences adequately develop the central or controlling idea of the paragraph. This central or controlling idea, usually stated in a topic sentence, is necessarily related to the purpose of the whole composition. A well-written paragraph has several distinguishing characteristics: a clearly stated or implied topic sentence, adequate development, unity, coherence, and an appropriate organizational strategy.

Parallelism Parallel structure is the repetition of word order or form either within a single sentence or in several sentences that develop the same central idea. As a rhetorical device, parallelism can aid coherence and add emphasis. Roosevelt's statement, "I see one third of a nation ill-housed, ill-clad, ill-nourished," illustrates effective parallelism.

Pathos A type of argumentative proof having to do with audience: emotional language, connotative diction, and appeals to certain values.

Personification See *Figures of Speech.*

Persuasion Persuasion, or persuasive argument, is an attempt to convince readers to agree with a point of view, to make a given decision, or to pursue a particular course of action. Persuasion appeals heavily to the emotions, whereas logical argument does not. For the distinction between logical argument and persuasive argument, see Chapter 13.

Point of View Point of view refers to the grammatical person of the speaker in an essay. For example, a first-person point of view uses the pronoun *I* and is commonly found in autobiography and the personal essay; a third-person point of view uses the pronouns *he, she,* or *it* and is commonly found in objective writing. See Chapter 7 for a discussion of point of view in narration.

Prewriting Prewriting encompasses all the activities that take place before a writer actually starts a rough draft. During the prewriting stage of the writing process, the writer selects a subject area, focuses on a particular topic, collects information and makes notes, brainstorms for ideas, discovers connections between pieces of information, determines a thesis and purpose, rehearses portions of the writing in the mind or on paper, and makes a scratch outline. For some suggestions about prewriting, see Chapter 2.

Process Analysis Process analysis is a type of exposition. (Definition, division and classification, comparison and contrast, and cause and effect analysis are the others.) Process analysis answers the question *how?* and explains how something works or gives step-by-step directions for doing something. See Chapter 8 for a detailed discussion of process analysis. See also *Exposition.*

Publication The publication stage of the writing process is when the writer shares his or her writing with the intended audience. Publication can take the form of a typed or an oral presentation, a photocopy, or a commercially printed rendition. What's important is that the writer's words are read in what amounts to their final form.

Purpose Purpose is what the writer wants to accomplish in a particular piece of writing. Purposeful writing seeks to *relate* (narration), to *describe* (description), to *explain* (process analysis, definition, division and classification, comparison and contrast, and cause and effect analysis), or to *convince* (argument).

Revision During the revision stage of the writing process, the writer determines what in the draft needs to be developed or clarified so that the essay says what the writer intends it to say. Often the writer needs to revise several times before the essay is "right." Comments from peer evaluators can be invaluable in helping writers determine what sorts of changes need to be made. Such changes can include adding material, deleting material, changing the order of presentation, and substituting new material for old.

Rhetorical Question   A rhetorical question is a question that is asked but requires no answer from the reader. "When will nuclear proliferation end?" is such a question. Writers use rhetorical questions to introduce topics they plan to discuss or to emphasize important points.

Rough Draft   See *Draft.*

Sequence   Sequence refers to the order in which a writer presents information. Writers commonly select chronological order, spatial order, order of importance, or order of complexity to arrange their points. See also *Organization.*

Simile   See *Figures of Speech.*

Slang   Slang is the unconventional, very informal language of particular subgroups of a culture. Slang, such as *bummed, coke, split, hurt, dis, blow off,* and *cool,* is acceptable in formal writing only if it is used purposefully.

Slanting   The use of certain words or information that results in a biased viewpoint.

Specific/General   *General words* name groups or classes of objects, qualities, or actions. *Specific words,* in contrast, name individual objects, qualities, or actions within a class or group. To some extent, the terms *general* and *specific* are relative. For example, *dessert* is a class of things. *Pie,* however, is more specific than *dessert* but more general than *pecan pie* or *chocolate cream pie.*

Good writing judiciously balances the general with the specific. Writing with too many general words is likely to be dull and lifeless. General words do not create vivid responses in the reader's mind as concrete, specific words can. However, writing that relies exclusively on specific words may lack focus and direction—the control that more general statements provide.

Strategy   A strategy is a means by which a writer achieves his or her purpose. Strategy includes the many rhetorical decisions that the writer makes about organization, paragraph structure, syntax, and diction. In terms of the whole essay, strategy refers to the principal rhetorical mode that the writer uses. If, for example, a writer wishes to show how to make chocolate chip cookies, the most effective strategy would be process analysis. If it is the writer's purpose to show why sales of American cars have declined in recent years, the most effective strategy would be cause and effect analysis.

Style   Style is the individual manner in which a writer expresses his or her ideas. Style is created by the author's particular selection of words, construction of sentences, and arrangement of ideas.

Subject   The subject of an essay is its content, what the essay is about. Depending on the author's purpose and the constraints of space, a subject may range from one that is broadly conceived to one that is narrowly defined.

Subjective   See *Objective/Subjective.*

Supporting Evidence   See *Evidence.*

Syllogism   A syllogism is an argument that utilizes deductive reasoning and consists of a major premise, a minor premise, and a conclusion. For example:

All trees that lose leaves are deciduous. *(Major premise)*

Maple trees lose their leaves. *(Minor premise)*

Therefore, maple trees are deciduous. *(Conclusion)*

See also *Deduction.*

Symbol   A symbol is a person, place, or thing that represents something beyond itself. For example, the eagle is a symbol of America, and the bear, a symbol of Russia.

Syntax Syntax refers to the way in which words are arranged to form phrases, clauses, and sentences as well as to the grammatical relationship among the words themselves.

Technical Language Technical language, or jargon, is the special vocabulary of a trade or profession. Writers who use technical language do so with an awareness of their audience. If the audience is a group of peers, technical language may be used freely. If the audience is a more general one, technical language should be used sparingly and carefully so as not to sacrifice clarity. See also *Diction.*

Thesis A thesis is a statement of the main idea of an essay. Also known as the *controlling idea,* a thesis may sometimes be implied rather than stated directly.

Title A title is a word or phrase set off at the beginning of an essay to identify the subject, to capture the main idea of the essay, or to attract the reader's attention. A title may be explicit or suggestive. A subtitle, when used, extends or restricts the meaning of the main title.

Tone Tone is the manner in which a writer relates to an audience—the "tone of voice" used to address readers. Tone may be described as friendly, serious, distant, angry, cheerful, bitter, cynical, enthusiastic, morbid, resentful, warm, playful, and so forth. A particular tone results from a writer's diction, sentence structure, purpose, and attitude toward the subject. See also *Attitude.*

Topic Sentence The topic sentence states the central idea of a paragraph and thus limits and controls the subject of the paragraph. Although the topic sentence most often appears at the beginning of the paragraph, it may appear at any other point, particularly if the writer is trying to create a special effect. Also see *Paragraph.*

Transitions Transitions are words or phrases that link sentences, paragraphs, and larger units of a composition to achieve coherence. These devices include parallelism, pronoun references, conjunctions, and the repetition of key ideas, as well as the many conventional transitional expressions, such as *moreover, on the other hand, in addition, in contrast,* and *therefore.* Also see *Coherence.*

Unity Unity is achieved in an essay when all the words, sentences, and paragraphs contribute to its thesis. The elements of a unified essay do not distract the reader. Instead, they all harmoniously support a single idea or purpose.

Writing Process The writing process consists of five major stages: prewriting, writing drafts, revision, editing, and publication. The process is not inflexible, but there is no mistaking the fact that most writers follow some version of it most of the time. Although orderly in its basic components and sequence of activities, the writing process is nonetheless continuous, creative, and unique to each individual writer. See Chapter 2 for a detailed discussion of the writing process. See also *Draft; Editing; Prewriting; Publication; Revision.*

Acknowledgments (continued from p. ii)

Sherwood Anderson. "Hands." From *Winesberg, Ohio.* Copyright © 1919 by B. W. Huebsch. Copyright © 1947 by Eleanor Copenhaver Anderson. Used by permission of Viking Penguin, a division of Penguin Putnam, Inc.

Roger Angell. "On the Ball." From *The Five Seasons* by Roger Angell. Copyright © 1972, 1973, 1974, 1975, 1976, 1977 by Roger Angell. Reprinted by permission of International Creative Management, Inc.

Maya Angelou. "Living Well. Living Good." From *Wouldn't Take Nothing for My Journey Now.* Copyright © 1993 by Maya Angelou. Used by permission of Random House, Inc.

Russell Baker. "The Plot against People." From the *New York Times,* January 1, 1968. Copyright © 1968 by The New York Times Company. Reprinted by permission.

Suzanne Britt. "Neat People vs. Sloppy People." From *Show and Tell* by Suzanne Britt. Copyright © 1982 by Suzanne Britt. Reprinted by permission of the author.

David Carkeet. "Take Me Out to the Counterfactual Present Time." Originally titled "Batting the Breeze: Take Me Out to the Counterfactual Ballgame" from the *New York Times Magazine,* July 23, 2000, pp. 20–22. Copyright © 2000 by the New York Times Company, Inc. Reprinted by permission.

Bruce Catton. "Grant and Lee: A Study in Contrasts." From *The American Story* by Earl Schenck Miers, editor. Copyright © 1956 by Broadcast Music, Inc. Reprinted by permission of U.S. Capitol History Society.

Judith Ortiz Cofer. "The Myth of the Latin Woman." From *The Latin Deli: Prose and Poetry* by Judith Ortiz Cofer. Copyright © 1993 by Judith Ortiz Cofer. Reprinted by permission of the University of Georgia Press.

Donna Woolfolk Cross. "Propaganda: How Not to Be Bamboozled." From *Speaking of Words: A Language Reader,* Third Edition by James Mackillop and Donna W. Cross. Copyright © 1986 by Holt, Rinehart and Winston. Reprinted by permission of the publisher.

Jacques d'Amboise. "I Show a Child What Is Possible." Originally published in *Parade* magazine. Copyright © 1989 by Jacques d'Amboise. Reprinted by permission of the author.

Annie Dillard. "Getting Caught." From *An American Childhood* by Annie Dillard. © 1987 by Annie Dillard. Reprinted by permission of HarperCollins Publishers, Inc.

Jim Dwyer, Peter Neufeld, and Barry Scheck. "When Justice Lets Us Down." Adapted from *Actual Innocence* by Jim Dwyer, Peter Neufeld, and Barry Scheck. Copyright © 2000 by Jim Dwyer, Peter Neufeld, and Barry Scheck. Used by permission of Doubleday, a division of Random House, Inc.

Lars Eighner. "On Dumpster Diving" from *Travels with Lizbeth* by Lars Eighner. © 1993 by Lars Eighner. Reprinted by permission of St. Martin's Press, LLC.

Sarah Federman. "What's 'Natural' about Our Natural Products?" Copyright © 2000 by Sarah Federman. Reprinted by permission of the author.

Thomas L. Friedman. "My Favorite Teacher." From the *New York Times,* January 9, 2001, Letters to the Editor. Reprinted by permission.

Nikki Giovanni. "Campus Racism 101." From *Racism 101* by Nikki Giovanni. Copyright © 1994 by Nikki Giovanni. Reprinted by permission of HarperCollins Publishers, Inc.

Natalie Goldberg. "Be Specific" from *Writing Down the Bones: Freeing the Writer Within* by Natalie Goldberg. © 1986 by Natalie Goldberg. Reprinted by permission of Shambhala Publications, Inc., Boston, www.shambhala.com.

Ellen Goodman. "The Company Man." © 1979 The Boston Globe Newspaper Co./Washington Post Writers Group. Reprinted by permission.

David Guterson. "San Piedro Island." From *Snow Falling on Cedars* by David Guterson. Copyright © 1994 by David Guterson. Reprinted by permission of Harcourt, Inc.

Sydney J. Harris. "A Jerk." From *Last Things First* by Sydney J. Harris. Originally titled "A Jerk Can't See Himself as Others Do." Copyright © 1957, 1958, 1959, 1960 by The Chicago Daily News and General Features Corporation. Copyright © 1961 by Sydney J. Harris. Reprinted by permission of Houghton Mifflin Company. All Rights Reserved.

Barbara Hattemer. "Cause and Violent Effect: Media and Our Youth." The article appeared in the July 1994 issue and is reprinted with permission from *The World & I*, vol. 19, #7, a publication of The Washington Times Corporation. Copyright © 1994.

Langston Hughes. "Salvation." From *The Big Sea* by Langston Hughes. Copyright © 1940 by Langston Hughes. Renewal copyright © 1968 by Arna Bontemps and George Houston Bass. Reprinted by permission of Hill & Wang, a division of Farrar, Straus & Giroux, L.L.C.

Jon Katz. "How Boys Become Men." Originally published in *Glamour,* January 1993. Copyright © 1993 by Jon Katz. Reprinted by permission of International Creative Management, Inc.

Martin Luther King Jr. Excerpt from "The Ways of Meeting Oppression" in *Stride Toward Freedom.* Copyright © 1958 Martin Luther King Jr. Copyright renewed 1986 by Coretta Scott King. "I Have a Dream" speech delivered on the steps at the Lincoln Memorial, Washington, D.C., August 28, 1963. Copyright © 1963 Martin Luther King Jr. Copyright renewed 1991 by Coretta Scott King. Reprinted by arrangement with The Heirs to the Estate of Martin Luther King Jr., c/o Writers House as agent for the proprietor.

Anne Lamott. "Polaroids." From *Bird by Bird* by Anne Lamott. Copyright © 1994 by Anne Lamott. Used by permission of Pantheon Books, a division of Random House, Inc.

Richard Lederer. "The Case for Short Words." From *The Miracle of Language* by Richard Lederer. © 1991 by Richard Lederer. Reprinted with permission of Pocket Books, a division of Simon & Schuster, Inc.

Judith Levine. "I Surf, Therefore I Am." From *Salon,* July 1997. Copyright © 1997 Judith Levine. Reprinted by permission of the author.

Tom and Ray Magliozzi. "Inside the Engine." From *Car Talk* by Tom and Ray Magliozzi. Copyright © 1991 by Tom and Ray Magliozzi. Used by permission of Dell Publishing, a division of Random House, Inc.

Nancy Mairs. "On Being a Cripple." From *Plaintext* by Nancy Mairs. Copyright © 1986 The Arizona Board of Regents. Reprinted by permission of the University of Arizona Press.

Kennedy P. Maize. "The Great Kern County Mouse War." From *Audubon,* vol. 79, November 1977. Reprinted by permission.

Malcolm X. "Coming to an Awareness of Language." From *The Autobiography of Malcolm X,* with the assistance of Alex Haley. Copyright © 1964 by Alex Haley and Malcolm X. Copyright © 1965 by Alex Haley and Betty Shabazz. Reprinted by permission of Random House, Inc.

Cherokee Paul McDonald. "A View from the Bridge." From *Sun Sentinel, Sunshine* magazine, Ft. Lauderdale, Fl. Reprinted by permission of the author.

Lorrie Moore. "How to Become a Writer." From *Self-Help* by Lorrie Moore. Copyright © 1985 by M. L. Moore. Used by permission of Alfred A. Knopf, a division of Random House, Inc.

Lance Morrow. "Why I Changed My Mind on the Death Penalty." From *http.//www.Time.com/* © 2001 Time Inc. Reprinted by permission.

Sherwin B. Nuland. "Cruel and Unusual." From the *New York Times,* November 11, 1999. Copyright © 1999 by The New York Times Company. Reprinted by permission.

George Orwell. "Shooting an Elephant." From *Shooting an Elephant and Other Essays* by George Orwell. Copyright © 1950 by Sonia Brownell Orwell and renewed 1978 by Sonia Pitt-Rivers. Reprinted by permission of Harcourt, Inc. Copyright © George Orwell 1936. Reproduced by permission of A.M. Heath & Co. Ltd. on behalf of Bill Hamilton as the Literary Executor of the late Sonia Brownell Orwell and Martin Seeker & Warburg Ltd.

Jo Goodwin Parker. "What Is Poverty?" From *America's Other Children: Public Schools Outside Suburbia* by George Henderson. University of Oklahoma Press. Reprinted by permission of the publisher.

Robert Ramírez. "The Woolen Sarape." Reprinted by permission of the author

Paul Roberts. "How to Say Nothing in 500 Words." From *Understanding English* by Paul Roberts. Copyright © 1958 by Paul Roberts. Copyright renewed. Reprinted by permission of HarperCollins Publishers, Inc.

Tom Rosenberg. "Changing My Name After 60 Years." From *Newsweek,* July 17, 2000. Copyright © 2000 Newsweek, Inc. Reprinted by permission. All rights reserved.

Scott Russell Sanders. "The Men We Carry in Our Minds." From *Paradise of Bombs* by Scott Russell Sanders. Copyright © 1984 by Scott Russell Sanders. Reprinted by permission of the author and the author's agents, The Virginia Kidd Agency, Inc.

Robert Scheer. "Violence Is Us." From *The Nation,* November 15, 1993. Reprinted with permission.

Charles Siebert. "An Audience with Dolly." From the *New York Times Magazine,* September 24, 2000, p. 62. Copyright © 2000 The New York Times Company. Reprinted with permission.

Leslie Marmon Silko. "Yellow Woman and a Beauty of the Spirit." From *Yellow Woman and a Beauty of the Spirit* by Leslie Marmon Silko. Copyright © 1996 by Leslie Marmon Silko. Reprinted by permission of Simon & Schuster.

Gary Soto. "Like Mexicans" appears in *The Effects of Knut Hamsun on a Fresno Boy: Recollections and Short Essays* by Gary Soto. Copyright © 1982, 1988, 2000 by Gary Soto. Reprinted by permission of Perseus Books, Inc. (New York).

Deborah Tannen. "How to Give Orders Like a Man." From *You Just Don't Understand* by Deborah Tannen. Copyright © 1990 by Deborah Tannen. Reprinted by permission of HarperCollins Publishers, Inc. "Sex, Lies and Conversation." From the *Washington Post,* June 24, 1990. Copyright Deborah Tannen. Reprinted by permission. This article is based in part on material from the author's book, *You Just Don't Understand* (Ballantine, 1990).

Ellen Ullman. "Needed: Techies Who Know Shakespeare." From the *New York Times,* July 8, 1998. Copyright © 1998 by The New York Times Company. Reprinted by permission.

Ernest van den Haag. "For the Death Penalty." From *The Death Penalty* by Ernest van den Haag. Copyright © 1963 by Ernest van den Haag and John P. Conrad. Reprinted by permission of Perseus Books Publishers, a member of Perseus Books, L.L.C.

Gore Vidal. "Lincoln Up Close." Originally published in the *New York Review of Books* (1991). Copyright © 1991 by Gore Vidal. Reprinted by permission of Janklow & Nesbitt.

Judith Viorst. "The Truth about Lying." Originally appeared in *Redbook.* Copyright © 1981 by Judith Viorst. This usage granted by permission of Lescher & Lescher, Ltd.

Alice Walker. "In Search of Our Mothers' Gardens." From *In Search of Our Mothers' Gardens: Womanist Prose.* Copyright © 1974 by Alice Walker. Reprinted by permission of Harcourt, Inc.

Barry Winston. "Stranger Than True." Copyright © 1986 by *Harper's Magazine.* All rights reserved. Reproduced from the December issue by special permission.

Cathy Young. "Sexism and the Death Chamber." From www.salon.com. Copyright © 2000 *Salon.* Reprinted by permission.

Index

Research and Writing Online

Whether you want to investigate the ideas behind a thought-provoking essay or conduct in-depth research for a paper, the Web resources for *Subjects/Strategies* can help you find what you need on the Web — and then use it once you find it.

The English Research Room
for Navigating the Web

www.bedfordstmartins.com/english_research

The Web brings a flood of information to your screen, but it still takes skill to track down the best sources. Not only does *The English Research Room* point you to some reliable starting places for Web investigations, but it also lets you tune up your skills with interactive tutorials.

- Do you want to improve your skill at searching electronic databases, online catalogs, and the Web? Try the ***Interactive Tutorials*** for some hands-on practice.
- Do you need quick access to online search engines, reference sources, and research sites? Explore ***Research Links*** for some good starting places.
- Do you have questions on evaluating the sources you find, navigating the Web, or conducting research in general? Consult one of our ***Reference Units*** for authoritative advice.

Research and Documentation Online
for Including Sources in Your Writing

www.bedfordstmartins.com/resdoc

Including sources correctly in a paper is often a challenge, and the Web has made it even more complex. This online version of the popular booklet *Research and Documentation in the Electronic Age,* by Diana Hacker, provides clear advice for the humanities, social sciences, history, and the sciences on —

- Which Web and library sources are relevant to your topic (with links to Web sources)
- How to integrate outside material into your paper
- How to cite sources correctly, using the appropriate documentation style
- What the format of the final paper should be